R

D0322824

Contemporary
Jewish Theology

LIBRARY
Tel: 01244 375444   Ext: 3301

Chester
A College of the
University of Liverpool

This book is to be returned on or before the
last date stamped below. Overdue charges
will be incurred by the late return of books.

Contemporary Jewish Theology

A Reader

❦

Edited by

Elliot N. Dorff
Louis E. Newman

New York   Oxford
Oxford University Press
1999

Oxford University Press

Oxford New York
Athens Auckland Bangkok Bogotá Buenos Aires Calcutta
Cape Town Chennai Dar es Salaam Delhi Florence Hong Kong Istanbul
Karachi Kuala Lumpur Madrid Melbourne Mexico City Mumbai
Nairobi Paris São Paulo Singapore Taipei Tokyo Toronto Warsaw

and associated companies in
Berlin Ibadan

Published by Oxford University Press, Inc.
198 Madison Avenue, New York, New York 10016
http://www.oup-usa.org

Oxford is a registered trademark of Oxford University Press

Library of Congress Cataloging-in-Publication Data

Contemporary Jewish theology : a reader / edited by Elliot N. Dorff
    and Louis E. Newman:
        p.   cm.
    Includes bibliographical references.
    ISBN 0–19–511466–3 (cloth). — ISBN 0–19–511467–1
(paper)
      1. Judaism—Doctrines. 2. Judaism—20th century.   I. Dorff,
Elliot. II. Newman, Louis E.
BM601,C66   1998
296.3—dc21   97–51341
                                                       CIP

Printing (last digit): 9 8 7 6 5 4 3 2 1

Printed in the United States of America
on acid-free paper

For Marlynn and Amy

Contents

Preface

This collection of essays is designed as a companion volume to our earlier *Contemporary Jewish Ethics and Morality* (Oxford, 1995). In the spirit of that volume, our purpose here is to introduce readers to the breadth of contemporary Jewish theology as it has developed over the last few decades. In our judgment, this has been an extraordinarily productive period for Jewish religious thought; a time when traditional issues have been addressed from new perspectives and when the circle of participants in theological discussion has widened considerably. No doubt readers will assess the success of these theological efforts in a variety of ways, and invariably not all the essays here will be equally persuasive or relevant to everyone who encounters them. Collectively, however, we believe that they testify powerfully both to the resourcefulness of contemporary Jewish thinkers and to the integrity with which they have approached the task of creating a theology appropriate to our times.

In making the always difficult decisions about what to include here, we have cast a broad net. Recognizing that Jewish theological reflection expresses itself in multiple idioms, and draws from multiple philosophical currents, we have attempted to be as inclusive as possible, given the constraints imposed by considerations of size. We have also attempted to juxtapose contrasting points of view on topics of perennial theological interest, thereby enabling readers to appreciate the scope of contemporary Jewish conversation on each issue. At the same time, we have organized these essays—from early twentieth-century works by the giants of modern Jewish thought to the most recent reflections by feminists and post-modernists—in categories that we hope underscore the continuities between modern Jewish theology and the long tradition of theological reflection to which it is heir.

We have benefited from the helpful suggestions of many colleagues, as well as from comments of the anonymous reviewers for Oxford University Press and its editors. At this point, we could never hope to thank individually all those who have had a hand in shaping this volume. Suffice it to say that the scope of the material we have included, and the clarity of the organizational scheme, have been enhanced considerably as a result of the input we received. We hope that all those who have given so generously of their time and insight will recognize the fruits of their efforts in this volume.

It is our hope that this book will both fairly represent the diversity and vitality of contemporary Jewish theology and make it accessible to a wide range of readers. We believe that this work is of interest to a number of constituencies. First, of course, this book should serve those within the Jewish community in search of sophisticated reflections on the meaning of their own religious life, those who until now have not had a single volume which presents a representative sampling of contemporary approaches to Jewish religious issues. In addition, theologians in other religious traditions may wish to learn from these authors just as, in fact, most of those included here have been informed by the work of those outside the Jewish tradition. At a time when the commitment to religious pluralism has increased dramatically, we hope that a collection of this sort will foster greater understanding of Judaism's theological underpinings, as these are currently understood by a range of Jewish thinkers. Finally, we trust that those who teach in academic settings will find this collection of essays helpful in introducing students to contemporary Jewish thought and to the continuing vitality of this religious tradition.

Martin Buber once wrote that "all real life is encounter" and that "extended, the lines of relationships intersect in the eternal You." We dedicate this volume to the people in our lives who have shown us most profoundly the connection between human intimacy and a relationship with the divine. In the deepest sense, they are a blessing, for they bring into our lives that sense of joy and deep contentment which are truly expressions of God's love.

Los Angeles, California   *E.N.D.*
Northfield, Minnesota   *L.E.N.*
11 Tammuz, 5757
July 16, 1997

Acknowledgments

The editors and publisher of this volume would like to thank the following authors and publishers for permission to reprint their articles or, in the case of four chapters, to publish them for the first time. The articles are listed here in the order that they appear in this reader, identified below by chapter number:

1. Byron Sherwin, "An Incessantly Gushing Fountain: The Nature of Jewish Theology," originally published in *Problems in Contemporary Jewish Theology* (Lewiston, NY: Edwin Mellon Press, 1991), pp. 43–68, and subsequently in Byron L. Sherwin, *Toward a Jewish Theology* (Lewiston, NY: Edwin Mellon Press, 1991), pp. 9–32. © Byron L. Sherwin, Spertus College of Judaica, Chicago, IL 60605.

2. Hermann Cohen, "God's Uniqueness," in *Religion of Reason Out of the Sources of Judaism*, second edition (Atlanta: Scholars Press, 1995), pp. 35–49. © Scholars Press, Atlanta, GA 30329.

3. Franz Rosenzweig, *The Star of Redemption*, trans. William W. Hallo (Boston: Beacon Press, 1972), pp. 380–92. © Henry Holt and Company, New York, NY 10011.

4. Martin Buber, *I and Thou* (New York: Simon and Schuster, 1958), pp. 3–6, 11–12, 33–34, 75, 77, 78–79, 80–81. © Simon and Schuster, New York, NY 10019. World rights: T & T Clark, Ltd., Edinburgh EH2 2LQ Scotland.

5. Abraham Isaac Kook, "A Thirst for the Living God" and "The Pangs of Cleansing" in Ben Zion Bokser, ed., *Abraham Isaac Kook*, (Mahwah, NJ: Paulist Press), pp. 250–52, 261–69. © Paulist Press, Mahwah, NJ 07430.

6. Mordecai Kaplan, "God as the Power that Makes for Salvation," in *The Meaning of God in Modern Jewish Religion* (New York: Reconstructionist Press, 1937), pp. 51–57, 61–69. © Jewish Reconstructionist Federation, Wyncote, PA 19095.

7. Abraham Joshua Heschel, *God in Search of Man* (New York: Farrar, Straus, and Cudahy, 1956), pages 114–24, 136–44, 311–13. © Farrar, Straus & Giroux, Inc., New York, NY 10003.

8. Louis Jacobs, "Belief in a Personal God: The Position of Liberal Supernaturalism," in his *God, Torah, Israel: Traditionalism Without Fundamentalism* (Cincinnati: Hebrew

Union College Press, 1990), pp. 3–19. © Hebrew Union College Press, Cincinnati, OH 45220.

9. Elliot N. Dorff, "In Search of God" (1990), published here for the first time, but subsequently developed in his book, *Knowing God: Jewish Journeys to the Unknowable* (Northvale, NJ: Jason Aronson, 1992). © Elliot N. Dorff, University of Judaism, Los Angeles, CA 90077.

10. Harold M. Schulweis, "From God to Godliness: Proposal for a Predicate Theology." *The Reconstructionist* 41:1 (1975), pp. 16–26. © Jewish Reconstructionist Federation, Wyncote, PA 19095.

11. Marcia Falk, "Toward a Feminist Jewish Reconstruction of Monotheism." *Tikkun Magazine: A Bi-Monthly Jewish Critique of Politics, Culture, and Society* 4:4 (July/August 1989), pp. 53–56. © Marcia Falk. "Further Thoughts on Liturgy as an Expression of Theology." Written for this volume. © Marcia Falk.

12. Ellen M. Umansky, "Jewish Feminist Theology," *Choices in Modern Jewish Thought*, second edition, in Eugene B. Borowitz, ed. (New York: Behrman House, 1995), pp. 314–17, 334–40. © Ellen Umansky.

13. David W. Weiss, *The Wings of the Dove: Jewish Values, Science, and Halachah* (Washington, D.C.: B'nai B'rith Book Service, 1987), pp. 81–87, 117–22. © B'nai B'rith Book Service, Washington, D.C. 20036.

14. Arthur Green, *Seek My Face, Speak My Name* (Northvale, NJ: Jason Aronson, 1992), pp. 53–70. © Jason Aronson Inc., Northvale, NJ 07647.

15. Emanuel Levinas, "Revelation in the Jewish Tradition," in *Beyond the Verse: Talmudic Readings and Lectures*, Gary D. Mole, trans. (Bloomington, IN: Indiana U. Press, 1994), pp. 129–50. © Indiana University Press, Bloomington, IN 47404.

16. Neil Gillman, *Sacred Fragments: Recovering Theology for the Modern Jew* (Philadelphia: Jewish Publication Society, 1992), pp. 25–34, 116–24. © Jewish Publication Society, Philadelphia, PA 19103.

17. Arthur A. Cohen, *The Natural and the Supernatural Jew*, second edition (New York: Behrman House, 1979), pp. 291–301, 306–11. © Behrman House, West Orange, NJ 07052.

18. Steven Schwarzschild, "On Jewish Eschatology," in *The Human Condition in the Jewish and Christian Traditions*, F. Greenspahn, ed. (New York: Ktav, 1986), p. 171–211. © Ktav Publishing House, Hoboken, NJ 07030.

19. Eugene Borowitz, "The Dialectic of Living in Covenant," Ch. 16 in *Renewing the Covenant* (Philadelphia: Jewish Publication Society, 1991), pp. 221–34. © Jewish Publication Society, Philadelphia, PA 19103.

20. David Novak, *The Election of Israel* (New York: Cambridge University Press, 1995), pp. 115–38. © Cambridge University Press, New York, NY 10011.

21. Michael Wyschogrod, "Love and Election," and "National Election," in *The Body of Faith* (New York: Harper Collins, 1983), pp. 58–70. © 1996, Jason Aronson Inc., Northvale, NJ 07647.

22. Judith Plaskow, "Torah: Reshaping Jewish Memory," in *Standing Again at Sinai* (San Francisco: Harper and Row, 1990), pp. 25–36. © Harper Collins Publishers, New York, NY 10022.

23. Elliot N. Dorff, "A Jewish Theology of Jewish Relations to Other Peoples," in *People of God, Peoples of God: A Jewish-Christian Conversation in Asia*, Hans Ucko, ed. (Geneva, Switzerland: World Council of Churches, 1996), pp. 46–66. © World Council of Churches Publications, 1211 Geneva 2 Switzerland.

24. Joseph Soloveitchik, *Halakhic Man*, trans. Lawrence Kaplan (Philadelphia: Jewish Publication Society, 1983), pp. 99–128. © Jewish Publication Society, Philadelphia, PA 19103.

25. Jakob J. Petuchowski, "Some Criteria for Modern Jewish Observance," in Alfred Jospe, ed., *Tradition and Contemporary Experience* (New York: Schocken/B'nai B'rith, 1970), pp. 239–48. © B'nai Brith Book Service, Washington, D.C. 20036.

26. Robert Gordis, *Dynamics of Judaism* (Bloomington, IN: Indiana University Press, 1990), pp. 63–68, 86–99, 105–7, 210–11. © Indiana University Press, Bloomington, IN 47404.

27. Rachel Adler, "Here Comes Skotsl: Renewing Halakhah," in *Engendering Judaism* (Philadelphia: Jewish Publication Society, 1997), pp. 21–23, 34–41, 51–59. © Jewish Publication Society, Philadelphia, PA 19103.

28. Eliezer Berkovits, *Faith after the Holocaust* (New York: Ktav, 1973), pp. 94–113, 128–37. © Ktav Publishing House, Hoboken, NJ 07030.

29. Richard Rubenstein, "Covenant and Divinity: The Holocaust and the Problematics of Religious Faith," in *After Auschwitz*, second edition (Baltimore: Johns Hopkins University Press, 1994), pp. 159–63, 171–76, 197, 200. © Johns Hopkins University Press, Baltimore, MD 21218.

30. Emil Fackenheim, *The Jewish Return into History* (New York: Schocken, 1978), pp. 19–24, and *To Mend the World* (New York: Schocken, 1982), pp. 294–302, 308–13.

31. Irving Greenberg, "Cloud of Smoke, Pillar of Fire," in *Auschwitz: Beginning of a New Era? Reflections on the Holocaust,* Eva Fleischner, ed. (New York: Ktav, 1977), pp. 7–9, 11–14, 15, 17–18, 19, 27–30, 31–33, 41–42, 44–52, 54–55. © Ktav Publishing House, Hoboken, NJ 07030.

32. A. B. Yehoshua, "Exile as a Neurotic Solution," in *Diaspora: Exile and the Contemporary Jewish Condition*, Etan Levine, ed. (New York: Steimatzky Publishing, 1986), pp. 15–35. © A. B. Yehoshua.

33. David Hartman, "The Third Jewish Commonwealth," in *A Living Covenant* (New York: Free Press, 1985), pp. 278–99. © Simon & Schuster, New York, NY 10019.

34. Yeshayahu Leibowitz, "The Religious and Moral Significance of the Redemption of Israel," in *Judaism, Human Values, and the Jewish State*, Eliezer Goldman, ed. (Cambridge: Harvard University Press, 1992), pp. 106–22. © Harvard University Press, Cambridge, MA 02138.

35. Marc Ellis, *Beyond Innocence and Redemption* (New York: Harper and Row, 1990), pp. 156–64, 177–90. © Harper Collins Publishers, New York, NY 10022.

36. Arthur Green, "New Directions in Jewish Theology in America," David W. Belin Lecture in American Jewish Affairs (Ann Arbor, MI: Jean and Samuel Frankel Center for Judaic Studies, University of Michigan, 1994), pp. 1–13. © Jean and Samuel Frankel Center for Judaic Studies, University of Michigan, Ann Arbor, MI 48109.

37. Rebecca T. Alpert, "Another Perspective on Theological Directions for the Jewish Future," published in this volume for the first time.

38. David Ellenson, "The Nature and Direction of Modern Jewish Theology," published in this volume for the first time.

39. Peter Ochs, "B'nei Ezra: An Introduction to Textual Reasoning," published in this volume for the first time.

Part I

Introduction

I. Theology in Judaism—Past and Present

Theology, from the Greek words meaning the "study of God," refers to reflection on the nature of ultimate reality and on the human condition in relation to it. As such, it encompasses a wide range of questions: How did the world and human life originate? What is the world destined to become, and what role do we have in shaping it? How do we come to know the ultimate reality we call "God"? What sort of relationship can and ought we have with God, and how are we to maintain such a relationship? In pondering these profound questions, theologians draw upon diverse resources—rational investigation, empirical study, individual and communal religious experience, and sacred literature, among others. Whatever the focus or form of theological discourse, its purpose is always the same. In Anselm's elegant formulation, theology is "faith in search of understanding." Through theological reflection, people of faith reflect on the meaning and values of their beliefs, probing the intellectual presuppositions of these beliefs and their implications for the life of individual believers and for members of religious communities. The persistence of theology, then, testifies to the depth of human faith in a supersensible reality, the felt need to orient one's life in relation to that reality, and the irrepressible desire to understand what that orientation means.

It is often claimed that, historically, Judaism has produced relatively little theology, properly speaking. In support of this contention, it has been noted that the classical literature of rabbinic Judaism—the Mishnah and the Talmuds of Babylonia and Palestine—contains dozens of tractates devoted to every aspect of life, but includes not a single volume devoted directly to matters of doctrine. The rabbinic mind apparently was drawn more to issues of orthopraxy, proper practice, than to orthodoxy, proper belief. Moreover, when the rabbis addressed theological issues in the midrash, they often expressed a variety of opinions without deciding among them.

The classical tradition is also portrayed as either indifferent or openly hostile to the use of philosophical reasoning to explain and investigate religious truths in abstract and systematic form. Consider the contrast with Christianity, which has produced a long line of systematic theologians—Augustine, Anselm, Aquinas, Luther, Calvin, and Barth, to name but a few. Jewish religious reflection more often takes the form of commentary to sacred texts (or commentaries on commentaries to those texts) and is embedded in the complex and sometimes arcane explication of legal rules and principles. The rabbis of ancient times and their successors down to the present, on this view, have been more concerned with maintaining a proper relationship with God than with articulating their understanding of that relationship in theological form.

Though it is not without an element of truth, this view minimizes the genuine significance of theological reflection in the history of Judaism. Within classical biblical and rabbinic literature itself (including both halakhah and aggadah, law and narrative) we find discussions of many standard theological topics: the nature of God, the ways in which we acquire knowledge of God, and the place of human beings in God's world. The fact that these discussions do not generally take the form of a Greek philosophical discourse does not detract from the seriousness of the theological questions the Bible and rabbis pose or from the philosophical sophistication of the answers offered. In many cases, the rabbis' theological reflections rely on literary devices, such as metaphor and simile, or contrived conversation, to explore a theological theme, such as the relationship of God to Israel. Undoubtedly their preference for textual exegesis reflected their view that ultimately all truth was already embedded in the text of Scripture and fundamentally only needed to be extracted from it through careful (or fanciful) reading. Perhaps, too, they eschewed philosophical modes of discourse because they were suspicious of any human claims to certain knowledge about ultimate realities, believing that our knowledge is inescapably indirect and incomplete, especially in contrast to God's omniscience. But this should not be mistaken for a lack of interest in theological matters. The question is not whether the rabbis felt the need to explore theological questions of ontology, cosmology, soteriology, or theodicy, but only what tools they used to fulfill that need.

In any case, since medieval times Jewish theology has often drawn heavily from both the content and form of the Greek philosophical tradition. Platonic and Aristotelian philosophy provided the intellectual currency for generations of Jewish (not to mention Islamic and Christian) philosophers. For Philo, Saadia Gaon, Maimonides, Gersonides, and Crescas, among others, the goal was to demonstrate that Jewish religious truths were consistent with the truths established by these Greek philosophers. The revelation in Torah could not contradict the truths evident through the use of human reason, and the God who spoke to the Israelites must be knowable, at least in principle, by all humankind. After all, truth being by definition universal, there could not be one version of it in Athens and another in Jerusalem. In the pursuit of this integrated system of truth, medieval Jewish theologians explored old religious questions using new tools borrowed from the surrounding culture. In doing so they simultaneously reassured themselves of the validity of their own religious truths and laid claim to the attention of intellectuals in the larger society.

Modern Jewish theologians, like their ancient and medieval predecessors, have continued to seek adequate ways of understanding basic elements of Jewish faith; moreover, they have used many of the same intellectual tools to do so. What has changed is the intellectual and social context in which they work. The distinctive challenges that modernity has posed to traditional Jewish belief and to the structures of the traditional Jewish community are well known and need not be rehearsed here in detail.

The onset of the Enlightenment brought a new emphasis on reason and empirical investigation, thereby challenging the traditional truth claims of both Judaism and Christianity, insofar as these were based on special revelatory events and miracles. Scripture, subjected for the first time to historical-critical investigation, could no longer stand as an irrefutable source of truth. Time-honored beliefs—for example, that God had chosen the Jews for a special mission and that history unfolded according to the will of God—were attacked as logically incoherent or empirically falsifiable, or both. In this new intellectual context, a new basis for Jewish religious faith was needed, one consistent with the dominant intellectual trends of the time.

In addition, the separation of church and state that led to the secularization of civil society meant that Jews could be welcomed into the larger society as equals for the first time without regard to their religious belief or practice. This acceptance opened the door for widespread assimilation (and sometimes the rejection of Jewish affiliation entirely), a trend that traditional religious authorities were essentially powerless to prevent. To be sure, many Jews resisted the pressure to assimilate and chose to remain connected with Jewish tradition and community. But now they needed to justify their decision to do so, both to themselves and to their non-Jewish fellow citizens. Praying to God, observing Jewish rituals, and fostering Jewish communal life were no longer self-evident ways of life reinforced both by rabbinic authority and by the social barriers separating Jews from non-Jews. Instead, commitment to Judaism could be maintained only insofar as it could be justified in relation to the very new intellectual and social realities of Jewish life.

Beginning with Moses Mendelssohn in the late eighteenth and early nineteenth centuries, modern Jewish theologians addressed these challenges, leaving behind an impressive body of work. Among the major works produced during the first century after Jewish emancipation were Nachman Krochmal's *Guide for the Perplexed of this Time*, Moses Hess' *Rome and Jerusalem*, Samson Raphael Hirsch's *Nineteen Letters* and *Horeb*, and Kaufman Kohler's *Jewish Theology*, to say nothing of the dozens of essays published in Zecharias Frankel's *Zeitschrift fuer die religioesen Interessen des Judenthums* and in Abraham Geiger's *Wissenschaftliche Zeitschrift fuer juedische Theologie*. While these authors represent a broad spectrum of intellectual commitments and addressed a wide range of theological topics, they shared elements of a common agenda. The twin challenges of natural and social science which threatened to undermine the supernatural foundations of Jewish faith required a response.

A wide range of responses was forthcoming. Some authors relied on the evolutionary thinking that dominated the last half of the nineteenth century. Others drew upon Hegelian, dialectical models of historical development. Still others were drawn to Kantian modes of thought, seeing in them the possibility for establishing a new foundation for religious belief and/or moral values. And, of course, there were those, influenced by European nationalism, who substituted national self-determination for religious commitment as a strategy for responding to the crisis in modern Jewish life. Whatever their predilections, nineteenth-century Jewish theologians variously reinterpreted (or jettisoned) components of their traditional faith in the effort to construct an intellectually defensible and socially viable religious life.

In the first half of the twentieth century, the legacy of these early efforts to reinterpret the nature of Jewish faith provided the foundation for new Jewish philosophical works. Some writers, like Hermann Cohen, drew heavily on the intellectual capital of the nineteenth century (especially neo-Kantianism), while others, like Martin Buber and Franz Rosenzweig, appropriated the existentialism that proliferated after World War I. Some, like Mordecai Kaplan, embraced the scientific spirit and saw in it a source of salvific power, while others, like Abraham Isaac Kook, drew on the long tradition of Jewish mysticism to fashion a response to modernity. Despite their differences, all these thinkers were acutely aware that the times had changed irrevocably; there was no going back to the pre-Emancipation, pre-Enlightenment world that had nurtured traditional Jewish life and thought. Instead, new ways of conceptualizing Jewish faith had to be formulated that were consonant with the intellectual and social realities of the twentieth century.

In the half century since the end of World War II, Jewish theology has followed in the footsteps of these major thinkers. Their orientations—toward rationalism or mysticism, idealism or naturalism—have been adopted and carried forward (in whole or in part) by virtually all subsequent Jewish religious thinkers. To be sure, there have been genuinely new developments. The rise of feminist thought, especially, and its pervasive influence in Western societies has forced a reassessment of many traditional (and even liberal) Jewish theological assumptions. In addition, the move toward "post-modernism" in contemporary intellectual circles has influenced some Jewish thinkers to reappropriate a text-based, exegetical approach to theological questions as opposed to the more abstract, philosophical approach that dominated earlier work in this century.

Finally, the devastation of the Holocaust coupled with the renaissance of Jewish national life in the State of Israel have exerted a profound effect on Jewish theologians in this period. These events have transformed the consciousness of contemporary Jews and have provided Jewish theologians with new questions—about power and powerlessness, history and salvation—on which to reflect. Yet, notwithstanding these epoch-making experiences, the essential challenges for Jewish theology have remained constant for more than a century: to identify those elements of life and of Jewish experience that are sacred, echoes of a divine, supernatural reality, and to distinguish these from the ordinary, mundane dimensions of life. How one understands God or Torah or Israel (people, land, and/or State) depends crucially on how one conceptualizes the relationship between the divine and the human, the eternal and the historical.

II. Scope and Organization

The foregoing reflections should serve to introduce the central concerns of contemporary Jewish theology. This volume is designed to survey the range of responses to these concerns that have been articulated by Jewish religious thinkers in the past few decades. It is our conviction that these have been extraordinarily fruitful times for Jewish religious reflection, and so we have chosen to include selections designed to illustrate the extent of the foment and creativity that have characterized these times.

As in all projects of this sort, it has not been possible to include every essay that has made an important contribution to contemporary Jewish theology or to showcase the work of every important thinker. Our criteria of selection have been similar to those employed in our earlier reader, *Contemporary Jewish Ethics and Morality* (Oxford, 1995). Our primary goal has been to represent accurately the breadth and diversity of contemporary Jewish theology. Hence, we have intentionally sampled the works of traditionalists who maintain a commitment to classical theological conceptions of God, Torah, and/or Israel, and who employ the vocabulary of modern thinkers only to clarify or justify those commitments. At the same time, we have included the work of those who have radically reformulated traditional categories—from any number of perspectives—thereby challenging time-honored beliefs and breaking new theological ground. Indeed, we have attempted to juxtapose sometimes strikingly different theological approaches and intellectual temperaments in the hope that this will serve to illustrate the range of options available to contemporary Jewish religious thought. Perhaps this volume, and the theological discourse it is intended to represent, can best be understood as a cacophany of voices—traditionalist and feminist, rationalist and mystical, philosophical and exegetical—all groping for the best way to understand what faith asserts, or to formulate a faith that these thinkers can honestly affirm.

Also, we have attempted to make this volume accessible to a general audience, as well as an academic one. Thus, while some of the essays here are more technical than others, we have given preference to articles that can be read on their own, without extensive background or acquaintance with the volumes from which they were excerpted. The selections from the works of early twentieth-century theologians at the beginning of the volume represent something of an exception to this principle. Because these essays presuppose that readers will be familiar with a range of philosophical views, and because many of these have been drawn from longer theological works, we have included a lengthy introduction to this section, placing these selections in proper context.

We have not attempted to represent the range of Zionist thought, either from the nineteenth or twentieth centuries. In the first place, Zionism incorporated within it many streams of thought, only some of which were explicitly religious. Indeed, many Zionist thinkers were openly hostile to the religious tradition, which they felt was antithetical to the goals of modern Jewish nationalism. In addition, Arthur Hertzberg's *The Zionist Idea* (Atheneum, 1975) remains the most comprehensive anthology of this material and obviates the necessity for us to try to represent this important current in modern Jewish thought here. In the section on Israel we have included several contemporary reflections on the religious meaning of the State of Israel, representing both Israeli and Diaspora perspectives.

Every anthology represents a kind of "snapshot" as it captures the "state of the field" at a particular time. The very vitality of a field ensures that the passage of time will render any collection "dated" and in need of revision. In the interests of minimizing this effect, we have given preference to work produced in the last decade or two, including older essays only when, in our judgment, they will still make worthwhile reading twenty or more years hence.

Throughout this book, we have intentionally included feminist voices alongside more traditional ones, rather than isolating feminist theology in a separate section. This reflects our dual conviction: first, that Jewish feminist thought has "come of age" and should be regarded as part of the mainstream, and second, that feminist voices can be understood best in juxtaposition with others addressing topics of common concern.

Finally, our collection is focused largely on work produced in the Anglo-American Jewish communities. Because English-speaking Jewish communities in the last half of this century have become the most numerous and, overall, the most highly educated in the world, it is here that most Jewish theological reflection has occurred. Israeli intellectuals, for complicated social and political reasons, have by and large not addressed issues of modern theology in a way that is generally accessible to the Western audience for whom this volume is intended. So while we have included some essays by Israeli and European authors, the thinkers represented here have by and large been trained in North American universities and have written for an English-speaking audience.

We have organized these essays in a way that we hope enhances their accessibility. The introductory essay by Byron Sherwin is designed to orient readers to the tasks that any modern Jewish theologian must take up, and so provides a fitting entré into the subject matter of this volume. The first large section of the book is devoted to the major Jewish thinkers of the early twentieth century whose work, as we mentioned above, has set the tone, if not the specific agenda, of contemporary Jewish religious thought. To provide a clear point of comparison among these theologians and to set the stage for the theological debates that follow, we have chosen selections that articulate their concepts of God.

The section that follows, "Contemporary Reflections on Traditional Themes," is subdivided into six topics. We begin with contemporary views of God, so as to carry forward the views already presented by theologians from before 1960. We next turn to the three ways in which God is traditionally understood to be related to the world—through acts of creation, revelation, and redemption. This matrix of relationships shapes Jewish religious identity, providing the context in which Jews explore the meaning of their own religious experience. Accordingly, this section of the book concludes with essays that address the themes most central to that experience: chosenness/covenant and law.

In the next major section of the volume, we focus attention on the two events that, perhaps more than any others, have shaped Jewish life in the second half of the twentieth century: the destruction of European Jewry and the establishment of the modern State of Israel. These events have called forth profound and unprecedented responses among both theologians and the Jewish community as a whole, and they will no doubt continue to do so for the foreseeable future. Thus, although some of these responses intersect with Jewish theological reflection on other topics, we believe the essays on these topics warrant a section of their own.

We conclude this volume with a symposium of responses to Arthur Green's provocative essay, "New Directions in Jewish Theology in America." In conjunction with the responses we have assembled here, this essay highlights some of the trends that have emerged in recent years and suggests some of the ways in which Jewish theology might take shape in the next few decades. The inconclusive character of this conclusion is intentional. No one forty years ago could have predicted the ways in which Jewish theology would unfold in the closing years of the twentieth century and, correspondingly, no one today can be certain what lies ahead. We can only take note of where we have come to and project some of the possibilities that might continue to be compelling for Jewish theologians into the twenty-first century.

1

An Incessantly Gushing Fountain: The Nature of Jewish Theology

BYRON SHERWIN

Judaism is a way of thinking, as well as a way of living.[1] The task of Jewish theology is to establish the nature and the parameters of Jewish religious thought, to articulate coherently the authentic views of Judaism, and to demonstrate how the wisdom of the Jewish religious teachings of the past can address the perplexities of contemporary Jewish existence in a manner that is compatible with the thought and life of the Jewish faith-community at a given juncture in time and space. The four criteria that characterize a valid Jewish theology are identical to those of any valid theology. These are: authenticity, coherence, contemporaneity, and, communal acceptance.[2]

Authenticity depends upon the nature and use of sources consulted, and to the faith commitment of the individual consulting them. Coherence relates to the cohesion, clarity, and communicability of a formulated theological perspective. Contemporaneity pertains to the successful application of past traditions to present situations. Communal acceptance refers to the ratification of a theological posture by committed members of a specific faith-community.

Should a theological stance not achieve communal acceptance, then it proves barren. When not contemporaneous, it then becomes anachronistic. If it lacks coherence, a theological position invites unintelligibility and hence proves unavailing. When a theology cannot claim authenticity, it is demonstrably spurious. While these four criteria for theological validity apply both to theology in general and to Jewish theology in particular, what follows addresses how and why these criteria relate to the formulation of a valid *Jewish* theology.[3]

Byron Sherwin, "An Incessantly Gushing Fountain: The Nature of Jewish Theology," originally published in *Problems in Contemporary Jewish Theology* (Lewiston, NY: Edwin Mellon Press, 1991), pp. 43–68, and subsequently in Byron L. Sherwin. *Toward a Jewish Theology* (Lewiston, NY: Edwin Mellon Press, 1991), pp. 9–32. © Byron L. Sherwin, Spertus College of Judaica, Chicago, IL 60605.

Authenticity

Jewish theology is not a _creatio ex nihilo_. A historical tradition, an extant canon of sacred literature, and a living faith-community precede each Jewish theologian's attempt to formulate a theology of Judaism. The challenge to the theologian is not to create, but to re-create tradition.[4]

To use a medieval analogy, the theologian is like a "dwarf riding on the shoulders of a giant."[5] The giant represents the cumulative corpus of the tradition that precedes the individual theologian. This analogy indicates that the coalescence of the wisdom of the past in the giant makes the stature of the giant necessarily higher and his vista broader than that of the dwarf who represents only his own wisdom and that of his particular generation. The giant represents the summation and the quintessence of tradition. But when perched on the giant's shoulders, the dwarf is provided an opportunity to see more, to exceed that which is attainable by the giant alone. Separated, the giant and the dwarf are destined each to his own individual fate. Together, the giant and the dwarf guarantee both the continuity and the development of tradition. Without the giant, there is no viable foundation for such development. Without the dwarf, the giant might become simply a relic of bygone days.

Tradition is a bequest of the ages available to the diligent theologian. It is a trust vouchsafed only to those who labor on its behalf. To be received, tradition must first be acquired. Study of the bibliographical menu of sacred texts is necessary, but not sufficient. Like food, the tradition must become incorporated as part of the theologian. It is not enough to know the sacred texts. The theologian must also absorb and become absorbed by them. As Shneur Zalman of Liady wrote:

> Seeing that through the knowledge of the Torah man's soul and mind encompass the Torah and are in turn encompassed by it, the Torah is called food and the sustenance of the soul. For just as material food sustains the body and enters it and is transformed in the body into flesh and blood, by virtue of which a man lives and endures, so it is with regard to knowledge of the Torah and its comprehension by he who studies with concentration until the Torah is grasped by the mind and becomes united with it.[6]

In this view, one must consume and be consumed by the Torah, the tradition. Study of the Torah is but a means; becoming Torah is the goal. Commenting on the phrase _"ve-zot torat ha-Adam"_ [literally: "and this is the Torah of man"] (2 Sam 7:19), Mordecai of Chernobyl explained it to mean that "the man himself _becomes_ the Torah."[7]

The theologian cannot be a passive voyeur, a casual tourist surveying the landscape of tradition. The scientist, the philosopher or the historian of religion can stand outside the arena of his or her inquiry as a disinterested observer. For the theologian, however, commitment precedes inquiry. Experience of the life of faith and participation in a faith-community anticipates theological investigation.[8] Only the well-springs of individual religious commitment can generate a viable theology. Only from the passion of faith can theology emanate. Theology is passionate faith seeking understanding.

Theology is not an intellectual parlor game but the articulation of a prior commitment. Observance of the commandments is an expression of that commitment. The Jewish theologian is not only obliged to _do_ what he or she _believes_, but to _believe_ what he or she _does_. _Halakhah_ is faith in the form of deeds. Performance of the commandments represents belief articulated as action. In a sense _halakhah_ may be considered the "practical theology" of Judaism, i.e., Jewish theological ideas expressed as specific concrete acts.

It would be an error to equate *halakhah* with Jewish theology. It would also be a mistake to detach Jewish theology from *halakhah*. *Halakhah* is predicated upon the most fundamental Jewish theological assumption: God gave the Torah to Israel. But theological premises not only underlie *halakhah*; theological ideas are also compressed within *halakhah*. A task of the Jewish theologian, therefore, is: to examine and to explicate the theological underpinnings of *halakhah*, to elicit the implicit theological issues pregnant within *halakhah*, and, to articulate the theological meaning of *halakhic* observance. For the Jewish theologian, *halakhah* is both a priori and a posteriori. Religious observance both precedes and flows from theological investigation.[9]

Study of the Torah, of the tradition, is a conclusion of which prior commitment is a premise. Study of the Torah without prior commitment is a conclusion without a premise, an embryo without a prior conception. Without both prior and subsequent commitment, study of the Torah becomes a stillborn. As a midrash observes, "If one studies (Torah) without the intention to observe it, it is better that he had not been born . . . it would have been better that he had been strangled by the placenta at birth, and had never ventured forth into the world."[10]

The rabbis read the verse describing the Torah as an inheritance (*morashah*) of Israel (Deut. 33:4) as denoting the betrothal (*me-orashah*) of the people of Israel and of each individual Jew to the Torah.[11] As Samuel of Uceda observed, commenting upon this rabbinic text, betrothal infers commitment, and commitment grants a license for intimacy. The person committed to the Torah, to the tradition, is granted entrée to her inner domain.[12] According to the Zohar, the true scholar is a lover of the Torah, invited by the Torah to penetrate her private precincts, to gain access through intimacy into her deepest mysteries, to uncover secrets she otherwise cloaks.[13] As Moses Hayyim Ephraim of Sudlykow wrote, "When one studies the Torah for its own sake, to keep it and perform it, then he brings all his limbs close to their source whence they originated and were generated, namely the Torah . . . and he becomes identical to the Torah like the unification of man and woman."[14] Speculating further on the already mentioned rabbinic text that compares the Torah to Israel's spouse, a commentator explains this analogy to mean that the Torah is caused to conceive by the sages of Israel, thereby assuring the continuous rebirth and development of the tradition.[15]

To a lover, his or her beloved is unique. Jewish theology focuses upon the specifically unique rather than upon the scientific tendency toward generalization.[16] Jewish theology posits its own sui generis nature. The formative events that concern it (such as the revelation at Sinai), the corpus of sacred literature that informs it, the people of Israel who live it, and the historical experience of that people which helps to shape it, are held to be unique. Consequently, a task of the theologian is to discern the particular categories of faith and thought that characterize and that are native to Judaism.

Unlike the historian of religion or the social scientist who seek to impose imported rubrics and generalizations upon Jewish faith, experience, and sacred literature, the theologian seeks to understand Judaism on its own terms, according to its own endemic categories, in its own particular language. Unlike the approach initiated by the *Wissenschaft des Judentums* (the Scientific Study of Judaism) that tried to surrender the uniqueness of Judaism into the vortex of the "universal human spirit," that advocated the application of an objective "value-free" universal scientific approach to Judaism, that attempted to reduce sacred Jewish literature to belles lettres, Jewish theology embraces Judaism in its uniqueness, on its own terms.[17] The Jewish theologian encounters Judaism as a living organism, as a beloved. The program of the Scientific Study of Judaism, as Gershom Scholem observed, aims at "the liquidation of Judaism as a living organism," and, as Zalman Shazar observed, its agenda inevitably leads to the "de-Judaization of Judaism" by divesting Judaism of that which is unique to it and of that which is vibrant about it.[18]

The historian of Judaism focuses dispassionately upon the anatomy of Jewish sacred literature and historical experience, scrutinizing individual limbs. But a minute examination of individual parts tends to eclipse the vision of the whole. The theologian seeks a total gestalt, unencumbered by historical considerations: "There is neither earlier nor later in the Torah."[19] For the theologian, the corpus of tradition is the body of his or her beloved. The theologian strives to know the personality of his or her beloved in ways unavailable to the historian of religion. The variety of knowledge available through anatomical research is not the kind of knowledge available through an act of love.

The historian of Judaism has access to Judaism on a surface level. But license to penetrate the deeper meaning of Judaism is vouchsafed only to one who already has received and accepted it, i.e., to the theologian. As a lover of the Torah, the theologian may have an access code to the text denied to the historian of religion or to the social scientist examining Judaism, or to the historian of Jewish experience. As the Torah is sui generis, its knowledge by its lovers is also sui generis. According to Samuel of Uceda, on the semantic level the Torah is only truly given and only truly gives herself to her lovers.[20]

As a lover embarks upon a never-ending quest for knowledge and experience of his or her beloved, the Jewish theologian embarks on the never-ending journey toward knowledge and experience of the Torah. While lust may be satisfied, deep abiding passionate love cannot ever truly be quenched.[21] In this regard, Samuel of Uceda noted, "even if a person would live 2,000 years, he could not grasp its [the Torah's] totality."[22] And as Judah Loew of Prague observed, the quest for Torah is itself Torah.

A blessing praises God for allowing us to be "preoccupied with the words of Torah" (*la-asok be-divrei Torah*).[23] Perpetual preoccupation with the Torah is required of the Jewish theologian. Like any love relationship, a modicum of mystery must prevail to stimulate the further pursuit of knowledge of the beloved.[24] Through continuous penetration of and preoccupation with the Torah, the Jewish theologian inevitably acquires erudition and understanding.

The Jewish theologian's knowledge of the Torah, coupled with the quest to understand Judaism in its own terms, grants license to the attempt to formulate a theology of Judaism. Here "Torah" is meant in its most generic and expansive sense: the teachings of Judaism as embodied in the literary works and oral traditions that have been held sacred by Jewish tradition.[25] In this sense, "Torah" is the entire canon of sacred Jewish literature. At its inner core is the corpus of biblical and rabbinic literature. At its periphery are the teachings of today's Torah-scholars: "Everything an erudite student will expound in the presence of his master was already spoken to Moses at Sinai."[26] For the Jewish theologian, the Torah is a single corpus, one organic conceptual unit. The Jewish theologian does not approach the Torah as if it were an archaeological dig requiring stratification and identification of its individual historical layers; that is the problem of the historian of religion. Rather, the theologian apprehends the Torah as a single organism, as if all of the texts that comprise it "were uttered in a single statement."[27]

Dining at the Banquet of Tradition

Once vested with erudition and learning, the Jewish theologian has gained entry into the banquet hall of tradition. An immense repast is set out before the theologian. Staple servings as well as exotic offerings grace the banquet table. The variety of available servings, the presence of unusual delicacies, the richness of seasonings and garnishments, and the quality of preparation and presentation of the menu all reflect the theologian's breadth and depth of learning. But, despite the cornucopia that he or she encounters, the bill of fare is not without limits; the banquet table has its borders, its perimeters. Rabbinic literature compares the Torah to a "multifaceted mirror," but the number of faces that may be reflected in the mirror, though widely diverse, nevertheless has limits: "the Torah has seventy faces."[28] In other words, though an expansive diversity of views characterizes the Torah, there are boundaries nonetheless. Just as the Jewish dietary laws permit a wide variety of foods to be eaten and proscribe that certain foods may not be eaten, the ideas that comprise an authentic Jewish theology and the texts that may be utilized in its formulation are diverse, but not without limits. Certain ideas, certain world-views, cannot legitimately appear on the menu of Jewish theology. Jewish theology embraces a broad but finite range. Tradition itself defines its own limits. In this regard, the *Ethics of the Fathers* encourages one to plumb the depths of the Torah, but even one who is "learned and virtuous" is enjoined from exceeding the limits, from "revealing faces of the Torah" that contradict tradition.[29]

In order for a meal to be complete, certain courses must be eaten, certain types of foods must be consumed. As no meal can be considered complete without the consumption of certain foods, no theology of Judaism can be considered complete without the incorporation of certain ideas such as God, revelation, messiah, providence, afterlife, and so forth.

As each person invited to partake of the offerings of an immense smorgasbord would emerge with a plate of food configured differently from another person, so each Jewish theologian would find his or her formulation of a theology of Judaism different from that of his or her fellow. Though in the final analysis, the choices of literary resources available to each Jewish theologian are identical, the form and presentation of each's theology of Judaism might nonetheless differ. This is precisely why each Jewish theologian is free to compose *a* Jewish theology while no Jewish theologian can offer *the* Jewish theology. Though ultimately making use of the same raw materials, each theologian will inevitably develop them in his or her own particular manner. To be authentic, each theology of Judaism must derive from the same diverse menu; nevertheless, each Jewish theology bears the singular stamp of its composer. Just as every symphony is composed of identical notes though the organization and presentation of these notes differs from composer to composer and from symphony to symphony, so is each authentic theology of Judaism a distinct aria of ideas. Thus, each authentic theology of Judaism simultaneously reflects the resources of a shared tradition as well as the particularity of an individual Jewish theologian and of the theology of Judaism he or she has elicited from that commonly affirmed tradition.[30]

Coherence

To be authentic, Jewish theological discourse must be expressed in its own native categories, in its own distinct vocabulary, and out of its own particular agenda. As Samuel S.

Cohen observed, "Attempts to cram Judaism into categories derived from other religions and theologies can lead only to grotesque results."[31]

As part of a religious minority in a predominantly Islamic or Christian culture, inevitably influenced by Western philosophical tradition, both the medieval and modern Jewish thinker becomes inevitably tempted to assimilate Judaism into alien and even inimical philosophies and theologies. Indeed, the Jewish thinker may remain oblivious to the "cultural conditioning" absorbed from his or her geographical environment, and may be led to articulate a theology of Judaism in a manner that does not cohere with authentic Jewish thought or with the inherent vocabulary of Jewish theological discourse.[32] In this regard, Solomon Schechter made a distinction between assimilating and being assimilated. An organism is able to assimilate and should assimilate that which strengthens and enriches it. However, an organism is always endangered by being assimilated into that which is inimical to it, into that which distorts its very nature.[33]

Three notions characteristic of medieval philosophical theology, derived from a profound attachment to the premises and methods of Western philosophy, are often found to have been assimilated by attempts to formulate a theology of Judaism, both in the medieval and modern periods. These are: the demand for a systematic formulation of theological ideas, the perceived need to reconcile religious and philosophical truth, and the rational demonstration of the convictions that theology asserts (i.e., "natural theology").[34]

Following Aristotle, who considered the validity of a system of thought as being affirmed by its logical consistency, "systematic theology" has often been embraced as the only valid variety of theological discourse. From this perspective, if logical consistency is a requirement for theological validity, then for a Jewish theology to be valid, it has to be systematic and internally logically consistent. Based upon these assumptions, numerous Jewish thinkers attempted to impose the rubric of Aristotelian systematic thinking upon Judaism in the attempt to articulate a valid theology of Judaism.

While it may be described as a religious system of thought or as a coherent "worldview," Jewish theology need not be systematic in order to be valid. Neither biblical nor rabbinic literature, for example, considered the systematization of ideas either necessary or desirable.[35] System offers structure and focus, but not necessarily theological validity. System provides a finality that can prove inimical to creative theological development.[36] A demand for internal logical consistency would smother the approach of classical Jewish religious thought that tends to articulate ideas in terms of complementary polar opposites; e.g., God as transcendent and immanent, human nature as simultaneously embracing both "the image of God" as well as "dust and ashes."[37]

Imposing a contrived system upon reality or upon Judaism would be like trying to lay a flat grid upon the Alps. Jewish thought, especially Jewish mystical thought, perceives reality as being characterized by polarity, contradiction, tension. "God created everything in pairs, one set against the other," says *Midrash Temurah*, such as good and evil, purity and impurity, echoes the Zohar.[38] "Everything that exists in the world is either of a certain essence or of its opposite," says Judah Loew of Prague.[39] Without one entity, its polar opposite is bereft of meaning. Jewish theological discourse is at home with "polar" thinking. Systematic thinking in the Aristotelian and scholastic fashion is foreign to its nature and to its native manner of discourse.[40] Logic and system may be vehicles to clarity, but they are not necessarily indicative either of coherence or of truth.

As Judaism is not wedded to Western philosophy, it has no endemic need to correlate or to identify its claims with those of philosophical discourse.[41] As Abraham J. Heschel observed, the categories and presuppositions that constitute the world-view of Judaism are so radically different than those of the Western philosophical world-view that any forthright attempt to reconcile one with the other would lead inevitably to the distortion of one or the other, or both. A deformed hybrid would be the inescapable result.[42]

The assumption, made by so many medieval and modern religious philosophers, that philosophy and religion are one mouth that speaks two languages that mean the same thing, that contradictions between philosophy and religion are merely apparent, is simply a fantasy. Once philosophical truth is affirmed, and religious teaching is required to become consistent with it, the perversion of religious teachings becomes inevitable, the assimilation of religion into philosophy unavoidably ensues. Religious teachings are compelled to speak a foreign language. Gersonides, for example, insisted that any "apparent" contradiction between the Torah and philosophy can be resolved through interpreting religious doctrine according to philosophical doctrine without "destroying the tenets of revealed religion."[43] Gersonides failed to appreciate, however, that conflicts between religious and philosophical doctrine can be actual and not merely apparent. He further failed to grasp how religious teachings can become distorted by subjecting them to conform to already affirmed philosophical doctrine.

Bahya ibn Pakudah expressed a typical formulation of the medieval Jewish philosophical approach when he described one who has faith only on the basis of tradition as the blind leading the blind, whereas the believer through reason is like a blind person who has learned how to see.[44] However, he neglects to consider the possibility that one who believes through reason can also be blind to truth.

While always encouraging the application of the divine gift of human reason to the quest for true belief, one nevertheless senses a hesitancy in classical Jewish thought automatically to equate the products of rationality with truth. That which is rational may be neither reasonable nor true.[45] In the quest for religious truth, rationality may become a "dead-end," or a faulty directional signal. Reason can offer acuity of vision, but it cannot grant sight itself. Reason is a necessary but not a sufficient aspect of the theological endeavor. It cannot demonstrate the validity of the convictions of theology, though it can clarify their meaning once they enter the purview of our vision. In theology, reason is a tool, a vehicle to be utilized for the clarification of what is already believed, but it is not truth personified. Like any tool, it can either improve or damage the entity to which it is applied.

While a Jewish theology need not be systematic, correlative with philosophy, or rationalistic to be valid, it does require coherence. A lack of coherence is a danger to the formulation of a valid theology. As Louis Jacobs observes, "loose and woolly thinking in the area of religion can lead to a glorification of the absurd . . . Holy nonsense is still nonsense."[46] While a theology can be personal and reflective of the particular style and approach of the individual theologian, it cannot become an exercise in abstract expressionism, comprehensible only to its author.

A major purpose of theological discourse is to communicate a vision, a stance, a perspective out of the collision between traditional wisdom and contemporary situations and events. A theology of Judaism that does not communicate is like a messenger who is unable to deliver the message. Such a theology proves mute and unavailing.

Contemporaneity

While the theologian is not charged with the initial creation of tradition, he or she is required to re-create the tradition from the raw materials bequeathed by the past. According to a midrashic analogy, the theologian is obliged "to derive flour from wheat, a garment from flax."[47] The theologian is challenged with vesting the bequest of tradition with new meaning, with liberating meanings implicit in pregnant sacred texts. The theologian is a midwife whose vocation is to bring forth new life from the womb of tradition.[48] For the Jewish theologian erudition is a vestibule, not a final destination. Medieval Jewish writers compared the erudite scholar who had amassed much learning but who had not grasped its meaning or its implications to a "donkey carrying books."[49]

In medieval Jewish literature, the consonants of the Hebrew alphabet are compared to a body and the vowels to a soul.[50] Yet, a Torah scroll is written only with consonants. Indeed, a vocalized Torah scroll is unfit for ritual use.[51] The Torah requires a *person* to supply the vowels, the vocalization, the soul, in order for it to become animate, alive, heard.[52] Without the person, the sacred text remains mute. Without the theologian to animate it, to provide it with a voice, tradition might otherwise remain inert. A task of the theologian is to provide the traditions of the past with a channel, with a means of speaking to the present, and with a vehicle for being transmigrated and transmitted into the future.

By providing the Torah with a voice, with animation, the theologian thereby becomes a co-author of the Torah, a collaborator with God in perpetuating and in helping to augment and to amplify in the present the voice once heard at Sinai.[53] As Meir Ibn Gabbai wrote, "Even the sages who arise in each generation receive that which is granted from Sinai. . . . If new teachings [regarding the understanding of the Torah] are produced daily, this proves that the fountain [of revelation] ever gushes forth and that the great voice [from Sinai] sounds forth without interruption."[54]

According to a midrash quoted by Ibn Gabbai, "Not only did all the prophets receive their prophecy at Sinai, but also each of the sages who arose in each generation received his wisdom from Sinai."[55] As a hasidic master put it:

> Everything depends upon the interpretation of the rabbis. . . . Until they had interpreted it, the Torah was not considered complete, but only half-finished; it was the rabbis, through their interpretations, who made the Torah whole. Such is the case for each generation and its leaders; they complete the Torah. The Torah is interpreted in each generation according to that generation's needs, and according to the soul-root of those who live at that time. God thus enlightens the sages of the generation in [the interpretation of] His holy Torah. He who denies this is as one who denies the Torah itself.[56]

Judah Loew of Prague observed that in the blessing over the Torah, God is not described as having *given* the Torah, but as *giving* the Torah (*notein ha-Torah*) because the Torah is continuously being given, is perpetually being revealed.[57] Judah Loew's brother, Hayyim ben Betzalel of Friedberg said further that "this blessing is stated all in the present tense because He is *still* giving us His Torah each day, since each person is able to introduce new meanings into it, provided they are correlative with the roots of observance and faith."[58] As Isaiah Horowitz wrote, "The scholars produce new words [in the understanding of the Torah] or derive them through the power of their insight. But all of it was contained in the power of that voice that was heard at the revelation; and now the time has come for them to bring it from potentiality into actuality through the efforts of their mediation. . . . It thus follows that while we say of God that 'He has *given* the Torah,' He can also be designated in every present time as 'the One who *gives* the Torah.' "[59]

According to some of the Jewish mystics, though the Torah that God gives is the same Torah for all, each individual may understand it in his or her own particular way, according to the manner peculiar to his or her individual "soul-root." From this perspective, the process of the re-discovery and re-creation of the initial revelation rooted at Sinai is a profoundly personal and individual endeavor.[60] As Louis Jacobs observes, "Every writer on the subject [of Jewish theology] can only repeat what the Jewish preachers of old were fond of saying when they squarely faced the question: Who am I to preach to others? They protested: I am speaking to myself. If others wish to overhear what I say, I cannot object. . . ." As Jacobs puts it, "While the historian asks what has happened in the Jewish past, the theologian asks the more personal question: what in traditional Jewish religion continues to shape my life as a Jew in the here and now . . . the task [of the theologian is] discovering what it is that a Jew can believe in the present."[61]

The individual human being is perpetually engaged in a process of self-understanding, self-discovery. The Jewish theologian is a person continuously engaged in the endeavor to understand his or her existence as a Jew. A critical component of this process is continuous understanding, discovery and re-discovery of the Torah, of that which is rooted in the initial revelation at Sinai. Once the Torah has been incorporated and assimilated into the self, the Jewish theologian's quest for understanding the Torah and his or her quest for self merge into a single endeavor. Since, as the Jewish mystics teach us, "God, Torah and Israel are one," the quest for self and for Torah is inextricably related to the quest for the divine.[62] Thus, the Jewish theologian is one engaged in the perpetual task of self-understanding within the context of the Torah—the tradition, as well as within the context of a specific moment in time and space. The theologian is charged with realizing the challenge posed by a midrash, "Let the Torah never be for you an antiquated decree . . . but as a decree issued this very day."[63] The theologian takes inherited notes and re-composes them into a new song for his or her own age. In so doing, the theologian heeds the words of the psalmist: "Sing unto the Lord a new song" (Ps. 96:1).

Theology as Artform

Study of the Torah aims not merely at a conveyance of information to its reader, but at the transformation of its reader. The transformed and re-created reader can engender a re-created and re-imagined theology of Judaism. From this perspective, it might be more appropriate to compare theology to art rather than to science. Science can examine the physical content of a piece of art, for example, but it is incapable of elucidating its continued meaning.[64]

To reduce aesthetics to subjectivity would be a mistake. Like the aesthetic dimension, the religious dimension is objectively present in the world. Like art, it requires a certain sensitivity to be appreciated and to be understood. It is objective and subjective at the same time. One must invest some of oneself to understand a great work of art. However, while one need not be an artist to be inspired by great art, one must become an artist in order to produce art. Similarly, one need not be a theologian to study or to understand the teachings of the Torah, but one must become a theologian in order to re-create Torah.

According to Scripture, Bezalel, who built the Tabernacle, was the first Jewish artist. The Talmud observes that Bezalel "knew how to combine the letters by which the heavens and the earth were created."[65] In other words, theological creativity derives from the ability to create new meanings from old texts. A Jewish theology offers new portraits, recreated visions, re-imagined descriptive narratives of the meaning of Judaism in general, and of specific issues of Jewish theological concern in particular. Out of the raw materials of tradition, the theologian must produce a narrative portrait of Judaism that is both authentic and communicable.[66]

While "descriptive theology" would constitute the major form of Jewish theological discourse, philosophical theology is also required. The task of philosophical theology would be to continuously refine, clarify, and sharpen the focus of "descriptive theology" in order better to convey to others the meaning of theologies composed by past and present Jewish theologians. In this view, theology operates simultaneously on three levels. The foundation level consists of the resources of sacred Jewish literature and the personal faith experiences of the individual theologian as a committed member of a faith-community. The primary level consists of the descriptive but authentic reformulation in a coherent and contemporary idiom of those resources and experiences.[67] The secondary level consists of the sharpening of the focus of the vision derived from the other two levels. In this sense, philosophical theology is derivative rather than primary. "Descriptive theology" rooted in faith and tradition remains primary. Without "descriptive theology," philosophical theology, despite its penchant for clarity, remains a roof hanging in air, destined to collapse for lack of a foundation.[68]

Communal Acceptance

Experience of the life of faith precedes theological speculation. The faith commitment and the experience of faith of the individual theologian ultimately derives from participation in a living faith-community. In the final analysis, it is that faith-community which will either incorporate or veto the theological views of a given theologian. Unless it acquires some form of communal acceptance, a theology of Judaism may prove to be authentic, coherent, and contemporaneous, but will nonetheless remain barren and ineffectual. Acceptance by the faith-community means inclusion into the ever-expanding canon of tradition.[69]

"Communal acceptance" does not infer acceptance by a consensus of the Jewish community as a social unit. In the biblical period, the consensus among Jews to worship the idol Baal did not mean that the authentic religion of biblical Israel was, or could ever be Baalism, for idolatry is outside of the boundaries of possible Jewish theological options. Rather, communal acceptance relates to acceptance by Jews who are not simply "Jewish" by birth, but by those who constitute the believing community, the *faith*-community, i.e., those committed to the vocation of the people of Israel. The vocation of the Jewish people as a faith-community is divine service as understood by the Torah. As Arthur Cohen put it, "Theology, of necessity, addresses the supernatural vocation of the Jew. When the Jewish vocation is abandoned, not theology but religious sociology takes over."[70]

Acceptance or rejection by the majority of Jews, or by the "organized" secular Jewish community which formulates "Jewish" views and policies by group consensus, is irrelevant to the Jewish theologian. Such acceptance or rejection is not germane to the validity of a theology of Judaism he or she may formulate. The communal role of the Jewish theologian today is more likely to be subversive than supportive of the Jewish communal agenda. The commitment of the Jewish theologian is not organizational but theological. The theologian's ultimate obligation, like that of Judaism itself, is service to God. When the theologian perceives Jewish communal existence to be out of sync with Jewish theological conviction, his or her subversive role becomes activated.

An End-Note

Finally, how can the uninitiated know upon whom to rely in the quest for a valid Jewish theology? In this regard, the Talmud provides what might be considered a tentative answer, a conclusion held in abeyance until the four criteria for a valid Jewish theology outlined above can be applied to an individual Jewish theologian's work. The Talmud advises:

> If someone tells you,
> "I have labored but not found,"
> do not believe him.
> If he says, "I have not
> labored, but I have found,"
> do not believe him.
> But, if he says, "I
> have labored and have found,"
> then believe him.[71]

Notes

1. On Judaism as a way of thinking, see e.g., Solomon Schechter, *Studies in Judaism* (New York: Meridian, 1958), p. 103; idem, *Seminary Addresses and Other Papers* (New York: Burning Bush Press, 1959), p. 200; Abraham Joshua Heschel, *The Insecurity of Freedom* (New York: Farrar, Straus and Giroux, 1966), p. 217; idem, *God in Search of Man* (New York: Harper and Row, 1955), p. 14.
2. Though these criteria for a valid Jewish theology are similar to those proposed by Jacob Neusner, my description and understanding of them differs from his. Furthermore, my proposed methodologies for composing a theology of Judaism differ substantially from those which Neusner suggests. See Jacob Neusner, "The Tasks of Theology in Judaism," *The Journal of Religion* 59:1 (1979): 71–86.
3. For want of a better English term I am obliged to use the term "theology" despite its inappropriateness when dealing with the nature and implications of Jewish faith. Etymologically, the term means "the study of God," or "divine discourse." However, Jewish teachings emphasize that the nature of God is beyond the ken of human understanding or analysis. We can only speak about the ideas, perceptions and experiences of God that we might have and that the classical sources discuss. The real subject of theology is not God per se, but the human relationship with the divine, and the nature and implications of religious faith. Compare St. Thomas Aquinas, *Summa Theologica* I,1 where theology is considered a way of knowing God as He knows Himself.

The medieval Jewish philosophers simply translated the Greek terms that considered theology "divine knowledge" or "divine science" into Hebrew, e.g., *limud elohi, hokhmah elohit, torat ha-elohut, mada ha-elohi*. In modern Hebrew, the term "theology" (*teiologica*) is used. A viable alternative might be use of the term suggested by Abraham Isaac Kook in his *Orot ha-Kodesh: "hokhmat ha-Kodesh*," "sacred knowledge" or "knowledge of the sacred." See Samuel S. Cohon, *Jewish Theology* (Assen: Royal Vangorcum, 1971), p. 9.

I believe it incorrect to maintain that theology is new to Judaism. See e.g., S. Daniel Breslauer, "Alternatives in Jewish Theology," *Judaism* 30:2 (Spring 1981): 234 and Cohon, p. 5.

4. On the issue of authenticity and tradition in Jewish theology, compare Gershom Scholem, "Reflections on Jewish Theology," in his *On Jews and Judaism in Crisis* (New York: Schocken, 1976), pp. 261–298.

5. On the use in Jewish literature of the expression "a dwarf on the shoulders of a giant," see e.g., Dov Zlotnick, *"Al Makor ha-Mashal ha-Nanas ve-ha-Anak ve-Gilgulav," Sinai* 77 (1975): 184–189; Hillel Levine, "Dwarfs on the Shoulders of Giants: A Case Study in the Impact of Modernization on the Social Epistemology of Judaism," *Jewish Social Studies* 40:1 (Winter 1978): 68–72; Byron L. Sherwin, *In Partnership with God: Contemporary Jewish Law and Ethics* (Syracuse, N.Y.: Syracuse University Press, 1990), pp. 1–5.

6. Shneur Zalman of Liady, *Lekutei Amarim [Tanya]* (Brooklyn: Otzar ha-Hasidim, 1965), chap. 5, pp. 18–19.

7. Mordecai of Chernobyl, *Lekutei Torah* (New York: Noble Printing Co., 1954), *"Le-Rosh ha-Shana,"* p. 22b.

8. See e.g., John Macquarrie, *Principles of Christian Theology* (New York: Scribner's, 1966), p. 5; D. S. Adam, "Theology," *Encyclopedia of Religion and Ethics*, 12 vols. (New York: Scribner's, 1908), vol. 12, p. 294; Cohon, p. 29; Louis Jacobs, *A Jewish Theology* (New York: Behrman House, 1973), p. 1; Bernard Bamberger, *The Search for Jewish Theology* (New York: Behrman House, 1978), p. 5.

9. On the relationship between Jewish theologies of revelation and approaches to Jewish law, see e.g., Sherwin, pp. 16–47; Jacobs, pp. 199–230. For a definitive study of theological issues discussed throughout the literature of halakhic responsa, see Louis Jacobs, *Theology in the Responsa* (London: Routledge and Kegan Paul, 1975). In his preface, Jacobs writes, "One result of this investigation is to give the lie to the view that Jewish theology is un-Jewish and that the Halakhist concentrates solely on the deed ignoring the beliefs that provide the deed with its sanction and infuse it with life."

10. See *P. Berakhot* 1:2; *Leviticus Rabbah* 35:7.

11. See *Berakhot* 57a, *Pesahim* 49b and *Sifre on Deuteronomy*, ed. Meir Friedmann (Vienna, 1865), para. 345 on Deut. 33:4.

12. Samuel of Uceda, *Midrash Shmuel* (Jerusalem: Brody-Katz, N.d.), pp. 61a–b.

13. Zohar II, 94b.

14. Moses Hayyim Ephraim of Sudylkow, *Degel Mahaneh Ephraim* (Jerusalem: Hadar, 1963), *"Aharei,"* p. 175.

15. See *Sifre on Deuteronomy*, para. no. 345, n. 8.

16. I obviously reject that longstanding view, rooted in Aristotle and developed in medieval and modern Christian theology, that considers theology as a science. See e.g., Adam, pp. 293–295.

17. For further discussion and documentation, see Sherwin, pp. 4–8.

18. See Gershom Scholem, "The Science of Judaism—Then and Now," chap. in his *The Messianic Idea in Judaism* (New York: Schocken, 1971), pp. 306–307.

19. *Pesahim* 6b.

20. Samuel of Uceda, pp. 61a–b. See also, José Faur, *Golden Doves with Silver Dots* (Bloomington, Indiana: Indiana University Press, 1986), p. 14.

21. In his *Dialoghi d'Amore*, Leone Ebreo distinguishes between lust which can be satisfied and

love which cannot. Lust can be quenched while love continues to regenerate itself. See Leone Ebreo, *The Philosophy of Love*, trans. F. Friedberg-Seeley and Jean H. Barnes (London: Soncino, 1937), p. 56.

22. Samuel of Uceda, p. 60b.
23. Judah Loew, *Netivot Olom*, 2 vols. (New York: Judaica Press, 1969), vol. 1, p. 32. The blessing derives from *Berakhot* 11a.
24. See Heschel, *God in Search of Man*, p. 280.
25. On "expansive" and "restrictive" notions of "Torah," see Abraham J. Heschel, *Torah min ha-Shamayim, vol. 2* (London: Soncino, 1965), pp. 220–264, 360–417.
26. See *Leviticus Rabbah* 22:1, and discussion of this text in Heschel, *Torah, vol. 2* pp. 236–237.
27. *Sifre on Deuteronomy*, para. 333. For parallels, see *Sifre*, ed. Louis Finkelstein (New York: The Jewish Theological Seminary, 1969), pp. 265–266, n. 13. Note, Faur, p. xv.
28. On the Torah as a multifaceted mirror, see *Pesikta Rabbati*, ed. Meir Friedmann (Vienna: Heraugebers, 1880), p. 100b. On the seventy "faces" of the Torah, see *Numbers Rabbah* 13:15. See also the discussion of Moshe Idel, "Infinities of Torah in Kabbalah," chap. in ed. Geoffrey Hartman and Sanford Budick, *Midrash and Literature* (London: Yale University Press, 1986), pp. 141–157. Idel maintains that beginning with late thirteenth-century Jewish mysticism the notion that the Torah has infinite meanings was introduced. Previously, the view that there are many but a limited reservoir of meanings pervaded. On infinite meanings, see also Gershom Scholem, "The Meaning of the Torah in Jewish Mysticism," chap. in his *On the Kabbalah and Its Symbolism* (New York: Schocken, 1965), pp. 50–86.
29. *Ethics of the Fathers* 3:15. For the notion of "principles" (*ikkarim*) as boundaries, see e.g., Julius Guttmann, "The Principles of Judaism," *Conservative Judaism* 14:1 (Fall 1959): 1–3; Seymour Siegel, "The Unity of the Jewish People," *Conservative Judaism* 42:3 (Spring 1990): 21–28. On "principles" as dogmas, see Menachem Kellner, *Dogma in Medieval Jewish Thought* (London: Oxford University Press, 1986).
30. As has been noted above, it is assumed that the Jewish theologian is committed to Judaism. This leads to the propriety of the theologian choosing among various theological options within the parameters of Jewish faith to design his or her own personal variation of Jewish theology. As Louis Jacobs puts it so well, "The whole question of whether one can choose within Judaism only arises if one has first chosen Judaism." See Louis Jacobs, *Faith*, (New York: Basic Books, 1968), p. 175.

The approach outlined above obviates the need for the type of "experiential" theology advocated by Breslauer, for the "open Jewish theology" advocated by Kaufman, and for the personalist "open traditionalism" advocated by Borowitz. Each of these authors, in my view, tends to see Jewish theology in its earlier sense as being too systematic, "closed," and monolithic. Kaufman, for example, calls for a "theology of clarification rather than a dogmatic [systematic] theology." But as is discussed here, Jewish theology need not be either systematic or dogmatic. Borowitz sets up a tension between traditionalism and existentialism, between Jewish tradition and individual choice. However, once the individual can act as the ultimate arbiter of what Jewish theology may be, then the authority of tradition is undermined and a claim to authenticity becomes problematic. My contention is that the broad boundaries offered by Jewish religious literature and the absence of a central theological authority like the Catholic curia, provide the means for variety and multiplicity for the formulation of an authentic though "open" Jewish theology. Moving blatantly outside its broad parameters would deny authenticity to a theological formulation of Judaism. Just as American constitutional law cannot admit the propriety of certain concepts and options and still remain valid and authentic, a Jewish theology cannot exceed its broad boundaries and continue to remain valid and authentic. In other words, a Jew cannot formulate any theology he or she wishes and consider it a valid Jewish theology. This would invite anarchy if not heresy. See Breslauer; William Kaufman, *Contemporary Jewish Philosophies* (New York: Reconstructionist Press,

1976), p. 7; Eugene Borowitz, *A New Jewish Theology in the Making* (Philadelphia: Westminster Press, 1968), pp. 208–209.

31. Cohon, Samuel S. *Jewish Theology* (Assen: Royal Vangorcum, 1971), p. 43.

32. For example, despite his legion attempts to distinguish Jewish theology from Christian theology, Kaufmann Kohler's pioneering work, *Jewish Theology: Systematically and Historically Considered*, originally published in 1918 (2nd ed.: New York: Ktav, 1968), is heavily influenced by contemporary Protestant thought. Despite his insistence that Jewish theology be systematic, he fails in the attempt to present it as such.

33. From a letter from Schechter to Max Heller, quoted in Sefton Tempkin, "Solomon Schechter and Max Heller," *Conservative Judaism* 16 (Winter 1962): 55.

34. On the historical function and present problematics of natural theology and on the role of reason in Christian theology, see Macquarrie, pp. 39–48.

35. See Solomon Schechter, *Aspects of Rabbinic Theology* (New York: Macmillan, 1909), pp. 13–14: "The rabbis show a carelessness and a sluggishness in the application of principles which must be most astonishing to certain minds which seem to mistake merciless logic for God-given truths. . . . It will, therefore, suggest itself that any attempt at an orderly and complete system of Rabbinic theology is an impossible task. . . ."

   On coherence without systematic thinking as a feature of rabbinic theology, see e.g., Max Kadushin, *Organic Thinking* (New York: Bloch, 1938), pp. 1–3, and, idem, *The Rabbinic Mind* (New York: Jewish Theological Seminary, 1952), pp. 11–26. According to Heschel, though rabbinic thought is not systematic, it nevertheless represents a cohesive world-view that must be elicited from the corpus of rabbinic literature. See Abraham J. Heschel, *Torah min ha-Shamayim, vol. 1* (London: Soncino, 1962), p. viii. It is significant that Heschel translated the title of this work as "*Theology* of Ancient Judaism." Compare Steven Schwarzschild's unsubstantiated contention that a systematic rabbinic theology is not only desirable but possible. See Menachem Kellner, ed., *The Pursuit of the Ideal: Jewish Writings of Steven Schwarzschild* (Albany: SUNY Press, 1990), p. 293, n. 64.

36. See Kaufman, p. 7.

37. On polarity in Jewish thought, see e.g., Heschel, *Insecurity of Freedom*, pp. 135–137.

38. See e.g., *Midrash Temurah*, printed in *Agadat Bereshit* (Warsaw: Levensohn, 1876), chap. 1, p. 49a; Zohar II, 69b (top). The Zohar's configuration of the *sefirot* articulates the polarity of "male" and "female" potencies. On the critical role of polarity in the thought of Judah Loew of Prague, see Byron L. Sherwin, *Mystical Theology and Social Dissent* (London: Oxford University Press, 1982), pp. 70–75 and sources noted there. Compare the notions of polarity as a way to apprehending truth in Morris Raphael Cohen, *Reason and Nature* (New York: Harcourt Brace, 1931), p. 165; Alan Watts, *The Two Hands of God* (New York: Collier, 1969).

39. Judah Loew, *Hiddushei Aggadot*, 4 vols. (New York: Judaica Press, 1969), vol. 2, p. 89.

40. See e.g., Bamberger, p. 30.

41. In this regard, Emil Fackenheim notes, "the attempted fusion of theology with either philosophy or science is a confusion. As regards the specific tasks of Jewish theology, it is apriori evident, not only that this is a confusion, but that it is a confusion fatal to the tasks of Jewish theology. For the categories of philosophy and science are, one and all, universal, but from such universal categories no conclusions can be derived which might be a theological justification of the particular existence of the Jewish people." See Emil Fackenheim, *Quest for Past and Future* (Boston: Beacon, 1968), p. 99.

42. Heschel, *God in Search of Man*, pp. 14–15, 23 n. 8.

43. Levi ben Gershon (Gersonides), *Milhamot ha-Shem* (Leipzig, 1866), p. 150. See Norbert Samuelson, "Philosophic and Religious Authority in the Thought of Maimonides and Gersonides," *Central Conference of American Rabbis Journal* 16:4 (October 1969): 31–43.

   Philosophy was considered superfluous at best and an entrée to heresy at worst by many Jewish thinkers. I hope elsewhere to demonstrate that if most of Jewish philosophical literature were discarded, it would have had little substantial impact on the development of Jewish religious thought. As a largely elitist endeavor, Jewish philosophical speculation had little lasting impact on Jewish life, unlike Jewish mysticism that did. The criteria discussed below of acceptance by the faith-community would historically disqualify much of medieval Jewish philosophical thought from claiming to be a valid expression of Jewish theology.

44. Bahya ibn Pakudah, *The Book of Direction to the Duties of the Heart*, trans. Menahem M. Mansoor (London: Routledge and Kegan Paul, 1973), p. 113.

45. "Rationality" has a wide variety of possible meanings. See e.g., Bryan Wilson, *Rationality* (New York: Harper and Row, 1971). See Bamberger, p. 4; Heschel, *God in Search of Man*, p. 20; Jacobs, *Faith*, pp. 41–65, 201–209.

46. Jacobs, *A Jewish Theology*, p. 5.

47. *Seder Eliyahu Rabbah ve-Seder Eliyahu Zuta*, ed. Meir Friedmann (Vienna: Ahiyasaf, 1904), "*Zuta*" chap. 2, p. 172.

48. See e.g., Faur, pp. 122–123; Moshe Idel, *Kabbalah: New Perspectives* (New Haven: Yale University Press, 1988), p. 215.

49. On the expression, "a donkey carrying books," see Israel Davidson, *Otzar ha-Mashalim ve-ha-Pitgamim* (Jerusalem: Mosad ha-Rav Kook, 1969), no. 2851, p. 171, n. 39.

50. See e.g., *Sefer ha-Bahir*, ed. Reuven Margaliot (Jerusalem: Mosad ha-Rav Kook, 1951), no. 115, p. 51. Note Judah Halevi, *Kuzari*, trans. Hartwig Hirschfield (New York: Schocken, 1964), 4:3, p. 202.

51. See e.g., Joseph Karo, *Shulhan Arukh–Yoreh Deah* 274:7.

52. See David ibn Zimra, *Teshuvot ha-Radbaz*, 4 vols. (Furth, 1781), vol. 3, no. 643, p. 43b. See discussion in Faur, pp. 136–138; Idel, *Kabbalah*, pp. 214–215, and sources noted there.

53. See, for example, the interpretation of the talmudic phrase "a partner in the work of creation" (*Sabbath* 10a) in the beginning of Jacob ben Asher's *Arba'ah Turim—Hoshen Mishpat* where scholars of any generation who correctly interpret the Torah and declare a correct legal judgment are considered God's partners in the work of creation. On the human being as co-author of the Torah, see Idel, *Kabbalah*, p. 215; Faur, p. 123.

54. Meir ibn Gabbai, *Avodat ha-Kodesh* (Jerusalem: Levin-Epstein, 1954), part 3, chap. 23, pp. 85b–86a.

55. *Exodus Rabbah* 28:6; see also *Midrash Tanhuma [ha-Nidpas]* (Jerusalem: Levin-Epstein, 1964), "*Yitro*," no. 11, p. 96.

56. Moses Hayyim Ephraim of Sudlykow, "*Bereshit*," p. 6.

57. Judah Loew, *Netivot Olom*, vol. 1, p. 32.

58. Hayyim ben Bezalel, *Sefer ha-Hayyim* (Jerusalem: Weinfeld, 1968), "*Sefer Zechuyot*," 1:1, p. 4.

59. Isaiah Horowitz, *Shnei Luhot ha-Brit* (Jerusalem: Edison, 1960), vol. 1, "*Beth David*," pp. 39a–b (pp. 25b–26a in the Amsterdam edition).

60. See e.g., Hayyim Vital, *Shaar ha-Gilgulim* (Jerusalem: Eshel, 1963), chap. 17, p. 48. Note Scholem, *On the Kabbalah*, p. 65 and sources noted there.

61. Jacobs, *A Jewish Theology*, pp. 6, 1. As Monford Harris notes, "an authentic Jewish theology always speaks in terms of specific historic situations." See Harris, "Interim Theology," *Judaism* 7:4 (Fall 1958): 305. For Harris (p. 302), "The existence in the world of Jewish existence and how each Jew is to link his private existence to Jewish existence sets into motion a *Jewish* theological enterprise."

62. On "God, Torah and Israel," see e.g., Abraham J. Heschel, "God, Torah and Israel," chap. in ed. E. L. Long and R. Handy, *Theology and Church in Times of Change* (Philadelphia: Westminster, 1970), pp. 71–90; Isaiah Tishbi, "*Kudsha Berikh hu, Oraita ve-Yisrael—had hu*," *Kiryat Sefer* 50 (1975): 480–492, 668–674.

63. *Pesikta de-Rav Kahana*, ed. Solomon Buber (Lyck: Mekitzei Nirdamim, 1868), p. 102a.

64. As in any analogy, there are similarities and differences between the two things compared. In

that theology demands commitment while aesthetics and art do not, the analogy cannot apply. See Bamberger, p. 87. On Judaism as an artform, see e.g., Alan Lazaroff, "Judaism as an Art," *Judaism* 30 (Summer 1981): 355–363; Sherwin, *In Partnership*, pp. 9–15.

65. *Berakhot* 55a.

66. Compare the similar model for Christian theology advocated by Macquarrie, p. 50. I believe that while for Christian theological discourse, descriptive theology is a departure (as Macquarrie suggests), for Jewish theology it would represent continuity with the past, particularly with regard to biblical, midrashic, kabbalistic, and late medieval and early modern East European traditional Jewish literature.

67. On the level of "unreflective faith," see e.g., Schechter, *Aspects of Rabbinic Theology*, p. 12; Heschel, "Depth-Theology," chap. in his *The Insecurity of Freedom*, pp. 115–126.

68. This approach reflects the influence of phenomenological method with its three levels of inquiry: the pre-reflective, the descriptive and the reflective. It also reflects the influence of my mentor Abraham Heschel who utilized phenomenological method. For a similar approach utilizing phenomenological method in Christian theology, see Macquarrie, pp. 30–36. In my view, this approach merely states in another way what many Jewish thinkers have been doing throughout the ages. However, while many Jewish thinkers not profoundly influenced by Jewish philosophy developed what is called here a "descriptive theology," Jewish philosophers utilized philosophical theology. The utilization of both would seem well advised. Cohon's, p. 27, observation that "even when employing the methods of philosophy, the theologian utilizes them in a somewhat different way and with a different object in mind," is relevant here.

69. See e.g., Faur, p. 108.

70. Arthur A. Cohen, *The Natural and the Supernatural Jew* (New York: McGraw Hill, 1964), p. 288. See also Cohen, "Theology," chap. in ed. Arthur A. Cohen and Paul Mendes-Flohr, *Contemporary Jewish Religious Thought* (New York: Charles Scribner's Sons, 1987), pp. 971–981. Neusner distinguishes between Jews and "Judaists," the latter term denoting members of the Jewish faith-community. See Neusner, p. 73.

71. *Megillah* 6b.

Part II

Classical Theologians in the Twentieth Century: Approaches to God

The Context and Topics of Modern Jewish Thought

The massive migration of European Jews to America, the Holocaust, and the establishment of the State of Israel were undoubtedly the most critical Jewish events during the first sixty years of the twentieth century, and many of the articles in this volume will attest that Jewish thinkers are still grappling with the impact of those events. Some of the major Jewish thinkers living during those years began to address the implications of those events—as, for example, Mordecai Kaplan's proposal to create an integrated Jewish community (a *kehillah*) in Western countries where religious affiliation and action were voluntary, and, as another example, the various Zionist theories of people like Ahad Ha-Am (Asher Ginzberg), A. D. Gordon, and Rav Kook. Much of the thinking on the State of Israel, though, and all of the serious thought about the Holocaust were to wait until the 1960s and thereafter.

When we look, then, at what occupied serious Jewish thinkers during the first six decades of the twentieth century, we find primarily the same topics that occur in the work of nineteenth-century thinkers—namely, the efforts to explain why and how one should be Jewish in a post-Enlightenment world, where Jews are politically and legally free to opt out of Judaism entirely. The authority and process of Jewish law figure heavily in such discussions, as do discussions of Jewish particularity versus Jewish universalism. These are both subtopics of the larger issue that affected every Jew of the time—namely, how am I supposed to understand myself and act in a non-Jewish world that will tolerate me as a Jew but will welcome me even more if I accept its invitation to give up Judaism and assimilate with the majority? To put this another way, the questions Napoleon posed to the French Sanhedrin that he convened in 1807—questions that asked French Jews to choose between being Jews *or* Frenchmen—continued to dominate Jewish thought throughout the nineteenth century and the first half of the twentieth.

Along with political and philosophical innovations, the Enlightenment brought with it a new emphasis on science. No longer was human inquiry to be fettered by church authorities or by devotion to the scientific ideas of Aristotle. Unbridled commitment to free and open inquiry became the rule of the age, with the new capturing the heart and the mind much more than the old. Along with this new confidence in the human ability to know and control nature came immense optimism, symbolized perhaps most clearly by the many utopian theories that shaped Jewish as well as non-Jewish thought at the end of the nineteenth century and the beginning of the twentieth, with Zionism being perhaps the most obvious. The old world was a thing of the past; the new world would embody political freedom, universalism, and scientific discovery.

In the meantime, several influential thinkers had all suggested in different ways that God is only a projection of something human. God does not exist as an independent, powerful Being; God is rather our superego writ large (Sigmund Freud), or a symbol of our yearnings and feelings (Ludwig Feuerbach), or the emblem of the community and its authority (Emile Durkheim). To add insult to injury, during the late nineteenth century Julius Wellhausen formulated and popularized the documentary hypothesis, according to which the Torah could not be seen as the direct word of God and therefore as evidence of such a Being; the Torah was rather composed of four documents written by human beings for political purposes. Thus belief in God was being attacked not only for scientific reasons, but also on psychological, sociological, and textual grounds.

Why, then, should anyone believe in God anymore? Was religion not, as Karl Marx had suggested, simply "the opiate of the masses," with belief in God one of its crutches? Even a defender of religion like William James insisted that people needed to be "tough-minded" to be part of the modern world. Increasingly, as the twentieth century brought major advances in science, thinking in the modern mode required people to draw conclusions only from what they could experience with the five senses, not from abstract things like ideas or from wishes about what one might like the world to be. The public and repeated observation embodied in scientific method could give you firm knowledge. In contrast, sentences about God were, for analytic philosophers like Ludwig Wittgenstein and A. J. Ayer in the 1930s, only expressions of emotions. Even those philosophers more sympathetic to religion—people like Whitehead and Dewey—managed to save the meaning and honor of theological language only by reducing it to descriptions of what happens in natural processes. The end of the nineteenth century and the first sixty years of the twentieth were, in other words, not only an age of science, but of scientism, where every aspect of life could remain credible only if it could be transformed and governed by the rules of scientific method. Truth could be found only in that way.

It is no wonder, then, that Jewish thinkers living in this milieu spent considerable effort in trying to define and defend some version of Jewish belief in God. In light of that, we, as editors of this volume, have decided to use that topic to introduce some of the major figures in Jewish thought in the first six decades of the twentieth century. While the bulk of this book consists of selections from the last four decades, all of Jewish thought during that time responds in significant ways not only to the events of the twentieth century, but to the thinking propounded by the philosophical giants writing between 1900 and 1960, the thinkers whose work has by now become "classical." The choice of belief in God as the topic to be studied is fair to them, for they each spent considerable time articulating and justifying an approach to God, and it also has the advantage of being a perennial subject that speaks to human beings in ever new ways over time.

It should be noted that Christian theologians during this period were grappling with the same issues. Karl Barth, Paul Tillich, Rudolf Bultmann, Reinhold Niebuhr, and others fashioned their Christian theologies to respond to these same factors of modernity that were influencing Jews. Their understanding of the world also, of course, reflects their Christian backgrounds and commitments, and the real differences born out of those beliefs should not be masked in noting the many similarities that exist between the Christian and Jewish thinkers of this time.

The theologians discussed in this section of the book differ, in part, in their concept of God. Mordecai Kaplan does not believe in a supernatural God altogether, and the rest, while affirming belief in a supernatural God, differ in the aspects of God they emphasize. These differences in the substance of their views are not only a matter of their individual personalities or predilections; they derive from the varying *methods* these thinkers use to come to knowledge of God in the first place. The various theological epistemologies espoused by the thinkers of this section reflect, in turn, the varying ways in which philosophers in general during this time period described the most effective ways to gain knowledge of anything. The views of God we shall meet in this section, in other words, are yet another example of a common feature of Jewish thought throughout the ages—namely, that Jewish thinkers learn from both Jewish and non-Jewish philosophers about new modes of thinking and then apply those methods to their own interpretation of Judaism.

While we shall not summarize each of the readings in this book in our introductions to each section, we thought it appropriate to explain at least some of the primary features of the thought of the major figures in the first six decades of the twentieth century so that their influence on the thought of the last four decades will be clear. This is especially important because while the selections in this section of the book will focus on the topic of God, that is certainly not the only subject that preoccupied these thinkers or influenced their successors. In what follows, page numbers for quotations that appear in the selections of this volume will not be cited, but references will be included for quotations from other parts of an author's work.

Hermann Cohen (1842–1918)

Hermann Cohen devoted his early writings to a critique of idealism as embodied in the thought of Plato and, especially, Kant. He developed a new interpretation of Kant's philosophy which came to be known as the Marburg School of neo-Kantianism, as Cohen himself was a professor of philosophy at the University of Marburg from 1865 to 1912.

Kant had maintained that empirical objects exist but we can only know the sensations we have of them, not the "thing in itself," and so the function of our mind is to organize the sensations we perceive according to the categories of our minds. Cohen, in contrast, put forth the extreme idealistic thesis that thought produces everything out of itself. According to his "principle of origin," objects are constructs of thought, and God is no exception. Cohen conceived of God as the idea that guaranteed the eternity of the world. He therefore distinguishes sharply between being and existence: we learn about the existence of things through our senses, but we know of being through reason. All objects of our senses come into being and pass away; only reason can produce thoughts about eternity. For God to be eternal, therefore, God must be a thought produced by reason. This also explains God's uniqueness; the Jewish fight against pantheism, anthropomorphism, and dualism; and the ethical nature of God.

Monotheism is the correct preparation for morality in that it declares "that nature, that man himself, has no original worth, no worth of its own. If nature and man should be able to attain any worth at all, it could only be derived from the unique worth of God's being." No idolatry of any part of existence is then possible, for all value resides in God.

This also guarantees that the ethical ideal will survive the foibles and even the demise of humanity and ultimately be fulfilled.

This does not prevent God from motivating moral human behavior; on the contrary, the correlations between God and humanity through reason should prompt us to imitate God. So, for example, in Jewish depictions of God and in rational conceptions of the Eternal, God loves the stranger, for there is no rational reason to elevate one's own family or people over other human beings. The slow progress of people living in historical time may require that individuals join communities in order to learn how to be moral and that some communities serve as moral models for others. But from the perspective of God's eternity, all people are equal in God's sight, for they all have derived from God the value of being created in the Eternal's image. Therefore even though Judaism begins with the particularistic Covenant tenet, the Jewish idea of God pushes Jews to work for the ultimate, universalistic unity of all humanity. This Jewish view of God clearly refutes the views of people like the historian Treitschke who pictured Jews as condoning theft and deception of non-Jews, for the very God that Jews worship forbids them to be that narrow-minded. Moreover, this view of God makes Messianism the central ideal and goal of Judaism; indeed, Messianism arguably plays a greater role in Cohen's vision of Judaism than in any other Jewish theologian's, for Cohen thinks that Judaism's messianic ideal provides the goal for all else within the religion.

Cohen's move from Marburg to Berlin in 1912, his contacts with the Jews of Warsaw and Vilna, and his efforts in Berlin and Poland to establish institutes for adult Jewish education also changed his views of religion. While he had until then embraced the Kantian idea that religion ultimately is the maidservant of ethics, providing the educational, emotional, and communal structure to teach moral values, in his waning years he described a new, independent role for religion. Ethics is concerned with mankind in general; it does not take into account the lives, fears, and aspirations of individual people. Religion, in contrast, addresses the individual and "saves" him or her from overwhelming feelings of anguish and guilt through its concepts of sin, repentance, and salvation. This theory is expressed in an early form in his 1915 book, *The Concept of Religion in the System of Philosophy*, but it gains its full expression in his last book, published posthumously by his wife in 1919, entitled *The Religion of Reason Out of the Sources of Judaism*—the book from which our selection comes. Now God is no longer simply a concept of reason, like everything else; on the contrary, all reality is now rooted in God, including even human reason.

Cohen had thus shifted from an anthropocentric system to a theocentric system. God is pure being—"I am that I am" (Exodus 3:14), or, in Cohen's translation, "I am the One that is, I am the One that can be named in no other way than by 'I am' "—while the world is always in the lesser ontological state of becoming. The world nevertheless can exist in God's reality through "correlation"—that is, the changing world physically depends upon, and logically requires, the divine world of being. Becoming could not exist if there were not eternal existence to guarantee its reality. On the other hand, being would have no meaning were it not manifested in the world of becoming. God and man are separated by a wide gap, as are God and the world and each human being from every other; but each part of existence gains its identity and significance by being related to the others.

This correlation Cohen dubs *Ruah ha-Kodesh*, the Holy Spirit. That is not part of the reality of either God or a human being; it rather emerges from their *relationship*. The correlation is especially evident in a person's attempt to imitate God, the model and source of holiness, and to become "God's co-worker in the work of creation." While Cohen held to a liberal interpretation of Judaism, which emphasized its moral teachings, he vigorously affirmed the value of Jewish law as the vehicle for enabling people to function as God's co-workers. His Kantian roots are clear in his doctrine that *mitzvah* (commandment) is both law and duty—law emanating from God and duty from the viewpoint of human beings. God issued commandments to human beings—in particular, Jews—and people, of their own free will, take upon themselves the "yoke of the commandments." Cohen's individualism and emphasis on Judaism's moral norms resonate with the Reform Judaism of his time, but his championing the role of Jewish law in the life of a Jew makes him considerably more traditional than the Reformers of his time. Cohen's students, Buber and Rosenzweig, later debate this aspect of Cohen's thought, differing markedly on whether individual autonomy can and should be integrated with a commitment to Jewish law.

The ultimate, divine task for human beings is to establish the messianic era, when all humanity would be united, when justice would be assured, and when the poor would be provided for in a socialist economic system. To prepare the way for that, individual communities living together in peace and harmony and shaped by the messianic ideals would have to be established to serve as models for the all-inclusive, messianic community of mankind. The Jewish people is, in Cohen's view, the first and clearest model. Cohen rejected Zionism because the Jewish people must live among non-Jews to serve effectively as models for them. Cohen cites the words of the biblical prophet Micah to support his view: "The remnant of Jacob shall be in the midst of the many peoples, like dew from the Lord, like droplets on grass . . ." (Micah 5:6). While the Jewish people were the first to take on this role of a model people for the messianic age, Cohen believed that the spirit of the German community of his time shared much with the spirit of Judaism—a painful, ironic piece of his theory to all who live after the Holocaust.

Cohen interprets Judaism as ethical monotheism. The selection included in this volume discusses what he thinks monotheism means and why it is so important to believe in one, unique God.

Franz Rosenzweig (1886–1929)

The approach Cohen adopted late in his life sowed the seeds for the existentialist ideas of his students, Rosenzweig and Buber. For both of them, as for Cohen, general concepts must give way to recognizing the surd reality of the individual human being, and meaning emerges out of relationship. Both, however, differed from their teacher in that while Cohen was a neo-Kantian rationalist, Rosenzweig and Buber were existentialists, basing their thought not on reason but rather on the concrete experiences of individuals. Their theologies, though, focus on different relationships: for Rosenzweig, our understanding of God comes from the ways in which God relates to us—namely, through creation, revelation, and redemption; for Buber, our understanding of God comes from the ways in which we relate to each other in personal, "I-Thou" interactions.

Rosenzweig's chief work is *The Star of Redemption*, which he wrote on postcards from the German front during World War I. That may explain some of the disjointedness of the work; but at bottom, Rosenzweig's terse, abstract style is most to blame for the *Star*'s difficulty. It will therefore be useful to outline his theory of God in clearer language here.

In Book One of the *Star*, Rosenzweig, writing from the reality of "the war to end all wars," points out that the experience of death is completely private: however much we may be accompanied by others when we die, ultimately each of us dies as an individual.

This demonstrates that the attempts of philosophers over the ages to generalize all people's experiences to arrive at a conceptual framework for understanding all of reality is based on quicksand, for human experience is not abstract and general, but rather concrete and individual. In asserting this, Rosenzweig and the other existentialists of his time (Camus, Sartre, Buber, etc.) were especially objecting to Idealism, an approach that had been popular in the late nineteenth century and the early twentieth.

For Rosenzweig, then, our experience reveals many individual elements (that is, our experience is "manifold"), with three components being the primary ones: humanity, the universe, and God. Any attempt to reduce these three factors to one basic element must be rejected on the grounds that this does not conform to reality as we know it through our experience.

Thus seeing the world as one, as philosophers and mystics are wont to do, or seeing the world as composed of many, unrelated objects and powers, as pagans do, are both wrong: the truth instead is that humanity, the universe, and God are distinct but related entities. They are related in three ways: through creation, revelation, and redemption, topics that he explores in the remainder of the book. The three "pagan" elements of God, humanity, and the world comprise one triangle; their interactions of creation, revelation, and redemption another triangle; and when superimposed one upon the other they form "the star of redemption."

Once the limits of philosophy (especially Idealism) have been demonstrated by a focus on the individual, revelation becomes intellectually defensible, a point that Rosenzweig develops in Book Two of the *Star*. Revelation, for Rosenzweig, is initiated by God in order to relate, first, God to humanity, and then humanity to God, and finally humanity to the world. So understood, revelation is not an historical event, but rather a continuous entry of God into the experience of each individual person. God's willingness to do this is a manifestation of God's love. This divine love evokes a response of love in us toward God and, in turn, of each of us to our neighbor. The relationship between Jews and God is framed by commandments, which Rosenzweig discusses in the remainder of Book Two, and which he expands upon in his later correspondence with Buber.

In Book III, Rosenzweig dubs people's desire for the repetition and permanent reality of the revelatory experience as the search for the kingdom of God. The People Israel entered into this kingdom of eternity from the outset, as evidenced by the themes of creation-revelation-redemption that frame the evening, morning, and afternoon services of each Sabbath and the sacred round of the three Jewish pilgrimage festivals. That covenant with eternity is also manifest, according to Rosenzweig, in the fact that Jewish identity is determined by birth, not by attachment to a land in defense of which people give up their blood. (Rosenzweig, while not nearly as sanguine about German culture as Cohen was, nevertheless was not a Zionist, lest a devotion to re-establishing a Jewish homeland in Israel sacrifice this eternal aspect of Jewish identity, as Jewish blood is lost in the cause of nationalism—a phenomenon he had witnessed all too clearly in World War I.) The Jew thus lives as part of an eternal people through his or her identity through blood, the sign of life, and through Jewish liturgy and the Jewish religious calendar. Israel is thus outside the stream of history, while Christianity attempts to bring people to the Kingdom of God within history. Each is equally valid for its community (Rosenzweig's "two covenant theory"), although, for Rosenzweig, Judaism's way is the one God has chosen for His chosen elite. In any case, the truth of both will be superseded by the absolute truth in the "end of days."

It is that absolute truth that Rosenzweig tries to hint at in the beginning of Book Three, the selection below, in which he expounds his understanding of God. Invoking the talmudic doctrine that "the seal of the Holy One, blessed be He, is truth" (B. *Shabbat* 55a; B. *Yoma* 69b; B. *Sanhedrin* 64a), Rosenzweig begins this book with: "God is truth. Truth is his signet. By it he is known. And will be [known] even when one day all has come to an end . . . in eternity." We human beings, however, are temporal; we are born, we live, and we die. It is from that concrete experience that we recognize that the eternity of God makes him totally different from us: "There is eternal life only in contrast to the life of those who pave the eternal way [i.e., human beings], which is always exclusively temporal."

Our awareness of our temporality and God's eternity stimulates in us "a desire for eternity [that] sighs forth out of the well-pits of this temporality." We must, though, acknowledge the truth that life as we know it disappears; this is the light of understanding that God imparts to us, the truth that changes the very nature of our lives as we confront our mortality. (Think of the verse in Psalms 90:10, 12: "The span of our life is seventy years, or, given the strength, eighty years . . . Teach us to number our days so that we may obtain a wise heart." That is, the awareness of our impending death should teach us to value our lives, moment by moment. That is Rosenzweig's divine "light" of understanding.)

At the same time, though, we also recognize that while death reminds us of the "mute darkness of the protocosmos"—that is, the world before being created—life reminds us of the love of God that created us. "God is not life: God is light." That is, God is neither living nor dead, for those are categories that apply to temporal beings like us; indeed, to employ them with regard to God is "pagan" since that would imply that God, too, is temporal. Instead, God is the lord of life, lovingly granting life to the dead—that is, creating living creatures from dead matter and therefore, presumably, able to promise us redemption in some future existence. God, though, is neither dead nor alive; He exists eternally, "that tender point where life and death touch and blend." " We experience his existence directly only by virtue of the fact that he loves us and awakens our dead Self to [be a] beloved and requiting soul." That is, we experience God directly when we become aware of our having been created out of dead matter. "The revelation of divine love is the heart of the All"—that is, the awareness we gain of God's love in creating us and in the future promise of redemption is the heart of God's being and nature.

While we become aware of God through his creative love for us, God himself is not love. Love is the aspect of God open to us to know, but God's internal essence is concealed from us. "We catch sight of the Creator and the Redeemer only from the vantage point of the God of love. . . . [but] The purely Prior, the protocosmos created from of yore, is too dark for us to be able to recognize the Creator's hand in it. And the purely Posterior, the redeemed hypercosmos, is too bright for us to be yet able to see the Redeemer's countenance in it . . . " That is, what came before the creation of the universe ("the protocosmos created from of yore") and what will come at some future time when the world will be redeemed ("the purely Posterior, the redeemed hypercosmos") cannot be known by us but only hinted at through the revelation of God's love in our lives. The Revelation of divine love in our lives is thus what connects Creation to Redemption, and the revelation of divine love through our creation reveals the Creator and Redeemer to us, "to the extent that such manifestation is vouchsafed [to us] at all."

Knowing God through his creative act of love is only knowing God indirectly, through his actions, but that is the most we can know: "Revelation extends only as far back as the

Creator. Its first word is 'in the beginning,' its second 'there created' " (Genesis 1:1). We cannot know God's essence in itself, apart from his acts, or even in his acts before creating the universe. "Before the beginning there may have been that inner vitality of God which grew out of divine self-creation, self-revelation, self-redemption; we could only depict it analogically—by analogy, that is, to the authentic creation, revelation, redemption" that we know from our own, human experience. "To answer honestly [from our own experience] what he [God] might be, we would have to say: Naught"—that is, nothing created in the way we experience created existence. Rosenzweig quotes the Psalmist, "the gods of the heathens are naughts," to say that any depiction of God apart from what we know of God in our experience is false, naught, because it is not based on anything we can know. The true God stands above and apart from all our human attempts to picture Him.

While we cannot know about any divine creative act before the creation of our universe, and while God's loving creative act reveals to us the nature of *our* Redeemer, God has also revealed to us the nature of God's own redemption—namely, when God "frees himself from having anything confront him that is not he himself." That is, in the ultimate state of redemption for God, there is nothing that exists except God. This is the day that the prophets speak of, when God is One and his Name is One—that is, when there is nothing besides Him. This is also God's day of rest, his great Sabbath, when He stops creating. Jews who know God's eternal name—YHWH—are not allowed to pronounce it precisely because in that day of God's own redemption nothing will exist outside of him and therefore there will be no naming at all, for naming assumes differentiation among disparate objects, and in that day all will be one. "For the sake of our eternity, we must anticipate the silence in which it and we together will one day sink. We must substitute for the name itself that which God is as long as he is still called upon as one name among other names, as Creator of a world of being, as Revealer of a language of souls: The Lord." We may say, like the Psalmist, that God is "like the living" in comparison to the dead, for that is how God is manifest to us in our lives, but we must know that ultimately God is One, beyond life and death, encompassing all.

"Only Naughts can reign over a multipartite Naught"—that is, only false gods, or partial depictions of God, can be believed to reign over the many sections of the created world—but "over that one All only a One who still has room beside and above it. But what else still has room beside the one All as the consummate reality except—truth?" Here Rosenzweig returns to the talmudic doctrine with which he began—that the signet of God is truth—and begins his explanation of the epistemology of religion—that is, how claims about God can be judged true or false.

God is truth, as the Rabbis say, but truth is not God, for "God has to be 'more' than the truth, just as every subject is more than its predicate, every thing more than the conception of it." Rosenzweig here is proclaiming his existentialist epistemology over that of Idealism—i.e., that individual things (including God) are real, not concepts of them. He attacks the doctrine of Idealism that truth authenticates itself on the grounds that we all recognize that error occurs; therefore if we stipulate that truth authenticates itself, we would also have to maintain that untruth authenticates itself, and that undermines all grounds for our claims of knowledge. The "ground on which truth places itself with its own two feet" must therefore instead be a fact—that is, part of our experience that we trust. The philosophers' confidence in the intellect can only be justified when the intellect rests its claims on individual, empirical reality as experienced by the "whole man," not by reason alone.

Truth is not God, for truth rests on concrete experiences, and God is beyond all such finite experiences. Rather, the reverse is true—namely, as the Rabbis say, that God is truth, for truth is from God. This does not tell us anything about the essence of God except that "he is the primeval ground of truth and that all truth is truth only by virtue of deriving from him." Indeed, the only thing that we can know of God's essence, according to Rosenzweig, is that "God is himself the lucid light which elucidates truth"—that is, God makes it possible for us to know anything by enabling us to receive revelation, and thus "that he is truth tells us in the final analysis none other than that he—loves." Similar to the messages of the second blessing before the Shema in the traditional morning and evening Jewish liturgy, and the fourth blessing in the weekday Amidah, a core prayer said three times daily, God's giving us the ability to know His instruction is, for Rosenzweig, the ultimate sign of God's grace and love for us. But "even if truth is really the last and the only thing one can still declare of God and his essence, still there remains to God a surplus beyond his essence."

Another way to articulate the same truth, according to Rosenzweig, is to say that "God is the Naught." By this he means that it is impossible to describe the essence of God. No predicate (= "the Naught") can capture God's essence.

Rosenzweig rejects the converse of this proposition—namely the Buddhist idea that the Naught is God—because to say that would be to say that nothingness precedes God and that God, once existing, comes from nothingness. The subject of a sentence, after all, is the beginning point of one's consciousness, and to make the Naught the subject is to make all that follows in the predicate of the sentence dependent upon the Naught. That is just as false, for Rosenzweig, as to say that the truth is God—i.e., that God comes from the truth. God does not derive from anything, but is rather the very first reality. Therefore what is correct to say is the converse of both propositions—namely, that God is truth and that God is the Naught, for the subject of both of those sentences is God. Making God the subject of the sentence indicates that all things—including the truth and the nothingness that characterized everything before God began his creative act—come from God.

To say both of these things—that God is the truth and that God is the Naught—is to indicate, correctly, that we cannot know God's protocosmic essence—that is, God before the world was created—or God's hypercosmic essence—that is, God's essence after the world ceases to be. We can only know God through his actions in the here and now, in the middle time between the beginning of creation and its end: "We find ourselves in this middle, and find Him, the 'First and the Last,' by our side, in immediate proximity, as a man finds his friend." We know God not by intellectually coming to some definition of his essence, but rather through experiencing God in the empirical facts of his deeds—just as a man finds his friend.

The Idealists had tried to unite God, man, and the world through arriving at an intellectual conception of them, generalizing over their separate characteristics until they all appeared as different manifestations of one essence. The mystics had tried to arrive at the same kind of essential unity of all things, although through their own method of turning inward and trying to divorce oneself from the diversity of real things. "Only the dishonest cognition of Idealism, or the unclear experience of mysticism, can delude itself with having comprehended it [the All]." When one recognizes, instead, that we cannot know things in their essence but only through the way they behave in the factual world, then God, man, and the world must be seen as ultimately distinct entities. In themselves, they are unknowable, but they *can* be known through their interactions: "God appears to be concealed, man secluded, the world enchanted. What does become visible is their recip-rocal interaction. That which is here immediately experienced is not God, man, and the world, but creation, revelation, and redemption." When we experience those interactions through prayer and the cycle of the Jewish liturgical year, we can get a glimpse of the Eternal behind those facts, but we can only really know the immediate interactions of God, man, and the world. Through experiencing those interactions we learn the truth em-bedded in the God-created empirical world rather than "the blasphemy of philosophy—the truth in us," as if that were all there was to know. Rosenzweig's star, then—God, man, and the world joined by creation, revelation, and redemption—becomes the key to accu-rate human knowledge and to the meaning and significance of Jewish life as a way to ac-quire and enact that knowledge in our lives.

Martin Buber (1878–1965)

Hermann Cohen had been a neo-Kantian, and both Rosenzweig and Buber, Cohen's stu-dents, accepted Kant's doctrine that one could not know something in itself but only in the way it manifests itself to us. They disagreed, though, as to how that happens. For Rosenzweig, as we have seen, the ultimate basis of knowledge is what God enables us to know through creation, revelation, and redemption, while for Buber the primary ground of knowledge is our human interactions with each other and with the world around us.

Buber, in his famous typology, distinguishes between I–It relationships and I–Thou re-lationships. I–It relationships are those of use, where I use the It. The "It" in such rela-tionships might be inanimate objects, animals, or human beings, as, for example, when I hire someone to paint my house for me. In that case, I am using the painter to have my house painted, and he, in turn, is using me as a means of earning money. There is noth-ing wrong with having such I–It relationships; on the contrary, without them none of the practical ends of life could be accomplished.

If human beings have I–It relationships exclusively, though, then they cease to be dis-tinctly human. What marks the human being as human is the ability to have I–Thou re-lationships, in which there is equality, mutuality, openness, and presentness. Even rela-tionships with one's family and one's closest friends must, at times and in some respects, become I–It relationships, as, for example, when I ask my friend to pick me up so that we can both enjoy a ball game together. The object of that interaction is to set the stage for many I–Thou encounters, but I am using him in the process for transportation. While interhuman relationships are the clearest kinds of I–Thou relationships, Buber maintains that a person might have such a relationship with animals (consider a pet) or even with inanimate objects like a tree or a piece of artwork.

With God, though, the Eternal Thou, it is impossible to have an I–It relationship; our relationships with God, if authentic, are the closest we can get to pure I–Thou relation-ships. Many people, of course, mistakenly think that they can inveigle God into serving their ends through petitionary prayer or other means. That, though, is transforming God into an idol, making God your own servant. God, who normally transcends us, can only be properly approached in an I–Thou way, in the hope that God will consent to become an equal to us for the duration of that encounter. God may refuse; to cite the Psalmist, as Buber does, God may "hide His face" to us, as He did in terrible moments like the Holocaust. God may, though, engage us, and then, by virtue of who God is and who we are, it could only be in an I–Thou way. Petitionary prayer might be included in such a relationship, but it would have to be without any expectation that one could use God to supply one's ends.

We come to know God through our own, human, I–Thou interactions: "Every particular Thou is a glimpse through to the eternal Thou." We do not find God by staying in the world through observing it at a distance or through using it in I–It relationships, and we do not find God by leaving the world in some attempt to transcend the world in a mystic trance. We find God, instead, by reaching out to other people in I–Thou encounters. This prepares us psychologically and epistemologically for the experience of the ultimate relationship with God. "The inborn Thou [in each one of us] is realized in each relation [with another Thou] and consummated in none. It is consummated only in the direct relation with the Thou that by its nature cannot become It"—namely, God.

It is no accident that Buber concentrated in his published studies of Judaism on the biblical Prophets and on the Hasidim—two groups of Jewish leaders who reported direct relationships with God. It is also no accident that while Buber was a staunch Zionist from as early as the late 1800s, his was not a political form of Zionism (he opposed Herzl on this) nor an Orthodox religious form, but a utopian socialist form, where, in Buber's vision, communities would live together in direct personal relationships so that Zionism's "holy way" would differentiate it from other forms of nationalism. Buber's dialogue theory led him to argue for Jews forming the community in Palestine actively to seek to accommodate the needs of the Arabs, but, on the other hand, it also led him to criticize Christianity as encouraging much too passive a relationship with God. Judaism, in his view, properly modeled and stimulated people to encounter God on an active, equal, interactive plane—a stance that later led a number of Catholic and Protestant thinkers to reformulate their own understanding of Christianity to mirror Buber's understanding of Judaism.

Abraham Isaac Kook (1865–1935)

Kook, appointed the first Ashkenazi Chief Rabbi of modern Israel when the chief rabbinate was established in 1921, was also unique in being a deeply religious mystic who nevertheless participated actively in the broader social concerns of his time. Unlike the majority of Orthodox rabbis in his time and ever since, Kook actively engaged and loved secular Jews and was, in turn, loved by them. He also advocated a broad curriculum for Jewish religious education so that religious Jews might understand not only rabbinic texts but also the breadth of Jewish and general culture. Kook's religious base led him to criticize secular Zionism, which, in his view, was too concerned with the material needs of the new Jewish community in Israel. At the same time, the warmth and openness of his personality and the broad sweep of his interests led him to criticize the Orthodox of his time for being too narrowly concerned with rabbinic authority and with Jewish religious life.

Kook's openness to ideas and people who lived life differently from the way he did also marks Kook's philosophy, in which mysticism becomes for him not, as for most mystics, the demand and the method to remove oneself from this world, but rather the insight into the nature of God and the universe that propels one to care for all people and for all just causes. Mystic souls who aspire "to the most luminous light" often "cannot be content with that light which shines in the quality of justice in the best of good deeds, or in the measure of truth in the most precise body of knowledge, or in the attribute of beauty in the most exalted of visions. It then sees the world as trivialized." Such souls become weary both in their quest for God and in trying to live in this concrete world. The proper way to think about God and the world, Kook says, is to perceive "the divine dimension disclosed in the world, in all its phenomena of beauty and grandeur, as manifested in every living thing, in every insect, in every blooming plant and flower, in every nation and state . . . in the talents of all creatures . . . in the feelings of every sensitive spirit, and in the heroic deeds of every person of valor." The sage is more important than the prophet precisely because while the biblical prophets stood on a high moral plane and condemned all those who fell short of perfection, the sages (that is, the Rabbis) began from the bottom up, seeing the divine potential in every human being for returning to God in small, but significant steps.

The quest to leap over the individual, concrete manifestations of life to know God's essence in its most abstract form can only lead to the spiritual troubles of the world—"grief, impatience, disillusionment, [and] despair." Such "confused notions" lead to an attitude of fear of God as a ruthless power and a corresponding sense of human debasement and insignificance. Atheism arises from such theologies, as people rebel against them, and it has a role in liberating people from such false ideas about God. Ultimately, though, both these paths—that based on the search for the transcendent essence of God on the one hand, and atheism on the other—are wrong; one should instead adopt a higher form of piety, enlightened by the Torah, where each aspect of our existence is a vessel for holding part of the divine light. One must not confuse any of the vessels with God Himself—that too would be idolatry; but one must also not fail to see the manifestation of God in each of the concrete ways (the "vessels") in which God becomes evident—through flowers, people of all sorts, instances of beauty, and acts of goodness.

Mordecai Kaplan (1881–1983)

While Cohen used neo-Kantian rationalism, Rosenzweig and Buber used different forms of existentialism, and Kook used mysticism to understand and interact with God, Mordecai Kaplan embraced naturalism and empiricism. Kaplan, in fact, reveled in the major advances of science in the mid-twentieth century, and he shaped his theology to appeal to scientifically minded people like him who nevertheless had a sense of the religious dimension of life. Even the style of his writing and of his teaching articulated his commitment to science: he was unfailingly demanding in his own thought and in that of his students for clarity, precision, and the empirically demonstrable.

Borrowing substantially from the thought of John Dewey, Kaplan identifies God as "the power that makes for salvation." As English is a Christian language, created by Christians and spoken as a native language primarily by Christians, it is crucial for English speakers to note at the outset that Kaplan has a distinctly Jewish understanding of "salvation" when he identifies "God as the Power that Makes for Salvation," the title of the chapter from which our selection is taken. While salvation for Christians means deliverance from sin, for Jews, as Kaplan explains, salvation means release from the limitations and frustrations of life—from hunger, poverty, insensitivity, meanness, and anomie. The sheer energy of the man, clear even in his style of putting complete sentences in italics, is evident more substantially in Kaplan's doctrine that God should be conceived as the Power in nature that saves us from feelings of hopelessness and insignificance. On the contrary, our awareness of the fact that nature supports our efforts to create and fix life's problems should stimulate in us the desire to be active, creative people in following the image of God.

Kaplan's doctrines of God as a power in nature and of salvation as being this-worldly were meant to appeal to the scientific spirit of the twentieth century, but they require major revisions in traditional Judaism—indeed, as Kaplan says, a "reconstruction" of Judaism in modern terms. In doing this, he claims that he is not changing the core of what Judaism has meant through the ages; he is only restating its tenets in modern, scientific terms. While even moderns might use metaphors, scientific thinking requires, for Kaplan, that we recognize that God is not supernatural or personal, as "the ancients" understood the Divine; God is rather a force in nature.

Similarly, salvation conceived as other-worldly was a product of the ancients' feeling of impotence vis-a-vis the world in which they lived. That factual assessment brought with it a moral implication: because salvation could only be achieved in another life, this traditional view of salvation encouraged passivity in one's life. Now that science has enabled us to understand and, in many cases, control the world, though, we should understand salvation in this-worldly terms as something within our reach and therefore something which we have the duty to try to promote.

If God is not personal or supernatural, what is the ground of authority for Jewish law? The moral aspects of Jewish law, according to Kaplan, have their own, self-evident authority. While he never explains this, one would expect that, given his grounding of the concept of God in nature, he would want to root morality in nature also, perhaps in some version of natural law theory. While Jewish sources may understand and apply moral norms in specific ways, the norms themselves are, for Kaplan, universal.

Jewish ritual laws are, by their very nature, not universal: they function, after all, to identify Jews as Jews. They also symbolize Jewish conceptions and values, as the selection included in this book demonstrates with regard to the Sabbath, but one prime goal of rituals is to give the Jewish community a sense of identity. Jewish ritual laws, then, are, for Kaplan, "folkways." Jews should abide by them in order to feel part of the Jewish people and in order to promote its vigor. As those are the ends of ritual laws, though, it would be counterproductive to see them as obligatory, imposed by some outside authority; one should rather see them as natural and healthy expressions of one's group identity.

That means that Jewish ritual laws will and should be observed to the extent that a Jew feels part of the Jewish people and their culture. Borrowing extensively from Ahad Ha'am, Kaplan understands Judaism as a civilization—the title of his first book (1934). In that book and in his many subsequent writings, he portrays Judaism as a civilization, with attachments to a specific land (Israel), language (Hebrew), art, music, dance, and literature. All of these aspects of Jewish identity, then, are important expressions of being Jewish, and Jews can latch on to their Jewish identity through any or all of these. Conservative Judaism, in which Kaplan's specific reconstructionist approach was housed until the founding of the independent, Reconstructionist Rabbinical College in 1968, has been heavily influenced by this philosophy in its formal and informal educational efforts, for spoken Hebrew, Zionism, and the cultural aspects of Jewish identity have been very much part of Conservative educational programs from Kaplan's earliest writings to our own time.

Like other civilizations, though, Judaism focuses on certain elements as its core. While the ancient Athenians concentrated on philosophy, drama, and architecture, the ancient Romans on military might and law, the modern Germans on music, science, and philosophy, the modern British on colonialism ("The sun never sets on the British empire") and fair play ("cricket"), and the Americans on individual liberty and technological know-how, the heart of the Jewish civilization is the Jewish religion. That means that while Jews might identify with any of the other elements of Jewish civilization, if they ignore its religious expressions, their Jewishness is skewed to something on the periphery of what it means to be a Jew rather than being rooted in its religious core. Therefore, even though Jewish ritual law in Kaplan's approach lacks the power of a personal God commanding it, as it has in traditional Jewish theologies, nevertheless Jewish religious expressions, including prayer, the round of Jewish rituals to mark the seasons of the year and of life, and Jewish ritual law such as the dietary laws all are centrally important for Kaplan as articulations of the core of what it means to be Jewish.

Abraham Joshua Heschel (1907–1972)

Although Heschel occupied a chair in Jewish ethics and mysticism at the Jewish Theological Seminary from 1945 to his death, he accurately described his own theology not as mysticism, but as phenomenology. That is, he concentrates in his thought on analyzing the phenomena within our experience that evoke in us an awareness of God. He specifically rejects both rationalism and empiricism as proper avenues to approach God. Rationalism borrows from non-Jewish sources to understand Judaism and substitutes philosophy for religion. Empiricism (of which Kaplan's thought is an example) ultimately substitutes psychology for religion, for it examines how religions function in serving people's needs. To penetrate to the heart of religion, for Heschel, one must instead be open to the ultimate questions that religion asks and to the ultimate reality, God, that it encounters.

Put another way, Heschel aims to examine not the content of Jewish faith—the *what* of Judaism—but the act of believing—*how* we come to faith in the first place. The core of Heschel's thought is that all religious faith is based on "an ontological presupposition"—that is, an experience of God that logically and educationally comes before all attempts to think about Him. Heschel wants to return to the "living reality" of the relationship with God that undergirds all conceptions of the Divine and all responses to God through prayer and law.

God, according to Heschel, can be encountered in three ways: through nature, through God's word in the Bible, and, most importantly, through sacred deeds. While Kaplan also encountered God in nature, Heschel's use of nature and his concept of God are radically different. While Kaplan concentrated on the creative forces of nature to find and identify God, Heschel instead focuses on the sublime, the mystery, and the glory of nature and the reactions that those aspects of nature engender in us—namely, wonder, awe, and faith.

The sublime "may be sensed in things of beauty as well as in acts of goodness and in the search for truth. . . . The sublime is that which we see and are unable to convey. It is the silent allusion of things to a meaning greater than themselves" (page 39 in *God In Search of Man*). The sublime provokes in us a response of wonder, of "Wow!"

By the quality of the world which is "mystery," Heschel does not mean merely the things we do not understand. That sense of mystery should properly prompt us to seek to understand, to do science. The religious category of "mystery" instead means the surprise that anything exists at all, "the essential mystery of being as being, the nature of being as God's creation out of nothing" (page 57). The proper response to this type of mystery is not inquiry, but awe—"Oh!"

The third aspect of our interaction with nature that Heschel uses as evidence of God is its glory. "The glory is the presence, not the essence of God; an act rather than a quality; a process not a substance. Mainly the glory manifests itself as a power overwhelming the world" (page 82). On that same page, Heschel connects that power with positive things—"it is a power that descends to guide, to remind. The glory reflects abundance of good and truth . . ." Those good manifestations of God's power lead us to respond in faith. Heschel's limitation of the manifestations of God in nature to positive things means that in his thought, as in Kaplan's, the experience of evil is not well accounted for.

All of these phenomena in nature, though, are not in themselves evidence of God to be used as building blocks for a rational proof of God, similar to the classical proofs of God in philosophy. These phenomena rather point beyond themselves to the "ontological presupposition" of all conceptions of God, the interactions with God that undergird all conceptions of God and all reactions to Him.

The second way of finding God, for Heschel, is through God's words in the Bible. Revelation and response through sacred deeds are, in fact, more direct ways of encountering God than trying to do that through nature: "The world, the word, as well as the sacred deed are full of His glory. God is more immediately found in the Bible as well as in acts of kindness and worship than in the mountains and forests" (pages 311–12). Heschel makes crystal clear, though, that he does not intend to take a fundamentalist position in his second way to God, through the Bible: "The surest way of misunderstanding revelation is to take it literally, to imagine that God spoke to the prophet on a long-distance telephone. . . . The cardinal sin in thinking about ultimate issues is *literal-mindedness*" (pages 178–79). Instead, one must understand that the Bible records the experience of being overwhelmed by God in the language of human beings. "As a report about revelation, the Bible itself is a *midrash*" (page 185), an interpretation by the human beings reporting their experience with God. Revelation is thus not simply a set of words spoken by God to the prophet: "The prophet is not a passive recipient, a recording instrument, affected from without, without participation of heart and will, nor is he a person who acquires his vision by his own strength and labor. The prophet's personality is rather a unity of inspiration and experience, invasion and response" (page 259). Revelation is therefore an ongoing process, in which the Bible gives each of us a clue of God's meaning for our lives each time we study it: "The word is but a clue; the real burden of understanding is upon the mind and soul of the reader" (page 183).

The third way of finding God is through sacred deeds (*mitzvot*): "In response to His will we perceive His presence in our deeds" (page 282). Piety, in fact, can be a vehicle by which we attain faith: "A Jew is asked to take a *leap of action* rather than a *leap of thought*" (page 283). Acts can help us go beyond our current understanding and feeling in an "ecstasy of deeds" (that is, literally, standing outside oneself in one's actions) in order to help us discover God and attach ourselves to Him. Heschel speaks eloquently against "religious behaviorism"—that is, a rigid adherence to the details of Jewish law without any sense of its goal to lead us to the Divine. While he stings the Orthodox that way, he also obliquely, but powerfully, attacks Kaplan's approach: civilization supplies our own needs as human beings (page 350), while "Judaism is *the art of surpassing civilization, sanctification of time, sanctification of history*" (page 418) in order to meet God. God is to be found, then, in the focused, intentional concentration of discovering God in nature, in the Bible, and in our deeds of prayer, ritual, and morality.

The Foundation for Contemporary Jewish Thought

These pivotal thinkers who wrote all or most of their work in the first six decades of the twentieth century paved the way for the contemporary Jewish theorists whose writings will occupy most of this volume. The issues, doctrines, and approaches formulated in the first part of the twentieth century have all stimulated some aspects of the topics, the convictions, and the methods of contemporary thinkers. While the increasing integration of Jews into Western democracies, the Holocaust, and the State of Israel have all raised new issues for Jewish reflection, or new forms of old issues, and while new approaches to religious issues generally and to Judaism in particular have arisen in the last four decades of the twentieth century, much of what has occupied contemporary Jewish thinkers finds its roots in these earlier giants.

The thought of those included in this section is thus important not only in its own right, but also as the foundation for contemporary Jewish theories. Much of what people have asserted and denied in the last four decades, represented by the writers in the other sections of this volume, stems from the writers discussed in this section who serve as their background and stimulus.

2

Religion of Reason Out of the Sources of Judaism

HERMANN COHEN

1. It is God's uniqueness, rather than his oneness, that we posit as the essential content of monotheism. Oneness signifies only an opposition to the plurality of gods. It is questionable whether this idea was the primary idea of monotheism, whether it by itself was capable of prevailing against polytheism. For in polytheism the point in question is not only the gods and their plurality but also their relation to the cosmos and its vast natural powers, in all of which a god first appeared. Therefore, if monotheism opposed polytheism, it also had to change God's relation to the universe in accordance with its new idea of God. From the point of view of the new notion of God, therefore, one cannot rest satisfied with the distinction between one God and many gods; rather, the oneness of God has also to be extended over nature, which manifests itself in many forces and phenomena.

Thus, from the very outset the concept of God's oneness involves a relation to nature. This oneness immediately acquires a significance that takes it beyond the opposition to plurality and elevates it even beyond mere opposition to the notion of *composition*. The notion of composition contains a relation to nature; therefore, with regard to nature also, the meaning of the oneness of God must ward off the notion of composition.

2. At this gateway to religion the biblical sources pose a methodological difficulty for us. It would seem that the thought of the oneness of God would alone unlock the gateway not to religion but rather to philosophy and metaphysics, especially if that oneness signified uniqueness. What does uniqueness mean in relation to the universe? And the uniqueness of God has to be thought of in relation to the universe, since the oneness of

Hermann Cohen, "God's Uniqueness," in *Religion of Reason Out of the Sources of Judaism*, second edition (Atlanta: Scholars Press, 1995), pp. 35–49. © Scholars Press, Atlanta, GA 30329.

God would suffice with respect to the plurality of gods. The uniqueness of God is therefore in opposition to the universe. What does this opposition mean?

The problem of philosophy arises as soon as one begins to think of a relation to the world. Religion is not philosophy. However, the religion of reason, by virtue of its share in reason, has at least some kinship with philosophy. It is therefore not surprising that this share in reason, akin to that of philosophy, begins to stir within religion, starting, it would seem, with its concept of God.

3. All objections against this idea do not originate in historical methodology that has to entertain complicated motivations of reason, even in its most primitive stages, in order to explain the basic concepts of human culture. The monotheistic principle possesses such a depth of culture that it is easily understood that all the problems of the natural world and its analogue, the moral world, were already present in its origins. Where and in what this origin of monotheism lies cannot be summarized into a formula of one concept, both because indeed God and the world always belong together and because the primeval theme of God cannot be determined without the primordial theme of nature.

Do not all spiritual creations contain in themselves the insoluble riddle of their origin? Supposedly one has to search for the conditions that prepare or make possible the historical appearance of these creations. One has to seek out the general historical conditions that further spiritual development. But even if the general historical atmosphere is illuminated, in the last analysis the spiritual impulse with which the spiritual movement in question begins, in such a way that it must recognize its origin in this impulse, will have to remain unexplained.

4. If it is true to say of the individual artist that it is his individuality alone that is the ultimate foundation for the intrinsic order of lawfulness his work exhibits, and if, with certain reservations, the genius at work in the production holds sway in every spiritual creation, then this secret of the spirit grows more mysterious in the case of the *national spirit*. Monotheism is not the thought of one man, but of the whole Jewish national spirit unfolding in the creation and development of this thought which impregnates the entire thinking of the people. One would have to be able to gather into one primeval word the whole history of this people if one were to attempt to formulate the primeval motive out of which monotheism originated.

The historical and political conditions do not offer a basis for sufficient elucidation either; they constitute the spiritual mystery of the people's character. However, the people have to have some relationship with other peoples, just as the one God does to the many gods. This necessary supposition is confirmed by the tradition itself; tradition does not question the existence of an original polytheism. The further development of polytheism leads to its self-dissolution in monotheism. The historical conditions could be summarized by one many-sided moment of historical experience: the people were originally inhabitants of Canaan, then emigrated to Egypt, and from there wandered back to the motherland.

Monotheism, therefore, comes to be not as a creation out of nothing but has its precondition in polytheism, which in Canaan was Israel's religion also. A further precondition is the emigration to Egypt, where the new seed of monotheism could have been conceived and nourished. And the political strength the people acquired to migrate back to their ancestral mother country could have had its germinating vigor in the new religious motivation of monotheism, so that both elements can be explained, one through the other: the wandering back and the origin of the new God.

These historical elements, however, are no more than preconditions lacking as yet the positive element for the new God, who originated in relation not only to the multiple gods but to nature as well. We must provisionally consider the possibility that the sources in their naiveté perhaps veil this original speculative relationship. We shall therefore have to attempt to give a preliminary orientation regarding the problem of the relation of the sources to their content.

5. It is already striking that Judaism presents its chief sources in *literary* documents, whereas polytheism possesses them above all in monuments of *plastic* art. Plastic art turns itself into an analogy of nature. The form of poetry, the original language of literature, however, can make thought more spiritually inward than plastic art. And Hebrew poetry limits itself to *epics* and *lyrics*. *Rhetoric*, instead of the drama, appears on the border of poetry and makes use particularly of the epic form.

This originally epic form of monotheistic thought explains the *naiveté* in the style of the Bible. This naiveté, moreover, embraces the innermost content of the thoughts expressed as well as the account and the redaction of the origins of national history. This redaction of the ancient sources follows a rule that is intelligible only through the original epic form of the national spirit. The original layers of thought are not covered up or smoothed over, much less eliminated, but another layer is superimposed upon them in such a manner that the lower layer can still be seen through the upper layer.

Owing to this peculiar style, the understanding of the sources of the Bible and its literary criticism become entangled in great difficulties. Against every routine approach the insight must prevail that progress in religious understanding has been accomplished through the revision and reinterpretation of the sources, while these themselves remain preserved in their individual layers and have been at most rearranged or given different emphasis. We shall have to confirm this view of exegetics in tracing the different states of the development within the monotheistic concept of God.

6. An almost insoluble riddle is already posed by the *plural* form of the name of God: *Elohim.* The routine explanation is that this name of God preserves the traces of an original polytheism, and that again and again polytheism breaks through against the new name *Yahveh,* as if there were a residue of polytheism that was not absorbed by monotheism. Contradictions and residues of duality are the usual aids of routine criticism of this sort, which, however, is unable to do justice to the problem of the style of a *national spirit* in its historical development.

If the preservation of the plural form, Elohim, seems to be a riddle, it is canceled out by an even greater riddle: that the *singular forms* of the adjective, as well as the tenses of the verb, are made to agree with this plural form. This psychological riddle is a logical monster that cannot exist. Therefore, logic here has to assist psychology. If the purport of this grammatical form is nonsensical and utterly absurd, psychology has to be taught by logic that the intention of this word in the plural form could not be plurality, but, as its connection with the singular form proves, singularity.

If this self-transformation of the plural form into a singular should still remain questionable despite the assistance of logic, then this question would be canceled by this insight: the new God was thought of as a unity, with such energy and clarity that the grammatical plural form could not impair this new content of thought. On the contrary, the preservation of the plural form testifies to the vigor of the new thought, which simply took no offense at all at the plural form. A literature that let come to be the "Hear, O

Israel" could unhesitatingly let the old name survive after the reinterpretation had been secured, even without adding the new name of God.

We abstain from entering into the discussion of the Elohistic and Yahvistic sources. Yet we may indicate that from the point of view of our method the unity of both sources cannot be considered entirely out of the question. It is in no way the case that only one source is monotheistic; rather, the Elohistic source also has its complete and certain share in the striving toward pure monotheism.

7. Another name of God is also given from of old: *El Shaddai*. With regard to the explanation of this name, we adhere to the disadvantageous position which holds that it is connected with *shed*, the general name for demons. The literary advantage of this name consists in its opposition to the new name Yahveh: "And I appeared to Abraham, Isaac and Jacob as El Shaddai, but my name Yahveh I did not disclose to them." Thus it is said (Exod. 6:3) at the summoning of Moses. There Yahveh is not only opposed to Elohim and to El but to El Shaddai. A later stage of interpretation, however, turned the Shaddai into the Almighty.

The positive idea of a creator and the negative idea of the destroyer are connected with this word throughout the biblical language, and it is characteristic of Job that he prefers to use this name of God, which designates God's primeval power. Therefore Maimonides' interpretation of this name exhibits a correct feeling for language: he starts out with the root די, which in the word expresses self-sufficiency, and at the same time he proves this self-sufficiency by stating, "that He is sufficient in himself to bring forth the world" (יש לו די להמצאת דברים זולתו).

8. Thus, even the oldest name relates God to the world, namely, as *creator*. Therefore the opinion that holds that the new name Yahveh contains this relation even more definitely is justified. Otherwise one would have to assume that the summoning of Moses and the revelation of God as Yahveh refer back to a name of God that is merely a magic name. If, however, the juxtaposition of both names properly signifies a development of the one name into the other, then this too shows that God's relation to the world is of primary origin and based on the essence of God. Thus every trace of artificial interpretation and unhistorical rationalization disappears when we assume that the share monotheism has in reason extends also to the *problem of being*, and when we try to derive this share of reason from the sources. In any case, the connection of the root of the word Yahveh with the word "being" (היה) is a philological fact. We shall have to observe how the first revelation clarifies this connection of God with being.

9. First, however, some information should be given about the general connection between the three concepts of being, unity, and God, which was also established in Greek philosophy and already realized in the philosophy of the Eleatics. Xenophanes was the first in the Eleatic tradition to establish this connection. He already conceived the cosmos under the concept of being. He was not brought to the idea of the unity of nature by the presupposition of some kind of matter and its transformation, but only through a presentiment of being could the idea of an ordered unity of the cosmos have originated.

In opposition to sensible appearances, which involve only change and motion, the being of nature had to be thought of as an object of thought, as opposed to perception. The distinction between thought and perception is determined by unity. One can hardly be certain whether unity or being is the first product of thought. They belong together, they originate in reciprocity. Without unity the cosmos could not be thought of as being; without being the cosmos could not be thought of as unity.

The reciprocity between being and unity is based on the efficacy of a third concept, the concept of God, which appears, according to Xenophanes, in unity with the other two. "With an eye on the whole cosmos," he said, "this unity is God." Be that as it may, the philosophical concept of God also originated in connection with the concepts of world and unity. But the difference between the philosophical and the religious concept of God soon becomes a power in the history of the mind. For here the case is not that the cosmos is thought of as unity, nor that God is thought as unity, but that both entities are one. Both, however, represent being, and both make it into *one* being. Thus, on the threshold of Greek philosophy, *pantheism* arises.

10. Within philosophy, therefore, the concept of unity makes manifest the connection of the concepts of God and the world, viz., the unity of the being of the cosmos and its identity with the unity of God. Here, too, the connection with being brought forth the notion of the one God; for the connection between being and the cosmos had as its consequence the connection between God and unity. But here the thought of God did not go beyond the conception of unity. Therefore this unity at once turns into the identity of God and the world. The unity of God is therefore basically nothing else than the unity of the world, and it is only the means through which the unity of the world was, if not discovered, at least confirmed.

The share religion acquires in reason should not be limited to this confirmation. Pantheism is not religion. This fundamental thought we shall have to clarify step by step. Thus, also, unity cannot be the deepest meaning of monotheism. Unity is always only the negative expression of monotheism, designating only its distinction from polytheism. Furthermore, it is the negative expression against pantheism, insofar as unity negatively opposes the idea of *composition* and therefore also excludes the identity of God with the world. Composition, however, would have been the characteristic of pantheistic thinking and would have been the characteristic of the cosmos, if God's unity had not brought about the unity of the cosmos. Thus unity, as opposed to the idea of composition, is in fact only a negative attribute. The Arabic philosophers admitted its validity in this capacity alone.

11. Uniqueness has positive meaning. It, too, gathers under its protection the concepts of being and God, but now the strict *identity* of both concepts sets in. Unity becomes identity, an advance in thought achieved by Parmenides in Greek speculation. Only God has being. Only God is being. And there is no unity that would be an identity between God and world, no unity between world and being. The world is appearance. This thought already flashes its light into the future: only God is being. There is only *one* kind of being, only one unique being: God is this unique being. God is the Unique One.

In the "Hear, O Israel" this uniqueness is designated by the word *Ehad*. In the rabbinical writings the more precise Hebrew word *Jihud* appears, as the designation of the uniqueness of God. It designates the Unique One, and through this meaning of the word the uniqueness of God is freed of the ambiguity which is connected with the word "unity." God's essence is also designated in rabbinic and religious-philosophical literature, in connection with this word, as *Jihud* (ייחוד).

The word *ahduth* (אחדות), which is connected with the word *Ehad* (אחד), is also used. However, it may not be correct to say that Arabic usage was the decisive motive for its adoption. For *Jihud* does not solely or chiefly mean the subjective act, through which the self achieves unity with God by devotion to him, by acknowledging his unity, but it can also mean God's causative act of bringing about unity. *Ahduth* represents the unity as actuality, as being; *Jihud*, on the contrary, represents the function through which this unity is achieved. What is of importance for us is this thought: throughout the development of religion unity was realized as uniqueness, and this significance of the unity of God as uniqueness brought about the recognition of the uniqueness of God's being, in comparison with which all other being vanishes and becomes nothing. Only God is being.

12. The difference between Jewish religion and Greek speculation, including pantheism, consists in the designation of this being as the *One Who Is Being*, in *the transformation of the neuter into a person*. This, to be sure, makes anthropomorphism unavoidable, and the decline of Jewish thought into myth would have been unavoidable if the *fight against anthropomorphism* had not proved from the very beginning of the oral teaching to be the very soul of Jewish religious education. It is perhaps possible to say that this fight already played a role in the compilation of the Canon of Scripture. We do not, therefore, at this stage of our exposition need to take offense at the transformation of an abstraction into a person, especially since its connection with *being* already at least diminishes the danger that is connected with the notion of the person. God is not that which is, nor is he only the one, but the Unique One that is.

13. Among all the wonders of style in the books of Moses, the greatest is perhaps the account of the *first* origin of monotheism. The first revelation of this God of being occurs at the Burning Bush. The mythical miracle of the fire that does not consume the bush merely constitutes the backdrop for one of the first acts of world history: the liberation of Israel from Egyptian bondage. Moses, who tended the sheep of Jethro, his father-in-law, is called upon by God from out of the bush. And the place where this call occurred is referred to as holy ground. God calls himself at first "the God of thy Father, the God of Abraham, the God of Isaac, and the God of Jacob" (Exod. 3:6). "I will send thee unto Pharaoh, that thou mayest bring forth My people, the Israelites, out of Egypt. . . . And Moses said unto God: Behold when I come unto the children of Israel and shall say unto them: the God of your fathers hath sent me unto you, and they shall say to me: what is His name? What shall I say unto them? And God said unto Moses: 'I am that I am' " [Exod. 3: 10-14].

The falsity of Kautzsch's translation is fatal: "I am who I am." It is scarcely intelligible, if not meaningless. The meaning of his error is disclosed in his annotation: "There is still considerable dispute about the original meaning of the name. It is only certain that the explanation of the name means . . . an imperfect *qual* form of the verb *hawa* (an older form of *haja*) in the sense of 'He is.' In this understanding He is hardly thought of as being the 'true being' in the philosophical sense of the word, but rather as the perpetual and unchanging One." The admission that God here reveals himself as the "perpetual and unchangeable One" is adequate for our "philosophical sense." In no way do we impose our philosophical explanation upon the text, but we undertake an explanation in order to throw light upon the original depth of the biblical word, and in order to make understandable the historical strength of its source. Moses asks by what name he should name God to the Israelites, and God answers: I am the One that is. I am the One, that can be named in no other way than by "I am." Thereby is expressed the thought that no other being may affirm about itself this connection with *being*.

Let us continue with the text that immediately after this says. "[and God said:] Thus shalt thou say unto the children of Israel; 'I am' hath sent me unto you' " [Exod. 3:14]. Thus it is not Yahveh who has sent Moses. But Moses is to name the name of God by this verb form of the first person in answering the question of the Israelites about the name of their God. In such a definite way *being* is named as that element in the name that designates the *person* of God. If this is not yet philosophy, it is certainly reason in the original sense of the word.

If the text then continues, "the Eternal, the God of your fathers, the God of Abraham, the God of Isaac, and the God of Jacob has sent me unto you," then this seems to contradict the objection Moses makes (verse 13): ". . . when I come unto the children of Israel and shall say unto them: the God of your fathers has sent me to you, and they shall ask me," etc. The text, however, says further (verse 15): "this is My name forever and this is My memorial unto all generations." The solemnity of these expressions in instituting God's name for all future times and the invocation of all future generations can only be explained by its relation to the new name of the One that is. The text, however, wants to exclude even a semblance of difference between the new name and the historical one. And the historical name in no way signifies a national God, but only the God of the fathers, who, moreover, was previously designated as "your God." Thus it becomes clear that God, as the One that is, is the God of Israel. He refers therefore to eternity and to all generations. Under this new name Moses has to awaken Israel's trust in the God of their fathers.

This is the content of the manifestation in the Burning Bush and its tremendous symbolism. The bush is not consumed. God is the One that is. The translation of God's name, Yahveh, as the Eternal One, corresponds to this basic source of God's revelation. The Eternal One designates the One that is as God, as God in distinction from the world, as the Unique One in comparison to whom the world is said to have no being. With this limitation of its sense, being here loses its philosophical meaning. However, we cannot rescue the latter by establishing an identity between the unique being that is and the being of the world.

The unique being, which is represented only by the unique God, in the first place negates the being of all other gods. "The gods of the nations are nothing" (אלהי העמים אלילים [Ps. 96:5]). This Hebrew word (אל) originates from a root that plainly means negation. The contempt that monotheism has for all kinds of polytheism is nourished by the insight that it is not only an erroneous concept that paganism assumes but a misconception that negates being. Being, however, has to be asserted, has to be understood correctly. This principle of reason guides monotheism. The plurality of gods is in contradiction to being.

In this way the Decalogue also becomes intelligible. "Thou shalt have no other gods before me." One should translate: thou shalt not take any other beings for God. The other is opposed to the Unique One. As far as true being is concerned, there is no other beside him and outside of him. Not only is there no other God, but there is no other being, beside this unique being. Isaiah does not merely say, "there is no God beside Me" (ומבלעדי אין אלהים[Isa. 44:6]); he also says "Nothing is beside Me" (אפס בלעדי [Isa. 45:6]). Nonbeing, as nothing, is opposed to the unique being.

14. Hence the uniqueness of God consists in *incomparability*. "To whom then will you liken Me, that I should be equal?" (ואל מי תדמיוני ואשוה [Isa. 40:25]). "There is none like unto Thee" (אין כמוך [Ps. 86:8]) is not a precise translation. For it must also mean: *nothing* is like unto Thee. The incomparability points as much to nature as to every other concept of God. Therefore the question above must refer to things (אל מה) as well as to person (אל מי).

15. Uniqueness, therefore, also entails the *distinction between being and existence*. The share of reason in monotheism is strongly confirmed in this distinction. For existence is attested by the senses, through perception. On the other hand it is reason which, against all sense-appearance, bestows actuality upon existence, discovers and elevates the non-sensible to being, and marks it out as true being.

This priority of reason in the original purity of monotheism can be seen negatively in the error that the *ontological* argument of the Middle Ages could not avoid. When this argument unites the *existence with the essence* of being, it in no way grants reason sovereignty, as it may appear, but it confuses thought and sensation, as if it were only through the recognition of sensation in its own peculiarity, in its sovereignty, that reason could achieve perfection; as if it were only sensation that grants reason its right. Thus one can grasp the argument of the *doctrine of attributes* that Islamic and Jewish monotheism raises against Christian ontology.

16. Uniqueness in this sense, therefore, is also distinguished from *simplicity*, since the latter is merely opposed to composition, which is the general characteristic of matter. This simplicity, however, is not sufficient to explain the being of God. The unique being of God is such that it does not admit any mixture, any connection with sensible existence. Ontology, which is based on this connection of being and existence, contains no safeguard against *pantheism*; indeed, pantheism bases itself on ontology and all its main representatives.

Monotheism can tolerate no such mixture, no such distortion of being by existence. In its eyes pantheism is nothing other than anthropomorphism. Moreover, all these problems disappear before the uniqueness of being. Not only does the thesis *Deus sive natura* contain a contradiction, but the ontological argument does so as well, insofar as it involves existence in essence. The unity of substance may thereby be defined, but its uniqueness is abolished. The position of monotheism leads to the consequence "Nothing is beside Me." Cosmos and nature are negated.

17. Must we not now ask: what could be the final meaning of God if he had no world, which is after all the human world? No offense should be taken at this question; a clear and satisfactory answer is required. God cannot remain without the world, without the human world. However, nature must not be set up in being together with God. Nature is subject to the limitations of space and time. These basic concepts of metaphysics also arise in the reasoning of monotheism. Space, however, cannot be a limitation of God's being. "The fullness," the whole "of the world is His glory." This is perhaps the meaning of the sentence in the vision of Isaiah (מלא כל הארץ כבודו [Isa. 6:3]). Although formerly the earth, the world was nothing; it should now contain in it the fullness, the infinitude of God's glory. The limitations of space have now fallen before the monotheistic view. Thus it becomes understandable that in the religious philosophy of the Middle Ages, as well as in the Talmud, *space* (מקום) becomes a name of God. This tendency is already recognizable in the warding off of anthropomorphism that is characteristic of even the oldest translations of the Bible.

18. There is still another expression for the godhead, which this surpassing of space makes intelligible: the *Shechinah*. The root of the word means "to lie" and "to rest." In this meaning it is generally connected with God. The use of this word as a name of God apparently is intended to describe being through rest. All change, all alteration, must be eliminated from God's being. The philosopher says: God is substance. Monotheistic religion says: God is Shechinah, absolute rest. Rest is the eternal prime cause of motion. This is also what is meant with regard to God. Motion, however, is to be excluded from his essential being. This in no way means that through the being of God motion is made impossible; rather, it is precisely through this being of rest that the being of motion becomes possible.

19. *Time*, like space, is not a limitation to the divine being. "I am the first and I am the last" (אני ראשון ואני אחרון). "I am He; I am the first, I also am the last" (Isa. 44:6; 48:12). It is not enough to say: "I am the first and I am the last"; it is also not sufficient if one adds "and beside Me there is no other God." One also has to add: "nothing *is* beside Me." Only through this is the *eternity* of God founded on his uniqueness.

20. By being opposed to time, God's being also excludes change. "I, the eternal One, do not change" (אני ה' לא שניתי [Mal. 3:6]). This determination of reason touches upon the boundary of ethics. The unchangeableness of God follows chiefly from the meaning of being as *continuance*. Continuance, however, is also the basis and presupposition of motion. Therefore, in order to distinguish God's being from all temporal *becoming*, the negative attribute of unchangeableness is necessary. "I am that I am." Being is here determined as the being of an I, and not of a substance that becomes the basis for the motion of matter. In this distinction between unchangeableness and continuance, the *ethical* meaning of God, as the Unique One, originates. The ground for this meaning is already prepared by the exclusion from God's being of all the characteristics that constitute *matter*.

21. This general opposition to *materialism* is analogous to monotheism's rejection of the philosophy of *idealism*. Philosophical idealism is based on the idealism of nature, and it is only on this basis, which justifies the natural sciences, that the idealism of ethics is established. Judaism rejects this idealistic basis. All the enthusiasm of thinking is limited to reflection on the unique being of God. Nature is nothing in itself. If through this limitation science is lost, compensation for this loss is to be sought in the depreciation of all earthly things in view of their irrelevance with regard to the knowledge of the *good*.

Oppostion to *eudaemonism* is therefore deeply rooted in monotheism. "Vanity of vanities, all is vanity," says Koheleth (Eccles. 1:2). One admires in Psalm 73 the lines: "Why should I care about the heavens? With the covenant with you I have no desire for the earth." Even without the positive completion of the sense that this verse provides, the basic idea of the unique being of God is already the confirmation of this frame of mind, of this fundamentally religious intention. There is no interest in heaven and earth: "They change, you remain." The psalmist and the prophet see in all change the symptom of annihilation, which can only be transitory. Only the One that is, is everlasting, is eternal, he cannot change.

The description of nature in Psalm 104, which Alexander von Humboldt so deeply admired, contains, along with the naiveté of its nature poetry, a primary feeling for a *sublimity that is beyond all the beauty of nature*, and maintains this mood as vigorously as it does the feeling for the sublimity of *nature*.

That this religious people, with the share its religion has in reason, should not have taken part in *science* would not be intelligible if its spirit had not been filled with this world-historical one-sidedness: there is only one unique being, and only this has to be thought through in all its foundations and consequences. Nature, however, is and remains nothing in comparison with the being of God's I. Only in this way could the metaphysics of monotheism be the origin of the unique God of ethics. Only in this way could the causality of nature be the origin of the teleology of morality.

22. Offenses against this rigid uniqueness were unavoidable, and God's unique being had to be defended against them. They were unavoidable at home, even without contact with foreign views. In Persia monotheism had to resist the doctrine of the *two* divine powers, which, to be sure, were related not only physically to *light* and *darkness* but directly to ethics, to *good* and *evil*. Monotheism had to affirm itself against this dualism. We shall see later how this affirmation was substantiated ethically; for the time being it suffices to point out that Isaiah, in opposing God to nothing, adds the following: "I form the light and create darkness; I make peace," etc. (Isa. 45:7). Peace is here coordinated to light, though one would expect it to be coordinated, instead, to the good, for immediately after this God declares himself, even according to the usual translation, to be the creator of evil. Peace, according to the Hebrew root of the word, means *perfection*.

Uniqueness stamps itself with this teleological perfection in order to strike down the thought of the *two* powers. The uniqueness of God's being exempts itself from any comparison not only to all worldliness but also to all imaginary world powers. There can as little be two equivalent kinds of being, as two governments of the world. All apparent existence is transitory, and as such, nil. It cannot have its own God, since it does not have its own true being.

23. Another contradiction arose in monotheism due to the operations of reason, and was even nourished by the Jewish spirit itself. The disdain for nature goes against Greek thought, and all mysticism, which arose there also, was unable to cripple this resistance. When the Jews in Alexandria took up, according to the talmudic image, "the beauty of Japheth into the tent of Shem," when they wanted to blend the Torah with "Greek wisdom," they took offense at the independence of nature for seeming to oppose its own being to God's being. If, however, God was to be responsible for the being of nature and, on the other hand, the Jews were not to fall into the Persian error of the two powers in the world, they had to find in reason itself a means of putting a similar, though not equal, being of nature alongside God's being. This was the origin of the mediating being of the *Logos*.

Uniqueness excludes any *mediation* between God and natural existence. The Logos, however, must inevitably become a second God, and yet there is no first, but only the one unique God. We will forthwith and also later have to draw out the consequences that the problem of the Logos has for the uniqueness of God; at this point we wish only to emphasize the contradiction which the idea of the Logos, in all its gradations, constitutes. There is no mediating being, not to mention a mediating person, that solves the problem of the origin or of the government of the world.

There is no change in this basic error if one transfers the mediation to reason instead of being in order to explain the being of nature. Reason can acknowledge only one unique kind of being, and therefore only one unique kind of God. The unique God wards off any mediating God, or God beside God. It is even a distortion of Plato, the ethical Plato, if the beyondness of the *good* is bridged by the Logos and connected to this-worldly being. In this manner one may develop at best the *Timaeus* with its Demiurge, but not the *idea* of the *good* in the *Republic*.

24. All other ideas of God originating from the notion of the Logos are also excluded; as expressions of "*partnership*" (שיתוף) they are distinguished from pure monotheism. The distinction between uniqueness and unity is the foundation of the distinction between monotheism and all dualism, as well as the belief in the *trinity*. The latter has its basis, as does dualism, in the recognition of another being beside the being of God. We cannot now judge the legitimacy of this claim, particularly since it does not base itself on science but, even in the most ideal interpretation, on morality alone. However, the correct *preparation* for morality should first be acquired. This preparation depends on one fundamental idea: that nature, that man himself, has no original worth, no worth of its own. If nature and man should be able to attain any worth at all, it could only be derived from the unique worth of God's being.

The *Logos*, with all its consequences, suffers from a basically erroneous idea. It overrates the importance of *existence* with regard to nature and the human spirit. It is characteristic of this idea that Philo, the Jew, establishes by the word for "reason" this other God beside God (*Nebengott*). Moreover, if it is possible to say that the trinity has its best objective and historical basis in the *immortality* of the human soul, then the reason for the falling away from pure monotheism shows itself here also: it is an exaggerated claim that man should possess eternal and therefore true being.

25. The Jewish notion of immortality culminates in this idea: "the spirit returns to God, who gave it." Only in God's being can the being of man be founded, and therefore only when "the dust returns to the earth, from which it has been taken," only when the form of human appearances passes away. Even immortality offers no excuse in monotheism for a comparison between God's being and any spiritual being. From this point of view, too, matter remains transitory dust. All natural poetry is shattered on the rock of the insight that allots sublimity to the unique God exclusively.

An important moment already comes to the fore, which lays down the bridge between the root of monotheism and its peak formed by Messianism: *the distinction between eschatology and Messianism.* The dignity of man is not grounded merely in the individual man but in the idea of humanity. The latter, however, escapes representation in plastic art almost as much as it remains denied to God's uniqueness.

3

The Star of Redemption

FRANZ ROSENZWEIG

The Eternity of Truth

God is truth. Truth is his signet. By it he is known. And will be even when one day all has come to an end by which he used to make his eternity known within Time—all eternal life, all eternal way—there where even the eternal comes to an end: in eternity. For not the way alone ends here, but life too. Eternal life, after all, endures only so long as life in general. There is eternal life only in contrast to the life of those who pave the eternal way, which is always exclusively temporal. The desire for eternity sighs forth out of the well-pits of this temporality; if it assumes the form of a longing for eternal life, that is only because it itself is temporal life. Of a truth, in truth, life too disappears. The way became vanity as the ocean of light engulfed it in its billows; life, though it does not thus become vanity, dissolves in the light. It is transformed, and having been transformed, is no more. Life has gone up in light. The mute darkness of the protocosmos had found speech in death. And something stronger, love, had over-powered death. Love had chosen life. And as the protocosmos had found its voice in death, so now life rallies in the silence of the hypercosmos and is transformed into light. God is not life: God is light. He is the lord of life, but he is no more living than dead. To say the one or the other of him, with the old [philosopher] that "God has life," or with the new one that "God is dead," reveals the identical pagan bias. The only thing which does not resist verbal designation is that neither/nor of dead and alive, that tender point where life and death touch and blend. God neither lives nor is he dead; rather he quickens the dead—he loves. He is the God of the quick and the dead, precisely because he himself is neither quick nor dead.

Franz Rosenzweig, *The Star of Redemption*, trans. William W. Hallo (Boston: Beacon Press, 1972), pp. 380–92. © Henry Holt and Company, New York, NY 10011.

We experience his existence directly only by virtue of the fact that he loves us and awakens our dead Self to beloved and requiting soul. The revelation of divine love is the heart of the All.

God (Theology)

The Manifest One

We learn that God loves but not that he is love. He draws too nigh to us in love for us to be yet able to say: he is this or that. In this love we learn only that he is God, not what he is. The What, the essence, remains concealed. It is concealed precisely by being revealed. A god who did not reveal himself would not permanently hide his essence from us, for nothing remains concealed from man's far-reaching learning, his capacity for conceptualization, his inquisitive intellect. But God pours forth over us in revelation; with us he turns from stationary to active God. Precisely thereby he forges the fetters of love around our free intellect, which is irresistible for everything stationary. Bound by such bonds, summoned thus by name, we move in the orbit in which we found ourselves, and along the route on which we are placed. We no longer reach beyond this except with the powerless grasp of empty concepts.

The Concealed One

If then the Manifest God dissolves in us, his concealed aspect remains with him all the more. True, we now recognize him in the dead and the living: he is the agent who creates the dead and re-creates it, transforms it until it comes to him and lets him quicken it; he is the agent who releases from himself the living, which had heard him summon it for life, and redeems it. But Creator and Redeemer we recognize in this way only after their connection in revelation. We catch sight of the Creator and the Redeemer only from the vantage point of the God of love. We can see what has been and what is to be only to the extent that the flicker of that moment of divine love shines. The purely Prior, the protocosmos created from of yore, is too dark for us to be able to recognize the Creator's hand in it. And the purely Posterior, the redeemed hypercosmos, is too bright for us to be yet able to see the Redeemer's countenance in it; he thrones above the annually recurring hymns of the redeemed. Only in the immediate vicinity of that heart and center of the All, of the revelation of divine love, is the Creator and Redeemer too manifested to us, to the extent that such manifestation is vouchsafed at all. Revelation teaches us to trust in the Creator, to wait hopefully for the Redeemer. Thus it allows us to recognize Creator and Redeemer too only as him who loves.

The First One

Thus it is the Loving God whom alone we see directly. As such a one, however, God is not the Lord. As such he is active. He is not above his deed. He is within it. He is one with it. He loves. Only as the Lord is God beyond that of which he is the Lord: the Lord of life and death is himself beyond life and death. It is beyond conceiving what he may be as Lord of death, his essence before creation. Revelation extends only as far back as the Creator.

Its first word is "in the beginning," its second "there created." Before the beginning there may have been that inner vitality of God which grew out of divine self-creation, self-revelation, self-redemption; we could only depict it analogically, by analogy, that is, to the authentic creation, revelation, redemption, by allowing God to experience within himself what emanates from him. The heathens knew of a God who had come to be in this fashion, and this perhaps gave us a hint that we were dealing with more than a mere analogy. But no word, no term derived from this hint. That vitality concealed within itself concealed this God from us too. The God-become became the God-concealed. To answer honestly what he might be, we would have had to say: Nought. For vitality in the Uncreated, in the realm of the dead, is nought. The heathen God is not dead, but he is Lord of the dead and only of the dead at that, only of Nought. This company of gods wields power only in the realm of the dead. Elsewhere they do not rule, they only live. But as Lords of the Nought they themselves become—Noughts. 'The gods of the heathen are noughts,' exclaims the Psalmist. They are not dead, far from it; the faith of their devotees testifies to that. Gods in whom a living world believes cannot be less alive than this world itself. But in all their vitality they are just as unsteady, just as ephemeral, just as subordinate to the almighty Perhaps as is this world, as are these devotees. They lack the framework of reality, the unambiguous orientation, the fixed position, the knowledge of right and left, above and below, which enters the world only with revelation. For all their vitality, they are thus "Noughts." And "those who make them are like them; so are all who trust in them." They are created, they live concealed in the shelter of their celestial fortress; and this the Psalmist counters with that which distinguishes his God from these Noughts: he had 'made the heavens.'

The Last One

What God, the true God, may have been before creation thus defies the imagination. Not so that which he would be after redemption. True, here too our living knowledge tells us nothing about God's essence beyond the Redeemer. That he is the Redeemer is the last thing that we learn by our own experience: we 'know that he lives' and that our 'eyes will behold him.' But God's redemptive function assumed a special importance even within this knowledge that is manifest to us. His creative power and his revelatory wealth both befell something else, something objective, juxtaposed to them. His redemptive function, on the other hand, has only an indirect effect on anything else, redeeming man by means of the world, the world by means of man. Its direct effect is confined to the redemption of God himself. For God himself, redemption is the eternal deed in which he frees himself from having anything confront him that is not he himself. Redemption frees God from the work of creation as well as from his loving concern for the soul. Redemption is his day of rest, his great Sabbath, the day which is but adumbrated in the Sabbath of creation. It is the day when, freed from all that is outside himself, from all that is ever and again compared to him, incomparable though he is, he 'will be one and his name: One.' Redemption redeems God by releasing him from his revealed name. In the name and its revelation there is consummated that delivery of revelation which had commenced with creation. Whatever happens thereafter, happens "in the name." Sanctification of the name or desecration of the name—since revelation there is no deed which does not bring about one or the other. The process of redemption in the world takes place in the name and for the sake of the name. The end, however, is nameless; it is above any name. The very sanctification of the name occurs only so that the name might one day be muted. Beyond the word—and what is name but the collective word—beyond the word there shines silence. There where no other names any longer confront the one name, where the one name is al(1)-one and all that is created knows and acknowledges him and him alone, there the act of sanctification has come to rest. For sanctity is meaningful only where there is still profanity. Where everything is sacrosanct, there the Sacred itself is no longer sacred, there it simply exists. This simple existence of the Highest, such unimpaired reality, omnipotent and solely potent, beyond any desire for or joy in realization, this is truth. For truth is not to be recognized through error, as the masters of the school think. Truth attests itself; it is one with everything real; it does not part in it.

The One

And such is the truth which, as God's signet, announces that he is One at the time when even the eternal people of the one God sank and disappeared. The One—this one name— outlives the people that acknowledges it. It outlives even the revealed name by which this outliving and more-than-living name will become known to the future. For the sake of this outliving which will be the lot of the One in the future, the revealed name must already be silent for the present and for every present. Precisely we Jews, we who know the name, who are called by it, and on whom the name is called, who know it and acknowledge it—we are not allowed to pronounce it. For the sake of our eternity, we must anticipate the silence in which it and we together will one day sink. We must substitute for the name itself that which God is as long as he is still called upon as one name among other names, as Creator of a world of being, as Revealer of a language of souls: The Lord. We call him the Lord in place of a name. The name itself falls silent on our lips and even beneath the silently reading eyes, just as it will fall silent one day when he is al(1)-one in all the world, when he is One.

The Lord

It is the ultimate silence which keeps silent in us there. This is the true depth of the deity. God himself is there redeemed from his own word. He is silent. Though the God of the protocosmos had not himself been dead, he was, as Lord of dead matter, himself like this a Nought. From creation we learn that the meaning of the protocosmos is death. Just so we learn, from redemption, that the meaning of the hypercosmos is life. The Lord of the hypercosmos is the Lord of life. As such he is not alive, far from it. But just as the Lord of dead matter, though not himself dead, was like the dead and thus nought, or more exactly a Nought, one of many Noughts, so too the Lord of the hypercosmos, though not himself alive, is like the living. That simile of the Psalm applies to him too: like him are those who trust in him. Since that which believes in him is what lives, therefore he must resemble that which lives. But what then is the nature of this living matter? What word can capture its essence? For we are aware that we have here made the leap beyond the world of words, just as we were still standing before its portals in the protocosmos. The realms of the dead lay before that portal, and we had recognized its Lord as a Nought there. For what could be the essence of an Aught prior to the world other than the Nought? And the Lord of dead matter, though he is not part of that matter, is in essence akin to it and thus a Nought like it. What then might be the essence of living matter, lying beyond the world of words on that side just as dead matter lay before it on this? The place of the

Nought would already be occupied; it is located before words. With what word, then, are we to designate that which would lie beyond words? It would have to be just as little at home among words as the Nought. The Aught is at home in the world of words. But above this world, as little a part of it as the Nought, there rests the All, to be precise the true All, the All which does not burst into pieces as in the world of the Nought, but rather the one All, the One-and-all.

This is the essence of living matter. Like death in creation, it is the last word in redemption. As such it points beyond words, like death. It designates redeemed matter as death designates uncreated matter. And as the Lord of life, God would be equal in essence to this essence. He would be the Lord of the one-and-all. And just this, this lordliness over the one-and-all, is meant by the sentence: God is truth.

Truth (Cosmology)

God and the Truth

Only Noughts can reign over the multipartite Nought, over the one All only a One who still has room beside and above it. But what else still has room beside the one All as the consummate reality except—truth? For truth is the only thing which is wholly one with reality and, while no longer separating in it, nevertheless is still distinguished from it as a whole. Truth is enthroned above reality. And is then truth—God?

No. Here we ascend the pinnacle seen from which the entire traversed path lies at our feet. Truth is not God. God is truth. To go on from the latter proposition first: it is not truth itself that sits enthroned above reality, but God, because he is truth. Because truth is his signet, he can be One above the one-and-all of reality. Truth is the scepter of his dominion. Life is consummated in the one-and-all; it becomes wholly alive. Truth is the essence of this wholly alive reality to the extent that it is one with it; to the extent that it can nevertheless separate itself from this reality—without in the least suspending the connection—truth is the essence of God.

Truth and Reality

If then God is truth, reality is nonetheless also truth. Even its ultimate essence is truth. The proposition "reality is truth" claims equal status with the other one, "God is truth." Thus truth is the essence of reality as well as of God. We recognized it as such in the all-embracing concept at the end of the course of reality. Already for this reason it would be impossible to reverse the proposition. One cannot say that truth is God, because it would then equally well have to be reality. In that case God would be reality, hypercosmos one with the world, and everything would be fused in one mist. Thus God has to be "more" than the truth, just as every subject is more than its predicate, every thing more than the conception of it. And even if truth is really the last and the only thing one can still declare of God and his essence, still there remains to God a surplus beyond his essence. How then does he compare to his essence? After all, the proposition "God is truth" differs from other propositions of the same kind, even from the proposition that reality is truth, since its predicate is not the general concept under which the subject is subsumed. But in that case what could the truth be? What is truth?

Questioning the Truth of Truth

Truth is supposed to be the only thing that cannot be gainsaid, cannot be doubted. Or so philosophy teaches. It is a fundamental notion of Idealism that truth authenticates itself. Every doubt about it is supposed to presuppose its indubitability. The proposition "There is truth" is supposed to be the sole indubitable proposition. If that was true, then obviously a proposition such as "God is truth" would be inadmissible, since it would tie truth to something else here when in fact it is only supposed to bind itself. Truth could only form the subject of a sentence, not its predicate. The very question "What is truth?" would constitute *lèse majesté*. Rather the proposition which we rejected above would be valid: that truth is God. What is then really the situation with regard to this self-authentication of truth?

The Fact of Truth

To begin with we must concede the fact that the validity of truth is indubitable. It would really not do to say that there is no truth, for then it would have to be true, at a minimum—that there is no truth. This will not do, in fact. But what have we admitted herewith except—a fact? And what is the basis for the respect which this fact enjoys? The respect is undeniable, so much so that philosophy does not hesitate to establish the certainty of this undeniability on it, on the mere fact that truth is undeniable. But is this factuality then even more deserving of respect than—the truth? Woe to "Idealism" if that be so! For Idealism set out to put the truth on its own two feet, and is it now to end by anchoring it to a—belief in a matter of fact?

The Trust in Truth

But what else is actually to be expected? Can anything stand without having something to stand on? And if it were to stand on itself would not then "itself" be the ground on which it stood? For then it would, after all, not be standing on its own standing, but on "itself." Only if it stood on its own standing, then it would indeed be without a whereupon. But the fact of the undeniable validity of truth is no such standing on its own standing at all. For one does not trust this fact of undeniability after the manner of matters of fact in general. If that were the case, then indeed the fact of the truth would stand on its own standing. But it is not the case. For otherwise why should one trust just in this fact? Just in this and none other. No one denies, after all, that there is error. Error is just as undeniable as truth. By admitting the fact that the existence of truth is undeniable, one also admits that there is untruth. As facts, the undeniability of truth and the undeniability of untruth are inseparable. Why then does one trust just the former undeniability while the undeniability of untruth is depressed to a fact of second rank? Because that undeniability of truth appears to us as a—true fact, and the undeniability of error is an—untrue one. The criterion of truth is directly connected with this fact, so directly that it appears to us as itself a fact. The undeniability of truth is a true fact, but a fact.

Thus it is not the fact in which we trust, but its trustworthiness. The fact as such, truth's standing upon itself, would mean little to us if it were only a standing on its own standing. It is, however, really a case of standing on itself: the undeniability of truth is itself true. It is not the fact of undeniability which already commands belief, but only the truth of this fact.

All trust in the truth thus rests upon an ultimate trust that the ground on which truth places itself with its own two feet is capable of supporting it. Truth is itself the ultimate presupposition of truth, not as truth which stands on its own feet, but as fact in which one trusts. Truth itself is a fact even before the fact of its undeniability. The fact of its undeniability would in and of itself still be a mere fact. But by virtue of the factuality of the truth which precedes it, sealed by the trusting Truly of belief, the fact of the undeniability of truth stands really established. The self-confidence of the intellect, which is customary with the masters of philosophy, is quite justified. But it is justified only because it rests on the confidence of the whole man, of whom intellect is but a part. And this confidence is no self-confidence.

Truth and God

Thus the factuality of truth is the last thing that truth itself has to tell us about itself. This last thing is that it demands confidence in itself as a fact. And thereby it acknowledges precisely this: that it is not God. Not truth is God, but God is truth. And for its truth, the truth must appeal to the fact—not that it be truth, let alone God, but that God is truth. Truth is from God. God is its origin. If truth is illumination, then God is the light whence springs its illumination. That God is the truth, the concept with which we had to designate the essence of God, is the last thing which we recognize in him as Lord of the Last, of the one life which is consummated in the All of the hypercosmos. And this last concept of his essence dissolves in our fingers. For if God is the truth—what does this tell us about his "essence"? Nothing but that he is the primeval ground of truth and that all truth is truth only by virtue of deriving from him. Thus truth becomes a concept which is anything but universal. It is not some concept of elucidating God's essence much as the essence of any given thing might be elucidated, by means of the universal concept under which it can be subsumed. Contrariwise, God is himself the lucid light which elucidates the truth. That which, being true, becomes clear and illuminating, derives its clarity and its illuminative power from him. The proposition "God is the truth" stands all alone among the propositions which seek to elucidate his essence. This divine essentiality is none other than God's revealing (manifesting) himself. Even the "ultimate" that we know of God is none other than the innermost that we know of him, namely that he reveals himself to us. God is the truth—this is the proposition with which we thought we had attained an uttermost of knowledge. But if we look more closely into what truth is, we find that this proposition merely brings us again in different words what we had already experienced as inmost confidence; the apparent knowledge concerning his essence becomes the proximate, immediate experience of his activity: that he is truth tells us in the final analysis none other than that he—loves.

At the Gate of Truth

Thus we grasp the ultimate knowledge of God's essence in the light of the hypercosmos only to recognize it as the very same discovery that we had already been able to make daily within the world as his creatures and children. If that be so, this ultimate cognition entitles us to venture one more time back into that pristine noncognition, that cognition of the Nought, which was our point of departure. In this Nought, paganism had directly found an All, the All of its gods, the fortress in which they concealed themselves from the eyes of the world. Paganism was satisfied with these gods and demanded nothing more. Revelation, however, taught us to recognize in these gods the concealed God, the concealed one who is none other than the not yet manifest one. Paganism really had found an All in that Nought. We, who recognized it as Nought, could only hope to find the All in it. The pagan world became protocosmos for us, the life of the pagan gods became for us the concealed prelife of God. Thus the Nought of knowledge of him became a Nought full of content for us, a mysterious prediction of what we have discovered in revelation. The darkness of the Nought loses its independent power, if ever it had it before. That God is the Nought becomes as figurative a proposition as that other one, that he is the truth. Just as the truth turned out to be simply the consummation of what we had already discovered with palatable and visible presentness in the love of God, namely his revelation, so too the Nought can be none other than the prophecy of that revelation. That God is "Nought" can no more hold out against the question into the essence, the question "What is?" than that God is "truth."

Discovering the Truth

What is Nought? The very question rules out the only answer which would allow the Nought to remain Nought, the answer: Nought. For Nought can never designate the essence, can never be predicate. Nought is no concept. It has neither dimension nor content. The concluding sentence of Schopenhauer's main work, "the world is—nought," is an absurdity in purely conceptual terms. At least it does not explain the world. With regard to the world it really says—nothing. The proposition about the Nought which Schopenhauer had in mind is another matter entirely. This is the Buddhist idea which one many formulate thus: the Nought is God. This proposition is no more absurd than that of Idealism to the effect that the truth is God. Only, like the latter, it is—false. For in the last analysis the Nought, exactly like the truth, is not an independent subject at all. It is a mere fact, the expectation of an Aught, a nought-yet. It is, in short, a fact which is still seeking the ground on which it stands. As the truth is truth only because it is from God, so the Nought is Nought only because it is toward God. Only of God can it be said that he is the Nought. This would be a first, nay the first cognition of his essence. For here indeed Nought may be a predicate, precisely because God is not recognized in his essence at all: the question "What is God?" is impossible. And precisely this impossibility is perfectly indicated in the true proposition: God is the Nought. This, apart from that other "God is the truth," is the only admissible answer to this question. As the answer "God is the truth" brings the mystical question concerning his hypercosmic essence, this ultimate question, back to the living discovery of his actions, so too the answer "he is Nought" leads the abstract question concerning his protocosmic essence, this pristine question, forward to the same discovery. In this discovery there thus is collected from both directions all that we may want to ask. There beginning and end arise out of their concealment into the manifest. We find ourselves in this middle, and find Him, the "First and the Last," by our side, in immediate proximity, as a man finds his friend. Thus the concealed becomes manifest. And seen from here, factuality, proximity, immediacy now fill all the ends of the world; it sleeps in every fragment of the protocosmos, it dwells on all the stars of the hypercosmos. Whether it be truth or Nought, God's essence has vanished in his deed, a deed wholly in-essential, wholly real, wholly proximate, in his love. And this, his wholly manifest act of loving, now enters space, freed as that is from the rigidity of essence, and fills it to every farthest corner. The Manifest becomes the Concealed.

At the Goal of Truth

Beginning, middle, end thus become equally immediate, that is, equally beyond mediating, beyond median-izing, became themselves already medial. With the beginning and end as immediate as the middle, the All that once broke in pieces has now grown back together again. By its immediacy, revelation provided the cement for healing the age-old breach. True, the pure reason of Idealism had ventured to rhyme the line which begins: "God, man and constellation, in that equalizing machine of cerebration." But these three, God, world, and man, cannot be "rhymed." Rather, the first requirement was to accept them as they were, in their unrhymed factuality. Here as in world history, revelation cannot open its mouth until authentic paganism—metaphysical, metalogical, metaethical—has preceded. By undertaking to equalize and adapt, to rhyme what is without rhyme and reason, Idealism only destroys the pure factuality in which the three originally stand each by itself. The stalwart figures of man, world, and God dissolve into nebulous images like subject, object, and ideal, or I, object, and law, or whatever other names may be vouchsafed to them. If, however, the elements are simply accepted, then they can come together, not for "rhyme and reason," but rather in order to produce a route in their mutual interaction. What becomes immediately visible in revelation is neither God nor man nor world. On the contrary, God, man, and world, which had been visible figures in paganism, here lose their visibility: God appears to be concealed, man secluded, the world enchanted. What does become visible is their reciprocal interaction. That which is here immediately experienced is not God, man, and world but rather creation, revelation, and redemption. In them we experience what it means to be a creature, to be child of the Name and its believing-disbelieving bearer through the world. But this immediacy of experience no more leads to an immediate relationship to the All than did that previous immediacy of cognition. Cognition had everything, true, but only as elements, only in its pieces. Experience got beyond the piecemeal; it was whole at every moment. But because it was always at the moment, it did not, though it was whole, have everything in any of its moments. The All, which must be everything as well as whole, can neither be honestly recognized nor clearly experienced. Only the dishonest cognition of Idealism, or the unclear experience of mysticism, can delude itself with having comprehended it. The All must be comprehended beyond cognition and experience if it is to be comprehended immediately. And precisely this comprehension takes place in the illumination of prayer. We have seen how the route here is rounded out to the cycle of the year and how, with the prayer for this rounding off, the All presents itself immediately to view. In this ultimate immediacy in which the All really approaches us completely, we are permitted to renew the name with whose denial we began our work, the name of the truth. We had been forced to reject the truth as it presented itself to us at the beginning of wisdom, namely as the appointed companion on the pilgrimage through the All. We denied that philosophy which rested on such a belief in the immediacy of cognition to the All and of the All to cognition. Now that our way has taken us from an Immediate via a Nighest to the immediate view of the structure, we find that the truth, which had wanted to press itself on us as the first, is the last there at the goal. In viewing it, we comprehend the eternal truth. But we do not view it, like philosophy, as basis—for us that is and remains the Nought—but rather as ultimate goal. And in seeing the truth there at the goal, it dawns on us at the same time that the truth is after all none other than the divine revelation which occurred to us too who hover in the middle between basis and future. Our Verily, our Yea and Amen with which we answered God's revelation—at the goal it stands revealed as the beating heart of the eternal truth as well. We find our way, find ourselves in the midst of the fire of the farthest star of the eternal truth, ourselves in the truth and not—to reject here for the last time the blasphemy of philosophy—the truth in us.

4

I and Thou

MARTIN BUBER

To MAN THE WORLD IS TWOFOLD, in accordance with his twofold attitude.

The attitude of man is twofold, in accordance with the twofold nature of the primary words which he speaks.

The primary words are not isolated words, but combined words.

The one primary word is the combination *I–Thou*.

The other primary word is the combination *I–It*; wherein, without a change in the primary word, one of the words *He* and *She* can replace *It*.

Hence the *I* of man is also twofold.

For the *I* of the primary word *I–Thou* is a different *I* from that of the primary word *I–It*.

❦

PRIMARY WORDS DO NOT SIGNIFY THINGS, but they intimate relations.

Primary words do not describe something that might exist independently of them, but being spoken they bring about existence.

Primary words are spoken from the being.

If *Thou* is said, the *I* of the combination *I–Thou* is said along with it.

If *It* is said, the *I* of the combination *I–It* is said along with it.

The primary word *I–Thou* can only be spoken with the whole being.

The primary word *I–It* can never be spoken with the whole being.

❦

THERE IS NO *I* TAKEN IN ITSELF, but only the *I* of the primary word *I–Thou* and the *I* of the primary word *I–It*.

Martin Buber, *I and Thou* (New York: Simon and Schuster, 1958), pp. 3–6, 11–12, 33–34, 75, 77, 78–79, 80–81. © Simon and Schuster, New York, NY 10019. World rights: T & T Clark Ltd., Edinburgh EH2 2LQ Scotland.

When a man says *I* he refers to one or other of these. The *I* to which he refers is present when he says *I*. Further, when he says *Thou* or *It*, the *I* of one of the two primary words is present.

The existence of *I* and the speaking of *I* are one and the same thing.

When a primary word is spoken the speaker enters the word and takes his stand in it.

❧

THE LIFE OF HUMAN BEINGS is not passed in the sphere of transitive verbs alone. It does not exist in virtue of activities alone which have some *thing* for their object.

I perceive something. I am sensible of something. I imagine something. I will something. I feel something. I think something. The life of human beings does not consist of all this and the like alone.

This and the like together establish the realm of *It*.

But the realm of *Thou* has a different basis.

When *Thou* is spoken, the speaker has no thing for his object. For where there is a thing there is another thing. Every *It* is bounded by others; *It* exists only through being bounded by others. But when *Thou* is spoken, there is no thing. *Thou* has no bounds.

When *Thou* is spoken, the speaker has no *thing*; he has indeed nothing. But he takes his stand in relation.

❧

IT IS SAID THAT MAN EXPERIENCES HIS WORLD. What does that mean?

Man travels over the surface of things and experiences them. He extracts knowledge about their constitution from them: he wins an experience from them. He experiences what belongs to the things.

But the world is not presented to man by experiences alone. These present him only with a world composed of *It* and *He* and *She* and *It* again.

I experience something.—If we add "inner" to "outer" experiences, nothing in the situation is changed. We are merely following the uneternal division that springs from the lust of the human race to whittle away the secret of death. Inner things or outer things, what are they but things and things!

I experience something.—If we add "secret" to "open" experiences, nothing in the situation is changed. How self-confident is that wisdom which perceives a closed compartment in things, reserved for the initiate and manipulated only with the key. O secrecy without a secret! O accumulation of information! It, always It!

❧

THE MAN WHO EXPERIENCES has no part in the world. For it is "in him" and not between him and the world that the experience arises.

The world has no part in the experience. It permits itself to be experienced, but has no concern in the matter. For it does nothing to the experience, and the experience does nothing to it.

❧

AS EXPERIENCE, the world belongs to the primary word *I–It*.

The primary word *I–Thou* establishes the world of relation.

❧

THE SPHERES IN WHICH THE WORLD OF RELATION ARISES are three.

First, our life with nature. There the relation sways in gloom, beneath the level of speech. Creatures live and move over against us, but cannot come to us, and when we address them as *Thou*, our words cling to the threshold of speech.

Second, our life with men. There the relation is open and in the form of speech. We can give and accept the *Thou*.

Third, our life with spiritual beings. There the relation is clouded, yet it discloses itself; it does not use speech, yet begets it. We perceive no *Thou*, but none the less we feel we are addressed and we answer—forming, thinking, acting. We speak the primary word with our being, though we cannot utter *Thou* with our lips.

• • •

THE *Thou* MEETS ME THROUGH GRACE—it is not found by seeking. But my speaking of the primary word to it is an act of my being, is indeed *the* act of my being.

The *Thou* meets me. But I step into direct relation with it. Hence the relation means being chosen and choosing, suffering and action in one; just as any action of the whole being, which means the suspension of all partial actions and consequently of all sensations of actions grounded only in their particular limitation, is bound to resemble suffering.

The primary word I–*Thou* can be spoken only with the whole being. Concentration and fusion into the whole being can never take place through my agency, nor can it ever take place without me. I become through my relation to the *Thou*; as I become *I*, I say *Thou*.

All real living is meeting.

THE RELATION TO THE *Thou* IS DIRECT. No system of ideas, no foreknowlege, and no fancy intervene between *I* and *Thou*. The memory itself is transformed, as it plunges out of its isolation into the unity of the whole. No aim, no lust, and no anticipation intervene between *I* and *Thou*. Desire itself is transformed as it plunges out of its dream into the appearance. Every means is an obstacle. Only when every means has collapsed does the meeting come about.

• • •

THE WORLD OF *It* is set in the context of space and time.

The world of *Thou* is not set in the context of either of these.

The particular *Thou*, after the relational event has run its course, *is bound* to become an *It*.

The particular *It*, by entering the relational event, *may* become a *Thou*.

These are the two basic privileges of the world of *It*. They move man to look on the world of *It* as the world in which he has to live, and in which it is comfortable to live, as the world, indeed, which offers him all manner of incitements and excitements, activity and knowledge. In this chronicle of solid benefits the moments of the *Thou* appear as strange lyric and dramatic episodes, seductive and magical, but tearing us away to dangerous extremes, loosening the well-tried context, leaving more questions than satisfaction behind them, shattering security—in short, uncanny moments we can well dispense with. For since we are bound to leave them and go back into the "world," why not remain in it? Why not call to order what is over against us, and send it packing into the realm of objects? Why, if we find ourselves on occasion with no choice but to say *Thou* to father, wife, or comrade, not say *Thou* and mean *It*? To utter the sound *Thou* with the vocal organs is by no means the same as saying the uncanny primary word; more, it is harmless to whisper with the soul an amorous *Thou*, so long as nothing else in a serious way is meant but *experience* and *make use of*.

It is not possible to live in the bare present. Life would be quite consumed if precautions were not taken to subdue the present speedily and thoroughly. But it is possible to live in the bare past, indeed only in it may a life be organised. We only need to fill each moment with experiencing and using, and it ceases to burn.

And in all the seriousness of truth, hear this: without *It* man cannot live. But he who lives with *It* alone is not a man.

. . .

THE EXTENDED LINES OF RELATIONS meet in the eternal *Thou*.

Every particular *Thou* is a glimpse through to the eternal *Thou*; by means of every particular *Thou* the primary word addresses the eternal *Thou*. Through this mediation of the *Thou* of all beings fulfilment, and non-fulfilment, of relations comes to them: the inborn *Thou* is realised in each relation and consummated in none. It is consummated only in the direct relation with the *Thou* that by its nature cannot become *It*.

. . .

To this end the world of sense does not need to be laid aside as though it were illusory. There is no illusory world, there is only the world—which appears to us as twofold in accordance with our twofold attitude. Only the barrier of separation has to be destroyed. Further, no "going beyond sense-experience" is necessary; for every experience, even the most spiritual, could yield us only an *It*. Nor is any recourse necessary to a world of ideas and values; for they cannot become presentness for us. None of these things is necessary. Can it be said what really is necessary?—Not in the sense of a precept. For everything that has ever been devised and contrived in the time of the human spirit as precept, alleged preparation, practice, or meditation, has nothing to do with the primal, simple fact of the meeting. Whatever the advantages in knowledge or the wielding of power for which we have to thank this or that practice, none of this affects the meeting of which we are speaking; it all has its place in the world of *It* and does not lead one step, does not take *the* step, out of it. Going out to the relation cannot be taught in the sense of precepts being given.

. . .

In relation with God unconditional exclusiveness and unconditional inclusiveness are one. He who enters on the absolute relation is concerned with nothing isolated any more, neither things nor beings, neither earth nor heaven; but everything is gathered up in the relation. For to step into pure relation is not to disregard everything but to see everything in the *Thou*, not to renounce the world but to establish it on its true basis. To look away from the world, or to stare at it, does not help a man to reach God; but he who sees the world in Him stands in His presence. "Here world, there God" is the language of *It*; "God in the world" is another language of *It*; but to eliminate or leave behind nothing at all, to include the whole world in the *Thou*, to give the world its due and its truth, to include nothing beside God but everything in him—this is full and complete relation.

Men do not find God if they stay in the world. They do not find Him if they leave the world. He who goes out with his whole being to meet his *Thou* and carries to it all being that is in the world, finds Him who cannot be sought.

• • •

God cannot be inferred in anything—in nature, say, as its author, or in history as its master, or in the subject as the self that is thought in it. Something else is not "given" and God then elicited from it; but God is the Being that is directly, most nearly, and lastingly, over against us, that may properly only be addressed, not expressed.

• • •

5

A Thirst for the Living God

ABRAHAM ISAAC KOOK

The spirit cannot find its stability except in a life oriented toward God. Knowledge, feeling, the imagination and the will, in their inner and outer manifestations, all condition people to center their lives in God. Then will they be able to find their fulfillment, their equitable and satisfying state. If a person should seek for himself less than this exalted state, he will at once become like a ship tossed about at sea. Stormy waves, raging in opposite directions, will continually rob him of peace. He will be thrown from wave to wave, and he will be unable to find himself. If he should be able to immerse himself in some crude and vulgar preoccupation, he may succeed for a time in reducing the perspective of his life, and it will seem to him that he has finally found peace. But it will not take long, and the spirit will break out of its imprisonment and the maddening agitation will begin to act in all its fury.

The place where we may find peace is only in God. God, however, transcends the existing world, making it impossible for us to grasp any aspect of Him in feeling or thought. This makes Him, as far as we are concerned, nonexistent, and the spirit cannot find contentment in what does not exist. It is for this reason that wise men who devote themselves to the quest for God are, for the most part, spiritually weary. When the soul aspires to the most luminous light it cannot be content with that light which shines in the quality of justice in the best of good deeds, or in the measure of truth in the most precise body of knowledge or in the attribute of beauty in the most exalted of visions. It then sees the world as trivialized. The soul has become so ascendent that the entire world, its material as well as its spiritual manifestations, appears to it as an imprisonment, gripping us in its choking atmosphere. Such men seek what is beyond their reach, what, in their condition, does not appear to exist, and to change the nonexistent to an existent is even beyond the will to enter-

Abraham Isaac Kook. "A Thirst for the Living God" and "The Pangs of Cleansing" in Ben Zion Bokser, ed., *Abraham Isaac Kook* (Mahwah, NJ: Paulist Press), pp. 250–52, 261–69. © Paulist Press, Mahwah, NJ 07430.

tain. It is for this reson that there is often a weakening of the will as well as of the other life-forces among people whose inner disposition is directed toward the quest for God.

It is necessary to show how one may enter the palace: by the way of the gate. The gate is the divine dimension disclosed in the world, in all its phenomena of beauty and grandeur, as manifested in every living thing, in every insect, in every blooming plant and flower, in every nation and state, in the sea with its turbulent waves, in the panorama of the skies, in the talents of all creatures, in the thoughts of writers, the imagination of poets and the ideas of thinkers, in the feelings of every sensitive spirit and in the heroic deeds of every person of valor.

The highest domain of divinity toward which we aspire—to be absorbed in it, to be included in its radiance—but which eludes all our longing, descends for us into the world, and we encounter it and delight in its love, and find peace in its tranquillity. At times, moreover, we are privileged with a flash emanating from the higher radiance, from that higher light which transcends all thought. The heavens open for us and we see a vision of God.

But we know that this is only a temporary state, the flash will pass and we will descend to dwell once again not inside the palace, but only in the courts of the Lord.

When the longing for the light reaches its highest point, it begins to draw a great profusion of light from the hidden radiance in our own soul through which is revealed the great truth, that all the worlds with all that is in them only appear to us particular effulgences but they are in truth manifestations of the higher light, and, seen in their essence, they make up one whole, a unitary manifestation in which is included all beauty, all light, all truth, and all good. These manifestations continually emerge and develop, they show themselves increasingly as in truth individual expressions of the all-good. The bounty that streams through all the good, that raises the soul to its highest, that, on the one hand, shrinks for us the significance of the existential world, the physical as well as the spiritual, in all its splendor and magnificence—this very bounty now renews for us all the worlds and all creatures, endowing them with a new image, and every sign of life stirs joy, and every good deed delights the heart and every discipline of study broadens the mind. The narrow boundaries of all these no longer oppress the soul, which at once realizes that all these tiny sparks continually ascend and become integrated into the comprehensive unity of all life. ❧

The Pangs of Cleansing

All the ideological controversies among people and all the inner conflicts that every individual suffers in his world outlook are caused by the confusion in the conception of God. This is an endlessly profound realm and all thoughts, whether practical or theoretical, are centered in it.

One must always cleanse one's thoughts about God to make sure they are free of the dross of deceptive fantasies, of groundless fear, of evil inclinations, of wants and deficiencies. Faith in God enhances human happiness only to the extent that the greatness of God is probed and studied by the elite elements of the human race, who are equal to it. Then is the soul illumined by the divine light, through cleaving in love and full understanding to Him who is the life of all life, and all feelings, all ideas and all actions, thus become refined. The attachment to God in feeling will have its effect in directing life on an upright path to the extent that this basic principle is operative in the soul, in a state of purity.

The foundation of religious faith is rooted in the recognition of the greatness and perfection of the Infinite. Whatever we conceive of it is insignificant in comparison with what by right we should conceive of it, and what we should conceive of it is not much more significant in comparison to what it really is. Whatever we may say of the good, of mercy, justice, might, beauty, of life and the beauty of life, or of religious faith, or of the divine—what the soul in its authenticity aspires for is above all these. All the divine names, whether in Hebrew or in any other language, give us only a tiny and dull spark of the hidden light to which the soul aspires when it utters the word "God." Every definition of God brings about heresy, every definition is spiritual idolatry; even attributing to Him intellect and will, even the term *divine*, the term *God*, suffers from the limitations of definition. Except for the keen awareness that all these are but sparkling flashes of what cannot be defined—these, too, would engender heresy. Among people who have lost this basic awareness they have indeed engendered gross heresy. If we become alienated from this basic perception, our faith will be impoverished and become valueless. There is no other alternative if our faith is to shine in a living light, but that it be linked to a level of enlightenment that transcends all particular values; and thus it will assure stability to all values. All teachings beyond this perception of the greatness of the Infinite are only explanatory aids to reach the essence of religious faith—they are in the category of "the limbs of the King" and some are in the category of "the garments of the King." One who is disdainful of the garments of the King is also guilty of irreverence. One must, however, draw a distinction between the essence of faith and the explanatory aids, as well as the different levels among the explanatory aids themselves.

The confusion of thought born of deficiencies in study and knowledge leads a person to focus his thought on the divine *essence*. The more he will immerse himself in the folly of this insolent and absurd preoccupation, the more he will think that he is thereby drawing closer to the exalted knowledge of God, to which he had heard that the world's leading spirits have always aspired. When this habit pattern is established over many generations various false notions are engendered, which lead to many tragic consequences. They beget a state of confusion that undermines the individual's material and spiritual vitality. The greatest impediment to the human spirit, on reaching maturity, results from the fact that the conception of God is crystallized among people in a particular form, going back to childish habit and imagination. This is an aspect of the offense of making a graven image or a likeness of God, against which we must always beware, particularly in an epoch of greater intellectual enlightenment.

All the troubles of the world, especially the spiritual, such as grief, impatience, disillusionment, despair, the truly basic troubles of man—they came about only because of the failure to view clearly the majesty of God. It is natural for a particular creature to feel insignificant before the whole, especially before the source of all existence, in which one senses infinite transcendence of the whole. There is no anguish or depression in such lowliness, but pleasure and pride, a sense of inner power adorned by every kind of beauty. When this perception of God's majesty develops in the soul, in all its dimensions, it reconciles life to its natural subjugation. It fills life with peace to the extent that the individual recognizes the greatness of the whole and the majesty of its source. As the soul diminishes itself before its Creator, the phenomena of existence ascend in power and beauty and become permeated with the touch of universality. This natural diminishing engenders greatness and dignity, distilling in the soul endless delight in its very being, and in its ever-widening role, reaching out to the Infinite beyond. But when is it natural? It is when the greatness of the divine is well perceived in the soul, in a pure conception, above considerations of the divine *essence*, but oriented toward the vision of the goodness of life. Then does the claim for self-diminishing emanate from every aspect of the soul, its universal as well as its particular dimensions.

The general failure of the spiritual disciplines to focus on studies pertaining to God has dimmed the conception of God; there is no rational service of God sustained by refined feelings. The outward fear, the natural faith and the feeling of lowliness remain in many hearts as an inheritance from earlier epochs when the divine perception and feeling were prevalent in an enlightened state in full force, when, because of their greatness, they naturally evoked humility from people. Since the thoughts concerning God in their basic elements are unclear, God's being, as conceived by the multitude and even by individuals who should be their leaders, is that of a ruthless power from whom there is no escape and to whom one must necessarily be subservient.

When one submits to a service of God on this empty basis, according to the confused notions that are engendered in the soul when one thinks about God without enlightenment and without Torah, we have here a lower form of piety severed from its source, which is the higher piety. The person increasingly loses the splendor of his world by orienting himself to a lower level of intellectual life. No grandeur of God is then manifest in the soul, but only the lowliness of wild imaginings, that conjure up a form of some deceptive, vague, angry deity that is dissociated from reality. It confuses everyone who believes in it, depresses his spirit, blunts his feelings, inhibits the assertion of his sensibilities, and uproots the divine glory in his soul. If such a person should repeat all day that this faith is the faith in the unity of God, his statement would be empty, and it would register nothing in his soul. Every sensitive spirit must turn his mind away from this. And this is the atheism which is due to arise prior to the messianic liberation, when the knowledge of God is due to run dry in the household of Israel—and in the entire world.

The tendency of unrefined people to see the divine *essence* as embodied in the words and in the letters alone is a source of embarrassment to humanity, and atheism arises as a pained outcry to liberate man from this narrow and alien pit, to raise him from the darkness of focusing on letters and expressions, to the light of thought and feeling, finally to place his primary focus on the realm of morals. Atheism has a temporary legitimacy, for it is needed to purge away the aberrations that attached themselves to religious faith because of a deficiency in perception and in the divine service. This is its sole function in existence—to remove the *particular* images from the speculations concerning Him who is the *essence* of all life and the source of all thought. When this condition persists for a period of several generations, atheism necessarily presents itself as a specific cultural expression, to uproot the remembrance of God and all institutions of divine service. But to what uprooting did divine providence intend? To uproot the dross that separates man from the truly divine light, and in the ruins wrought by atheism will the higher knowledge of

God erect her Temple. To cleanse the air of the arrogant and evil aberration of focusing thought on the divine *essense*—a preoccupation that leads to idolatry—a thoroughgoing atheism arises, in itself no better than the former but opposed to it in absolute terms. Out of the clash of these two opposites will mankind be aided greatly to reach an enlightened knowledge of God, which will bring near its temporal and eternal happiness. In place of the presumptuous and vain preoccupation with the divine *essence*, the human heart will be oriented to concern itself with pure morality, and the heroism for higher things, which emanate as flashes from the divine light and are at all times connected with its source, showing man the way of life and placing him in the light of God. The mighty wind will come from the four corners and will raise in its surge, against their will, the anguished victims of the conception of God contrived by the sick imagination. "And you will know that I am the Lord when I have opened your graves." "And I will bring you up from your graves, O my people, and bring you to the land of Israel" (Ezek. 37:13, 12). The violence of atheism will cleanse away the dross that accumulated in the lower levels of religious faith, and thereby will the heavens be cleared and the shining light of the higher faith will become visible, which is the song of the world and the truth of the world.

Whoever recognizes the essence of atheism from this perspective embraces the positive element in it and traces it back to its origin in holiness. He glimpses the awesome splendor in the ice-like formations upon the celestial horizon (Cf. Ezekiel 1:22).

When one discovers the stern protest embodied in rebellion and atheism, which seeks to repudiate the good of our ancestral inheritance in pursuit of some new vision, one finds the element of good inherent in it. It is in truth a general aspect of penitence stirring the heart. It is the kernel of repentance that seeks to redress everything lowly and defective, and as a result of it one also comes to redress the defect that is represented in its destructiveness. Then there will be a general return to God, and redemption will come to the world. The perfection of the world that will be effected by the influence of the Jewish people is found in the ideal of penitence. As long as a person orders his life on the basis of a fixed pattern he will not be able to escape his intellectual, moral and practical deficiencies, and how will he be able to mend himself? We must therefore not permit habit to be the primary factor in our social or personal life. The individual person as well as society at large must always seek to correct itself and to mend its spiritual and practical defects. All reformations of life and all revolutionary proposals that aim to change the order of things so as to improve it are all paths of repentance. Repentance must always be at the summit of all efforts to improve the world.

From time to time there is exposed the admixture of the pure belief in one God with the obfuscation of ascribing corporeality to Him, and whenever an aspect of anthropomorphism falls away, it appears as though religion itself has fallen. Soon, however, it turns out that religion has not fallen, but has become clarified. In the recent turn of the human spirit toward pure faith the last subtle shell of anthropomorphism is giving way, which consists in ascribing the attribute of general *existence* to God, for truly whatever we ascribe to the term *existence* is immeasurably remote from the divine. This denial has the sound of atheism. It is, however, the highest expression of religion when it becomes well clarified, and the human spirit grows accustomed to hearing the message of religion in terms of actions and influences, the phenomena of existence and the phenomena of the Torah and of morals—the recognition that *the divine is the activating influence on existence and is, therefore, obviously above existence.* What looks like atheism, cleansed of its defilement, thus returns to the highest realms of pure religion. But this denial of *exis-*

tence [in God], which is a return to the vision of God as the source of all existence and to the most ultimate essence of the majesty of all existence, requires the most scrupulous understanding. Each day it must be traced back to its authentic purity.

Religion is corrupted through the decline of the higher Torah, through which one gains the recognition of the greatness of God, the higher perfection that is infinite and beyond assessment. Thus our religion does not yield the noble fruit it ought to yield, it does not raise the souls from their lowly state and the numbers of those who dishonor it and desecrate it increase. However, the Jewish religion is rooted in the Infinite, which transcends every particular content of religion, and for this reason the Jewish religion may truly be considered as the ideal of religion, the religion of the future, the "I shall be what I shall be" (Exod. 3:14), what is immeasurably higher than the content of religion in the present. The ideal essence descends many levels to become the Jewish religion as a corporate religious establishment rather than the ideal essence of religion. The aberration of atheism arises against religion as an established institution, but atheism does not affect the ideal essence of religion, which is beyond atheism as it is beyond institutional religion. Atheism is without a true ideal; as the Zohar put it (Mishpatim, II, 103a), "The alien deity is sterile, it bears no fruit." Despair and chaos contribute nothing, and therefore there is no place for an ideal contrary to the religious ideal. Though there is a conception [in the Cabbalah] of a negative counterforce paralleling institutional religion, the ideal essence of religion, which corresponds to what the Talmud calls the "fiftieth level of understanding" that was not revealed to Moses (Rosh Hashanah 21b), has no counterpart in the realm of the negative. The influence of this fiftieth level of understanding, the ideal essence of religion, infuses life to all other levels and subdues the negative aspect of atheism, which is devoid of an ideal, before the holiness of religion, which remains attached to an eternal ideal. "With You is the source of life" (Ps. 36:14).

On seeing such convulsions people believe that religion is dying, that the world is being overturned. In truth, however, the shadows are stirring, they are in flight in order to make room for the light. If religious faith is to be revitalized, a great effort is needed to deepen the knowledge of God, to follow the most subtle paths of mystical thinking through which one rises above every kind of limitation in God. As it is a case of folly and weakness to ignore "revealed" knowledge, the beauty and might exemplified in empirical existence, so is it foolish to detach our minds from the inclination to pursue the promptings hidden in the depths of the soul, without which one cannot discern anything sublime that transcends our dull senses, which have been dulled by much defilement and affliction. It is only thus that the soul can be filled with knowledge and sensibility, and it is only through such subtlety of thought that the world will be filled with the light and the dew of revival, that the dormant will be awakened and the dead return to life. The best among the *zaddikim*, the sages most informed in the knowledge of God, must bestir themselves greatly to stimulate the interest in studying the greatness of God through all methods, the rational and the ethical. Then will religion regain its strength, it will rise out of its darkness toward a great light, and it will become the life-giving force to the highest and the most sensitive of souls, even as it is in its authentic nature. Thus will it necessarily regain its respect among all sections of humanity. For the Jews this is the anchor of the nation's rescue in this epoch—to restore to it the preciousness of religious faith in its purity, which is the entire basis of their existence.

But it is precisely when the lights are in convulsion, and the vessels that have housed them seem about to break, that there is need to proclaim that indeed the letters, the words, the actions, are not the essence of the light, but they are vessels, the organs of a living body, which bears within itself a soul. But alas for anyone who denies them even the role of vessels. Whoever denies the holiness of the letters, the words, the actions and the forms within their own domain, will render himself speechless, without utterance, without any inner conceptual image, and altogether without the power to act, flooded by various forces that will disturb him altogether, body and soul.

Raise up religion, elevate thought, acclaim the real life, lived according to the conceptual forms and the practical actions in which the imagination has robed the higher light. It is a divine service through life, through the Torah and through the commandments.

6

God as the Power that
Makes for Salvation

MORDECAI KAPLAN

What Salvation Must Mean in Our Day

Although faith in other-worldly salvation no longer functions as it did in the past, this does not mean that we can dispense with the faith that the world affords men an opportunity for salvation, or with the institution of the Sabbath that expresses and confirms this faith. However conditions of life may have changed and however different our modern conception of the cosmos may be from that held by our fathers, the need for a faith that will save us from a sense of the vanity and futility of human life remains with us. For man is not a self-sufficient entity. His interests cannot be confined in space or time to his immediate physical environment and the brief span of his life. And it is these larger interests that, above all, he identifies with his selfhood or personality.

Man's immediate unconscious responses to the physical stimuli of his environment, while indispensable to his life, do not spell for him the meaning of life; they are not the experiences that make him want to cling to life. It is of his purposive acts, his awareness of wants and his attempts to satisfy them that a man thinks, when he thinks of his life. The summoning of all our resources of memory and imagination in response to consciously felt needs gives us our sense of personality. As part of the process of satisfying our wants we conceive a future situation in which these wants shall have been satisfied; and we endeavor to affect our environment or our own behavior in ways that conform to that concept. Such concepts are what we mean by ideals.

The fact of human mortality puts no temporal limit to the objectives of our idealization. Men are concerned that, even after their death, their world be a safe one for their

Mordecai Kaplan, "God as the Power that Makes for Salvation," in *The Meaning of God in Modern Jewish Religion* (New York: Reconstructionist Press, 1937), pp. 51–57, 61–69. © Jewish Reconstructionist Federation, Wyncote, PA 19095.

children to grow up in. But the fact of human mortality does put an end to the opportunity of men to achieve the purpose that the ideal expresses; it is this which often overwhelms men with the sense of human impotence and the futility of living. This sense of frustration can be counteracted only by faith in a God of salvation, faith that inherent in the world as it is constituted is the Power that makes for the fulfillment of all valid ideals. We shall learn in the sequel what constitutes validity.

We cannot today think of salvation in the same other-worldly terms as did our fathers. But in the terms in which we can think of it, it remains an indispensable element of our religion. Fortunately, the very forces that have destroyed the illusion by which the medieval mind saved itself from despair and weariness of life give us a substitute for our lost paradise. The extent to which man has, by scientific techniques, changed the face of nature for the satisfaction of his own physical needs has released him from feeling the helplessness in the face of other obstacles to the satisfaction of his desires and purposes. True, psychology and the social sciences have lagged behind the physical sciences in their development, and we are not yet able to change our social environment in conformity with human needs with the same facility with which we have changed our physical environment. "Knowledge comes but wisdom lingers." Nevertheless, we look to these sciences to point the way to the eventual abolition of the inveterate evils of human life.

The salvation that the modern man seeks in this world, like that which his fathers sought in the world to come, has both a personal and a social significance. In its personal aspect it represents the faith in the possibility of achieving an integrated personality. All those natural impulses, appetites and desires which so often are in conflict with one another must be harmonized. They must never be permitted to issue in a stalemate, in such mutual inhibition as leaves life empty and meaningless, without zest and savor. Nor must they be permitted to issue in distraction, in a condition in which our personality is so pulled apart by conflicting desires that the man we are in certain moments or in certain relations looks with contempt and disgust at the man we are in others. When our mind functions in such a way that we feel that all our powers are actively employed in the achievement of desirable ends, we have achieved personal salvation.

This personal objective of human conduct cannot, however, be achieved without reference to a social objective as well. Selfish salvation is an impossibility, because no human being is psychologically self-sufficient. We are impelled by motives that relate themselves to the life of the race with as imperative an urge as by any that relate themselves to the preservation of our individual organism. "Love is strong as death,"[1] and frequently sacrifices life itself for the object of love. Although to every individual the achievement of personal salvation is his supreme quest and responsibility, it is unattainable without devotion to the task of social salvation. The thought, "If I am not for myself, who will be for me?" in this striving for salvation always carries with it the implication, "If I am but for myself, what am I?"[2] because we cannot even think of ourselves except in relation to something not ourselves.

In its social aspect, salvation means the ultimate achievement of a social order in which all men shall collaborate in the pursuit of common ends in a manner which shall afford to each the maximum opportunity for creative self-expression. There can be no personal salvation so long as injustice and strife exist in the social order; there can be no social salvation so long as the greed for gain and the lust for domination are permitted to inhibit the hunger for human fellowship and sympathy in the hearts of men. There is a sense in which it is still true that salvation is of the world to come, for its attainment is clearly not of today or of tomorrow. That it will ever be attained can never be demonstrated, but faith must assume it as the objective of human behavior, if we are not to succumb to the cynical acceptance of evil, which is the only other alternative.

The goal to be reached need not necessarily be conceived as a static and final goal. Life can always be depended upon to create new wants that call for satisfaction and give birth to new ideals. But the measure of our self-fulfillment as individuals and as a society will ever be the extent to which our lives are oriented to valid ideals. In this sense the center of gravity of our lives remains in the world to come, for it is ever the potentialities of the future that redeem the efforts of the present from futility, and that save our souls or ethical personalities from frustration. The self-indulgent sensualist who spiritually lives a hand-to-mouth existence can never find self-fulfillment, because such a life does not begin to bring into play all the latent faculties and powers that inhere in human nature. Only the individual whose purposes in life relate themselves to objectives that lie in the future can experience that sense of well-being and aliveness which comes when all our powers are enlisted in the pursuit of some desired end.

In the light of all that, *salvation must be conceived mainly as an objective of human action, not as a psychic compensation for human suffering*. Though it is absurd to charge religion as such with being an opiate, the truth is that other-worldly religion did function as an opiate. But this fact by itself does not count even against other-worldly religion. In the two thousand years preceding the Enlightenment, religion had to function as an opiate, for so acutely aware had man become of evil which seemed to him irremediable that he might have been driven into despair, had he not been able to hope for salvation in the hereafter. By preserving the ideal of salvation, so to speak, in heaven, man could bring that ideal down to earth as soon as he learned enough about himself and the world he lived in to be able to improve both. But religion owes a genuine debt to those who have called attention to the danger in our own day of drugging the human with the opiate of other-worldliness. The effect of such an opiate at the present time is to keep us from the attainment of salvation on earth. This is equally true whether we think in terms of personal salvation or of social salvation.

In regard to personal salvation, the habit of conceiving it as coming from the grace of God has made men seek salvation by a withdrawal from the world and the flesh, and by resort to prayer, meditation and ascetic self-mortification. In the light of modern science, however, such measures defeat their own purpose. Man has a physical organism not unlike that of the lower animals, and the healthy functioning of that organism is a prerequisite to mental and spiritual hygiene. The effort to suppress any natural instinct is more likely to lead to a dangerous psychosis than to that serene, tranquil and happy state which we associate with salvation. Withdrawal from the world must result in an intense introversion and exaggerated egocentricity which inhibit those impulses to fellowship, friendship and love that for most of us express what we feel to be best and truest in our natures. Excessive prayer, too, often represents the verbalization of interests that should express themselves in deeds, not in words. Preoccupation with the sense of sin may result in such self-contempt as to emphasize rather than heal the breach between the crude appetites of men and their deeper, more stable and more significant social emotions. The masochism of self-mortification leads inevitably to the sadism of fanaticism.

We cannot hate human nature in ourselves and love it in others. "Be not righteous overmuch,"[3] and "Be not wicked in thine own esteem"[4] are injunctions, the significance of which other-worldly religion has too frequently overlooked. The self-righteousness which makes us withdraw in holy horror from contact with the wicked world, and the self-contempt which believes personal salvation impossible except by the intervention of some miracle of grace, are alike dangers inherent in the other-worldly viewpoint. The religion of the future will, therefore, turn from most of these practices and avail itself of such guidance as the science of psychology affords for the training of character, with personal salvation as its goal.

With respect to social salvation, other-worldliness has been, if that is possible, an even greater obstacle to its attainment. Indeed, it is the obvious failure of religion in this respect that is responsible for its condemnation by the class-conscious laboring masses. Other-worldly religion, by regarding patient resignation to social evil as a method of achieving merit and ultimate salvation in the world to come, definitely aligned religion with the forces of social reaction. To bear one's yoke was considered more virtuous than to rebel.[5] Revolution against the social order, no matter how tyrannical and oppressive that order might be, was condemned. This played so directly into the hands of ruling powers that these tended further to corrupt religion by State subsidies and special privileges. The State made itself the secular arm for enforcing Church discipline, and the Church made itself the religious arm for inculcating loyalty to the status quo. Although the multiplication of religious sects since the Protestant Reformation has in a measure pried loose this unholy alliance, nevertheless the role played by the churches during the World War shows that, on the whole, organized religion is still counted upon to defend the status quo against attack.

That religion may be a force for revolution or social reconstruction is best evidenced by the prophetic movement in Israel. Because the Prophets conceived of the scene of the Kingdom of God as on this earth, because they meant by it the manifestation of God's government of Israel through the establishment of righteousness and justice, they were almost always antagonistic to the existing regime. Contrast the attitude of Hosea expressed in the words: "I give thee a king in mine anger and I take him away in My wrath,"[6] with the medieval doctrine of the divine right of kings. Religion must no longer betray the hopes of men for the abolition of poverty, oppression and war on this earth by regarding these evils as mere "trials and tribulations" or "chastisements of love," for which we shall be compensated in another world. It must cease waiting for an act of miraculous intervention to remove these evils "in the end of days." It must encourage men with faith and hope to apply human intelligence and good-will to the removal of these evils in the achievement of the social salvation of mankind.

· · ·

God as the Creative Life of the Universe, the Antithesis of Irrevocable Fate and Absolute Evil

The idea of creativity, which makes of the Sabbath a *zeker lema'aseh bereshit*, "a memorial of the creation," has functioned in Jewish life as an antidote to the pessimism which experience with the evils of life tends to engender. We are so accustomed to think of God as the creator of the world that it is hard for us to associate the idea of godhood with any being not conceived as endowed with superlative powers of creation. It is, nevertheless, a fact that in primitive religion, and even in the more developed religions of polytheism, the notion of godhood was seldom closely associated with the power to create. The psychological origin of the belief in God as creator is undoubtedly wish-fulfillment of man's desire to transform his environment when he realized his own impotence to do so. The realization of that impotence marks considerable progress in human development, and may be recognized by the rise of creation myths.

Before the age of philosophy, creation was always synonymous with transformation, or making over some pre-existing substance. Even in the philosophies of Plato and Aristotle, the existence of primeval matter is likewise assumed. That primeval matter was regarded as coeternal and coexistent with the divine principle of creativity. The human mind, as Kant has shown, cannot really solve the problem of absolute beginnings, and identifying creativity with transformation marks the limit of its capacity. But the theologians who were intent upon maintaining the historicity of the miracles recorded in the Bible felt that the power merely to transform was not adequate for the performance of miracles, for such power was limited by the inherent nature of reality. Only the power to create out of nothing could comport with the performance of miracles. This line of reasoning made the belief in *creatio ex nihilo* the apple of discord among thinkers for centuries. To the modern way of thinking, its connection with spiritual life is remote, if not altogether irrelevant.

Only the moral aspect of that belief is nowadays of vital import. *The moral implication of the traditional teaching that God created the world is that creativity, or the continuous emergence of aspects of life not prepared for or determined by the past, constitutes the most divine phase of reality.* A modern equivalent of the notion of creativity, which tradition regarded as the very essence of godhood, would be the concept of the latent and potential elements in the universe as making for the increase in the quantity and quality of life. Since a spiritual conception of life is consistent only with a world-outlook which counts on the realization of much that is still in the womb of possibility, it implies the belief that both man and the universe are ever in a state of being created.

The Sabbath is regarded in Jewish tradition as celebrating the creation of the world. The modern equivalent of that interpretation of the day would be the use of it as a means of accentuating the fact that we must reckon with creation and self-renewal as a continuous process. The liturgy speaks of God as "renewing daily the works of creation." By becoming aware of that fact, we might gear our own lives to this creative urge in the universe and discover within ourselves unsuspected powers of the spirit.

The belief in God as creator, or its modern equivalent, the conception of the creative urge as the element of godhood in the world, is needed to fortify the yearning for spiritual self-regeneration. That yearning dies down unless it is backed by the conviction that there is something which answers to it in the very character of life as a whole. *There can hardly be any more important function for religion than to keep alive this yearning for self-renewal and to press it into the service of human progress.* In doing that, religion will combat the recurrent pessimism to which we yield whenever we misjudge the character of the evil in the world. It will teach us to live without illusion and without despair about the future, with clear recognition of the reality of evil and creative faith in the possibility of the good.

We should not minimize in the least the pain, the agony, the cruelty and the destruction that deface the world. But we should not go to the extent to which the ancients and moderns have gone when they interpreted all that evil as inherent and eternal in the very constitution of the world. Of what avail to strive to improve the conditions of life when we know beforehand that life must ever remain the same? Koheleth's conclusion "All is vanity" derives from the premise, "There is nothing new under the sun." Religion should indicate to us some way whereby we can transform the evils of the world, if they are within our control, and transcend them, if they are beyond our control. If we give heed to the creative impulse within us which beats in rhythm with the creative impulse of the cosmos, we can always find some way of making our adjustment to evil productive of good. It is not given to us, with our necessarily limited vision and understanding, to know how the effects of this creative adjustment can withstand the ravages of time. It is enough that in the act of achieving such adjustment we experience self-fulfillment, as though that act were eternal and an end in itself.

To effect an adjustment which shall partake of the nature of faith and hope, it is essential to guard against the fatal error into which men have always fallen with regard to the place of evil in the scheme of things. We must avoid the tendency to interpret our own despair as the collapse of the moral order. The error has consisted mainly in personifying, dramatizing or apotheosizing evil. Instead of being treated as mere negation, chance or accident which is inevitable only in the logical and passive sense that darkness is the inevitable concomitant of light, evil has been raised to the same level of intention and power as God. At times it has been represented as superior to God and whatever is associated with God; at other times as coordinate with God and as engaged in frustrating his purposes. This is not a question merely of metaphysics, but of world-outlook and attitude toward life. Misleading interpretations of evil have always dominated the human mind and found expression in the classic literatures, in the oracles of scientists, and even in the great religions of the past. Their unwholesome and paralyzing effects may be noted in the ordinary conversations and actions of the average man and woman of today. As a first step in affirming and eliciting the creativity, that latent and potential good in the world which spells God, it is necessary to identify for the purpose of deprecation the conceptions of evil which obstruct the realization of the good.

One interpretation of life, which western civilization has inherited from ancient Greek culture, is that human life is the inevitable working out of a dire doom from which there is no escape. Man may delude himself with the belief that he is free to make of his life what he will, but in actuality he is trapped by a destiny which is deaf to his most heart-rending appeals. The very antithesis of that is the version of life implied in the Jewish religion. According to that version, human life is part of the process of creation which God initiated, a process in which the future always somehow redeems the past, and man is always being tested as to how long he can hold out in awaiting that future.

The idea of Fate, or Necessity, which in one form or another is to be found in every civilization, became a veritable obsession with the Greeks. It attained a depth and pathos unknown to any other people. It is writ large on almost every page of their great literature. In a variety of ways unparalleled in any other language, the Greeks sounded the threnody of man's impotence in the face of "Anankē," "Moira," or "Kēr." The idea of fate was the keynote of Greek tragedy. Euripides put it clearly in *Orestes*:

> "Ye tear-drowned toiling tribes
> Whose life is but a span,
> Behold how fate, or soon or late,
> Upsets the hopes of man!
> In sorrow still your changing state
> Must end as it began."

The pattern of the world as the ancient Greeks conceived it may be said to have been that of a huge spiderweb, at the center of which Fate, or Necessity, like a great spider, feeds on the victims caught in the filaments of the web. In his ignorance man worships these very filaments as gods, praying to them to help him in his struggle against Fate, forgetting that they themselves are nothing but the very ooze of Fate. "Ah me! if Fate, ordained of old, held not the will of gods, constrained, controlled," sings the Chorus in Æschylus' *Agamemnon*. "Pray not at all, since there is no release for mortals from predestined calamity," says the Chorus in Sophocles' *Antigone*.

Although western civilization has long repudiated the Greek mythology and the Greek religion, it is dominated by the Greek mood and has come under the spell of the Greek view of life. In spite of the western man's acceptance of the religion that came from the East, he is the western man still and cannot free himself of the habit of thinking in terms of cold, impersonal and iron law which is relentless and unchanging. At bottom, this is nothing more than a resurgence of the belief in Fate. The idea of nature and natural law is the empire of Fate, conceived as extending into the innermost depths of the human soul.

This fatalism with which the western mind has always been obsessed has acted like a canker which disintegrates the soul of every people it has attacked. In ancient Hellenic culture the dread of Fate at least begot great epic and dramatic art. The plays of the great tragedians elicited from Aristotle the observation that they had the effect of purifying and exalting the emotions. They helped to give man a sense of his own worth and dignity. Because Fate was conceived as external to man himself, a power operating upon him but not inherent in his makeup, his attempt to measure himself against Fate rendered him morally victorious. He remained, like Prometheus, a defiant Titan, chained to the rock but unsubdued. It is otherwise with the modern elaboration of fatalism into scientific law. All human values dissolve under the scrutiny of scientific self-analysis. When fatalism is thought out to its logical conclusion, and the human being is shown up to be nothing but a congeries of wild and uncontrollable hates and passions that inhere in the blood, then the last shred of human worth and dignity disappears, and all that is left is abject self-pity. This is always the swan song of art; this marks its decadence.

The reiteration of this decadent note in the serious literature of contemporary America has led some writers to question whether our whole American civilization with all its fierce energy and activity is characterized less by youthful verve and vigor, as optimists would have us believe, than by a pathological restlessness that suggests a dangerous maladjustment to life. In the tragedies of Eugene O'Neill, in the novels of Dreiser, Anderson, and Lewis, the most poignant theme is the struggle of characters, preconditioned by circumstances against a healthy adjustment to life, falling slowly victims to the inevitable consequences of their conditioning. But this note is no more characteristic of America than it is of other nations of the western world. It cannot be considered, as has been suggested, to be due to some racial compulsion. Rather is it to be ascribed to an intellectual compulsion, to the compulsion that inheres in the assumption of the occidental mind. The incubus of curse and calamity, bred of the elemental fear expressed in the belief that some irrevocable Fate has set its seal upon the career of the universe, has lain altogether too long on the mind of the western man. It must be shaken off, if western civilization is to survive.

According to the version which the Jewish civilization at its best has always given to man's place in the world, life is conceived not as the working out of a doom but as the fulfillment of a blessing. The process of that fulfillment is continually interrupted by all manner of evil. Evil is an interference; it is not Fate. "The die is cast," says the occidental man; and Jewish religion retorts, "But the final issue is with God." For God is the creator, and that which seems impossible today he may bring to birth tomorrow.

Once we learn to regard evil as the chance invasion of sheer purposelessness, and learn to identify all meaningful factors in the world with good and blessing, we become adjusted to whatever befalls us, not in the spirit of desperate resignation, but of hopeful waiting. Thus, for example, the Jews have been taught to regard their national history in the light of the blessing which God had bestowed upon Abraham. Though every page of that history records unparalleled suffering and tragedy, the Jews as a people never for one moment surrendered their faith in the blessing. The suffering and the tragedy have always been viewed merely as interruptions which have postponed the fulfillment of the blessing. They were never thought of as the fulfillment of some irrevocable doom. It is only Christianity, which has assimilated a great deal of the Greek spirit, that has made the doctrine of original sin a fundamental teaching. Calvinism, with its crystallization of Jewish thought into the fixed molds of western logic, has gone so far as to make of God a cosmic monster who delights in the tortures of the eternally damned.

According to Jewish traditional teaching, man is not trapped but tested. His vicissitudes should serve as a challenge to his faith, and patience in the face of the retardation of that blessing which he has a right to expect with the gift of life. To deny the worth of life and to fall into despair because the promise is slow of fulfillment is to fail in the test. This is the main point in the cycle of Abraham stories, which culminates in the account of the test to which God put Abraham when he commanded him to offer up Isaac. At first sight, it appears that in the Jewish religion, too, the notion of some inexorable doom hanging over mankind is present; for what else is the meaning of the curse imposed upon Adam and Eve for their having eaten the forbidden fruit? But the fact is that from the standpoint of the Torah the curse inflicted on mankind is not treated as irrevocable. On the contrary, the assumption throughout Scriptures is that God has revealed to the descendants of Adam the means whereby they may nullify the effects of the original curse.

Yet it would be untrue to say that Jewish civilization has always managed to steer clear of the idea of Fate. Time and again some of the wisest in Israel fell under the influence of Greek thought, and were so thrilled by their newly acquired teachings that they prated of them with the glib cocksureness of converts. One such wise man was Koheleth. He states that the doctrine of Fate in the well-known verses: "Everything has its appointed time, and there is a time determined for every occurrence under the sun. There is a time appointed to be born, a time to die; there is a time appointed for planting and a time for uprooting.[7] The sons of men are snared in an evil time, when it falleth suddenly upon them."[8] No wonder life was nothing to him but a series of vanities. His book was taken into the Bible only because it has been reinterpreted to harmonize with the traditional outlook of Judaism. Note, for example, what the rabbis did with the verse, "There is no new thing under the sun,"[9] which evidently contradicts the religious faith in man's power of self-renewal. "The Sages said to Solomon," we read in *Pirkē de R. Eliezer*,[10] "the righteous and all their works will be *renewed*, but the wicked will not be renewed, and 'no new thing' shall be given to all who worship and trust *under* the sun. Therefore it is said, 'There is no new thing under the sun.'"

The present condition of western civilization, with its failure of nerve, may be traced to the sense of frustration which man now experiences. This frustration is the outcome of man's failure to attain that happinesss to which he had looked forward by reason of his increased knowledge of nature and his ability to manipulate its forces. He has discovered to his consternation that there are forces within him, selfishness, greed and lust, which rage within his soul and work with the same inevitability as the mechanical forces about him, but which he finds himself unable to bring under control. He feels himself more trapped than ever. Out of this realization nothing good can come, only despair and disillusionment. There is an urgent need for a renewal of that faith in life which Jewish religion proclaimed when it identified God with creation.

Notes

1. Cant. 8:6.
2. *Abot.* I, 14.
3. Ecc. 7:16.
4. *Abot.* II, 13.
5. *Cf.* Cant. *R.* on 2:7.
6. Hos. 13:11.
7. Ecc. 3:1, 2.
8. *Ibid.,* 9:12.
9. *Ibid.,* 1:9.
10. Ch. LI.

7

God in Search of Man

ABRAHAM JOSHUA HESCHEL

An Ontological Presupposition

Moments of Insight

But how can we ever reach an understanding of Him who is beyond the mystery? How do we go from the intimations of the divine to a sense for the realness of God? Certainty of the realness of God comes about

As a response of the whole person to the mystery and transcendence of living.

As a response, it is an act of raising from the depths of the mind an *ontological presupposition* which makes that response intellectually understandable.

The meaning and verification of the ontological presupposition are attained in rare *moments of insight.*

The Encounter with the Unknown

It is the mystery that evokes our religious concern, and it is the mystery where religious thinking must begin. The way of thinking about God in traditional speculation has been *via eminentiae*, a way of proceeding from the known to the unknown. Our starting point is not the known, the finite, the order, but *the unknown within the known*, the infinite with the finite, *the mystery within the order.*

All creative thinking comes out of *an encounter with the unknown*. We do not embark upon an investigation of what is definitely known, unless we suddenly discover that what we have long regarded as known is actually an enigma. Thus the mind must stand beyond its shell of knowledge in order to sense that which drives us toward knowledge. It is when we begin to comprehend or to assimilate and to adjust reality to our thought that the mind returns to its shell.

Indeed, knowledge does not come into being only as the fruit of thinking. Only an extreme rationalist or solipsist would claim that knowledge is produced exclusively through the combination of concepts. Any genuine encounter with reality is an encounter with the unknown, is an intuition in which an awareness of the object is won, a rudimentary, *preconceptual* knowledge. Indeed, no object is truly known, unless it was first experienced in its unknown-ness.

It is a fact of profound significance that we sense more than we can say. When we stand face to face with the grandeur of the world, any formulation of thought appears as an anticlimax. It is in the awareness that the mystery which we face is incomparably deeper than what we know that all creative thinking begins.

Preconceptual Thinking

The encounter with reality does not take place on the level of concepts through the channels of logical categories; concepts are second thoughts. All conceptualization is symbolization, an act of accommodation of reality to the human mind. The living encounter with reality takes places on a level that precedes conceptualization, on a level that is responsive, *immediate*, *preconceptual*, and *presymbolic*.[1] Theory, speculation, generalization, and hypothesis, are efforts to clarify and to validate the insights which preconceptual experience provides. "To suppose that knowledge comes upon the scene only as the fruit of reflection, that is generated in and through the symbols and sign manipulations, is, in principle, to revert to that very idol of sheer rationalism against which the whole vigorous movement of modern empiricism has lodged such effective and necessary protest."[2]

All insight stands between two realms, the realm of objective reality and the realm of conceptual and verbal cognition. Conceptual cognition must stand the test of a double reference, of the reference to our system of concepts and the reference to the insights from which it is derived.

Particularly in religious and artistic thinking, the disparity between that which we encounter and that which is expressed in words and symbols, no words and symbols can adequately convey. In our religious situation we do not comprehend the transcendent; we are present at it, we witness it. Whatever we know is inadequate; whatever we say is an understatement. We have an awareness that is deeper than our concepts; we possess insights that are not accessible to the power of expression.

Knowledge is not the same as awareness, and expression is not the same as experience. By proceeding from awareness to knowledge we gain in clarity and lose in immediacy. What we gain in distinctness by going from experience to expression we lose in genuineness. The difference becomes a divergence when our preconceptual insights are lost in our conceptualizations, when the encounter with the ineffable is forfeited in our symbolizations, when the dogmatic formulation becomes more important than the religious situation.

The entire range of religious thought and expression is a sublimation of a presymbolic knowledge which the awareness of the ineffable provides. That awareness can only partly be sublimated into rational symbols.

Philosophy of religion must be an effort to recall and to keep alive *the meta-symbolic relevance of religious terms*. Religious thinking is in perpetual danger of giving primacy to concepts and dogmas and to forfeit the immediacy of insights, to forget that the known is but a reminder of God, that the dogma is a token of His will, the expression the inexpressible at its minimum. Concepts, words must not become screens; they must be regarded as windows.

Religion Is the Response to the Mystery

The roots of ultimate insights are found, as said above, not on the level of discursive thinking, but on the level of wonder and radical amazement, in the depth of awe, in our sensitivity to the mystery, in our awareness of the ineffable. It is the level on which the great things happen to the soul, where the unique insights of art, religion, and philosophy come into being.

It is not from experience but *from our inability to experience* what is given to our mind that certainty of the realness of God is derived. It is not the order of being but the transcendent in the contingency of all order, the allusions to transcendence in all acts and all things that challenge our deepest understanding.

Our certainty is the result of wonder and radical amazement, of awe before the mystery and meaning of the totality of life beyond our rational discerning. Faith is *the response* to the mystery, shot through with meaning; the response to a challenge which no one can for ever ignore. "The heaven" is a challenge. When you "lift up your eyes on high," you are faced with the question. Faith is an act of man who *transcending himself* responds to Him who *transcends the world*.

To Rise Above Our Wisdom

Such response is a sign of man's essential dignity. For the essence and greatness of man do not lie in his ability to please his ego, to satisfy his needs, but rather in his ability to stand above his ego, to ignore his own needs; to sacrifice his own interests for the sake of the holy. The soul's urge to judge its own judgments, to look for meaning beyond the scope of the tangible and finite—in short, the soul's urge *to rise above its own wisdom*— is the root of religious faith.

God is the great mystery, but our faith in Him conveys to us more understanding of Him than either reason or perception is able to grasp.

Rabbi Mendel of Kotsk was told of a great saint who lived in his time and who claimed that during the seven days of the Feast of Booths his eyes would see Abraham, Isaac, Jacob, Joseph, Moses, Aaron, and David come to the booth. Said Rabbi Mendel: "I do not see the heavenly guests; I only have faith that they are present in the booth, and to have faith is greater than to see."

This, indeed, is the greatness of man: to be able to have faith. For faith is an act of freedom, of independence of our own limited faculties, whether of reason or sense-perception. It is *an act of spiritual ecstasy*, of rising above our own wisdom.

In this sense, the urge of faith is the reverse of the artistic act in which we try to capture the intangible in the tangible. In faith, we do not seek to decipher, to articulate in our own terms, but to rise above our own wisdom, to think of the world in the terms of God, to live in accord with what is relevant to God.

To have faith is not to capitulate but to rise to a higher plane of thinking. To have faith is not to defy human reason but rather to share divine wisdom.

Lift up your eyes on high and see: Who created these. One must rise to a higher plane of thinking in order to see, in order to sense the allusions, the glory, the presence. One must rise to a higher plane of living and learn to sense the urgency of the ultimate question, the supreme relevance of eternity. He who has not arrived at the highest realm, the realm of the mystery; he who does not realize he is living at the edge of the mystery; he who has only a sense for the obvious and apparent, will not be able to lift up his eyes, for whatever is apparent is not attached to the highest realm; what is highest is hidden. Faith, believing in God, is attachment to the highest realm, the realm of the mystery. This is its essence. Our faith is capable of reaching the realm of the mystery.[3]

Ultimate Concern Is an Act of Worship

The sense of wonder, awe, and mystery does not give us a knowledge of God. It only leads to a plane where the question about God becomes an inescapable concern, to a situation in which we discover that we can neither place our anxiety in the safe deposit of opinions nor delegate to others the urgent task of answering the ultimate question.

Such ultimate concern is *an act of worship*, an act of acknowledging in the most intense manner the supremacy of the issue. It is not an act of choice, something that we can for ever ignore. It is the manifestation of a fundamental fact of human existence, the fact of worship.

Every one of us is bound to have an ultimate object of worship, yet he is free to choose the object of his worship. He cannot live without it; it may be either a fictitious or a real object, God or an idol.

It is a characteristic inversion to speak of the "problem of God." At stake in the discussion about the problem of God is the problem of man. *Man is the problem.* His physical and mental reality is beyond dispute; his meaning, his spiritual relevance, is a question that cries for an answer. And worship is an answer. For worship is an act of man's relating himself to ultimate meaning. Unless man is capable of entering a relation to ultimate meaning, worship is an illusion. And if worship is meaningless, human existence is an absurdity.

Since our concern with the question about God is an act of worship, and since worship posits the realness of its object, our very concern involves by implication the acceptance of His realness.

Just as supreme worship of an ultimate object is indigenous to human existence, so is explicit denial of the realness of an ultimate object absurd. Let man proclaim his denial over a loud-speaker that would bring his voice to the Milky Way a hundred million light-years from now and how ludicrous he would be.

There can be no honest denial of the existence of God. There can only be faith or the honest confession of inability to believe—or arrogance. Man could maintain inability to believe or suspend his judgment, if he were not driven by the pressure of existence into a situation in which he must decide between yes and no; in which he must decide what or whom to worship. He is driven toward some sort of affirmation. In whatever decision he makes he implicitly accepts either the realness of God or the absurdity of denying Him.

We Praise Before We Prove

Understanding God is not attained by calling into session all arguments for and against Him, in order to debate whether He is a reality or a figment of the mind. God cannot be sensed as a second thought, as an explanation of the origin of the universe. He is either the first and the last, or just another concept.

Speculation does not precede faith. The antecedents of faith are the premise of wonder and the premise of praise. Worship of God precedes affirmation of His realness. We *praise* before we *prove*. We respond before we question.

Proofs for the existence of God may add strength to our belief; they do not generate it. Human existence implies the realness of God. There is a certainty without knowledge in the depth of our being that accounts for our asking the ultimate question, a preconceptual certainty that lies beyond all formulation or verbalization.

An Ontological Presupposition

It is *the assertion* that God is real, independent of our preconceptual awareness, that presents the major difficulty. Subjective awareness is not always an index of truth. What is subjectively true is not necessarily trans-subjectively real. All we have is the awareness of allusions to His concern, intimations of His presence. To speak of His reality is to transcend awareness, to surpass the limits of thinking. It is like springing clear of the ground. Are we intellectually justified in inferring from our awareness a reality that lies beyond it? Are we entitled to rise from the realm of this world to a realm that is beyond this world?

We are often guilty of misunderstanding the nature of an assertion such as "God is." Such an assertion would constitute a leap if the assertion constituted an addition to our ineffable awareness of God. The truth, however, is that to say "God is" means less than what our immediate awareness contains. *The statement "God is" is an understatement.*

Thus, the certainty of the realness of God does not come about as a corollary of logical premises, as a leap from the realm of logic to the realm of ontology, from an assumption to a fact. It is, on the contrary, a transition from an immediate apprehension to a thought, from a preconceptual awareness to a definite assurance, from being overwhelmed by the presence of God to an awareness of His existence. What we attempt to do in the act of reflection is to raise that preconceptual awareness to the level of understanding.

In sensing the spiritual dimension of all being, we become aware of the absolute reality of the divine. In formulating a creed, in asserting: God is, we merely bring down overpowering reality to the level of thought. Our thought is but an after-belief.

In other words, our belief in the reality of God is not a case of first possessing an idea and then postulating the ontal counterpart of it; or, to use a Kantian phrase, of first having the idea of a hundred dollars and then claiming to possess them on the basis of the idea. What obtains here is first the actual possession of the dollars and then the attempt to count the sum. There are possibilities of error in counting the notes, but the notes themselves are here.[4]

In other words, our belief in His reality is not a leap over a missing link in a syllogism but rather *a regaining*, giving up a view rather than adding one, going behind self-consciousness and questioning the self and all its cognitive pretensions. *It is an ontological presupposition.*

In the depth of human thinking we all presuppose some ultimate reality which on the level of discursive thinking is crystallized into the concept of a power, a principle or a structure. This, then, is the order in our thinking and existence: The ultimate or God comes first and our reasoning about Him second. Metaphysical speculation has reversed the order: reasoning comes first and the question about His reality second; either He is proved or He is not real.

However, just as there is no thinking about the world without the premise of the reality of the world, there can be no thinking about God without the premise of the realness of God.

The Disparity of Experience and Expression

Certain assertions, particularly those that intend to describe the functional aspects of reality, the aspect of power, do not suffer from the incongruity and inadequacy of expression. What can be measured, weighed, or calculated can be exactly formulated. But assertions that intend to convey the essence of reality or the aspect of mystery and grandeur are always understatements; inadequacy is their distinct feature. Thus we have no adequate words or symbols to describe God or the mystery of existence.

The divergence between what we think and what we say is due to the necessity of the adjustment of insight to the common categories of thought and language. Thus, more serious than the problem of how should the religious man justify his creed in terms of philosophical thinking is the problem of how should the religious man justify his concepts, his creed in terms of religious insight and experience? There is a profound disparity between man and reality, between experience and expression, between awareness and conception, between mind and mystery. Thus the disparity of faith and creed is a major problem of the philosophy of religion.

Maimonides urges the reader of his *Guide of the Perplexed* to acquire an adequate understanding for the "unity of God" and to become one of those "who have a notion of, and apprehend the truth, even though they do not utter it, as is recommended to the pious, *Commune with your own heart upon your bed and be still perpetually* (Psalms 4:5)."[5] Why should one be "still perpetually"? Why is silence preferable? The reason, we believe, lies in Maimonides' experience of the inadequacy of all our categories. Following the statement that God's unity is not something superadded to His essence ("He is One without unity"), Maimonides says: "These subtle concepts, which almost pass the comprehension of our minds, are not readily expressed by words. Words are altogether one of the main causes of error, because whatever language we employ, we find the restrictions it imposes on our expression extremely disturbing. We cannot even picture this concept by using inaccurate language."[6] And all language is inaccurate.

In order to speak we must make concessions and compromises. We must therefore remember that ultimate ideas can never be expressed. "Since it is a well-known fact that even that knowledge of God that is accessible to man cannot be attained except by the way of negations, and that negations do not convey a true idea of the Being to which they refer, all men . . . declared that God cannot be the object of human comprehension, that none but Himself comprehends what He is, and that our knowledge consists in knowing that we are unable truly to comprehend Him. . . . The idea is best expressed in the book of Psalms: *Silence is praise to Thee* (65:2). It is a very expressive remark on this subject; for whatever we utter with the intention of extolling and praising Him, contains something that cannot be applied to God, and includes derogatory expressions. It is, therefore, more becoming to be silent, and to be content with intellectual reflection. . . . Commune with your own heart upon your bed, and be still (Psalms 4:4)."[7]

Silence is preferable to speech. Words are not indispensible to cognition. They are only necessary when we wish to communicate our ideas to others or to prove to them that we have attained cognition.[8]

In concluding his discussion of the nature and attributes of God, Maimonides writes: "Praise be to Him who is such that when our minds try to visualize His essence, their power of apprehending becomes imbecility; when they study the connection between His works and His will, their knowledge becomes ignorance; and when our tongues desire to declare His greatness by descriptive terms, all eloquence becomes impotence and imbecility."[9]

We said that God is an ontological presupposition, and that all statements about Him are understatements. But what is the meaning and content of that ontological presupposition? We believe that there is another source of certainty of God's existence and one which is more capable of giving us an understanding that goes beyond our mere awareness. To explore that source of certainty is the object of the following inquiry.

• • •

God in Search of Man

"Where Art Thou?"

Most theories of religion start out with defining the religious situation as man's search for God and maintain the axiom that God is silent, hidden and unconcerned with man's search for Him. Now, in adopting that axiom, the answer is given before the question is asked. To Biblical thinking, the definition is incomplete and the axiom false. The Bible speaks not only of man's search for God but also of *God's search for man*. "Thou dost hunt me like a lion," exclaimed Job (10:16).

"From the very first Thou didst single out man and consider him worthy to stand in Thy presence. This is the mysterious paradox of Biblical faith: *God is pursuing man*. It is as if God were unwilling to be alone, and He had chosen man to serve Him. Our seeking Him is not only man's but also His concern, and must not be considered an exclusively human affair. His will is involved in our yearnings. All of human history as described in the Bible may be summarized in one phrase: *God is in search of man*. Faith in God is a response to God's question.

> Lord, where shall I find Thee?
> High and hidden in Thy place;
> And where shall I not find Thee?
> The world is full of Thy glory.
>
> I have sought Thy nearness:
> With all my heart have I called Thee,
> *And going out to meet Thee*
> *I found Thee coming toward me.*
>
> Even as, in the wonder of Thy might,
> In holiness I have beheld Thee,
> Who shall say he hath not seen Thee?
> Lo, the heavens and their hosts
> Declare the awe of Thee,
> Though their voice be not heard.[12]

When Adam and Eve hid from His presence, the Lord called: *Where art thou* (Genesis 3:9). It is a call that goes out again and again. It is a still small echo of a still small voice, not uttered in words, not conveyed in categories of the mind, but ineffable and mysterious, as ineffable and mysterious as the glory that fills the whole world. It is wrapped in silence; concealed and subdued, yet it is as if all things were the frozen echo of the question: *Where art thou?*

Faith comes out of awe, out of an awareness that we are exposed to His presence, out of anxiety to answer the challenge of God, out of an awareness of our being called upon. Religion consists of *God's question and man's answer*. The way *to* faith is the way *of* faith. The way to God is a way of God. Unless God asks the question, all our inquiries are in vain.

The answer lasts a moment, the commitment continues. Unless the awareness of the ineffable mystery of existence becomes a permanent state of mind, all that remains is a commitment without faith. To strengthen our alertness, to refine our appreciation of the mystery is the meaning of worship and observance. For faith does not remain stationary. We must continue to pray, continue to obey to be able to believe and to remain attached to His presence.

Recondite is the dimension where God and man meet, and yet not entirely impenetrable. He placed within man something of His spirit (see Isaiah 63:10), and "it is the spirit in a man, the breath of the Almighty, that makes him understand" (Job 32:8).

Faith Is an Event

Men have often tried to give itemized accounts of why they must believe that God exists. Such accounts are like ripe fruit we gather from the trees. Yet it is beyond all reasons, beneath the ground, where a seed starts to become a tree, that the act of faith takes place.

The soul rarely knows how to raise its deeper secrets to discursive levels of the mind. We must not, therefore, equate the act of faith with its expression. The expression of faith is an affirmation of truth, a definite judgment, a conviction, while faith itself is *an event*, something that happens rather than something that is stored away; it is *a moment* in which the soul of man communes with the glory of God.[13]

Man's walled mind has no access to a ladder upon which he can, on his own strength, rise to knowledge of God. Yet his soul is endowed with translucent windows that open to the beyond. And if he rises to reach out to Him, it is a reflection of the divine light in him that gives him the power for such yearning. We are at times ablaze against and beyond our own power, and unless man's soul is dismissed as an insane asylum, the spectrum analysis of that ray is evidence for the truth of his insight.

For God is not always silent, and man is not always blind. His glory fills the world; His spirit hovers above the waters. There are moments in which, to use a Talmudic phrase, heaven and earth kiss each other; in which there is a lifting of the veil at the horizon of the known, opening a vision of what is eternal in time. Some of us have at least once experienced the momentous realness of God. Some of us have at least caught a glimpse of the beauty, peace, and power that flow through the souls of those who are devoted to Him. There may come a moment like a thunder in the soul, when man is not only aided, not only guided by God's mysterious hand, but also taught how to aid, how to guide other beings. The voice of Sinai goes on for ever: "These words the Lord spoke unto all your assembly in the mount out of the midst of the fire, of the cloud, and of the thick darkness, with *a great voice that goes on for ever.*[14]

A Flash in the Darkness

The fact that ultimately the living certainty of faith is a conclusion derived from acts rather than from logical premises is stated by Maimonides:

> "Do not imagine that these great mysteries are completely and thoroughly known to any of us. By no means: sometimes truth flashes up before us with daylight brightness, but soon it is obscured by the limitations of our material nature and social habits, and we fall back into a darkness almost as black as that in which we were before. We are thus like a person whose surroundings are from time to time lit up by lightning, while in the intervals he is plunged into pitch-dark night. Some of us experience such flashes of illumination frequently, until they are in almost perpetual brightness, so that the night turns for them into daylight. That was the prerogative of the greatest of all prophets (Moses), to whom God said: *But as for thee, stand thou here by Me* (Deuteronomy 5:28), and concerning whom Scripture said: *the skin of his face sent forth beams* (Exodus 32:39). Some see a single flash of light in the entire night of their lives. That was the state of those concerning whom it is said: *they prophesied that time and never again* (Numbers 11:25). With others again there are long or short intermissions between the flashes of illumination, and lastly there are those who are not granted that their darkness be illuminated by a flash of lightning, but only, as it were, by the gleam of some polished object or the like of it, such as the stones and [phosphorescent] substances which shine in the dark night; and even that sparse light which illuminates us is not continuous but flashes and disappears as if it were the *gleam of the ever-turning sword* (Genesis 3:24). The degrees of perfection in men vary according to these distinctions. Those who have never for a moment seen the light but grope about in their night are those concerning whom it is said: *They know not, neither will they understand; they walk on in darkness* (Psalms 82:5). The Truth is completely hid-

den from them in spite of its powerful brightness, as it is also said of them: *And now men see not the light which is bright in the skies* (Job 37:21). These are the great mass of mankind. . . .[15]

Only those who have gone through days on which words were of no avail, on which the most brilliant theories jarred the ear like mere slang; only those who have experienced ultimate not-knowing, the voicelessness of a soul struck by wonder, total muteness, are able to enter the meaning of God, a meaning greater than the mind.

There is a loneliness in us that hears. When the soul parts from the company of the ego and its retinue of petty conceits; when we cease to exploit all things but instead pray the world's cry, the world's sigh, our loneliness may hear the living grace beyond all power.

We must first peer into the darkness, feel strangled and entombed in the hopelessness of living without God, before we are ready to feel the presence of His living light.

"And it shall come to pass, when I bring a cloud over the earth, that the bow shall be seen in the cloud" (Genesis 9:14). When ignorance and confusion blot out all thoughts, the light of God may suddenly burst forth in the mind like a rainbow in the sky. Our understanding of the greatness of God comes about as an act of illumination. As the Baal Shem said, "like a lightning that all of a sudden illumines the whole world, God illumines the mind of man, enabling him to understand the greatness of our Creator." This is what is meant by the words of the Psalmist: "He sent out His arrows and scattered [the clouds]; He shot forth lightnings and discomfited them." The darkness retreats, "The channels of water appeared, the foundations of the world were laid bare" (Psalms 18:15–16).[16]

The essence of Jewish religious thinking does not lie in entertaining a concept of God but in the ability to articulate a memory of moments of illumination by His presence. Israel is not a people of definers but a people of witnesses: "Ye are My witnesses" (Isaiah 43:10). Reminders of what has been disclosed to us are hanging over our souls like stars, remote and of mind-surpassing grandeur. They shine through dark and dangerous ages, and their reflection can be seen in the lives of those who guard the path of conscience and memory in the wilderness of careless living.

Since those perennial reminders have moved into our minds, wonder has never left us. Heedfully we stare through the telescope of ancient rites lest we lose the perpetual brightness beckoning to our souls. Our mind has not kindled the flame, has not produced these principles. Still our thoughts glow with their light. What is the nature of this glow, of our faith, and how is it perceived?

Return to God Is an Answer to Him

We do not have to discover the world of faith; we only have to recover it. It is not a *terra incognita*, an unknown land; it is a forgotten land, and our relation to God is a palimpsest rather than a *tabula rasa*. There is no one who has no faith. Every one of us stood at the foot of Sinai and beheld the voice that proclaimed, *I am the Lord thy God.*[17] Every one of us participated in saying, *We shall do and we shall hear.* However, it is the evil in man and the evil in society silencing the depth of the soul that block and hamper our faith. "It is apparent and known before Thee that it is our will to do Thy will. But what stands in the way? The leaven that is in the dough (the evil impulse) and the servitude of the kingdoms."[18]

In the spirit of Judaism, our quest for God is a return to God; our thinking of Him is a recall, an attempt to draw out the depth of our suppressed attachment. The Hebrew word for repentance, *teshuvah*, means *return*. Yet it also means *answer*. Return to God is an answer to Him. For God is not silent. "Return O faithless children, says the Lord" (Jeremiah 3:14).[19] According to the understanding of the Rabbis, daily, at all times, "A Voice cries: in the wilderness prepare the way of the Lord, make straight in the desert a highway for our God" (Isaiah 40:3). "The voice of the Lord cries to the city" (Micah 6:9).[20]

"Morning by morning He wakens my ear to hear as those who are taught" (Isaiah 50:4). The stirring in man to turn to God is actually a "reminder by God to man."[21] It is a call that man's physical sense does not capture, yet the "spiritual soul" in him perceives the call.[22] The most precious gifts come to us unawares and remain unnoted. God's grace resounds in our lives like a staccato. Only by retaining the seemingly disconnected notes do we acquire the ability to grasp the theme.

Is it possible to define the content of such experiences? It is not a perception of a thing, of anything physical; nor is it always a disclosure of ideas hitherto unknown. It is primarily, it seems, an enhancement of the soul, a sharpening of one's spiritual sense, an endowment with a new sensibility. It is a discovery of what is in time, rather than anything in space.

Just as clairvoyants may see the future, the religious man comes to sense the present moment. And this is an extreme achievement. For the present is the presence of God. Things have a past and a future, but only God is pure presence.

A Spiritual Event

But if insights are not to physical events, in what sense are they real?

The underlying assumption of modern man's outlook is that objective reality is physical: all non-material phenomena can be reduced to material phenomena and explained in physical terms. Thus, only those types of human experiences which acquaint us with the quantitative aspects of material phenomena refer to the real world. None of the other types of our experience, such as prayer or the awareness of the presence of God, has an objective counterpart. They are illusory in the sense that they do not acquaint us with the nature of the objective world.

In modern society, he who refuses to accept the equation of the real and the physical is considered a mystic. However, since God is not an object of a physical experience, the equation implies the impossibility of His existence. Either God is but a word not designating anything real or He is at least as real as the man I see in front of me.

This is the premise of faith: Spiritual events are real. Ultimately all creative events are caused by spiritual acts. The God who creates heaven and earth is the God who communicates His will to the mind of man.

"In Thy light we shall see light" (Psalms 36:10). There is a divine light in every soul, it is dormant and eclipsed by the follies of this world. We must first awaken this light, then the upper light will come upon us. In Thy light which is within us will we see light (Rabbi Aaron of Karlin).

We must not wait passively for insights. In the darkest moments we must try to let our inner light go forth. "And she rises while it is yet night" (Proverbs 31:15).

• • •

The Immanence of God in Deeds

Where is the presence, where is the glory of God to be found? It is found in the world ("the whole earth is full of His glory"), in the Bible, and in a sacred deed.

Do only the heavens declare the glory of God? It is deeply significant that Psalm 19 begins, "The heavens declare the glory of God," and concludes with a paean to the Torah and to the mitsvot. The world, the word, as well as the sacred deed are full of His glory. God is more immediately found in the Bible as well as in acts of kindness and worship than in the mountains and forests. It is more meaningful for us to believe in the *immanence of God in deeds* than in the immanence of God in nature. Indeed, the concern of Judaism is primarily not how to find the presence of God in the world of things but how to let Him enter the ways in which we deal with things; how to be with Him in time, not only in space. This is why the mitsvah is a supreme source of religious insight and experience. The way to God is a way of God, and the mitsvah is a way of God, a way where the self-evidence of the Holy is disclosed. We have few words, but we know how to live in deeds that express God.

God is One, and His glory is One. And oneness means wholeness, indivisibility. His glory is not partly here and partly there; it is all here and all there. But here and now, in this world, the glory is concealed. It becomes revealed in a sacred deed, in a sacred moment, in a sacrificial deed. No one is lonely when doing a mitsvah, for a mitsvah is where God and man meet.

We do not meet Him in the way in which we meet things of space. To meet Him means to come upon an inner certainty of His realness, upon an awareness of His will. Such meeting, such presence, we experience in deeds.

To Be Present

The presence of God is a majestic expectation, to be sensed and retained and, when lost, to be regained and resumed. Time is the presence of God in the world.[23] Every moment is His subtle arrival, and man's task is *to be present*. His presence is retained in moments in which *God is not alone*, in which we try to be present in His presence, to let Him enter our daily deeds, in which we coin our thoughts in the mint of eternity. The presence is not one realm and the sacred deed another; the sacred deed is the divine in disguise.[24]

The destiny of man is to be a partner of God and a mitsvah is an act in which man is present, an act of participation; while sin is an act in which God is alone; an act of alienation.

Such acts of man's revelations of the divine are acts of redemption. The meaning of redemption is to reveal the holy that is concealed, to disclose the divine that is suppressed. Every man is called upon to be a redeemer, and redemption takes place every moment, every day.

The meaning of Jewish law is disclosed when conceived as sacred prosody. The divine sings in our good deeds, the divine is disclosed in our sacred deeds. Our effort is but a counterpoint in the music of His will. In exposing our lives to God we discover the divine within ourselves and its accord with the divine beyond ourselves.

Notes

1. W. von Humboldt's celebrated statement that "man lives with his objects chiefly . . . as language presents them to him" (see Ernst Cassirer, *Language and Myth*, New York, 1946, p. 9) does not apply to creative thinking. Intuition and expression must not be equated. Thought contains elements that cannot be reduced to verbal expression and are beyond the level of verbalization. Nonobjective art may be characterized as an attempt to convey a preconceptual, presymbolic encounter with reality. Compare also Philip Wheelwright, *The Burning Fountain*, Bloomington, 1954, p. 18f. For an analysis and critique of symbolism in religion and theology, see A. J. Heschel, *Man's Quest for God*, pp. 117–144.
2. George P. Adams, "The Range of Mind" in *The Nature of Mind*, Berkeley, Cal., 1936, p. 149. Compare J. Loewenberg, "The Discernment of Mind," ibid., p. 90f.
3. Rabbi Loew of Prague, *Netivot Olam*, netiv haavodah, ch. 2.
4. See *Man is Not Alone*, p. 84f.
5. *The Guide of the Perplexed*, vol. I, p. 50.
6. Ibid., p. 57.
7. Ibid., p. 59.
8. Ibid., Book II, p. 5.
9. Ibid., Book I, p. 58. *Lift up your eyes on high and see: who created these?* "Are we to imagine from this that by lifting his eyes upward a man can know and see what is not permitted to know and see? No, the true meaning of the passage is that whoever desires to reflect on and to obtain a knowledge of the works of the Holy One, let him lift his eyes upwards and gaze on the myriads of hosts and legions of existence there, each different from the other, each mightier than the other. Then will he, while gazing, ask: who (*mi*) created these? 'Who created these?' amounts to saying that the whole of creation springs from a region that remains an everlasting *who?* in that it remains undisclosed." *Zohar*, vol. II, 231b.
10. The liturgy of the Day of Atonement.
11. "Said Rabbi Yose: Judah used to expound, *The Lord came from Sinai* (Deuteronomy 33:2). Do not read thus, but read, *The Lord came to Sinai*. I, however, do not accept this interpretation, but, *The Lord came from Sinai*, to welcome Israel as a bridegroom goes forth to meet the bride." *Mechilta, Bahodesh* to 19:17. God's covenant with Israel was an act of grace. "It was He who initiated our delivery from Egypt in order that we should become His people and He our King," *Kuzari* II, 50. "The first man would never have known God, if He had not addressed, rewarded and punished him. . . . By this he was convinced that He was the Creator of the world, and he characterized Him by words and attributes and called Him *the Lord*. Had it not been for this experience, he would have been satisfied with the name *God*; he would not have perceived what God was, whether He is one or many, whether He knows individuals or not." *Kuzari*, IV, 3.
12. See *Selected Poems of Jehudah Halevi*, translated by N. Salamon, Philadelphia, 1928, pp. 134–135.
13. *Man is Not Alone*, p. 87f.
14. Deuteronomy 5:19, according to the Aramaic translation of Onkelos and Jonathan ben Uzziel and to the interpretation of *Sanhedrin*, 17b; Sotah, 10b; and to the first interpretation of Rashi.
15. *More Nebuchim*, introduction, ed. J. Ibn Shmuel, Jerusalem, 1947, pp. 6–7. *The Guide of the Perplexed*, translated by Ch. Rabin, London, 1952, p. 43f. In a somewhat similar vein, we read in the *Zohar*, the Torah reveals a thought "for an instant and then straightway clothes it with another garment, so that it is hidden there and does not show itself. The wise, whose wisdom makes them full of eyes, pierce through the garment to the very essence of the word that is hidden thereby. Thus when the word is momentarily revealed in that first instant those whose eyes are wise can see it, though it is soon hidden again." *Zohar*, vol. II, p. 98b. See also Plato, *Epistles*, VII, 341.

16. Rabbi Yaakov Yosef of Ostrog, *Rav Yevi*, Ostrog, 1808, p. 43b.

17. *Tanhuma*, Yitro, I. The words, according to the Rabbis, were not heard by Israel alone, but by the inhabitants of all the earth. The divine voice divided itself into "the seventy tongues" of man, so that all might understand it. *Exodus Rabba*, 5, 9.

18. *Berachot*, 17a.

19. According to Rabbi Jonathan, "Three and a half years the *Shechinah* abode upon the Mount of Olives hoping that Israel would return, but they did not, while a voice from heaven issued announcing, Return, O faithless sons." *Lamentations Rabba*, proemium 25.

20. According to *Masechet Kallah*, ch. 5, ed. M. Higger, New York, 1936. p. 283, these passages refer to a perpetual voice.

21. "This call of God comes to him who has taken the Torah as a light of his path, attained intellectual maturity and capacity for clear apprehension, yearns to gain the Almighty's favor, and to rise to the spiritual heights of the saints, and turns his heart away from worldly cares and anxieties." Bahya, *The Duties of the Heart, Avodat Elohim*, ch. 5 (vol. II, p. 55).

22. Rabbi Mordecai Azulai, *Or Hachamah*, Przemysl, 1897, vol. III, p. 42b.

23. A. J. Heschel, *The Sabbath*, p. 100.

24. "Shechinah is the mitsvah," *Tikkune Zohar*, VI; see *Zohar*, vol. I, p. 21a.

Part III

Contemporary Reflections on Traditional Themes

As the theologian's task is to explain the meaning of the religious faith shared by a community, Jewish theologians are necessarily preoccupied with those aspects of Jewish religious experience that make it distinctive. From biblical times on, the cornerstone of Jewish faith has been the belief in a transcendent God who created the natural order, who elected the people of Israel to be the bearers of a special divine revelation, and who controls human history and will ultimately redeem the world from the evils that beset human existence. This framework of religious beliefs about God's relation to the world has shaped Israel's self-understanding as a "chosen people," bound to God through a special covenant, and therefore obligated to observe God's law (Torah) for all time. These motifs—creation, revelation, and redemption, chosenness, covenant, and law—are like the themes in a musical composition, weaving their way throughout the tradition and giving it coherence. Over the centuries, many variations on these themes have been expounded, and not every theologian has paid equal attention to each of them. Yet taken together, they represent the central categories of Jewish life and thought, the issues that no Jewish theologian can possibly ignore.

In this section we offer a survey of contemporary reflections on these classical themes. We begin with concepts of God, logically the first topic for theological investigation. Louis Jacobs defends the traditional theistic conception of God against the challenges of atheism, agnosticism, and religious naturalism. At the same time, he places himself firmly within the tradition of those who have been exceedingly modest in the claims they have made about our knowledge of God. Elliot Dorff focuses on the multiple ways in which we come to know God—through contemplation, action, the revelation of God, prayer, and observance of Jewish law. Only by attending to all of these media can we gain the fullest possible understanding of God. Harold Schulweis argues that we need to shift our thinking from God as subject to godliness as predicate. Following in the tradition of Kaplan's naturalism, he believes that what we call God is a set of qualities that we encounter in certain aspects of our experience. Marcia Falk challenges the traditional conception of God as male and of the God/human relationship as hierarchical, or even personal. In its place she offers us alternative ways of conceiving God, as "wellspring of life," or "breath of all living things," images which are either (grammatically) feminine or gender neutral. Ellen Umansky offers a summary of the most important aspects of Jewish feminist theology as it has developed in recent years, together with a statement of the contributions it is making to contemporary Jewish religious thought generally. She sees feminist theology as fundamentally relational and experiential, self-consciously re-

sponsive to its historical context and attentive to the personal situation of women theologians.

In the last few decades, scientific inquiry, especially in the areas of physics and biology, has increasingly dominated intellectual life in many spheres. Jewish views of creation reflect that influence. David Weiss tackles head on the supposed conflict between
scientific perspectives and traditional Jewish understandings of divine creation. As a scientist himself, he regards science and Judaism as complementary, not antithetical, interpretations of reality. Arthur Green, drawing from Judaism's mystical tradition, offers an
interpretation of creation as an emanation of God, of the One becoming many through a
process that unfolds over time. Such a view does not so much negate scientific approaches
to the universe as set them aside, looking instead to a myth about the divinity inherent in
the cosmos.

For Jews, the concept of God's revelation of Torah to Israel has always been an article of faith. Emanuel Levinas, a French post-modern Jewish philosopher, explores the category of revelation as presupposing the possibility of a "breach in the closed order of totality" and a challenge to the self-sufficiency of reason. He argues, however, that in
Judaism revelation takes the form of commandment, especially the ethical commandment
which implies infinite responsibility for the other. As such, it is not an intrusion from another order of reality into this one, but arises from openness to a transcendent Infinite
Other which does not negate reason, but transforms it. Neil Gillman analyzes the traditional view of revelation as a kind of myth which is neither verifiable nor easily falsifiable. Like classical Jewish midrash, such myths are ways of "reading" or understanding
the world around us that shape our perceptions and structure our experience.

The issue of redemption turns on the relationship of the eternal (God) to the temporal
(human history). What are the implications of living and acting in history when one believes that history is itself being guided by God to a culmination of God's own choosing?
For Arthur Cohen, this assures the divine significance of human life, for "time is the
medium and history the substance of divine actualization." History, then, is never merely
a concatenation of events, but rather the means by which "divine possibility is realized"
in the world. Steven Schwarzschild focuses on the twin doctrines of the Messiah and the
resurrection of the dead. He sees in these tenets of traditional Jewish belief an ethical
thrust, that we are called upon both to live in this world and to live for the sake of a future world; ultimately, we are to make these two worlds one. Eschatology, then, is the
cornerstone of ethics, for in holding before us the image of a perfected world, we are
called to recognize the essential incompleteness of this as yet unredeemed world.

We have decided to treat the concepts of chosenness or election and covenant in a single section, for in classical Jewish theology they are inextricably bound together—Israel
is chosen by God to stand in a covenantal relationship. Indeed, taken together, Israel's
election by, and covenant with, God are arguably the central theme in all Jewish theology. The use of covenant as a metaphor for God's relationship with Israel has its origins
in the Hebrew Bible and has been a component of Jewish theology from its beginnings.
In recent years, however, interest in covenant has grown considerably, perhaps because
this concept appears to offer a way to capture the dialectical quality of the divine-human
relationship.

No one in this generation has offered more sustained reflection on the covenant concept than Eugene Borowitz. In the piece included here he explores the ways in which the
Jewish covenant with God bridges the gap between the individual and the community, as

well as between particularism and universalism. The concept of Israel's chosenness has proven to be among the most difficult aspects of classical Jewish theology to analyze rationally. How can a universal God have a special and exclusive relationship with one national group? That question stimulates David Novak to reflect on the relationship between God's love of Israel and the people's own choice to embrace that love, not once and for all, but in each successive generation. He concludes that the revelation of God to Abraham signals a new, distinctive understanding of the Jews' place in God's world and of their moral relationships with others.

For Michael Wyschogrod, the key to the concept of chosenness is that God's blessings are transmitted to and through a corporeal entity, the people of Israel. The fact that God's love is directed toward a nation suggests that it is the whole human being, political as well as spiritual, whose devotion God wants. Accordingly, the love between God and Israel is not an abstract, spiritualized love, but the very sort of passionate, vulnerable love that ebbs and flows within human relationships. Judith Plaskow offers a feminist critique of the traditional view of covenant, which, in the scriptural account, explicitly includes only men. We need to find ways of bringing women into the covenant, which necessitates both recovering the history of women's experiences of relationship with God and also reading women's stories into the biblical text.

Finally, Elliot Dorff discusses what covenant implies for the relationships between Jews and the larger non-Jewish world, including the non-Western world. In Dorff's view, the particularism of the Jews' covenant with God is balanced within the tradition by belief in a God who treasures the diversity within humankind and who relates to non-Jews as well as to Jews, albeit in different ways.

We conclude this section with recent reflections on the law, which for Jews has represented the primary content of revelation, as well as the primary means through which Jews demonstrate their covenantal commitment to God. Joseph Soloveitchik, the most renowned American Orthodox thinker of this generation, reflects on the worldview that the halakhah (Jewish law) entails and the way in which it shapes the religious consciousness of those who observe it. Jakob Petuchowski offers a Reform approach to the law, offering criteria by which liberal Jews can determine those aspects of the traditional halakhah that they should feel bound to observe from those that are no longer compelling.

Robert Gordis, an eloquent spokesperson for one Conservative approach to Jewish law, maintains that Judaism's survival has depended on the creative adaptation of the law to the changing circumstances in which Jews have lived. The law, while divine in origin, ultimately belongs to the people and is shaped by them as they attempt in each successive generation to determine what God demands of them. Rachel Adler addresses the fact that women traditionally were both excluded from expounding the law and were disadvantaged by many of its provisions. Her essay boldly envisions how including women's stories in the process of law-making will necessitate a re-thinking of the nature of law itself, including the relationship between norm setting and the narrative dimensions of our lives.

These essays, taken together, should demonstrate the richness of these theological themes and the diversity of approaches to them represented by contemporary Jewish thinkers. At the same time, we believe they amply attest to the vitality and creativity of Jewish theology at the close of the twentieth century.

SECTION A.
GOD

8

Belief in a Personal God: The Position of Liberal Supernaturalism

LOUIS JACOBS

At the beginning of this century in the United States, debate raged furiously in Protestant circles between liberals and fundamentalists. The liberals, accepting the findings of biblical criticism and the conclusions of modern science, held that the Bible could no longer be seen as completely accurate and infallible and that, consequently, the whole question of divine inspiration needed to be reconsidered in the light of the new knowledge. The fundamentalists retorted that the inerrancy of Scripture is a *fundamental*, to jettison which is to abandon the faith completely. In traditional Judaism, this position takes a slightly different turn: It has been argued that there cannot be a Jewish fundamentalism since traditional Judaism does not take the Bible literally; this is a mere quibble, however, in that then the rabbinic interpretation is adopted in a fundamentalistic way. Unless you believe, Jewish fundamentalists declare, that God conveyed directly to Moses that interpretation of the Bible found in rabbinic literature, you might as well reject Judaism in toto. . . . I shall argue that there is nothing in modern thought to demand the rejection of the traditional theistic view that God is a real Being, involved in nature but other than and beyond nature. *Liberal supernaturalism* is that attitude which affirms the being and transcendence of a personal God while remaining open to the fresh insights regarding the manner in which God becomes manifest in the universe He has created.[1]

Israel Zangwill once said of the ancient Rabbis that while they were the most religious of men they had no word for religion. Of the Jewish religious thinkers in the premodern age (before the French Revolution and Jewish Emancipation), it can similarly be said that, while they undoubtedly believed in a personal God, they had no word for "person." To be sure, the medieval thinkers, in particular, had a highly sophisticated and extremely ab-

Louis Jacobs, "Belief in a Personal God: The Position of Liberal Supernaturalism," in his *God, Torah, Israel: Traditionalism Without Fundamentalism* (Cincinnati: Hebrew Union College Press, 1990), pp. 3–19. © Hebrew Union College Press, Cincinnati, OH 45220.

stract conception of the Deity: they preferred, in Pascal's famous terminology, "the God of the philosophers" to "the God of Abraham, Isaac and Jacob." For all their stress on God's ineffability, however, they too believed that God really *is*. As the medieval thinkers—Jewish, Christian and Moslem alike—discussed God in the vocabulary they had adopted from the Greeks, He is both transcendent and immanent, in space and time and yet beyond space and time, His essence defying any attempt at comprehension, yet capable of human apprehension through His manifestation, the glory of which fills the universe. Of course, no one who thinks of God as a person is unaware that personhood is associated with the human condition and is totally inappropriate when applied to God; but then, so is all human language. The description of God as personal is meant to imply that there is a Being (this term, too, is totally inadequate) by whom we were brought into existence and whom we encounter and who encounters us. To affirm that God is a person, or, better, not less than a person, is to affirm that He is more than a great idea the emergence of which, like the invention of the wheel and of writing and the discovery of electricity, has shaped civilization.[2]

What are the causes of the decline in theistic belief—that is, belief in a personal God? Ever since the Renaissance, human ingenuity has tended to replace a God-centered universe with a universe the center of which is man. The existence of God has, as a consequence, not been so much denied as it has been considered increasingly irrelevant to a world which is constantly reminded of *mankind's* impressive achievements in art, literature, music, science, and technology. At the same time, the religious mind, always in need of the transcendence that only theism can satisfy, has begun to be haunted by a terrible question: What if theism, desirable though it may be, is not true? Once Darwin offered an explanation of how species developed by the process of natural selection, once astronomers uncovered the vastnesses of a universe in which our whole solar system is no more than a speck in outer space, once Marx pointed to the economic motivation behind religious belief and Freud to the possibility that religion is a collective neurosis, belief in the God who cares for each individual has become highly problematical.[3]

Some religious thinkers, notably Paul Tillich and the "Death of God" theologians on the Christian scene, Mordecai Kaplan and his Reconstructionist school on the Jewish, reluctant to allow victory to the bleak philosophy of atheism, have argued that the only way to meet the challenge is to give up not the idea of theism but the understanding of God as a divine person. Yes, these thinkers concede, after Darwin and the others, it is impossible to believe in the God who creates and fashions, who intervenes in the affairs of the universe, who loves His creatures and listens to their prayers, who can endow the human soul with immortality, and who can guarantee that evil will ultimately be vanquished. That personal God, they maintain, is dead because, we now see, He never existed in the first place. But if God is understood as the power in the universe that makes for righteousness, if belief in God means that, by faith, we affirm that the universe is so constituted that goodness will ultimately win out, then God, far from being dead, is truly alive, the most vital reality for the enrichment and ennoblement of human life.[4]

For Jewish thinkers who espouse this doctrine of naturalism, prayer and ritual are still of the highest value.[5] Prayer is not, however, an exercise in trying to beseech an undecided deity to grant our desires; it is, rather, a reaching out to the highest in the universe and in ourselves. In the life of prayer, our attention is called to the eternal values and this, in itself, makes their realization in our lives more feasible. Similarly, the Jewish rituals are still mitzvot and serve the same purpose as prayer. They link our individual strivings to the strivings of the Jewish people towards the fullest realization of the Jewish spirit. Even for the naturalist, then, the mitzvot are divine commands, but these commands arise from the experiences of the Jewish people in its long collective trek through history rather than as the dictates of a divine lawgiver.

This attitude should be treated with respect: In the past it has saved many Jews from abandoning a religious outlook on life, and many today still find it the only tenable approach to Judaism in the modern world. It cuts across the usual divisions in Jewish life, with devotees in the Orthodox as well as in the Conservative and Reform movements— though Orthodox Jews are less likely to admit openly to it. The trouble with religious naturalism, however, is that it does not deliver what it promised, a God capable of being worshiped. How can a vague belief that there is a mindless something "out there" be a real substitute for the traditional theistic belief that there is Mind behind and in the universe? The appeal of theism in its traditional form lies precisely in this, that the universe makes sense because it has an Author who continues to guide and watch over His creatures. The traditional argument for the existence of God—pointing to the evidence of order and design in the universe as proof that there is a Master Designer—provides powerful support for the liberal supernaturalist's position but has no weight at all as an argument for naturalism.[6] Indeed, how can one sustain the conviction that there really exists the supposed power that makes for righteousness in the world when, based on the naturalistic premise itself, that power is mindless?

The advocates of religious naturalism, influenced by science, appear to imagine that to describe God as an impersonal force or power is more philosophically respectable today than to think of Him as a person. Is it? As the medieval thinkers never tired of saying, all human descriptions of God are really inadmissible; yet since the object of worship, to be worshiped, has to produce some picture in the mind, it is necessary to use halting human language, the only language we have, always with the proviso that the reality is infinitely more than anything we dare utter. We must perforce use in our description terms taken from the highest in our experience and then add "and infinitely more than this." A force or power, precisely because it is impersonal and hence mindless, is inferior in every way to the human personality. To use the demolition job done by the scientists as a reason for preferring the force or power metaphor is to overlook the obvious fact that scientists themselves operate through their human minds. Of course, from one point of view, it is absurd to speak of God as a *person*, a term laden with all too human association. But it is even more absurd to speak of God as an *It*, which is what speaking of Him as a force or power involves. William Temple was on surer grounds, philosophically and religiously, when he said that to speak of God as *He* is to say that *He* is more than a *He* but not less. An *It*, however, is less than a *He*.

Here it can be objected, is not to take such a position to ignore the real challenges that have been presented to traditional theism? Is it not a cowardly retreat into fundamentalism? Not so. Your fundamentalist does not face the challenge: He simply denies that there is one. For him, the evolutionists were wrong; the findings of the astronomers were known all along to the Rabbis; Freud's contention that religion has its origin in the irrational fears of primitive man was an "illusion," as is the notion that there has ever been such a creature as primitive man. The liberal supernaturalist, on the other hand, has an open mind on the question of how the idea of God came into the human mind and will be prepared to acknowledge that often a religious outlook is no more than wishful thinking. He will, moreover, make the additional distinction between the question of whether God exists and the very different question, If God exists, what are the mechanics He uses? On the question of the mechanics, for example, Darwin and Freud may well be right. Who are we to say that God, in His infinite wisdom, did not choose these and other great thinkers as His instruments to convey to other humans the way in which He works?

The failure to consider both of these questions has led to a soulless scienticism. Freud, for example, was convinced that God does not exist and that religion is an illusion. Since there is no God, Freud asked, how did the idea that there is one come into the human mind? And since belief in God is an illusion, why does it persist among the human race? That the theist denies that there is any cogency to Freud's basic premise does not mean that he must reject the ensuing Freudian explanations. If he becomes convinced by what Freud had to say, he will go on to conclude that, thanks to Freud's insight, we now have a better understanding of how God chose to make Himself known in the infancy of the human race and how He uses man's natural fears in a hostile environment to cause man to rely on God as his sole refuge.

Rabbi A. I. Kook in his essay "The Pangs of Cleansing" holds that the believer ought not to be too disturbed by attacks on his belief. These attacks are often directed against crude notions of deity which all but the most naive believers do not themselves entertain. When believers are tempted to adopt unworthy and unrefined ideas about God, the atheistic attacks, by exposing the crudities, pull the believers back.[7] This *via negativa*, the negation from the idea of God of anthropomorphic associations, has respectable antecedents in Jewish thought, and we can now look at these. What must be said at the outset, however, is that the way of negation is very different from the reductionism of the religious naturalists. The way of negation affirms that we know nothing and can say nothing about God's essence. At the same time, however, it also affirms that the unknown God can be apprehended in His manifestation. For the reductionist, on the other hand, what the supernaturalist sees as God's manifestation *is* God—that is to say, there is no Being manifesting Himself in creation.

Maimonides and other medieval thinkers have developed the idea of negative attributes. Regarding God's essential attributes, those of existence, wisdom, and unity, one can only speak in negative terms. Thus to say that God exists is not to say anything about His actual nature for that is unknowable. All it means—a very big *all*—is that He is not nonexistent, that there really is an unknowable God. Similarly, to say that god is wise is to say that whatever else He is He is not ignorant. And to say that He is One is to negate multiplicity from His Being.[8] There is a real difficulty here, however. Logically, what difference is there between negating a negation and a positive affirmation? The two are surely the same. It would seem that the issue for the medieval thinkers is not so much a matter of semantics as it is a matter of psychological need.[9] To pray to God, the worshiper must have some picture of God in his mind. As we have argued, the most effective picture is drawn from human personality, the most significant construct available to man in his universe. But the picture in the mind must never be accepted as the reality; the mental reservation must always be present. As the famous Kabbalist Moses Cordovero puts it: "The mind of the worshiper must run to and fro, running to affirm that God is (and for this the picture is essential) and then immediately recoiling lest the mental picture be imagined to be all that is affirmed."[10]

The Kabbalists speak of God as He is in Himself as *En Sof*, "That which has no limits."[11] Of this aspect of deity nothing at all can be said. Even the way of negation is impermissible when applied to *En Sof*. This does not mean that the Kabbalists believe in two gods, one revealed, the other hidden. *Deus absconditus* is *Deus revelatus*.

The liberal supernaturalist will not, of course, consider himself necessarily bound to accept the formulations of Maimonides or of the Kabbalists. Because he has a liberal approach, he will tend to see these and similar formulations in historical terms—that is, as conditioned by the thought patterns of the age in which the particular thinkers lived. What he gains from their speculations is the appreciation that the true nature of God is bound to be a mystery beyond the grasp of the human mind. As the sage quoted by Albo has it: "If I knew Him I would be He."[12] That there has been a considerable degree of freedom in the Jewish tradition to speculate on the mystery is comforting to the liberal supernaturalist, who is thus encouraged to engage in his own speculations. But because he believes in the God of the tradition (the speculations and the freedom to speculate are themselves part of the tradition), he will always stop short of reductionism. He will steadfastly refuse to refine God out of existence, so to speak.

There are thus three attitudes on the question of God for the modern Jew: He can be an atheist, he can be a religious naturalist, or he can be a religious supernaturalist. In other words, he can deny that God exists, he can reinterpret the idea of God in terms of the force or power that makes for righteousness, or he can believe in the personal God of the Jewish tradition. It all depends on which attitude makes the most sense of human life and is the most coherent philosophy of existence. One man's coherence is another's incoherence. Subjectivity is no doubt an element in the choice for all three philosophies. This is presumably what Kierkegaard and the other religious existentialists refer to when they speak of "the leap of faith," a rather overworked concept in contemporary Jewish religious thought but useful in calling attention to this element of freely choosing one's philosophy. Let us examine briefly why the liberal supernaturalist prefers this attitude to the other two.

To think of God as a person is first to justify coherence itself. For if, as the atheist maintains, the universe is just there as brute fact, and if, as the religious naturalist maintains, the force that works for righteousness is similarly just there, how does one explain that feature of coherence in the universe by which science operates—indeed, by which all human reasoning operates? Taylor's famous illustration is germane in this connection.[13] In some English railway stations near the Welsh border, small pebbles are arranged to form the words "Welcome to Wales." A skeptical passenger in the railway carriage may decide that, somehow, the pebbles just happened to have gotten there, coincidentally, to form these words by accident. What that skeptic cannot reasonably do, based on his perception, is to turn to his fellow passengers and inform them that they are entering Wales. The liberal supernaturalist would not mistake the welcome sign for an accidental formation of pebbles, but neither does he attempt to explain everything in this strange and mysterious universe, which he believes has been created by a benevolent Mind. He cannot understand why there is evil in the universe, for instance. But he can explain why humans have this constant urge to explain, the human mind exploring the workings of Infinite Mind behind the universe. In the other two hypotheses, all is random development. But randomness implies that all is fortuitous and coincidental so that ultimately there is no meaning to meaning. Unless there is a personal God, whence came personality? Unless there is Mind behind the universe, whence came human reasoning powers? Unless righteousness is written large in the universe, whence came the power that makes for righteousness—indeed, whence came the very concept of righteousness? If everything just happened to be, it would not only be religion that was wishful thinking. All thinking would be wishful.

The poet bravely and stoically declares:

It fortifies my soul to know
That though I perish truth is so.

But without belief in God in the traditional sense, what *is* this soul fortified by the truth? And where and what is that truth that those poor souls who are doomed to perish may proclaim it? Similarly, when W.E. Henley rejoices in his "unconquerable soul," he has to offer his thanks to "whatever gods may be." Ultimately, there is no escaping the "Hound of Heaven." Faith in reason is ultimately faith in God; faith in goodness is ultimately faith in God.

The Christian understanding of theism is, with few exceptions, to stress that God is personal. Indeed, in the classical Christian doctrine of the Trinity, there are three persons in the Godhead. Jews, naturally, have rejected the Christian dogma as incompatible with pure monotheism. And while the Jewish supernaturalist takes issue with the naturalistic idea because it is too impersonal, he rejects the Christian idea because it is too personal. In his polemic against Christianity, the seventeenth-century Venetian Rabbi, Leon Modena, is not convinced that the doctrine of the Trinity per se is totally incompatible with the Jewish position. He points out that the Kabbalistic doctrine of the *Sefirot*, the ten powers or potencies in the Godhead through which *En Sof* becomes manifest, resembles, to some extent, the Christian Trinity.[14] (Even though the Kabbalists were devout Jews, opponents of the Kabbalah accused them of being, as they put it, "worse than the Christians" in that the Kabbalists spoke of ten, rather than three, aspects of the divine unity.)[15] It is the affirmation of the three *persons* in the Trinity that has made Christianity offensive to Jews—specially the Christian doctrine of the Incarnation in which one of the three assumes human flesh. The author of an article in the journal *Judaism* a few years ago maintained that Jews have not argued against the doctrine of the Incarnation because of the impossibility of God assuming human form, but only because this did not, in fact, happen.[16] Such a position is absurd. Jews have held that God, being God, cannot assume human flesh. In the Jewish doctrine, it is as impossible for God to do so as it is for Him to deny Himself or to wish Himself out of existence. Contradiction, as Aquinas said, does not fall under the scope of divine omnipotence. The sober fact is that Jews throughout the ages have held the Christian doctrine to be idolatrous and have laid down their lives rather than embrace Christianity, although some Jewish teachers have qualified this by stating that Christianity is an idolatrous faith for "us"—that is for Jews, but not for "them"—that is, for Gentiles, who are enjoined by the Torah to reject idolatry, but who do not offend against the Noachide Laws by adopting the Christian faith.[17]

The Jewish supernaturalist obviously rejects agnosticism as he rejects atheism. The term agnosticism, which was coined by T.H. Huxley in the last century, was intended to convey the idea that there can be no "gnosis," no knowledge, about God.[18] He was not saying, as many agnostics do nowadays, that he could not decide whether or not God exists, but rather that since the whole subject is not amenable to proof, it is *impossible* to decide one way or the other. There is thus a "hard" and a "soft" agnosticism. The "hard" agnostic holds that one can never know whether or not God exists. The "soft" agnostic cannot make up his mind on the question. The fallacy in the "soft" option is that belief in God profoundly affects a person's life, the whole quality of which is different from the life of the atheist. As Chesterton rightly said: "Show me a man's philosophy and I'll show you the man." One can adopt an agnostic attitude towards certain questions with little consequence: one can, for example, live perfectly well without ever knowing whether there are intelligent beings on other planets. But a man and a woman may agonize for a lifetime over whether they really love one another and thus never marry. And by leaving the matter in abeyance, by not deciding whether or not he believes in God, the agnostic, in fact, has decided to live without God. To remain undecided all of one's life, then, is, in effect, to decide against.

As for "hard" agnosticism, it is difficult to understand on what grounds it is affirmed that one can never know whether or not God exists. How does the agnostic *know* that he can never know? All the pros and cons have been presented to him. Why should the human mind be incapable of deciding one way or the other on this question as it decides on other questions?

For all that, the liberal supernaturalist, while ruling out agnosticism on the basic question of God's existence, may well adopt an attitude of reverent or religious agnosticism on other questions. Because of his liberal stance, he will weigh dogma in the light of history and of reason and may come up with views that are less traditional but more coherent to him in the light of new knowledge; or he may feel that the problem is too complicated for a tidy *yes* or *no* to be given and must be left to God.

Finally, we must consider the idea of a limited personal God. Among many other thinkers, Gersonides in the Middle Ages, John Stuart Mill,[19] E.S. Brightman,[20] and Charles Hartshorne[21] in modern times, have presented a view of theism in which the idea of God's omnipotence is qualified. Saadiah Gaon, in his *Beliefs and Opinions*[22] argued, as did Aquinas centuries later,[23] that God, who can do that which is impossible for us to do, cannot do that which is logically impossible. For instance, says Saadish, God cannot pass the whole world through a signet ring without making either the world smaller or the ring larger. Actually, here it is not a question of whether God can or cannot do something. The statement "To pass the whole world through a ring without making the world smaller or the ring larger," is a self-contradictory and hence logically meaningless jumble of words. To pass A through B means that B is larger than A so that the statement is as logically meaningless as "to make the world smaller or the ring larger without making the world smaller or the ring larger." When one asks questions of this kind, one is really asking "Can God. . .?" without completing the sentence.

The doctrine of omnipotence, however, can be qualified in still other ways. There is the classic problem of predetermination, for example. Gersonides, bothered by the old question of how God's foreknowledge is compatible with human freedom, holds that what God knows beforehand is all the choices open to each individual; He does not know, however, which choice the individual, in his freedom, will make.[24] Other thinkers similarly qualify God's omnipotence. God has all the power there is, but He is limited by what is called "The Given," that is, by things as they are. Such ideas are not a form of dualism, a belief in two gods. In dualism there are two powers, one good, the other evil, contending for supremacy: that view is certainly incompatible with Jewish monotheism. In the idea of God as personal but limited, He has no rival; there is only One God who is all powerful in some respects but lacking a degree of power in other respects because that is how things are.

Take the problem of evil, often expressed in the form: Either God can prevent evil and does not choose to do so, in which case He cannot be good. Or he wishes to prevent evil but cannot do so, in which case He cannot be omnipotent. An answer often given is that God does have the power to banish evil but does not do so because in some way evil serves the cause of good; for example, a universe in which there was no evil would be a universe in which freedom to choose the good would be impossible.[25] Exponents of the limited God idea, however, see no dilemma. God is good and would prevent evil if He could but He cannot. He is not, in fact, omnipotent, and evil is simply there. Of course God can and does mitigate the banefulness of evil, and He can and does urge His creatures to fight evil and be on the side of good.

Although I find this whole notion incoherent, it is possible for a supernaturalist Jew to adopt such a position without finding himself outside of Judaism. On a surface reading of the Jewish tradition, the picture which emerges is indeed one of God struggling, as it were, with that in the universe which frustrates His will. Gersonides, in his work *The Wars of the Lord* (in which he puts forward his view on God's limited foreknowledge) holds that only such a view does complete justice to the biblical record. The abstract term "omnipotence," after all, was coined by thinkers influenced by Greek thought. Neither the term nor the idea of an *all*-powerful God is found in the Bible or in the rabbinic sources. In the Lurianic Kabbalah, the first stage in the divine creative processes is that of *tzimtzum*, the withdrawal of *En Sof* "from Himself into Himself" in order to make room, as it were, for the finite universe. Thus, in this view, the universe could only have come into existence through God's self-limitation, through His allowing finitude to encroach on His Infinity; thus, there is a doctrine of a limited God in manifestation, though not in essence, in this theology of Judaism. In an even more radical version of the Lurianic Kabbalah, *En Sof* purges Himself of the evil within Himself by His withdrawal to leave room for the universe. This version of the Kabbalah is careful to stress that the evil was only present in infinitesimal quantity, "like a grain of salt in a vast ocean."[26]

For all the attempts of some to rename Gersonides' work "Wars *Against* the Lord" the limited God idea, unlike atheism, agnosticism, dualism, and the doctrine of the Trinity, is not necessarily incompatible with monotheism as understood by Judaism. The question is not, however, Is the idea Jewish? but rather, Is it convincing?

Isaac Husik dubbed Gersonides' idea that God does not know the contingent "a theological monstrosity."[27] That might be an overstatement, but every radical qualification of the idea of God's power results in severe theological difficulties, even if it is otherwise philosophically attractive. The problem with the notion of "The Given," for example, is that it is extremely difficult to entertain the notion of a God who has to work with poor material not of His own making. And what is to become of the whole idea of a purposeful God if, by definition, He can know the future only in general terms and does not know the particular choices individuals will make—choices which may very well result in the frustration of His purpose. To reply that, indeed, God depends on His creatures for the fulfillment of His purpose is to turn God into a divine experimenter and that, surely, is a distortion of the Jewish faith, popular though the notion might be with the poetic mind. This is very different from the typically Jewish idea that God *uses* His creatures as coworkers for the realization of a purpose He knows will ultimately be realized.

A different and even more radical understanding of the personhood of God is provided in some versions of Hasidic thought, in which God is not a Being totally above His creatures but the One who embraces the All in the fullness of His Being. This notion is best called panentheism, "all is in God," though the Hasidim themselves used no such abstract term for their doctrine. In this view, from God's point of view, as it were, only God enjoys ultimate existence. It is only from the point of view of God's creatures that they and the universe they inhabit enjoy existence independently of God.[28] If by a "Jewish" doctrine is meant a doctrine held by Jews, then Hasidic panentheism is undoubtedly Jewish—although opponents of Hasidism like the Gaon of Vilna believed the notion to be rank heresy.[29] That the Vilna Gaon declared it to be heresy would not make it such for the liberal supernaturalist but here, too, there are severe difficulties, chief of which is, how can it be said that the universe and its creatures only enjoy existence from their point of view and not from God's point of view? Either they exist or do not exist.

In this lecture we have tried to consider the meaning of the doctrine of a personal God and have contrasted it with rival theological formulations. I have argued that liberal supernaturalism is both the closest in approximation to the traditional Jewish view, or, at least, to the implications of that view, and that it scores over its rivals in its coherence. The mystery remains, however, and, God being God, must remain. It was a religious man who composed the salutory doggerel:

> Dear God, for as much as without Thee
> We are not even able to doubt Thee.
> Lord give us the grace
> To convince the whole race
> We know nothing whatever about Thee.

This takes us to the heart of the matter. The sophisticated theist can address God as *Thou* and can pray to Him and yet, in that very prayer, admit, as he must, that God is unknowable. But there is all the difference in the world between the ineffability of God as conceived of by the theist and the mysterious force that makes for righteousness of the religious naturalist. In the former, the true nature of God cannot be uttered or known by the human mind because God is too great to be encapsulated in human expression. In the latter, all that is affirmed is that somehow we live in the faith that the universe is so constituted that goodness will ultimately win out. No theist will seek to deny that there are difficulties in the theistic position. If he, nonetheless, opts for theism against atheism or agnosticism it is because theism, for all its difficulties, makes more sense of the universe and of human life. It is this "making sense" that is the appeal of theism. The mystery lies in the concept of the Being whom thought cannot reach; it is not a falling back on the idea of "we do not know" and leaving it at that. The whole race has to continue to live without knowing anything about God and yet countless human beings have lived and still live in the conviction that there is a *Thou* infinitely more that an *It* in charge of the universe.

While there does not seem to be any convincing midway position between theism and atheism on the theoretical level, there is, of course, an ebb and flow in the life of faith: there are times when the believer has complete conviction, other times when he is not so sure, other times again when his faith is completely shattered. But the content of belief in God does not allow for semantic confusion for the believer or the nonbeliever. All of the arguments for and against theism can be debated at length, but the discussion must not center on the meaning of the *term* God. The theist is convinced that God exists; the atheist denies it. In trying to be theist and atheist at the same time, the religious naturalist seems to be involved in semantic sleight of hand when he reduces the *term* to mean only that power that makes for righteousness in the world. This is a very different approach from postulating two hypothetical views of the same Being as one does in considering the idea that God is omnipotent and the idea that He is limited in some respects. When the religious naturalist defends his use of the term to link his concept with Jewish tradition, this is precisely the question: Does not such a radical reinterpretation of theism sever that link entirely? It is no way to meet the real challenges to belief in modern times to say that theism is now to be understood in a different sense from that in which it has to be understood throughout history. It is rather like saying that antisemitic allegations no longer have any force because the people hitherto considered to be Jews are not Jews at all. The believer in a personal God, because he is a believer, should be ready to express his doubts and speculate on the mystery. He may then emerge from the struggle with his faith fortified and enriched.

Notes

1. For the history and resurgence of fundamentalism in Christianity see James Barr, *Fundamentalism* (London, 1977). One of the best defenses of Christian fundamentalism is J. L. Packer, *"Fundamentalism" and the Word of God* (London, 1958). The placing of quotation marks around the word in Packer's title is indicative of the tendency, to be observed on the Jewish scene as well, of fundamentalists to be uneasy with the term because of its pejorative connotations. I have discussed the topic in the Jewish context in: "World Jewish Fundamentalism," *Survey of Jewish Affairs* 1987, ed. William Frankel (London, 1988), pp. 221–34. I used the term "liberal supernaturalism" to describe my theological position in the symposium *Varieties of Jewish Belief*, ed. Ira Eisenstein (New York, 1966), pp. 109–22. The editor of this symposium observes that his purpose in assembling this collection of essays is to present the views of a diversified group of contemporary theologians. He goes on to remark:

   > The second purpose (for the editor, at least, equally important) is to demonstrate the validity of the Reconstructionist contention that, in the Judaism of today and tomorrow, diversity of theologies must be recognized as both inevitable and desirable. . . .We have reason to hope that the encouragement of diverse conceptions of Jewish religion will stimulate creative thought, and help to render the tradition relevant, and even exciting.

   It can be questioned whether the naturalists in the symposium, in view of their radical understanding of what God means, should better be seen as philosophers of Judaism rather than theologians. Cf. the too sweeping but not entirely irrelevant remarks of Bernard J. Heller, "The Modernist Revolt Against God," *Proceedings of the CCAR* 40 (1930): 323-57.

   > We need not fear the atheist and the skeptic. He has adopted a philosophy and has taken a definite position. He tells unequivocally what he believes or disbelieves and where he stands. He calls a spade a spade. This makes it easy for us to comprehend his views and appraise them and point out what seem to be their inadequacies. It is, however, not so with the Jewish humanists. They vacillate and equivocate. They negate the cardinal affirmations and attitudes which religion demands and implies, and yet they persist in using the term "God."

   Of course, this broadside, uttered over fifty years ago, begs the question. The religious naturalists have replied to this kind of critique by stating that, on the contrary, theirs is an attitude that religion demands or implies, and that theirs is the concept behind all the more sophisticated formulations of theism in the past. Yet this lecture has as its main aim to point to the religious inadequacy of the naturalist view.

2. The following two formulations, separated by several centuries, one by a great religious rationalist, the other by a determined religious antirationalist, can be quoted in this connection.

   a) Maimonides, *Mishneh torah, Yesodey ha-torah* 1:1–3. It is the basis of all foundations and the pillar on which all wisdom rests to know that there is a Prime Being [*matzuy ri-*

shon] who brought into being everything that exists and that all creatures in heaven and earth and between them only enjoy existence by virtue of His existence. If it could be imagined that He did not exist, then nothing else could have existed. But if it could be imagined that all beings other than He did not exist, He alone would still exist and He would not suffer cessation in their cessation. For all beings need Him but He, blessed be He, needs not a single one of them. It follows that His true nature [*amitato*] is unlike the nature of any of them [i.e. His is necessary being, whereas theirs is contingent].

b) Zevi Elimelech of Dinov (1785–1841), *Derekh pikkudekha* (Jerusalem, n.d.) no. 25, p. 125. The nature of this command [to believe in God] is to believe in the heart in very truth that God exists. He, blessed be He, it is who, out of nothing, has brought all creatures into being. By His power and will, blessed be He, there has come into existence everything that was, is and will be and nothing exists except by His will and desire. His providence extends over all, in general and in particular, so that even the natural order is the result of His desire to use nature as the garment of His providence.

Maimonides believed that, as he goes on to say, belief in God's existence can be attained by the exercise of human reasoning. The Hasidic master relies on the truth as taught by the tradition and considers speculation harmful to faith, as he goes on to say in this passage. But, differ though they do on how faith is to be attained, the object of faith is conceived of by both in almost identical terms, insofar, at least, as personhood is concerned, though neither, of course, uses the term.

3. On the conflict between science and religion and the Darwin controversy there is, of course, a vast literature. Helpful summaries are provided in the older work by Andrew D. White, *A History of the Warfare of Science and Theology* (London and New York, 1897), pp. 65ff. and in the more recent works Harold K. Schilling, *Science and Religion* (London, 1963); and D.C. Goodman, ed., *Science and Religious Belief* 1600-1900 (Dorchester, 1973). For the Marxist attack on theistic faith see James Collins, *God in Modern Philosophy* (London, 1960), pp. 249–257; *K. Marx and F. Engels on Religion* (Moscow, 1957); David Elton Trueblood, "The Challenge of Dialectical Materialism," in *Philosophy of Religion* (London, 1957), chap. 12, pp. 161–70. There is an immense literature on Freud and religious belief. Freud's own negative views on religion are contained chiefly in his *Totem and Taboo* (London, 1915); The *Future of an Illusion* (London, 1928); and *Moses and Monotheism* (London, 1939). Two helpful examinations of the way religous belief can face and overcome the Freudian critique are Leslie D. Weatherhead, *Psychology, Religion and Healing* (London, 1952); and H. L. Philp, *Freud and Religious Belief* (London, 1956).

4. For Tillich see his *Dynamics of Faith* (London, 1957). A severe critique of Tillich is found in the symposium *Religious Experience and Truth*, ed. Sidney Hook (Edinburgh, 1962). Here Howard W. Mintz (pp. 254–60) faults Tillich's reductionism for lack of clarity and goes so far as to suggest that while the beliefs of a Billy Graham may not be true, they are more philosophically and logically tenable than those of Tillich. K. Nielson, in the same symposium (p. 278) remarks that when Tillich equates belief in God with "ultimate concern" he makes the atheist, who also has "ultimate concern," into a theist. Nielson calls this "conversion by redefinition." See my book: *Faith* (London, 1968), p. 22 n. 2. "Conversion by redefinition" is precisely my accusation of the religious naturalists in this lecture. For the "Death of God" controversy, now somewhat old-hat, see the books of John Robinson, the Bishop of Woolwich, *Honest to God* (London, 1963); *The New Reformation* (London, 1965); and, with David L. Edwards, *The Honest to God Debate* (London, 1963). Cf. also Daniel C. Jenkins, *Guide to the Debate About God* (London, 1966); C. D. Moule and others, *Faith, Fact, and Fantasy* (London, 1964). Don Cupitt, *The Sea of Faith: Christianity in Change* (London, 1984), is a more recent statement of religious naturalism and is open to the same critique on grounds of reductionism. It should be noted that Mordecai M. Kaplan anticipated all of these theories without receiving credit for them. Kaplan's classical work is *Judaism as a Civilization* (New York, 1936), but

his main work on our theme is *The Meaning of God in Modern Jewish Religion* (New York, 1947). Cf. Kaplan's *Questions Jews Ask* (New York, 1958); and Ira Eisenstein (Kaplan's son-in-law and disciple), *Judaism Under Freedom* (New York, 1956). Also, Max Arzt, "Dr. Kaplan's Philosophy of Judaism," *Proceedings of the Rabbinical Assembly of America, 5* (1938):195–219. In the same naturalistic vein from the Jewish side are Richard L. Rubenstein, *After Auschwitz* (Indianapolis, 1966); *idem., The Religious Imagination* (Indianapolis, 1968); and Harold M. Schulweis, *Evil and the Morality of God* (Cincinnati, 1984). Schulweis develops the novel idea of "predicate theology" but does not succeed in showing how one can have divine predicates without a divine subject and how such thinking qualifies as theology.

5. For a defense of the naturalistic view of prayer, see Eugene Kohn, "Prayer and the Modern Jew," *Proceedings of the Rabbinical Assembly of America*, 17 (1954):179–91. The same volume incudes A. J. Heschel's "The Spirit of Prayer," pp. 151–77, on the supernaturalist understanding. See the discussion of both papers, pp. 198–217.

6. Recent accounts of the arguments for the existence of God and their refutation include Leszek Kolakowski, *Religion* (Oxford, 1982); E.C. Ewing, *Value and Reality: The Philosophical Case for Theism* (London, 1973); Richard Swinburne, *The Existence of God* (Oxford, 1979); and J.L. Mackie, *The Miracle of Theism: Arguments For and Against the Existence of God* (Oxford, 1982). An important question is whether it is logical to proceed inductively in building up the case for theism by an accumulation of the traditional arguments, each of which is inadequate in itself but which gains conviction when combined with the others. Swinburne (p. 13 n. 1) refers to Antony Flew, *God and Philosophy* (London, 1966), p. 62f., who remarks that "if one leaky bucket will not hold water there is no reason to think that ten can." Swinburne, however, notes that arguments that are not deductively valid are often inductively strong, and if you put three weak arguments together you may often get a strong one. Thus if ten leaky buckets are placed together in such a way that the holes in one rest against the solid part of another, the ten buckets may hold water where one will not. There is a comprehensive bibliography on the arguments in Paul Edwards and Arthur Pap, *A Modern Introduction to Philosophy* (Glencoe, Illinois and London, 1957), pp. 619–21. On p. 447 the argument is advanced that, in denying the existence of God, an atheist does not necessarily claim to know the answers to such questions as "What is the origin of life?" or "Where does the universe come from?" He merely rules out theological answers to these questions. The illustration is given: "If somebody asked me, 'Who killed Carlo Tresca?' I could answer, 'I don't know and it will probably never be discovered,' and I could then quite consistently add, 'But I know some people who certainly did not kill him—Julius Caesar or General Eisenhower or Bertrand Russell.'" This analogy is totally misleading. The man who says that he does not know who killed Carlo Tresca knows that Carlo Tresca was killed. The question "Who killed him?" is logically meaningful even though the answer may never be known. On the other hand, the atheist does not say that we may never know the origin of the universe but we know it was not brought into being by God. The atheist does not deny the solution; he denies the very question, since there is no middle ground between the statement that the universe just happened and the statement that it was created by God. Ultimately, it is a question of whether the search for meaning has any meaning.

7. Rabbi A. I. Kook, "The Pangs of Cleansing," in *Abraham Isaac Kook*, trans. Ben Zion Bokser (New York, Ramsey, Toronto, 1978), pp. 261–69. [Cited in this volume, chapter 5.]

> Atheism has a temporary legitimacy, for it is needed to purge away the aberrations that attach themselves to religious faith because of a deficiency in perception and in the divine service. This is its sole function in existence—to remove the *particular* images from the speculations concerning Him who is the *essence* of all life and the source of all thought. When this condition persists for a period of several generations, atheism necessarily presents itself as a specific cultural expression, to uproot the remembrance of God and all institutions of divine service. But to what uprooting did divine providence intend? [i.e. in al-

lowing atheism to emerge as a philosophy] To uproot the dross that separates man from the truly divine light, and in the ruins wrought by atheism will the higher knowledge of God erect her Temple.

8. For a good account in English of the Maimonidean doctrine of divine *attributes*, see Isaac Husik, *A History of Medieval Jewish Philosophy* (Philadelphia, 1940), pp. 261–66. The main discussion by Maimonides is in his *Guide* I:51–60.

9. See Bahya Ibn Pakudah, *Duties of the Heart*, trans. Moses Hyamson (Jerusalem and New York, 1978), vol. I, chap. 10, pp. 98–123.

10. *Elimah rabbati* (Lemberg, 1881), I:10, p. 4b.

11. For an account of the Kabbalistic doctrine of *En Sof* see I. Tishby, *Mishnat ha-zohar* (Jerusalem, 1957), vol. I, pp. 98–130. Cf. Gershom G. Scholem, *Major Trends in Jewish Mysticism*, 3rd ed. (London, 1955), p. 12:

> The latter designation [*En Sof*] reveals the impersonal character of this aspect of the hidden God from the standpoint of man as clearly as, and perhaps even more clearly than, the others. It signifies "The infinite" as such; not, as has been frequently suggested, "He who is infinite" but "that which is infinite".

It should be noted, however, that among later Kabbalists the expression *En Sof, blessed be He* occurs frequently.

12. Joseph Albo, *Sefer ha-ikkarim*, trans. Isaac Husik (Philadelphia, 1946), vol. II, chap. 30, pp. 96–97.

13. Richard Taylor, *Metaphysics* (Englewood Cliffs, 1963), pp. 96–97. Taylor's is basically a new argument from design. If it just so happened that our minds have come together at random and the world just happened by chance, how can we use our minds in order to discover an order or design in the universe? Taylor's version of the argument from design has been assailed; see Barry Kogan, "Judaism and Contemporary Scientific Cosmology: Redesigning the Design Argument," in *Creation and the End of Days: Judaism and Scientific Cosmology*, ed. David Novak and Norbert Samuelson (Lanham, New York, and London, 1981), pp. 97–155. I do not quote Taylor's as an irrefutable argument but as an indication that the relentless search for proof for the existence of God is for the God who endows human reasoning with its significance, not a blind force which, by definition, has no mind.

14. *Magen va-herev*, ed. S. Simonsohn (Jerusalem, 1960), part II, chap. 4, pp. 25–27.

15. See Isaac b. Sheshet Perfet, *Responsa Ribash*, ed. I.H. Daiches (New York, 1964), no. 157. Abraham Abulafia seems to have been the first critic to compare the Sefirotic doctrine to Christian beliefs about the Trinity; see Moshe Idel, *Kabbalah: New Perspectives* (New Haven and London, 1988), p. xii and notes.

16. Michael Wyschogrod, "A New Stage in Jewish-Christian Dialogue," *Judaism*, 31 (1982):355–65.

17. See the sources cited in my article "Attitudes Towards Christianity in the Halakhah" in *Gevurat haromah (Jewish Studies Offered at the Eightieth Birthday of Rabbi Moses Cyrus Weiler)* (Jerusalem, 1987), pp. XVII–XXXI.

18. Huxley's coinage of the term agnosticism is described in a famous passage:

> When I reached intellectual maturity, and began to ask myself whether I was an atheist, a theist, or a pantheist; a materialist or an idealist; a Christian or a freethinker, I found that the more I learned and reflected, the less ready was the answer until at last I came to the conclusion that I had neither art nor part with any of these denominations, except the last. The one thing in which most of these good people were agreed was the one thing in which I differed from them. They were quite sure they had attained a certain "gnosis"—had more or less successfully solved the problem of existence; while I was quite sure that I had not, and had a pretty strong conviction that the problem was insoluble. [T. H. Huxley, *Collected Essays*, vol. 5, (London, 1893-94) pp. 239–40]

19. John Stuart Mill, *Three Essays in Religion* (London, 1874).

20. E.S. Brightman, *The Problem of God* (New York, 1930).

21. Charles Hartshorne, *Man's Vision of God* (New York, 1941).

22. Saadiah Gaon, *The Book of Beliefs and Opinions*, trans. Samuel Rosenblatt (New Haven, 1948), II:13, p. 134.

23. Thomas of Aquinas, *Summa Theologica*, part I, quest. 25, 4.

24. Gersonides, *Milhamot*, III:6. See Harry Slonimsky, *Essays* (Cincinnati, 1967). Slonimsky has developed a limited God theology on the basis of midrashic statements. There is no doubt that a surface reading of both the Bible and the rabbinic literature give the impression of a God who needs man to help Him in His struggle against that which is simply "given" and not of His making.

25. The best statement of the free-will defense of theism is that of John Hick, *Evil and the God of Love* (London, 1966). Hick develops the argument that the existence of evil makes the universe into an arena in which man, by freely choosing the good, makes the good his own for all eternity. See Roland Puccetti, "The Loving God—Some Observations on John Hick's *Evil and the God of Love*," *Religious Studies*, II (1967):255-68. Puccetti argues against Hick that there is evil in the universe which can in no way contribute to human moral advance—the suffering of little children, for instance. Hick defends his views in "God, Evil and Mystery," *op. cit.*, 539–46. An apparent random element in nature is essential, for if it were always possible to discover the teleological necessity of each kind of suffering this would interfere with man's free choice.

> The contingencies of the world process are genuine; though the existence of the whole process, with its contingencies, represents a divine creative act, the purpose of which is to make it possible for finite creatures to inhabit an autonomous world in which their creator is not involuntarily evident and in which, accordingly, their moral and spiritual nature may freely develop.

See on this Richard Swinburne, *Existence of God*, pp. 200-24. On the Jewish side see L. Carmel, "The Problem of Evil: The Jewish Synthesis," *Proceedings of the Association of Orthodox Jewish Scientists*, I (1966):92–100. See also in the same volume, G.N. Schlesinger, "Divine Benevolence" pp. 101–103, and Schlesinger's "Suffering and Evil," in *Contemporary Philosophy of Religion*, ed. Steven M. Cahn and David Shatz (Oxford, 1982), pp. 25–31.

26. The best study of the Lurianic doctrine is I. Tishby, *Torat ha-ra ve-hakelipah be-kabbalat ha-ari* (Jerusalem, 1942).

27. *op. cit.*, p. 346

28. See my translation of Dov Baer Schneersohn, *Kuntres ha-hitpa-alut, Tract on Ecstasy* (London, 1963) and my study *Seeker of Unity* (London, 1966), for an account of this doctrine.

29. See the letters of anathema against the Hasidim in E. Zweiful, *Shalom al yisrael* (Zhitomer, 1868-9), vol. II, pp. 37–60; and in M. Wilensky, *Hasidim u-mitnaggedim* (Jerusalem, 1970), vol. I, pp. 187–90.

9

In Search of God

ELLIOT N. DORFF

A. Coming to Terms with God

For a long time, the Jewish belief in God, as I understood it, was an embarrassment to me. As Camp Ramah was having its effect on me, I came to know Judaism as a religion that probed the very meaning of life in an open and challenging way and that, in the meantime, provided a sensible, sensitive, supportive, and beautiful pattern for living. My increasing commitment to Judaism, however, was based on the inherent wisdom and value that I sensed in the tradition and not its own structure of authority based on God. By nature I am a skeptic, and I could not see why one needed to believe in God or why one should do so in the absence of the usual, empirical evidence for belief and, indeed, the presence of some cogent grounds for doubt.

And yet I knew that being a practicing Jew while being unsure of the tradition's fundamental premises was an inherently unstable condition. Consequently, I have been in search of a strong epistemological basis for belief ever since. I do not pretend that the thoughts that follow are that, but they have made me more comfortable in thinking and speaking theologically and thus increasingly at home in the tradition's conceptual structure.

B. Epistemological Moorings

I begin with one fundamental belief concerning the human ability to know. I am deeply convinced of both the value and the limitations of human knowledge. I honor and pursue

---

Elliot N. Dorff, "In Serach of God" (1990), published here for the first time, but subsequently developed in his book, *Knowing God: Jewish Journeys to the Unknowable* (Northvale, NJ: Jason Aronson, 1992). © Elliot N. Dorff, University of Judaism, Los Angeles, CA 90077.

knowledge, pushing reason as far as it will take me in understanding my experience; in that sense I am a rationalist. At the same time, I assume from the beginning that ultimately there will be features of my experience that will not fit into a neat, intellectual system, sometimes because of my own individual failings to understand, and sometimes because no human being does or can understand them. I therefore do what I think the Rabbis, in contrast to the Greeks, did—that is, I entertain and pursue any explanation that sheds light on an issue; I expect that conflicting analyses may each be true and helpful to some degree, conflicting though they be; and I prefer to live with inconsistency rather than distort or ignore features of my experience that do not fit into a given theory, however helpful that theory may be in explaining other facets of my experience. Keeping the limitations of human knowledge in mind does not make me abandon the effort to know, but it does afford me a healthy sense of epistemological humility and humor; I must let go of the human quest for certainty and adopt instead a mellow, almost playful, posture vis-a-vis earnest human attempts to understand everything.[1]

In practice, what that means with reference to God is that I am a "constructivist"; that is, I think that we human beings have no unmediated knowledge of God but that we rather have to construct our conceptions of God on the basis of the experiences we have. Like most other conceptions (except perhaps more so), our understanding of God will therefore be built not only upon those experiences that we all share but also upon those that are unique to each one of us. Hence the benefit of discussing God with each other and the concurrent necessity of recognizing the limits that each person's perspective will impose on that discussion.[2]

C. God in Contemplation versus God in Action and Prayer

If that is my fundamental methodological belief in these matters, my root experience is that "God" is a term that means one thing to me in moments of thought and another in moments of prayer and action. When *thinking* about God, "God" signifies, among other things, the superhuman (and maybe supernatural) powers of the universe; the moral thrust in human beings; the sense of beauty in life; and the ultimate context of experience. While these phenomena do not offer proof of God, they persuade me that theological language is appropriate in describing experience and ultimately more adequate than a totally secular conceptual framework.[3]

The depictions of God produced by reason, however, are very abstract. That, I have come to recognize, is more a result of the character of reason than it is a reflection of God.[4] Reason by its very nature seeks to generalize over specific phenomena and draw analogies among them. In contrast, when I experience God in prayer or action, the God I encounter is a unique personality who interacts with the world, most especially in commanding everyone to obey the laws of morality and the People Israel to observe the *Mitzvot*. It is the one, unique God who cannot be reached by generalization.

This is similar to the distinction made by Halevi, and later Pascal, between the God of the philosophers and the God of Abraham, Isaac, and Jacob;[5] but, unlike them, the evidence of personal experience does not convince me that philosophy is hopelessly useless in explicating religious experience. On the contrary, the more we can not only report a given experience but integrate it into our knowledge of other areas of life, the stronger and clearer our claim to have knowledge of that experience, for then we not only know the experience first-hand but also its relationship to our other experiences. Therefore, if our experiences of God have a strongly personal element to them, and if, besides, the Jewish tradition speaks in terms of a personal God, we must revise our philosophic conceptions of God to include that personal element.[6]

This has led me in recent years to examine personal interactions with God—not "kooky" or even mystic experiences (I am too much of a rationalist for that), but evidence of a personal God in everyday experience. We learn most about other people and we foster relationships with them through doing things together and through talking with them. Observation and cogitation have limited value in such contexts. Since God in the Jewish tradition is both personal and unique, human experience would suggest that we use common action and verbal communication in seeking knowledge about God. Moreover, the Jewish tradition would suggest that, for historically Jews have experienced God not so much in thinking about God but rather in the process of carrying out God's commandments, in revelation, and in prayer.

D. Acquiring Knowledge of God through Action

How can action provide knowledge? Acquiring knowledge is most often conceived as a combination of verbal and mental processes, but in fact we gain knowledge from our actions too. We may need some ability to generalize over our actions to enable them to generate knowledge in any proper sense of that term; but actions are necessary to make us sensitive to given areas of experience in the first place, and they often remain the most important part of the process of acquiring some types of knowledge.

Technical skills are probably the clearest example of this. "Book learning" is often not necessary and usually not sufficient to impart a skill. We do not have the skill until we can actually perform it, and we learn to do that primarily through practice.

Our emotional maturity and sophistication are similarly dependent upon our life experience. "You do not know what it feels like until you have done it," as people commonly say. One cannot understand the joy of having a child or the pain of a parent's death, for example, unless one has experienced those events personally, and the ability to empathize with people involved in such experiences is limited if you yourself have not had them. Jewish law gives poignant expression to this when it requires that all judges in a capital case be people who have children of their own;[7] only then does one know fully the stakes involved, for the defendant is, after all, somebody's child.

Similar considerations apply to morality. Children learn about right and wrong through the reactions of their family and friends to their behavior. To understand that such reactions are not just whims peculiar to a given occurrence but rather an evaluation of all such behavior, children must be able to generalize to some degree, but their resulting knowledge must be based upon their original actions and the reactions of others. Although adults may learn moral norms from reading or discussion, they still learn much about the intricacies of morality through interacting with others.

But it is not only technical, emotional, and moral knowledge that we acquire through action; we gain factual knowledge as well. I learn, for example, what happens to skin if I sit in the sun too long—however painful that lesson may be! I may learn that ahead of time (and without the pain) from books or discussions, but that detached learning is really only a substitute for my own, first-hand suffering, a substitute which is available to me because somebody was sunburned before and warned me about the consequences of too much exposure to the sun. In effect, much of our knowledge about ourselves, other people, and the world around us is gained through our own actions or those of others.

The Rabbis suggested that we come to know God that way too. An oft-quoted Rabbinic Midrash says the following:

> "They have deserted Me and have not kept My Law." (Jeremiah 16:11) God says, "Would that they had deserted Me and kept My Law, for if they had occupied themselves with the Law, the leaven (or, perhaps, the light) in it would have brought them back to Me."[8]

The boldness of God's willingness to be forgotten on condition that the People Israel observe His Law accounts for the renown of this passage, but that unfortunately obscures the epistemological point that the last clause makes: practice of the law can be a method of coming into contact with God.

The Jewish tradition makes that point emphatically through its insistence on not only observing Jewish law, but understanding it as God's commandments. Thus "greater is one who is commanded and observes than one who is not commanded and observes," for, among other reasons, the commanded one acts out of deference toward, and relationship with, God.[9] Similarly, Rabbi Joshua ben Korha explains the order of the *Shema* on the basis of the need to accept the kingship of God before accepting the responsibility to obey God's commandments.[10] Rabbi Reuben makes the converse point with reference to the order of the Decalogue: "Nobody proceeds to commit a transgression without first having denied Him Who prohibited it."[11] Even non-Jews, according to Maimonides, fulfill the Seven Laws of Noah correctly only if they do so not because the laws make rational sense but because God commanded them.[12] The Law is thus not only a set of rules; it is a format for relating to, and learning about, God.[13]

Discovering the nature of God through obeying the commandments is, of course, not a proof of the existence or nature of God. The knowledge we gain from observing God's commandments is not easily confirmable by other modes of gleaning information, such as first-hand sensory experience or the reliable reports of others. I can never observe God's reactions to my observance and must instead rely on my own inferences and reactions. It is as if the child is blind and the parent is mute, and neither has a sense of touch; in such circumstances how can the child's actions ever afford knowledge of the existence or nature of the parent? But I am *not* trying to *prove* the existence of God—an impossible project—but rather to *construct* a view of God adequate to my experience. The insight of the Jewish tradition is that action is, in many ways, a better way to discover and relate to God than the usual alternatives based on observation and reasoning.

That is true for several reasons important to the objectives of religion. Actions are concrete and more easily learned than complex theological argumentation. Therefore, this type of learning is available to the young and uneducated as well as the mature and learned. Moreover, actions are repeatable, especially if they are short and specific, as many of the commandments of Judaism are. That is important if the knowledge gained is to become an integral part of our lives and not just a piece of our intellectual storehouse. Actions also involve in an active way the body, emotions, and will as well as the mind, and that is important if the knowledge of God is to influence our whole being and not just a part of us. Since religions aim to affect our actions as well as our thoughts, and since our cognitive knowledge all too often has little effect on our behavior, teaching directly through rules for action is an especially appropriate form of learning about God.

Even if we restrict our attention to the cognitive claims of religion, learning through action is no more problematic as a way to God than is learning through observation and thought. We do, after all, learn about the existence and nature of other people by doing things with and for them—more, probably, than we do through observing them or think-ing about them. Applying that mode of learning to God clearly involves an extension of our normal experience, but it is an extension of the method by which we gain the type of knowledge in human affairs closest to the type of knowledge that we seek in regard to God, i.e., knowledge of a personal being.

I can learn most about another person by varying my experiences with him or her. The system of *mitzvot*, however, puts much stock in limiting the nature of our actions; there is a regularity to them. I am supposed to do the same thing each time I eat a piece of bread. Only in that way can the *mitzvot* afford the Jewish people the continuity and co-herence it expects from its legal system.

That, however, does not preclude the *mitzvot* from serving an epistemological function as well. While the *mitzvot* may remain relatively stable, the situations in which they are observed change, making observance of each *mitzvah* an opportunity for a new experi-ence of God. The Sabbath, for example, changes in significance and tone as one moves from childhood through high school and college to the various stages and circumstances of adulthood. It is also a different experience from week to week, even if the people with whom it is spent are the same, for each person brings a new week's experiences to its celebration and can derive new meaning from the liturgy, Torah reading, sermon, and so-cializing. Similarly, returning a lost object, while a fairly simple and well defined *mitz-vah*, introduces a new dimension into a person's life and thus an enriched understanding of God each time he or she observes it. I observe *mitzvot* in response to my experiences of God, but the process of observing them, in turn, reveals new aspects of God. Action thus provides knowledge of God that must be integrated into my developing conception of Him.

E. Acquiring Knowledge of God through Words: Revelation

We also learn about other people through verbal communication. The religious phenom-ena parallel to that are revelation and prayer. Both are highly problematic from a philo-sophical point of view primarily because one of the communicators, God, is not available for direct, reciprocal communication in the same way human beings are to each other when they have a conversation. That raises many questions. How do we know that it is indeed God communicating with us through revelation? On what basis do we accept one revelation over others, or one record of a revelation over others? When we speak to God through prayer, how can we ever be sure that God hears? Is it really communication or only an extended monologue?

These problems of knowing God through revelation and prayer are immediately ap-parent to us. When we investigate our knowledge of other human beings through our com-munication with them, however, we find that some of the same questions apply. We as-sume, for example, that most speakers identify themselves correctly and tell us the truth when they speak to us, but some do not. If we do not know a person through any previous contact, it is hard to determine whether the person is telling the truth about anything, even about who he or she is.

The chances of being deceived are even greater when the verbal communication takes place over the telephone or in some other way which prevents the hearer from checking the speaker's identity and intent through seeing him or her. We learn to identify the voices and intonations of the people we know, but sometimes even they can trick us into thinking someone else is talking as part of a practical joke.

The problems grow worse still when the verbal communication is in written rather than oral form. Handwriting is an identifying mark, but even that is sometimes open to dispute. Hence the existence of contested wills and the need for notary publics. When the written words are typed or written by someone else, or when the document is unsigned, the reader's ability to identify the author and his or her intent diminishes yet further.

Even when verbal communication is articulate and accurate, we do not depend upon it alone because we recognize that it only gives us partial knowledge of the other person. So, for example, people who have been pen-pals for years may know much about each other, but they often feel that they do not really know one another until they communicate in non-verbal ways by meeting and doing things together. We are somewhat different people in writing than we are in person because writing lacks the immediacy and spontaneity of personal contact. We learn to account for possible deceptions in verbal communication and to compensate for its insufficiencies through other means of contact so that we can then use words as one means to learn about other people and interact with them.

When we apply these considerations to our knowledge of God, the problems that we have with revelation and prayer become less awesome and less peculiar to religion. Specifically, we do not rely exclusively on biblical revelations for our knowledge of God; on the contrary, those accounts have meaning for us precisely because Jews throughout the centuries have found that their own experience confirms the world-view and value system of those documents and is, in turn, illuminated by them. In fact, the very meaning of the Bible has been constantly changed through the process of *midrash* (interpretation)—so much so that Judaism is really the religion of the Rabbis more than it is the religion of the Bible. That process provides a formal mechanism whereby the ongoing experience of the people is invoked to confirm, disconfirm, and modify biblical revelation. Moreover, the Rabbis themselves narrowed the domain of revelation by refusing to recognize the legitimacy of revelations much after the destruction of the First Temple and by stressing the primacy of the revelation to Moses over the others that they did legitimate.[14]

Does this process reduce revelation to a wholly human phenomenon? Has it effectively become simply the record of human experience with God, phrased in language that makes it seem as if God is talking? That depends on one's view of revelation and on the source and nature of its authority.[15]

My own view is based on a keen awareness that I do not know what happened at Sinai. I accept the arguments of modern biblical scholars to the effect that the Torah itself is not a direct transcription of events at Sinai but rather represents a compilation of sources from a variety of times and places. Moreover, even if the Torah were a direct recording of words spoken there, it would be a record by human beings according to their own understanding of those events, and that limits its credibility. As William Temple has pointed out,[16] classical theories of revelation claim that we can gain especially authoritative knowledge about God and His will through a direct revelation from Him, but all of the major religions (even the fundamentalist ones) assert that that revelation must be *interpreted*. As soon as one says that, however, one has lost the claim to special authority that the revelation was supposed to afford, because its interpretations will inevitably represent a *human* understanding of its contents.

These considerations lead me to the following position:[17]

1. Human moral, intellectual, and aesthetic *faculties* are a touch of the divine within humanity, because those faculties distinguish human beings from other animals, in degree if not in kind.

2. The structure of the world is an objective base which sets a limit to possible alternatives in thought and practice and which serves as a criterion for the evaluation of any philosophic or moral code. Homosexuality, for example, can become the norm for humanity only on pain of extinction of the human species, and wanton use of atomic weapons carries the same price. Since I hold that the world was divinely created in the sense that its creation involves powers beyond our control, I would be willing to say that God informed us about Himself and the world and gave us the Law in an *indirect* way, i.e., by creating the world in such a way that certain formulations of thought and practice fit the pattern of creation much better than others.

3. I would aver, however, that the specific *content* of our theological ideas and codes of practice is of human creation and hence subject to error and change. For me revelation occurs in events *which human beings interpret to be revelatory* of truths or norms of conduct, and therefore any event could be a source of revelation, although some may be more impressively so than others. I would want to stress that within Judaism, it is the Jewish *community* of the past and present that decides which events are revelatory and what the content of that revelation is. This communal check prevents revelation from being simply the figment of one person's imagination, and it preserves the tradition's insistence that revelation must be affirmed by the Rabbis so that there will not be multiple Torahs.[18]

4. I would then observe Jewish law (i.e., Jewish law would attain its authority for me) because it is the way *my people* have understood *the demands of God*. Since that involves attention to God, the Jewish people, and the interaction between them, Jews must be taught sensitivity to the religious dimension of life and commitments to the Jewish People and its moral mission—no small order!

This approach also means that when a particular Jewish law is not moral or wise, I must be prepared to change it in consort with the rest of the community, taking due regard of the weight of tradition in the process. On the other hand, my position does not necessarily entail rejection of those truth statements and norms on which reason, morality, and experience are neutral or indecisive. On the contrary, I would be interested in affirming the necessity to abide by the rationally unnecessary rules (*hukkim*) and the decisions of the tradition in rationally ambiguous areas, because those are precisely the laws that identify the Jewish group most strongly, as the Rabbis recognized.[19]

5. This view enables me to make a serious knowledge claim for revelation. Revelation adds to our knowledge of God by framing and informing our present experience with God through the insights and experiences of our ancestors. Neither the original revelation, nor its traditional interpretations, nor the continuing testing of that tradition with our own experience is alone sufficient: the key to using revelation as a source of knowledge of God is the *interaction* between the original revelation and its ongoing interpretation. But this is exactly parallel to the intersubjective mark of objectivity in other areas of knowledge, where truth emerges from the repeated testing of any proposed theory by a variety of people. Consequently, even though the differing focuses of religion and science produce disparate levels of verifiability, the logic of religious discovery is structurally similar to the logic of scientific discovery, making it possible to assert for my understanding of the Jewish concept of revelation a claim to knowledge in a strict sense of the term.[20]

F. Acquiring Knowledge of God through Words: Prayer

The other side of learning about God through verbal communication is prayer. On a personal level, prayer is often difficult; on a philosophical level, it is complex. And yet in both the personal and philosophical realms it can be highly enriching.

Like all other people, there are times when I am in the mood to pray and times when I am not. I clearly try to generate at least some *kavannah* (intention, devotion) for prayer, but I also pray when I cannot, for on those occasions I am at least affirming my connection to God, Judaism, and Jewish values—connections that I consider and feel more deeply at other times.

When I can concentrate on my prayers, their meaning can be both great and varied. I like to think of prayer as a baseball game, in which one strikes out more often than one would like, but one can also get a hit for one or more bases and sometimes even a home run. Moreover, there is a variety of ways in which one might get on base or hit a home run. Similarly, the level and nature of the meaning of prayer can vary for each individual from day to day. "Home runs" in prayer include, but are not limited to, new moral insights or intellectual knowledge of the tradition; increased sensitivity to nature and/or human beings; relief of guilt feelings together with resolve to do better; expression of feelings of sadness or joy; and/or a stronger sense of one's connectedness to God, nature, the People Israel, and other human beings.[21]

At its root, however, prayer is communication with a personal God. The traditional God hears our praises and appeals. People as simple as Tevye, the milkman, can talk with Him. Prayer is a format by which the community is brought together for purposes of comradeship, education, celebration, mourning, sensitivity training, and moral stimulation, but if there is no personal Being to interact with us in prayer, then all of these noble functions are not enough to sustain our interest. Without a personal God, prayer loses its soul.

This persistent facet of our worship must be given serious philosophical weight in forming our conceptions of God. Our interpersonal experiences with each other give intersubjective evidence of the reality of human personality, and our attempts to relate to God seem to follow the same pattern. Halevi was certainly correct in affirming that the religious experience is not abstract and cerebral but rather concrete and total, involving the whole of a person's personality as an individual and as a member of a group.[22] In Buber's terminology, the religious person forms a bipolar relationship with God, such that God is no longer a distant, absolute Being but the partner who influences us as we influence Him.[23] Although conceiving of God in this way may be a manifestation of our tendency to anthropomorphize rather than a feature of reality, many in the Western traditions have found that their relationship with God is best expressed in personal terms, that the reality of God itself seems to require personal categories of thought and language. This view may be a misinterpretation of our experience or even a total delusion, but the number of people involved and the commonality of their descriptions mean that the religious experience of a personal God can and does serve as a basis for serious knowledge claims.

Oriental experiences, of course, are very different, especially in Hinduism and Hinayana Buddhism, but I would suggest that that is due to the fact that personality (especially its element of free will) is viewed as an illusion and an entrapment in the East, while it is a reality and a blessing (indeed an imprint of the divine) in the West. This contrariety produces totally different kinds of religious experience and worship: in the East religious training and practice is designed to rid people of their sense of individuality as much as possible, while in the West they are taught to relate to God in an active and intensely personal way in both word and deed. If we are to maintain the Western evaluation of personality in non-theological matters, then we should not be embarrassed to include it in our theology as well.

On the contrary, we should feel ourselves compelled to do so. For Halevi, the God of the philosophers and the God of Abraham were radically distinct because philosophy was understood to include only the knowledge gained in trying to *describe* experience in as detached a manner as possible. But since we learn objective facts about the world when we *interact* with it as well, it is *intellectually justifiable* to include that element of our experience in our concept of God. Moreover, it is *intellectually necessary* to do so because otherwise our image of God neglects a major part of our experience. Indeed, it may be the case that experiences of love, anger, hope, fidelity, and the like are logical prerequisites to an adequate understanding of God; it is certainly true that sensitive souls have told us as much about the nature of God as great minds have. Both the abstract God of the intellect and the personal God of action, revelation, and prayer are legitimate and complementary conceptions of God, and we need both to be true to the totality of our experience as human beings and as Jews.[24]

Notes

I would like to thank Drs. Neil Gillman and Gordon Tucker for their helpful comments on a previous draft of this paper. The position expounded herein is clearly mine and not theirs, but they have helped me see and articulate it more clearly.

In the following notes, M. = Mishnah; T. = Tosefta; B. = Babylonian Talmud; M.T. = Mishneh Torah.

1. Cf. Walter Kaufmann, *Critique of Religion and Philosophy* (Garden City, NY: Doubleday, 1958, 1961), pp. 13–16, where he points out how the lack of proper epistemological humility produces philosophers without a sense of humor.

2. I am, in other words, a "soft perspectivist." Cf. Van A. Harvey, *The Historian and the Believer* (New York: Macmillan, 1966), pp. 205–30; James Wm. McClendon, Jr., and James M. Smith, *Understanding Religious Convictions* (Notre Dame: University of Notre Dame Press, 1975), pp. 6–7.

3. Milton Steinberg has taken a similar approach. Cf. his *A Believing Jew* (New York: Harcourt, Brace and Company, 1951), pp. 13–31; and his *Anatomy of Faith*, Arthur A. Cohen, ed. (New York: Harcourt, Brace and Company, 1960), pp. 73–79.

4. I first articulated this in "Two Ways to Approach God," *Conservative Judaism* 30:2 (Winter 1976), pp. 58–67; reprinted in Seymour Siegel and Elliot Gertel, eds., *God in the Teachings of Conservative Judaism* (New York: Rabbinical Assembly, 1985), pp. 30–41.

5. Judah Halevi, *Kuzari*, Book IV, pars. 3, 13, 15–17; Book V, pars. 16, 21; Blaise Pascal, *Pensees*, #555; cf. #430.

6. Will Herberg, *Judaism and Modern Man* (Cleveland and New York: World Publishing Company, and Philadelphia: Jewish Publication Society of America, 1951, 1959), ch. 7, pp. 57–68 has been especially important for me on this score.

7. T. *Sanhedrin* 7:3; cf. B. *Sanhedrin* 36b and M.T. *Laws of Courts (Sanhedrin)* 2:3.

8. Pesikta d'Rav Kahana, Ch. 15. Although the manuscripts have *se'or*, "leaven," Prof. Robert Gordis has pointed out that that is probably an error. "Leaven" is not applicable to Torah, since its metaphoric use refers to sinfulness. The reading should probably be *ma'or*, "light."

9. B. *Kiddushin* 31a; *Bava Kama* 38a, 87a; *Avodah Zarah* 3a.

10. M. *Berakhot* 2:2.

11. T. *Shevuot* 3:6.

12. M.T. *Laws of Kings* 8:11.

13. Cf. Franz Rosenzweig's differentiation between law and commandment—the former devoid of the express theological linkage in the latter—in his essay, "The Builders," in Franz Rosenzweig, *On Jewish Learning*, Nahum Glatzer, ed. (New York, NY: Schocken, 1955), pp. 75ff; reprinted in Elliot N. Dorff, *Jewish Law and Modern Ideology* (New York: United Synagogue of America, 1970), pp. 112–20.

14. On the cessation of prophecy: B. *Sanhedrin* 11a; *Numbers Rabbah* 14:4. On the primacy of the revelation to Moses: B. *Megillah* 14a; *Exodus Rabbah* 28:6; 42:8; *Leviticus Rabbah* 1:14.

15. For a thorough discussion of the Rabbinic and major contemporary positions on the nature and authority of revelation, cf. my *Conservative Judaism: Our Ancestors to Our Descendants*, (New York: United Synagogue Youth, 1977, second edition, 1996), Chapter III, Sections C and D.

16. William Temple, *Nature, Man, and God* (New York: St. Martin's Press, 1934), Lecture XII, pp. 304–18; reprinted in John Hick, ed., *Classical and Contemporary Readings in the Philosophy of Religion* (Englewood Cliffs, N.J.: Prentice-Hall, 1970), pp. 271–81.

17. I delineate it more extensively in "Revelation," *Conservative Judaism* 31:1–2 (Fall-Winter, 1976–77), pp. 58–69, from which the previous paragraph and the rest of this section are a selection. This also formed the basis for part of the chapter on revelation in my book *Knowing God: Jewish Journeys to the Unknowable*, pp. 91–128.

18. B. *Shabbat* 31a; B. *Rosh Hashanah* 25a–b; B. *Sotah* 47b; B. *Bava Metzia* 59b. The same is true for practices of the masses, even if embodied in formal legislation; cf. Menahem Elon, "Minhag," *Encyclopedia Judaica* 12:23–25; "Takkanot Ha-Kahal," *ibid.* 15:732–35.

19. B. *Yoma* 67b; cf. *Sifra* 86a.

20. Cf. my article, "Revelation," cited above at note 17, for more on this.

21. I develop this more fully in my monograph, "Prayer for the Perplexed," *University Papers #5* (Los Angeles: University of Judaism, 1982), which formed the basis for part of the chapter on prayer in my book, *Knowing God: Jewish Journeys to the Unknowable*, pp. 149–208.

22. Halevi, *Kuzari*, Book IV, pars. 3, 13, 15–17; Book V, pars. 16, 21.

23. Martin Buber, *I and Thou* (New York: Charles Scribner's Sons, 1958), especially pp. 81–83; *Eclipse of God* (New York: Harper and Brothers, 1952, 1957), pp. 42–46.

24. I develop this in a somewhat different way in "Two Ways to Approach God," cited in note 4 above.

10

From God to Godliness: Proposal for a Predicate Theology

HAROLD M. SCHULWEIS

In a paper presented at the Rabbinical Assembly in June, 1909, Mordecai M. Kaplan set forth in Kantian fashion his "Copernican revolution." He argued there that a deeper understanding of Judaism, and a more effective way to deal with the challenges to Judaism, call for an inversion of the claim that the Jewish people exists for the sake of Judaism. To the contrary, Kaplan maintained, Judaism exists for the sake of the Jewish people. That proposal reveals both the descriptive and prescriptive elements of Kaplan's reconstructionism. Kaplan's new perception directs us to ask not simply what Judaism *is* but ask what Judaism ought to be.

Theology with a New Perception

In this paper I want to take advantage of Kaplan's methodological principle (and for Kaplan reconstructionism is more methodology than doctrine) by applying it to our understanding of God. To paraphrase Kaplan's inversionary principle, I will be arguing that, better to understand the God-idea and more effectively overcome the obstacles to the acceptance of God in our lives, we must view theology with a new perception. Elohut, Godliness, the divine predicates do not exist for the sake of Elohim, God, the Subject, but vice versa. It is not the attributes of a divine Ego, but the divinity of the attributes which demands our allegiance. What I propose for consideration is adoption of a "Predicate Theology" as a viable alternative for those who are not persuaded by the arguments and claims of traditional "Subject Theology." I am convinced that for many who intellectually and temperamentally are blocked

Harold M. Schulweis, "From God to Godliness: Proposal for a Predicate Theology," *The Reconstructionist* 41:1 (1975), pp. 16–26. © Jewish Reconstructionist Federation, Wyncote, PA 19095.

from expressing their religious sensibilities because of the formulations and presuppositions of Subject theology, Predicate theology offers a way to relate positively to divinity, and its celebration in prayer and ritual. My proposals differ from Kaplan's theological claims in a number of important areas, but I believe they are in consonance with his orientation. While Dr. Kaplan cannot be held responsible for my errors, he is responsible, in larger measure than he can know, for encouraging my own theological reconstruction.

Two Ways of Seeing

God did not create theology. Men differ in temperament, in needs and wants, and their theologies reflect those needs. This should not mean the denigration of theology, but it should introduce a necessary measure of theological modesty in our claims. I have argued the importance of the God-idea before many diverse groups, especially in college circles, and for many years. I have noted an interesting response to two different ways of formulating the God-idea. In one form I ask how many could subscribe to the belief that God is just, merciful and good; that it is He who uplifts the fallen, heals the sick and loosens the fetters of the bound. The question is generally met with reluctance, at best with agnostic reserve and frequently with strong denial.

The other formulation asks how many would affirm that justice, mercy and goodness are godly; that uplifting the fallen, healing the sick and loosening the fetters of the bound are divine. Here the response is largely positive and most often enthusiastic. What is the meaning of these different reactions? Is it a response to style or to religious substance? Is it the aim of the theologian to prove the existence of the Subject God or to convince others of the reality of the divine predicates? Does my religious interest lie in persuading others that the divine Subject possesses certain qualities, or is it to identify, exhibit and name those qualities as themselves divine? Is the theological task to encourage faith in the Subject or to elicit faith in the Predicates of divinity? Which is more important religiously, morally and liturgically—to endorse faith in the "who" or in the "what" of divinity, fidelity to Elohim or to Elohut? And what difference does there appear to be in the minds of those who are willing to affirm (a) that that which heals the sick is godly while denying (b) that it is God who heals the sick?

The Grammar of Subject Theology

Theological statements are traditionally expressed in terms of subject-predicate relations. However God is portrayed, whether as Person, Being, Power or Process, one speaks of Him as a Subject to which there is attached a number of qualities. Here Orthodox, Reform, Conservative and Reconstructionist prayer books alike follow the same subject-predicate formula: "Blessed art Thou, O Lord our God who. . . ." The very language of our theological and liturgical forms focuses attention upon the Subject who brings forth the bread from the earth, establishes peace in the heaven, reveals, rewards, punishes, judges and forgives. The language of Subject theology rivets our attention upon the divine Subject and frames the way we look for and at divinity.

The very grammar of our ordinary language is biased towards Subject theology. To say "God" is to use a concrete noun which insinuates the naming of some separate entity. George Berkeley long ago warned that it is only grammatical convention which makes us "apt to think every noun substantive stands for a distinctive idea that may be separated from all others: which hath occasioned infinite mistakes." Despite Berkeley's strictures against the ontologizing bewitchment of language, for most people, "God" is a concrete noun which suggests a corresponding substance, something or someone which underlies the predicates assigned to Him. The Subject is independent of the predicates as the noun is of its adjectives. Modern philosophers have noted that this grammatical prejudice played an analogous role in classical philosophy which favored substantives over verbs and prepositions. Bertrand Russell argues that such linguistic bias led to the erroneous notion that "every proposition can be regarded as attributing a property to a single thing, rather than as expressing a relation between two or more things." It is to avoid such theological limitations that Kaplan insists that God be considered as a functional, not a substantive noun, a correlative term which implies relationship, e.g., as teacher implies pupil and king implies subjects.

Yet, the inherited language of traditional theology and prayer reflects the dominance of the Subject. And it is the Subject, whether described through the categories of classic or modern metaphysics or the biblical notion of a divine Personality, which is regarded as alone unqualifiedly real, objective and independent, and worthy of worship.

The Depression of the Predicates

What happens to the predicates of divinity within the systems of traditional theology? They live under the shadow of the Subject and at its mercy. Characteristically, theologians have qualified them out of their independent and affirmative meaning. They may be analyzed away as negative qualities, puns (homonyms), equivocal or essentially incomprehensible. All that is known for sure is that God is, or that God is He who is, i.e., that God is Subject. But as to His character, His attributes, these must be accepted with a grain of salt. The caution over ascribing literal meaning to the predicates of divinity derives from a sensitivity to the charge that in so doing we are projecting our own human values upon the Subject. Even the Biblical theologians, who will have nothing to do with the bloodless negative theology of the philosophers, tend to suppress the moral predicates of the living God. For they sense that to hold firmly to the moral connotation of the divine predicates, to cling to the positive and humanly comprehensible meaning of such attributes as goodness and justice and mercy is to risk playing havoc with the Subject.

Theodicies Defend the Subject

Most especially when confronting the gnawing problem of evil and the suffering of innocence, the traditional theologian feels compelled to mute the original moral meaning of the predicates. To defend the Subject, and that is the core concern of all theodicies, the moral predicates must be rendered inapplicable to the Subject. Reciprocal divine human covenant or not, moral *imitatio dei* or not, confronted by the patent immorality of events, the theologian grows aware that the danger to the Subject comes from the moral predicates within. For the Jobian outrage with which the theological defenders of God must deal is based upon earlier belief in the moral predicates of divinity. Reluctantly but invariably the theodicies of Subject theology feel compelled to raise the divine Subject beyond the reach of the moral predicates. The underlying strategy of traditional theodicies is to render the Subject invulnerable from the internal attack of the moral predicates. The warm and full-blooded intimacy with a personal moral God must be cooled. The moral attributes originally ascribed to the divine Subject are now discovered to be *qualitatively* other than the same moral attributes ascribed to human conduct. The meaning of God's goodness is not simply "more than" human goodness, it is "wholly other," apart from the connotation it possesses in the domain of human affairs. Over and again, relief is found in the assertion that the Subject's ways are not the ways of man, nor Its thoughts ours. It is a costly defense. For the denial of the human comprehensibility of the moral attributes of God is accompanied by the denial of human competence to make moral judgment. If "good and evil" in the eyes of God are construed as qualitatively different from that understood by man, then man's judgment and emulation of God's moral traits are invalidated.

Moral Predicates Challenge the Subject

Karl Barth articulates the root case for Subject theology in bold fashion. "Strictly speaking" he asserts, "there is no divine predicate, no idea of God which can have as its special content *what* God is. There is strictly speaking only the Divine Subject as such and in Him the fitness of His divine predicates." While few Biblical theologians flaunt the absolute autonomy and independence of the divine Personality as openly as Barth does, in the last analysis, and particularly before the onslaught of innocent suffering, they too resort to the same argument. God's ultimate retort to the Jobian plaint draws upon the inscrutability and freedom of He who is. The moral predicates normally assigned to Him must fade away. For faith in the moral predicates would mean the right to challenge the Subject. But it is the Subject who judges the predicates and who assigns it meaning. The divine Subject's disclosures cannot be questioned or held to any single, constant meaning by the standards of the moral predicates.

With Subject theology, faith in God is faith in the Subject itself, independent of the attributes. The love of God is not justified by man's appreciation of His qualities, for that would set man above God and limit the freedom of God. The unconditional love of God is for the divine Ego, for the Personality. However God may appear to act, whatever moral contradictions may appear in His conduct, the height of faith demands acceptance of the Subject beyond the predicates.

The Schism Within Divinity

Inadvertently traditional theology is compelled to sever the Subject from the predicates of Divinity. For it, the proper subject of theology is the Subject. The moral predicates seem all too human. This separation of Subject and predicate is reflected in the growing tension between faith and morality, the divine and the human. In his *Meaning of God* and throughout his works, Kaplan expresses his sensitivity to the schism we have described by warning against the erroneous theological view which conceives of God and man as separate and distinct, "with man, on the one hand, enslaved by his physical self, by his fellow man, or by his own tools, and on the other hand, God completely transcendent, in Himself absolutely, free, dispensing the gift of freedom."

The "Why" and the "Who"

The mind-set which allows the Divine personality to swallow up the moral predicates and frames God as the Subject, conditions the believer to see the world in a particular fashion, to raise certain questions and to accept only certain answers. To draw some of the implications of this orientation, let us examine a typical benediction informed by Subject theology. The prayer which proclaims "God heals the sick" entails a number of presuppositions. The liturgical language suggests a linear causal relationship between the Subject and the patient. In recovery, all praise is due the Subject. Should the patient fail to be healed or indeed die, theological explanation of the tragic event again must refer to the Subject alone. For however the competences of the physician and attendants may be involved in the cure or the failure, these are secondary factors which for satisfactory explanation must be traced to the sole agent who directly or obliquely heals or restrains the hands from healing. Which rabbi has not experienced the series of "whys" in such crises! "Why did he die?" "Why did he have to suffer?" "Why did it happen to him?" No explanation of the tragedy in terms of congenital or contagious disease, ignorance, neglect or accident is acceptable to the questioner. For these explanations are regarded as secular, naturalistic, human accounts which ignore the divine Subject who ultimately controls the destiny of men. "Why" questions are the consequence of "Who" formulations; and the latter legitimates only certain kinds of explanations.

Theodicy Subject Leads to Religious Masochism

Only answers which refer to the will or design of the Subject may put an end to the limitless "whys." And, insofar as many of the events to be explained patently violate the moral expectations expressed in the moral attributes of divinity, the situation can be saved only by mind-reading the intention of the inscrutable God. Somehow we are to be persuaded that the affliction is not truly bad or else that it is deserved. Our predicates are not His, but whatever His are they must be good. It is not for naught that so much of the theodicies of Subject theology lend themselves to exercises or religious masochism.

As a consequence of such Subject theodicy, the identification of the "acts of God" with those phenomena which are unpredictable, uncontrollable and inimical to man is irresistible. For it is precisely where men are incompetent and impotent to act that God's hand appears to be unmistakably revealed. Hurricane, earthquake and whirlwind appear as the unambiguous bearers testifying to the divine Subject's free will. Contrariwise, where men participate in the curative process, the acts of healing are merely human, at best derivative. The acts of God are not the acts of men, else we flirt dangerously with humanism.

The Perception of Predicate Theology

How different is it to invert the prayer that God heals so that it reflects the belief that that which heals is divine? The newer formulation directs our attention to the natural realm in which transactions between man and his environment take place in the process of healing the sick. The vertical relationship between Subject and patient is horizontalized. We no longer look for "Elohut" in the unknowable designs of a supra-moral personality, but in the activities whose qualities we experientially discover as sacred. We learn that healing is dependent upon the nonhuman givenness of energies, the potentially curative powers which remain dormant without the will, competence and moral purpose of men. We come to recognize that actualization of these potencies depends upon the training, skill and dedication of researchers, medical practitioners, nurses and the manner in which a society chooses to dispense these powers. These activities manifest qualities of intelligence, cooperation, and responsibility which are not dismissed casually as merely human or simply secular or only natural. They are the significant signs which are daily with us, morning, noon and evening, and testify to the reality of "Elohut."

Good and Evil Not Personalized

In what sense are these signs of divinity? What makes them divine is not their lodging in some alleged Subject. They are sacred not because they inhere in any person or supra-person, but because they are instrumentally or intrinsically good. The discovered qualities of Godliness reside in no single thing but in relationships through which they exhibit their sacred character. Elohut or Godliness, then, describes the way the predicates of divinity are organized and coordinated. Sickness, suffering, death, according to the predicate view of divinity, are real, but their origin stems neither from a benevolent or a malevolent Subject. Good and evil are not personalized in the form of a God or a Satan. They are neither rewards nor punishments visited upon us by a mysterious Subject. The painful reality of accident, negligence, greed are neither divinized nor demonized. Blame, responsibility, guilt are not foisted upon another realm wherein the Subject needs be either exonerated or condemned.

Suffering and evil, fault and responsibility are taken seriously by predicate theology; but the latter invites different expectations and demands different human responses from those which are generated by Subject theology. The Job of predicate theology is sensitive to the evils which beset man, but his questions are not directed towards a plotting, purposing, supra-human Ego nor are his friends raised in a theological atmosphere which prompts them to decipher the hidden motives of a morally remote Subject. The Job of predicate theology and his friends look elsewhere for explanation and for response. They would examine the "how" and "where" and "what" which brought forth the pain of the situation, in order to call upon the powers of Elohut in and between them and the environment so as to bind the bruises and to act so as to avoid repetition of the tragedy.

Predicate Prayer

To reverse the Subject and Predicate of theology is no idle grammatical inversion. It proposes that we reflect upon the predicates of divinity as the proper subject of our theological concern. Not the attribute of the Divinity but the divinity of the attribute requires our attention. The form of our traditional Subject liturgy is focused upon an It or Thou or He. In the coin of the traditional benediction it is a "who" to whom all praise is due; a "who" brings forth the bread from the earth. Predicate liturgy would invert the formula so that religious attention and appreciation is directed to the givenness of earth and seed and sun and water, to the preparation of the soil, the weeding, ploughing and nurturing of the field, the reaping, winnowing, grinding of the wheat, the kneading, seasoning and baking of the dough and to the equitable distribution of bread to those in need. "Brukhah elohut hamotziah lehem min haaretz." Blessed is Elohut which brings forth bread from the earth. The prayer form celebrates the reverent acknowledgment of those values and qualities which through human effort unite to satisfy the needs of man.

These divine qualities are not invented but are discovered in society. They are revealed not by or through some hypostatized existence above or beyond or beneath the world in which we live, but in and through our transactions with each other. They are located in the this-worldly hyphenated realm of I-thou-we which Buber has called "betweenness." They are disclosed in the values discovered through the relationship "between" self and other, "between" self and community, "between" self and the environment. The discovered attributes are as real as living, as objective as our social agreement and our community's acceptance of the consequence of their use, as significant as love, justice and peace are for our lives. And because discovery and confirmation of divine attributes are an on-going process coterminous with the life of our people, Elohut is not fixed forever. As long as the community of faith is open to life, no predicates reign immutable, no set of predicates can exhaust the changing and expanding character of Godliness.

The Category Mistake

But where is Godliness in all this discussion? Where is "Elohut" located? The question is itself inherited from the vertical view of Subject theology. On our analysis the question stems from what philosophers have termed a category mistake. Gilbert Ryle's questioner also sought to know where exactly the "university" is, even after being shown the faculties and facilities, the student-body and alumni. His query could not be answered, not because the "university" is not real or important or objective, but because "university" does not function logically like the term gymnasium which can be inventoried as an item alongside the laboratory. The university is not illusory, an imaginary, arbitrary invention. One can not point to the university because the university is simply not a thing among things but the way in which all that has been pointed out is organized and interrelated. The university is no mysterious entity beyond those events which have been exhibited. Analogously, Elohut or Godliness refers to the way the predicates a tradition discovers, accepts and names as divine are related. Elohut, like university, has a unitive function. Elohut, Godliness is One in that it unites and relates the godly attributes. Unlike Subject theology, the unity of the predicates is not maintained by virtue of their belonging to some independent Subject. The oneness of Elohut is found in the common relationship of all the predicates to goodness. Intelligence, compassion, justice, peace, etc., are named divine when they serve ends which the community of faith judges to be good.

Predicate Theology in a Post-Holocaustal World

Predicate theology is not for all persons. Some may think it too prosaic, too natural, too human. Others may think it denies the mystique of the wholly other Subject. But for many others, living in a post-holocaustal world, the older consolations and mysteries of traditional theologies and theodicies take too high a moral toll. In this Nietzsche spoke for the modern consciousness: "To look upon nature as if it were proof of the goodness and care of a God; to interpret history in honor of a divine reason, as a constant testimony to a moral order in the world and a moral final purpose; to explain personal experiences as pious men have long enough explained them, as if everything were a dispensation or intimation of Providence, something planned and set on behalf of the salvation of the soul: all that is passed; it has conscience against it."

For too many the alternative to the traditional presuppositions and forms of Subject theology is simply the abandonment of the God-idea together with all of religious sensibilities. The twists and turns of traditional theology before the face of Auschwitz appear to them as desperate rationalizations, worse, as a betrayal of the moral stance. For them, to save God the Subject at the expense of faith in the moral attributes of divinity is to be left standing before a naked God. To have faith in the Subject alone strikes them as at least amoral. Feuerbach warned that devils too believe in God. What is important then is not faith in a Subject God but in the character of divinity which serves as a model for our own lives. The criterion of theological meaningfulness remains that of C.S. Peirce. The serious theologian must ask, "Suppose this proposition were true, what conceivable bearing might it have on the conduct of our lives?" After the traditional theodicies are over we are left with a God beyond morality. Belief in such a God, for many, makes no moral difference. Following Peirce's criterion, William James concluded "a difference that makes no difference is no difference." Predicate theology deserves to be considered by those who require a conceptualization of God which will reflect the primacy of a moral ideal respectful of man's moral capacities, one recognizing divinity in his creativity and demanding his responsibility. This is entailed in the shift from Subject to Predicate, from noun to adjectival characterization of divinity, from substantival entity to transactional process of the idea of God.

Two Difficulties

Aside from the problems which some have in identifying divine qualities as real without some substantival base, there appear two ancillary blocks to predicate theology. One of these is apprehension over its emphasis upon the moral essence of divinity which seems to reduce religion to ethics. The other difficulty questions the legitimacy of employing such terms as godly, divine and godliness to describe what are primarily ethical qualities.

I would answer the first question by pointing out that, while ethical concern and behavior must lie at the heart of the God-idea and of religion, there is far more in belonging to a community of faith than belief in a moral deity. Judaism includes ritual and liturgical reflection, an entire gamut of affective, cognitive and celebratory activities and a central fidelity to the career and destiny of our world people. Our discussion of the God-idea in no way is meant to reduce the religious phenomenon to ethical culture or philosophy.

As far as the use of terms such as divinity, Elohut and godliness, these are chosen for three reasons.

(a) There is a commonality of interest and value between traditional and modern conceptions of divinity which is expressed by allegiance to certain sacred terms. Godliness, godly, Elohut express the nexus between my ancestors and myself. However critically different the many forms of Jewish theology may be, what they hold in common, and thus what is the essential core which unites them, are the moral predicates which are to be lived out in our lives. Analogously, the myths of the Bible, e.g., the Garden of Eden episode, the deluge and Tower of Babel, the miracles in Egypt, are differently interpreted by different generations. Although I may question their historical accuracy, they remain significant because the common moral intention of their telling can be translated in non-miraculous terms. Does a non-Orthodox interpretation of the Torah lose thereby its legitimation as a sacred text? The diverse theological forms in which the divine qualities are posited ought not eclipse the sanctity of the attributes which express our faith and direct our behavior.

From Secular to Sacred

(b) The briefest rehearsal of the history of Jewish theology from Philo to Kaplan will offer evidence that each reflective thinker of Judaism has proposed conceptions of God quite other than that which is found in the Biblical text. Maimonides' reconstruction of the God-idea might have been, and indeed was challenged, on the grounds that his notions of an incorporeal deity and of negative attributes were foreign to the Scriptural text. To establish monopoly on the use of God-terms would serve only to arrest theological freedom. To submit to a monolithic semantics would stymie theological response to the intellectual and moral demands of our people and would put a halt to theological progress.

(c) Terms like godly or divine are emotionally charged. They are used to express the ultimate significance which a community of faith attaches to certain qualities. The identification and naming of such predicates as divine mean to raise them out of the ordinary, "merely" secular into the realm of the sacred. The incorporation of values into the realm of Elohut, into the liturgical vocabulary of our faith-language is no casual act. The naming acts which call "peace" or "justice" divine are critical in articulating the conscious spiritual tasks and purpose of a people.

In his haunting novel *The Accident,* Eli Wiesel portrays the tortured spirit of Sarah, the prostitute-saint of the death camp. His hero cries out that "whoever listens to Sarah and doesn't change, whoever enters Sarah's world and does not invent new gods and new religions, deserves death and destruction."

Wiesel is a traditionalist, but he cannot endure the thought of theology and religion as usual after Auschwitz. Theological and liturgical sameness is not of itself a tribute to tradition, especially when that tradition records so much courage and audacity in propounding new ideas of God and new ways to commune with the divine.

Our proposals for predicate theology and predicate liturgy, despite the dispassionate and analytic character of its presentation, is one response to Wiesel's challenge. Its intention is to help those embittered by the absurdity of the Holocaust, and upset by the amoral tones of the defense of God after Auschwitz, to look again and differently at the face of Elohut. It is meant for those who cannot go home again using the old routes, but who may learn to believe and pray and celebrate again through another way. We are an old-new people and we require old-new ways to renew our connection with our ancestors' faith. From Elohim to Elohut is not a path away, but towards our spiritual renewal and reconciliation.

11

Toward a Feminist Jewish Reconstruction of Monotheism

MARCIA FALK

The dilemma of monotheism for feminist Jews is more profound than at first we may have thought. It is not just that monotheism has been perverted, throughout Jewish (as well as Christian and Moslem) history, to mean male monotheism; this problem would be relatively easy to correct. We would add female images to our language, change "he" to "she" and "God" to "Goddess" (at least part of the time), and substitute *Shekhinah* for *Adonai* in our prayers—or come up with new feminine names for Divinity. Would that it were so easy! Unfortunately, the rather obvious gender problem in our God-language is the surface manifestation of a deeper and more complex difficulty.

Nor is it just that in Jewish theology oneness has been confused with singularity. Elsewhere I have argued that any single-image monotheism is idolatrous, since all images are necessarily partial and the exclusive use of any part to represent the whole is misleading and theologically inauthentic. I have gone on to suggest that only with a great number of images can we come close to an authentic expression of the monotheistic principle. Authentic monotheism, I have suggested, entails "an embracing unity of a multiplicity of images." Such multiplicity not only celebrates pluralism and diversity; it diminishes the likelihood of unconscious forms of idolatry, such as "speciesism" (I use this term to refer to human devaluation and domination of other species of life). I have specifically argued that anthropocentrism in Jewish God-language is as idolatrous as sexism: that we cannot have an authentic imaging of a monotheistic Divinity that uses exclusively personal terms, even if those terms include female representations. By taking the idea of *tzelem elohim*—humanity as created in the image of God—too literally, and deducing

Marcia Falk, "Toward a Feminist Jewish Reconstruction of Monotheism," *Tikkun Magazine: A Bi-Monthly Jewish Critique of Politics, Culture, and Society* 4:4 (July/August 1989), pp. 53–56. © Marcia Falk. "Further Thoughts on Liturgy as an Expression of Theology." Written for this volume. © Marcia Falk.

from it that *we alone* bear within us the spark of Divinity, we contribute to the belief that our human species is "godlier" than the rest of creation, and we give license to humanity's domination of the planet.

But all these caveats are still not enough. What I want to examine here is a problematic premise that underlies many of our theological images, even new images born of feminist re-visioning: the postulation of Divinity (any Divinity) "out there" that is not coextensively "in here," in the *entirety* of here.

Although Judaism sometimes speaks *conceptually* of God's immanence—in much Hasidic teaching, for example—the theological *imagery* in Jewish worship is overwhelmingly the imagery of transcendence. In the theology of the traditional prayerbook God is portrayed, vividly and dramatically, not as part of the world but as apart from and above it. God is sovereign, the world is God's dominion; God is creator, the world is God's creation. Because I believe—as Nelle Morton eloquently argues in *The Journey is Home*—that ideas are what we think and images are what we live by, I am convinced that this imagery of transcendence accurately reflects historical Jewish perceptions of the relationship between God and world. I would venture to say that for most religiously concerned Jews "God" is a term that, in a deep though not necessarily conscious way, applies to something "out there"—be it concerned or apathetic, personal or impersonal, powerful or impotent. Indeed, the definition of theism as the belief in a deity above and beyond the world has probably determined for many Jews whether they call themselves theists or atheists.

Even today, our efforts at imaging immanence are very limited. At most, we have tried to picture God as within *us*—that is, within the *human* individual or community—not within the whole of creation. And when we image God as within us, as some new feminist and other "alternative" Jewish liturgies commendably try to do, we still often conceive of God as *separable* from us—as in this example from the Kehilla Community Synagogue *Prayerbook for the High Holidays:* "Our Guide deep within us, / O hear us and give us / compassion and mercy and peace." Thus, when we speak of God as inside us, we still tend to envision God not as something *permeating us* but rather as something *other than us,* someone or something we can localize and isolate, petition and address.

In Judaism, this definition of God as *other than the world* is so ingrained that it may even seem self-evident, tautological. Yet, from a feminist perspective, it is problematic. Because Judaism sees God as perfect and the world as imperfect, the dualism of God and world is always one of inequality, and ultimately one of hierarchy. Thus, this theological premise supports and perhaps even spawns the hierarchical dualisms that split the world into two unequal halves.

The basic sexist dualism of male and female is the most pervasive and perhaps most fundamental representation of this problem. In Judaism's stories of the relationship between God and world, God is consistently imaged as male, the world (earth, people of Israel) as female. Thus maleness is associated with creativity, power, knowledge, and will; while femaleness is identified with object, matter, weakness, and even evil. The otherness of God in Judaism extends beyond sexism, however; it underlies a complex organization of reality that everywhere sanctions polarized relationships of inequality and domination.

Consider for a moment the following *piyyut* (liturgical poem), which is found in the traditional *makhzor* (High Holiday prayerbook), and from which I translate, as literally as possible:

O God and God of our fathers,
  forgive us, pardon us, grant us atonement—
For we are your people (nation) / you are our God
We are your sons / you are our father
We are your slaves (servants) / you are our lord
We are your congregation / you are our fate (lot, portion)
We are your inheritance (possession) / you are our destiny
We are your flock / you are our shepherd
We are your vineyard / you are our watchman
We are your work (the product of your labors) / you are our creator
We are your female lover / you are our male lover
We are your special one (treasured property) / you are our relative (close one)
We are your people (nation) / you are our king
We are your favored (exalted) one / you are our favored (exalted) one

The first thing that strikes us as we sing or chant this poem is its incantatory structure, built on the repetition of *anu / atah*—we are this, you (masculine) are that. This emphatic repetition works its theme on our ears and into our psyches, our imaginations: humanity and Divinity (here represented specifically as the people of Israel and God) are two, separable, *related through opposition.* The long list of metaphors employed here to describe the relationship between God and Israel is drawn from many aspects of societal life and structure: peoplehood, family or patrilineage, slavery or servitude, community, inheritance, animal breeding, agriculture, artistic creation, sexual love, property ownership, government, and even friendship. In every realm, the relationship is symbolized by a hierarchically linked pair (or a pair that we are supposed to understand as hierarchically related): people and God (this is the central metaphor, and the one least recognized *as metaphor,* that is, the "dead metaphor" that controls the series), sons and father, slaves and lord, community and fate (as case of concrete and abstract), inheritance and destiny (another such case), sheep and shepherd, vineyard and watchman, artifact and artist, woman and man, property and owner, subjects and king. Only in the final line of the poem do we find an equal, reciprocal relationship—favored one and favored one—although we should also note that this line, more explicitly than any other line in the poem, implies an unequal relationship between Israel and the other peoples of the world (since this God may conceivably have other children, other subjects, other flocks, other possessions; but he can have only one favorite).

Thus the distinction between God and world which is reflected in this *piyyut*—and which, I would argue, has been at the core of Jewish theology until the present day—sets a pattern that does not allow us to see the distinction between self and other in a positive or even neutral way. Rather, this distinction becomes the basis of hierarchy and domination. When the self is hierarchized (not just differentiated) from the other, it *must* see itself as superior—or else inferior. Just as we see ourselves as inferior in relation to God, so we view ourselves as superior in relation to others. The self projects negativity outward, onto the other, so that the self (like God) remains all-good, while the other (like the world) is the source of badness. This type of projection, which is rooted in our theological model, forms the psychological basis of pernicious social structures, including sexism, homophobia, racism, classism, anti-Semitism, and Jewish anti-Gentilism (chosenness).

Yet Judaism teaches a passion and commitment to justice, through a central and significant body of teachings that have been inspirational for many feminist Jews, and that have even, for some of us, parented our feminist concerns. "Justice, justice you shall pursue, so that you may live" says the biblical voice of God, words that embrace both process and ideal in an ever-renewing commitment to *tikkun olam,* repair of the fragmented world. Where does this idea come from? If Judaism is built on a theology of domination, where is the theological source for the principle of justice? Where can one turn for theological support for the passion to make the world whole?

Despite all I have said about Jewish theology, I believe that the source of justice and of the passion for justice is to be found in monotheism—in *authentic* monotheism, not that which is imaged in the standard Hebrew prayerbook. For what does monotheism posit? Monotheism posits a single, infinite Divinity that embraces and extends beyond all that is knowable. What does monotheism mean? What are its true implications? I believe monotheism means the *affirmation of unity* in the world. Within the human family, monotheism means that, *for all our differences*—differences that I celebrate and honor— I am more like you than I am unlike you. It means that a single standard of justice applies to us equally. It means that we—with all of creation—participate in a single source and flow of life.

How, then, does monotheism come to support the patriarchal order? It seems that monotheism supports patriarchy by *deviating* from its own primary insight. When patriarchy takes the principle of unity and splits it into two—when God is removed from the world and set above it, when Divinity is no longer inherent in us but exists as an ideal outside ourselves—both God and world are exiled. The problem, in other words, is not the oneness of Divinity but the otherness of Divinity. The problem is in our imagery of transcendence, through which we disempower ourselves as we portray God as power over us.

As a feminist Jew, then, I seek a return to the fundamental insight of the religion—the perception of unity in the world. Unity of all elements of creation, unity of creation with creative source and power. This perception can be restored only through radical re-visioning, *re-imaging* that brings us back to the root of the monotheistic idea.

• • •

My own journey as a poet to enact this feminist Jewish vision has led me to write new Hebrew *b'rakhot* (blessings) to substitute for the traditional, formulaic ones that have idolized the image of a male lord/God/king ruling over the world. I begin with the traditional formulations, seeking what is meaningful in them as links to Jewish culture and history. Although I reject the traditional naming of God as *adonai eloheynu melekh ha-olam,* "lord our God king of the world," I find other elements of the *b'rakhot* moving. For example, I like the picture found in the second phrase of the most common Hebrew blessing, the *motzi,* which is said before beginning a meal: *Barukh atah adonai eloheynu melekh ha-olam / ha-motzi lekhem min haaretz,* "Blessed are you, lord our God king of the world / who brings forth bread from the earth." The image here of bread being drawn out of the earth calls to mind important associations between the earth and our food, the earth and ourselves. As we are made of the stuff of the earth, so the earth provides our nourishment. As we care for the earth, so it provides for us.

But with what sense of Divinity do I connect this image, this moment? Surely not with God as sovereign, which is the image embodied in the formulaic address that appears in all traditional Hebrew blessings (a formula known as *shem u'malkhut*). Rather, I feel connected at this moment to nurture, source, home. And so the biblical word *ayin,* "well" or "fountain," with the figurative meaning of "source," an image rooted in the earth, rises to my consciousness. And I make the image *eyn ha-khayyim,* "wellspring or source of life," to point toward Divinity here.

Now that I have my images, where do I begin my *b'rakhah* (blessing)? Perhaps the most important element of change in my *b'rakhah* is that, instead of using the traditional opening, the passive form which states God's "blessedness," I take back the power of blessing. Instead of *barukh atah,* "blessed are you [masculine]," or even *b'rukhah at,* "blessed are you [feminine]," I say *n'varekh,* "let us bless," active and gender-inclusive. My wish is to reaffirm the living community of voices, to remind us of our own power to bless. To affirm the Divinity *in* our voices even as it flows out beyond us, the Divinity that is us and also greater than us, the whole that is greater than the sum of its parts. The whole within which we wish to create mutual and reciprocal relation. And so my blessing for the meal becomes: *N'varekh et eyn ha-khayyim / ha-motziah lekhem min ha-aretz.* "Let us bless the wellspring of life / that brings forth bread from the earth."

I create and use new images—images such as *eyn ha-khayyim,* "wellspring or source of life," *ma'yan khayyenu,* "fountain or flow of our lives," *nishmat kol khai,* "breath of all living things," and *nitzotzot hanefesh,* "sparks of the inner, unseen self"—to serve as fresh metaphors for Divinity. With these images and still others, composed of all the basic elements of creation—earth, water, wind, and fire—I hope to help construct a *theology of immanence* that will both affirm the sanctity of the world and shatter the idolatrous reign of the lord/God/king. Today I find that every blessing I write journeys toward yet another image of the Divine, and embarks on a fresh search for the hidden places in my life where Divinity may be awakened.

At the same time, the specific language of my images and the structure of my prayers are drawn from traditional Jewish sources, which give historical connection to my labor and, I hope, to the products of my labor. The desire for this connection is deep; being a Jew feels almost as fundamental to my self-definition as being female. Yet it is not just a matter of early-formed identity; I continue, as a feminist, to choose Judaism, despite its problems, because I know that all real relationships entail struggle—and my relationship to Judaism is one through which I continue to grow.

In the end, Judaism's emphasis on unity is a crucial source of awareness for me: it is the foundation of empathy and connectedness; it is the principle that expresses the integrity of existence. As a poet in pursuit of images to affirm both diversity and unity, I know that the journey is just—ever—beginning. As a feminist Jew, I hope that if, through community, we support and continue such pursuits, embracing all our truths as parts of a greater whole, we may approach a truly whole and diversified, inclusive and pluralistic, vision—and give voice to authentic monotheism. ❦

Further Thoughts on Liturgy as an Expression of Theology

MARCIA FALK

One of the more heated debates that have arisen in response to my creation of alternatives to the traditional blessing form concerns the fact that my blessings do not directly address God in the second person. The question of whether Jewish prayer *needs* to address God as "you" is a highly charged one, perhaps even more provocative than the feminist challenge to the gendered God. Vigorous protests arise when one questions the exclusive authority of the "I–Thou" address of divinity; there is a widely held assumption that this is the only legitimate mode for Jewish prayer. Why this assumption should prevail is not clear. There are certainly people for whom the direct address of God requires a breath-holding suspension of disbelief; while for some this may be an acceptable fiction, for others it feels more like a lie. That one may have an experience of the divine that does *not* assume "otherness" is attested to by many people, Jews clearly among them; this has been true in the past as well as today. The sixteenth-century mystic Moses Cordovero, for example, articulated a nondualistic Jewish theology: "Do not attribute duality to God. . . . Do not say, 'This is a stone and not God.' . . . Rather, all existence is God, and the stone is a thing pervaded by divinity."[1] Speaking personally, I would describe my own experience of the divine as an awareness, or a sensing, of the dynamic, alive, and unifying wholeness within creation—a wholeness that subsumes and contains and embraces me, a wholeness greater than the sum of its parts. Is it reasonable to exclude experiences like this, or formulations like Cordovero's, from the range of conceptualizing that might properly be considered Jewish theology?

Indeed, the modern movement of Reconstructionism, founded by Rabbi Mordecai Kaplan, is explicitly based on a theology that denies that God is either personal or "supernatural."[2] While Kaplan did not seek to abolish the direct address of God in prayer, his eminent disciple Rabbi Ira Eisenstein, President Emeritus of the Reconstructionist Rabbinical College and an editor of the first Reconstructionist prayer book, has recently called for just that. Eisenstein writes: "Prayer does not necessarily require a 'Thou.' In several cultures, prayer is experienced without reference to a personal being or a Thou. . . . When I pray, I confine myself to the kind of text that enables me to achieve what Walter Kaufman called 'passionate reflection.' . . . I suggest that traditional Jewish values become the central theme of passionate reflection." Eisenstein goes on to say that prayer today must be "our own, couched in our own idiom, emerging out of our sense of the world."

This essay, which is a follow-up to "Toward a Feminist Jewish Reconstruction of Monotheism," is adapted from the introduction to the Commentary in *The Book of Blessings: New Jewish Prayers for Daily Life, the Sabbath, and the New Moon Festival.*

136

Arguing that "a dialogue with some Other" does not constitute authentic prayer, he urges Reconstructionists to try to pray "without the Thou."[3]

Yet the position that God *must* be viewed and addressed as an Other is held today by many Jews, including some liberal theologians and scholars with whom I share dialogue (and with whom I am often in agreement on other issues). Thus feminist theologian Rachel Adler writes: "Eradicating otherness, breaking down all boundaries between self and other, self and God, God and world, simultaneously eradicates relatedness. . . . God's otherness, God's difference from us, is what makes possible relationship and exchange."[4] And liturgy scholar Lawrence A. Hoffman, arguing for the importance of maintaining God's otherness in our prayer, states that "God can be known only in relationship and can never be adequately described outside of relationship."[5]

While I would agree that relationship is an important element of theology, I do not see why it is necessary to envision God as a transcendent Other in order to affirm relationship. This view certainly fails to account for the deep sense of connectedness I personally feel when I am in touch with my participation in the greater Whole of creation.[6] Moreover, the conception of God as transcendent Other is based on a hierarchical construct of God and world that can be highly problematic for modeling relationships, especially from a feminist perspective, since it provides theological underpinning for the hierarchical dualisms—including the foundational dualistic construct of female and male—that characterize and plague Western culture. It hardly seems coincidental that, when the relationship between God and world is depicted in the tradition in sexual terms, God is envisioned as male and the world—often represented by the human community or the people of Israel—is depicted as female.

Of course, not all liberal theologians maintain the need to preserve God's otherness; one contemporary scholar who has made a point of challenging the dominant view is Arthur Green. Green writes: "We seek a religious language that goes beyond the separation of 'God,' 'world,' and 'self' that seems so ultimate in most of Western theology. The God of which we speak here is not the 'wholly other,' so widely familiar in our thought and yet so little tested by real understanding. We refer rather to a deity that embraces all of being, a single One that contains within it all the variety and richness of life, yet is also the Oneness that transcends and surpasses all. . . . But where do we allow room for the truth that all is One if our religious language is that of 'Self' and 'Other'?"[7]

Green makes a stirring case here; and indeed, the importance of speaking honestly of the experience of divine immanence is a central premise of his book. How odd it is, therefore, to find that he declines to abandon the address of God as Other in prayer—in fact, he *insists* upon the use of a personal "you." As he puts it: "For the nondualist, speaking *to* God is as much a betrayal as speaking *of.* Though I insist on using the dualist language in prayer ('blessed are You . . .'), I know that I do not mean it in its simplest sense. This language is a way of addressing the One as though it were possible for me to stand outside that One in such a moment, as though there really were an 'I' who could speak this way to a 'Thou.' But if such prayer is betrayal of our deepest consciousness, it is there to keep faith with our ordinary experience as human beings."[8]

I cannot help but wonder whose "ordinary experience" is being referred to and why we must betray our "deepest consciousness" in order to "keep faith" with it. Why should we be willing to hold one set of beliefs as our truths while we articulate something very different in our worship? If we do not try to touch our deepest faith—our most truthful truths—in prayer, then where?

Striking as it seems, this discrepancy between what one believes and what one is willing to say in prayer is not unique to Green; rather, I would suggest, it reflects an entrenched conservatism on the part of the Jewish community at large in regard to liturgical change. The reasons for this conservatism are open to speculation: the role of nostalgia should perhaps not be underestimated in explaining why people cling to the words they remember (whether accurately or not) from childhood. Still, most people are quite willing to do things differently from their grandparents; this seems to be at least as true in the arena of religion as it is in other areas of life. I would venture to guess that few if any liberal Jews today observe traditional religious customs and laws as their grandparents did. It seems that only when it comes to the actual words of prayer is innovation resisted so fervently. While I cannot adequately explain what causes this phenomenon, I believe I can point to some of its effects. Although liturgical change is often seen as a threat to the continuity of tradition, I would suggest that resistance on the part of the established Jewish community to bringing its prayer in line with its theological, moral, and sociopolitical beliefs has caused many individuals to feel isolated and uncomfortable in synagogue settings, and has dissuaded others from attempting to pray at all. Because communal worship and celebration of the liturgical calendar are central aspects of synagogue experience, many people decline synagogue affiliation and as a consequence have little involvement in Jewish community of any kind. And, as has been documented in recent years, many Jews today pursue spiritual paths in other traditions, such as Buddhism, that seem to speak more authentically to their beliefs. It is my conviction that we *can* articulate our beliefs authentically in a Jewish idiom and a Jewish context, and that it is essential that we try to do so in our prayer if we hope to keep Jewish liturgical tradition alive.

Related to the position that God must be viewed as an Other is the belief that God must be conceptualized and addressed as Person. Thus Lawrence Hoffman states emphatically: "Indeed, it is essential to retain a conception of God as Person, since it is primarily as Person that we know God in the first place."[9] Feminist theologian Judith Plaskow maintains that we need to use personal imagery for God, at least some of the time, for the following reason: "Because relationships among human beings are unique in containing the potential for the full mutuality and reciprocity that form the foundations of the moral life, it is important that we use anthropomorphic imagery [for God], and that we broaden it as far as possible. But our moral responsibility extends to the entire web of creation, all of which manifests and can symbolize divine presence and activity."[10]

Despite these challenges from thinkers I respect and from whom I have learned a great deal, I have to say that the image of God as Person is not one I find helpful, and I believe that, in this regard, I speak for many others. It is not at all true for me that "it is primarily as Person" that I know God; I experience the divine in many ways, ways that are better represented by nonpersonal images, as well as by other, less direct modes of expression that do not attempt to locate divinity in specific images at all. Moreover, I am seriously troubled by the overwhelming predominance of anthropomorphic imagery in traditional Jewish prayer; it seems to me that this emphasis has led us as a culture into dangerous forms of anthropocentrism (what some call "species-ism"), that is, the belief that the human species is "godlier" than the rest of creation. The detrimental effects of this point of view have been widespread and lasting; one could make the case that this theological perspective buttresses an ideology responsible in large measure for the ecological crisis we face today. With this in mind, I would hold that we ought to explore more fully and more creatively other ways to imagine and conceptualize divinity, and that we should hesitate before adding more anthropomorphisms to our prayer books.

In further response to Plaskow, I would say that I do not believe an anthropomorphic view of the divine is necessary for the foundations of a moral life. While I appreciate Plaskow's desire to represent human relationships in our liturgy, I would stress that this needn't take the form of creating images of God as Person (even if that Person is Friend rather than Lord, female rather than male). Instead, I would suggest that we bring human relations *directly* into our liturgy by explicitly affirming in that liturgy our interpersonal values, and by using prayer as an occasion to make commitments to live according to those values. This approach is, I believe, in keeping with the model of "passionate reflection" on traditional Jewish values that Eisenstein is calling for, which he describes thus: "appreciation of the marvels and the mysteries of the universe, dedication to the ideas of human perfectability, individual and social concern for the downtrodden and the stranger, as well as a sense of gratitude for whatever well-being one enjoys. Passionate reflection should revive one's resolution to strive for ethical heights, to resist evil, to engender love and respect for fellow persons—and, finally, to rekindle love of and loyalty to the Jewish people, to Torah in its broadest and deepest sense."[11] I offer examples of moral commitments in various parts of my liturgy, found in my new prayer book, *The Book of Blessings.*[12] Other offerings in that book provide direct address between human beings and attempt, through this form, to model the reciprocity and respect that Plaskow and Eisenstein urge us to seek. The book as a whole offers numerous alternatives to the direct address of divinity that is found in the traditional blessing form because, in the end, there is no single answer to the question of how to speak authentically in prayer.

Notes

1. Moses Cordovero, *Shi'ur Komah,* Modena Manuscript, 206b, as cited in translation in Daniel C. Matt, *The Essential Kabbalah* (San Francisco: Harper San Francisco, 1995), p. 24.
2. Kaplan believed that God was "the Power that makes for Salvation," that is, a force that runs through us and allows us to achieve redemptive goals. For Kaplan, God was neither a Person who acted on the world nor an outside force, but rather the organic interrelationship of all the laws of the universe, which act not upon us but through us. See *Judaism as a Civilization: Toward a Reconstruction of American-Jewish Life* (New York: Macmillan, 1935) and Emanuel S. Goldsmith and Mel Scult, eds., *Dynamic Judaism: The Essential Writings of Mordecai M. Kaplan* (New York: Schocken Books/Reconstructionist Press, 1985).
3. Ira Eisenstein, "Prayer as 'Passionate Reflection,' " *Reconstructionism Today* 2:2 (Winter 1994–95): 9–10.
4. Rachel Adler, "And Not Be Silent: Towards Inclusive Worship," in *Engendering Judaism* (Philadelphia: Jewish Publication Society, 1997).
5. Lawrence A. Hoffman, "A Response to Marcia Falk," *Tikkun* 4:4 (July–August 1989): 57.
6. For me, theology begins with personal experience; this approach is one I share with other feminist theologians. In an insightful essay providing an overview of Jewish feminist theology, Ellen M. Umansky writes: "What differentiates feminist theology from many theologies of the past, and some of the present, is both a willingness to acknowledge openly the autobiographical nature of experience and a consequent reluctance if not refusal either to assert universal truths or to make universal claims" (Umansky, "Jewish Feminist Theology," chap. 13 in Eugene B. Borowitz, *Choices in Modern Jewish Thought: A Partisan Guide,* 2d ed. [West Orange, NJ: Behrman House, 1995], p. 314). [Chapter 12 in this volume.]

7. Arthur Green, *Seek My Face, Speak My Name: A Contemporary Jewish Theology* (Northvale, NJ: Jason Aronson, 1992), pp. 8–9.

8. Ibid., pp. 16–17.

9. Hoffman, "Response," p. 57.

10. Judith Plaskow, "Spirituality and Politics: Lessons from B'not Esh," *Tikkun* 10:3 (May–June 1995):32. Plaskow discusses the issue of anthropomorphic "God-language" in chap. 4 of her groundbreaking work *Standing Again at Sinai: Judaism from a Feminist Perspective* (San Francisco: Harper & Row, 1990); see especially pp. 154–69. In the same chapter, pp. 128–34, she critiques the image of God as dominating Other.

11. Eisenstein, "Prayer," p. 9.

12. *The Book of Blessings: New Jewish Prayers for Daily Life, the Sabbath, and the New Moon Festival* (San Francisco: Harper San Francisco, 1996).

12

Jewish Feminist Theology

ELLEN M. UMANSKY

Attempts to create a Jewish feminist theology—or Jewish feminist theologies—have been fairly recent. Most of these attempts have been articulated in articles and public addresses rather than in full-length books. Thus, a summary of the published writings of Jewish feminist theologians is limited by the fact that, with the exception of Judith Plaskow, none has yet written a major theological work. What's more, some of those currently engaged in writing Jewish feminist theology are graduate students whose doctoral work has been presented at academic conferences but has not yet been published. The reader, then, needs to keep in mind the following: Jewish feminist theology is not only a new field but also a growing one. New articles are continually being published and one can hope that a number of book-length theological works soon will appear. This chapter therefore represents an early step in the delineation of both the nature and content of Jewish feminist theological thought.

Jewish Feminist Theology as Responsive and Contextual

While, as we shall see, the specific theological concerns articulated by Jewish feminist theologians differ from one another, all seem to share an understanding of theology as rooted in personal experience. All, in other words, recognize that theologians have always drawn on their experiences in developing both a theological language and a theological system. What differentiates feminist theology from many theologies of the past, and some of the present, is both a willingness to acknowledge openly the autobiographical nature of theology and a consequent reluctance if not refusal either to assert universal truths or to make universal claims. The goal of feminist theology is not to persuade others to share

Ellen M. Umansky, "Jewish Feminist Theology," *Choices in Modern Jewish Thought,* second edition, in Eugene B. Borowitz, ed. (New York: Behrman House, 1995), pp. 314–17, 334–40. © Ellen Umansky.

any one feminist vision. Rather, its goal is to articulate the theologian's own understanding of the self, God, and the world and, within a Jewish context, to view these realities through the lens of Jewish feminist experience.

This does not mean that all Jewish feminists share the same experiences of the self, God, and the world. What it does mean is that Jewish feminists approach theology with an a priori commitment to writing a theology that is both feminist and Jewish. By feminist, I mean that which is consciously rooted in the theologian's own experiences of self. These experiences, not limited to those of gender, are shaped by specific cultural, historical, and economic factors. As a perspective, feminist theology calls into question any theology that views male experience as universal. It begins with the presupposition that traditional Jewish theology—like traditional Christian theology—has been androcentric. That is, it has placed men in the center, using the experiences of Jewish men as a lens through which the world is viewed. Thus, one still finds some Jewish theologians referring to the "613 commandments that Jews traditionally are obligated to perform" even through it is only men who are obligated to perform 613, while other theologians refer to "the study of religious texts and participation in regularly scheduled public worship" as *the* central expressions of Jewish piety when in fact only men have been obligated to study and to participate in public worship. Consequently, in the writings of such theologians, the ways in which the piety of Jewish women traditionally gained expression are minimized if not ignored.

Jewish feminist theology, *as feminist theology,* thus begins with what the Christian feminist theologian Elisabeth Schüssler Fiorenza, in her work on the New Testament, has labeled a feminist hermeneutics of suspicion. As Schüssler Fiorenza has written, the feminist theologian begins her study of biblical texts and their interpretations with the assumption that they are androcentric and also serve patriarchal functions. The Jewish feminist theologian, then, like the Christian feminist theologian, approaches traditional texts suspecting that the experiences of women will either be peripheral to the text or simply will not be recorded. When they are recorded, such experiences are most likely described in such a way as to reinforce male power or to justify the traditional roles to which women have been assigned by men. While Jewish feminist theologians, then, may advocate making such liturgical changes as "*Elohei avoteinu v'imoteinu*" ("God of our fathers and mothers") to replace the traditional "*Elohei avoteinu*" ("God of our fathers"), there is still the recognition of how difficult it is to talk of God as the God of our fathers *and* mothers when the only known stories are male stories and the Jewish experiences read about have been solely the experiences of men.

Having recognized that sources of Jewish theology, including the Written and Oral Torah, philosophical and mystical texts, and traditional liturgy, were largely (if not exclusively) created by and for men, the first task of the Jewish feminist theologian is thus to recognize that the visions we have received are incomplete. Before the feminist theologian can reform or transmit Judaism's traditional visions, she needs to receive these visions herself. She needs to hear her own voice and feel her own presence within the sources of Jewish tradition. Before she can shape the content of religious expression, she must discover what women's religious experiences have been. To do so may require reading between the lines, filling in stories, writing new ones, making guesses. Consequently, Jewish feminist theology, *as Jewish theology,* can be described as a theology that by definition is "responsive."

As defined by Daniel Breslauer in an essay entitled "Alternatives in Jewish Theology" (1981), responsive theology is that which emerges out of an encounter with "images and narrative from the Jewish past" and from the experiences of the theologian. Unlike normative theology, response theology does not begin with a set of norms delineating what is authentically Jewish. Rather, it begins with the "subjective response of the theologian to a set of experiences," encouraging, therefore, a "more fluid view of Judaism and the Judaic experience itself."

If Jewish feminist theology is responsive theology, its a priori commitment to Jewish tradition need not be a commitment either to the past norms of that tradition or to the current articulations of those norms as expressed by Judaism's major religious movements. Rather, its commitment is to the sources and fundamental categories of God, Torah, and Israel. Jewish feminist theology, then, is a theology that emerges *in response to* Jewish sources and Jewish beliefs. These responses are shaped by the experiences of the theologian as woman and as Jew. What may emerge is a transformation not only of Jewish theology but of the sources the feminist uses in transmitting her visions.

What's more, because Jewish feminist theology is rooted in the experiences of the theologian, it can also be understood as contextual theology, that is, a theology self-consciously rooted in the context of the theologian's own life. Rather than attempting to create theological systems that transcend personal experience, feminist theologians have firmly grounded their theologies in the realities of their own lives. The similar concerns and at times the similar visions of many contemporary Jewish feminist theologians can thus be attributed not to their having arrived at some universally attainable ontological truth but rather to their writing in a similar context—for example, as white, middle-class, religiously liberal, university-educated, U.S. feminists writing during the last three decades of the twentieth century. This does not mean, however, that feminist theological claims have relevance only for the theologian herself. On the contrary, it is the hope of the feminist theologian that by drawing on her experiences and sharing her stories, she will encourage others to draw on their experiences as well. In so doing, the feminist theologian offers women and men a means of formulating their own articulated and unarticulated responses to the categories of God, Torah, and Israel. She also offers women and men a means of viewing their own experience as Jewish experience, enabling them to recognize, as Rabbi Laura Geller has written, "that to be a Jew means to tell my story within the Jewish story." Acknowledging the importance of personal experience as a source of wisdom and truth, the feminist theologian leads others to discover, sharing Laura Geller's sentiments if not her terminology, that there is a "Torah of our lives as well as the Torah that was written down. Both need to be listened to and wrestled with: both unfold through interactive commentary."

• • •

A Personal Assessment

Much of the constructive theological work in which I myself have been engaged owes a great deal to Jewish feminist theologians. I have learned a great deal from reading their works and have been spiritually challenged by the many theological debates and discussions that we have had with one another. While not identifying my objective as the creation of a feminist Judaism, this demurral may be less ideological than communal, stemming from the fact that the Jewish community with which I most strongly identify is the liberal Jewish community and even more specifically the Reform movement, of which I have been a member my entire life.

It is primarily with other liberal Jews, both laity and clergy, that I am most actively engaged in working toward the kinds of feminist transformations that I shall in a moment detail. My goal is not some universal transformation of Judaism nor is it the creation of a new religious movement or denomination. Rather, it is the transformation of Reform Judaism in ways that reflect feminist insights and values while at the same time honoring and maintaining the insights and values of Reform. While many, if not most, of my concerns share many commonalities with those articulated by other liberal Jews, including Reconstructionists, many within the Conservative movement, and those who identify themselves as New Age, *havurah,* or feminist Jews, the religious language that I speak is very much the language of Reform Judaism. It includes such phrases as "ethical monotheism" and "ongoing revelation," the belief that "one serves God best by serving others" (a phrase rooted in nineteenth-century Classical Reform taken from the writings of George Eliot), and the conviction that observance in and of itself does not make one holy. Perhaps the reason I most often identify myself as a liberal Jewish theologian (and not a Reform theologian) is that I recognize the great extent to which my religious language is also indebted to Mordecai Kaplan, whose understanding of Judaism as a civilization, call for "unity in diversity," allowing *halachah* a "vote but not veto," great commitment to change, and love for *klal Yisrael* (i.e., the Jewish community and all that has shaped and nurtured it in the past, as well as that which shapes and nurtures it in the present) have greatly influenced my understanding both of what Judaism is and of what it might be.

Torah, as I understand it, refers to Jewish teachings and values that reflect the ongoing covenantal relationship between God and the Jewish people. Like Rachel Adler, with whom my theology has a great deal in common, I envision God as a personal Being capable of commanding and of revealing religious teachings. Similarly, my source of authority is rooted in both personal and communal experience as well as in sacred texts. While applauding Adler's efforts to revision *halachah,* I question whether progressive Jews (and Reform Jews in particular) can be persuaded to forfeit their autonomy even for the best of causes, that is, for a *halachah* that gives meaning to their actions and helps transform Reform Judaism from a way of thinking into a way of life. Indeed, because autonomy has been so central to Reform Judaism, talking about a Reform *halachah* may well be premature.

Drawing on the values of relationship and connectedness, my interest is in creating a theology of peoplehood that is rooted in the experiences of American Reform Jews. In the recognition that feminism as a philosophical perspective has already had a great impact on the liberal Jewish community and that the Reform commitment to social action has long underscored relationship and connection as Jewish values (a point that Drorah Setel also makes in her writings), this theology begins with the rejection of classical Reform's identification of Judaism with personal religion. It suggests that the Jewish self exists in covenant not as a "single soul in its full individuality" (to quote Eugene Borowitz) but as a relational soul in community with others. Rather than beginning with the autonomous self who chooses to become a Jewish self, my theology, deeply infused with Jewish and feminist values, begins with the recognition that no self is fully autonomous. As Martin Buber wrote long ago, we always exist in relationship to others and to the world in which we live.

To date, most of my own theological writings have focused on my relationship to God and on God's relationship with all creation. Essays written in the early 1980s focused on the importance of reimaging the Divine as male and female, both to underscore the Jewish

conviction that all of us—men and women—have been created in the image of God, and
to eliminate the theological justification for male political and social power that exclusively masculine images of Deity provide. These essays also suggested, though these views
have yet to be developed at length, that one possible solution to the problem of theodicy
(the existence of evil in light of God's being all-knowing, all-powerful, and all-good) may
be that God is neither all-powerful nor all-good but in fact has both an evil and a good
nature, as do we, those beings created in the Divine image. God therefore cannot always
prevent human tragedy because God is not only strong but also weak. Drawing on Heinrich
Zimmer's study of Indian myths and symbols which suggests that a deity is great only if
that deity can display "mutually antagonistic attitudes and activities," one essay concludes
that Zimmer may well be right; by limiting God, we have in fact limited God's greatness.

More recent theological works have emphasized that God's metaphorical gender is less
important than the kinds of images through which God is envisioned. Insisting that there
is a direct connection between the ways in which we envision the Divine relationship and
the ways in which we actually relate to the world and its creations, they maintain that using images of hierarchical domination in imaging the Divine—such as King, Lord,
Queen—encourages an envisioning of the human-Divine relationship as one of domination and submission. It establishes this relationship as a model of how things really are,
encouraging us, even if unintentionally, to set ourselves over and against both the earth
and other people—especially over those to whom we may feel superior by virtue of our
gender, race, socioeconomic class, age, religious affiliation, nationality, or other qualities.
Believing that God is both immanent and transcendent, I am at present working to create
new images of Divinity that will encourage myself and others to work with God rather
than under God's authority.

At the same time, I am continuing to create *midrashim* that give expression to my theological visions. Like the intent of those Rabbis who created classical *midrashim,* my intention is to enable biblical texts to speak to me, that is, meaningfully to ground and give
expression to my own understanding of Judaism. Such *midrashim* begin with a feminist
hermeneutics of suspicion. Focusing on biblical women whose actions the text minimizes
or ignores, they then attempt to view biblical texts through the lens of feminist experience (in this case, my own). *Midrash* clearly is an important resource for Jewish feminist
theology, for if, as Laura Geller has written, to be a Jew means to tell one's story within
the Jewish story, then *midrashim* written in story form (as mine and those recently created by other feminists have been) are particularly effective means of seeing women not
as objectified Others but as normative Jews whose experiences of God, Torah, and Israel
can add to, challenge, and transform previously held theological convictions.

But Is It Jewish?

Jewish feminist theology may be described as a contextual theology that responds to
Judaism's fundamental categories of God, Torah, and Israel. Nonetheless, one may ask—
as some critics have already—whether this theology is in fact Jewish. To this non-Orthodox
Jew who believes in the authenticity of liberal Judaism, the answer is clearly yes. As this
chapter has indicated, the sources on which Jewish feminist theologians have drawn and
continue to draw are Jewish ones (though not exclusively so), as are the religious communities out of which each sees her theology emerging. At the same time, most Jewish

feminist theologians, including those referred to in this chapter, acknowledge that there may be personal or communal boundaries beyond which they as Jews cannot go.

Though some Jewish feminist theologians (myself among them) seem to be more concerned with boundaries than others, even Judith Plaskow, who has maintained that an insistence on predetermined boundaries may confine the creativity and resources of Jewish feminists, admits that monotheism *is* a boundary for her. Indeed, it seems to be a crucial boundary for all of the Jewish feminist theologians whose works have been mentioned here. Other boundaries that emerge in the work of Jewish feminist theologians include the following: an a priori commitment to placing one's experiences of the Divine within a specifically Jewish framework; an understanding of Judaism that retains a sense of legal integrity; and a refraining from using names for Divinity (such as Elilah) that in the biblical text not only are names for a deity other than the Hebrew God but also, in Hebrew, equate such worship with idolatry.

For Women Only?

To the extent that Jewish feminist theology is grounded in the experiences of Jewish women, it is by definition a theology that can be created by women only. At the same time, however, because Jewish feminist theology can also be seen as a theology rooted in feminist and Jewish values, so its insights can be reflected upon and shared by women and men. Indeed, there are a growing number of male rabbis and academics—among them Daniel Boyarin, Howard Eilberg-Schwartz, David Ellenson, Lawrence Hoffman, Lawrence Kushner, Zalman Schachter-Shalomi, and Arthur Waskow—who have openly acknowledged their indebtedness to feminist theology. Just as many Jewish feminists have drawn on their work, so in their writings and teachings have they drawn on the works of Jewish feminists. At the same time, they have understood the importance of speaking with and to feminist theologians rather than speaking for them.

Contributions of Feminist Theology

Undoubtedly, one of the greatest contributions that Jewish feminist theology has already made has been to demonstrate that it is possible for diverse groups of people to talk seriously about Jewish theology outside of a *halachic* framework. While religiously liberal rabbis have long discussed the creation of a non-*halachic* Jewish self-identity, they have not taken the theological basis for this identity seriously enough. Certainly, in the twentieth century there have been a handful of liberal Jewish theologians who have taken the Jewish theological enterprise seriously, Eugene Borowitz among them, but feminist theologians have been the first to create, however loosely, a network of religiously liberal theologians who have seriously examined together, both formally and informally, traditional and liberal Jewish theological claims.

Further, in attempting to ground this theology in their experience as women, feminist theologians have called into question not only traditional theological language (for example, the concept of a Father, rather than a Mother, God, who gives birth to creation), but also the ways in which theology is done. Through the creation of new blessings, *midrashim,* poems, rituals, and the like, feminist theologians have added a vibrancy to the liberal Jewish theological enterprise. While it is hoped that more fully developed Jewish feminist theologies will be written in the future, the many questions raised and the many theological directions pursued have already awakened in a significant number of American Jews both an intellectual and a personal interest in theological exploration.

It is too early to identify, much less assess, all of the lasting contributions of Jewish feminist theology. It is hoped that among them will be the encouragement of growing numbers of Jewish women to reclaim the power of naming themselves, the world, and God. In so doing, it will have helped to create a more inclusive Judaism, for as Judith Plaskow has written, "Only when those who have had the power of naming stolen from us find our voices and begin to speak will Judaism become a religion that includes all Jews—will it truly be a Judaism of women and men."

13

The Wings of the Dove: Jewish Values, Science, and Halachah

DAVID W. WEISS

Judaism and the World of Science

It is a prevalent contemporary supposition that religious belief and scientific knowledge are incompatible. The roots of this supposition lie with the assumption that science explains, or potentially can explain, all events and phenomena in the cognizance of man. There is no room, accordingly, for other interpretations of the world. Science and religion are seen as laying competing, contradictory claims to the truth of reality. Where scientific evidence clearly refutes specific religious assertions whose acceptance is demanded on an acquiescence of faith alone, the contradiction is unyielding.

In a confrontation between demonstrable facts and religious profession, persons who think and question will tend to opt for the former. The tragedy of the loss to Judaism of many of the most talented members of the Jewish people is compounded by the needlessness of the choice. There may, indeed, be an irreconcilable conflict between modern science and the basic credo of some religions; there is none for Judaism.

The assumption that science can explain the world is mistaken. Moreover, there is no dogma in Judaism that relates to cause and effect in the existing, material universe. Far from standing in contention with science, Judaism impels scientific inquiry and investigation; scientific understanding can only support, not negate, the cardinal allegations of Jewish belief.

David W. Weiss, *The Wings of the Dove: Jewish Values, Science, and Halachah* (Washington, D.C.: B'nai B'rith Book Service, 1987), pp. 81–87, 117–22. © B'nai B'rith Book Service, Washington, D.C. 20036.

The Limits of Scientific Explanations

Scientific explanations are attempts to show that a particular phenomenon is a special instance of one or more general principles. Basic principles are at times deduced directly from accumulated cognate experience. More often, they are at first inferred, or predicted, on the strength of suggestive but limited data. In either event, principles, or laws, must be validated both by strict reasoning from other, established principles, and by the consistency of extensive observations in the field or laboratory. However, in numerous instances it is impossible to know definitely the nature of a phenomenon. Where our information can be obtained only in indirect, imprecise ways, many details remain obscure, and the truth can only be approximated. In these cases, mental constructs, or theories, are formulated to intimate a cohesive picture. Theories must fit the known facts and subsume their most likely deductions and inferences.

In many areas of science, spanning the science of the very large (cosmology) and the science of the very small (elementary particle physics), we can make sense of observed phenomena only by advancing propositions that in themselves are not subject to the empirical methodologies of scientific investigation. Scientific knowledge is most certain when it accrues from rigorously controlled experimentation. It is the experimental confirmation of ideas and experience that delimits and distinguishes the natural sciences from other areas of ideation, from philosophy, religion, and artistic intuition. Yet, such confirmation is often unattainable in the sciences. Certain postulates may be obligatory elements in our conceptual constructs for explaining order in the universe, but where they are not objectively measurable, they fall into the category of the intangible or abstract, beyond the strict boundaries of the natural sciences. Theories in the natural sciences thus often demand the inclusion of premises that are intrinsically not in the realm of science.

It is often impossible, moreover, to ascertain whether a scientific theory, even if it is in agreement will all known facts and reasonable premises, represents the whole or sole truth. Not infrequently, diverse theories "explain," to seemingly equal satisfaction, a body of experimental results and observations.

Theories are also limited by the repertoire of visual images with which we are equipped.[1] As a physicist wrote sixty years ago, "All our pictures are built out of things with which we are familiar. In picturing material things, we use matter *as we see it*. But we see matter only in gross assemblages. It is not probable that the fundamental entities of matter look or seem familiar to gross matter, or even have the same properties. Hence it is not surprising that our physical pictures of the atom and of the electron do not always fit. A good example is our inability to form a picture of an electron which is consistent with all its apparent properties. Sometimes it behaves as if it were a wave, and at other times as if it were a tiny dense particle."[2] The advances in mathematical physics and other areas of the basic sciences during the past half century have underlined the veracity of this caveat of limitations.

There is a further reservation to the incisiveness of scientific explanation. Explanation is often more descriptive than analytical, even apart from our enforced resort to untestable assumptions. Thus, science cannot explain the infinitely complex, ordered universe in terms of the behavior of atoms and molecules. It does not easily bridge the gap between unit and aggregate structure. Science could predict chaotic disorganization rather than consistent order on all levels, from atom to cosmos, on the basis of the properties of the universe's primary constituents of matter and energy. We can indeed "comprehend" certain phenomena retrospectively, having identified and characterized their constituent components, and then finding similar arrangements of building blocks and similar qualities of the integrated whole in all identical phenomena. However, given the properties of each component to begin with, but without knowing the invariable uniformity of the qualities of the whole, we could often imagine—theorize—very different outcomes of their deterministic or probability interactions: i.e., a non-uniformity of attributes of the resultant entity—disorder.[3]

Science cannot account for the generation of the universe from its composite elements. The postulate of random collisions between these is inadequate. Taking the age of the universe as approximately eighteen billion years, that span of time seems insufficient by far to allow for all the requisite convergences at random, and for the maintenance by chance of fragile intermediate entities.

Science can delineate subsequent events as they take place, but it often fails to offer reasons for the sequence. For instance, science can trace the evolution of species. It cannot quite explain why it occurred, why higher forms developed from well-adapted "lower" ones.[4]

Most importantly, science can address itself neither to the origin of the primary constituents of the universe, nor to the causes of their distinctive qualities of structure and function. They are as they are, givens, and scientific inquiry can proceed only from there. This is stated eloquently by the cosmologist Weisskopf in the concluding passages of a recent article on the origin of the universe: "What existed before the Primal Bang?. . . The question of what happened before has no concrete content. Scientific description and explanation apply only to the events that happened afterward. This answer may seem unsatisfactory, but it is the only scientific answer that can be given to this question. . . . The origin of the universe can be talked about not only in scientific terms, but also in poetic and spiritual language, an approach that is complementary to the scientific one. Indeed, the Judaeo-Christian tradition describes the beginnings of the world in a way that is surprisingly similar to the scientific model."[5]

The *scientific* answer that questions of ultimate origin have no concrete content seems unsatisfactory precisely because it is those questions that lie at the heart of our search for meaning of the universe and of our place in it. It is unsatisfactory, too, because we cherish the faith that science, and only science, can bring the light of reason to the quest. This faith is an illusion. The grasp of science is limited to certain dimensions in time and certain aspects of the reality we know. It is religion that advances hypotheses for the primal origin, evolvement, order and purpose of the universe. To these, science does not attest. Science and religion cannot possibly clash if the scope of each is defined correctly. Discordance results only when either assumes provenance over alien territories. Mainstream Judaism, in contradistinction to many other religions, has avoided such false arrogation. It rejects the hubris of science that would aspire to an inclusive view of the cosmos; but it unhesitatingly mandates to science the full freedom of search into all that can possibly yield to scientific exploration.

Jewish Belief and Scientific Knowledge

The irreducible axiom of Judaism is belief in a Creator concerned with His creation. The fundamental revelation of science is that existence is indescribably complex, and is governed by a measure and consistency of order that defies material interpretation. It is the scientist who knows best that the universe does not exist by playing dice with itself, nor by the throwing of dice by an extrinsic force. The scientist can leave it at that; he can restrict his inquires to what the tools of natural science enable, and leave untouched the questions of origins and harmony. If he chooses, however, to entertain these, he is compelled to the supposition of a creative intelligence by the same dictates of scientific logic that pertain to the formulation of all theories of physical processes whose features or etiology are not fully given to cognitive analysis. Scientific knowledge thus affords a powerful argument for the being of an unseen, constant architect of the otherwise inexplicable universe, and hence for a principle at the epicenter of Jewish belief. Science and Judaism hold complementary interpretations of reality. Affirmation of an unceasing, guiding intelligence above nature is an inference drawn far more reasonably and convincingly on the basis of scientific knowledge than in ignorance of the world.[6] Where scientific reasoning alone can intimate only an unnamed power that is incumbent in the equation of existence but that remains forever wholly abstract, detached, and unknowable, Judaism assigns qualities to this guiding force—the God of Israel—and avers that *cognito dei* is within reach in *imitatio dei*.[7]

Sacred Texts and the Facts of Science

A fundamentalist reading of sacred writings often clashes with scientific fact. However, the sacred literature of Judaism—Scripture, *Talmud*, and the ensuing Rabbinic tradition—is concerned exclusively with spirituality and morality. Allusions to phenomena and events in nature—for instance the stories of creation and of the exodus from Egypt—are not intended as finite material depictions binding on faith. From the *Talmud* on, Judaism's authoritative commentators have proposed a variety of explanations of the textual accounts, some allegorical, many naturalistic. The *mechanisms* of the world's functioning are irrelevant to Judaism's message, and no conception is forbidden that does not deny the essential belief in a Creator heedful of His works. For Judaism, the laws of nature, however comprehended, are a manifestation of the Divine will, not a constraint. Their study represents no threat to the faith. Indeed, it can bring man closer to an approximation of one facet of the infinite. Understanding of the processes of nature enlarges, rather than diminishes, the mystery and wondrousness of being, of progressive development, of human sentience.[8] Science leads to materialism only when the most fundamental questions are dismissed out of hand, and where the eventuality of an underlying value substrate is discarded as "unscientific."

Judaism and the Uses of Science

For at least two thousand years, Judaism has emphasized the merit of scholarship, and Jewish society has been distinguished by its preoccupation with traditional study, both for its own sake and as a directive for action. Engagement with the knowledge of *Bible, Talmud*, and the commentaries has been accorded the highest esteem by Jewish communities the world over. The roots of this thrust lie in the Judaic conception of man and the world. Man enters, collectively and individually, an imperfect world. Its perfection is his responsibility. In the religious idiom of Judaism, man becomes partner with the Creator in the work of creation when acting towards its completion. Man's partnership is relentlessly demanded. The *Mishnah* puts it succinctly: "It is not incumbent on you to complete the work, neither are you free to desist from it."[9] It is only by his constant "involvement" with the material universe and with the betterment of mankind that the human being can attain to his *raison d'etre*. Knowledge provides the means for the attainment. "An ignorant person cannot be righteous," holds the *Mishnah*.[10] The great Medieval philosopher and physician, Maimonides, summed up the position of Judaism definitively: ". . . A person ought therefore to devote himself to the understanding and comprehension of those sciences and studies that will inform him concerning his Master, as far as it lies in human faculties to understand and comprehend."[11]

Although Jewish society today is predominantly secular, it is reasonable to suspect that the classical Judaic tradition of learning has been a major generative element in the Jewish contribution to science. It is also reasonable to assume that it is because understanding and human well-being are so closely linked in Judaism's ethos, that Jews have been especially drawn to those scientific pursuits that hold out most directly the hope of advancing the human situation. It would seem not to be coincidence that Jewish scholars have been so outstandingly prominent in laying the foundations of modern biology and biochemistry, medicine, much of physics, psychology, psychiatry, and sociology. Their representation in these fields has towered above the proportional population of Jews in the countries in which they have made their contributions. Neither is it by chance that the participation of Jewish scientists has been far less disproportionate in the more static fields of science, such as geology, paleontology, and descriptive botany and zoology. The conclusion would seem inescapable that the way to Jewish achievement in the basic, dynamic sciences has been paved by the seminal influence of normative Judaic values.

Randomness and Determinism in Nature: A Consideration

A scientific approach to natural phenomena is, in certain religious circles, regarded as suspect if not indeed heretical. The antagonism to the study of nature originates in no small part from a misunderstanding of the concepts of randomness and determinism. It is thought that these concepts clash with the belief in a divine Creator and Master of the universe. What place does God have if the events of nature transpire at random? Where do we find Him if they are manifestations of blindly deterministic natural laws? In light of this threat to belief, the pursuit of science is discountenanced as a hazardous occupation for the faithful.

The fear is unwarranted. There is no conflict between a scientific view of nature and normative Judaism;[12] there is, rather, a mutuality of these perspectives of reality.

Judaism and science speak distinct languages of ideas; both are required for a comprehensive understanding of the world. However, their semantics often overlap, and words that are common to both are invested with meaning that differs with the observer's frame of reference. They thus generate misapprehension and contradiction when used or read indiscriminately. It is necessary to identify the conceptual frameworks within which common terms are applied, and in each context to define accurately the events denoted by them. Clarification of the meaning and implications, for both science and Judaic belief, of randomness and determinism demonstrates the complementarity of Judaism and scientific knowledge.

In the context of science, the behavior of an individual natural unit—an integer—can be predicted in many instances with near absolute certainty. Laws of causality are seen to apply inclusively, to given effect in given circumstances, to each similar unit in a field of units. For example, a particular arrangement of chromosome constituents invariably controls production by a cell of the same, corresponding molecular product. The behavior of the integer is framed in a deterministic model. In statistical terms, it can be specified reliably in advance by a single value derived from the appropriate equation. Phenomena and transactions that follow patterns of such determinism are distinguished, individually and collectively, by the qualities of surety and constancy.

Deterministic consistency derives from the inherent attributes of each reactant, attributes that are identical, or sufficiently similar, for each analogous integer under scrutiny to make for equivalent function under the influence of particular conditions. Philosophically, the matter can be left to stand at that, leaving untouched the questions of ontogenesis of the primary properties involved, and of their integration into larger, multifactorial domains of transaction. Such a stance by the observer is safe—and truncated; the analysis remains descriptive. If, however, the range of inquiry is extended, questions of both ultimate causality and of larger order must be confronted. The confrontation leads perforce to the topic of purpose as well.

The Judaic response is categorical: The forces, attributes, and transactions discerned are manifestations and evidence of a master plan of creation and supervision of the cosmos. One way of phrasing this conclusion—and the conclusion is one to which many an observer has been driven inescapably by the evidence of nature itself—is to say that matter and its constituent components and energies are so fashioned and endowed as to make for all the eventualities and potentials that we perceive in the cosmos. God's agencies for unfolding of the creative design, and for intervention in the affairs of the world, are every created thing. There is no constraint on Divine creativity and managership in the determinism of natural events: Nature is God's daughter. God's hand;[13] the laws of nature are a disclosure of the manner in which He has chosen to govern the universe. *Within* the matrix of determined natural law, the Creator acts as a conductor. He actuates the integration of discrete sets of phenomena into progressively larger, co-ordinated constructs; the realization of intrinsic potentials for larger order does not come about automatically, solely through the properties of the primary components. The Creator sets the conditions and *co-incidences* in which reactions, individually deterministic, will proceed along a purposeful course. Shallow waters, for example, will predictably recede under a sustained wind from a certain quarter, but the physics of the situation alone cannot explain the salvation of Israel at the crossing of the Red Sea. It is the Creator who modulates the circumstances of environment in place and time so that there can survive and develop whatever is meant to. For Judaism there is no philosophical contradiction between determinism of natural processes and the omnipotence of the Deity. From the appropriate perspective, they are interacting. As every created thing can be the means of God's intent, so can it also be a tool by which man exercises the responsibilities of free will, and of partnership in the perfection of creation, that are incumbent on him.

In contrast to the determinism that holds for some natural occurrences, it is in the nature of individual events within a related set often to take place at random (at certain levels of organization, in some regards, and in some circumstances). Thus, the quantum position and velocity of a single electron orbiting an atomic nucleus cannot be forecast, for a given point in time; neither can the precise locus and nature of a spontaneous mutational change in a given chromosomal region. As pointed out in the preceding chapter, foreknowledge of the precise fate of an integer in a field of seemingly identical integers is uncertain; conclusive laws of causality cannot be formulated. Stated statistically, many natural occurrences, and especially those of a biological nature, that involve complex relationships between distinct units, do not fit deterministic models; they must be analyzed, instead, as probability (or, "stochastic") processes:

> Any description of . . . possible changes . . . with time must take account of the fact that things could turn out quite differently . . . a probability model is essential to describe the pattern of happenings that could occur with their relative chances of occurrence. We must therefore envisage the existence at any one point of a probability distribution . . . instead of the single value specified by a deterministic model.[14]

We can say with near certainty for such events that a particular transaction shall take place involving one of many seemingly equivalent units; and we can often closely approximate its frequency and timing. But we cannot pinpoint the particular integer to be so affected within the set. Such individual "randomness" applies frequently in nature, in different instances, over a range of matter's organizational strata. In the dimension of human demeanor, with its unique elements of will, choice, and conscience, foresight of individual action is certainly not given, even where the pertinent variables appear to be known and "controlled."

Moreover, in certain cases where deterministic laws do appear to fit phenomena in nature, they in fact pertain to the cumulative consequences of individually random transactions.

What are the possibilities of philosophic perception of such randomness? For one, the particular reaction can be designated as indeed wholly chance—"it just so happened"; analysis of causality in the aggregate set within which the particular event transpired is restricted to the seemingly relevant forces immediately at play. Questions of primary ontogenesis, integrative permutation, and purpose are, again, not touched.

The conceptualization can be less shallow, however. The single event that is, by any criterion, random within a family of related phenomena can be perceived nonetheless as a requisite component of a *comprehensively* embracing blueprint. The behavior of a given integer may be wholly fortuitous, but that of the composite whole guided. In that orchestration there are subsumed all necessary eventualities for the revelation of Divine will and the expression of human volition.

A further consideration may be added. The individual unit's behavior that is supposedly the result of chance may, in effect, not evince randomness at all. It may rather represent the consequence of some attribute, unknown to the observer, that distinguishes that integer from similar ones and makes it subject to the relevant rules of causality. It is always difficult to exclude such a possibility categorically. Invoking it shifts the discussion away from randomness and places it within the framework of determinism.

There is no need, however, from the philosophic position of Judaism, to cast doubt on the de facto randomness, by scientific yardsticks, of discrete natural occurrences. Quite the contrary. That which is, in scientific terms, a truly haphazard event can be read in theological ones as decreed, reflective of the determination of a force standing above nature. The man descending the ladder falls, and strikes and kills the passerby beneath.[15] Nothing in the constellation of tangible factors can reveal a design in the chain of events—that man on the ladder, slipping at that instant, that person below at the fatal second. By all the rules that govern natural reactions it is happenstance. But from another conceptual vantage point, it is not coincidence at all, but ordained retribution. Absence of a discernible natural cause for a specific occurrence in time, large or small, is an inference germane to one dimension of reality. The conclusion does not impinge on the truth of another. What took place did, when it did, because it was so directed by the Designer whose hand is nature. That conclusion derives from a different, coexistent dimension of reality.

Essence and meaning of material phenomena are, at least in part, as they are inferred by the beholder; they take form as cognition filters through the prism of his a priori conception of existence. The multifaceted grasp of reality can be given voice only by resort to distinct ideational languages, each suited to the facet it proclaims. In the paucity of words, however, the same nomenclature is often used in connoting decisively distinct apprehensions and valuations. Special care must then be taken to specify the purport and salience of each appellation. "Determinism" and "randomness" bear a wholly different import as they relate, on the one hand, to scientifically demonstrable causality and predictability of material phenomena and, on the other, to questions of superior authority and significance in the occurrence. There is no randomness in nature in the sense of chance disconnected from the will and potency of God to act. There is no determinism in the sense of an autonomous natural order, independent of, and in conflict with, Divine intent. In all events, whether they fit by the material standards of natural science's deterministic or probability-stochastic models, the Jew can recognize the purposeful instrumentation of the Creator and Master.

Notes

1. Edelman, Gerald M., and Mountcastle, Vernon B., *The Mindful Brain: Critical Organization and the Group-Selective Theory of Higher Brain Function* (MIT Press, Cambridge, 1982).
2. Stewart, Oscar M., *Physics* (4th Edition, Ginn and Company, N.Y., 1944) p. 759.
3. Weiss, David W., "Randomness and Determinism in Nature: Language and Perspectives," *Tradition*, 20 (1982), pp. 101–105. [Reprinted at the end of this chapter.]
4. Weiss, David W., "Judaism and Evolutionary Hypotheses in Biology: Reflections on Judaism by a Jewish Scientist," *Tradition*, 19 (1981), pp. 3–27.
5. Weisskopf, Victor F., "The Origin of the Universe. An Introduction to Recent Theoretical Developments that are Linking Cosmology and Particle Physics," *American Scientist*, LXXI (1983), pp. 473–480.
6. Weiss, David W., "The Forces of Nature, The Forces of Spirit," *Judaism*, 32 (1983), pp. 477–487.
7. Weiss, David W., "Reflections on the Law of the Rabbis: Matrices and Dimensions (Part 1)," *Tradition* 20, (1982), pp. 205–227.
8. Eccles, John C., *The Human Psyche* (Springer International, Heidelberg, 1980).
9. Mishnah *Avot*, 2:21.
10. Mishnah *Avot*, 2:6.
11. Maimonides, *Mishneh Torah, Book of Knowledge*, Ch. X.
12. Weiss, David W., "Judaism and Evolutionary Hypotheses in Biology: Reflections on Judaism by a Jewish Scientist." *Tradition*, 19(1) (Spring 1981) pp. 3–27.
13. Meir Simchah Hacohen of Dvinsk (*Meshech Chochmah*). Commentary on *Pentateuch*, on *Leviticus* 26:3.
14. Bailey, N. T. J., *The Mathematical Approach to Biology and Medicine* (Wiley & Sons, N.Y., 1967), ch. 2.
15. *Makkot*, 10b.

14

Seek My Face, Speak My Name

ARTHUR GREEN

The fact is that we Jews have largely abandoned Creation as a theological issue. Convinced as we are that the origin of species—and of the universe itself—is something to be explained by scientists rather than theologians, most of us have seen no value in attempting a defense of ancient Jewish views on Creation. If Jews have asked theological questions in this century (one in which theology has surely not been our forté), they are mainly those of revelation ("Did God give the Torah?"), authority ("Then why keep the commandments?"), and providence ("Where was God during the Holocaust?"), but not of Creation. We have left Genesis I in the hands of the so-called Creationists among fundamentalist Christians, circles from which we are quite alienated, both socially and theologically.

But the issue of Creation will not disappear so quickly. The search for meaning and the question of origins do not readily separate from one another. When we ask ourselves what life is all about, why we live and why we die, we cannot help turning to the question of how we got here in the first place. When we try to understand our place in the universe, and especially the relationship of humanity as a whole to the world of nature, we find ourselves returning to the question of Creation. As we seek to extend our notion of community and fellow-feeling to include all *creatures*, seeking out the One within the infinite varieties of the many, we discover that we are still speaking the language of Creation.

We have no essential argument with an evolutionary approach to the tale of life's origins. But we see evolution itself as the greatest of all religious dramas. The history of our universe is the ongoing account of how Y-H-W-H, source of life, reached forth into the world of form, became manifest in the infinite variety of species, and finally became articulate in the consciousness and language of humanity. No blind process is this, but rather the great striving of the One to be manifest in the garb of the many.

Arthur Green, *Seek My Face, Speak My Name* (Northvale, NJ: Jason Aronson, 1992), pp. 53–70. © Jason Aronson Inc., Northvale, NJ 07647.

More than one voice within contemporary science seems open to describing the origin and evolution of species, in some sense, as the expression of a singular universal force, or as the growth and development of an underlying single organism. While such a force could be conceived as an external Creator, it is more generally seen as a drive within existence that strives relentlessly, though by no means perfectly, toward greater complexity and consciousness. The evolutionary process would then be conceived in a unitive way as the halting, struggling self-assertion of such a singular force or presence, rather than as the endless war of creatures against one another. Such a vision would explain the ongoing emergence of "higher" and more conscious life-forms as evidence of this struggle's emerging success, instead of as the "survival of the fittest."

We recognize that a new Creation story is emerging in our day, one that begins with the origin of matter and reaches onward through the beginnings of plant, animal, and human life. This tale is still unfolding, to be sure, and we nonscientists understand it imperfectly. But we Jews, as bearers of the old Creation tale that for so long nourished and sustained the West's sense of origins and self-understanding, have a special interest in the emerging new story. We are concerned that its ultimate message be one of harmony, one that brings creatures to appreciate their oneness, and does not serve to justify endless conflict. We hope it will retain the strengths of our ancient tale, one that gave each creature its dignity as God's handiwork, gave us humans a special sense of stewardly responsibility, and glorified our rest, our sense of being at peace with all of God's Creation.

We are urgently in need of ways to renew our sense of human responsibility for preserving the natural world around us. As we call for less abusive treatment of earth's resources and a more reverent protection of air, soil, and water, for the preservation of species in both plant and animal realms, we need a theological language that will serve as the basis for such a change in human attitude. The age in which we live cries out for a religious language that speaks of the underlying *unity* of all existence, a unity that is manifest within life's diversity, rather than of the struggle of species against species. This unity is that of Creation, of the sense that all beings emerge from a single source.

We are also tied to Creation and to our ancient tale in the most basic cycle of our religious lives as Jews. I recite the Friday night *kiddush*, which begins with the words "The sixth day; Heaven and earth were completed, they and all their hosts." As the week draws to a close, I know that the creation cycle has happened in my life once again. With the beginning of Shabbat, I bear witness to God's world, whole and created anew. On Friday evening, I testify that I am present to the ongoing word and rest of Y-H-W-H as Creator. This act is an important, even vital one to me. It affirms more than Judaism for me; it affirms my essential humanity, my sense of belonging in this God-filled world, my creation and constant re-creation in God's image.

Creation and the Struggle for Faith

I thus find myself living in an active and symbolically deeply connected way with a story that says God created the world in seven days. I know that I don't believe that story in the literal sense. Neither do I believe in the seven-day Creation, nor am I particularly attracted to the notion that the seven days should be reinterpreted as seven time periods, as seven stages of evolution, or in any other way that seeks to save the literal truth of the text. No, I do not believe it in any ordinary intellectual sense of that term. I also know with all my being that I find this tale both deeply attractive and irresistibly powerful. It draws me to itself, sustains me through the week, and expresses my existence and its meaning. It has become *my own*, so that I choose to live with it in this regular and ever-reaffirming way.

Thus, the simple act of reciting *kiddush* on Friday night leads me to theological crisis. How do I *affirm* that which I do not *believe?* What is the nature of this affirmation in the face of my disbelief? How do we learn to live at peace with these two realities? Rabbi Nahman tells the tale of a prince, well born and noble of character, whose mind was led astray by the intellectual temptations offered him by his royal tutors. Whenever he exercised his mind, he was skeptical of the ancient wisdom on which he had been raised. But when he set that rational mind aside and allowed his heart to speak, he knew that it was true, perhaps true with a depth that he could never articulate in words that would convince his own inquiring mind.

Nahman's prince was still a rare creature in his author's early nineteenth-century universe. But by now, nearly all of us have become that prince. Are we, who refuse to choose between modernity and religious language, condemned to live our lives in constant conflict between heart and mind? Or will we be able to give birth to a new tale of Creation, one that sanctifies our rest and our humanity while also satisfying our search for truth and nourishing our scientific imagination? Can such a new tale, told in other words, come to bear the old tale within it? Or can the old tale be retold in such a way that it contains the new? The real task may be that of integrating our two tales, the one inherited from ages past, and the one emerging from our own spiritual understanding of contemporary science. For a century, these accounts of life's origin have been presented in opposition to one another. The time has come to end that opposition, *to see the two tales as versions of the same story, representing two stages in humanity's own evolving self-understanding.* The time has come when we need to raise our cups over the old tale, aware that it contains the new one being born within it, a drawing together of ancient, contemporary, and timeless truth.

What Comes "First"?

Somewhere within us we intuit that stillness precedes motion. Perhaps this comes as a projection of our own human experience. We imagine silence existing before sound, serving as the *background* from which sound emerges. Darkness seems to us as the condition *prior* to light. There is no inherent reason why any of these should be the case; each of them could as well be reversed. In this same way we see the One as existing *before* the many: unformed being seems simpler than multiplicity. Thus, it intuitively seems *prior* to the countless specific forms that being takes.

This priority is essentially one of primitive logic or of the structure of our thought, rather than one of time. It is in this way that Y-H-W-H of the "upper" unity, the undefined, endless One, precedes Y-H-W-H of the "lower" unity, or God as manifest in the garments of this world. *Sovev,* God in stasis, is still from eternity מעולם ועד עולם. אתה אל —"From world unto world You are God"—alone, unchanging. *Memale,* God in motion, "begins" the dance at some point, sets out on the path that leads through evolution, development, history.

The tale of Creation places this relationship of precedence into a *temporal* framework that is essential to its expression in the language of narrative or myth. Myth is a narrative about that which is beyond narration; in order to bring it into words, it has to be "told" as story. We understand that the story, if it is to work as such, needs *time*. That's the way stories are: some things happen first, other things happen later. There is a temporal order that is essential to the narrative plot. *Once we speak about the relationship of the transcendent unmoved One and the immanent ever-flowing Life Force in narrative terms, we have to invoke time.* Thus we come to Creation. "God created the world" is our Jewish-mythic way of saying "The One precedes—and enters into—the many."

This view essentially sees Creation as emanation: the "act" about which we speak is really a process, a flowing forth of the divine self, rather than the creation of a wholly other out of nothing. It is divinity *becoming* universe, or pure being garbing itself in forms, rather than a specific deity *creating* a universe outside itself. We also understand that this emanation process is a timeless one: to speak of Y-H-W-H before emanation is to construct a reality truly beyond our understanding. Our religious *language* continues to be that of Creation, just as our liturgy continues to speak of god in personal metaphors. But its meaning has shifted in this significant way.

From the time our sages encountered the philosophy of Greece, they insisted that God had created the world *Yesh me-ayin*, "being out of nothingness." Against Aristotle's view that matter could be neither created nor destroyed, and was therefore eternal, Jewish thinkers held fast to that which they considered the biblical faith. They did so even though the Bible had no clear position on the nature of Creation, except that it was a freely willed act of Y-H-W-H, effected by the power of divine speech. Many interpreters of the Torah had long claimed that the *tohu va-bohu* ("formlessness and void") of Genesis 1:2 in fact referred to some "prime matter" or earlier state of being, out of which Creation took place. The early rabbis seem to have had such views; they spoke of "the treasuries of snow beneath God's Throne of Glory" as the stuff of which the world had been formed. But all these views were set aside, or even condemned as folly, in the drive to purify our view of Creation, to say that Y-H-W-H did it all alone, with no prior existence to help Him, and out of pure nothingness. Such was the philosophers' selective reading of the older rabbinic sources. But then the mystics of Judaism undertook a truly remarkable reversal of language and meaning. The *ayin* (or "nothingness") out of which being emerged, they claimed, was in fact *God's own deepest self*. God's act of Creation begins with a turning inward. It is within the divine *nihil*, the nothingness that is God, that Creation takes place. The divine nothing (perhaps better "No-thing"), so called because it had been utterly empty, without form, beyond reach, beyond description, in the moment of Creation reveals itself also to be the "All-thing," the source from which all being emerges and the flowing fount by which all is sustained.

Two Tales

The traditions of Israel offer us two tales of Creation that may come to be placed on a more equal footing in the Judaism we pass on to future generations. First is the biblical tale in Genesis I, in which God *speaks* the world into being. The universe is divine articulation, the unspoken inner self of divinity put into reality by means of language or the creative word. The oneness of silence becomes the multiplicity of words or things, both referred to as *devarim* in Hebrew. This multiplicity begins with the first *yehi*, "let there be," a word closely related to the name of God. From there it becomes all words, all language, all the variety of life, seen as the unending verbalization of the great divine silence. Once the well of that silence is plumbed, the gush of *devarim*, of constant creation through language, never ceases. Were the flow of divine speech to be halted even for an instant, some hold, the entire cosmos would return to nothingness. The power of this account in the formation of the Jewish psyche is well known. We are a civilization of language, one that bears endless respect and affection for the written or spoken word.

Side by side with this ancient tale, the kabbalists offer another. According to this account, the world is *born*, rather than spoken, out of God. Here we are called to take note of the first letter *Heh* of the divine name. This letter is associated with the inner divine womb and the act of birth. This face of God is that of primal mother, the divine as life giver, as nourishing and sustaining source. It is from this God-womb that all variety is born. The primal point of *Yod* has here revealed itself to be an ever-giving font of life in *Heh*. This *Heh* is the womb of oneness out of which all the multiple varied offspring will be born. Variety emerges first in the multiple faces of God, but flows onward to include all faces and all bodies of the universe. Each of us comes out of this single source in the One, and all of us ever turn back to it. *Teshuvah*, or return to Y-H-W-H, as we shall see later, is also an eternal movement, an ongoing return to the womb of God. Contemplation, says the father of all kabbalists, is an act of nursing at the divine breast.

Whichever of these two accounts we use, we want to be careful to articulate it in a way that keeps faith with our vision of oneness: the word as spoken is never fully separate from its speaker; the child remains deeply connected to and nourished by the one who gives it birth. Here, perhaps unlike the human analogy, separation is only superficial. We think that we are separate in order to function as separate minds and beings. But, in a deeper sense, we know that there has been no separation at all. We remain a part of that divine source that spoke us into being or gave us birth.

The One and the Many

In this theological context, to ask the question "Why did God create the world?" is to ask too fully within the framework of the myth. In Yiddish, this is called *a kashe oif a mayse*, "an objection to a story." Stories should be allowed to stand on their own merit as stories, free from intellectualized objections. The question assumes not only the temporal precedence of God to world but also a will of God in an overly anthropomorphic sense. The question should better be put, in our context: "Why is reality the way it is? Why does human consciousness experience itself as separate, but bear within it intimations of a greater oneness? *If all is one, on some deeper or truer level of existence, why do we experience life as so fragmented? Why are there many faces, rather than just the one?*"

In seeking to answer these questions, we have to enter into the dialectics of what Jewish writers call *tsimtsum* and *hitpashtut*, or divine contraction and divine flow. In discussing Creation while holding fast to oneness, we cannot help but speak the language of paradox. Creation may be depicted as the first act of divine self-revelation, Y-H-W-H coming out of hiding, the One revealing itself in the garb of nature. But this revelation takes place through an act of hiding, for the One is now cloaked within the many. This two-sided process, a self-revelation of God that comes about through the hiding or cloaking of the divine Self, begins in the first moment of Creation, and repeats itself constantly in each moment that Creation is renewed.

The God of stillness begins to enter into the dance of motion. The undefined One puts on the coat of many colors. In this, the One is seeking, as it were, to enter into a world of infinite variety so that its oneness might be attested to the ultimate degree. *Only in that garbing does the Divine sufficiently hide itself that it might be revealed.*

Within being, there is an endless drive for manifestation in ever new and varied forms, a drive we see manifest as a life force, but that exists beyond the bounds of what we call "animate" as well. As that force drives ever forward for growth and change, the oneness that it bears within it is stretched ever further. Thus is the One renewed in its singularity, as each new form turns out to be naught but itself once again. The One renews itself by stretching forth into the realm of the many. This drive toward self-extension, ever testing the limits of selfhood, as it were, is the One's search for its "other." The inherent tendency toward variety and diversity, combined with the constant reaching toward more complex forms of life, culminates, according to our ancient tale, in the creation of humanity, the crowing achievement of the "sixth day." Only when a self-conscious human being has emerged, one who can both acknowledge the One and insist on the separateness of individual identity, has the test of self-extension begun to reach its goal. We humans are thus the divine helpmate; the *ezer ke-negdo*, both the partner and the one who stands "over against," or "as opposed to." In the very "otherness" of our self-conscious minds, we serve to confirm the existence of the One.

The fact that procreation throughout the higher forms of life, animal as well as human, requires the partnership of male and female, is nature's representation of this essential quality of searching for the other, of longing for fulfillment in union-reunion, which lies at the very base of all existence. In seeing ourselves as living in need of partnership with another for true fulfillment (a man without a wife is called "half a body" by the Zohar), we represent, in human form, the search of the eternal One. This is yet another way in which we are "God's image," though here the likeness is shared with other living creatures as well.

To say it differently, the testimony that God is One requires the presence of an other. Who else can bear witness to that Oneness? But God has no other, no one to whom to be revealed, no one to say "There you are!" The divine One seeks out an other for reasons that we do not fully understand; the One that is beyond division becomes divided and enters into this universe of fragmentation so that there is one who can respond to it, one who can affirm its reality, one who can both know it as real and love it as "other." Self-revelation requires encounter between self and other; the revealer needs an other to whom to be revealed. The flow of divine energy, which we experience as God's love for the world, needs to step outside itself. Love needs another. There must be someone to witness, to appreciate, even to respond. Hide-and-seek just doesn't work as solitaire! But how can there be such an other if life is naught but an infinite coloring of varied manifestations of the One? The God who is all can have no other. Here the divine light has to hide itself that it might be revealed. It withdraws itself from being in order that it might be seen, in order to allow for us to exist as "other," so that we might see and bear witness to it. This paradox of divine self-withdrawal is what the Jewish sages call *tsimtsum*.

The intensity of divine light is so great that it allows for the existence of no other. Were this light to be revealed fully, all sense of separate identity would pass away, and "we" would be naught but part of the endless One. But the "other" is the very purpose of that flow of life in the first place. The immortal and eternal seeks to be known by its opposite, the mortal and temporal. But what room is there for the mortal and temporal to exist if all is the flow of divinity? Therefore, divine light has to be withheld, and we are given the gift (however illusory) of existence as separate beings, individual mortals, who struggle and rejoice our way through a transitory life. In order to be God's "other," we have to be all that the eternal One is not: transitory, corporeal, mortal. God, as it were, seeks out an opposite—and a partner—in us.

Who Is at the Center?

But do we really want to say that "God creates the universe *in order* to create the human being?" In our tradition, the debate between advocates of the theocentric and the anthropocentric universe has existed for a long time. Maimonides, in view of the evidence of science and philosophy in his time, rejected the anthropocentric worldview of the early rabbis, one that claimed clearly that God had created the world for the sake of humans, and indeed for the sake of Israel, or "the righteous." The kabbalists responded to Maimonides by reasserting the anthropocentric point of view in new terms. Maimonides' universe was the one that left no room, they felt, for the significance of human action. What difference could it make to the abstract Maimonidean God whether we existed or not, whether we fulfilled the *mitsvot* or not? They created an image of the universe in which God is incomplete without human action, in which the role of humanity in the process of *tikkun* (cosmic restoration), or the establishment of divine sovereignty, is a crucial one.

Recent discussions of this subject, largely in the environmentalist community, have tried to speak for a *biocentric* rather than either a theocentric or an anthropocentric worldview. Both of these views, it is claimed, for different reasons, have led to human neglect of responsible action with regard to protecting and preserving life as a whole. The anthropocentric view has tended toward human arrogance, a view that only human life and human creations are worthy of serious attention, whereas the theocentric view is anti-worldly altogether, not seeing in material existence itself a fit object for true or urgent concern. Both of these critiques are somewhat simplistic, using as "straw men" highly reductionist versions of these religious outlooks. The fact is that theocentrism, at least as represented in Judaism, has also led to a strong sense of religious obligation to act, a heteronomous ethic in which we are commanded by the One "above" to act in a responsible manner. It is the anthropocentric view, seeing humans as the "crown" of creation, that gives birth to the notion of stewardship and guardianship over the divine creation. Both of these are potentially valuable allies in the fashioning of a more responsible human viewpoint. *Rather than fight or denounce these parts of our human legacy, our job is to see that they are used in ways that increase, rather than diminish, our sense of collective responsibility.*

In a nondualistic worldview, the sharp edges are taken off this debate. If the One is the center of the cosmos, that hardly means that the human or the natural is at the periphery of significance. Still, we must somehow take our place in this ancient conversation. The question is given new focus in our time because the magnitude of the universe has made us so much smaller. We speak of a world that is not 6,000 years old, but whose age reaches into billions of years. We speak of a universe not of one planet with a *raki'a*—firmament—above it, and God sitting on a throne just beyond it, but of one with infinite numbers of stars in infinite numbers of galaxies, set in a space so vast it can hardly be measured or imagined. How hard it is to say, in such a world, that the purpose of it all was this speck of earth and this brief moment of transitory human life!

Here too, we may be guided by an alternative voice from within our own tradition. The tale of Creation, as told in Genesis, indeed seems to view human beings as the final goal, created in the moment just before God enters into rest and celebrates the world's completion. Later versions of that story make the point even more explicit. Adam and Eve are like the guests at a banquet; everything is prepared for them before they arrive. But other parts of the Bible itself seem to take issue with this view of humanity's place in the universe. The Psalmist sees a great chorus of beings singing hallelujahs to their God. Humans are just part of this symphony of praise, one where "elders and youths, young men and maidens" take their place together with "mountains and hills, fruit-trees and cedars; wild beasts and cattle, creeping things and winged birds." Another Psalm describes the great panorama of Creation as beginning when God spread forth the heavens like a garment of light. In this luminous cosmos, each creature is given its particular place, human alongside stork, mountain-goat, hare, and young lion. Of all of them together, the author exclaims, "How manifold are your works, O Y-H-W-H, You have made them all in wisdom."

Nowhere is this view more fully expressed than in the closing chapters of the Book of Job, the great biblical testimony to the struggle with life's meaning and divine justice. Job's challenge to God is finally answered, and God's speeches there are truly among the most elevated religious documents of all time. But the answer given to Job is not one that defends God as a just actor on the stage of human history. Job is given no reason for his suffering, no explanation of his children's deaths, or his own affliction. Rather, he is shown the magnificence of God's universe, the great and wondrous creatures that extend far beyond human reach or human understanding. He is shown that the human world is but an infinitesimal part of this universe, one far too vast and too magnificent to be embraced by the mind of mortals. It is in seeing these, and realizing both his own smallness and his own place within a vast and glorious cosmos, that God's challenger finds his consolation.

15

Revelation in the Jewish Tradition

EMANUEL LEVINAS

The Content and Its Structure

The Problem

I think that our fundamental question in these lectures concerns less the content ascribed to revelation than the actual fact—a metaphysical one—called the Revelation. This fact is also the first and most important content revealed in any revelation. From the outset this revelation is alleged to be unusual, extra-ordinary, linking the world in which we live to what would no longer be of this world. How is it thinkable? What model do we use? Suddenly, by opening a few books, there would enter into a positive world, open in its consistency and steadfastness to perception, to enjoyment and to thought, a world given over in its reflections, metaphors and signs to reading and science, truths that come from elsewhere—but from where?—and dated according to a 'chronology' called holy History! And, as in the case of the Jews, a holy History against which stands, without a break in continuity, a 'History for historians', a profane History! That the holy History of the Christian West is, in its greater part, the ancient history of a people of today, retaining a still mysterious unity, despite its dispersion among the nations—or despite its integration into these nations—is undoubtedly what constitutes the originality of Israel and its relation to the Revelation: of its reading of the Bible, or its forgetting of the Bible, or of the memories or the remorse that remain from this very act of forgetting. Against the transfiguration into myth that threatens, with degradation or sublimation, this 'far and distant past' of the Revelation, is the surprising present existence of Judaism, a human collec-

Emanuel Levinas, "Revelation in the Jewish Tradition," in *Beyond the Verse: Talmudic Readings and Lectures*, Gary D. Mole, trans. (Bloomington, IN: Indiana U. Press, 1994), pp. 129–50. © Indiana University Press, Bloomington, IN 47404.

tivity, albeit small and continuously sapped by persecution, weakened by half-heartedness, temptations and apostasy, yet capable, in its very irreligiosity, of founding its political life on the truths and rights taken from the Bible. And indeed, chapters of holy History are reproduced in the course of profane History by trials that constitute a Passion, the Passion of Israel. For many Jews who have long since forgotten or never learnt the narratives and the message of the Scriptures, the signs of the Revelation that was received—and the muted calls of this exalting Revelation—are reduced to the trauma of lived events long after the completion of the biblical canon, long after the Talmud was written down. (The Talmud is the other form of the Revelation, distinct from the Old Testament which Christians and Jews have in common.) For many Jews, holy History and the Revelation it entails are reduced to the memories of being burnt at the stake, the gas chambers, and even the public affronts received in international assemblies or heard in the refusal to allow them to emigrate. They experience the Revelation in the form of persecution!

These are the 'history-making events' of which Paul Ricœur spoke in taking up Emil Fackenheim's expression. Do they not refer us to the Bible that remains their living space? Does not the reference materialize in reading, and is not reading a way of inhabiting? The volume of the book as a form of living space? It is in this sense, too, that Israel is a people of the Book, and that its relation to the Revelation is unique of its kind. Its actual land is based on the Revelation. Its nostalgia for the land is fed on texts. It derives nothing from belonging in some organic way to a particular piece of soil. There is certainly in this a presence to the world where the paradox of transcendence is less unusual.

For many Jews today, communities and individuals alike, the Revelation is still in keeping with the conception of a communication between Heaven and Earth, such as the plain meaning of biblical narratives would have it. It is accepted by many excellent minds that cross the deserts of the religious crisis of our time by finding fresh water in the literal expression of Sinaitic Epiphany, of the Word of God calling to the prophets, and in the confidence in an uninterrupted tradition of a prodigious History that testifies to it. Both orthodox people and communities, untouched by the uncertainties of modernity, even when they sometimes take part professionally in the fever of the industrial world, remain, despite the simplicity of this metaphysics, spiritually attuned to the noble virtues and most mysterious secrets of divine proximity. Men and communities thus live, in the literal sense of the term, outside History where, for them, events neither come to pass nor relate to those that have already passed. It is nevertheless true that for modern Jews—and they are the majority—to whom the intellectual destiny of the West, with its victories and its crises, is not borrowed clothing, the problem of the Revelation insistently arises and demands new conceptions. How are we to understand the 'exteriority' particular to truths and revealed signs striking the human mind which, despite its 'interiority', is a match for the world and is called reason? How, without being of the world, can they strike reason?

Indeed, these questions arise acutely for us, for anyone among men today still sensitive to these truths and signs, but who, living in modern times, is more or less troubled by the news of the end of metaphysics, by the victories of psychoanalysis, sociology and political economy; to whom linguistics has taught the significance of signs without signifieds and who, in the light of this, confronted with all these intellectual splendours—or shadows—sometimes wonders if he is not present at a magnificent funeral for a dead god. The ontological status or regime of the Revelation is thus worrying essentially for Jewish thought, and its problem should come before any presentation of the content of this Revelation.

The Structure of a Revelation: The Call to Exegesis

However, we shall devote this first section to explaining the structure presented by the content of the Revelation in Judaism. Certain inflections in this structure will already, in fact, suggest the sense in which the transcendence of the message can be understood. I think that this explanation will also be useful because the forms of the Revelation as they appear to Jews are not well known to the general public. Ricœur has given a brilliant account of the organization of the Old Testament which Judaism and Christianity have in common. This will certainly save me having to go back over the various literary genres of the Bible: prophetic texts, the narration of founding historical events, prescriptive and sapiential texts, hymns and thanksgiving. Each genre is said to have a revelatory function and power.

But for the Jewish reading of the Bible these distinctions are perhaps not established with the same steadfastness as in the lucid classification proposed to us. Prescriptive lessons that are above all to be found in the Pentateuch, in the Torah—the 'Torah of Moses', as it is called—are privileged in Jewish consciousness for the relation they establish with God. They are required in every text; certain psalms would allude to figures and events, but also to commandments: 'I am a sojourner on earth; hide not thy commandments from me!' says Psalms 119:19 in particular. The sapiential texts are prophetic and prescriptive. Between the 'genres', then, allusions and references visible to the naked eye circulate in multiple directions.

One further remark: There is a vital search, throughout, to go beyond the plain meaning. This meaning is, of course, known and acknowledged as plain and as wholly valid at its level. But this meaning is perhaps less easy to establish than the translations of the Old Testament lead one to suppose. It is by going back to the Hebrew text from the translations, venerable as they may be, that the strange or mysterious ambiguity or polysemy authorized by the Hebrew syntax is revealed: words coexist rather than immediately being co-ordinated or subordinated with and to one another, contrary to what is predominant in the languages that are said to be developed or functional. Returning to the Hebrew text certainly and legitimately makes it more difficult than one thinks to decide on the ultimate intention of a verse, and even more so on a book of the Old Testament. Indeed, the distinction between the plain meaning and the meaning to be deciphered, the search for this meaning buried away and for a meaning even deeper than it contains, all gives emphasis to the specifically Jewish exegesis of Scripture. There is not one verse, not one word of the Old Testament—read as a religious reading, read by way of Revelation—that does not half-open on to an entire world, unsuspected at first, which envelops what was easily read. 'R. Akiba went as far as to interpret the ornamentation of the letters of the sacred text', says the Talmud. The scribes and scholars who are said to be slaves of the letter attempted to extract from the letters, as if they were the folded-back wings of the Spirit, all the horizons that the flight of the Spirit can embrace, the whole meaning that these letters carry or to which they awake. 'Once God has spoken; twice have I heard this': this part of Psalms 62:11 proclaims that innumerable meanings dwell in the Word of God. At least if we are to believe the Rabbi who, already in the name of this pluralism, scrutinizes the very verse that teaches him this right to scrutinize! This is the exegesis of the Old Testament called *Midrash*, or search, or interrogation. It is at work well before grammatical research, which came late, although it was well received, and was added to the decipherment of enigmas locked away in a quite different mode to the grammatical in the grammar of Scripture.

The diversity of styles and the contradictions of the text of the Old Testament did not escape this awakening attention. They became the pretexts for new and more penetrating readings, for renewing meanings that measure the acuteness of the reading. Such is the breadth of Scripture. A Revelation that can also be called a mystery; not a mystery that dispels clarity, but one that demands greater intensity.[1]

But this invitation to seek and decipher, to *Midrash*, already constitutes the reader's participation in the Revelation, in Scripture. The reader, in his own fashion, is a scribe. This provides us with a first indication of what we might call the 'status' of the Revelation: its word coming from elsewhere, from outside, and simultaneously dwelling in the person who receives it. More than just a listener, is not the human being the unique 'terrain' in which exteriority can appear? Is not the personal—that is, the unique 'of itself'—necessary to the breach and the revelation taking place from outside? Is the human as a break in substantial identity not, 'of itself', the possibility for a message coming from outside not to strike 'free reason', but to take on the unique figure that cannot be reduced to the contingency of a 'subjective impression'? The Revelation as calling to the unique within me is the significance particular to the signifying of the Revelation. It is as if the multiplicity of persons—is not this the very meaning of the personal?—were the condition for the plenitude of 'absolute truth'; as if every person, through his uniqueness, were the guarantee of the revelation of a unique aspect of truth, and some of its points would never have been revealed if some people had been absent from mankind. This is not to say that truth is acquired anonymously in History, and that it finds 'supporters' in it! On the contrary, it is to suggest that the totality of the true is constituted from the contribution of multiple people: the uniqueness of each act of listening carrying the secret of the text; the voice of the Revelation, as inflected, precisely, by each person's ear, would be necessary to the 'Whole' of the truth. That the Word of the living God may be heard in diverse ways does not mean only that the Revelation measures up to those listening to it, but that this measuring up measures up the Revelation: the multiplicity of irreducible people is necessary to the dimensions of meaning; the multiple meanings are multiple people. We can thus see the whole impact of the reference made by the Revelation to exegesis, to the freedom of this exegesis, the participation of the person listening to the Word making itself heard, but also the possibility for the Word to travel down the ages to announce the same truth in different times.

A text from Exodus (25:15), prescribing the making of the holy Ark of the Tabernacle, makes provision for poles to be used in transporting the Ark: 'The poles shall remain in the rings of the Ark; they shall not be taken from it'. The Law carried by the Ark is always ready to be moved. It is not attached to a point in space and time, but is continuously transportable and ready to be transported. This is also indicated by the famous Talmudic apologue relating the return of Moses on earth at the time of R. Akiba. He enters the Talmudic scholar's school, understands nothing of the master's lesson, but learns from a celestial voice that the teaching he has not understood at all comes, however, from himself. It was given 'to Moses at Sinai'. This contribution of readers, listeners and pupils to the open-ended work of the Revelation is so essential to it that I was able to read recently, in a quite remarkable book by a rabbinical scholar from the end of the eighteenth century, that the slightest question put by a novice pupil to his schoolmaster constitutes an ineluctable articulation of the Revelation which was heard at Sinai.

However, how is such a call to the person in his historical uniqueness—and this means that the Revelation requires History (which means, outside all theosophical 'wisdom', a personal God: is a God not personal, before all other characteristics, inasmuch as he appeals to persons?)—how is such a call to the diversity of people insured against the arbitrary nature of subjectivism? But perhaps there are crucial reasons why a certain risk of subjectivism, in the pejorative sense of the term, must be run by the truth.

This in no way means that in Jewish spirituality the Revelation is left to the arbitrariness of subjective fantasies, that it desires to be without authority and that it is not highly characterized. Fantasy is not the essence of the subjective, even if it is its by-product. Without recourse to any doctrinal authority, the 'subjective' interpretations of the Jewish Revelation have managed to maintain the awareness of unity in a people in spite of its geographical dispersion. But, what is more, a distinction is allowed to be made between the personal originality brought to the reading of the book and the pure play of the fantasies of amateurs (or even of charlatans); this is made both by a necessary reference of the subjective to the historical continuity of the reading, and by the tradition of commentaries that cannot be ignored under the pretext that inspirations come to you directly from the text. A 'renewal' worthy of the name cannot avoid these references, any more than it can avoid reference to what is known as the oral Law.

Oral Law and Written Law

The allusion to the oral Law leads us to point out another essential feature of the Revelation according to Judaism: the role of the oral tradition as recorded in the Talmud. It is presented in the form of discussions between rabbinical scholars that took place in the period between the first centuries before the Christian era and the sixth century after Christ. From the point of view of historians, these discussions continue more ancient traditions and reflect a whole process in which the centre of Jewish spirituality was transferred from the Temple to the house of study, from cult to study. These discussions and teachings are principally concerned with the prescriptive part of the Revelation: rituals, morality and law. But they are also concerned in their fashion, and by way of apologues, with the whole spiritual universe of men: philosophy and religion. Everything is bound up around the prescriptive. Outside Judaism, or within de-Judaized Judaism, the picture that one has of the prescriptive—which is reduced to the pettiness of rules to be respected, or to the 'yoke of the law'—is not a true picture.

Contrary to what is often thought, the oral Law is not just a matter, moreover, of commentary on the Scriptures, whatever the eminent role incumbent upon it on this level may be. It is religiously thought as deriving from its own specific source of Sinaitic Revelation. Here, then, is an oral Torah, next to the written Torah and of at least equal authority.[2] This authority is claimed by the Torah itself. It is accepted by religious tradition and agreed upon by the philosophers of the Middle Ages, including Maimonides. For Jews it is a Revelation that complements the Old Testament. It is able to enunciate principles and to give information lacking in the written text or passed over in silence. The Tannaim, the oldest scholars of the Talmud, whose generation comes to a close towards the end of the second century after Christ, speak with sovereign authority.

Clearly, the oral teaching of the Talmud remains inseparable from the Old Testament. It orientates its interpretation. This reading—scrutinizing the text in the literal mode described above, to which the Hebrew of the original of the Bible miraculously lends itself—is precisely the way the Talmud works. The entire prescriptive part of the Torah is 'reworked' by the rabbinical scholars, and the entire narrative part is expanded and clarified in a specific way. In such a way that it is the Talmud that allows the Jewish reading of the Bible to be distinguished from the Christian reading or the 'scientific' reading of the historians and philosophers. Judaism is definitely the Old Testament, but through the Talmud.

The spirit guiding this reading, which is said to be naively 'literal', perhaps consists, in actual fact, in maintaining each specific text in the context of the Whole. The connections that may appear verbal or attached to the letter represent, in fact, an effort to let the 'harmonics' of one verse resound within other verses. It is also a question of keeping the passages that appeal only to our taste for spiritualization and interiorization in contact with tougher texts, in order to extract from these, too, their real truth. Yet it is a question too, in extending the remarks that may seem severe, of bringing together the generous vital forces of harsh realities. The language of the Old Testament is so suspicious of the rhetoric which does not stutter that its chief prophet was 'slow of speech and of tongue'. There is undoubtedly more to this than just the avowal of being limited in this defect: there is the awareness of a kerygma which does not forget the weight of the world, the inertia of men, and the deafness of understandings.

The freedom of exegesis is upheld at this Talmudic school. Tradition, running through history, does not impose its conclusions, but the contact with what it sweeps along. Does this constitute an authority on doctrinal matters? Tradition is perhaps the expression of a way of life thousands of years old which conferred unity on the texts, however disparate the historians claim their origins may have been. The miracle of confluence, which is as great as the miracle of the common origin attributed to these texts, is the miracle of that way of life. The text is pulled tight over what tradition expands, like the strings on a violin's wood. The Scriptures thus have a mode of being that is quite different from the exercise material for grammarians, entirely subject to philologists; a mode of being whereby the history of each piece of writing counts less than the lessons it contains, and where its inspiration is measured by what it inspires. These are a few of the features of the 'ontology' of the Scriptures.

We have said that the oral Torah was written down in the Talmud. This oral Torah is thus itself written. But its writing down came late. It is explained by contingent and dramatic circumstances of Jewish History, external to the nature and specific modality of its message. Even written down, however, the oral Torah preserves in its style its reference to oral teaching; the liveliness provided by a master addressing disciples who listen as they question. In written form, it reproduces the diversity of opinions expressed, with extreme care taken to name the person providing them or commenting upon them. It records the multiplicity of opinions and the disagreement between the scholars. The great disagreement running all through the Talmud between the school of Hillel and the school of Shammai (in the first century before Christ) is called the discussion or disagreement 'for the glory of Heaven'. Despite all the care it takes to reach an agreement, the Talmud never ceases to apply to the differences of opinion between Hillel and Shammai—and to the flow of divergent ideas which proceed from them through the successive generations of scholars—the well-known phrase: 'These and those alike, are the words of the living God'. A discussion or dialectic which remains open to readers, who are worthy of this name only if they enter into it on their own account. Consequently, the Talmudic texts, even in the physiognomical aspects that their typography takes on, are accompanied by commentaries, and by commentaries on and discussions of these commentaries. The page is continuously overlaid and prolongs the life of the text which, whether it is weakened or reinforced, remains 'oral'. The religious act of listening to the revealed word is thus identified with the discussion whose open-endedness is desired with all the audacity of its problematics. To the extent that Messianic times are often designated as the epoch of conclusions. Not that this prevents discussion, even on this point! One text from Berakoth (64a) says: 'R. Hiyya b. Ashi said in the name of Rab: The disciples of the wise have no rest either in this world or in the world to come, as it says, *They go from strength to strength, every one of them appeareth before God in Zion* (Psalms 84:7)'. This going from strength to strength is attributed pre-eminently by R. Hiyya to the scholars of the Law. And it is the eleventh-century French commentator, Rashi, whose explanations guide every reader, even the modern one, through the sea of the Talmud, who adds by way of commentary: 'They go from one house of study to another, from one problem to another'. The Revelation is a constant hermeneutics of the Word, whether written or oral, discovering new landscapes, and problems and truths fitted into one another. It reveals itself not only as the source of wisdom, the path of deliverance and elevation, but also as the nourishment of this life and the object of the particular enjoyment that goes with acquiring knowledge. To the extent that Maimonides, in the twelfth century, was able to attach to the hermeneutics of the Revelation the pleasure or happiness that Aristotle attached to the contemplation of pure essences in Book 10 of the *Nicomachean Ethics*.

As the 'people of the Book' through its land which extends the volume of in-folios and scrolls, Israel is also the people of the Book in another sense: it has fed itself, almost in the physical sense of the term, on books, like the prophet who swallows a scroll in Ezekiel Chapter 3. The remarkable digestion of celestial food! As we have said, this excludes the idea of a doctrinal authority. The strict formulas which, in the shape of dogmatic principles, would bring the multiple and sometimes disparate traces left in Scripture by the Revelation back to unity, are absent from the spirit of Judaism. No Credo brings together or orientates the reading of texts, according to the method in which even the renewal of the reading and of the meanings given to the verses would still be like a new wine poured into old goatskins and preserving the old forms and even the bouquet of the past. In Judaism, the formulation of articles of faith is a late philosophical or theological genre. It does not appear until the Middle Ages—that is, after an already well-ordered religious life of two thousand years (to go by historical criticism, which is always making the spiritualization of texts more recent while looking much further back for their genealogy anchored in the mythical). Between the first formulations of the Jewish Credo— which is to vary as to the actual number of essential points—and the opening out of the prophetic message of Israel situated in the eighth century before Christ (the period in which many of the Mosaic elements of the Pentateuch are said to have been composed), two thousand years have already passed; more than a thousand years separated these formulations from the completion of the biblical canon, and several centuries from the writing down of the Talmudic teachings.

Halakhah *and* Aggadah

But if there is no dogmatism in the Credo to summarize the content of the Revelation, the unity of this Revelation is concretely expressed for Jews in another form. Indeed, crossing the distinction between written Revelation and oral Revelation which is particular to Judaism is the distinction, to which we have already alluded, between the texts and teachings relating to conduct and formulating practical laws, the *Halakhah*—the actual Torah in which can be recognized what Ricœur qualified as prescriptive—and, on the other hand, the texts and teachings of homiletic origin which, in the form of apologues, parables and the development of biblical narratives, represent the theologico-philosophical part of tradition and are collected together under the concept of *Aggadah*. The first gives to the Jewish Revelation, both written and oral, its own physiognomy, and has maintained as an orthopraxis the unity of the very body of the Jewish people throughout dispersion and History. From the outset Jewish revelation is commandment, and piety is obedience to it. But an obedience which, while accepting practical decrees, does not stop the dialectic called upon to determine them. This dialectic continues and is valid by itself in its style of open-ended discussion.

The distinction between oral Law and written Law on the one hand, and *Aggadah* and *Halakhah* on the other, constitute, as it were, the four cardinal points of the Jewish Revelation. The motivations of the *Halakhah* remain, let me repeat, under discussion. This is because, through the discussion of the rules of conduct, the whole order of thought is present and living. It gives access to the exercise of the intellect from the obedience and the casuistry it entails. This is very significant: the thought that issues from the prescriptive goes beyond the problem of the material gesture to be accomplished; although, right in the heart of the dialectic, it also enunciates what conduct is to be kept, what the *Halakhah* is. A decision which is not, therefore, strictly speaking, a conclusion. It is as if it were based on a tradition of its own, although it would have been impossible without the discussion which it in no way cancels out. The antinomies of the dialectic that are the waves of the 'sea of the Talmud' are accompanied by 'decisions' or 'decrees'. And very soon after the completion of the Talmud, 'decision manuals' appeared which fixed the form of the *Halakhah*. A work of several centuries which culminated in a definitive code entitled *Shulchan 'Arukh*, 'Prepared Table', in which the life of the faithful Jew was fixed down to the smallest details.

Jewish revelation is based on prescription, the *mitzvah*, whose strict accomplishment was taken, in the eyes of Saint Paul, to be the yoke of the Law. It is in any case through the Law, which is in no way felt as a stigma attached to being enslaved, that the unity of Judaism comes about. On the religious plane, this unity is clearly distinct from any doctrinal unity which, in any case, is the root of all doctrinal formulation. Rashi's first rabbinical commentary, which opens the 'Jewish editions' of the Pentateuch, expresses the surprise caused by the first verse of the Torah: why begin with the account of Creation, when the prescriptions begin in Exodus 12:2: 'This month shall be for you the beginning of months'? The commentator thus endeavours to explain the religious value of the account of Creation. It is observance which gives unity to the Jewish people. In contemporary Judaism this unity is still alive through the awareness of its ancient status and is still accorded respect even when the Law, in the strict sense, is poorly observed. It would not be wrong to claim that it is this unity, conferred upon the Jews by the Law—observed in the past by everyone—which nourishes, without them actually knowing, those Jews who no longer practise, yet still feel a sense of solidarity with Jewish destiny. Finally, it is worth noting that the study of the commandments—the study of the Torah, that is, the resumption of the rabbinical dialectic—is equal in religious value to actually carrying them out. It is as if, in this study, man were in mystical contact with the divine will itself. The highest action of the practice of prescriptions, the prescription of prescriptions which equals them all, is the actual study of the (written or oral) Law.

Besides these halakhic texts we have just discussed, which unite the prescriptions of the Law, and where strictly ethical laws are placed side by side with ritual prescriptions, immediately positing Judaism as an ethical monotheism, there are the apologues and parables called *Aggadah* which constitute the metaphysics and philosophical anthropology of Judaism. In the Talmudic texts they alternate with the *Halakhah*. The *Aggadah* also contains special collections, of diverse antiquity and quality, which have given life to Judaism and which, without being aware of historical perspective, are treated as if their wisdom were of the same order as the *Halakhah* which unifies the religion. In order to know the system of thought on which Judaism has lived as a unity throughout the centuries of its religious integrity (which is not the same as knowing its historical development), it is necessary to consider these texts from various epochs as contemporaneous. The lucid work of historians and Jewish and non-Jewish critics—who can reduce the Jewish miracle of the Revelation *or* that of national spirit to a multiplicity of influences that they have undergone—loses its spiritual importance at the critical hours which have frequently struck in the course of two thousand years for post-exilic Judaism. What we called earlier the miracle of confluence takes on a voice that is immediately recognizable, and reverberates in a sensibility and a thought which hear it as if they were already expecting it.

The Content of the Revelation

But up until now we have spoken about the form or the structure of the Revelation in Judaism, without saying anything of its content. It is not a matter of attempting to give a body of dogma, a task that resisted the Jewish philosophers of the Middle Ages. What we wish to do, in an empirical way, is to list some of the relations that are established between, on the one hand, Him whose message the Bible carries, and, on the other, the reader, when he agrees to take as the context of the verse being examined the whole of the biblical text—that is, when he takes the oral tradition as the point of departure for his reading of the Bible.

This will undoubtedly be an invitation to follow at all times the highest path, to keep faith only with the Unique, and to distrust myth which dictates to us the fait accompli, the constraint of custom and land, and the Machiavellian State with its reasons of State. But to follow the Most-High is also to know that nothing is greater than to approach one's neighbour, than the concern for the lot of the 'widow and orphan, the stranger and poor'; and that to approach with empty hands is not to approach at all. The adventure of the Spirit also takes place on earth among men. The trauma I experienced as a slave in the land of Egypt constitutes my humanity itself. This immediately brings me closer to all the problems of the damned on earth, of all those who are persecuted, as if in my suffering as a slave I prayed in a prayer that was not yet oration, and as if this love of the stranger were already the reply given to me through my heart of flesh. My very uniqueness lies in the responsibility for the other man; I could never pass it off on to another person, just as I could never have anyone take my place in death: obedience to the Most-High means precisely this impossibility of shying away; through it, my 'self' is unique. To be free is to do only what no one else can do in my place. To obey the Most-High is to be free.

But man is also the irruption of God into being, or the explosion of being towards God: man is the rupture of being which produces the act of giving, only giving with one's hands full rather than bringing struggle and plunder. Hence the idea of election which can deteriorate into pride, but which originally expresses the awareness of an indisputable summons which gives life to ethics and through which the indisputability of the summons isolates the person responsible. 'You only have I known of all the families of the earth; therefore I will punish you for all your iniquities' (Amos 3:2). Man is called upon in the judgement of justice which recognizes this responsibility. Mercy—the *rachamim* (the trembling of the womb[3] where the Other is in gestation in the Same, maternity within God, so to speak)—attenuates the rigours of the Law (without suspending it in principle; yet it can go so far as to suspend it in reality). Man can do what he must do. He will be capable of mastering the hostile forces of History and realizing a Messianic reign foretold by the prophets. Waiting for the Messiah is the actual duration of time. Or waiting for God. But now waiting no longer testifies to an absence of Godot who will never come. It testifies, rather, to the relation with something that cannot enter into the present, because the present is too small for the Infinite.

But the most characteristic aspect of Jewish difficult freedom lies perhaps in the ritual that governs all the acts of daily life, in the famous 'yoke of the Law'. In ritual, nothing is numinous. There is no idolatry. In ritual a distance is taken up *within* nature *in respect of* nature, and perhaps therefore it is precisely the waiting for the Most-High which is a relation to Him—or, if one prefers, a deference, a deference to the beyond which creates here the very concept of a beyond or a towards—God.

The Fact of the Revelation and Human Understanding

I come now to the main question: how might a Jew 'explain' to himself the very fact of the Revelation in all its extraordinariness, which, if the Scriptures are taken literally, tradition presents to him as coming from outside the order of the world? It will not have escaped the reader that the exposition of the content and above all of the structure of the Revelation presented so far has allowed us to take a few steps towards this question.

A Few Particulars

Let us confine ourselves for a moment to the literal meaning. Here are a few significant remarks. The Bible itself tells us of the supernatural quality of its origin. There were men who heard the celestial voice. The Bible also warns us against false prophets. So much so that prophecy is suspicious of prophecy, and a risk is run by the person associated with the Revelation. In this there lies a call to vigilance which undoubtedly belongs to the essence of the Revelation: it cannot be separated from anxiety. A further important point is when Moses recalls the Sinaitic Epiphany in Deuteronomy 4:15: 'Therefore take good heed to yourselves. Since you saw no form on the day that the Lord spoke to you at Horeb out of the midst of the fire'. The Revelation is a saying which outlines, without mediation, the uprightness of the relation between God and man. In Deuteronomy 5:4 we read: 'The Lord spoke with you face to face'. These expressions will authorize the rabbinical scholars to confer prophetic dignity on all the Israelites present at the foot of Sinai, and therefore to suggest that in principle the human spirit as such is open to inspiration, that man as such is potentially a prophet! Let us look, too, at Amos 3:8: 'The Lord God has spoken; who can but prophesy?' Prophetic receptivity already lies in the human soul. Is not subjectivity, through its potential for listening—that is, obeying—the very rupture of immanence? But in the text quoted from Deuteronomy, the Master of the Revelation insists on the fact that the Revelation is word, not a visible image. And if the words in

Scripture designating the Revelation are borrowed from visual perception, God's appearance is reduced to a verbal message (*devar elohim*) which, more often than not, is a command. Commandment rather than narration constitutes the first movement in the direction of human understanding; and, of itself, is the beginning of language.

The Old Testament confers upon Moses the dignity of being the greatest of prophets. Moses has the most direct contact with God, called a 'face to face' (Exodus 33:11). And yet he is not allowed to look at the divine face; according to Exodus 33:23, only the 'back' of God is shown to Moses. In order to understand the very spirit of Judaism, it is perhaps of some interest to mention the way in which the rabbinical scholars interpret this text on the Epiphany: the 'back' that Moses saw from the cleft of the rock from which he followed the passing of divine Glory was nothing other than the knot formed by the straps of the phylacteries on the back of God's neck! A prescriptive teaching even here! Which demonstrates how thoroughly the entire Revelation is bound up around daily ritual conduct. This ritualism suspends the immediacy of the relations with Nature's given and determines, against the blinding spontaneity of Desires, the ethical relation with the other man. To the extent that this ritualism does this, it confirms the conception of God in which He is welcomed in the face-to-face with the other and in the obligation towards the other.

The Talmud upholds the prophetic and verbal origin of the Revelation, but it already lays more stress on the voice of the listener. As if the Revelation were a system of signs to be interpreted by the listener and, in this sense, already revealed to him. The Torah is no longer in heaven, but is given: henceforth it is at men's disposal. A famous apologue from the Tractate Baba Mezia (59b) is significant on this point: R. Eliezer, disagreeing with his colleagues on a problem of *Halakhah*, is supported in his opinion by miracles, and finally by a voice or an echo of a heavenly voice. His colleagues reject all these signs and the echo of a voice, on the irrefutable pretext that the heavenly Torah has been on Earth since Sinai and appeals to man's exegesis, against which the echoes of heavenly voices can no longer do anything. Man is not, therefore, a 'being' among 'beings', a simple receiver of sublime information. He is simultaneously him to whom the word is said, but also him through whom there is Revelation. Man is the place through which transcendence passes, even if he can be described as 'being-there', or *Dasein*. In the light of this situation the whole status of subjectivity and reason must perhaps be revised. In the event of the Revelation, the prophets are succeeded by the *chakham*: the sage, or scholar, or man of reason. In his own way he is inspired, since he bears the oral teaching. He is taught and he teaches, and he is sometimes suggestively called *talmid chakham*: the disciple of a Sage or disciple-sage who receives, but scrutinizes what he receives. The Jewish philosophers of the Middle Ages, in particular Maimonides, admittedly trace the Revelation back to prophetic gifts. But instead of thinking of them in the heteronomy of inspiration, they assimilate them, to varying degrees, to the intellectual faculties described by Aristotle. Like Aristotelian man, Maimonidean man is a 'being' situated *in his place* in the cosmos. He is a part of being which does not go outside being and in which there never occurs the rupture of the same, the radical transcendence that the idea of inspiration and the whole trauma of prophecy seem to entail in the biblical texts.

Revelation and Obedience

Let us now come to the main problem. It is certainly not a problem of an apologetic nature requiring the authentication of the various revealed contents, confessed by the religions described as revealed. The problem lies in the possibility of a rupture of a breach in the closed order of totality, of the world, or of the self-sufficiency of its correlative, reason. A rupture which would be caused by a movement coming from outside, but a rupture which, paradoxically, would not alienate this rational self-sufficiency. If the possibility of such a fissure in the hard core of reason could be thought, the most important part of the problem would be resolved. But does not the difficulty come from our habit of understanding reason as the correlative of the possibility of the world: a thought which is equal to its stability and identity? Can it be otherwise? Can a model of intelligibility be sought in some traumatic experience in which intelligence is broken, affected by something that overflows its capacity? Certainly not. Unless, however, it were a question of a 'Thou shalt' which takes no account of what 'Thou canst'. The act of overflowing here is not insane. In other words, is not the rationality of the rupture practical reason? Is not the model of revelation an ethical one?

In the light of this, I wonder whether there are not aspects in Judaism which indicate the 'rationality' of a reason less turned in upon itself than the reason of philosophical tradition. For example, there is the primordial importance in Judaism of the prescriptive, in which the entire Revelation (even the narrative) is formed according to both the written teaching (the Pentateuch) and the oral teaching. Or the fact that the revealed is welcomed in the form of obedience, which Exodus 24:7 expresses in the phrase: 'All that the Lord has spoken we will do, and we will be obedient [we will listen to it]'. The term evoking obedience here ['we will do'] is anterior to that which expresses understanding ['we will listen'], and in the eyes of the Talmudic scholars is taken to be the supreme merit of Israel, the 'wisdom of an angel'. The rationality here would not appear as that of a reason 'in decline', but would be understood precisely in its plenitude from out of the irreducible 'intrigue' of obedience. This obedience cannot be reduced to a categorical imperative in which a universality is suddenly able to direct a will. It is an obedience, rather, which can be traced back to the love of one's neighbour: a love without eros, without self-complacency and, in this sense, a love that is obeyed, the responsibility for one's neighbour, the taking upon oneself of the other's destiny, or fraternity. The relation with the other person is placed at the beginning! Moreover, Kant himself, in the statement of the second phrase of the categorical imperative, hastens towards this relation through a regular or irregular deduction from the universality of the maxim. Obedience, which finds concrete form in the relation with the other, indicates a reason that is less centred than Greek reason, the latter having as its immediate correlative something stable, the law of the Same.

The rational subjectivity which we have inherited from Greek philosophy—and not to begin with this inheritance does not mean that we are rejecting it, or that we shall not have recourse to it later, or that we are 'sinking into mysticism'—does not entail the passivity which, in other philosophical essays, I have been able to identify with the responsibility for the other. A responsibility which is not a debt limited by the extent of a commitment that has been actively made, for such a debt can be settled; whereas, without compromising my thought, we can never pay our debt to the other. This is an infinite responsibility, a responsibility against my will, one that I have not chosen: the responsibility of the hostage.[4]

Admittedly, it is not a matter of deducing from this responsibility the actual content of the Bible: Moses and the prophets. We are concerned, rather, with formulating the possibility of a heteronomy which excludes subservience, an ear retaining its reason, an obedience which does not alienate the listener; and with recognizing, in the ethical model of the Bible, the transcendence of understanding. This opening on to an irreducible transcendence cannot occur within the conception of reason that prevails in our philosophical profession today. Here, reason is solid and positive; it begins with all meaning to which all meaning must return in order to be assimilated to the Same, in spite of the whole appearance it may give of having come from outside. Nothing in this reason can cause the fission in the nuclear solidity of a thought which thinks in correlation with the world's positivity, which thinks from its starting point of the vast repose of the cosmos; a thought which freezes its object in the theme, which always thinks to its measure, which thinks *knowingly*. I have always wondered whether this reason that remains closed to the excessiveness of transcendence is capable of expressing the irruption of man into being or the interruption of being by man or, more exactly, the interruption of the alleged correlation of man and being in ess*a*nce[5] in which the figure of the Same appears. I have wondered, too, whether the anxiety that the Other causes the Same is not the meaning of reason, its very rationality: the anxiety of man caused by the Infinite of God which he could never contain, but which inspires him. This inspiration is the originary mode of anxiety, the inspiration of many by God which is man's humanity. Here the 'in' of the 'excessiveness in the finite' is made possible only by the 'Here I am' of man welcoming his neighbour. Inspiration's original mode is not in listening to a Muse dictating songs, but in obedience to the Most-High as an ethical relation with the other.

This is what we have said right from the outset: the subject of our enquiry is the fact of the Revelation, and a relation with exteriority which, unlike the exteriority with which man surrounds himself whenever he seeks knowledge, does not become simply the content of interiority, but remains 'uncontainable', infinite and yet still maintaining a relation. The path I would be inclined to take in order to solve the paradox of the Revelation is one which claims that this relation, at first glance a paradoxical one, may find a model in the non-indifference towards the other, in a responsibility towards him, and that it is precisely within this relation that man becomes his 'self': designated without any possibility of escape, chosen, unique, non-interchangeable and, in this sense, free.[6] Ethics is the model worthy of transcendence, and it is as an ethical kerygma that the Bible is Revelation.

The Rationality of Transcendence

What we would also like to suggest and—albeit very briefly—to justify is that the openness to transcendence, as it appears in ethics, does not mean the loss of rationality, that which gives significance to meaning. Rational theology is a theology of being where the rational is equated with the identity of the Same, suggested by the firmness or positivity of the firm ground beneath the sun. It belongs to the ontological adventure which led the biblical God and man, understood from the standpoint of the positivity of a world, towards the 'death' of God and the end of the humanism, or the humanity, of man. The notion of subjectivity coinciding with the identity of the Same and its rationality meant the connection of the world's diversity and the unity of an order which left nothing outside; an order produced or reproduced by the supreme act of Synthesis. The idea of a passive subject and one which, in the heteronomy of its responsibility for the other, differs from all other subjects, is a difficult one. The Subject which does not return to itself, which does not join up again in order to settle, triumphantly, into the absolute repose of the earth beneath the vault of heaven, is unfavourably treated as a product of Romantic subjectivism. The opposite of repose—anxiety, questioning, seeking, Desire—is taken to be a repose that has been lost, an absence of response, a privation—a pure insufficiency of identity, a mark of self-inequality. We have wondered whether the Revelation does not precisely restore the thought of inequality, difference, and irreducible alterity which is 'uncontainable' in gnoseological intentionality; the thought which is not knowledge but which, overflowing knowledge, is in relation with the Infinite or God. We have wondered too whether intentionality, which in its noetic and noematic correlation thinks 'to its measure', is not, on the contrary, an insufficient psyche, one that is more impoverished than the question which, in its purity, is directed towards the other, and is thus a relation with something that can never offer an investment. And finally, we have wondered whether seeking, desire and questioning, far from carrying within themselves the emptiness of need, are not the explosion of the 'more in the less' that Descartes called the idea of the Infinite, a psyche that is more awake than the psyche of intentionality and the knowledge adequate to its object.

The Revelation, as it is described from the standpoint of the ethical relation and where the ethical relation with the other is a modality of the relation with God, denounces the figure of the Same and of knowledge in their claim to be the only place of signification. This figure of the Same and this knowledge are only a certain level of intelligence where it is dulled, becomes middle-class in the satisfied presence of its place, and where reason, always being brought back to the search for repose, calm and conciliation—which imply the ultimateness or priority of the Same—is already absent from living reason. Not that the lack of plenitude, or self-inadequacy, is worth more than coincidence. If it were just a matter of the self in its substantiality, then equality would be better than lack. It is not a question of making the Romantic ideal of dissatisfaction preferable to full self-possession. But does the Spirit end in self-possession? Is there not good cause to think of a relation with an Other which would be 'better' than self-possession? Does not a certain way of 'losing one's soul' signify a deference to what is more, or better, or 'higher' than the soul? It is perhaps in this deference that the very notions of 'better' or 'high' are uttered only as a sense, and that seeking, desire and questioning are thus better than possession, satisfaction and response.

Should we not go beyond the awareness which is equal to itself, or which seeks this equality through assimilating the Other, in order to emphasize the act of deference to the other in his alterity, an alterity which can occur only by way of an awakening by the Other of the Same sleeping in his identity? And, as we have suggested, is not obedience the modality of this awakening? And is it not possible to think of this awareness, in its self-adequacy, as a modality of modification of this awakening, this disturbance that can never be absorbed, of the Same by the Other, in his difference? Rather than being seen in terms of received knowledge, should not the Revelation be thought of as this awakening?

These questions concern the nature of the ultimate, and bring into question the rationality of reason and even the possibility of the ultimate. Should not stupor and fossilization be feared in the identity of the Same to which thought aspires as if to a repose? The other is thought of only quite improperly as an enemy of the Same, his alterity leading not to a dialectic play but to an incessant questioning, without the ultimateness, the priority and the tranquillity of the Same, like an inextinguishable flame which burns yet consumes nothing. Is not the prescriptive of Jewish revelation, in its unfulfillable obligation, its very modality? An unfulfillable obligation, a burning that does not even leave any ash, which would still be, in some respect, a substance based on itself. There is always this explosion of the 'less', incapable of containing the 'more' that it contains, in the form of 'the one for the other'. 'Always' signifies here in its native force: the sense of great patience, of its dia-chrony and temporal transcendence. A sobering up that is 'always' deeper and, in this sense, the spirituality of the spirit in obedience. We may well ask questions about the manifestation of these things in what is said. But can transcendence as such be converted into answers without being lost in the process? And is not the question, which is also a calling into question, the distinctive feature of the voice commanding from beyond?[7]

Notes

1. An invitation to intelligence which at the same time, by the mystery from which it comes, protects it against the 'dangers' of the truth. Here is a Talmudic apologue commenting on Exodus 33:21-2 ('And the Lord said, "Behold, there is a place by me where you shall stand upon the rock; and while my glory passes by I will put you in a cleft of the rock, and I will cover you with my hand until I have passed by" '): 'Protection was needed, for complete freedom had been given to the destructive forces to destroy'. The moment of truth is the one in which all interdicts are lifted, where the enquiring mind is permitted everything. Only the truth of the Revelation gives protection at this supreme moment against evil, which, as truth, it also risks leaving free.
2. The written Torah refers to the twenty-four Books of the Jewish Biblical Canon and, in a narrower sense, to the Torah of Moses, the Pentateuch. In the broadest sense, Torah means the whole of the Bible and the Talmud with their commentaries and even with their collected works and homiletic texts called *Aggadah*.
3. On this subject, see also Chapter 3 in my *Autrement qu'être, ou Au-delà de l'essence* (The Hague: Martinus Nijhoff, 1974) [*Otherwise than Being, or Beyond Essence*, trans. by Alphonso Lingis (The Hague and London: Martinus Nijhoff, 1981)], and the study 'Sans identité' in my *Humanisme de l'autre homme* (Montpellier: Fata Morgana, 1972).
4. Cf. *Autrement qu'être, ou Au-delà de l'essence*.
5. We are writing this as *essance*, as an abstract noun designating the verbal sense of the word 'being'.
6. Freedom would therefore mean the hearing of a vocation to which I alone am capable of responding; or even the capability-to-respond right there, where I am called.
7. The ideas presented in these final pages have already been put forward in 'De la conscience à la veille', *Bijdragen*, 3–4 (1974).

16

Sacred Fragments: Recovering Theology for the Modern Jew

NEIL GILLMAN

The Jewish Myth

We have come full circle. We opened our discussion of revelation by noting that our three subissues—the principle, the fact, and the content—of revelation were inextricably intertwined, that the way we dealt with any of the three issues would inevitably predetermine how we would deal with the other two. Our review of the various attempts to define the content of revelation indicates that at least for three of our thinkers—Kaplan, Rosenzweig, and Heschel—the only way of approaching all of these questions is to reject the literalness of the biblical account of revelation and to posit that no human characterization of God and His activity can be understood as objectively true. Rather, all such characterizations have to be understood as metaphorical attempts to capture what is inherently beyond the range of human experience.

The primary metaphor, the metaphor on which the status of Torah rests, is the claim that God "spoke" to Moses and the children of Israel at Sinai. Acknowledge the metaphorical nature of that claim and you redefine Torah as to some extent the creation of a human community. That is precisely what Kaplan, Rosenzweig, and Heschel have done, each in his distinctive way. Each, then, has to struggle with redefining the uniqueness and authoritative character of Torah. But we should never minimize the gravity of the step that these thinkers have taken. The gap between these three positions and the traditionalist position is genuine and irreparable.

Yet a third version of the middle position—the position that strives to balance the complementary contributions of God and the human community in shaping the content of rev-

Neil Gillman, *Sacred Fragments: Recovering Theology for the Modern Jew* (Philadelphia: Jewish Publication Society, 1992), pp. 25–34, 116–24. © Jewish Publication Society, Philadelphia, PA 19103.

elation—stems from the contemporary preoccupation with the status of theological language and conceptualization. The seminal statement of this position is in the writings of the preeminent Protestant philosopher/theologian of this century, Paul Tillich (1886–1965) who proposed that all religious language has to be understood as "symbolic" and "mythical." In popular parlance, a "myth" is understood to be either a fiction (the "myth" of the invincibility of the New York Yankees) or a legendary tale (the "myth" of Oedipus). But scholars in the social sciences and in religion use the term in a different, more technical way.

A myth should be understood as a structure through which a community organizes and makes sense of its experience. The world "out there" does not impinge itself on us in a totally objective way, tidily packaged and organized into meaningful patterns. Our experience of the world is a complex transaction between what comes to us from "out there" and the way we structure or "read" it. Myths are the spectacles that enable us to see order in what would otherwise be confusion. They are created, initially, by "reading" communities, beginning with their earliest attempts to shape, explain, or make some sense out of their experience of nature and history. Gradually, as the mythic structure seems to work, to be confirmed by ongoing experience, it is refined, shared, and transmitted to later generations. It becomes embodied in official, "canonical" texts and assumes authoritative power. In its final form, it becomes omnipresent and quasi-invisible, so much has it become our intuitive way of confronting the world.

Take, for example, the myth of the human psyche that is at the heart of Freudian psychoanalytic theory. Before Freud, students of human functioning were confronted by a confusing array of behaviors without any clear idea of how they were connected, what patterns they assumed, what meaning they had, which were pathological and which normal, and why people behaved the way they did. Scientists of human behavior didn't even know what to look for, which data were worth noting and which were irrelevant, or what constituted the "facts" that needed interpretation.

Freud's contribution was to organize this data into patterns. He identified what constituted the significant facts. He showed how these various behaviors assumed certain predictable forms. Finally, through his picture of the human psyche with its id, ego, and superego, its conscious, preconscious, and subconscious, its oedipal drive, and the rest, he proceeded to explain how and why people behave the way they do. To this day, even with all of its revisions, we invariably use the Freudian myth as a set of spectacles that enables us to "read" and understand human behavior.

Leaving aside, for a moment, the differences between the ways myths function in science and in religion, the Freudian example is instructive. A myth orders experience, explains how it reveals specific shapes, forms, and meaningful patterns. In general it explains overt experience by constructing an invisible or covert world that lies behind ordinary experience and is not itself directly accessible—that's why the myth often appears to be subjective or fictional. Is there really such a thing as an id or an ego? Is the subconscious a real dimension of the psyche? In short, did Freud invent these entities or did he discover them?

In fact, he did both. He was able to see certain patterns in human behavior because they were there in the first place, along with many other apparent patterns and much that didn't fit into any clear-cut scheme. But his creative, inventive, or imaginative contribution was to select and identify those patterns that were significant, and show how they cohered with each other to form a meaning-laden whole.

The more global the myth—the more it tries to explain—the more inventive and imaginative it seems, and hence the more fictional it appears to be. But though a myth has an inherently subjective quality—for it can never be directly compared to the reality it represents, and objectively confirmed to be true or false—it is far from a deliberate fiction. We may never be able to stand outside of the myth to measure its correspondence with reality, for we can never have a totally a-mythical perception of that reality. The issue is never myth or no myth but which myth, for without a myth our experience would be literally meaningless. But every myth is dictated by experience, however much it shapes that experience in the very process of being constructed.

Myths are intrinsic to communities. In fact, myths create communities. When they assume narrative form, they recount the community's "master story," explaining how that community came into being, what distinguishes it from other communities, how it understands its distinctive history and destiny, what constitutes its unique value system. A myth provides a community with its distinctive raison d'etre.

Religious myths do all of this for a religious community. They also convey the community's distinctive answers to ultimate human questions: Why am I here? What is the meaning or purpose of my existence? How do I handle guilt, suffering, sexuality, interpersonal relations? What happens when I die? Myths promote loyalty to the community, motivate behavior, generate a sense of belonging and kinship. Because they emerge from and speak to the most primitive layers of our being, they are capable of moving or touching us in the most profound way. People die for their myths, so coercive is their hold.

Religious myths are canonized in Scripture, in the sacred books that record the authoritative version of the communal myth and become the test for communicating it to succeeding generations. They inspire liturgies, poetic recitations of portions of the myth, to celebrate significant events in the life of the community and its members. They also generate rituals, dramatic renderings of the myth, this time in the language of the body. Frequently, liturgy and ritual merge to create elaborate religious pageants which bring the myth into consciousness and give it a concrete reality in the life experience of the community. The Passover *seder* and the Jewish rites of passage are superb examples of such pageants.

If myths are subjective, impressionistic human constructs, in what sense are they "true"? Why should one be preferred to another? There is no simple answer to these questions. Myths are clearly not objectively true in the sense that they correspond to some reality out there. We simply do not have an independent picture of that reality against which we can measure the myth, for we literally can not see the world except through the spectacles of our myth.

But myths are also not capricious inventions. They emerge originally out of our experience of natural and historical patterns. They may select, identify, and organize these specific patterns, but they can do all of this because the patterns are there to be seen, selected, and organized in the first place. They can then be seen to be roughly consistent with our experience of the world. To use our earlier language, we are able to falsify some mythic claims. For example, many of us would not want to account for the death of six million Jews in the Nazi Holocaust by invoking the traditional mythic explanation of suffering as God's punishment for sin. That explanation has been falsified for us; it does not cohere with our experience. It does not provide an adequate explanation. We may not be able to produce a better explanation, but we know this one can not be true.

It is one thing to falsify a myth but quite another to verify or confirm one. Though no single mythic claim may capture reality in a totally accurate way for everyone, some claims may be more or less accurate than others. Again an example. There is a clear difference between the Jewish and Christian explanations of why people behave in evil ways. The dominant Christian image is of the human being as forever tainted by the "original sin" that stems from Adam and Eve's rebellion in Eden and is transmitted throughout the generations by procreation. Judaism, in contrast, sees the human being as the arena of a conflict between two warring impulses, one good and the other evil, with the individual free and responsible for determining which dominates. This is an admittedly crude presentation of a complex issue, but it shows how two communities produce two different mythic explanations for a complex pattern of human behavior. Judaism's consistent rejection of the doctrine of original sin reflects this community's continuing intuition that its own explanation is closer to the real state of affairs.

Beyond this, myths can be subject to a pragmatic test that determines whether they work, whether they do what they are supposed to do: explain, motivate, generate loyalty, create identity, and so forth. The pragmatic test is frequently invoked by scientific myths. Freud's psychoanalytic theory, for example, will be judged "true" to the extent that it works to predict human behavior and cure pathology. It will be replaced if and when another equally mythic theory does all of this more effectively.

Finally, myths can be verified existentially. Existential truth is ineluctably personal and subjective. The more a mythic claim touches upon my personal, concrete existence, the less it can be "true in general," "true for everyone," "objectively true"—and the more it has to be "true for me" or "true for us." Mathematical truth, within a specific set of axioms, is objective; it is "true for everyone." But the further we move toward the issues that impinge deeply upon our humanness, the more our truths become personal and subjective. In effect, we make these existential claims true by living them, by committing ourselves to them, and by risking our lives for them.

Revelation in the Torah Myth

Freud's efforts were directed to understanding one small corner of our experience of the world, human behavior. In the course of its earliest experience as a people, the biblical community tried to do much more: understand the world in its entirety and its own place in that world. The classic Torah myth, embodied in Scripture and celebrated in liturgy and ritual, is the result of that inquiry. The only way our ancestors could make sense of their experience of the world was by invoking a supernatural, personal God who created the natural order, entered into a uniquely intimate relationship with a man, his family, and ultimately his progeny. He delivered this people from slavery, entered into a covenant with them whereby they pledged to constitute themselves into a holy people devoted exclusively to Him and His revealed will, punished them for their disobedience, rewarded them for their loyalty, guided them through the desert to their promised homeland, exiled them, and subsequently returned them there again. It is nothing less than astonishing that this classic mythic structure, elaborated and refined throughout the generations—notably by the addition of a vision of the end of days as the ultimate fulfillment of this community's hopes for itself and for mankind—remains in place to this day.

Is this structure objectively true? There is no way of establishing that. We can not prove, objectively, that God did or did not take our ancestors out of Egypt, destroy Jerusalem, save the Maccabean army, or, for that matter, guide the reestablishment of the modern State of Israel in 1948. But there is no denying that in large measure, the myth has withstood the attempts to falsify it. Nor is there any doubt that it has passed both the pragmatic and existential tests of truth for close to three thousand years.

As for revelation, if we are serious in affirming that no myth is a fiction, then we have in the same breath affirmed both the principle and the fact of revelation. Since there is an objective dimension to the myth, since the patterns are discovered, not invented, however much they may be shaped or "read" by the community, that objective dimension is what we call "revelation." In fact, the very use of that term is the best indication that the myth is at work.

The thesis that Torah contains the classic Jewish mythic explanation of one community's experience of the world, is clearly still a third version of what we have called the middle option on revelation. It most closely resembles Heschel's position that Torah is a *midrash*, but it uses a different idiom. A *midrash* is usually understood to be a reading of a text, but in an extended sense, it can also be taken as a reading of the world, of human experience. In this extended sense, myth and *midrash* share many characteristics. Both are culturally conditioned, human renderings of realities that lie beyond direct human apprehension. Both exhibit startling continuities and equally surprising discontinuities as they move through history. As long as the community that shapes them remains vital, it will determine what it wishes to keep and what it prefers to discard and reshape in the light of its ongoing experience.

Five Options: How Do We Choose?

Decisions between theological options should never be made on the basis of one issue alone, even as central an issue as revelation. It may yet be helpful, in a preliminary way, to suggest how various criteria figure in reaching such decisions.

In the course of this chapter, we have appealed to four such criteria: theological coherence, historical authenticity, programmatic implications, and psychological adequacy. First, is the position theologically coherent on its own terms? Second, does it have an authentically Jewish ring? Third, what are its implications for the decisions that face the Jewish community today? Finally, does the position meet the psychological needs of the individual believer?

It should not be disturbing that theological decisions are rarely made on the basis of internal theological criteria alone. The expectation that they should is neither realistic nor reflective of how human beings operate. The middle two criteria are invoked because we want our theology to resonate Jewishly because our context remains Judaism, and because theology is not an intellectual game. Its purpose is to make it possible for Jews to belong to the community and to function Jewishly.

Finally, since everything we do is informed by our individual psychic constitutions, we will naturally gravitate to religious positions that best meet our psychological needs. A person who looks to religion as a source of authority, who wants final and absolute answers to issues of belief and practice, who is impatient with pluralistic or indecisive answers to ultimate questions, will embrace the traditionalist position and view Torah as literally and verbally revealed. In contrast, someone who is prepared to live with ambiguity and indecision, who accepts the inevitability of different points of view on complex moral, theological, and spiritual issues, and who is prepared to become engaged in the issues and evolve a position that is personally adequate, however much it may differ from that of the religious establishment, will embrace one of the other options.

How any one of these options fares in regard to the four criteria remains a highly individual judgment. This author finds both the traditionalist option and Mordecai Kaplan's position problematic both on theological and programmatic grounds—though clearly for very different reasons. The middle position, though far from unassailable, remains the most satisfying of the group. It is this position, particularly in its third version, that will inform the remainder of this volume.

Religion is an extraordinarily complex affair. It is an organic unity of historical memories, theological doctrines, behavioral patterns, communal bonds, myths, rituals, and liturgies, all of which touch various levels of our being: intellectual, emotional, aesthetic, and psychological. What distinguishes the "insider" from the "outsider" is that for the former, the whole coheres in an ultimately satisfying way. Any one of us may feel vaguely dissatisfied with any of these dimensions; we may, for example, find some of the liturgy anachronistic, some rituals meaningless, or the approach to suffering thoroughly inadequate. Sometimes many small dissatisfactions will accumulate and outweigh the positives. But most of the major religions are rich and variegated enough—and/or have evolved procedures for discarding and replacing the outworn and the unsatisfactory—that as a whole, the tradition still works for many, though clearly not for all, in the community.

The process is messy and hardly quick and easy. One person may want intellectual sophistication, another, explicit guidance in ethical decision making. A third may seek emotionally and aesthetically pleasing worship experiences, a fourth, psychological support in traumatic life situations. How all of this works itself out in the life experience of any one individual is subtle and complex. But this is probably an accurate picture of how most of us do, in fact, reach decisions of this kind.

One final note. The decision can not be made from the outside. Religious commitments are probably the most existential issues we face. We have to be prepared to jump in and live within a tradition before we can appreciate its strengths and weaknesses. The convinced skeptic may be unwilling to take this initial step but this is a failure of will, and it is not our failure. Our responsibility is to address those who feel the urgency of the issues and are willing to struggle to find the answers.

• • •

When a believer speaks of experiencing the world religiously, he may well be echoing the kind of "seeing" that Job achieved. What makes this experience "religious" is first its global quality and then its integrating capacity, its reach for a pervasive sense of order and harmony throughout, and the sense of belonging that this conveys. My life acquires meaning when the world as a whole has meaning. Ultimately it is God who is either the source of this cosmic order or, in a more pantheistic framework, is Himself that order.

An experience, then, can be "religious" in four possible ways: either because of the object of the experience, "what" is actually experienced—God, Jesus of Nazareth, angels, or the saints; or because of the interpretation that is given to the experience—the patterns of nature and history are interpreted as revealing God's presence; or because of the emotion that the experience and/or its interpretation inspires—typically a feeling of awe, dependency, guilt, or salvation; or because of the global, perspective-yielding quality of the experience, the sense of a cosmic order through which my life acquires meaning. Most frequently, two or three of these components will come together. In Jewish sources, for example, the last three factors usually coincide. But, invariably, one will be dominant. As we shall soon see, that dominant factor will determine how the experience is to be understood and what theological significance it will assume.

The Problem of Subjectivity

Our definition of religious experience shifted from pure sense experience to a more interpretive kind of sense experience; to interpretive sense experience transfigured with emotion; to a more inward, intense, personal, and mystical experience; and, finally, to experience as yielding a global, integrated perspective on the world as a whole. It is clear that in the process the subjective character of the experience increased steadily. Most of us would agree that the patch out there is red. The members of a jury will frequently agree to interpret the pattern of evidence in a complex business case as revealing fraud rather than legal business practices. But when the emotional dimension of the experience becomes dominant, we are being asked to accept an experience that is ineluctably personal as legitimate and valid for all. And when the yield of the religious experience is the perception of an order that pervades all things, we sense that we are dealing with a vision that can neither be proven nor disproven, but represents an individual's or a community's most intuitive stance toward the world as a whole.

In all of our three approaches to God, certain basic questions must be asked: First, how does the approach deal with what we called "the escape clause" of the experience, the factor that enables someone to refuse to see, or not to be able to see, to forget what has been seen, or to be unwilling or incapable of interpreting what has been seen as the believer does? Second, how does the approach deal with the problem of illusory or hallucinatory seeing? Third, how does it prove, verify, or establish the truth of its claims while at the same time disproving or falsifying contrary claims? Finally, how does it handle the charge that the claims are mere wish-fulfillments, far from objective reports of anything out there but, rather, statements about the state of mind and soul of the believer himself?

If there is one characteristic stance of the religious experientialist on the issue of subjectivity, it is this: Subjectivity is an inevitable component of all religious experience; but religious communities, especially those with a long and continuing historical experience, have worked out ways of minimizing its impact.

The most fruitful analogy for the approach of the experientialist is that of the jury in a complex business case. The evidence is provided by the records of the corporation over a decade. The task of the prosecuting attorney is to review the records, highlight the instances of apparently fraudulent activity, connect these instances into a pattern, draw that pattern to the attention of the jury, and convince it that this pattern is sufficiently dominant to constitute grounds for conviction. The defense attorney will seek to highlight the evidence of acceptable and legal business practice, connect that into a pattern, draw that pattern to the attention of the jury, and try to persuade it that this pattern is sufficiently convincing to warrant acquittal. Each of the attorneys will simultaneously do some disconnecting or try to unravel the pattern that the other has shaped. The jury will weigh the conflicting patterns and, in most instances, reach a decision.

Of course, the process is more complicated than we have described. The attorneys will pay careful attention to jury selection, trying to anticipate what factors may predispose one juror to see the evidence in one way over the other. Sometimes these factors may not even be conscious to the juror; they may be issues of innate disposition, education, or personal style. Witnesses will be chosen with an eye to their general credibility and persuasiveness. In their summations, the two attorneys will use rhetorical devices that will appeal to the emotions of the jurors and influence how they read the evidence.

But the core of the process is the presentation and sharing of complex patterns in time and space. This is essentially a social or communal experience; it takes place in the context of a group. In the privacy of the jury room, members of the jury will share their reading of the data with each other and try to convince each other of the persuasiveness of one or the other outcome. They will retrace the connections made by each of the attorneys and weigh the strength of the emerging patterns. They will also retrace the attempts of each attorney to disconnect or destroy the opposing patterns. They will examine the conflicting readings of the evidence. They will attempt to explain or integrate apparently discordant data. Eventually, in most instances, the process works—a consensual reading emerges and a verdict is reached. Sometimes the process is inconclusive. In American law, with its presumption of innocence, the burden is on the prosecutor to prove the dominance of his pattern. If he fails to do this, or if the defense is successful in unraveling the pattern, the jury will acquit. If the patterns seem to have equal weight, the jury will be "hung" and the defendant remain innocent.

The process of evolving a religious reading of experience is similar to that used in a court of law, but the evidence is infinitely more complex, the jury is much larger, the time required for the process stretches over centuries, and the record of the deliberations is rarely available to us. It is very much a social process; it takes place in the context of a community of believers. But a good part of the process is completed before it emerges into the light of history. We become aware of it, for example, when we have a Bible, or even one of the documents or books that became part of the biblical canon. But the very fact that a biblical document exists indicates that the process has been largely completed and that it has worked successfully. The Bible represents the verdict, the consensual decision of a centuries-old community to choose one specific reading of the pattern over another. From that point on, the Bible becomes the textbook through which each successive generation within the community is instructed in the community's reading of its experience.

That function is shared with the later texts that the community accepts as canonical—preeminently in the case of Judaism, talmudic literature and the daily, Sabbath, and Festival liturgies. That there is a post-biblical, canonical literature in the first place—indeed that the Bible itself includes earlier and later strata—indicates that the community's reading of its experience has a certain plasticity, that it is never entirely closed.

Jews use the term *midrash* to denote the process of modifying, expanding, or, at times, deleting and recreating portions of their consensual pattern. For example, the Bible says almost nothing about the afterlife of the individual, while postbiblical literature is positively voluble about the immortality of the soul and the resurrection of the body. Another example is suffering. The dominant biblical explanation for suffering is that it is God's punishment for sin, but Job repudiates that explanation. In a striking piece of intrabiblical *midrash*, Jonah 4:2 rewrites Exodus 34:6–7 because the author of Jonah no longer believes that God must inevitably punish us for our sinfulness; the possibility of repentance is now introduced into the pattern.

Then there are those instances when the community refused to accept a proposed extension of their consensual pattern. Most first-century C.E. Jews refused to go along with Paul's proposal that Jewish messianic expectations had now been fulfilled in the life and career of Jesus of Nazareth. They would not, or could not, interpret and integrate that series of events into their consensual pattern.

The analogy of the jury's decision-making process works well when the religious experience is directed to patterns in nature and history. In these instances, there is clearly something out there that can be "seen," however much interpretation the seeing requires. The social context works to direct the seeing and its interpretation, to screen out idiosyncratic (i.e., illusory or hallucinatory) interpretations, to achieve consensus. What is gained through the experience can be accepted as "true," where truth is understood to mean that which corresponds to reality. Because the data are so infinitely more complex, we do not hold religious truths to as high a standard as we do most scientific truths. They can not be verified by repeatable experiments. But they are roughly comparable to the scientific truth of the more global and abstract of scientific theories, those that deal not with the immediate data of scientific experiments but more with the underlying nature of reality, such as in quantum mechanics or astronomy.

The less the religious experience is directed to something that is even vaguely identifiable as "out there," the more the experience is inner-directed, the greater the emotional dimension of the experience, or the greater the very personal nature of the experience (as in mysticism), the analogy of the jury becomes progressively less helpful. In fact, this is the point where experientialism shades into existentialism and the subjective quality of the experience is not only accepted but even extolled.

Typically, at this point the believer will refer to his experience as "self-verifying." This is simply a polite way of dismissing the subjectivity questions as irrelevant. The believer knows beyond question that the experience is true because it is true *for him*, and this personal conviction is the single most important condition of the truth of the experience. But then we have redefined what we mean by truth in religion. We no longer even aim for objectivity. "True" means "true for me" and the experience carries its own warranty. Just about any religious claim based on a personal experience of this kind is implicitly acceptable as legitimate. However, if the preeminent religious experience is only personal, then the very possibility of a religious community is called into question. Small wonder, then, that most religious traditions have been wary of relying on experiences of this kind.

Actually, most religious communities have been able to make room for and even to welcome their mystics, and that for two reasons. First, the community exercises powerful control over the shape of its mystics' experiences, accepting those that reflect the specific religious tradition. Jewish mystics will never have mystical experiences of Jesus of Nazareth or of his mother Mary, or of the Christian saints; they will, instead, invoke themes and symbols that emerge out of the classical texts of the Jewish tradition, such as Ezekiel's vision of the divine chariot (Ezekiel I), or Isaiah's vision of the heavenly host praising God (Isaiah 6). Or a classical Jewish institution such as the Sabbath becomes personified as a bride or a queen, and then becomes the channel for a mystical experience. Though a Jewish mystical experience may strain the parameters of the *halakhah*, it will never deliberately seek to undermine its authority. Effectively, then, the mystical ex-

perience, however idiosyncratic and personal it may be, can enrich the emotional coloration of the traditional pattern and thereby strengthen its appeal.

It can do even more. It can infuse the everyday experience of the community with a
mystical dimension. The late Max Kadushin's study of rabbinic Judaism, *The Rabbinic
Mind*, employs the felicitous term "normal mysticism" to capture what Kadushin considers to be the normative way in which the rabbinic Jew experiences the world. It is "mysticism" because God's presence in the world is experienced directly. But it is "normal"
because this experience is never private, esoteric, ecstatic, or incommunicable. It is, rather,
very much a communal experience and an experience of ordinary, everyday things and
events. The food that we consume, the normal functions of our bodies, sunrise and sun-
set, the cycles of the seasons—all of these become infused with a sense of the mystical
that makes us aware of God's immediate presence in the world. The *halakhah* serves to
structure and communalize the experience, and the liturgy, specifically the *berakhot* (the
benedictions that we recite, e.g., before and after we eat), directs our attention to God's
presence in the experience.

Finally, what of those religious experiences that perceive a cosmic order pervading all
things? Here, if anywhere, the questions that the subjectivity issue poses appear irrelevant. These cosmic configurations are neither provable nor disprovable. They emerge in
the earliest stages of a community's awareness and are solidly in place long before they
assume literary form. Genesis 1–3 records the classic Jewish description of that order, describes how it came to be, and, subsequently, how it was disrupted by the behavior of primordial and paradigmatic human beings—Adam and Eve, and Cain. Essentially, these
chapters provide the Jewish account of why things are as they are in nature and in human
life. The Exodus/Sinai narrative explains why the Jewish people is the way it is. Not un-
expectedly, these accounts are couched in metaphorical terms; how else can human beings portray events and realities that lie beyond human perception? But once in place, the
metaphor determines everything else about the community's experience. Cosmic
metaphors of this kind effectively define the community. They shape the community's
most primitive or intuitive sense of its role and destiny, and they are well nigh invulnerable.

Cosmic metaphors of this kind share many of the qualities we earlier ascribed to a
community's myth. In fact, a myth should be understood as a literary rendition of the
community's metaphor. The metaphor itself has a more pictorial quality; it is more the
result of "seeing." It is a visual prefiguration of the myth, the source of the dramatic and
poetic quality that is characteristic of a great myth. To put this another way, the myth is
a discursive rendering of the community's metaphor. The metaphor is also the source of
the inherent subjectivity that is characteristic of myths, the quality that makes them easily identified as fictions. But as we have seen, neither myths nor their underlying metaphors
are fictions. They emerge out of a community's most primitive confrontation with the
world. They carry their own distinctive kind of truth, for they have been verified many
times over, as witnessed by the community's continued vitality through centuries. They
are "true" because they have enabled the community to maintain its integrity and its members to live satisfying and fulfilling lives; thus, what we have called the singular "invul-
nerability" of these structures. The community will cling to its picture of the world, come
what may, for what is at stake is the community's very existence.

Note also the emotional component of these cosmic metaphors, or, indeed, of any religious experientialist reading of events. Some forms of the religious experience have a

direct emotional component. But even the more low-key perception of those patterns in nature and history carry an emotional charge. This is what distinguishes them from more scientific readings of experience. Religion is expected to engender pervasive moods in the community of believers. The moods are not always congruent. One believer may feel a sense of "all's right with the world"; another, a sense of guilt or imminent disaster; a third, a sense of authenticity, of having been "saved" for all time. A religious reading of the world should also motivate behavior, engender a sense of loyalty to the community, and enable its members to cope with the normal stresses of everyday life.

What emerges from the religious experience? A certain body of knowledge about the world, an awareness that certain patterns prevail. To a significant degree, it understands religious faith as "belief that . . ."—belief that the world out there reflects these patterns. In this mode, it tends to view the atheist as "blind," incapable of seeing the patterns or of understanding them as the community does. Here, the believer and the atheist can still speak to each other and examine the evidence of lack thereof.

But when experientialism begins to emphasize the highly personal and self-verifying nature of the experience, religious faith tends to become "belief in . . ."—an instinctual, emotional, gut conviction that the believer's experience is veridical. In this mode, atheism represents more a failure of will than of vision, for now the evidence is irrelevant, for or against. The atheist refuses to take the step that the believer has taken. At this point, the atheist and the believer speak past each other.

17

The Natural and the Supernatural Jew

ARTHUR A. COHEN

Reflections Upon a Metaphysics of History

The image of Exile has, like the cord of Theseus, passed through each chamber of the historic Jewish mind, imparting unity and continuity to disparate and seemingly unrelated moments of creation and despair.

The Exile has been not only a rationalization of historical events, an effort to elevate disaster into national triumph, a neurasthenic sublimation of pain and defeat; it has been a source of permanent meaning. To be sure, the naturalization of the Exile, accompanying as it did the naturalization of the Jew—his rejection of supernatural vocation and destiny and his conventional, frequently unresisting, acceptance of the hostility of the non-Jewish world—has made of Exile and physical diaspora an opprobrious reality for both Zionists, who revile the Exile, and Diaspora Jews, who would willingly exchange it for adjustment.

It is not our purpose, however, to prolong the war with Jewish nationalism or with Jewish assimilationism. That war is really over. It raged passionately in the last century and was continued in the present, but it is now over. The rhetoric of Zionist repudiation of the Exile lingers on, a reminder of this dead but eloquent war. It is a dead war because Zionism is now triumphant and yet millions of Jews are unwilling either to go up to the Land or to be assimilated. The situation of the modern Jew is substantially as it was before. There is limbo, an indeterminate stasis, where nothing appears changed, other than the fact that the present situation is clearer, more sharply etched, false and inadequate alternatives having been removed by the outcome of historic events.

It would appear that however much the controversies of the nineteenth century have been silenced by decisive historical fortune, the perpetual crisis of Jewish survival con-

Arthur A. Cohen, *The Natural and the Supernatural Jew*, second edition (New York: Behrman House, 1979), pp. 291–301, 306–11. © Behrman House, West Orange, NJ 07052.

tinues. Jewish survival is nevertheless an historical problem. It is a problem formed out of the pull and drag of events. It is a natural problem in the most immediate and meaningful of senses, for the issue of Jewish survival, so seen, is an issue of population and numbers. To be sure, Jewish survival is qualitative as well, since one would not be willing to settle for Jews in name only. But let us be equally clear that we will not be asked to settle for Jews in name only, if Jews indeed survive. It is hardly thinkable that the Jewish communities of the Dispersion could survive if every Jew intermarried, if there was no interest in raising one's children as Jews, if those powerful "symbols" of identification—Sabbath, the High Holy Days, the Kaddish of praise and mourning—were all discarded. Since we are not a race, marked off by ineffaceable physical characteristics, we cannot rest confident that race will enable us to survive; nor are we simply an ethnic community whose cultural artifacts are so agreeable, harmless, and undivisive that they can be perpetuated as links of sentimental continuity. No racial or ethnic unity—unless so minimally defined as to be all but worthless—helps us to survive. We are destined to disappear if our existence depends solely upon the slow action of history. The ethnic ties fray and rot, the cultural artifacts are abandoned, and our religion, cut off and separated from the whole of our life, becomes a formal piety—itself a fashion of history to be abandoned when the climate of opinion heralds the time of abandonment.

It is exceptionally difficult to articulate the lines of Jewish intellectual history from the beginnings of the Hellenistic world to the present day. The stages of Jewish history do not conform to the stages of Western history. Its middle ages were not followed by a renaissance, a reformation, an enlightenment, and an age of scientific rationalism and political ideology. Such historical periods have at best contingent validity. They reflect, not merely man's assessment of himself in the moment of his renaissance or enlightenment, but more intensely, the retrospective appraisal of later ages, seeking either to praise or blame, to epitomize and condense, to adjudge, define, and transmit their characteristics and accomplishments to later ages. Historical generalization apostrophizes an age, setting forth its emphases and directions; but it cannot report with accuracy the daily life which textured and gave relief to what men actually thought and felt. Systems of historical tagging, at best mnemonic devices, are useless to the historian, particularly to the historian of Christianity or Judaism! To lay the history of Judaism over the history of the West in the hope that it will fit is vain exertion and profitless history. It assumes that the intellectual history of Judaism and the development of European thought pass through identical stages. It assumes moreover that the history of Israel is similar to the history of the nations of the world. The first assumption is rendered implausible by the fact that the conditions of European history were relevant to the life of the Jew only recently and then only when his Judaism had radically changed or disappeared. Marx and Freud, whatever their Jewish syndromes, reacted to conditions which the West defined, not to presuppositions which the religion and culture of Israel imposed. Jewish culture cannot be said to exist *wherever* one finds Jews (though to be sure we may learn much about how the Jew considers himself in separation from Judaism by reflecting upon the Jewish genius sundered from his Judaism). Jewish culture can be said to exist only where one finds the Jew whose Judaism is the energizing center of his life and activity. It is equally implausible for the Jew to consider his own history to be like that of the nations. The scientific historian (who has problems enough of his own) may be unable to tolerate such a metaphysical bias; but the historian of Judaism cannot interpret many of the most shocking and scandalous assumptions of the Jewish religious mind unless he acknowledges that the

Jew considered his own history to be the central event of a divine drama—a drama of covenant, sin, and purgation; a drama of divine dispersion and promised ingathering; a drama in which natural history was raised up to God and relocated within the order of providential causation.

If natural history does not supply the medium of Jewish survival, it is to sacred history that we must turn. If ours is not a history according to nature, then it must be considered as history according to God. Having affirmed this, we should nevertheless beware the sundering of all connection, indeed all intimacy and interaction, between natural and supernatural history. To determine our history according to God is not to repudiate our history according to nature. It is merely to suggest that history according to nature—separated from God—and time—independent of eternity—are insufficient. History cut off from its transcendent source and arbitration becomes either historicist phenomenalism, where all of life becomes history without the Archimedean point of judgment, or else a passionless and formal recurrence of events with which past history has already prepared and bored us.

History and the metaphysics of history are indispensable to the Jew. We need not expand upon the Greek indifference to history and the Hebraic preoccupation with history. History was meaningless to the Greek for the reason that concrete and immediate events were essentially meaningless; it was possible, as Ernst Troeltsch suggested, for the Greek to adumbrate a science of history precisely because the laws of fate (*vide* causality) were rigid, but it could not ask the question of meaning because such would be a metaphysical question inappropriate to nature and its animated presentation in history.[1] The Greek only began "providential" history when he had succeeded, paradoxically, in escaping it. He could discern meaning in his historical life, as did the Stoics, only when he had removed himself from history and affirmed his detachment and disengagement from it. But to be detached from history, to become as an object of nature, is to become unaware of time. Without the apprehension of time there can be no meaning in history. The Hebrew on the contrary could not escape time—every event that mediated divinity in time was sanctified and preserved in the historical memory.

History does not occur until selective judgments are pronounced upon the discrete events of the past. There is no history other than to him who remembers. In some sense, therefore, history is a myth of memory. The history of historians, no less than the history of metaphysicians of history, is a myth—the former more reticulated by evidence, proofs, and confirmation, the latter more dangerously patterned by ideologies and theses. The history of historians, quite as profoundly as the history of metaphysicians of history, attempts to do more than recount faithfully the phenomenal display of connected events. Both wish to elicit their own meaning, to explain why this particular past invades their present. The contemporary historian cannot prevent himself from relating the past to our present, for he is of our present and addresses us—and not as did a slightly mad German scholar of this century, who preferred to discourse to the busts of Roman emperors who ringed his study rather than to his students. The historian is always locating in the past his own fixities, his own truths, and his own eternity, for as R. G. Collingwood observed, the historian, even the historian without metaphysical interests, is only interested in self-understanding. The metaphysician of history is but a more bizarre and unavoidably pretentious synthesis of the working historian; for where the scientific historian wishes to identify a portion of the whole, to describe the hazy limits of a single moment within the flow of history, the metaphysicians of history—Augustine, Hegel, Marx—wish to locate nothing less than the meaning of all history.

The philosophy of history is, therefore, the greatest myth-making. It stands in the great tradition which begins in early Christian times with the sacramental transformation of late Jewish and Apostolic eschatology and proceeds through a neutralization and finally, in the nineteenth century, a secularization of the doctrine of the end of history. The philosophy of history is as well an asking of the most crucial of human questions: What is that whole which comprehends time and eternity, death and life, being and the perfection of being? To be preoccupied with history as such is to confront an essentially religious problem: the relation of history to God and the meaning of God in history.

Man is not a bystander of history who records the weathering of the past and observes the maturation of the future. If such be a view of history, it is one which cannot help but destroy all that is meaningful in it. Indeed, it is possible to speak of ages and times in which man was so serenely integrated into nature that time and history vanished, that history became a distortion of purity, and contemplation the most significant form of human activity. Inescapably our own concentration upon historical reality—that the past is our own past and the future our own future and memory the eternal link which defines the substance of history—is the consequence of disquiet. What the Greek called *hybris*, the sin of excessive and arrogant pride, can be read as little more than the presumption of some men that they were capable of effecting their destiny rather than submitting to their fate. As such, *hybris* was the presumption of the historical. Such presumption was not a sin to the Hebrew, but a requirement. It was a requirement because the Hebrew believed himself, his community, and his universe to have a beginning and a consummation.

Man can only have a destiny if he has a beginning which originates outside of time and an end which will transcend it. Time, we believe, is but an epoch in eternity. The false infinity of time, as Hegel describes a history without origin and fulfillment, is never broken unless time is construed as an outcropping of eternity. So viewed, history is not a succession of events in time and historical knowledge is not simply the recognition of pattern or the delight in novelty. Historical reality becomes an occasion for the spirit and the historical memory enacts the drama of eternity. In our view—and we acknowledge much in it which is painfully obscure and difficult to explain—the essential nature of God is freedom. The freedom of God is not to be understood as being the unruly and capricious option of the tyrant. The unlimited freedom of God is what gives meaning to the Biblical understanding of divine pathos and divine potency. The completeness of God is to be understood as the completeness of potency—all is possible to God, but all is not actualized. Indeed, there could be *nothing* but potency in the divine nature were eternity God's only habitation. The outpouring of God into time—in creation, revelation, and redemption—is the process of actualization. This is not to say that man is the actualization of divinity; it is only to say that man is that creature through whose life the endless richness and variety of divine possibility is realized. Time is the medium and history the substance of divine actualization.

We can only suggest—as Lurianic mysticism has done, as Jacob Boehme has done, as Nicholas Berdyaev has done—what we understand to be the incredible drama of God's life. Process within God is providence for man; unceasing actualization in God is destiny for man. We can do little more, at this moment in our thinking, than propose that our age and our aeon are but moments in eternity; that what we know as history is but an epoch in God's "history"; that our beginning and our end mean not the beginning and end of the only revelation and the only truth, but the beginning and end of the only truth which has been vouchsafed to us. Our history may not have been the first and our history may not be the last, but it is *our* history and therefore the only one with which we can be concerned.

It is foolish to speak of human destiny unless we speak of creation and consummation. This is the religious postulate of any metaphysics of history. Destiny "can exist," Berdyaev has written, "only if man is the child of God and not of the world."[2] Freedom of potency in the divine nature is freedom to good and evil in history. Only as potency is life, and eternal potency is eternal life, can we speak of God as good. Only the advent of death and corruption possesses the reality of evil. It is unimportant that the realized nature of God is as self-evident as his potency. What counts is that we *believe* the fixities of his eternal nature, but *live* in the face of his potency; that we are committed to his perfection, but pass our life in the shadow of *his* passion to consummation. We can know little or nothing of what God is in himself; we can only known what it is that God has made us and to what destiny we are appointed in the service of his freedom.

In the image of God's freedom we were created; but from God's realized perfection we are departed. This is the schism in our nature which is not present in God's. There could be no movement in our world if the freedom of God and the goodness of God were allowed to determine us. The interval which separates the beginning from the end is the interval of history in which faith makes the dead live, in which memory redeems the past and trust invests the future with novelty and hope.

Were history perfection it would be impossible to speak of incompletion, meaninglessness, waste, or distortion. History would contain its own fulfillment, its ends would be immanent in its unfolding; its process would be essentially good, even if it were obliged to press on through inadequacy to greater adequacy, through partial truth to consummate truth. Whether or not one's view of history is that of Vico or Condorcet (making reason the arbiter of progress) or Comte and Saint-Simon (viewing science and technology as the instruments of a continually self-perfecting man), the result is the same: history becomes a unity encompassing its own ends. For optimistic interpreters of history, history passes through evil to good. Good overwhelms evil as surely as reason overcomes superstition, science improves society, and technology enhances the comfort of man. In such views evil is not the foundation but the impediment of history.

It is our contention, however, that *within* history there is no meaning other than the self-illumination which the historian derives from the discernment of pattern and rhythm. Grand meaning does not exist, because grand meaning presupposes purpose and an end which uncreated and eternal history cannot allow. History becomes meaningful only when it is seen to commence and to conclude; and even though its commencement may be remote and unavailable to confirmation and its end but an image of an indefinite future, what passes between both points must be the inconclusive struggle of man to overcome the demonic. To consider the reality of evil as the foundation of history is never to say that history is evil *as such*; it is only to say that evil makes history significant, for in the evil which is possible to man our freedom and our finitude, our community with God and our estrangement from him are authenticated. We are not God's myth, but his creation; he created good and evil, said Isaiah, and we are both.

A metaphysics of history depends, therefore, for its significance upon the freedom to do evil—indeed, the reality of evil is the foundation of history.

It is in the presence of evil that we address ourselves again to the vocation and destiny of the Jews. Exile—that long and unbridged chasm which separates the Jew from his fulfillment—is a spiritual reality. To be sure, it is also a reality well founded upon the history and conduct of the nations. It is a spiritual reality of enormous importance, because it accords perfectly with that particular "freedom to evil" which is appropriate to the Jew. What the sin of Adam was to every man, the Exile of the Holy Spirit, the Exile of the community of Israel, the Exile of the faithful remnant of Zion, is to the Jew. The special destiny of the Jew is to witness to the evil which man does, not alone to the individual, but to providence. The election of Israel—that remarkable instance of God's unceasing pursuit of consummation—is degraded by the Exile of Israel; the good action of God is offset by the freedom to do evil which is at the root of history.

The Exile of Israel is, in the order of spiritual history, the first moment and the advent of the true Messiah is the last. God creates, man falls; God elects, the community sins; God disperses, the nations ravish. There is no center to history, no mid-point. There are innumerable centers, partial adumbrations; but the final word is indeed a final word. There can be no penultimate finalities, such as Jesus Christ. In the order of history Jesus is one among many centers, but if he be called Christ, the Messiah, he can be called such only by those who knew not the nature of history and discovered it through him. Jesus may be Christ for the Greek, but not for the Jew. Through Him the pagan discovered what had been known to the Jews: that God is present in history, that providence riddles time with possibility, and that no moment is ever the last until the final moment has come.

The rediscovery of sacred history is the first stage in the rejuvenescence of the Jewish theology. It was known to Scripture, known to the rabbis, known throughout the Middle Ages, known indeed until the dawn of modern history; but it was lost when history was disconnected from faith and the consummation of history was abandoned through the withering of trust.

• • •

Messianism and the Consummation of Culture

Actually there can be no constructive thinking respecting history apart from culture. Since history is always the history of a people, it is reasonable that the historical event—a political movement, a style of art, a technological innovation, a scientific discovery—should be prepared by the ambience of culture. It is only possible to speak, therefore, with generality of the contours of culture, but not to fix them with finality, for culture is the latency of history, the actuality given and the possibilities implicit but unrealized.

The relation of Judaism and the Jewish people to the realities of culture has always been intimate and intense. Judaism was not matured independently of the formative and tributary cultures of the West. Judaism lived in profound and unbroken connection with the world that surrounded it, whether Near Eastern paganism, Hellenistic syncretism, Roman internationalism, pan-Islamism, or European Christianity. The Jewish people could not be sufficient to itself; its natural life was founded upon reaction and intermingling with the nations of the world. Were this condition *fact* alone it would only enable us to develop an argument based upon the historical involvement of Judaism with the West, and to define natural imperatives for the renewal of Jewish participation in the culture of the West. However, it is possible—as we have done throughout this study—to do more than adduce the compulsions of history as justification. It is not simply that Judaism can do no other than relate itself—for reasons of historical necessity, the urgencies of survival, or the requirements of ethnic pride—to the cultural life of the nations; it is rather that Judaism, theologically understood, cannot properly stand aloof from the world.

The vitality of Jewish culture is to be measured by the intensity with which it undertakes *galut* (Exile) as a cultural demand; indeed, as the living of its messianic vocation.

God witnesses the suffering of Israel, yet it is only to the natural eye of man that this suffering is suffering without purpose. The suffering is not ordained, nor, we believe, does God will our destruction. But if we are set among the nations who see themselves redeemed—whether through a God-Man or, as in the East, from the shambles of time—we are to them a mystery and a reproof. The role of Judaism, therefore, is not to create culture *as such*, but to be the critic of culture—to make culture the partial consummation of history and the anticipation of the Kingdom of God.

Culture is, we are increasingly aware, a precarious and indefinable phenomenon. As often as not culture is not discerned until it is past, until the new culture is born and the past may be accounted good or evil, productive or wasteful. The intellectual may call the culture of the moment popular and vulgar (and therefore inauthentic) and the historian who succeeds him in time may call it authentic (however popular and vulgar). The popular culture of Florence in the days of the Medicis was possibly no more exalted than the popular culture of contemporary America or England, but it is rather hard at this moment to set the prodigies and achievements of contemporary culture side by side with the culture of fifteenth-century Italy. It is our impatience to historicize that makes so many of our ventures into cultural appraisal risky; and yet such impatience is justified by the fact that our time and our history are not leisurely, that our age is covered with the veil of apocalypse and finality, and that many people—the best people of the West—are trying to locate the source of conservation and endurance.

The role of Judaism in the cultural enterprise is not different in kind from that of any other religion, although its role may be somewhat less precise and somewhat more oblique and tendentious. Any high culture—one that involves the amalgamation and fusion of well-articulated spheres of independent life and authority—results from the synthesis of different cultural traditions. It is not, as in primitive societies, the articulation of a unified whole, reflecting the penetration of primary myth into every aspect of life. In primitive society, the myth is so overwhelming as to transmute all activity into the bearer and fulfillment of the myth. The economy, the social organization, the family are all specific extrusions of myth, every aspect of life testifying to the psychic and spiritual claims of the regnant mythology. In the evolution of civilizations multiple cultural traditions are blended—not without pain to both the victor and the captive culture—independent spheres of authority are evolved, and individual and self-contained worlds of thought are refined and sustained. Where the culture succeeds, containing its diversity, the historic function of religion has been to conserve the vision toward which that unity is directed. Such societies are few and they have all declined, for the price of unity fashioned from the synthesis of discrete and individual centers of authority is that the vision is conventionalized by its conserving institutions and the rebellion of the diverse principalities of the mind and society which it once contained. The Kingdom of God on earth is always shattered when the vision is institutionalized; for the finite cannot routinize the infinite without tricking those whom it subjects, and the subjected finally rebel against the pretension of the conserving authority. It was the destiny of the medieval Church to pass and of the Holy Roman Empire to dissolve; it was the destiny of medieval Islam to decline in the face of the routinization of prophecy.

In our day the task of religion in culture is not to conserve the vision but to dislocate those who pretend to institutionalize *less* than the vision. In a disintegrating culture the task of religion is prophetic.

The paradox of God in time is always witnessed most acutely in the cultural consequences of the religious vision, for religion corrupts God when it would commit him now and forever to a single institution in time and yet it loses God when there is no institution at all through whom he speaks. This paradox drives us again to the unique vocation of Israel—neither committed nor aloof, neither rooted nor alien, neither of this world nor of any other. The Jew may stand astride time and eternity. Of needs he must! In the age of synthesis the cultural obligation of the Jew is to learn from culture that it may strengthen his prophecy, and in an age of prophecy to recapture tradition that the false prophet may not arise. So said, Judaism is the bearer of true prophets in ages of idolatrous self-sufficiency and the destroyer of false prophets in ages of dislocation.

The present obligation of religion to culture differs somewhat from its past, for the alternatives are no longer that religion either reigns or disintegrates. There is no religion; there is only religious sentiment. The real powers of our time are beyond the appeal of religion. This is, as Rosenzweig has said, the age of the Johannine gospel, which is beyond church and nation. There is no culture, as we have previously defined it; there are but the diverse authorities of society and the mind. There is profession; there is family; there are neighborhood and community; there are state, nation, and world—but there is little connection or communication between them. The spheres of authority are mute and inarticulate and, in the neutrality of the "between-sphere," the emptiness may be seen. There is neither vision nor the loss of vision; there is only ambiguity and the abyss.

The present task of the religious is neither to sustain nor to prophesy, but to begin again, to make new. It is here that Judaism is once more of the greatest importance, for Judaism has been committed neither to sustaining this world nor to prophesying the imminency of the next. Ours is the position of the "between" because we do not believe that redemption has come.

If Israel is "chosen," it is chosen for a distinguished task—to outlast the world and its temporizing solutions, to be borne up to the end of time as his alone, to strain and winnow the pride of the world, to demonstrate that the burden of this incomplete time and this imperfect history is indeed insupportable, whereas all the ideologies of this world would render them bearable, indeed good and sufficient. This is unavoidably an aristocratic mission.

The messianic view of culture is not as the Rabbi of Prague said at the moment of the coming of the pretender savior, Sabbatai Zevi: We do not believe, for the world is not yet changed. The Rabbi of Prague was an insufficient messianist and a too committed mystic. But messianism is not mysticism; it is rather historical realism. It is the urging of undespairing realism toward this world. The transformation of the world is not demonstrated by the righting of wrongs, the justification of injustice; it is only partially this, for the transformation of the world consists in more than that the wolf and the lamb shall lie down together or that war shall cease from the world. This is the social image of salvation which is true enough as far as it goes. The change in the world that comes in the wake of the Messiah is not only social change, for social change requires but the restructuring of relations, the reordering of patterns. Social change assumes that the ultimate structure of the world, its being, is essentially perfect, but that its accidental historical arrangements are awry.

God does not work social change, attend diplomatic conferences, listen to political invocations, or bother with grace at charity banquets. He does not improve good will; rather he works on a universe in which society and man participate. Society does not reject God. The individual must first turn Him out of his life. It is the insufficiency of man that he should be unable to follow after God. A man may follow after his beloved, or seek after beauty, but to follow after God is a task of infinite difficulty. This is a condition of our world—and to such a world the Messiah comes not as reformer.[3] The Jew is the "between-man," between time and eternity, between the sadness of the world and the joy of redemption. He neither believes that in this time and history has the Kingdom of God been foretasted nor does he know when it is that God appoints this time and history for redemption.[4] For this reason the Jew is not bound to the stabilities of the world: he can create in ages when others would destroy and destroy in ages where others create—for he is the leaven of history. And this, we would think, is the messianic relation of the Jew to culture.

Notes

1. Clearly this is a partial statement of the Greek view of history. If we were to undertake a more thorough treatment many refinements would emerge. It is true, however, that for Greek philosophy history was but an instructor of the natural fatality of events. History demonstrated only the limits of human power. It set the limit to expectation. It could not open the prospect of a transcendence acceptable to the gods, because man, nature, and the gods were all in competition and the gods invariably won. The Stoics were wise to counsel calm, serenity, and indifference.
2. Nicholas Berdyaev, *The Meaning of History*, trans. by George Reavey (London, Geoffrey Bles, 1936), p. 77.
3. Indeed, the acute and critical disease from which Jewish messianic thinking suffers is that it has not perceived the enormous relevance which Rudolf Bultmann's demythologizing of Christianity has for Judaism. Jewish messianic thinking is beclouded by ethnic mythologies—the national restoration of Zion, the political rejuvenation of Israel, the punishing of the persecutors of the Jews, the miraculous return of all Jews to the Holy Land. Only if these limiting mythological conceptions are abandoned is it possible to discern what prophetic and rabbinic messianism really stands for—namely, the completion of one order of time and history and the inauguration of another. The regnancy of Israel is but a mythological symbol of a metaphysical transformation; for if the spiritual kingdom of the world is built again, that kingdom shall be the kingdom of the Jewish spirit.
4. See a variety of the author's essays dealing with various aspects of the problem of messianism and the Jewish attitude toward Christian affirmation: "The Encounter of Judaism and Christendom," *Cross Currents*, Vol. I, No. 3 (Spring, 1951), pp. 91–95; "Messianism and the Jew," *Commonweal*, Vol. LXII, No. 15 (1955), pp. 367–69; "Moses, Mystery, and Jesus," *The Jewish Frontier*, Vol. XXIII, No. 6 (June, 1956), pp. 24–28; "Three We Have Lost: The Problem of Conversion," *Conservative Judaism*, Vol. XI, No. 4 (1957), pp. 7–19; "Semite According to the Flesh," *The Christian Century*, Vol. LXXIV, No. 38 (Sept. 18, 1957), pp. 1097–89; "The Jewish-Christian Contradiction," *Worldview*, Vol. 1, No. 2 (1958), pp. 3–5; "The Natural and the Supernatural Jew," in Philip Scharper, ed., *American Catholics: A Protestant-Jewish View* (New York, Sheed & Ward, 1959), pp. 127–57.

18

On Jewish Eschatology

STEVEN SCHWARZSCHILD

Introduction

Jewish eschatological doctrine was classically and canonically formulated in the last two of Maimonides' "Thirteen Principles."[1] I quote them here in their foreshortened creedal and liturgical form.[2]

> 12. I believe with full faith in the coming of the Messiah, and, though he tarry, I anticipate him, nonetheless, on every day, when he may come.
> 13. I believe with full faith that there will be a resurrection of the dead at the time that the Creator, may His name be blessed, wills it . . .

A limited explication of these two principles will launch us on our outline of classical Jewish eschatological teachings as a whole.

Messianism

First of all, it is, of course, clear (however wide the ignorance of this in non-Jewish and often even Jewish circles) that classical Judaism authoritatively teaches both Messianism and resurrection. Secondly, as far as this formulation of Messianism is concerned, four points of detail deserve notice. One is fairly obvious—namely, that on Jewish teaching the Messiah has not yet come. Indeed, since the Jews of all generations recite the Maimonidean credo every day of their lives,[3] as will those of all future generations, the logic of this formulation entails that—if one may put it like this—the Messiah will al-

Steven Schwarzschild, "On Jewish Eschatology," in *The Human Condition in the Jewish and Christian Traditions*, F. Greenspahn, ed. (New York: Ktav, 1986), pp. 171–211. © Ktav Publishing House, Hoboken, NJ 07030.

ways not yet have come, into all historical eternity. It is his coming, or rather the expectation of his coming, not his arrival, his "advent," that is obligatory Jewish faith. In Maimonides' own words, "Set no time limit to his coming!"[4] (Isaac Abrabanel even makes an argument against Maimonides out of this: a "principle of the faith" would have to be nontemporally true, once the Messiah has come one would no longer "believe" in and "anticipate" his coming; *ergo* . . .)[5]

This leads straight into the strikingly unusual phrasing of the last part of the twelfth principle, taken from Habakkuk 2:3: "*achakeh lo bechol yom sheyavo.*"[6] This is usually translated to the effect that "I will await him on any day on which he may come." But the Hebrew is at best awkward if this is to be the sense of it—namely, that we do not know on which particular day he may come, and we must, therefore, be ready for him, as it were, on any day. The wording does not lend itself to this explication. What the text says is not that the Messiah may come on any day but that he does come, conditionally, on every day, on all days. Into all eternity the Messiah comes, conditionally, on every day.[7] "As sustenance comes every day, so does redemption come every day."[8]

The significance of this conception is well caught in the talmudic *aggadeta*, that Rabbi Joshua ben Levi found the Messiah sitting at the gates of Rome, constantly rebinding his wounds, and asked him when he would "come." The Messiah answered: "Today" (*hayom*, lit. "the day").[9] Joshua was flabbergasted at this apparent and extreme adventism, so the son of David explained: "Today—if ye keep God's commandments" [i.e., if all of you transform into actuality all of God's will for the world—this is, or this causes, the Messianic advent).[10]

We can thus also better understand the verb in the imperfect tense—*achakeh*. It is usually translated as "await," but there are several Hebrew terms for this notion. *Lechakkot* is different from, to use the colloquialism, "sitting on one's backside and awaiting developments." It is a very active verb without any quietistic connotations. When one *mechakkeh*, one is doing something very energetically. Compare it to a runner in the starting position of a sprint: he is not running yet; he looks stationary; in fact, however, all his muscles and nerves are highly tensed, so that he can get the fastest possible start the second the gun sounds. "Anticipate," therefore, perhaps comes closest in English to the meaning of the term—anticipate actively and joyfully, the way one makes practical and emotional preparations for the return of a wife who has been away on a long trip, or, in the words of Maimonides, describing the practice of omer, "as is done by one who waits for the coming of the human being that he loves best and counts the days and the hours."[11]

Finally, still dealing with vocabulary, this is, of course, also the strong implication of the introductory phrase to every one of the Thirteen Principles—'*ani ma'ameen be'emunah shlemah*. In English we cannot readily say, "I believe with full belief," or "I have faith with full faith," but this is exactly what the Hebrew does here. "Full" might, in any case, be better rendered as "integral" or something like that. Above all, as Martin Buber taught our age, *emunah* is different from *pistis*.[12] Buber tends to translate it as "trust," rather than "belief" or "faith"; "active interaction between at least two parties" might be a somewhat fuller rendering of the notion in English.

How could we then best, though also somewhat circumlocutorily, translate the meaning of the twelfth principle? "I am totally and actively committed to the postulate of the coming of the Messiah; and, although he will always delay his coming, I will always bend every effort to prepare his coming, for he is on the way on every day into eternity." The religious power of such a proposition was once again, and unforgettably, demonstrated when the Jews in the ghettos, concentration camps, and extermination camps, in Warsaw and among the partisans and the survivors, made Maimonides' twelfth principle their universal anthem.[13]

We ought to dwell for another moment on my earlier assertion that, Jewishly, the Messiah not only has not come but also will never have come—that he will always be coming. This is, to be sure, a radical assertion. It must scandalize Christians, for it flies in the face of the central Christian theologumenon that the Messiah has, in fact, come—at least the first time.[14] (I am leaving aside the even more fundamental deification of the person of the Messiah.) The eternal futurity of the Messiah, translated into operational language, asserts that no smallest time-unit nor any smallest space-unit in the universe is as yet, or will ever have been, redeemed. Indeed, what is asserted is that the universe is always infinitely different from what God wants it to be and what we must, therefore, make it, insofar as this lies within and perhaps beyond our power.

But my radical assertion also scandalizes most Jews. Popularly it is believed by most Jews that, though the Messiah has not yet come, one day, "at the end of days" (better actually: *be'acharit hayamim*—i.e., "in the after-time"), he will have come. In what I daresay was the classical controversy of our century on this score, Franz Rosenzweig had a bit of an argument with Hermann Cohen. Cohen formulated, philosophically and religiously, the doctrine of the eternal delay of the advent.[15] Rosenzweig asserted, to the contrary, that anything that happens in eternity never happens,[16] and, in a beautiful commentary to a Messianic poem by R. Yehudah HaLevy he said that all humanity (or at least all Jews) can be divided into those who have more faith than they have hope, who always figure that very shortly the Messiah will have come; and those who have more hope than they have faith, who always figure that the end-time is still far away.[17] Up to now, says Rosenzweig, the latter have always been right. But someday, on "the day," they will be wrong. Therefore, be very watchful!

Rosenzweig, despite the persuasiveness of the poetic imagination which he shared with R. Yehudah HaLevy, was, I think, wrong. The eternity of the pre-Messianic "interim" is necessary, as Cohen rightly recognized, for at least two reasons: it prevents the mythologization to which, above all, Christianity has fallen prey, of any man or all men ever deifying themselves, and it makes humanity's ethical (and, indeed, scientific) tasks not an interim obligation but a perpetual (if you please, metaphysical) destiny.

Permit me a piece of metahistorical speculation. An entrenched characteristic of very many Christian millenarian movements has always been celibacy; after all, the end is near, and to have children under such circumstances is at best de trop. I know of not a single Jewish counterpart to this![18] History is simply not expected to terminate.

The eternal moral striving that is produced by the eternal delay of the Messianic advent can be deftly summarized here in two ways. Akiba Ernst Simon has written: "After having always again said our no to every claim of redemption that has been proffered to us, we have gone on our long way, the Law on our shoulders and backs, thus remaining with that beloved and endured burden in an unredeemed world—the unredeemed people of redemption and witness of its coming."[19] Nora Levin's full title tells the same story: *While Messiah Tarried: Jewish Socialist Movements 1871–1917.*[20]

Resurrection

Let us move on to the last of Maimonides' principles.[21] The most notable feature of the creedal formulation of the doctrine of resurrection is that it concentrates exclusively on the divine act of volition that is to bring it about. This is also entirely in keeping with Maimonides' own systematic teaching. We must, then, take a glance at his way of handling the tenet of resurrection.

The Thirteen Principles were, as is well known, formulated by Maimonides at the end of the introduction to his commentary to chapter 10/11 (*perek chelek*) of the Mishnah's tractate *Sanhedrin*. This was early in his career (1168). The purpose of formulating such a credo (revolutionary as such an act was at the time and has remained in Judaism)[22] was to make it possible for *hoi polloi* to hold the beliefs which are actually the conclusions of highly sophisticated and esoteric philosophic studies but which are *heilsnotwendig*, i.e., salvifically prerequisite to the (Neoplatonic/Aristotelian) "conjunction" of the human "acquired intellect" with the divine "active intellect," through which alone immortality is achieved.[23] There is thus so early in the exfoliation of Maimonides' systematic views a strikingly paradoxical relationship between the doctrine of resurrection and the doctrine of immortality: you have to believe in resurrection in order to achieve immortality. Curious as such a philosophical tenet may be, it is in fact an entirely accurate restatement of the Mishnaic text which he is here expositing—that anyone who does not believe in the resurrection of the dead, or who, while believing it, does not believe that it is a biblical doctrine,[24] fails to achieve immortality (his "share in the world to come").

In his magnum opus, the *Guide for the Perplexed*, Maimonides never even broaches the doctrine of resurrection. (Thus, immortality is not mentioned in the Thirteen Principles, his popular exposition, and resurrection is not mentioned in the *Guide*, his technical exposition.) This is, however, in no way incompatible with the position we have seen him take in his *Commentary to the Mishnah*, for not talking about resurrection does not, of course, necessarily imply not believing in it, and, in any case, we have seen that for him resurrection, or at least belief in resurrection, is a propaedeutic to immortality. With immortality, in the sense in which we have earlier seen him define it, he does deal in the *Guide*.[25]

Nevertheless, Maimonides had a lot of troubles with his contemporaries.[26] He was accused of heresy for not teaching resurrection. A formal inquiry sent to him became the occasion for his writing the *Treatise on Resurrection*. Here he made his position quite clear, though he gave away nothing either stylistically or substantively. On the one hand, he publicly affirmed belief in resurrection. On the other hand, he made a theological move which is rarely paid attention to: he stipulated two immortalities—the first, between a person's death and his resurrection, and the second, after the death of the resurrected body, for eternity. In other words, resurrection is still an intermediate stage toward immortality.[27]

It must be kept in mind that the problem we are looking at is not one concocted by the high scholasticism of Maimonides. Maimonides here, as almost always, correctly formulates authentic, classic, rabbinic doctrine.[28] The paramount liturgy, the Eighteen Benedictions, recited three times a day by the Jew, dates back to the mishnaic era and always includes the second benediction: "Thou art mighty forever, O Lord—resurrecting the dead. Thou art great to save. Thou sustainest life with grace, resurrectest the dead with great mercy . . . and He upholdeth His faithfulness to those who sleep in the dust. Who is like unto Thee, Lord of might. . . . the King who resurrecteth the dead and maketh salvation sprout . . . Thou art trusty to resurrect the dead. Praised be Thou, O Lord, who resurrecteth the dead." The "first comprehensive Talmud commentary," by R. Chananel b. Chusiel (d. after 1053), already stipulated belief in the Messiah and in the world to come as "great foundations" (*pinnot*).[29] Clearly here, too, the theological emphasis is placed on the proposition that resurrection is not the result of some kind of natural or divine or even ethical law but that it is a matter of gratuitous, "gracious," beneficence by God. This is the reason that statements about resurrection are always collocated with references to divine power, mercy, and grace (*chesed verachamim*) in relevant Jewish texts.[30]

What in the religious texts is called divine grace is what Maimonides calls God's "will."[31] Such philosophical rather than theological language permits Maimonides to follow an extremely sophisticated set of moves: in the first place, "divine will" may justly be taken to mean, as the rabbis intended, a stipulation beyond natural, rational law; in the second place, however, the cognoscenti will understand that ultimately "will," too, is rationalized by Maimonides: it implies the scholastic identity of will and intellect in the deity, and thus it comes to mean what Kant later was to call "the primacy of practical reason." (This is why Maimonides systematically rejects all miraculous claims, even those in the Bible and the Sinaitic revelation itself, while maintaining the possibility of miracles—as a formulation of the ultimacy of "will" = ethics in the universe.) In other words, Maimonides wants to hold on to both horns of the dilemma: physical existence in any form is bound to be finite and perishable (thus mortal), but it is also prerequisite to infinite, human, moral striving (thus postulatorily resurrectable); he, therefore, teaches a first temporary resurrection on earth and a second resurrection in the "spiritual body" toward and into eternity (which is really indistinguishable from personal immortality).[32] Also in his legal *Code* (intermediate between his *Commentary to the Mishnah* and his *Guide*) he actually implies precisely this doctrine in the climactic last paragraph: in the Messianic age all humanity (Jews and Gentiles, those then living as well as those then resurrected) will live lengthily and in material comfort—thus enabled to study Torah thoroughly and able to achieve the *conjunctio*: "In those days perfection will be widespread, with the result that men will merit the life of the world to come."[33] And a few paragraphs earlier Maimonides declares: "People should never busy themselves with the legends or expatiate on the *midrashim* that deal with these matters [details of the Messianic age] and similar things, and they should not regard them as fundamental, for they engender neither awe nor love" (the two basic religious categories of Maimonides).[34] The last phrase states categorically that, according to Maimonides, eschatology is to be done exclusively as a function of its human heuristics.

Clearly, we find ourselves, via Maimonides, in the very eye of the storm that continues to rage to this day about the dichotomy between the biblical/Jewish doctrine of resurrection versus the Greek doctrine of immortality.[35]

A careful survey of the history of Jewish eschatology would make it clear, I believe, that such controversies, both before and in Maimonides' time as well as in our own, are due to a perennial failure to do with this subject what Maimonides did do with, for example, the subject of divine attributes (anthropomorphism, etc.)[36]—rigorous linguistic analysis of the terminology of Jewish eschatology (e.g., *olam haba* ["the coming world"], *atid lavo* ["the future to come"], *acharit hayamim* ["the after-time"], *ge'ulah* ["redemption"], *yeshu'ah* ["salvation," "help"], *yemot hamashiach* ["the days of the Messiah"], *malchut shamayim* ["the kingdom of heaven"], etc.), followed by conceptual reconstruction based on such linguistic analysis,[37] but what he did only more spottily in the Code with respect to the eschatological vocabulary.[38] What is needed is, in Karl Rahner's phrase, a thorough "hermeneutics of eschatological assertions."[39] I can here only summarize, even in diagrammatic form, what the result of such an unpacking would be.

Man exists in the material world. By ethicizing his life, he incrementally "spiritual-izes" himself and thus approaches the (ethical) spirituality of God's world ("the coming world"), which always exists and "comes" to man.[40] He cannot, however, actually attain that infinite (infinitely moral, spiritual) world in the material world by himself. Therefore, at the end of an individual's lifetime his infinite human potential ("soul") is eternalized— on a number of conditions: God's gracious will, whether he or she is a Jew ("All Israel have a share in the world-to come"),[41] or whether he or she is a "righteous non-Jew" ("All the righteous of the nations of the world have a share in the world to come"),[42] etc. That is what is called "immortality." The striving toward total human morality on earth ("the Messianic kingdom") continues beyond any and all individual human lives: this is what we call "history," and it consists of the infinite and, therefore, never-completed spiritual-ization of the human universe. The regulatively postulated completion of that infinite his-torical process of spiritualization is what is called "the coming of the Messiah."[43] At this point a new kind of history ensues—call it posthistorical history or intra-Messianic his-tory or, with Karl Marx, human instead of zoological history: all sorts of things continue to happen (the wars of Gog and Magog, other Messianic events, the reinstitution of the purified Law and what it provides for, etc.).[44] We are then here talking about something far different from an undifferentiated "eternity." By the —per impossibile (hypothetical)— time that all of these intra-Messianic events have taken place, the dichotomy between mat-ter and spirit, body and soul will be dissolved (i.e., the soul is body and the body is soul). Men will be "spiritual bodies" or "quasi-physical souls" (*gufot ruchaniyot*—cf. Paul's *soma pneumatikos*)[45]—and this is what is called "resurrection."[46] (Up to this time, i.e., until after both "normal history" and post-Messianic history are consummated, only the immortality of the soul, not [contra fundamental Christian doctrine] a single resurrection,

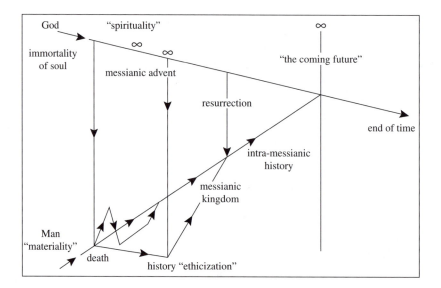

obtains).[47] At this (regulatively) final point God's world to come will, in "the coming future," indeed, have come, even as the immortal souls and the resurrected bodies will be of the same nature. Saadia Gaon thus held that during the four hundred to five hundred years that the Messianic kingdom would last, men would so spiritualize themselves that, without having to die again, they would slip into the eternal world to come.[48]

Of course, all of this is a radically tenuous synthesis between resurrection and immortality. It could not be maintained indefinitely. Ex-Christian Marranos like Uriel d'Acosta and Spinoza rejected all resurrection together with Christianity and, therefore, subsequently also Judaism. For them religious truth was totally rational and thus excluded all "positivity"—not only history but also temporality as such: the end time is the same as present time. What could be aspired to was, then, what the medievals had called *conjunctio*, the absorption of the rational individual within the infinity of the divine substance. (Though it must be remembered that for Spinoza that substance is both thought and extension = soul and body, and "immortality" is, therefore, for him not totally immaterial.)[49] Under the impact of both Spinoza and Leibniz, Moses Mendelssohn, the first great exponent of Jewish thought under the impact of modernism, then expounded a peculiarly ambivalent conception. His metaphysical rationalism discerned an injustice in the belief that people who happened to live later, say in the Messianic age, should be better off than those who lived earlier, regardless of their moral deserts (as his friend Lessing's conception of history as the education of the human race implied),[50] and he, therefore, sloughed off the Jewish commitment to Messianic progress, resurrection, etc., adding to his translation of Maimonides' Thirteen Principles, among others, the principle of immortality.[51] On the other hand, his Leibnizian monadology let him claim that the immortal soul would have some "quasi-body."[52] After Kant in particular, such ambiguities were bound to fall apart, and thus Jewish religious "liberalism" in the nineteenth and twentieth centuries discarded resurrection in favor of immortality on allegedly scientific and rationalistic grounds.

My own view, for what it is worth, is that Maimonides was, as usual, wiser than modernity. I would want to argue that we require the doctrine of resurrection, therewith to assert what is nowadays called the psychosomatic unity, or the embodied-soul/ensouled-body, of the human individual and the infinite ethical tasks incumbent on him or her. (Some current philosophical argument to the effect that spatiotemporal continuity is prerequisite to personal identity reaffirms the traditional affirmation of "quasi-physical" immortality for the purpose of justifying resurrection.)[53] Individual rights as well as duties follow from such "supernatural," i.e., absolute, status: the *Halacha* of respect for human beings is enshrined in the laws of respect for corpses.[54] This is why and how Kant also stipulated what he still (wrongly, by his own standards) called "immortality" in the First and Second *Critiques*. Like Kant, we, too, cannot derive any metaphysical asseverations from such regulative, functional reasons for the belief in resurrection. If we want, religiously, to make such assertions, we have to make them as *theologumenoi* (thus returning to the rabbinic proclamation of God's power and grace as its ground),[55] while philosophically limiting ourselves to regulative, ethical explanations.

Even within the limits of philosophical regulativity we can go a bit further, though. When speaking of the world of resurrection, we are implying some sort of materiality on two scores—that "world" itself and the "spiritual" bodies of the resurrected. Each of these instances of "bodily-ness" is, however, to be taken, even terminologically (in the hermeneutics of eschatology) as strongly homonymic. Whether *olam haba* ("the *world* to come") is to be taken spatially as "world" or temporally as "aeon" needs to be analyzed.

By the same token, whether "spiritual body" is to be understood as a body whose substance is spirit (whatever this might mean) or as an entity which acts "spiritually," i.e., morally, also ought to be analyzed. (Consider the transformation of the very notion of "substance" into that of "function" in Ernst Cassirer's book by that title.)[56] In both instances, bodily-ness is translated into terms of "action in time." Thus the regulativity of the entire doctrine is put in the brightest light, and "life eternal" (life always in the "now") is seen to be a quasi-temporal, not a quasi-spatial, conception.

At least two of the most sophisticated philosophical, neoMarxist, and atheist intellectuals of the last generation arrived at precisely our conclusion. J.-P. Sartre ended his life with an interview by Benny Lévy in which he practically declared himself (justly) an honorary Jew and specifically expressed endorsement of the doctrine of resurrection as part of Jewish messianism.[57] And Theodor W. Adorno, in an extraordinarily impressive while typically sophisticated passage in *Negative Dialectic*, sums up our point in the sentence: "Hope clings, as in Mignon's song, to the transfigured body."[58]

Eschatology as Ethics

The two eschatological doctrines, Messianism and resurrection, have all along been seen to interjibe. "Will" has turned out to be the central word and concept that underlies them both. The creedal formulation of the thirteenth principle turned on it explicitly (resurrection as an act of divine will), and the eternal futurity of the Messianic advent (which entails the resurrection) has for its purpose the activation of the human will (as "the image of the similarity of God's structure")[59] in the form of the moralization of the (human) universe. (The fact is that, as we have seen, the [regulative] realization of morality is identical with the resurrection.) "Will" is short for "rational will," and "rational will" is, for Maimonides and Jewish philosophy in general as it is for Kant, another way of saying "morality."[60] In brief, Jewish eschatology is the metaphysical as well as ethical absolutization of morality.

Eschatology as a fundamental operator in ethical discourse calls for some, however limited, further unpacking.[61] Messianism as an ethical operator simply declares that, since humanity is to strive to imitate God and thus to endeavor to become like Him, and since they are to undertake these efforts in this world, the ultimate goal of ethics is to establish what is then called "the (Messianic) kingdom of God" on earth. This is, of course, an infinite goal, infinitely (or as Kant and H. Cohen like to say, asymptotically) to be approached. Far from implying a bracketing of Messianism ("utopianism"), as irrelevant to the daily, historical occurrences of moral problems (i.e., a postponement *ad calendas Graecas*), Messianism in fact operates, therefore, as a direct producer of moral values and as an intermediate criterion of proper action in any and every situation. When men ask themselves how to behave or, indeed, what the standards are to be of their proper behavior, the Messianic end defines the means by which that end can and is to be attained. (This is the point of Kant's *Religion Within the Bounds of Reason Alone*). As Solomon Schechter put it by way of example: "If the disappearance of poverty and suffering is a condition of the Kingdom of the Messiah, or, in other words, of the Kingdom of God, all wise social legislation in this respect must help toward its speedy advent."[62]

Here once again the avant-garde of *contemporary* technical philosophy is trying to catch up as best it can with the entrenched methodologies of Jewish culture (and of

Hermann Cohen's Judaistic neo-Kantianism). G.H.v. Wright, in stipulated agreement with Jaakko Hintikka, defines deontic logic as "the study of logical relations in deontically perfect worlds . . . concerned with logical relations between the ideal states the descriptions of which are implicit in norms," and norms " 'bridge the gap' between Is and Ought."[63] *Ethics* in turn is the producer of such norms.[64]

Halacha is then the formalization of the required actions which will take mankind from where we are to where we ought to get—"to 'bridge the gap' between Is and Ought." At this point of the analysis one would have to go into the complexities of Halachic jurisprudence. One of them I will explicate to some extent shortly, namely: does Jewish law enjoin us to act entirely in accord with perfectionist Messianic values or incrementally with the goal of Messianism in view? To mention only two others: what is the notion of a "Messianic Torah," and how does it relate to "the Torah in our hands"?[65] Secondly, what is the status—more importantly, what, if anything, is the function—of *hilcheta dimeshicha*?[66] But these are complicated, technical issues that we cannot go into here. Suffice it to recall the large number of laws that are explicitly defined as possessing Messianic functions: "he who quotes something in the name of its author brings redemption";[67] if Israel observed two Sabbaths, or only one Sabbath, or anyone one of a number of other commandments, just once perfectly—if Israel repented properly only one day[68]—the Messiah would come,[69] etc. The principle of the matter is "to bring near the end" (*lekarev et haketz*). "Great is justice, for it brings redemption near."[70] And the entire complex subject of "*Messianic Halacha*" arrives at the bottom line that it may be dealt with only insofar as currently actionable consequences flow from it.[71] Martin Buber once put it like this: "A drop of Messianic consummation must be mingled with every hour; otherwise the hour is godless, despite all piety and devoutness."[72] All this can be reduced to the formula that Judaism is actionable Messianism.[73]

The theoretical ("aggadic") substructure of the Halachic function of Messianism was paradigmatically formulated in a midrashic passage that is worth quoting at length (and which stands far from alone).

> "There is no God like Jeshurun. who rides the heavens for your help" [Deut. 33:26]: Who, indeed, is like God? Jeshurun—the goodly and praiseworthy ones among you. Said Rabbi Berachya in the name of Rabbi Judah b. R. Simon, who said: "You will find that everything that the Holy One, praised be He, will in the future do in the world to come He has anticipated and done through the righteous ones in this world: the Holy One, praised be He, revives the dead—and Elijah revives the dead; the Holy One, praised be He, restrains the rains and Elijah restrains the rains; the Holy One, praised be He, blesses the diminutive—and Elijah blesses the diminutive; the Holy One, praised be He, redeems the barren women—and Elijah redeems the barren women; the Holy One, praised be He, sweetens the bitter—and Elisha sweetens the bitter [2 Kings 4]; the Holy One, praised be He, sweetens the bitter by means of the bitter—and Elisha sweetens the bitter by means of the bitter" [Exodus 15 and 2 Kings 2].[74] R. Berachya in the name of R. Simon said: " 'There is none like God.' and 'who is like God?' Jeshurun,' the people of Israel, for what the Holy One, praised be He, has written about Himself, 'God is elevated by Himself [Isa. 2:11]. is also applied to Jacob: 'And Jacob remained by himself [Gen. 32:25].[75]

The Talmudic *midrash* reports:

> Rabban Gamliel sat and taught: "Woman is destined [in the Messianic time] to give birth every day, as it is written [Jer. 31:7]: 'She shall conceive and immediately bear

child.' " But a certain disciple scoffed at him, quoting Eccles. 1:9: "There is absolutely nothing new under the sun." Rabban Gamliel replied: "Come, and I will show you an example of this in this world." He went out and showed him a hen. Again R. Gamliel sat and taught: "Trees are destined [in the Messianic age] to yield fruit every day, as it is written [Ezek. 17:23]: 'And it shall bring forth twigs and bear fruit': just as there are twigs every day so shall there be fruit every day." But that pupil scoffed at him, saying: "It is written: 'There is absolutely nothing new under the sun.' " R. Gamliel replied: "Come, and I will show you an example of this in this world." He went out and showed him a caper bush. Again R. Gamliel sat and taught: "The Land of Israel is destined [in the Messianic time] to bring forth Lesbian cakes [a pastry] and robes of Melat [fine garments], as it is written [Ps. 72:18]: 'There shall be an abundance of grain in the land.' " [There is an intricate Hebrew wordplay at work here.] But that pupil scoffed at him, saying again: "There is absolutely nothing new under the sun." R. Gamliel replied: "Come, and I will show you an example of this in this world." He went out and showed him morels and truffles, and for robes of Melat he showed him the bark of a young palm tree.[76]

If we may interpret just briefly, Rabban Gamliel clearly expounds the following: the Messianic society is one of universal economic abundance; this will constitute a real novum, a miracle, a qualitative, revolutionary leap. To those who claim that "there are absolutely no nova in the world," he points out that the whole real, even pre-Messianic, world consists, naturally, of nova: life and nature, as over against the inanimate world, are indeed characterized by constant novelty. The whole passage occurs in the context of a polemic against the somewhat Hellenistic book of Ecclesiastes and is part of an extended affirmation of the special nature of human life.[77]

The Messianic doctrine has produced one of the perennial splits in the ethical (and general) outlook of Judaism. One of the entrenched interpretations of the schism between Hillel and Shammai is that the latter's rigorism legislates that people must completely act today as they will in Messianic times, whereas Hillel's leniency formulates the accommodations which people are forced to make under prevailing circumstances in their incremental approximations of the kingdom of God. (Thus it can be true that "these and those are the words of the living God.")[78] One of the counterintuitive results of that interpretation is that ethical rigorism, *mishnat hassidut*—"supererogatory morality," *lifnin mishurat hadin*—"acting within the line of the law" (i.e., not beyond its widest circumference but in its deepest core), etc.,[79] are manifestations of the stern Shammaite spirit, not first or foremost of the humane Hillelite spirit, although also the danger of premature Messianism is thereby run.

This split with regard to the enactment of Messianism in history can be shown to be operative generally in Jewish history and ideology, not excluding the present: one view is that the only, or the best, way in which the universal rule of the Messiah can be established is in situation A to bring about totally Messianic conditions, then to do the same thing in situation B, etc., until the whole world "is filled with the spirit of God as the waters cover the sea" (i.e., to turn every local moral situation into a forward bastion of Messianic conquest), while the other view is that the only, or the usual, practical way of bringing about "the kingdom" is to make situation A a little more Messianic today, even more Messianic tomorrow, etc., to do the same with situation B, etc., until the same result is achieved.

There are many further intra-Messianic problematics: How is the advent to be calculated (if at all)? Is that advent in time or beyond time/history (i.e., in "eternity")? Is there an intra-Messianic, extrahistorical time? And so on. All these apparently metaphysical, eschatological questions can be shown, by dint of "the Jewish twist," to have ethical and even moral functions.[80]

In the *midrashim* quoted at some length above, the function of Messianism slides almost imperceptibly into the ethical function of the doctrine of the resurrection. In the latter the ethical question is raised: What is immortal life like, and how must I act in this life if I am to approximate immortal life as much as possible? (Compare Kant on immortality in the First and Second *Critiques*.) Now, eternal life is, of course, so totally nonempirical that the rabbis could have dogmatically stipulated anything whatever for it without fear of refutation. That they described it in only certain ways implies that these ways are ethically desirable, imitatable ways. For example, perfect justice obtains in the world of eternity. When our earthbound notions and experiences of justice conflict with that perfect justice, we have strong reasons to puzzle, and puzzling values are very weak models for imitation—or none at all.[81] For another example, resurrection is denied to usurers.[82] Z. Shapiro uses the revelation at Sinai as an historical instantiation of resurrection: in both instances men die, in order literally(?) to be resurrected by and in divine truth.[83] As a result the chief classical texts in Jewish ethical (*musar*) literature are built on *M. Sota* 9:15, that morality leads to goodness, goodness leads to holiness, holiness to the holy spirit, and the holy spirit to resurrection.[84]

The function of the Messianic doctrine in Jewish ethics is to be clearly distinguished, I think, from what has come to be called "eschatological verification" in philosophy of religion in our time.[85] The difference resides, it seems, in the following.

"Eschatological verification"—developed from positivism via "analysis"—stipulates the verification of theological statements by some experiential, i.e., in the Kantian sense "sensuous," or at least by some (whatever that might mean) "quasi-sensuous," criterion in the "afterlife"; therefore, the entities referred to, "God," "the personal individual," etc., would have to be sensuous, i.e., material, or at least quasi-material, entities. If, on the other hand, one holds that "the world to come" and all that this comprises are totally immaterial, then (a) such verification is by definition impossible, and (b) to people who accept the notion of such "eschatological verification" is applicable what Maimonides said about ignorant and foolish Moslems who expect a material afterlife.[86]

The eschatological doctrine, as here used, says something else. To use the Kantian distinction, we are making statements that are synthetic a prioris—i.e., they are judgments which cannot themselves be empirically verified but which are, in the first place, logically, analytically true, and which also, as regulatives, make other statements that are a posteriori, synthetically, empirically true logically possible. In other words, we are dealing with "transcendentals" or with "possible-worlds theorizing." Thus, here, statements about life in the Messianic era or in the world to come are not logically self-contradictory or morally counterproductive and, in addition, produce this-worldly ethical injunctions which can both function empirically and be approved of morally.

In our analysis of Jewish eschatology we have hitherto concentrated on its human, ethical significance. This is proper, but it is, of course, also one-sided. It will be remembered that in our diagram the arrows of action go in two directions—one upward set, representing human, moral striving, and the other set downward (the acts of bestowing immortality, sending the Messiah, bringing about resurrection, etc.—all of which are summarized under the theological conception of "grace"), representing divine activities; and it is the dialectical interaction of these two sets of movements in their totality which, alone, leads to the *eschaton*. Thus, humanity and its morality are a necessary but not a sufficient condition for the attainment of the life of the world to come (what Emil Brunner, in Christian terms, called *Anknuepfungspunkte*—i.e., human occasions which God requires for the bestowal of grace), and, by the same token, God's work is a necessary but, for ethical reasons, not in turn a sufficient condition.

This sounds like the extraethical, theological, dimension of Jewish eschatology. It is that. But even this extraethical dimension can be shown, in the hermeneutics of Jewish eschatological assertions, to be of pervasively ethical significance.

It should be noted, in the first place, that all human striving in our diagram—individual life, history, even the Messianic kingdom—is finally consummated by divine action. This is logically necessary once that striving is seen to be a divine norm—divine norms are, by definition, infinite—and human beings cannot, of course, either individually or collectively, attain infinite goals. Thus, "grace" here means: do more, for you have never done enough![87] In the second place, even finite, inadequate, human morality is held to be impossible without divine grace. We are all inextricably and totally embroiled in the necessities of nature—the struggle for survival, the physical and social forces that make us what we are. How then can even one individual, not to speak of a group of individuals (however small), lift itself by its own bootstraps out of that morass?[88]

The paradigm of the indispensability of divine grace for the enactment of even very limited acts of human morality is taken from the Bible, but typically enshrined in the Jewish liturgy. Thus, before the Jew begins to recite the Eighteen Benedictions every day, he silently prays Psalm 51:17: "O Lord, open Thou my lips, so that my mouth may speak Thy praise."[89] In other words, the one smallest thing that it would appear man can do by himself, namely utter God's praises and ask for His help (the mere activity of making sounds)—even this he cannot do without prevenient grace. Or the liturgy often uses Lamentations 5:21 (and its repetition after v. 22 as the conclusion of the book): "Return Thou us, O God, so that we may [be able to] return; create our days anew as Thou didst create them newly at the outset." "Return" here is the Hebrew term *teshuvah*, usually translated as "repentance." It does mean "repentance" in the narrower sense, but more widely it means "humanly initiated, autonomous, i.e., moral action, *praxis*," of which "repentance" is then only one, though the most characteristic, instantiation. Here again, then, the one human activity which, by its very definition, must be humanly initiated turns out to require prevenient divine grace. This is the point of the extended classical debate between R. Eliezer and R. Joshua as to whether "repentance" (moral action) or God's grace will bring redemption;[90] as Emmanual Levinas points out, the debate remains dialectically open-ended at its conclusion.[91]

Of course, the dialectic of this type of situation is endlessly complex. If I have to pray to be divinely moved to pray and yet I cannot pray until God has moved me to pray, the He and I are in a classical "Mexican stand-off"; neither of us can move until the other has moved first—and nothing can happen. The very fact that these stand-off situations occur in obligatory liturgical contexts throws the first move to the human side: logically I can't pray;[92] I just do. I drop out of the logical situation by taking (moral) action; in this particular situation, I pray. The unsalvageable theological situation is transcended and salvaged by autonomous, human, moral action.[93] Emil Fackenheim put it like this: "Viewed in the light of faith, history is a dialectic of the doing of man and the doing of God. . . . In moments of grace the tension is overcome."[94] Hermann Cohen liked at this point to quote the end of Goethe's *Faust*: "The indescribable—here it is done."[95]

Human beings cannot, of course, know where the curve of their moral striving will be met by the curve of divine grace. They, therefore, have to push the only line under their (partial) control as far as, and further than, they really can. Yet the *hybris of Werkheiligkeit*, of which historic Christian theology has always accused Jewish ethicism,[96] is never even a temptation for at least two reasons. For one thing, as we have already noted, grace is held to be prerequisite for the beginning and certainly for the completion of the infinite moral enterprise. For another, we were careful in our diagram to draw the line of human history, up to the advent of the Messiah, in a number of different possible directions— upward, downward, and going every which way. Rabbinic Judaism is far from wedded to any notion of automatic or necessary progress in history. History may very well go, and (as Jews know only too well) often has gone, in regressive directions. The point is that, as the rabbis classically put it, "the son of David will come in a generation which is either totally guilty or totally innocent."[97] But, of course, for human purposes only the alternative of the "wholly innocent generation" can serve as a regulative. To strive to become a "wholly guilty generation," for the purpose of thus forcing God's hand to send the Messiah at the ultimate nadir of history, ails of a whole slew of terrible sins:[98] (1) it constitutes Sabbateanism, the worst of all Messianic heresies;[99] (2) it violates the fundamental injunction not to rely on miracles;[100] and (3) it obviously is the antithesis of ethics. Still, God's hand cannot be stopped: if and when that nadir of human, historical existence should ever, in God's judgment, have been reached—i.e., when the world has fallen so low that no self-rehabilitation is possible any longer—then God may have to take salvific action. (The descriptions of the condition of the world that would trigger such redemption from the extreme of evil are truly apocalyptic.)[101] Indeed, God's saving hand may force the end at any time that He determines—for example, as Isaac Abravanel canonically formulated this conception, by forcing Israel into an historical situation where it is constrained, rather than morally motivated, to act out the final *Anknuepfungspunkt* of the Messianic advent.[102]

The final upshot, then, of the dialectic of grace and ethics in Jewish eschatology is this: salvation may come about by works or by grace, but, in the first place, grace is indispensable to works themselves, and, in the second place, salvation by grace alone would be such a horrifying experience—morally atrocious and experientially painful—that humanity will not choose it as the way to the goal: "May he [the Messiah] come, but let me not see it!"[103] Thus, ethics remains as the only actionable course. M. Buber puts this by way of saying that men improve the world, while God transforms it. " 'Turning' and 'redemption' belong together. God knows how. I don't need to know."[104]

The meaning of the entirety of the Jewish eschatological vision is then perhaps best summarized in the liturgical phrase: *letakken olam bemalchut shaddai*—"to repair/perfect the world by means of the kingdom of God." This is an infinite task in individual human life, in history, beyond history into the kingdom of the Messiah, and even into the life of the world to come of the resurrection. "The Torah of life and of the love of grace, of righteousness and blessing and compassion and life and peace," i.e., the moral enterprise, is operative into that eternity of the holy God.[105]

Notes

1. For the sake of compactness I shall here omit consideration of principles 10 and 11 (individual providence and reward/punishment), though they obviously are of one piece with their

successors. (Maimonides handles them with the same sophistication as the others, see n. 105 below.) The full English text of the Thirteen Principles is found in A. J. Wolf, trans., "Maimonides on Immortality and the Principles of Judaism" *Judaism* 15 (1966): pp. 96 ff., 213 ff. (= I. Twersky, *A Maimonides Reader* [New York: Behrman House, 1972] pp. 422 f.). Maimonides' "catechism" possesses universal Jewish authority (the Yemenites inserted Maimonides' name into the *Kaddish* prayer for early redemption: "In your life and in the life of our teacher Moses ben Maimon" [*Kovetz Teshuvot haRambam* (Leipzig, 1859), pp. 8 f.])— which is not to say that it cannot be or has not been disputed (cf. M. M. Kellner, "R Isaac Abravanel on the Principles of Judaism," *JAAR 45*; n. 4, Supplement [December 1977]: n. 1); it does say that no one can fail to consider it with the highest degree of seriousness. For the place of the Thirteen Principles within Maimonides' total philosophical system, see S. Schwarzschild, "Moral Radicalism and 'Middlingness' in Maimonides' Ethics." A brief history and a very good historical theology of all of Maimonides' Thirteen Principles is Louis Jacobs, *Principles of the Jewish Faith: An Analytic Study* (New York: Basic Books, 1964); for our principles, see chaps. 12–14 (cf. also Jacobs, *A Jewish Theology* [New York: Behrman House, 1973], chaps. 22–23). See also M. M. Kellner, *Dogma in Medieval Jewish Thought* (Oxford: Oxford University Press, 1986), in Hebrew as *Torat ha-Ikkarim . . .* (Kibbutz-Me'uhad, forthcoming), chap. 1 on Maimonides.

2. I translate these two sentences as literally as possible and with an eye toward their most sophisticated explication. Seligmann Baer (*Siddur Avodat Yisrael* [Berlin, 1937], p. 154) adduces Samuel David Luzzatto (introduction to Mahzor Roma, p. 18) to attribute the *Yigdal*, a hymnal formulation of Maimonides' Principles, to Daniel b. Judah Dayyan early in the sixteenth century; the credal formulation here used appears first in the 1566 Venice Haggadah (cf. A. Altmann, "Articles of Faith," *Encyclopaedia Judaica*, 3:656). Zalman S. Shapiro (*Treatise on the Thirteen Principles* [Hebrew, Denver, CO, 1959], pp. 24, 27) interestingly assigns the credal form to use by the masses, the philosophically more technical hymnal form to potential students, and *Adon Olam* (another hymnal version of considerable technical sophistication) to the scholars, thus "rationalizing" the liturgical repetitiousness of all three versions in the prayer book.

3. Cf. Baer, loc. cit.: "They are accepted in all the dispersions of Israel." See also the legal code of my family's hometown, Frankfurt o/M, *Joseph Ometz*, §60: "In Germany the custom is to recite *Yigdal* after every prayer, for it is a beautiful hymn, structured according to the thirteen principles of our faith. Therefore, it is good to learn its grammatical explanation and to recite it with devotion."

4. Wolf, op. cit., p. 341. Maimonides here recapitulates the classic Talmudic prohibition of predicting the time of the Messiah's advent: B. Sanh. 97b: "Perish all those who calculate the 'end'!" (Cf. also ibid., 99a–b.) This is a prohibition which has, however, been violated more frequently than one can count—with all sort of excuses—even by Maimonides himself. S. Zeitlin ("Maimonides," *American Jewish Yearbook*, vol. 37 [1935], pp. 78 ff.) even suggested that Maimonides codified the laws that would be operative again only in Messianic times because he expected those times imminently. Cf. also A.J. Heschel, "Did Maimonides Believe That He Was Worthy of Prophecy?" *Louis Ginzburg Jubilee Volume* (New York: American Academy of Jewish Research, 1954), Hebrew sec., pp. 159–188.

5. *Rosh Amanah*, chap. 5, objection 8.

6. Cf. Rashi's extended treatment of Hab. 2:3, in which he summarizes the bulk of classical Jewish speculation regarding the Messianic advent, and also E. Urbach, *The Sages* (Hebrew) (Jerusalem: Magnes Press, 1969), p. 607.

7. Cf. the fifteenth benediction in every Amidah recited by the Jew; ". . . for upon Thy salvation we do hope all the day/on every day," and also S. Schwarzschild, "The Messianic Doctrine in Contemporary Jewish History," in *Great Jewish Ideas* (Washington, D.C.: B'nai B'rith, 1964), p. 246.

8. *Gen. Rab.* 97, 94a.

9. *B. Sanh.* 98a, *Targum Jonathan* to Gen. 35:21 and Exod. 13:43. Cf. also A. Berger, "Captive at the Gate of Rome: A Messianic Motif," *Proceedings of the American Academy for Jewish Research* 44 (1977), and the intellectualized interpretation of this *'aggadeta* by R. Isaac b. Yedaiah (13th cent., Provencal) in Marc Saperstein, *Decoding the Rabbis: A 13th Century Commentary on the Aggadah* (Cambridge, Mass.: Harvard University Press, 1980). pp. 102–117.

10. Compare Maimonides, Code, Laws of Repentance 7:2. In the *Star of Redemption*, Franz Rosenzweig uses this text for his particular theological purposes—namely, that Israel, in its religious life, lives outside of time/history, i.e., in eternity at all times [New York: Holt, Rinehart & Winston, 1971], pp. 289–293.

11. *Guide of the Perplexed* 3:43, ed. S. Pines (Chicago: University of Chicago Press, 1963), p. 571.

12. *Two Types of Faith* (London: Routledge & Kegan Paul, 1957). Wilfred Cantwell Smith picks up this Buber-categorization, although he gives only passing credit (*Faith and Belief* [Princeton, N.J.: Princeton University Press, 1979], p. 325, n. 65), and he universalizes and quite unduly exaggerates it.

13. Cf. Schwarzschild, "Messianic Doctrine," pp. 237 ff.

14. Hegel's perpetual haranguing of "bad infinity" in favor of "good (i.e., completed, or completable, 'actual') infinity" and all its subsequent philosophical as well as even mathematical (e.g., Georg Cantor) ramifications are modernist reformulations of this Christian doctrine. Cf. my "The Religious Stake of Modern Philosophy of Infinity," *Annual of Bar Ilan University* 22–23 (1987), pp. 63–84.

15. Cf. S. Schwarzschild, "The Personal Messiah—Toward the Restoration of a Discarded Doctrine." "The Democratic Socialism of Hermann Cohen," *Hebrew Union College Annual* 27 (1956): 436f.; and my introduction to Cohen's *Ethik des reinen Willens* (Hildesheim and New York: G. Olms, 1981), pp. xxiff. (M. Buber, too, says: "In our [Jewish] view redemption occurs always, and none has yet occured"—cf. Maurice Friedman, *M. Buber's Life and Work: The Late Years, 1945–1965* [New York: Dutton, 1983], 3:50.) It should be noted that the assertion of the personhood of the Messiah, as over against the notion of "the Messianic age," is logically and theologically independent of the affirmation that one day he will have, in fact, come; cf. S. Schwarzschild, "Personal Messiah," p. 17. What I wish to confess in repeating this point is that, with respect to the article just cited, which has often been reprinted, translated, and used (recently, for example, in Ze'ev Lévy, *On the Relationship Between Jewish and General Philosophy* [Hebrew] [Tel Aviv: Hakibbutz Hamme'uchad, 1982], pp. 247 f.), I have been forced to change my mind. I continue to argue for the personhood of the Messiah, as I did there, but I have come to see that the other argument there (actually Rosenzweig's argument—cf. nn. 13 f.), that the Messianic advent has to be in time rather than "in infinity," is erroneous for at least two reasons: (1) it is philosophically mistaken (H. Cohen was, after all, right [cf. *Ethik*, pp. xxiv f.]), and (2) it is historically invidious (for example, the pseudoMessianism of Zionism and the State of Israel is precluded by the doctrine of the Messiah's eternal coming). I am, indeed, now prepared to argue that even the denial of the expectation of the personal Messiah in the classical Jewish sources (for example, the silence about this in several biblical books and the statement of the amoraic Rabbi Hillel that "he had already been consumed" [*B. Sanh.* 99a, Rashi ad locum = *Midr. Ps.* 107, and I. Abrabanel, *Yeshu'ot Meshiho* (Königsberg: 1861), pp. 26a ff.; cf. A.H. Silver, *A History of Messianic Speculations in Israel* (New York: Macmillan, 1927), p. 197, Rav's statement that "all the 'ends' have been exhausted, and the matter now depends solely on repentance and good deeds." B. Sanh., 97b, etc.]) and the derogation of the whole doctrine, one way or the other (for example, by Albo, *Ikkarim* I/4, IV/35:1; cf. Urbach, op. cit., p. 612, n. 10; Schwarzschild, "Personal Messiah," p. 20; and Kellner, *Dogma*, chap. 1, n. 244, who here comes to the con-

clusion that "Maimonides' emphasis on the dogmatic importance of belief in the Messiah is unique in the literature of medieval Jewish dogmatics") ought to be understood in the same way: these teachers, too, really want to say that such an advent is not to be counted on as an operational factor in Jewish ethics of history. I am always puzzled why it is that Julian the Apostate's concrete attempt to restore the Jerusalem Temple left no traces in rabbinic literature. (Cf. Y. Levi, "Caesar Julianus and the Building of the Temple" [Hebr.], Zion 6 (1940–1941): 1–32 and F. Blanchetière, "Julien Philhéllène, Philosémite, Antichrétien: L'affaire du Temple de Jerusalem [363]," *Journal of Jewish Studies*, 31, no. 1 [Spring 1980]: 60–81.) None of the historical experts comes up with any solutions. It may be a weak, *e silentio*, argument, but I like to think that the rabbis did not take Julian seriously because, since he had come, he could not be the Messiah.

16. Cf. Schwarzschild, "Personal Messiah," p. 21 and "F. Rosenzweig's Anecdotes about H. Cohen," in *Gegenwart im Rueckblick—Festgabe f.d. jüdische Gemeinde zu Berlin 25 Jahre nach dem Neubeginn*, ed. H. Strauss and K. Grossman (Heidelberg, 1970), pp. 210 f.

17. *Jehuda Halevy—92 Hymnen und Gedichte deutsch* (Berlin: L. Schneider, n.d.), p. 239.

18. Cf. S. Schwarzschild, "Jenseits von Sein und Zeit" (review), *International Studies in Philosophy* 14, no. 1 (1981): 102 ff.

19. *Entsheidung zum Judentum—Essays und Vorträge* (Suhrkamp, 1980).

20. (New York: Schocken, 1977). Her English title reproduces the Yiddish locution of not using an article with the name "Messiah": after all, the name of any other individual also does not take an article.

21. Maimonides himself refers back to his entire introduction of the Principles for the doctrine of resurrection. He is right: his entire exposition there deals with eschatology.

22. Cf. Kellner, *Dogma*, loc. cit.

23. Cf. Maimonides' *Code*, Laws of Repentance 8:3, and Schwarzschild, "Moral Radicalism," pp. 143 f.

24. *M. Sanh.* 10:1 (It seems actually, on the latest evidence, that the phrase about having to believe resurrection to be "taught in the Bible" is not part of Maimonides' own text in his *Commentary to the Mishnah*; cf. ibid., ed. R. Joseph Kafich [Jerusalem: Mossad HaRav Kook, 1963], vol. 4 ["Nezikin"], p. 165). Or in the vernacular: if you don't believe in it, you won't get it. Presumably this Talmudic dogma contradicts both Sadduceeanism and Greek spiritualism. Note carefully Maimonides' wording (Wolf, op. cit., p. 31): "We are to believe as a fact that . . . " Such a formulation is significantly different from saying "it is a fact that . . . " Also, it leads straight into Maimonides' logic of what he calls "necessary truths," themselves a component of the complex history of *pias fraus* and "fiction." (Cf. S. Schwarzschild, "Introduction," p. x in Cohen, *Ethik*; Moshe Silberg, *Talmudic Law and the Modern State* [New York: Burning Bush, 1975], chap. III, "Evasion of the Law"; and my late teacher, Samuel Atlas, *Pathways in Hebrew Law* [Hebrew] [New York: American Academy of Jewish Research, 1978], "Evasion and Fiction," pp. 265 ff., esp. pp. 267 f., for the philosophy of fiction, and "Whatever the Rabbis Sanctify is Sanctified" [Hebrew], *Sinai* 75 [Sivan—Tammuz 1974]: 135 f., 141; Y.S. Zuri, "Legal Conceptualization in Jewish Law," [Hebrew], *Festschrift for B.M. Levin* [1940], pp. 174–195; M.A. Amiel, "The Concept of Potentiality in the Halakhah" [Hebrew], *Sinai* 7 [1943]: 20–33; A. Karlin, "Ex Post Facto Law" [Hebrew], *Sinai* 14 [1951]: 129–142 and "De Jure Personality," *Sinai* 2 [1939]: 445–452; Solomon Goldman, "The Legal Fiction in Jewish Law," in *Presentation Volume to William Barron Stevenson*, ed. C.J. Mullo Weir, (Studia Semitica et Orientalia 2 [Glasgow, 1945]).

25. Arthur Hyman ("Maimonides' Thirteen Principles," in *Jewish Medieval and Renaissance Studies*, ed. A. Altmann [Cambridge: Harvard University Press, 1967], pp. 134 ff.) argues that Maimonides does not deal with the subjects of principles 12 and 13 because he does not regard them as philosophical, i.e., rational. Kellner (*Dogma*, chap. 1, nn. 239–241) convincingly argues that Hyman is mistaken about this by pointing out that principle 13 is the only one of

all of them that employs all three of the epistemic terms of Maimonides' vocabulary—"knowledge," "faith," and "sincere affirmation."

26. Cf. esp. Rabad *ad* "Laws of Repentance" 8:1 ff.; D. Silver, *Maimonidean Criticism and Maimonidean Controversy* 1180–1240 (Leiden: E.J. Brill, 1965), pp. 109–135; Jacobs, *Principles*, pp. 407 f.; and Z.S. Shapiro, *op. cit.*, p. 13: "The heavens and the earth have long quaked with the arguments against the Thirteen Principles."

27. Cf. "Moral Radicalism," pp. 154f. Saadiah Gaon and Ibn Ezra (ad Dan. 12:2) make similar stipulations. The purpose is in each case the distinction between normally physical existence in the Messianic realm, on the one hand, and existence in a "spiritual body" in the world-to-come, on the other hand (cf. below). Gersonides, as usual, exponentializes Maimonides' rationalism. He does not mention the Messiah at all in his magnum opus, *The Wars of the Lord*. He, too, makes the will central to the Jewish enterprise (M. Kellner, "Gersonides on Miracles, the Messiah and Resurrection," *Da'at* 5 [Winter 1980]: 33, n. 114), and, therefore, Jewish morality brings the Messiah (ibid., pp. and 30, nn. 106 and 109). One might note with curiosity that Euridice is resurrected twice in Gluck's *Orfeo and Euridice*.

28. On rabbinic doctrine cf. Arthur Marmorstein, "The Redemption-Idea in The Teachings of the Tannaites and Amoraites" in his *Studies in Jewish Theology: The A. Marmorstein Memorial Volume*, ed. J. York (Oxford University Press, 1950), pp. 17–76; see also pp. 145–161 ("The Doctrine of the Resurrection of the Dead in Rabbinic Theology") and pp. 162–178 ("Participation in Eternal Life in Rabbinical Theology and Legend"); S. Lieberman, "Some Aspects of After Life in Rabbinic Literature," in *Texts and Studies* [New York, 1974], pp. 235–272, and H.J. Matt, "An Outline of Jewish Eschatology," *Judaism* 17 (Summer 1968): 186–196. (The article on "Eschatology" in vol. 6 of the *Encyclopedia Judaica* has a good summary of the subject in biblical literature—and next to nothing else!)

29. Cf. Altmann, op. cit., col. 655.

30. Cf. Schwarzschild, "Messianic Doctrine," pp. 254f.

31. Cf. S. Schwarzschild, "The Lure of Immanence—The Crisis in Contemporary Jewish Thought."

32. Cf. S. Schwarzschild, "Moral Radicalism," n. 122, and Maimonides, Laws of Repentance 8:7 and 9:1.

33. *Code*, Law of Kings 12:5; cf. Twersky, op. cit., pp. 414 f. The continuity of Maimonides' thought throughout his life is thus reconfirmed. (Cf. Twersky, op. cit., p. 387.)

34. Ibid., 10:5.

35. Cf. Oscar Cullmann, "Immortality of the Soul and Resurrection of the Dead," in *Immortality and Resurrection: Death in the Western World: Two Conflicting Currents of Thought*, ed. K. Stendahl (New York: Macmillan, 1965), pp. 9–53. I think Cullmann's dichotomy is valid. I also think, however, that his claim to the doctrine of resurrection in the New Testament and early Christianity misfires (cf. J.D. Tabor, "Resurrection and Immortality," in *Christian Teaching: Studies in Honor of LeMoine G. Lewis* [Abilene: Abilene University Press, 1981]).

36. *Guide*, I.

37. There is a beginning of this in Joseph Klausner, *The Messianic Idea in Israel* [London, Allen & Unwin, 1956], especially pt. III, and in S. Forstein, "The Law in Talmudic Eschatology" (diss., Hebrew Union College—Jewish Institute of Religion, 1965).

38. Laws of Repentance 8:4 re "soul," 8:5 re "perishing," and 8:8 re "coming."

39. *Theological Investigations* (Baltimore: Helicon, 1966), 4:323–346.

40. Cf. *Code*, Laws of Repentance 8:1 ff. and 8:8.

41. *M. Sanh.* 10:1.

42. T. *Sanh.* 13:2 Cf. S. Schwarzschild, "Do Noachites have to Believe in Revelation?" and "An Eschatological Liturgy," *CCAR Journal 23*, no. 4 (Autumn 1976): 22–26; Jacob Katz, "The Vicissitudes of Three Apologetic Passages" (Hebrew), *Zion* 23–24, nos. 3–4 (1958–59): 174–181.

43. The Hebrew word for "coming" (as in *olam haba, bechol yom sheyavo,* etc.), here needs to be unpacked in its eschatological usage. (Cf. nn. 37 ff. above.)

44. Aggadic literature is full of the things that God does in His eternity and, indeed, of the things that people do in their eternal lives. Above all, the latter continue to "strive"—i.e., they "grow"—intellectually and morally; cf. Maimonides' interpretation of the rabbinic dictum (*B. Ber. 17a*) that, though "there is no eating or drinking or sexual intercourse in the world to come, the righteous will sit, wearing crowns on their heads"—i.e., there will still be something beyond themselves, namely, the "Idea" of God and immortality—and, therefore, "they will drink in the effulgence of the presence of God"—i.e., they will enjoy greater, namely spiritual, pleasures: study of Torah. (Twersky, op. cit., pp. 411 f. and Laws of Repentance 8:2, "the crowns" are "knowledge.") Cf. also Emanuel Levinas, "Temps messianiques et temps historiques dans le chapitre xi du Traité 'Sanhedrin,' " in *La Conscience Juive*, ed. E.A. Lévy-Valensi and J. Halpérin (Paris, 1963). (For an adumbration of Levinas' eschatology cf. S. Schwarzschild, "S. Strasser, 'Jenseits von Sein und Zeit,' " *loc. cit.*, last paragraph.) Cf. Kant's *Religion Within the Bounds of Reason Alone* in *Immanuel Kants Werke* ed. H. Cohen et al. (Berlin: B. Cassirer, 1923), vol. 6, ed. E. Casirer, p. 283: "This notion of a history of after-life, which is itself historical, is a beautiful ideal of the . . . future epochs of the world, . . . toward which we look forward in continuous progress and approximation."

45. 1 Cor 15:44 (cf. J.T.A. Robinson, *The Body: A Study in Pauline Theology* [London, 1952], p. 28, on *sarx* ["flesh"] vs. *soma* ["body" = person].) Cf. also Klausner, op. cit., p. 270 on the Wisdom of Solomon; ibid., p. 300 for the Book of Enoch: the "spiritual bodies" are bestowed like "the garments in the wilderness"; Albo, *Ikkarim* II/1 on Saadiah; Maimonides' *Guide* 2.30, and the end of the Rabad's (typically vehement but suddenly conditional) polemic against Maimonides' Code, Laws of Repentance 8:2; B. Safran, "Rabbi Azriel . . . " in I. Twersky, ed., *Rabbi Moses/Nahmanides (Ramban): Explorations in His Religious and Literary Virtuosity* (Cambridge: Harvard University Press, 1983) p. 86; Manasseh b. Israel, Nishmat Hayyim, chap. 1; G. Scholem, *Shabbetai Zvi* (Tel Aviv: Am Oved, 1956/57), p. 57, on "spiritual body" (English trans., p. 73).

46. Cf. Nachmanides, *Gate of Reward* in the *Zohar*, on "spiritual bodies." Also cf. E. Urbach, *The Sages*, p. 591, about the "intermixed," rather than metaphysical, character of *olam haba* and about the distinction between individual salvation and historical or posthistorical redemption.

47. *B. Shab.* 152b f. and Rashi *ad locum*; also on Maimonides' Code, Laws of Repentance 8:7.

48. *Book of Beliefs and Opinions*, trans. S. Rosenblatt (New Haven: Yale University Press, 1948), pp. 218, 431, 433. f. Cf. *B. Niddah* 61b, *Tosfot*, where the Messianic age and eternal life are collapsed into one. The rabbinic split of the Messiah into two Messiahs, the Son of Joseph and the Son of David, also basically expresses the two dimensions of this single eschatological entity—the physical and the spiritual. Max Brod, a goodly man who is too little known in this country for all but his relationship to Kafka, devoted, in our time, the whole second volume of his *Diesseits und Jenseits* (Winterhur: Mondial-Verlag, 1947), which was written in a very personal vein in Palestine during World War II, to "The Immortality of the Soul, the Justice of God, and a New Politics." (Brod's philosophizing is, unfortunately always rather amateurish and quasi-pantheistic.) His doctrine of immortality, attached to the rabbinic doctrine of "death by God's kiss" and to Maimonides' "conjunction" (chap. 6, M), is heavily ethical, even politically socialist (ibid., p. 334). Yet even he raises the possibility of a quasi-material immortality (i.e., resurrection), which eventually would gravitate toward God (ibid., pp. 294 ff.).

49. Cf. *Ethics*, 3.11f. and 5.20 to the very end and climax of the work; compare H.A. Wolfson, *The Philosophy of Spinoza* (New York: Meridian books, 1965), 2:284–325, 349F. (On d'Acosta, pp. 323f.).

50. For Kant's argument against Mendelssohn on this score cf. his "On the Old Saw: This May Be Right In Theory But Won't Work in Practice," in *Kant's Gesammelte Schriften* (Berlin:

Reimer, 1907), 6:392 f., and "Ideas for a Cosmopolitan History in Pragmatic Perspective," "Third Thesis," as well as H. Arendt, *Lectures on Kant's Political Philosophy* (Chicago: University of Chicago Press, 1982), p. 77. There is an extraordinary current debate among neo-Marxists, which duplicates this discussion and which owns up to its deeply Jewish character: cf. Helmut Peukert, *Wissenschaftstheorie-Handlungstheorie-Fundamentale Theologie* (Duseldorf: Patmos, 1976), pp. 280 f., and *Habermas: Critical Debate*, ed. J.B. Thompson and D. Held (London: Macmillan, 1982), pp. 246 f., as to whether an ideal society can be happy remembering or forgetting the suffering of the past.

51. Cf. Isaac Heinemann *Ta'amay haMitzvot beSifrut Yisráel* (Jerusalem, 1961), 2:15 and A. Altmann, *Moses Mendelssohn: A Biographical Study* (Philadelphia: Jewish Publication Society, 1973), pp. 171–186. Cf. E. Schweid, "The Educational and Political Justification of Commandments of Belief According to Maimonides" (Hebrew), *Táam veHakashah* (Ramat Gan: Massada, 1970), pp. 80–104.

52. Altmann, *Moses Mendelssohn*, p. 183.

53. Cf. T. Penelhum, *Survival and Disembodied Existence* (London: Routledge & Kegan Paul, 1970) and A.G.N. Flew, "Is There a Case for Disembodied Survival?" *Journal of the American Society for Psychical Research* 66 (1972): 129–144.

54. Cf. C.Z. Reines, "*Kvod haMet*" (Hebrew), *Sinai* 53 (Tammuz-Av, 1936): 193 ff., esp. p. 193, n. 6: "This myth (of resurrection) entered, as is known, into Christianity, which assigned a mythological-mystical meaning to 'resurrection,' whereas Judaism assigned to it moral and symbolic meaning, connected with the Messianic conception." Reines concentrates so much on the moral significance that he, Orthodox Jew that he was, nonetheless somewhat neglects the sheer physical integrity of corpses; for this cf. Y.Y. Greenwald, *Kol Bo'al Avelut* (Hebrew) (New York: Feldheim, 1956).

55. S.L. Steinheim distinguished between the naturalistic doctrine of immortality, offered by reason, and the doctrine of immortality by grace, offered by revelation: cf. N. Rotenstreich, "S.L. Steinheim—Philosopher of Revelation." *Judaism* 2, no. 4 (1953): 332f.

56. Chicago: Dover, 1953 (really *Substantial Concept and Functional Concept* [Berlin: Cassirer, 1910]). "Dimensionless bodies" is a notion used by the Kalam, which is rehabilitated in Leibnitz's monads—mathematized at that time in the infinitesimal calculus (cf. S. Schwarzschild "Two Lives in the Jewish 'Frühaufklärung'," *Leo Baeck Institute Year Book* 29 [1984], pp. 102 and 104)—taken further in Marburg neo-Kantianism in the form of "intensive magnitudes," and surely a legitimate scientific problematic at this time both epistemologically as well as in the burgeoning field of subatomic physics. The realms of ethics and of science must, to be sure, be carefully distinguished, but not sealed off, from one another.

57. Cf. *Telos* 44 (Summer 1980): 179 (compare S. Schwarzschild, "J.-P. Sartre as Jew."

58. Frankfurt, 1966, pp. 389–392. Generally, the role of the "Frankfurt School" in contemporary, avant-garde Messianism is a subject that cries out for full explanation. E.g., T.W. Adorno even gets to resurrection: "Thus the center of Benjamin's philosophy is the idea of the salvation of the dead as the restitution of deformed life through the perfection of its objectification." (*Über W. Benjamin* [Suhrkamp, 1970], p. 29.) Jewish Messianism is this-worldly, social. "Utopia is the center of his theory" (p. 79). As for Adorno himself, cf. his *Minima Moralia* (Suhrkamp, 1951): "Philosophy as it can only be seen responsibly done in the face of depair would be the attempt to regard all things from the perspective of redemption" (p. 113). Walter Benjamin's part in the school and the importance of his freindship with Gershom Scholem are well known: Benjamin's "Theological-Political Fragment" (*Schriften*, ed. T.W. Adorno [Frankfurt, 1955], 1:511 f.)—Adorno dates this fragment ca. 1920 (*Über W. Benjamin*, p. 168, n. 19). G. Scholem, on the other hand, dates it as the very end of Benjamin's life (Scholem, *On Jew and Judaism in Crisis* [New York: Schocken, 1976], pp. 180, 199, 231). I cannot decide this issue between Adorno and Scholem. Each of them, no doubt, thinks that it has something to do with his respectively more Marxist or more Kabbalistic reading of Benjamin. (Cf. Über W. Benjamin,

pp. 91 ff.) I think they both overdo their respective theses. (Cf. also Benjamin's famous "Angelus Novus," *Illuminations*, ed. H. Arendt (New York: Harcourt, Brace, & World, 1968], pp. 12f., 257 f., and Scholem, *op. cit.*, "Walter Benjamin and His Angel.") is perhaps the most profound and relevant formulation of Jewishly, radically pessimistic Messianism in our tragic century. Ernst Bloch's *The Principle Hope* (Suhrkamp, 1959), occupies an even more curious position in contemporary thought: Bloch himself and Jews and Judaism have been only dimly aware of one another and their inner connections, while Christian "theology of hope" (Möltmann, etc.), "theology of liberation," etc., are, in turn, only dimly aware of the (partial) Judaization which they underwent in the process of learning from Bloch. (Cf. Michael Landmann, "Das Judentum bei E. Bloch und seine messianische Metaphysik" in *Jüdische Miniaturen* [Bonn: Bouvier Verlag Grundmann, 1982], 1:161–182.)

59. B. *Ket* 8a. Compare the third benediction of the wedding ceremony (and its many commentaries). The whole benediction fits our present concern: "Praised be Thou, O Lord, our God, King of the world, who created man in His image, in the image of the similarity to His structure, and perfected for him therefrom a timeless edifice." Cf. S. Atlas, *"Dina D'Malchuta* Delimited," *Hebrew Union College Annual* 46 (1975): 280, n. 9, and Boaz Cohen, "Law and Ethics in the Jewish Tradition," in *Law and Tradition* (New York: Jewish Theological Seminary, 1959), p. 187, n. 28, middle.

60. Cf. Kant's distinction between *Wille* and *Willkühr*: L.W. Beck, *A Commentary on Kant's Critique of Practical Reason* (Chicago: University of Chicago Press, 1960), pp. 176–208.

61. For a discussion of the contemporary Jewish philosopher E, Levinas's ethics as an eschatological "optics," cf. Steven G. Smith, *The Argument to the Other: Reason Beyond Reason in the Thought of K. Barth and E. Levinas* (Chico, Calif.: Scholars Press, 1983), pp. 85, 168.

62. *Some Aspects of Rabbinic Theology* (New York: Behrman, 1936), p. 114.

63. "Is and Ought," in *11th World Congress of Philosophy of Law and Social Philosophy* (Helsinki, 1983), "Plenary Main Papers and Commentaries," pp. 16–17.

64. Ibid., p. 25. (Fundamental disagreement still separates me from Hintikka.)

65. Cf. Schwarzschild, "Jewish Eschatological Liturgy," pp. 25 f.

66. Cf. the article *"Hilkheta dimeshicha,"* *Encyclopedia Talmudit* (Hebrew), 9:388 f. The material here would have to be carefully conceptualized.

67. *B. Meg.* 15a.

68. *Exod. Rab.* 25:16.

69. *B. Sabbath* 118b, *B. Sanh.* 97b f., *B. Abod. Zara* 3a, *B. Ber.* 57b; *Midr. Psalms*, ed. Braude, 2.137; Klausner, op. cit., pp. 427 f.; A.J. Heschel, *The Sabbath* (Philadelphia: Jewish Publication Society, 1952).

70. *B.B. Bat* 10b.

71. Cf. article *"Hilkheta dimeshicha,"* *Encyclopedia Talmudit* (Hebrew), loc. cit.

72. Will Herberg, ed., *The Writings of Martin Buber* (New York: Meridian Books, 1956), p. 311; cf. also R. Isaac Hutner, *Pachad Yitzchak*, vol. "Day of Atonement" (Hebrew) (Brooklyn, N.Y.: Gur Aryeh, 1978), lecture 5, pt. I, par. 2: "The belief in the end-time perceives anticipations of the future in the present" (see also my "Two Lectures of R.I. Hunter," *Tradition* 14, no. 4 [Fall 1974]: 93, and "Introduction to the Thought of R. I. Hunter," *Modern Judaism*, [Fall 1985], pp. 225–227), Ernst Bloch, "Resistance and Peace" in Z. Batscha, ed., *Materialien zu Kantz Rechtsphilosophie* [Suhrkamp, 1968], p. 374: "Therefore, distant goals must be present in every nearby goal more than implicitly—namely, they must emerge as more than *sine qua non* and as participatory"; Benjamin, "Theses about the Philosophy of History," op. cit., AB appendix to thesis 18: "Every second is the narrow portal through which the Messiah may enter."

73. For a detailed example of Messianic expatiation of *Halachah* cf. S. Schwarzschild, "A Note on the Nature of Ideal Society—A Rabbinic Study in Menahem Kellner, ed., *The Pursuit of the Ideal* (Albany: State University of New York, 1990).

74. Cf. *B. Ta'anit* 2a f.: "God has kept three or four keys to himself—the keys to rain, birth, res-

urrection . . . and has not handed them over to a messenger" (*shaliach*; Rashi ad locum repeats the phrase three times: *velo shaliach!* [Compare the repeated refrain, "God Himself—not a messenger,' " etc., in the *midrash* to Deut. 26:5–8 in the Passover Haggadah.]) *Tosfot* ad locum reconciles this statement with ours by saying that Elijah did, as a matter of fact, have the keys to rain and resurrection—he did not hold on to them permanently. Rashi reconciles the two passages by saying that no one human being ever shall have all three keys.

75. *Gen. Rab.* 76:1 and the parallels there cited.

76. *B. Shab.* 30b., cf. *B. Ket.* 111b.

77. If J. Klausner is right, this *midrash* is especially titillating, for he claims that "the certain disciple" or R. Gamliel was Paul of Tarsus (*Messianic Idea in Israel*, p. 107). See also *Pirke deRabbi Eliezer*, ed. Friedlander, pp. 415 f., for a similar argument: again it is a matter of the novum of the resurrection against the "Greek" doctrine that "there is nothing new under the sun"; again the identity of one of the polemicists is left in doubt, but this time the later, medieval, Aristotelian concept of the sublunar world is invoked, so that the righteous will be resurrected "above the sun," while the wicked will cease to exist "under the sun," where there is really nothing new.

78. Cf. *M. Eduyot* 1:13, where Shammai insists Messianically that there can be no half-slaves, whereas Hillel, "for the sake of the (gradual) improvement of the world," permits them meanwhile; Shammai famously would light all eight Chanukkah candles immediately on the first night, whereas Hillel (and we) "build up" to them; Shammai insists on a total, rigorous, Messianic Sabbath (cf. M. Buber, *To Hallow This Life*, ed. J. Trapp [New York: Harper & Brothers, 1958], p. 97) rather than treating the Sabbath as "a foretaste" of the world to come (*B. Abod. Zara* 3a, *B. Ber.* 57b), and stolen property has to be returned to its rightful owner, regardless of invidious consequences (*B. Gitt.* 55a).

79. Cf. S. Greenberg, "And He Writes Her a Bill of Divorcement," *Conservative Judaism* 24, no. 3 (Spring 1970): 132.

80. Cf. S. Schwarzschild, *On Jewish Meta-Ethics*, chapter "Messianism," forthcoming.

81. Cf. S. Schwarzschild, "Justice," in *Encyclopaedia Judaica* (Jerusalem: Keter, 1971). For the ethicization of the Jewish vision of the world to come, see idem, "Eschatological Liturgy," p. 26.

82. Cf. S. Schwarzschild, "K. Marx's Jewish Theory of Interest," *Gesher* (New York: Yeshiva University, 1978), n. 53. Also the doctrine of reincarnation, which pops up in Jewish mysticism, is in fact a doctrine of renewed opportunities for self-remortalization (cf. "Eschatology: Kabbalah," *Encyclopaedia Judaica*, loc. cit.).

83. Shapiro, "Treatise," p. 16.

84. Maimonides' *Eight Chapters*, beginning; *Sefer Chassidim* (S. A. Singer, *Medieval Jewish Mysticism: The Book of the Pious* [Northbrook, Ill., 1971], p. 15); M. H. Luzzatto, *Mesillat Yesharim*, etc.

85. Cf. John Hick, *Philosophy of Religion*, 2d ed. (Englewood Cliffs, N.J.: Prentice-Hall, 1973), pp. 90–95, and idem, "Eschatological Verification," in *The Logic of God/Theology and Verification*, ed. M. L. Diamond and Litzenberg Jr. (Indianapolis: Bobbs-Merril, 1975), sec. 6.

86. *Code*, Laws of Repentence 8:6.

87. This need for grace in the performance of even a single, limited moral action is expressed, for example, in the rabbinic principle, variably instatiated, that the fulfillment of one important commandment is accounted as though it were the fulfillment "of the whole Torah" (*B. Kidd* 40a. for the denial of idolatry; *B. Chullin* 4a for Sabbath observance). See nn. 68–70 above.

88. Cf. S. Schwarzschild, "On the Theology of Jewish Survival," in Kellner, ed. *Pursuit of the Ideal*, p. 97 and S. H. Bergman, *Faith and Reason* (Washington, D.C.: B'nai B'rith Hillel, 1961), p. 50, on Hermann Cohen's "correlation": "correlation is . . . the narrow ridge between two dangerous abysses: man's activism, his trust in his own power, his confidence that heaven is not needed . . . and an attitude exemplified, for instance by Luther who makes man the passive recipient (or non-recipient) of divine grace. . . . Cohen, in rejecting both extremes, fol-

lows the tradition of classical Jewish thought." Compare also R. Yehuda HaLevy's dialectic of grace and works: the influx of grace must be prepared, even on the part of Jews who are metaphysically equipped for this, by the fulfillment of the commandments.

89. Cf. *B. Ber.* 4b.

90. *B. Sanh.* 97bf. = *Y. Ta'anit* 1:1, 63d.

91. "Temps messianiques," loc. cit.

92. Sometimes Ps. 65:2 and Deut. 32:3 are added to Ps. 51:17. I suspect that Ps. 65:2 is expected to be the overtone to Ps. 65:3: "Unto Thee [O God] silence is praise." (N.B. the recurrence of the word "praise" in Ps. 65:2 and Ps. 51:17.) Thus prayer somehow emerges out of the necessary silence between man and God that precedes and underlies prayer. (Cf. S. Schwarzschild, "Speech and Silence before God," in *Understanding Jewish Prayer*, ed. J. Petuchowski [New York, 1972], pp. 84–99 and 167–170). Indeed, at their end the Eighteen Benedictions fade back into the silence out of which they emerged, in the words of the coda, also silently recited by the individual: "Let my soul be silent and like dust unto all" (*B. Shabb.* 88b, *Tosfot* to *B. Ber.* 17a). N.B. the use of the word "my lips" at the end, as at the beginning. Cf. also I. Frimer, "The Recital of 'O Lord, open my lips . . .' *Or Hamizrach* 34/1–2 (120–21"; September 1985), pp. 87–93.

93. The dialectics does not, of course, dissolve so simply. Man takes autonomous action (by praying), but he gets this prayer from the Bible, which is "graciously" revealed. Many similar liturgical situations occur. For example, "Our Father, merciful Father, merciful One, be merciful by putting it into our hearts . . . to keep, to do, and to fulfill in love all the words of learning of Thy Torah."

94. *Quest for Past and Future* (Bloomington, 1968), pp. 90, 202; cf. also ibid., "Judaism and the Idea of Progress," pp. 83–95, and "Human Freedom and Divine Power."

95. *Ethics of the Pure Will* (Berlin: Cassirer, 1904), p. 407.

96. There is, in any case, a pervasive hybris ("counter-snobbery") in "salvation by grace": the *ecclesia triumphans* boasts of being saved because it is poor in works!

97. *B. Sanh.* 97a and *Midr. Pss.* 45:3. The "or" in the Hebrew sentence should probably be taken as an inclusive, not as an exclusive, i.e., "and/or." Cf. S. Schwarzschild, "From Critical to Speculative Idealism" (review), *Journal of Bible and Religion* 34 (January 1966): 65 f.

98. Cf. S. D. Goitein, " 'Meeting in Jerusalem': Messianic Expectations in the Letters of the Cairo Geniza," *AJS Review* 4 (1979): 52 ff.

99. Scholem, op. cit., pp. 76 f. (Nathan Shapiro, in Spinoza's and Shabbetai's time).

100. *B. Pesah*, 64b.

101. Cf. *B. Sota*, end, the biblical notion of "the terrible day of God," and the rabbinic notion of "the birth pangs of the Messiah." Cf. also R. Aron Rote, as exposited in S. Schwarzschild, "Speech and Silence before God," *Judaism* 10, no. 3 (Summer 1961): 199.

102. Cf. Schwarzschild, "Survival," p. 97.

103. *B. Sanh.* 98b.

104. Maurice Freidman, *Martin Buber's Life and Work: The Late Years 1945–1965* (New York: E. P. Dutton, 1984), p. 103.

105. We can finally integrate principles 10 and 11 into Maimonides' eschatology. Principle 10 asserts, against then current Aristotelianism, divine *providentia individualis* for human beings alone, through the reason that God and humanity share (cf. *Guide* 3.17 f.). Principle 11, "reward and punishment," can then draw the conclusion that reward consists of immortality (by virtue of the *conjunctio* of the human spirit with the divine), while punishment consists of the absence or reward (*theologia negativa*) (cf. Twersky, op. cit., p. 412—Laws of Repentance 8:5). Albo makes the doctrine of reward and punishment (i.e., the ultimacy of moral responsibility) fundamental to Judaism (unlike the Messianic doctrine, cf. n. 15, end, above) and inserts the Messianic kingdom on earth and physical resurrection as intermediate stages between normal life and immortality (just like Maimonides) only so that immortality can follow the elimination of the guilt/punishment phenomenon. (*Ikkarim* 1:23, 4:30, and 31:9).

19

Renewing the Covenant

EUGENE BOROWITZ

I have been critical of the modern notions of the solitary self and self-validating univer-salism in the hope of permitting the consciousness of our particularity to make itself felt and make its proper claim on our selfhood. At the same time I have tried to insist that this strong religious particularism must allow for self-determining persons and a central regard for humankind entire. Let me now indicate something of the proper balance I en-vision between these potentially clashing Covenant commitments. How shall we live with the conflicts that arise between the Jewish self and the Jewish polity? And then, how shall our people be true to itself without losing its proper involvement with humanity?

I begin by restating the first premise of this position: The self gains its inestimable worth neither by the self-evident nature of its quality nor our willing it, but by being covenanted to God. It cannot then demand a Kantian or Sartrean radical autonomy or self-legislation without regard to God, the Source of our freedom and the Standard of all value. We employ our will rightfully when God serves as its limiting condition, better, as our partner in decision making.

Today, with selfhood fundamental to our philosophic theories and political practice, we cannot as easily indicate why human collectives ought validly exercise significant sway over us. Let us set aside the extreme possibilities: totalitarianism and the absolute primacy of the group, and a radical individualism that proceeds without primary in-volvement with others. Practically, most of us will accept group authority for the sake of simple social order or group functioning, but we retain the right of conscience to dissent or withdraw from a beloved community should an exceptional issue arise. We face our greatest perplexity when our dialectical commitments pull us in two directions.

Eugene Borowitz, "The Dialectic of Living in Covenant," Ch. 16 in *Renewing the Covenant* (Philadelphia: Jewish Publication Society, 1991), pp. 221–34. © Jewish Publication Society, Philadelphia, PA 19103.

The Group's Rightful Authority over Autonomous Selves

Acknowledging a certain primacy of selfhood, I begin my analysis of this problem with a repudiation of the self as a monad. God makes us individuals but also an inseparable part of humanity. Our finitude also makes each of us necessarily dependent upon others and inevitably bonds us more closely to some people than others. We therefore stand under a religio-moral charge to live in communities and to exercise our personal autonomy with social concern. In turn, our communities may justifiably require us to curtail our freedom so that they can function and persevere. Moreover, because certain of them such as country, family, and religion substantially make us who we are, they can also legitimately make exceptional demands on us. They can rightly insist that we curb the free exercise of our consciences when their promptings conflict with the group's central affirmations.

Our postmodern humility about selfhood also requires us to grant our group's greater esteem than the modern ethos did. People having shown themselves to be far less rational, selfless, and morally competent than we once thought, we can freshly appreciate how community standards and traditions can benefit the mature self. They often embody a sagacity far more profound, comprehensive, and time-tested than anything we might create. In conflict with a community that still shapes us, we cannot assume, as we once imperiously did, that modernity has given us far greater insight into our duty and destiny than it has. Rather, we now often find that we must bow to what, after initial rejection and open reconsideration, we concede to be its superior wisdom.

I do not mean by strongly arguing for the sociality of the self and thus of its self-legislation to also make a case for Dostoevski's Grand Inquisitor. But I am regularly exasperated by an American Jewry that, wallowing in freedom, prates piously of the sanctity of personal choice and uses it mainly to sanction casual nonobservance and flabby ethics. I seek only to restore a proper tension between our autonomy and social responsibility, one the contemporary idolization of the self has grossly distorted. I too equate all human dignity with self-determination, but only within the context of a Covenant with God that gives us our personal significance and makes all God's covenant-partners an essential element of our selfhood.

That being understood, when an institution suggests that I should regularly rely on its judgment rather than on my own, I will reassert the sanctity of personal autonomy and oppose its effort to diminish my personhood. I concede that in any such controversy my community may legitimately ask for my social bona fides and ask what sacrifices I, as more than a selfish self, have in fact made for its/our welfare. As long as I can present reasonably satisfactory credentials, I will then unabashedly ask for its bona fides. What sacrifices has it made of its power, its ambition, and its self-serving nature for me and others of its adherents, we who are not merely its beneficiaries but independent centers of worth and wisdom, and not infrequently the source of its authority? Most institutions still function without essential regard for the rich personhood of those they serve. Their leaders seek compliance by quickly reverting to paternalism, punishment, or tyranny. In the dialectical arrangement of living in covenant, just as autonomous individuals must live in responsible sociality, so our institutions must structure and activate themselves in elemental respect for the God-given dignity of their participants. We properly yearn for the messianic day when the common course will fully represent the common will. Until then, we must ask for its practical equivalent: that our organizations manifest a major, activist commitment to achieving true community and make regular progress toward that goal.

I cannot specify a rule by which we can settle serious confrontations between these valid authorities or even identify the signs that indicate we have reached reasonable limits of individual sacrifice or institutional patience. But we have an old-new model for such open, unsettled, but mutually dignifying relationships, namely, "covenant," now less a contract spelled out from on high than a loving effort to live in reciprocal respect. As the pain of trying to create egalitarian marriages indicates, we cannot know early on what forms and processes most people will find appropriate to such relationships. We can, however, accept covenantal relationships as a central ethical challenge of our time and pragmatically learn how we might sanctify ourselves by living it. For some such reason, I take it, God has given us freedom and opened history to our determination.

The Special Responsibilities of Religious Groups

I believe the foregoing analysis applies to secular as to religious social structures, but it takes somewhat altered form when applied to the corporate life of a biblical religion, most specifically, of course, Judaism.

In the Bible and Talmud the interests of the Covenant people heavily outweigh concern for its individual members. True, individual Jews have extraordinary religious scope in Judaism. Simply by knowing and willing, any Jew may do what God requires of Jews. Even the legal authorities who determine the details of our obligations do so not by institutional selection but by an authority invested in them by an informal community recognition of their personal religious attainment. Yet classically, this heady Jewish recognition of individuality functions only within our folk contract with God.

Non-Orthodox thinkers have broadly extended the role of individual autonomy in Judaism, all the while insisting that our Jewish legitimacy also requires ongoing interaction with the Jewish community. I link the social, the theological, and the personal levels of our Jewishness by utilizing the existentialist metaphor of relationship. In my view, Jewish autonomy becomes the use of our freedom in terms of our personal participation in the people of Israel's Covenant with God as the latest expression of its historic tradition.

Two intensifications of general human sociality arise from this conception of the Jewish self. As in all religions, living in Covenant involves a human being's most utterly fundamental relationship, namely, that with God. Hence our religious communities and duties cannot be peripheral to our lives but must be at their center; anything less than profound devotion and commitment profanes our professions of Jewish faith. Moreover, because the Covenant was made primarily with the Jewish *ethnos* and only secondarily with the Jewish *autos*, the Jewish people, its local communities, families, and progeny, remain the immediate channels through which we Jews sacralize existence. Since modern life immerses us in an individualistic ethos, all contemporary Judaisms must stress the sociality of Jewish spirituality so that we may live in proper Covenantal duality.

For their part, we must admit, our religious leaders bear impossible burdens. Does anyone truly know how to transform impersonal institutions into humanely interactive communities and not lose the stability that enables a religion to survive? Not every individualizing change we have advocated or they have initiated has proved entirely beneficial. Others, which they have resisted, have shown only ambiguous value when implemented elsewhere. Besides, in recent years tradition has often held up well against modernity.

Surely the accumulated wisdom of centuries should not easily be surrendered for what may announce itself as our fulfillment but what the passage of time will show to have been one period's passion. Moreover, our leaders must guide us in terms of what they believe God wants God's people to be doing now. Though they know they cannot speak as God's special intimates, they also may not evade the special obligation created by their preeminence, for it inevitably invests their decisions or their inaction with something of God's own authority.

Jewish leaders find these theoretical problems exacerbated by the persistent threats to our existence. With our people requiring vigilant defense against its foes, how can it easily tolerate vigorous critics and conscientious dissenters? At the same time, our community knows and practices so little, believing even less, that its indifference alone threatens meaningful Jewish continuity. Then shall what has been preserved of our tradition be further vitiated for the sake of individual conscience?

Though our religious leaders can find strong warrant for resisting further experiments in personalizing our faith, they should not expect that we will passively accept significant disregard of human autonomy. We not only expect religious institutions to model the humane values God demands of us as individuals, we expect them to do so in exemplary fashion. Though we cannot demand perfection of our religious leaders and institutions, we can and must expect them to demonstrate more corporate righteousness than the unconsecrated, for we can find individual holiness by ourselves. They legitimate their communal roles under the Covenant only as they make it possible for us to fulfill the necessary social dimension of our responsibility to God.

Most Americans today apparently do not find that their religious institutions meet these spiritual expectations. Against everything sociologists keep saying about secularization, pollsters regularly find that the overwhelming majority of Americans continue to profess belief in God and a broad range of other traditional beliefs. Yet they do not greatly involve themselves in organized religion and its practices—and that is more true of Jews than any other religious sample. Of course, this picture of a massive Lincolnesque defection from religious institutions stems in part from the limitations of polling people about religion. But I think it tells us much about our righteous intolerance of religious bodies that do not clearly exemplify their vaunted values.

Here too I can adumbrate no rule for resolving discord between the conscientious self and Jewish religious leadership seeking to be true to God. Though our tradition has honored obedience more than innovation, inspirited Jews have continually enriched our heritage in amazingly diverse fashion. Today, with individual creativity a primary cultural good, we may expect that those who achieve intimacy with God will make quite unpredictable demands upon our institutions. But if these innovative spirits also know themselves to stand in Israel's Covenant with God, they must also acknowledge a summons to live by the discipline of the Covenant community. We will initially assess the Jewish authenticity of their demands upon our institutions by asking how they have met their obli-gations to our people. What do they know of the tradition they have brought into judgment? What sacrifices of self have they made for Judaism's continuity? What place does the people of Israel have in their personal vision of the proper Jewish sevice of God? Does their individual version of Judaism give promise of continuing Israel in faithful corporate service to God until the Messiah comes?

Only when they have satisfied these social claims can individual Jews claim that their prophetic protests against our institutions arise from a Jewish ground. Then they may rightly ask: How have our organizations used their power in relation to individuals and in pursuit of their corporate aims? How much dissent and pluralism have they tolerated or encouraged? How far have they sought to lead us and our society toward a more humane existence rather than merely mirror or modify its present virtues and vices?

Our special contemporary difficulties with this clash between self and community derive from our need to refashion the relationship that once shaped our institutional life. Heretofore it involved only two centers of authority: God and the folk pledged to God. Now our commitment to the religious significance of the autonomous self requires us to factor into this alliance a new and demanding third partner, the self-determining individual. This must not be taken to mean that God's primacy in the Covenant ought in any way be diminished. The existence of the people of Israel corporately and of Jews as individuals devolves from God and they therefore ought to be dedicated, beyond all else, to God. I am only saying that our religious experience requires that our religious institutions recognize that the individual Jew is neither bereft of God's presence nor insensitive to God's present command. So each Jewish self must now be factored into our understanding of the community's obligations under the Covenant. This means to me that we require more help from our institutions than we have commonly received as we seek to work out the meaning of our personal existence in Covenant. That will likely mean tolerating greater dissent in ideas and divergence in practice than they have previously found congenial, but that alone can make it possible for us to become more the persons as well as the people of God.

God's Uniqueness Demands a Universal Horizon

Broadening our horizon from the intra- to the extracommunal arena of Covenant responsibility essentially recapitulates the clash of self and community in the tension between devotion to our people and to humanity. Again I wish to redress the imbalance I may have created in stressing Jewish uniqueness by offering an appreciation of the Jewish roots of universalism.

The modern Jewish dedication to humanity has often been scanted as an apologetic ideology created by nineteenth-century modernizers. Clearly, it became an explicit, major motif in the non-Orthodoxies that appealed to many Jews because, among other reasons, their universal teaching justified giving high Jewish priority to the non-Jewish problems and ideals in which they now happily found themselves involved. However, this development had a considerable basis in some of the underpinnings of classic Jewish belief, namely, its doctrines of first and last things.

The Torah does not begin with the first Jew or the first *mitzvah*. For eleven chapters it tells how everything began and how world history gained its sorry character, thus eliciting the call to Abraham and its consummation at Sinai. Messianism, too, has universal significance, as in the dramatic prophetic vision of all nations living in peace and everyone dwelling in security. Of course, the Bible and the Talmud both have more dominant particularistic eschatologies, which strikes me as reasonable for a people highly conscious of its eccentric, minority status among the nations. But what normal ethnic development explains the accompanying Hebrew national self-transcendence? And why did it persist over the centuries? I can explain it only as a logical consequence of Israel's experience with its unique God, the entailments of which took considerable time to work out.

Consider the implications of God's stature, uniqueness, and goodness. Creation establishes God's sole right to rule and any effort to establish another ultimate authority must be resisted to the point of martyrdom. Every other center of power in human history therefore derives its legitimacy from God. No clan, tribe, nation, class, party, or race can call for unconditional allegiance without becoming idolatrous.

God's uniqueness integrally complements God's sovereignty. Asserting oneness alone might leave God unified but cosmically insignificant. Proclaiming God the only real God gives God's commands unchallengeable, irreplaceable, imperative quality. The ubiquitous old, now troublesome, political metaphor, "King," once aptly symbolized all this: Only God sets the order of creation and God alone has ultimate authority in all that follows. Moreover, being good, God cares about human beings and the quality of their action. God wills that singly and collectively they sanctify their lives by their deeds, manifest God's goodness in their character, and direct their freedom by God's behests. Therefore, the supreme, unique God of the universe makes a covenant with humankind, all humankind.

Were the notion of God covenanting not paradoxical enough, the picture of the resulting relationship makes the behavior predicated of creation's sole Sovereign even odder. God creates beings who are free enough to say "No" to the One who made them. Then, apparently because of this distinctive power, God summons these creatures into an alliance of mutual responsibility. For whatever reason, people refuse to fulfill their part of the ennobling pact. Yet the scorned God does not abandon, overpower, or—except in one unsatisfactory experiment—destroy them. Rather, the Ultimate now manifests a tenacious purposiveness. Creatively, God tries numerous ways—revelation, prophecy, punishment, a Covenant with a special people—to save the unique creatures from their obduracy and to realize the divine rule on earth. Messianism is the logical culmination of this view of God, and though the dialectic of Jewish faith makes it possible to assert Israel's sole salvation, God's universal concern must in due course also be voiced.

Surveying the extent to which Judaism's implicit universalism became explicit over the centuries suggests that only when exclusion eased have Jews been moved to articulate their comprehensive ideal. The literatures of the Jews of Hellenistic Alexandria and, later, the Moslem-Jewish symbiosis give ample evidence of this. So, in turn, the more complete social equalization of the Jews in the Emancipation motivated its expression with a fullness theretofore unknown. Assimilationists, Marxists, and others made universalism their exclusive faith and scorned Jewish particularity as superfluous, a charge most Jews rejected, dialectically reaffirming the lasting importance of Jewish particularity. More recently, the Holocaust and its resonance in subsequent threats to Jewish continuity have reminded us of the preciousness of this specific folk. So we live in the uneasy tension created by simultaneous devotion to our people and to humankind.

The Sovereign God and the Proper Authority of Nations

Much of our theology of clashing group loyalties derives from our understanding of nationhood, whose *locus classicus* is Genesis, chapters 10 and 11.

Had humankind remained simply Noahide, we could speak of the historic reality of universalistic existence, but the Torah realistically acknowledges that we meet humankind entire only in the form of "tongues, languages, lands, and nations." It appears to transmit two different traditions about the division of a universal, Noahide humanity into diverse nations. In Genesis 10, ethnicity evolves as a natural consequence of the postdiluvian population explosion. Genesis 11, however, depicts the division of languages and the scattering to many lands as punishment for seeking to build a tower into heaven, God's abode, and to wrest a (divine?) name. In consequence, God creates divisions among people to diminish their united power to do evil. Elsewhere biblical authors say God assigned a particular folk character to each nation, implying that their number and culture are fixed for all time.

The sages had little difficulty integrating these views. The differences among people emerge "naturally" as a result of their customary sinfulness, attested by their decreasing longevity in the generations after the flood. God divided them into their various groups to turn their blasphemous self-assertion against one another and only the superior rule of the Messiah will bring them to live with one another as God's faithful servants. What the rabbis observed of the paganism that surrounded them simply confirmed the biblical judgment: Nationhood is a natural expression of the human will-to-do-evil, for collectivity intensifies individual lust. When the rabbis speak of "the nations" one may be reasonably certain that their point will be derogatory. Despite this, they did not renege on the belief that God had made a covenant with all humankind. This allowed them to rule that a righteous individual gentile could attain the life of the world to come, a judgment they never made of a collective other than Israel. Seeing "the nations" behave abominably, they, like the prophets, confidently expected God would one day punish them drastically.

Until recently, Jewish thinkers have been too overjoyed at being granted citizenship to say much about the dark side of nationhood. They have responded to existence in freedom with messianic fervor, believing that the enlightened acts of their states showed them reaching moral stature. In the latter part of the nineteenth century, Isaac Mayer Wise described American democracy in eschatological terms while Hermann Cohen argued, about World War I, that the German nation enshrined humanity's highest ideals. Today political realism has become such a burden that one can easily become wistful at their naiveté. Nations still show themselves to be a pretty ugly bunch, exponentially exemplifying our human will-to-do-evil. History remains God's problem—and ours. Theologically, rabbinic realism carries as much conviction on the social as on the individual level. While all human beings stand in covenant with God and some individuals live up to it, the nations and peoples generally do not. Collectivity distorts and displaces our personal sense of Noahide covenantship. I mean this not as a Rousseauistic description of society as the despoiler of our congenital individual goodness. Without our collectives, we still would not be back in Eden—something anarchists do not understand. I am only saying, with the rabbis, that as we organize our nations we empower and give scope to our will-to-do-evil.

But God has not made a covenant with humankind for nothing. Without violating the freedom that makes us possible covenant partners, God still proposes to bring us to covenant holiness and therefore does not abolish the alliance with the Noahides. Instead, God makes a new, more involving Covenant, the one announced to Abraham and consummated at Sinai.

The Unique Character of the Nation Covenanted to God

The Torah accounts specify God's repeated promises to turn Abraham's descendants into a great nation and thus they assert a unique origin for the Hebrews: a divine summons to special obedience to replace arrogance and its punishment. So too the Hebrews do not begin with a land of their own, only the promise of one as God's Covenant partner. Even as they approach it, Moses warns them that they can occupy it only as long as their behavior reflects loyalty to God. For Covenant reciprocity entails Israel's life-and-society-transforming acceptance of God's rule and rules. By the new multiplicity of deeds commanded by God, Israel shows itself to be God's partner without parallel.

In this nation, the Transcendent uniquely grounds the collective enterprise and character. Realistically, and with an absence of the defensiveness we expect of institutional documents, the biblical authors do not claim that the will-to-do-evil no longer functions among the Hebrews. They sin, sometimes egregiously, but they also know it to be a special responsibility of their odd nationhood to keep the nation in thrall to the true sovereign, God. In the stories of the kings who embody Israelite responsibility we find the model of our people's intuition of its idiosyncratic, sacred nationhood. Being human, the kings demonstrate the will-to-do-evil; being rulers, they do so on a grand scale. But their political preeminence does not exempt them from God's reproof and judgment by those extraordinary figures, Israel's prophets. That the Israelites remembered and transmitted as sacred teaching the history and messages of the prophets attests to the perception of Covenant-distinctiveness that came to animate this unusual nation.

The incongruity of Israel's political behavior in the light of its Covenant ideals prompts the theological wonder that God did not choose another social form for them rather than subject them to the awesome risks of collective power. Two suppositions—one substantive, one functional—respond to this query.

God makes Abraham's family a nation in history in order to show that collective power can be sanctified through subordination to God's rule. This does not, however, require Israel to fulfill its Covenantal responsibilities through political autonomy or any other given social structure. The specific form in which the people should organize itself devolves from the historical circumstances in which it finds itself. Thus, Israel could be content with a loose federation and occasional charismatic leaders until the Sea Peoples threatened its existence, bringing about a shift to monarchy. In their extended Middle Ages, the Jews had no hope of political independence and carried on their corporate career through autonomous community existence. In our time, a numinous combination of tragedy, international guilt, and Jewish will made it possible for us to renew Jewish statehood, this time in democratic, secular form. And world Jewry has acknowledged its vital role in keeping our people alive and providing us with new opportunities to pursue our millennial quest.

Being organized as an ethnic group also has functional value in the Covenant. Israel must live in intense fealty to God amidst nations who will ignore or spurn God's behests for them. The Jews have therefore had to bear an uncommon burden of contumely and suffering, a human condition the Covenant does not proclaim a virtue and Jewish prayer often asks God to end. God's redemptive power manifesting itself only sporadically, the nations remaining obdurately perverse, the Messiah tarrying, Israel lives in jeopardy and continues its service in history with difficulty. Where other groups may seek a future out of biological drive, social inertia, or ethnic self-assertion, Israel fights to live so that God's reality will become known to all humankind.

The multiple ties that ethnicity engenders help the imperiled people endure. Bound to one another and their Covenant memories by land, language, customs, heroes, jokes, foods, gossip, and other aspects of folk life, the Jewish people can defend itself from history's blows clothed in a many-layered ethnic armor. Infusing its folkways with Covenant sensibility, it can powerfully transmit, reinforce, and renew Israel's lasting purpose. This socialization carries such power, Israel can for some period continue being Israel despite times of relative indifference, illiteracy, and faithlessness.

In sum, Jewish ethnic individuality has a universal telos that affects and directs it, but since that purpose must be accomplished in history, it can only be achieved in premessianic times by this particular group in quite local ways. The dialectic of telos and means can be sinfully distorted at either pole. Modern Jews giddily believed that benign politics would imminently realize universalism and sought to sublimate their particularity to it. And the nations have often so abused us that self-concern has blinded us to our involvement with humanity. But we cannot avoid the dialectic of duty imposed on us by our people's Covenant with God, which teaches us of God's covenant with all human beings.

The Theological Context of Jewish Politics

I have spoken in the generalities appropriate to reflective discourse but it would be a denial of Jewish responsibility to avoid applying them to the critical locus of our contemporary clash of values, the State of Israel.

The Holocaust searingly made plain that the Jewish people must never again surrender to others our responsibility to do all that we can to assure our people's survival. We can no longer blithely expect the nations of the world to take up our cause because of their moral progress. During the Middle Ages we could often count on the popes to save us from local despots and fanatics (and then be appropriately compensated). Our sorry experience with Christianity during the Holocaust and our ambivalent relations with it since make it a questionable support in a time of great Jewish trial. Perhaps nations occasionally act out of moral considerations and religion can still affect political decisions. Nonetheless, it does not hurt that we are remarkably loyal and productive citizens worldwide and effectively self-reliant in the State of Israel. For all that we can and must do, the future of our various communities remains in the hands of others, and only as democracy functions truly can there be some hope of Jewish security—another indication of the intertwining of ethnic self-assertion and involvement with humanity at large.

Having returned to independent ethnic status as a sovereign nation, we do not wish ever again to be denied corporate dignity. Though our forebears found ways to sanctify ghetto existence, they considered it the epitome of exile, a metaphysical as well as a political debasement. Having tasted the rights of self-determination and self-expression, we wish, like all the other peoples of the earth, to make our contribution to humankind by being allowed to be ourselves in our own way.

The State of Israel came into being on some such surge of particularism and since its existence has so continually been threatened, one might reasonably feel that it fulfills its role as a Jewish state merely by keeping our people alive. That continues to be all many Israelis and some Diaspora Jews feel ought to be asked of it. Many other Israelis and much of world Jewry, though agreeing on the necessity of Jewish survival, also press our corollary Covenant commitment to high humane standards. For many years they took special Jewish pride in the State of Israel's exceptional moral accomplishments, which are made all the more impressive as a conscious ingredient of Israeli national purpose despite requiring special sacrifice from the citizenry. In recent years, as the West Bank remained under military administration, as Jewish irredentism increased, as the incursion into Beirut helped destabilize Lebanon, as the Intifada expressed a Palestinian will for independence, the discord between Jewish self-interest and universal values split Israelis into opposing camps of near equal size. Diaspora Jews, reflecting their less ethnic, more humanistic situation, began exhibiting a new sense of distance from the State of Israel. Remarkably, in this excruciatingly difficult situation, few Jews could argue that particularity or universality alone could satisfy the demands of Jewish responsibility. The double entailment of the Covenant remained that clear but also, therefore, unresolvable by any one-sided proposal for action. The dialectical understanding of our duty does not remove us from the indeterminacy of history and its testing, but helps us to understand why we are torn—and that too may incline us toward one practical decision or another. At least it helps us to be more responsible about our decisions. To say more than that, I believe, is to pass from theology into politics.

20

The Election of Israel

DAVID NOVAK

Creation and Election

In the narrative of Scripture the election of Abraham, the progenitor of the covenanted people of Israel, comes suddenly and without warning. It seems to catch us unprepared.

> The Lord said to Abram: "You go away from your land, from your birthplace, from your father's house to the land that I will show you. I will make you a great nation and bless you; I will make your name great and you will be a blessing. I will bless those who bless you and those who curse you I will curse. Through you (*vekha*) all the families of the earth will be blessed. And Abram went as the Lord had spoken to him." (Genesis 12:1–4)

In this elementary text there seems to be no clue as to why God elects Abraham and his progeny or why Abraham obeys the call to respond to being elected by God. Unlike in the case of Noah, who is elected to save humankind and the animal world from the Flood "because (*ki*) I have seen that you are righteous (*tsadiq*) before Me in this generation" (Genesis 7:1), and who obviously responds to God's call because of the biological drive for self-preservation, there is no reason given here for either God's choice or Abraham's positive response to it. Any righteousness attributed to Abraham is seen as subsequent, not prior, to God's election of him.[1] It is thus a result of, not a reason for, election. And unlike Noah, Abraham does seem to have the alternative of staying where he already dwells. He seems to have a reasonable alternative to obedience to God's call. From the text of Scripture itself it seems as though Abraham could have stayed home. In his case, there is no destruction like a universal flood on the imminent horizon.

David Novak, *The Election of Israel* (New York: Cambridge University Press, 1995), pp. 115–38. © Cambridge University Press, New York, NY 10011.

Simply leaving the matter at this mysterious level, is not speculation about the deeper meaning of the covenant established by this election and its acceptance thereby precluded? In the case of God's reason for electing Abraham and the people of Israel his progeny, the answer seems to be yes. At that side of the covenant, Scripture itself seems to imply "My thoughts (*mahshevotai*) are not your thoughts" (Isaiah 55:8) when it states,

> For you are a people consecrated to the Lord your God; the Lord your God chose you (*bekha bahar*) to be unto him a treasure people from out of all the peoples on the face of the earth. It was not because you were more numerous than all the other peoples that the Lord desired you (*hashaq bakhem*) and chose you, for you are the least (*ha-me'at*) of all the peoples. It was because of the Lord's love for you (*me'ahavat adonai etkhem*) and his keeping the promise (*ha-shevu'ah*) he made to your ancestors. (Deuteronomy 7:6–8)

Of course, taken by itself this statement is a tautology: God loves you/chooses you/desires you because God loves you/chooses you/desires you. For there is no reason given as to why he made his promises to Abraham, and to Isaac and Jacob in the first place.[2] And the people of Israel themselves cannot claim any inherent qualities that could be seen as reasons for their election by God.[3]

This is consistent with the logic of creation. In Scripture, unlike other ancient sagas, we are not told about any life of God prior to creation. Indeed, only the God to whom "all the earth is mine" (Exodus 19:5), to whom "the heavens and the highest heavens" (Deuteronomy 10:14) belong, only this God has such absolute freedom from any natural necessity to create a singular relationship like the covenant with Israel. There is nothing that could be considered a divine a priori from which one could infer the possibility of a nondivine world, much less the reality of any such world. All of God's relations with the world are, therefore, a posteriori. From revelation we learn some of the things God wants to do with the world, most especially what God wants his human creatures to do with the world along with him, but we do not learn why he made the world the way he did in the first place or, indeed, why he made it at all. So, too, we do not learn why God chose the people of Israel or, indeed, why he chose any people at all. All we learn, a posteriori, is what God wants to do with this people. "The secret things (*ha-nistarot*) are for the Lord our God; but the revealed things (*ve-ha-niglot*) are for us and our children forever: to practice all the commandments of this Torah" (Deuteronomy 29:28).

However, on the human side of this relationship of election, it is not only Abraham who is to respond to election. Election is primarily generic and only secondarily individual. Abraham is elected as the progenitor of a people. Every member of this people is elected by God, and every member of this people is called upon to respond to his or her generic election. So, even if Abraham's individual reasons for accepting God's call could well be left alone as his own private and inscrutable business, speculation about his generic reasons for accepting it is our business as well inasmuch as his response is archetypal for all of us who follow after him.[4] For a communal response is a public matter, one whose reasons have to be rooted in continuing common experience before they can enter into personal reflection. This, then, calls for our reflection on our own human situation and what conditions in it enable us to respond to God's electing presence without caprice. Projecting our own reflection on the human conditions for election back to Abraham retrospectively is essential midrashic thinking.[5] Without it, we would lose our singular connection to the text of Scripture. It would become merely *a* datum among other data rather than *the* datum for us.

Of course, at the most original level, the prime reason for obeying God is that God is God. In Scripture, God's original presence is explicitly normative: his first contact with humans in the Garden is set forth in the words: "The Lord God commanded (*vayitsav*) the humans (*al ha'adam*)" (Genesis 2:16).[6] Norms are a necessity for human life because humans are beings who must consciously order the conflicting parts of their experience if they are to survive and cohere. That ordering requires a primary point of authority. (One can only be a moral relativist when looking at someone else's choices from afar, not when one is required to make his or her *own* choices at hand.) A human life without an ordering hierarchy of authority could only be that of an angel: an infallible life without conflict.[7] So it follows that any rejection of God's norms presupposes the substitution of God's authority by the authority of one who is not-God being made into God. The prime authority wherever is always taken to be God. There can be no normative vacuum.[8] That is why the first temptation to disobey God is the temptation that "you will be like God" (Genesis 3:5). You, not God, will become the prime authority. Without absolute authority, the creator would no longer be the creator; he would be forced to abdicate, as it were.

The relationship with God the creator at this original level is essentially negative, however.[9] It only consists of prohibitions that function as divine limitations of human illusions of self-sufficiency and autonomous authority. So far there is nothing positive between humans and God. It is with Abraham's call that we begin to see the establishment of a substantive relationship of humans *with* God. And in order for any such positive relationship to be sustained, there must be the discovery of positive reasons by humans *within* themselves for them to want to accept and maintain this relationship. Thus, whereas resistance to the idolatrous temptation to substitute the authority of not-God (the world or the human person) for God involves the affirmation of truth, the response to the covenant involves the desire for good.[10] By obeying God, what good did Abraham desire? What did his response intend?

The covenant itself must be the object of human desire. This desire for it as good is an essential component of it. Hence in presenting the positive covenantal norms. Moses appeals to the desire of the people for what is their good.[11] "The Lord commanded us to practice (*la asot*) all these statutes, to fear the Lord our God, which is good for us (*tov lanu*) all times for our vitality (*le-hayyotenu*) as it is today. And it will be right (*tsedaqah*) for us to be careful to do this whole commandment before the Lord our God as he has commanded us" (Deuteronomy 6:25). And shortly before this passage, each one of the people is commanded to "love the Lord your God with all your heart, with all your life, and with all your might" (6:5). But can there be any love without desire? And is not desire experienced, inchoately to be sure, even before its desideratum comes to it?[12] "For you O Lord is my whole desire (*kol ta'avati*)" (Psalms 38:10).[13] And does not desire entail hope, which is essentially an anticipation of something in itself unknown in the present? Moreover, can there be any desire that does not intend good for the one in whom it stirs?[14] Or as the Psalmist puts it, "Who is there for me in heaven, and besides you I desire (*lo hafatsti*) no one on earth . . . As for me, the nearness of God, that is my good (*li tov*) . . ." (Psalms 73:25, 28). Is not God to be served by a "desiring soul" (*nefesh hafetsah*) (I Chronicles 28:9)?

It seems to me that the reasons for Abraham's answering the electing call of God, and thus the paradigm for all subsequent Jewish answering of it, can be seen in the promise made in the initial call itself that Abraham and his progeny will be the source of blessing for all humankind. Accordingly, Abraham's relationship with God is correlative to his relationship with the world. And the precise presentation of that correlation is found in Abraham's dialogue with God over the judgment of the cities of Sodom and Gomorrah. God justifies including Abraham in this dialogue as follows:

> How can I conceal what I am doing from Abraham? And Abraham shall surely become a great and important (*atsum*) nation, in whom all the nations of the earth shall be blessed. For I know him, so that (*le-ma'an*) he will command his children and his household after him to keep the way of the Lord to do what is right (*tsedaqah*) and just (*mishpat*). (Genesis 18:17–19)

The question now is to determine the connection of the blessing of the nations of the earth to Abraham and his people keeping the way of the Lord to do what is right and just.

The first thing to note is that God's statement of his knowing does not seem to be a noetic prediction. The text does not say "I know that," but rather "I know him (*yed'ativ*)."[15] Abraham is the direct object of God's knowing, and the result of his being aware of God's knowing him will be that he will be able to keep the way of the Lord. Without God's knowing him and his being aware of it, Abraham would not be able to recognize the way of the Lord and keep it.[16]

Here "knowing" is not a judgment of a state of affairs drawn from the objects of past experience and then projecting from them into the future. This knowing is, rather, a relationship of direct and intimate personal contact. It is presence. Thus in the Garden the "tree of the knowledge (*ets ha-da'at*) of good and bad" is a symbol for the direct contact with all the experience the world now has to offer and which the first human pair desire.[17] Since they were able "to judge favorably (*va-tere*) that (*ki*) the fruit of this tree is good to eat and delightful in appearance" (Genesis 3:6) even before they ate it, their judgment preceded their experience or "knowledge." Their judgment is in essence a prediction of what they think they will experience. This is why "knowledge" is used to designate the intimacy of sexual contact—"And the man knew (*yada*) Eve his wife and she conceived" (Genesis 4:1)—although it is not limited to sexual contact.[18] It is something that can be judged desirable based on one's desire of it in advance, but it can only be experienced directly in the present.

In connection with the election of Israel, the prophet Amos conveys to Israel God's announcement: "Only you have I known (*raq etkhem yad'ati*) of all the families of the earth" (Amos 3:2). Now, the prophet could not be saying that God is unaware of the other nations inasmuch as he himself has already been called to prophesy about them by God.[19] What the prophet is saying is that God shares a unique intimacy with Israel that is the basis for the unique claims he makes upon her. The claims are because God cares for Israel. Since these claims are made in the context of covenantal intimacy, the prophet then says in the very next verse, "Can two walk together if they have not met each other (*no'adu*)?"[20] Israel is intimately known by God and is to act based upon her intimate experience of that knowing. The relationship here is not a noetic relation of a subject and an object. It is the divine I reaching out to embrace a human thou who then chooses to be so embraced.[21] Thus at the very beginning of God's regeneration of the covenant with Israel in Egypt, Scripture states:

> And the children of Israel groaned from their toil and cried out, and their cry reached up to God from out of their toil. Then God took notice (*va-yizkor*) of his covenant with Abraham and Isaac and Jacob. And God looked with favor (*va-yar*) at the children of Israel and God cared (*va-yeda*). (Exodus 2:23–25)[22]

As for Abraham's response to God's election, it is initially a response to being in intimate contact with God. That is what he desires. That intimacy is, as we shall soon see, the main characteristic of the covenantal life of the Jewish people in the present. Those commandments of the Torah that specifically celebrate the historical singularity of the covenantal events give that life its rich substance.

What we must now see is how the experience of being known by God leads Abraham and his progeny to practice the way of the Lord. That can be better understood if we remember that the act of election is first a promise. Thus the covenant itself is founded in a promise. But why does Abraham believe the promise of God? Is his response anything more than a "leap of faith"?

In terms of the sequence of the biblical text itself, it is important to remember that the promise of God to Abraham is not the first promise God has made. After the Flood God promises that "I shall uphold my covenant with you . . . and there will be no further deluge (*mabul*) to destroy the earth" (Genesis 9:11). The Rabbis were very astute in insisting that unconditional divine promises are made as oaths. Any oath made by God could not be annulled by God thereafter inasmuch as the annulment of an oath (*shevu'ah*) can only be done by a higher authority than that of the one who made it. But there could be no higher authority than God to annul it. God must keep his own word, then; if not, his credibility would be totally undermined.[23] Moreover, the connection between the promise made to Noah and the promise made to Abraham is explicitly made by Deutero-Isaiah. "For this is to me like the waters of Noah: just as I promised (*nishba'ti*) that the waters of Noah would never again pass over the earth, so do I promise . . . that even if the mountains be moved and the hills be shaken, my kindness shall not be moved and my covenant of peace (*u-vriti shalom*) shall not be shaken—so says the Lord who loves you" (Isaiah 54:9–10). Furthermore, we learn that God's relation to the world is the correlate of his relationship with Israel, and Israel's relationship with the world is the correlate of her relationship with God.

I think that one can see the inner connection of these two promises in the term used to characterize the "way of the Lord" that Abraham is to teach his progeny: "what is right and just" (*tsedaqah u-mishpat*). But this requires that we look upon the two words in the term as denoting two separate but related acts. The usual interpretations of them sees them as denoting one single act, namely, correct justice, which is the standard whereby the distinction between the innocent and the guilty is consistently maintained in adjudication. This interpretation of the term is appropriate to the immediate context of the dialogue between God and Abraham in which Abraham indicates that consistency in judgment is the bare minimum to be expected from God who has chosen to be "the judge of all the earth" (Genesis 18:25). This interpretation concentrates on the ethical issues in the text.[24] However, looking at the even deeper theological issues in the text, one can take *tsedaqah* as one term and *mishpat* as another. Along these lines, one can interpret *tsedaqah* as the transcendent aspect of God's relation to creation and *mishpat* as the immanent aspect of it. The elect people, then, are to imitate both the transcendent and the immanent aspects of God's relation to the world.

Tsedaqah is the transcendent aspect of God's relation to creation because it is something totally gracious. God's creation of the world is an act of grace; there is nothing that required that there be something created rather than nothing. And after the Flood, the renewal of creation in the covenant with the earth is even more gracious inasmuch as God's human creatures—made in his own image—were so ungrateful for the gift of their existence and that of the world.

God's *tsedaqah* is the ultimate explanation of the contingency of existence. As such, it could only be expressed in a promise, which extends from the present into the future. For the past by itself never guarantees any continuity or permanence. Its immanent order is itself contingent.[25] So, to use a current metaphor, reliance on this order in itself might be nothing more than "arranging deck chairs on the *Titanic*." But a primary promise in and of itself has no antecedents; indeed, if it did, it would be the process of making an inference and then a prediction based upon that inference. It would, then, designate a relation *within* the world already there. A primary promise, conversely, is infinitely more radical, infinitely more originating. Accordingly, it could not come from the world itself, whose real existence (rather than its abstract "Being") is no more necessary than real, mortal, human existence.[26] It could only come from the One who transcends both the world and humankind.

Yet despite its ultimate contingency, worldly existence has structure and continuity. The primal event of creation founds existence as an orderly process. That is because the divine promise is itself covenantal. The structure and continuity of existence, its essential character, is what is meant by *mishpat*. It is through *mishpat* that existence coheres. Minimally, that coherence is seen in the principle of contradiction, by which things maintain their distinct identities in relation to each other. Abraham's challenge to God that the judge must act justly and consistently distinguish between the innocent and the guilty is the biblical presentation of this basic principle of all reason. *Mishpat*, then, is the standard whereby the boundaries between things and between acts are maintained. *Mishpat* is violated when those boundaries are not respected. That is why *mishpat* is basically negative. It functions as a limit. Indeed, it is not inappropriate here to use Spinoza's formula: *determinatio negatio est*.[27] *Mishpat* is that fundamental *determinatio* that makes an ordered approach to existence possible. Nevertheless, *mishpat*, precisely because it is essentially negative, can never guarantee the facticity of existence; it always presupposes that existence is being maintained by God's *tsedaqah*. Expressions of *mishpat* are always ultimately conditional, namely, *if* there is a world, *then* it must have certain structures to cohere. As Jeremiah puts it, "Without my covenant by day and by night, I would not have put the laws (*huqqot*) of heaven and earth in place (*lo samti*)" (Jeremiah 33:25).[28] Essence in biblical theology follows from existence, but existence is never derived from essence.[29]

That is why truth (*emet*) is God's faithfulness before it is external correspondence and before it is inner coherence. Truth is first God's faithful promise that created existence will abide. "He makes heaven and earth, the sea and all that is in them, keeping faith (*hashomer emet*) forever" (Psalms 146:6).[30] Only when nature is "your faithful seasons (*emunat itekha*)" (Isaiah 33:6) can it function as a standard to which human judgment can truly correspond. And human judgment and action can only cohere fully, can only "do justly and seek fidelity (*emunah*)" (Jeremiah 5:1) when it is aware of the coherence of cosmic *mishpat*. That complete awareness only comes when the Torah functions as the "true witness (*ed emet*)" (Proverbs 14:25) of creation and its order in both nature and history.

The world until the time of Abraham was certainly aware of cosmic *mishpat* and the necessity to practice it in society. Thus after the Flood and the reconstruction of human life on earth, the basic moral law prohibiting bloodshed and establishing its commensurate punishment—"one who sheds human blood shall have his blood shed by humans" (Genesis 9:6)—is directly preceded by the affirmation of the cosmic order: "For as long as the earth endures (*od*), there will be seedtime and harvest, cold and heat, summer and winter, day and night, they shall not cease" (Genesis 8:22). That cosmic order, in which both the human and the nonhuman participate, is its *mishpat*. Thus Jeremiah employs an analogy between human and nonhuman *mishpat* to make the following point: "Even the stork in the sky knows her seasons, and the turtledove, the swift, and the crane keep the time of their coming; but my people do not know the law (*mishpat*) of the Lord" (Jeremiah 8:7). Clearly, the "seasons" (*mo'adeha*) of the stork and the regular cycles (*et bo'anah*) of the other birds are their *mishpat*.

Mishpat, however, is known only as a negative, limiting force. Because of that, the violation of it is considered a denial of the fear of God, which is in effect restraint before the highest authority, the epitome of *mishpat*, the pinnacle of cosmic justice. Thus when Abraham assumes that there is no respect for the boundaries of the marital relation in the Philistine city of Gerar, specifically assuming that his wife Sarah will be abducted into the harem of the city's ruler Abimelech, he justifies his lying about Sarah being his wife by saying, "surely (*raq*) there is no fear of God (*yir'at elohim*) in this place" (Genesis 20:11). In other words, there is no *mishpat* there.[31]

What is not recognized, though, until the time of Abraham, is the reality who is the source of this cosmic order, this *mishpat*, the reality who created and sustains the cosmos in which *mishpat* is to be operative as its norm.[32] But the philosophical questions to be asked now are: What difference does it make whether we know or do not know the source of this cosmic order? Indeed, why does it have to have a source at all to be appreciated theoretically and implemented practically by us? And, furthermore, why does this source have to reveal his presence to Abraham, which is simultaneously an act of election, as biblical revelation always is? And if there is such a cosmic source, why can't this source be discovered by ratiocination, which is universal in principle?

Only when the cosmic order is perceived by those who suffer enough philosophical unrest can the most basic existential question be asked authetically: What is my place in the world? That question lies at the heart of Abraham's desire for God's presence.

This question arises from our experience of the phenomenal order of things we immediately and regularly experience around us through our bodily senses. What we soon learn from this order is our own mortal vulnerability, our superfluity in the world. When we "eat of the tree of knowledge of good and bad" (Genesis 2:17)—which is the acquisition of worldly experience—we simultaneously discover the imminence of our own death.[33] "Dust you are and to dust you shall return" (Genesis 3:19). "All is futile (*havel*). What advantage (*yitron*) is there for man in all his accomplishments (*amalo*) under the sun? One generation goes and another comes and the earth remains the same forever" (Ecclesiastes 1:2–4). Therefore, throughout human history, perceptive persons have become aware that their place is not immanently available as an animal-like instinct. As a result of this existential predicament, the transcendent desire that goes beyond immanent need arises.[34]

The first possibility is for us to discern with the intellect a higher noumenal order undergirding the phenomenal order initially perceived by the senses. Our motivation is to subordinate ourselves to this order. It alone offers us a transcendent end for our participation.[35] This is the attitude of scientific (understood as *scientia* or *Wissenschaft*, that is) *homo spectator*. The second possibility is for us to despair of ever finding the higher noumenal order "out there" and thus to look within our human selves for an order of our own device with which to use and control as much of the world as we can. This is the attitude of technological *homo faber*. The third possibility is for us to cry out for the person who stands behind this cosmic order to reveal himself to us; since the presence of persons can never be inferred from something nonpersonal, it must always be self-revelation.[36] This is the attitude of *homo revelationis*, the person of faith. For the Bible, Abraham is the first *homo revelationis*.[37]

In the biblical narrative preceding the emergence of Abraham, we find hints of both the first and the second possibilities and their attendant human attitudes. And both are seen as being in essence idolatry.

As for the first possibility, Scripture notes that during the time of Enosh, the grandson of the first couple, "the name (*shem*) of the Lord began (*huhal*) to be invoked" (Genesis 4:26). Rabbinic interpretation notes that the word for "begin" is etymologically similar to the word for "profane" (*hol*).[38] Thus it sees the time of Enosh as the beginning of idolatry, not the worship of the true God. The question here is: If this interpretation is accepted, what did the idolatry consist of?

Maimonides, in introducing his comprehensive treatment of the specifics of Jewish tradition concerning idolatry, speculates that at this time human beings were so impressed with *what* they perceived, namely, the cosmic order, the highest manifestation of which is the astronomic order, that they forgot *who* so ordered it.[37] Their worship, then, was transferred from the creator to his most impressive creations. In an earlier discussion of the essence of idolatry, Maimonides speculates that the worship of the cosmic order itself inevitably leads to a situation where some people understand this order much better than others by virtue of their greater powers of discovery. As such, they translate their noetic power into political power by convincing the masses that they should be given absolute authority, being the effective conduits of that cosmic power. They alone can channel it for the public weal.[40] Here we have the rule of the philosophical guardian.[41] In Maimonides' reading of Scripture, tyranny is the practical result of theoretical idolatry.

As for the second possibility, Scripture is more explicit. During the time of the Tower of Babel, humankind despaired of ever discovering the cosmic order, much less making peace with it in order to live *within* its limits. The cosmic order is now the enemy to be conquered by technological means. "And each man said to his neighbor, 'come let us make bricks and fire them in a kiln . . . come let us build for ourselves a city, and a tower with its head into heaven, and we will make a name (*shem*) for ourselves, lest we be scattered over the face of all the earth' " (Genesis 11:3–4). In response to all this, the Lord says, "this they have begun (*hahillam*) to do, and now nothing they are plotting (*yazmu*) to do will be withheld from them" (Genesis 11:6). An important thing to note here is that in the preceding passage, dealing with what we might in modern terms call "heteronomous idolatry," the *name* sought is still something external to humans themselves. Here, however, dealing with what we might in modern terms call "autonomous idolatry," the *name* sought is one of human making.

The connection between this idolatry and political tyranny is even more obvious. Here we have the rule of the technocrat.[42] Here the exercise of power becomes an end in itself. There is no longer even the pretense of a higher justification and purpose for the exercise of human power. Thus in rabbinic interpretation, Nimrod is the true founder of Shinar, the place where the Tower of Babel was built.[43] About Nimrod it is said, "He began (*hehel*) to be a mighty man on earth. He was a mighty warrior (*gibor tsayid*) before the Lord" (Genesis 10:8–9). And in rabbinic tradition, Abraham's quest for God quickly challenged the tyranny of Nimrod and was taken as a mortal threat by Nimrod.[44] And, finally, since I am following rabbinic insights, it should be noted that in the case of Enosh, in the case of the Tower of Babel, and in the case of Nimrod, the word that the Rabbis saw as connoting idolatry (*hallel*) is found.[45]

As for the third possibility, which is the cry for the person behind the cosmic order to reveal himself, we only have our speculation that God's call to Abraham is in truth a response to an existential question. And there is a long tradition of speculation about just what this question is. In this tradition, Abraham begins his career as a philosopher.[46] The error, however, of many in this tradition was to assume that Abraham *found* God through what is called "the argument from design," namely, that the perception of order leads one to *conclude* that there is an orderer who brought it about.[47] But as many philosophers have argued, no such conclusion is necessary. One can take the order itself as ultimate.[48] And if there is such an orderer, then the most one can rationally conclude is that the orderer and the order are essentially identical, and that the orderer cannot be understood as transcending his order in any way, as in Spinoza's view of God as *causa sui*, as we have already seen.[49] In other words, the orderer need not be taken as a person, that is, one consciously engaged in transitive acts, let alone mutual relationships.

Abraham's cry for the master of the universe to reveal himself, to follow the speculation of a well-known midrash, is not an exercise in inferential thinking.[50] Without the revelation whereby God personally elects him through a promise and establishes a perpetual covenant with him and his progeny, without that, Abraham's cry would have been the epitome of futility, an unheard cry in the dark, a dangerous gamble, an exercise in wishful thinking. The free choice of God, his liberty to be when he will be, where he will be, with whom he will be, cannot in any way be the necessary conclusion by any inference whatsoever.[51] The most Abraham or any human person can do is to prepare himself or herself for the possibility of revelation, to clear the ground for God, but without any immanent assurance that God will ever come.

One can speculate, from philosophical reflection on the human condition itself, that Abraham could not accept the first and second approaches to the cosmos (that of *homo spectator* and that of *homo faber*) because neither of them could establish the cosmos as the authentic dwelling-place for humans. Abraham the bedouin is looking for his home.[52]

To regard order itself as ultimate, as does *homo spectator*, is to regard humans as souls from another world, souls whose task is to "escape and become like God."[53] And in this view, God is eternal and immutable Being. But there is no relationship *with* Being; there is no mutuality between Being and anything less than itself. There is only a relation *to* Being. God dwells with himself alone. That is why in this view of things, the highest achievement of humans is to reach the level where they can only silently gaze on that which is eternal. The philosopher, like God, is ultimately beyond human community and beyond the world.[54] And to regard the cosmic order as mere potential, a resource for its own use, as does *homo faber*, something to be ultimately outsmarted, is to regard the cosmos as ultimately disposable. All being is engulfed *by* human *technē*. There is, then, no authentic being-at-home in the world.[55] One is in constant struggle *against* the world. Humans dwell with and among themselves alone, but that brings them no rest. For the struggle against the world is extended into their struggle with each other for mastery.[56] For *homo faber*, there is not enough trust of either the world or one's fellow humans for him to be able to enjoy the vulnerability of a Sabbath.

Only an authentic relationship with the creator God who made both world and humankind enables humans to accept the world as their dwelling-place. Without that, the world becomes either our prison that we are to escape *from*, or our prison *against* whose walls we battle, striving to tear them down. "For so says the Lord, the creator of heaven, he is the God who formed the earth, who made it and established it, who did not create it to be a void (*tohu*), but who formed it to be a dwelling (*la-shevet*)" (Isaiah 45:18). "God brings the lonely homeward (*ha-baitah*)" (Psalms 68:7). All true dwelling-in is a dwelling-with more than ourselves. But it is only the case when we prepare the world from our singular place for God's descent into the world to dwell with us therein in covenantal intimacy. "They shall make for Me a holy place (*miqdash*) and I shall dwell in their midst" (Exodus 25:8). "Surely the Lord is here (*yesh*) in this place (*ba-maqom ha-zeh*) . . . it will be the house of God (*bet elohim*)" (Genesis 28:16, 22).[57]

Here the propensity for tyranny we noticed in the first and second human approaches to the cosmos (that of scientific *homo spectator* and that of technological *homo faber*) is less. For here is where everyone in the covenant is to be directly and equally related to God. Even the quintessential modern apostate from Judaism, Baruch Spinoza, was impressed by this political aspect of the covenant, as we saw earlier.[58] Here is where the prophet can say, "O were it so (*mi yiten*) that all the people of the Lord would be prophets, that the Lord would place his spirit upon them" (Numbers 11:29).[59]

Thinking along these lines, one can see why Scripture requires the people of Israel, when they are at home in the land of Israel and satiated with an abundant harvest, to remember their bedouin origins by declaring about Abraham (and perhaps the other patriarchs too): "a wandering Aramean was my father" (Deuteronomy 26:5).[60] Indeed, even in the land of Israel, which is at the same time as Abraham's election itself elected to be the homeland, the dwelling-place of his people, this people is reminded in Scripture that "the land is Mine, that you are sojourning tenants (*gerim ve-toshavim*) with Me" (Leviticus 25:23).[61] Indeed, the purpose of a home is to be the location for persons to coexist, a place for authentic *mitsein*. It is not a part of them, and they are not parts of it as is the case with the first two attitudes we have detected above. Although God dwells with the people of Israel wherever they happen to be, the most complete dwelling-together of God and his people is only in the land of Israel.[62] The rest of the earth is created; the land of Israel like the people of Israel is elected in history. It is selected from among multiple possibilities.

On the basis of this theology, time and space are to be constituted as abstractions from event and place.[63] Time is ordered by the events in which Israel is elected and the covenant with her given its content. These events are the prime point of temporal reference; they are not in time, but all time is related to them. As Scripture puts it in the first creation narrative itself: "And God said, 'let there be light in the expanse of the sky to divide between day and night, and to be for signs and seasons (*le'otot u-le-mo'adim*), for days and for years'" (Genesis 1:14).[64] And space is ordered by its relation to the land of Israel. It is the *axis mundi*, the prime point of spatial reference.[65] It is not in space, but all space is related to it. As Scripture puts it just before the people of Israel entered the land of Israel: "When the Most High gave nations their homes (*be-hanhel*) and set the divisions of man, he fixed the boundaries (*gevulot*) of peoples in relation to the numbers (*le-mispar*) of the children of Israel" (Deuteronomy 32:8).[66]

Getting back again to Abraham's keeping of "the way of the Lord to do what is right (*tsedaqah*) and just (*u-mishpat*)," we are now in a better position to discern the reason for his—and our—acceptance of God's election. It must be immediately recalled that Abraham's concern with *tsedaqah u-mishpat* is in connection with the nations of the world which are to be blessed through him. Indeed, his concern here is that justice be done to the people of Sodom and Gomorrah, whom Scripture shortly before described as "exceedingly wicked sinners (*ra'im ve-hat'im*) against the Lord" (Genesis 13:13). Abraham is concerned that justice be done to these people as the due process of law that even they deserve, whether the final verdict be guilt or innocence. His response to his being known-and-chosen by God is to want to imitate in microcosm the way God relates to the whole world in macrocosm. Both God and Abraham are now concerned with the earth and especially with all the peoples in it. Thus Abraham's concern is that *mishpat* be done. That in itself is an act of justice; he acts as their defense attorney seeking some merit in them. And the very fact that he involves himself in their case, when he owes them nothing, is an act of *tsedaqah*. Knowing that he is known by God, Abraham is now in a position to act truly as *imitator Dei*.[67] His being known by God is not only something he enjoys and can celebrate; it is something he can act on.

As *homo revelationis*, Abraham desires to dwell *with* God *in* and *for* the world. Conversely, the desire of *homo spectator* is for absorption *into* God *outside* the world; and the desire of *homo faber* is to be God *against* the world. Only the right relationship with God founds one's rightful place in the world. And only the acceptance of one's rightful human place in the world prevents one from intending either absorption into God or the replacement of God.

Finally, in the covenant, the relation of existential *tsedaqah* and essential *mishpat* is not only one of originating event and subsequent process. Sometimes, *tsedaqah* is subsequent to *mishpat* and not just the origin behind it. *Mishpat*'s world is never so tightly constructed that *tsedaqah* cannot on occasion intrude into it. Indeed, the contingency of created existence would be eclipsed if even God's *mishpat* were to be taken as an impermeable total order, as a system perfect in itself. There always remains the possibility of miracle. *Tsedaqah* can be directly experienced at rare times in history/nature (time/space). For a miracle is the unpredictable exception to ordinary, normal order, and it is beneficial to those for whom it is performed. In fact, outside the singular experience of the faithful, illuminated by revelation, a miracle can soon be explained by more mundane categories.[68] Thus the splitting of the Red Sea for Israel was seen by them as the "great hand" (Exodus 14:31) of the Lord. But precluding the presence of God, one could see the act as that of "a strong east wind" (Exodus 14:21). Israel's redemption from Egyptian slavery illumined by revelation is because "the Lord took us out of Egypt with a mighty hand" (Deuteronomy 26:8). But precluding the presence of God, one could see it as an escape by fugitives: "It was told to the king of Egypt that the people had escaped (*barah*)" (Exodus 14:5).

The election of Israel is assumed to be the greatest intrusion of divine *tsedaqah* into the usual order of nature and history.

> You have but to inquire about bygone ages that came before you, ever since God created humans (*adam*) on earth, from one end of the heavens to the other: has anything as great as this ever existed or has it ever been heard of? Has any people ever heard the voice of God speaking out of fire, as you have and are still alive? Or has God ever so miraculously (*hanissah*) come to take for himself one people out of another? (Deuteronomy 4:32–34)

This notion of intrusive *tsedaqah*—miraculous grace—became the background for explaining how God can mercifully cancel the inevitable consequences of sin by forgiveness and atonement. For the Rabbis, the world could not be sustained if strict justice (*mish-*

pat as *din*) were always maintained consistently by God.[69] And the covenantal community could not be sustained without periodic infusions of grace by those in legal authority, at times ruling "deeper than the limit of the law (*lifnim me-shurat ha-din*)."[70] The theological import of all of this is enormous.

Also, in terms of our philosophical retrieval of the biblical doctrine of election, no philosophical reflection can ignore the outlook and findings of its contemporary science. At this juncture in history, the outlook and findings of Quantum Theory can be helpful. For unlike earlier modern science, where a totally interconnected universal causal model was required, Quantum Theory only requires a statistical model. Here phenomena in general, but not each phenomenon, have a causal explanation.[71] Furthermore, here the intrinsic role played by scientific observers themselves makes the total abstraction of scientific objects impossible.[72] Thus Quantum Theory constitutes a physical universe in which the unusual and the subjective are not precluded in principle. And it is the unusual datum plus the integral role of the one for whom it is performed that is the ontological *sine qua non* for a philosophical acceptance of the possibility of miracles. It is not that Quantum Theory "proves" any miracle or even engenders the concept of miracle at all. What it does for us, however, is to present a natural science that does not contradict what revelation teaches about miracles. That is enough for our theology.

Notes

1. See Gen. 26:5, Neh. 9:7–8.
2. See R. Judah Loewe (Maharal), *Netsah Yisra'el* (Prague, 1599), chap. 11; *Gevurot Ha-Shem* (Cracow, 1582), chaps. 24, 39, 54.
3. See H. Wildberger, *YHWH's Eigentumsvolk* (Zurich, 1960), 111; N. W. Porteous, "Volk und Gottesvolk in Alten Testament," in *Theologische Aufsätze: Karl Barth zum 50. Geburtstag* (Munich, 1936), 163. Cf. H. H. Rowley, *The Biblical Doctrine of Election* (London, 1950), 38–39, n. 2. Rowley sees Israel's election being based on teleology (35ff.), that is, God chose Israel because she had qualities useful for universal divine purposes. However, Rowley's supercessionist assumptions lie just beneath the surface of his scholarship. For when Israel fails God, then her election is annulled (49ff). The implication, of course, is that the Church will have better qualities, so that it will replace Israel in and for God's universal plan. Porteous and Wildberger, conversely, being under the influence of Karl Barth (and it seems Calvin too), see God's electing promise and covenant to Israel as unconditional and never annulled or to be annulled. (See Barth, *Church Dogmatics*, 2/2, sec. 34, trans. G. W. Bromiley *et al.* [Edinburgh, 1957], 195ff.; Calvin, *Institutes of the Christian Religion*, 2.10.1ff., trans. F. L. Battles [2 vols., Philadelphia, 1960], 1:428ff.) Whatever differences Calvinist and Barthian Christians have with Judaism over the ultimate meaning of election—and they are crucial—these Protestants are not offended by the Jewish doctrine of the unconditional election of Israel, which is not the case with most of their more liberal co-religionists. Along these lines, see K. Sonderegger, *That Jesus Christ was Born a Jew* (University Park, Pa., 1992), 161ff.
4. See Isa. 41:8–10; 51:1–2.
5. See Isaak Heinemann, *Darkhei Ha'Aggadah*, 2nd ed. (Jerusalem, 1954), 21ff.
6. See B. Sanhedrin 56b re Gen. 2:16 and Exod. 32:8 (and, esp., the view of R. Judah; see the view of R. Meir on B. Avodah Zarah 64b); also, Maimonides, *Mishneh Torah*: Melakhim, 9.1.
7. See *Shir Ha-Shirim Rabbah*, 8.13 re Lev. 15:25 and Num. 19:14; B. Kiddushin 54a and parallels. In rabbinic theology, angels are seen as monads with only one function to perform for which they are programmed by God (see *Bere'sheet Rabbah* 50.2). The primary human need

for conscious ordering is coeval with the need for communicative community because that ordering finds its locus in the *public* nature of speech. See Gen. 2:18; B. Yevamot 63a re Gen. 2:23; B. Ta'anit 23a. Cf. Aristotle, *Politics* 1254a20.

8. That is why God's most generic name is *elohim*, "authority," which is first divine and then human. See B. Sanhedrin 56b re Gen. 2:16 and Exod. 22:7; also, D. Novak, "Before Revelation: The Rabbis, Paul, and Karl Barth," *Journal of Religion* (1991), 71:58.

9. Thus the Noahide laws, stipulating the minimal relation of humankind to God, are essentially prohibitions. See B. Sanhedrin 58b-59a and Rashi, s.v. "ve-ha-dinin" re Lev. 19:15.

10. See Novak, *Jewish Social Ethics*, 14ff.

11. See *ibid.*, 27ff.

12. There is an important debate about the role of *eros*, i.e., desire, in the God–human relationship between Christian theologians that I venture to enter here because it helps one gain a better philosophical perspective on the role of desire in the biblical covenant itself (see M. Avot 4.1 re Ps. 119:99 and Maimonides, *Commentary on the Mishmah*: intro., trans. Y. Kafih [3 vols., Jerusalem, 1976], 1:247). The main protagonists are Augustine and Paul Tillich, who emphasize the erotic component, and Karl Barth and Anders Nygren, who deny it. I would say that without the factor of inherent human desire for God, the covenantal relationship between God and humans can only be seen as essentially one of God with himself rather than one between God and his nondivine covenantal partners. So it seems to me that Jewish covenantal theologians have more in common with Augustine and Tillich than they do with Barth and Nygren on this key point. See Augustine, *Confessions*, 7.10; Paul Tillich, *Systematic Theology* (Chicago, 1951), 1:282; Karl Barth, *Church Dogmatics*, 2/2, sec. 37, pp. 555ff.; Anders Nygren, *Eros and Agape*, trans. P. Watson (Chicago, 1982), 160ff.; also, Novak, *Jewish Social Ethics*, 51ff.

13. Following R. Judah Halevi, "Adonai Negdekha Kol Ta'vati," in *Selected Religious Poems of Jehudah Halevi*, ed. H. Brody (Philadelphia, 1924), 87.

14. See Aristotle, *Nicomachean Ethics* 1094a1; *Metaphysics* 1072a25. For the recognition of the universal desire for God, see Mal. 1:11 and R. Solomon ibn Gabirol, "Keter Malkhut," in *Selected Religious Poems of Solomon ibn Gabirol*, ed. I. Davidson (Philadelphia, 1924), 86. The kabbalists called human *eros* for God *it'aruta dil-tata* ("awakening from below"—see *Zohar*: Vayetse, 1:164a). But without an adequate theology of revelation, the God so desired becomes trapped as an eternal object like the intransitive god of Aristotle (see *Metaphysics* 1072a2off.) or something similar to *it*.

15. For this epistemological distinction, see Bertrand Russell, "Knowledge by Acquaintance and Knowledge by Description," in *The Problems of Philosophy* (Oxford, 1959), 46ff. Although there are significant differences between Russell's empiricism and my phenomenology, his essay is still useful for making my point here.

16. "He [R. Akibah] used to say that man (*ha'adam*) is beloved (*haviv*) being created in the image (*be-tselem*); even more beloved in that it is made known to him that he is created in the image of God . . . Israel is beloved being called children of God; even more beloved in that it is made known (*noda'at*) to them" (M. Avot re Gen. 9:6; Deut. 14:1). Thus human knowledge/awareness is subsequent to God's knowledge/care (in the sense of *Sorge* in German, meaning care/concern/attention/interest/involvement, etc.). Revelation, then, brings the truth of being elected to conscious mutual relationality. The creation of humans in the *imago Dei* is also election; hence the Torah is "the book of human history (*toldot ha'adam*)" (Gen. 5:1; see Nahmanides' comment thereon). It brings the meaning of being created in the image of God to human awareness and action. And the *tselem elohim* itself is the human capacity for a relationship with God (see D. Novak, *Law and Theology in Judaism* [2 vols., New York, 1974, 1976], 2:108ff.; *Halakhah in a Theological Dimension* [Chico, Calif., 1985]). It is not a quality humans have any more than the election of Israel is due to any quality she has. For a quality can be discovered through solitary introspection or inferred by ratiocination. Although felt inchoately by desire in advance, the meaning of this capacity only comes to knowledge/experience when her desideratum

presently reveals himself to her. For the relation of humankind and Israel indicated in the above *mishnah*, see R. Israel Lipschütz, *Tif'eret Yisra'el (Bo'az)* thereon.

17. See Maimonides, *Guide of the Perplexed*, 1.2.

18. See Martin Buber, "The Election of Israel: A Biblical Inquiry," trans. M. A. Meyer in *On the Bible*, ed. N. N. Glatzer (New York, 1968), 80–81.

19. See Amos 1:3ff.

20. Whether the roots *yod daled ayin* and *yod ayin daled* are etymologically related or not, there seems to be a literary relation between them being made by this juxtaposition. (I thank my colleague Prof. Gary Anderson for pointing this out to me.)

21. See Abraham Joshua Heschel, *Man is Not Alone* (Philadelphia, 1951), 125ff.; *God in Search of Man* (New York, 1955), 136ff.

22. Note how the Passover Haggadah connects this "knowing" with the sexual "knowing" of the people themselves, the essential connection between the two being the factor of intimacy. See M. M. Kasher, *Haggadah Shlemah*, 3rd ed. (Jerusalem, 1967), pt. 2, p. 41. That is how R. Akibah could see the eroticism of Songs of Songs as the holiest intentionality (see *Shir Ha-Shirim Rabbah*, 1.11). And whereas in Songs of Songs human sexuality suggests God's love of Israel, here God's love of Israel suggests human sexuality. Along these lines, see Novak, *Jewish Social Ethics*, 94ff.

23. See, esp., B. Berakhot 10a re Exod. 32:13; also, Novak, *Halakhah in a Theological Dimension*, 116ff.

24. So I too argued in *Jewish Social Ethics*, 41, n. 48.

25. See David Hume, *A Treatise of Human Nature*, 3.1.2, ed. L. A. Selby-Bigge (Oxford, 1888), 473ff.

26. See Novak, *Law and Theology in Judaism*, 2:19ff.

27. *Epistola*, no. 50, in *Opera*, ed. J. van Vloten and J. P. N. Land (The Hague, 1914), 3:173: "Haec ergo determinatio ad rem juxta suum esse non pertinet: sed econtra est ejus non esse . . . et determinatio negatio est."

28. In the Talmud, that covenant is seen as the covenant between God and Israel (B. Pesahim 68b; also *Ruth Rabbah*, petihah, 1 re Ps. 75:4). Indeed, the divine *tsedaqah* that creates the world and maintains its existence is most immediately experienced in the covenant with Israel. See *Mishnat Rabbi Eliezer*, sec. 7, ed. Enelow, 1:138; R. Judah Halevi, *Kuzari*, 1.25 re Exod 20:2.

29. See Heschel, *God in Search of Man*, 92.

30. For two important discussions of truth as faithfulness (*emet vemunah*), see Martin Buber, *The Knowledge of Man*, ed. M. Friedman (New York and Evanston, 1965), 120; Eliezer Berkovits, *Man and God* (Detroit, 1969), 253ff.

31. See B. Baba Kama 92a. For the distinction between universal *mishpat* and local custom, cf. Gen. 29:26 and 34:7.

32. See Novak, *Jewish Social Ethics*, 163–164.

33. See Nahmanides' comment thereon.

34. Along these lines, see Hannah Arendt, *Lectures on Kant's Political Philosophy*, ed. R. Beiner (Chicago, 1982), 12–13.

35. See Plato, *Republic* 476Bff.

36. See D. Novak, "Are Philosophical Proofs of the Existence of God Theologically Meaningful?," in *God in the Teachings of Conservative Judaism*, ed. S. Siegel and E. B. Gertel (New York, 1983), 188ff.

37. See B. Berakhot 7b re Gen. 15:8.

38. *Bere'sheet Rabbah* 23.7.

39. *Mishneh Torah*: Avodah Zarah, 1.1. See also T. Boman, *Hebrew Thought Compared with Greek*, trans. J. L. Moreau (London and New York, 1970), 117.

40. *Commentary on the Mishnah*: Avodah Zarah, 4:7; also, *Mishneh Torah*: Avodah Zarah, 11.16.

41. See Karl Popper, *The Open Society and its Enemies* (2 vols., Princeton, 1962), 1:138ff.

42. See Jacques Ellul, *The Technological System*, trans. J. Neugroschel (New York, 1980), 145ff.

43. See Louis Ginzberg, *The Legends of the Jews* (7 vols., Philadelphia, 1909–1938), 5:199ff., nn. 81ff.
44. See *Pirqei De-Rabbi Eliezer*, chap. 26.
45. See *Bere'sheet Rabbah* 23:7.
46. See Ginzberg, *Legends of the Jews*, 5:210, n. 16; also, Maimonides, *Mishneh Torah*: Avodah Zarah, 1.3 and *Guide of the Perplexed*, 3:29.
47. The first to make this argument was Josephus in *Antiquities*, 1.155–156. Cf. Novak, *Law and Theology in Judaism*, 2:21–22.
48. See Plato, *Euthyphro* 10e.
49. See H. A. Wolfson, *The Philosophy of Spinoza* (2 vols., Cambridge, Mass., 1934), 2:346, who sees the deity of Spinoza as a return to Aristotle's deity, "an eternal paralytic," in Wolfson's colorful words.
50. *Bere'sheet Rabbah* 39.1: "Abraham used to say, 'could it be that the world has no leader (*man-heeg*)?' God peered out and said to him, 'I am the leader and the lord (*adon*) of all the world.'"
51. See Exod. 3:13 and the discussion of its philosophical career by D. Novak, "Buber and Tillich," *Journal of Economical Studies* (1992), 29:161ff.
52. See Rashbam, *Commentary on the Torah* and Hizquni, *Commentary on the Torah*: Gen. 20:13.
53. Plato, *Theaetetus* 176A–B. See also *Republic* 501B; *Timaeus* 68E–69A; *Philebus* 63e; *Laws* 716C.
54. See Aristotle, *Nicomachean Ethics* 1177b25ff. For Plato's struggle with this problem, see *Republic* 516cff.; also, D. Novak, *Suicide and Morality* (New York, 1975), 21ff.
55. See Novak, *Jewish Social Ethics*, 133ff.
56. See, e.g., Ginzberg, *Legends of the Jews*, 1:179.
57. See B. Pesahim 88a and Rashi, s.v. "she-qara'o bayit."
58. See D. Novak, *The Election of Israel*, pp. 31–38.
59. Cf. Exod. 20:15–18. That is why, it seems to me, the Rabbis had to impugn the motives of Korah's rebellion against the authority of Moses (e.g., *Bemidbar Rabbah* 18.1ff.), namely, the argument "you have taken too much for yourselves, for the entire assembly is holy and the Lord is in their midst. So why do you elevate yourselves above the congregation of the Lord?" (Num. 16:3). The premise of the argument is surely valid *prima facie*. Indeed, there is always a suspicion of too much human authority in the covenantal community (see, e.g., Jud. 8:22–23; I Sam. 8:7ff).
60. See the comments of Ibn Ezra and Rashbam thereon.
61. See Ps. 119:19; I Chron. 29:15.
62. See Nahmanides, *Commentary on the Torah*: Deut. 8:10; also, Novak, *The Theology of Nahmanides*, 89ff.
63. "And even as prayer is not in time but time in prayer, the sacrifice not in space but space in the sacrifice—and whoever reverses the relation annuls the reality" (Martin Buber, *I and Thou*, trans. W. Kaufmann [New York, 1970], 59).
64. See Rashi's comment thereon.
65. See Nahmanides, *Commentary on the Torah*: Gen. 14:18; Deut. 16:20.
66. See *Targum Jonathan ben Uziel* thereon.
67. See B. Shabbat 133b re Exod. 15:2 and 34:7; Maimonides, *Guide of the Perplexed*, 3.54 re Jer. 9:23 and D. Novak, "Maimonides' Concept of Practical Reason," in *Rashi 1040–1990: hommage à Ephraim E. Urbach*, ed. G. Sed-Rajna (Paris, 1993), 627ff.
68. See Nahmanides, *Commentary on the Torah*: Gen. 14:10.
69. See, e.g., *Bere'sheet Rabbah* 12.15 re Gen. 2:4; B. Rosh Hashanah 17b; also, Ephraim E. Urbach, *Hazal* (Jerusalem, 1971), 400ff.
70. See T. Shekalim 2.3; B. Baba Metsia 30b. For the use of the term *lifnim me-shurat hadin* re God's merciful overriding of his own created *mishpat*, see B. Berakhot 7a; also Y. Makkot 2.6/31d re Ps. 25:8 and R. Moses Margolis, *Penei Mosheh* thereon. Cf. W. Eichrodt, *Theology of the Old Testament*, trans. J. A. Baker (2 vols., Philadelpiha, 1961), 1:244.
71. See Bernard Lonergan, *Insight*, 3rd ed. (San Francisco, 1970), 97ff.
72. See M. Sachs, *Einstein versus Bohr* (La Salle, Ill., 1988), 235ff.

21

The Body of Faith

MICHAEL WYSCHOGROD

Love and Election

Why does God proceed by means of election, the choosing of one people among the nations as his people? Why is he not the father of all nations, calling them to his obedience and offering his love to man, whom he created in his image? More fundamentally, why must the concept of nation intrude itself into the relation between God and man? Does not God address each individual human being as he stands alone before God? Because those questions are so fundamental, we must answer them with caution.

We must avoid an answer that does too much. Any answer that would demonstrate that what God did was the only thing he could have done or that it was the right thing to do would be too much of an answer. God must not be subject to necessity or to a good not of his own making. He is sovereign and his own master, and must not be judged by standards external to him. Much of religious apology misunderstands this fundamental point and therefore defeats itself just as it succeeds because it limits God's sovereignty as it proves that he could not have done anything other than what he did or, more usually, that what he did measures up to the highest standards of morality. Having thus succeeded in providing the best possible reasons for God's actions, the apologist does not realize that he has subjected God to judgment by criteria other than his free and sovereign will and that, however much he has justified God's actions, he has infringed his sovereignty and is therefore no longer talking of the biblical God. We must avoid this sort of justification at all cost and therefore begin our answer to the questions posed by noting that God chose the route of election, and of the election of a biological instead of an ideological people, because this was his free choice. He could have acted otherwise. He could have dispensed completely with election or he could have constituted the elected group in some other

Michael, Wyschogrod, "Love and Election," and "National Election," in *The Body of Faith* (New York: Harper Collins, 1983), pp. 58–70. © 1996, Jason Aronson Inc., Northvale, NJ 07647.

way, and had he done so, we would have praised those choices as we now praise these. Rarely has any theology come to grips with the contingency that follows from God's freedom. Christian theology has rarely conceded that God could have decided to save all men without the need for an incarnation, crucifixion, and resurrection. The vast preponderance of Christian thought makes it seem that given man's fall, only the sacrifice of God's only begotten son could have served as atonement for man's sin. The Christian faith ought to contend that the way of the incarnation was the way chosen by God, though he could have chosen another. Correspondingly, we will assert the same of the election of Israel, dispensing with all claims of necessity or that this was the best possible course for God to take.

Having said this much, we must also permit the praise of God. There is hardly any literary activity more prevalent in the Bible than the praise of God. The Bible is first and foremost the word of God, in which man is told what God wants him to know. But the Bible is also the word of man as man responds to the word of God. This response takes a number of forms. There is the direct response of those, like Abraham, Moses, and others, whom the Bible reports as being addressed by God and whose responses are reported as part of the dialogue. There is the biblical Wisdom literature most prominent in Proverbs, which, in a sense, is the form that most closely resembles philosophy because it seems to consist of the insights of human experience distilled over the centuries. There is also the praise of God that we find in Psalms as well as many other places in the Bible. The human encounter with God that is expressed in praise is the one response most difficult for modern man, and particularly for the contemporary Jew, to understand. For post-Auschwitz Jewry it is the voice of Abraham contesting the justice of the divine decree against the corrupt cities of man that speaks most recognizably of the human condition. There has crept into our consciousness a profound anger at God, and this anger is shared by all Jews, even those who will not permit this anger to become conscious. Yet we must recognize that there was a time when men in general and Jews in particular were overwhelmed by a deep emotion of gratitude for the wonderful favors bestowed by God. In Psalms this is rooted in David's unshakable faith in his election and the divine protection that insured triumph over those wishing God's anointed ill. Praise of God is thus rooted in gratitude and wonder at the complexities and beauty of creation. Most important for our purpose is the recognition that praise does not involve measuring God's creation and conduct by external standards and declaring them good because they live up to those standards. Praise is an act of gratitude that is totally focused on God to whom we are grateful. Gratitude rises in the human soul when an act of love is bestowed that is felt not to be deserved. It is difficult to be grateful for what is owed one. When, however, man is dealt with kindly without deserving it, it is natural for him to be grateful. In gratitude there is a feeling of loving dependence on the other because gratitude makes it necessary for man to feel his vulnerability, in the absence of which he would not need the favor that has been bestowed on him. Israel must therefore praise God. This will not justify God's election of Israel, but it will enable us to express our wonder and gratitude for the election of Israel.

All this has been preliminary to our discussion of election, which we will not justify but which we might come to understand somewhat from the standpoint of praise. The question we asked was, Why does God proceed by election rather than by being the impartial father of all peoples? Behind these questions lurks the pain of exclusion. If God elects one individual or group, there is someone else whom he does not elect and that other is left to suffer his exclusion. With exclusion comes envy of the one elected and anger, perhaps even hatred, of the one who has done the exclusion. David's love for God reaches great peaks because he is so deeply grateful for his election, but the modern reader finds it difficult not to have some sympathy for his enemies, whose downfall is so certain because they have not been chosen and have dared to conspire against the elect of God. We begin to feel the pain of exclusion and ask why it was necessary for pain to be caused by love. Would it not have been better for God not to have favored Israel, so as not to hurt the other peoples of the world?

This leads us to think about the wonder of love. Western man has, as we have seen, distinguished between *eros* and *agape*. *Eros* is sensual love, the love of man for woman, where jealousy is a possibility. In *eros* the other is a means toward the pleasure of the self, so that *eros* is really self-love. *Agape* is the love of parent for child. Sometimes this love is distorted where children are made into appendages of the parents and used for self-gratification. True *agape* demands nothing in return because it is a love truly directed to the other, to his welfare and prosperity, to what is good for him rather than the pleasure of the one who loves. *Agape* is thus charity in the purest sense but without condescension and any sense of superiority. The love of the Greek world, it has further been said, is *eros*, while that of the Judeo-Christian, *agape*. The question we have posed is thus a question about *agape*. God's love for man is surely *agape* rather than *eros*. How, then, can it exclude? Does a parent who loves one child exclude another? Is not equal love of all children the essence of parental love?

There is something wrong about the distinction between *eros* and *agape*. It resembles the distinction between body and soul. *Eros* seems to be a bodily love and *agape* love of and by the soul. Such a distinction would be valid if the distinction between body and soul were. But in the biblical view, body and soul are aspects of the one being that God created in his image. Human love, correspondingly, must not be bifurcated into the *agape-eros* mold or any similar scheme. There is no doubt that there are imperfect examples of human love, as there are imperfect human beings. But it is simply not true that love as charity applies equally to all and makes no distinctions as to person. This would be conceivable if charitable love were primarily an emotion within the person who loves, with the recipient of the love being a dim image at the periphery of consciousness serving as an occasion for the activation of love. If this were the case, we would be dealing with an I-It relationship in Buber's sense, hardly the model of true love in charity. Love that is in the realm of the I-Thou is directed toward the other who is encountered in his being and on whom we do not impose our preconceptions. Undifferentiated love, love that is dispensed equally to all must be love that does not meet the individual in his individuality but sees him as a member of a species, whether that species be the working class, the poor, those created in the image of God, or what not. History abounds with example, such fantastic loves directed at abstract creations of the imagination. In the names of these abstractions men have committed the most heinous crime against real, concrete, existing human beings who were not encountered in their reality but seen as members of a demonic species to be destroyed. Both the object of love and that of hate were abstract and unreal, restricted to the imagination of the lonely dreamer who would not turn to the concretely real persons all around him. Unlike such fantasies, the divine love is concrete. It is a genuine encounter with man in his individuality and must therefore be exclusive. Any real love encounter, if it is more than an example of the love of a class or collectivity, is exclusive because it is genuinely directed to the uniqueness of the other and it therefore follows that each such relationship is different from all others.

But difference is exclusivity because each relationship is different, and I am not included in the relationship of others.

And it also follows that there must be a primacy of relationship. The authentic person is open to all. When he is with a particular individual, he devotes himself to that person completely, listening with all of his being to the presence of the other. Such listening cannot be a technique that succeeds equally in all cases at all times. The counterfeit of such listening could presumably be standardized and applied with regularity to person after person. But it would then clearly not be a real encounter but a clever imitation of real relationship. In any true I-Thou encounter, nothing can be controlled, no certainty of result can be preordained. It is for this reason that those who live with the possibility of meeting find that it happens with some and not with others. Instead of lamenting this fact, they pray for the continuing possibility of meeting, while recognizing the inherent exclusivity of those meetings that have happened. There is no denying a dimension of guilt in the knowledge that the primacy of relationship with a few cannot be repeated with many others who thus remain strangers. Even among the small circle of persons with whom there is an ongoing relationship, some are loved more than others because each is who he is and because I am who I am. The only alternative is a remote, inhuman love, directed at universals and abstractions rather than real persons.

Our praise of God expresses our gratitude that he loves man in a human way, directing his love to each one of us individually, and that by so loving he has chosen to share the human fate such love involves. The election of Israel is thus a sign of the humanity of God. Had he so willed it, he could have played a more godly role, refusing favorites and loving all his creatures impartially. His love would then have been a far less vulnerable one because impartiality signifies a certain remoteness, the absence of that consuming passion that is a sign of need of the other. Herein resides the inhumanity of *agape* and the humanity of *eros*. *Agape* demands nothing in return. It asks only to give, never to receive. However noble this sounds at first hearing, it must quickly be realized that it also implies an incredible person of strength. To be able only to give, never to need, never to ask for anything in return for what we give, is a position that truly befits a God. And to need something from the other, to need the body of the other for my satisfaction, is the misery of human being. Human being is need, the state of incompleteness within myself and therefore the longing for what the other can give. The *eros* of Don Juan is therefore a more human condition than the *agape* of the saint who needs nothing and no one and distributes his gifts from the height of his Olympian self-sufficiency. The truth is that human love is neither *eros* nor *agape*.

Both are caricatures because reality is a combination of the two, which are not different kinds of love but aspects of human love with a constantly changing composition of elements. No human love is totally indifferent to the reaction of the other. If the relationship is a human one, if the person loved is not perceived as an object to which things are done but a person to whom one speaks and whose answer one awaits, then the response received must be an important element in the direction of the developing relationship. This does not mean that a rebuff necessarily results in the termination of concern or even love. It is possible to love—and here is the truth of *agape*—in spite of rebuff or absence of response. But such absence is never a matter of indifference and plays an important role in the relationship because response is always sought, needed, and hoped for. Similarly, there is no erotic relationship without an element of concern. The sexual, even in its most exploiting and objectifying form, reveals a glimmer of gratitude and affection. If totalitarian states find it necessary to repress the sexual, it is because they are dimly aware that the person to whom the sexual is a reality is a person whose humanity has not been totally deposited with the state and who is therefore untrustworthy for the purposes of a system whose presupposition is dehumanization. All this is not to deny that there are loves in which *agape* predominates and those in which *eros* does. But none is exclusively one or the other because man is created in the image of God as a being constituted by need who gives and also asks to be given in return.

The love with which God has chosen to love man is a love understandable to man. It is therefore a love very much aware of human response. God has thereby made himself vulnerable: he asks for man's response and is hurt when it is not forthcoming. For the same reason, God's love is not undifferentiated, having the same quality toward all his children. God's love is directed toward who we are. We are confirmed as who we are in our relationship to God. And because God is so deeply directed toward us, because his love is not self-love (in spite of Plato, Neoplatonism, and the tradition flowing from these) but true meeting of the other (and there is an other for God; this is the mystery of creation), there are those whom God loves especially, with whom he has fallen in love, as with Abraham. There is no other way of expressing this mystery except in these terms. God's relationship to Abraham is truly a falling in love. The biblical text tells us this when it fails to explain the reason for the election of Abraham. The rabbis, of course, were aware of this omission and perplexed by it. They supplied reasons, making of Abraham the first natural philosopher who saw through the foolishness of the idol worship of his time and reasoned his way to the one God. In the Bible, it is not Abraham who moves toward God but God who turns to Abraham with an election that is not explained because it is an act of love that requires no explanation. If God continues to love the people of Israel—and it is the faith of Israel that he does—it is because he sees the face of his beloved Abraham in each and every one of his children as a man sees the face of his beloved in the children of his union with his beloved. God's anger when Israel is disobedient is the anger of a rejected lover. It is above all jealousy, the jealousy of one deeply in love who is consumed with torment at the knowledge that his beloved seeks the affection of others. To much of philosophical theology, such talk has been an embarrassment in urgent need of demythologization. But theologians must not be more protective of God's dignity than he is of his own because God's true dignity is the sovereignty of his choice for genuine relation with man.

What, now, of those not elected? Those not elected cannot be expected not to be hurt by not being of the seed of Abraham, whom God loves above all others. The Bible depicts clearly the suffering of Esau. The Bible is, after all, the history of Israel and could therefore be expected to be partial to the Jewish cause. And yet, in recounting the blessing of Jacob and the exclusion of Esau, no careful reader can fail to notice that the sympathy shown Esau is greater than that for Jacob. God shows Esau compassion even if Jacob does not. The consolation of the gentiles is the knowledge that God also stands in relationship with them in the recognition and affirmation of their uniqueness. The choice, after all, is between a lofty divine love equally distributed to all without recognition of uniqueness and real encounter, which necessarily involves favorites but in which each is unique and addressed as such. If Abraham was especially loved by God, it is because God is a father who does not stand in a legal relationship to his children, which by its nature requires impartiality and objectivity. As a father, God loves his children and knows each one as who he is with his strengths and weaknesses, his virtues and vices. Because a father is not an impartial judge but a loving parent and because a human father is a human being with his own personality, it is inevitable that he will find himself more compatible with some of his children than others and, to speak very plainly, that he love some more than others. There is usually great reluctance on the part of parents to admit this, but it is a truth that must not be avoided. And it is also true that a father loves all his children, so that they all know of and feel the love they receive, recognizing that to substitute an impartial judge for a loving father would eliminate the preference for the specially favored but would also deprive all of them of a father. The mystery of Israel's election thus turns out to be the guarantee of the fatherhood of God toward all peoples, elect and nonelect, Jew and gentile. We must, at the same time, reiterate that none of this amounts to some sort of demonstration of the "necessity" of election in any sense. It can be understood only from the point of view of man's gratitude for the fatherhood of God, since only the invocation of the category of "father" and the divine permission we have to apply this category to God enable us to begin to fathom the mystery of election. When we grasp that the election of Israel flows from the fatherhood that extends to all created in God's image, we find ourselves tied to all men in brotherhood, as Joseph, favored by his human father, ultimately found himself tied to his brothers. And when man contemplates this mystery, that the Eternal One, the creator of heaven and earth, chose to become the father of his creatures instead of remaining self-sufficient unto himself, as is the Absolute of the philosophers, there wells up in man that praise that has become so rare yet remains so natural.

National Election

There still remains the problem of the national election of Israel. Even if we see the election of Abraham as flowing from the fatherhood of God, we can still remain in the darkest of puzzlement in regard to the election of a whole people, the seed of Abraham, unto all eternity. What is the meaning behind the spontaneous emergence of the nation at the moment God enters into romance with Abraham? What is the "great beast" of national existence (to use Simone Weil's phrase) doing in the inner sanctum of man's relationship with God? Is this not properly the domain of the "single one," the man who stands alone before God and is able to hear God only because he has escaped the power of the crowd, which drowns out the voice from above? Finally, and perhaps above all, why a covenant with the carnal instead of the spiritual seed of Abraham? Is it physical relationship that is essential? Are there not those who are Abraham's children in the spirit who are more dear to God than a crass, perhaps unbelieving, Jew who is related to Abraham in the flesh but whose spiritual illumination is quite dim? Are not the real elect the aristocrats of the spirit, who derive from all peoples, cultures, and races? These are the questions that are hurled at Israel. Most often, they are not real questions because no answer is expected, since none is thought possible. The faith of Israel is dismissed as prespiritual, a carnal and early phase of human consciousness destined to be outgrown in the maturation of the race. Christianity's self-understanding as the new Israel of the spirit expresses this conviction and so does, though proceeding from sharply different premises, modern historical scholarship, which is determined to find early and late stages in everything, with the early always inferior to the later. Against all of these, Israel reaffirms its election in its physical descent from Abraham, a physical bond every Jew who is not totally alienated from his being experiences every day of his life as he moves among men, all of whom are his brothers—in whom he perceives the image of God—but all of whom are not Jews—in whom he perceives a family kinship unique to Jews. It is this that we must try to understand.

The nature of God is spiritual. This is the almost unanimous, and not untrue, wisdom of most religions, East and West. As spirit, God's natural kinship is with the spiritual man, with his soul and mind, which is uniquely capable of grasping the reality of the spiritual God. Man's relationship with God therefore comes to be centered in the spiritual and, more particularly, in the ethical, which is spiritualized by the elimination of law and the substitution of love as the dominant theme. The difficulty with this spiritualization of the God-man relationship is that it is untrue to man's nature, which is largely carnal. The division of man into the spiritual and the material is itself an act of abstraction that has a limited validity but that must not obscure the basic unity of human existence. This unity must not be conceived as a coupling of the spiritual and the material because any coupling presupposes an original separation, which is simply not warranted. Man is not a coupling of the spiritual and material but a creature who thinks and runs, grieves and cries, is amused and laughs. He is, in short, what he is: a being with an identity and a world in which he lives. Here, again, God could have played a godly role, interested in certain features of human existence, the spiritual, but not in others, the material. He could even have assigned man the task of wrenching himself out of the material so as to assume his spiritual identity, which is just what so many religions believe he did.[1] Instead, the God of Israel confirms man as he created him to live in the material cosmos. There is therefore no possibility of a divine requirement for the discarding of a part of human existence. Instead, there is a requirement for the sanctification of human existence in all of its aspects. Israel's symbol of the covenant is circumcision, a searing of the covenant into the flesh of Israel and not only, or perhaps not even primarily, into its spirit. And that is why God's election is of a carnal people. By electing the seed of Abraham, God creates a people that is in his service in the totality of its human being and not just in its moral and spiritual existence. The domain of the family, the most fundamental and intimate human association, is thereby sanctified, so that obedience to God does not require hate of father and mother.[2] It is also true that simple, undialectical attachment to the natural can be incompatible with a hearing of the divine command. Abraham is commanded to leave his land, birthplace, and father's house and follow God to a place that he will show him. The man who hears God's word is therefore wrenched away from his natural setting, from the bonds that tie him to his parents, brothers, sisters, and the whole world into which he was born and that gives man his natural security. If the divine command went no further, if it merely instructed him to leave his birthplace and then preach a moral vision or religious discovery, then the natural would have been slain once and for all and Kierkegaard would be right in saying that a real relation with God excludes real relations with human beings.[3] But the divine command does not stop there. After commanding Abraham to leave his father's house, it promises to make a great nation of his seed. The natural is now reinstated, projected into the future instead of rooted primarily in the past, and, above all, sanctified as a natural community. The divine does not, therefore, destroy the natural but confirms it by placing it in its service.

And very much the same is true of the national order. Simone Weil is far from wrong in speaking of society and the nation as the "great beast" to which men sacrifice their individuality,[4] so that they never dream it possible to become a "single one" before God.

No one who has read the prophets of Israel can be unaware of the extent to which Israel's faith fears the arrogance of the collective. But the question is, What to do? Shall the domain of the state be written off as the domain of the Devil, beyond the hope of sanctification, or shall it be seen as the most difficult challenge of all, which must be won for the holy precisely because of its remoteness from it? Israel attempts to sanctify national existence in obedience to the divine election, which is a national election. And it is a national election precisely because the nation is most remote from God and is therefore commanded to be the most proximate. To believe that the individual can be lifted out of his nation and brought into relation with God is as illusory as to believe that man's soul can be saved and his body discarded. Just as man is body and soul, so man is an individual and member of a nation. To save him as an individual and to leave the national social order unredeemed is to truncate man and then to believe that this remnant of a human being is the object of salvation. The national election of Israel is therefore again a sign of God's understanding of the human predicament and the confirmation of and love for that humanity. By sanctifying the nationhood of Israel, God confirms the national order of all peoples and expresses his love for the individual in his national setting and for the nations in their corporate personalities. In the case of Israel, the relationship that started with Abraham, the individual, soon becomes a relationship with a nation that becomes the elect nation. The promise of salvation is thus not held out to man as an individual but as a member of his nation. It is held out to the complete man and therefore to all nations, without which we have a part rather than all of man. In addition, by taking the national order seriously, redemption of the historical order becomes a possibility. History pertains to nations and if only the individual is real, history is not real. Purely spiritual religions, those that do not hesitate to address only the spiritual in man, do not take history seriously. This tendency is pronounced in early Christianity, which distanced itself from the political order because its citizenship was in the heavenly city that was not of this world. The salvation that Israel awaits must occur in the historical order, and it therefore is forced to continue to wait as long as that order is unredeemed. Israel cannot believe that in the midst of an unredeemed world there is an island of redemption, the Church, to which men can flee from the sorrows of the world. But this tenacity in its hold on reality flows from God's confirmation of that reality in refusing to exclude from the promise of redemption those structures that the spiritual religions have no hesitation in discarding but that, because they are real, defeat their purely spiritual visions.

We were led into an exploration of Jewish existence as a national family from our discovery that philosophy has played a less central role in Judaism than in Christianity. Judaism, we said, was not first a set of ideas but an existing people on whom commands are imposed and from whom ideas are generated but whose own being is the existential soil from which everything else emerges. Before we can explore this relationship between soil, or ground, and idea, we must allude to another fundamental reason for the different roles played by philosophy in Judaism and Christianity. Christianity sees before it a completed salvation history. Creation to resurrection constitutes a totality of promise and fulfillment that is available to viewing and therefore to thought. Israel's story is incomplete. It is replete with great peaks and deep disappointments, but it is, above all, incomplete. The redemption implicit in the very first promise to Abraham is still in abeyance. The Exodus, Sinai, the Temple are all peaks and previews of what is in store for Israel and humanity in the fulfillment. But that fulfillment has not yet occurred, and we are therefore dealing with an uncompleted tale whose outcome we know because of our trust in the source of the promise. Nevertheless, however great our trust, we must not confuse promise with fulfillment, especially for man, who lives in time and for whom the future is shrouded in darkness.

Because this is so, the philosophical cannot now be central for Judaism. Philosophy demands a revealed and therefore knowable object that it can investigate. It requires stable categories by means of which it can grasp its object. Philosophy, as a form of knowledge, is therefore most comfortable with the past and least secure with the future, about which it knows little. Because Judaism—though this is often forgotten—is so much a venture into the future, the mode of knowledge will never be as natural to it as to a faith that is fulfilled. It is by no means a coincidence that Maimonides, the greatest Jewish philosopher, is also the man who had the most profound problems with the resurrection and the messianic idea as a whole. In regard to the resurrection, it is the materiality of it that causes him difficulty. With the Messiah, it is the apocalyptic dimension that must be toned down, so that the future not be made too dissimilar to the past. All these are expressions of the incompatibility of the philosophic standpoint with a genuinely transformed future whose dissimilarity to the past is a premise of prophetic thinking. A Judaism that remains true to its messianic faith can only place provisional trust in categories of thought derived from an unredeemed world destined to pass away. If the future is decisive, reason must be prepared to see itself transcended by developments that cannot yet be dreamt of. But no reason worthy of itself can be that modest, since it would then be untrue to its essence, which consists in confidence in the power of its illumination. In its own way, reason participates in the illusion of redemption for which Judaism is prepared to hope but the reality of which it is not prepared to proclaim. Because it is therefore still on the way, Judaism cannot easily express itself in the philosophical idiom, much of which is rooted in a metaphysics of completion.

Notes

1. Especially Gnostic religions. See Hans Jones, *The Gnostic Religion: The Message of the Alien God and the Beginnings of Christianity* (Boston: Beacon Press, 1958).
2. See Luke 12:53 ("They will be divided, father against son and son against father") and 14:26 ("If any one comes to me and does not hate his own father and mother and wife and children and brothers and sisters, yes, and even his own life, he cannot be my disciple"). Such ideas do not seem to have Jewish origins.
3. Lowrie quotes Hanna Mourier, who writes that "Kierkegaard's motive in this breach was the conception he had of his religious task; he did not dare to bind himself to anything upon earth lest it might check him in his calling; he must offer the best thing he possessed in order to work as God required him." See Walter Lowrie, *Kierkegaard* (Gloucester, Mass.: Peter Smith, 1970), 1:5.
4. Simone Weil, *Gravity and Grace* (New York: Putnam, 1952), pp. 216–22.

22

Standing Again at Sinai

JUDITH PLASKOW

Entry into the covenant at Sinai is the root experience of Judaism, the central event that established the Jewish people.[1] Given the importance of this event, there can be no verse in the Torah more disturbing to the feminist than Moses' warning to his people in Exodus 19:15, "Be ready for the third day; do not go near a woman." For here, at the very moment that the Jewish people stands at Sinai ready to receive the covenant—not now the covenant with individual patriarchs but with the people as a whole—at the very moment when Israel stands trembling waiting for God's presence to descend upon the mountain, Moses addresses the community only as men. The specific issue at stake is ritual impurity: An emission of semen renders both a man and his female partner temporarily unfit to approach the sacred (Lev. 15:16–18). But Moses does not say, "Men and women do not go near each other." At the central moment of Jewish history, women are invisible. Whether they too stood there trembling in fear and expectation, what they heard when the men heard these words of Moses, we do not know. It was not their experience that interested the chronicler or that informed and shaped the Torah.[2]

Moses' admonition can be seen as a paradigm of what I have called "the profound injustice of Torah itself."[3] In this passage, the Otherness of women finds its way into the very center of Jewish experience. And although the verse hardly can be blamed for women's situation, it sets forth a pattern recapitulated again and again in Jewish sources. Women's invisibility at the moment of entry into the covenant is reflected in the content of the covenant which, in both grammar and substance, addresses the community as male heads of household. It is perpetuated by the later tradition, which in its comments and codifications takes women as objects of concern or legislation but rarely sees them as shapers of tradition and actors in their own lives.

Judith Plaskow, "Torah: Reshaping Jewish Memory," in *Standing Again at Sinai* (San Francisco: Harper and Row, 1990), pp. 25–36. © Harper Collins Publishers, New York, NY 10022.

It is not just a historical injustice that is at stake in this verse, however. There is another dimension to the problem of the Sinai passage without which it is impossible to understand the task of Jewish feminism today. Were this passage simply the record of a historical event long in the past, the exclusion of women at this critical juncture would be troubling, but also comprehensible for its time. The Torah is not just history, however, but also living memory. The Torah reading, as a central part of the Sabbath and holiday liturgy, calls to mind and recreates the past for succeeding generations. When the story of Sinai is recited as part of the annual cycle of Torah readings and again as a special reading for Shavuot, women each time hear ourselves thrust aside anew, eavesdropping on a conversation among men and between men and God.[4] As Rachel Adler puts it, "Because the text has excluded her, she is excluded again in this yearly re-enactment and will be excluded over and over, year by year, every time she rises to hear the covenant read."[5] If the covenant is a covenant with all generations (Deut. 29:13ff), then its reappropriation also involves the continual reappropriation of women's marginality.

This passage in Exodus is one of the places in the Tanakh where women's silence is so deeply charged, so overwhelming, that it can provoke a crisis for the Jewish feminist. As Rachel Adler says, "We are being invited by Jewish men to re-covenant, to forge a covenant which will address the inequalities of women's position in Judaism, but we ask ourselves, 'Have we ever had a covenant in the first place? Are women Jews?' "[6] This is a question asked at the edge of a deep abyss. How can we ever hope to fill the silence that shrouds Jewish women's past? If women are invisible from the first moment of Jewish history, can we hope to become visible now? How many of us will fight for years to change the institutions in which we find ourselves only to achieve token victories?[7] Perhaps we should put our energy elsewhere, into the creation of new communities where we can be fully present and where our struggles will not come up against walls as old as our beginnings.

Yet urgent and troubling as these questions are, there is a tension between them and the reality of the Jewish woman who poses them. The questions emerge out of a contradiction between the holes in the text and the felt experience of many Jewish women. For if Moses' words came as a shock and affront, it is because women have always known or assumed our presence at Sinai; the passage is painful because it seems to deny what we have always taken for granted. Of course we were at Sinai; how is it then that the text could imply we were not there?

It is not only we who ask these questions. The rabbis too seem to have been disturbed at the implication of women's absence from Sinai and found a way to read women's presence into the text. As Rashi understood Exodus 19:3—"Thus shall you say to the house of Jacob and declare to the children of Israel"—"the house of Jacob" refers to the women and "the children of Israel" refers to the men. The Talmud interprets Exodus 19:15 ("Do not go near a woman") to mean that *women* can purify themselves on the third day after there is no longer any chance of their having a discharge of live sperm.[8]

Apparently, women's absence was unthinkable to the rabbis, and this despite the fact that in their own work they continually reenact that absence. How much more then should it be unthinkable to us who know we are present today even in the midst of communities that continue to deny us? The contradiction between the Torah text and our experience is crucial; for, construed a certain way, it is a potential bridge to a new relationship with the tradition. To accept our absence from Sinai would be to allow the male text to define us and our connection to Judaism. To stand on the ground of our experience, on the other hand, to start with the certainty of our membership in our own people is to be forced to re-member and recreate its history, to reshape Torah. It is to move from anger at the tradition, through anger to empowerment. It is to begin the journey toward the creation of a feminist Judaism.

Give Us Our History

Jewish feminists, in other words, must reclaim Torah as our own. We must render visible the presence, experience, and deeds of women erased in traditional sources. We must tell the stories of women's encounters with God and capture the texture of their religious experience. We must expand the notion of Torah to encompass not just the five books of Moses and traditional Jewish learning, but women's words, teachings, and actions hitherto unseen. To expand Torah, we must reconstruct Jewish history to include the history of women, and in doing so alter the shape of Jewish memory.

The idea that Jewish feminists need to reenvision the Jewish past requires some explication, for it is by no means generally accepted. There are many Jewish feminists who feel that women can take on positions of authority, create new liturgy, and do what we need to do to create communities responsive to our needs in the present without dredging around in sources that can only cause us pain or lifting up little sparks of light as if they were sufficient to guide us. As the simple daughter asks in Esther Broner's Passover Seder, "If Miriam lies buried in sand,/ why must we dig up those bones?"[9] On this view, we need to acknowledge and accept the patriarchal character of the Jewish past and Jewish sources and then get on with issues of contemporary change. Studying our past can only cause us bitterness. "Mother, asks the wicked daughter,/ if I learn my history,/ will I not be angry?"[10]

But while the notion of accepting women's past invisibility and subordination and attending to the present has some attractiveness, it strikes me as untenable. If it is possible within any historical, textual tradition to create a present in dramatic discontinuity with the past—and I doubt that it is—it certainly seems impossible within Judaism. For the central events of the Jewish past are not simply history but living, active memory that continues to shape Jewish identity and self-understanding. In Judaism, memory is not simply a given but a religious obligation incumbent on both Israel and God.[11] "Remember this day, on which you went free from Egypt, the house of bondage, how the LORD freed you from it with a mighty hand" (Ex. 13:3). "I will remember my covenant which is between me and you and every living creature among all flesh" (Gen. 9:15). "We Jews are a community based on memory," says Martin Buber. "The spiritual life of the Jews is part and parcel of their memory." Many visions of the past feed and sustain Jewish existence, but memories expanded and slightly reshaped with each generation have for centuries been handed down from parent to child, and with them a certain set of attitudes toward the past and toward the world.[12] It is in telling the story of our past as Jews that we learn who we truly are in the present.

Perhaps the best example of the significance of memory in Jewish life is the Passover Seder. On this most widely celebrated of Jewish holidays, families gather together not to memorialize the Exodus from Egypt but to relive it. As the climactic words of the Seder say (slightly transformed!), "In every generation, each Jew should regard her or himself as though she or he personally went forth from Egypt. . . . It was not only our ancestors which the Holy One redeemed from slavery, but us also did God redeem together with them." But even this reliving would be pointless, or simply a matter of momentary experience, were it not meant to shape our wider sense of identity and obligation. Indeed, the experience and memory of slavery and redemption are the very foundations of Jewish religious obligation. "You shall not wrong or oppress a stranger, for you were strangers in the land of Egypt" (Ex. 22:20, altered). "I the LORD am your God who brought you out of the land of Egypt, the house of bondage" (Ex. 20:2). All the commandments follow. In the modern era, the memory of slavery in Egypt has also taken on more specifically political meaning. It has fostered among some Jews an identification with the oppressed that has led to involvement in a host of movements for social change—and has fueled the feminist demand for justice for women within Judaism.[13]

The past as depicted in Jewish sources can be used not simply as a warrant for change, however, but also as a bulwark against it. If we need any further proof of the power of memory in Jewish life, we need only consider the ways in which the past is used against the possibility of innovation. Arguments against the ordination of women as rabbis, for example, are rooted not so much in any real legal impediment to women's ordination as in the fact that historically rabbis have been men. The notion of a woman as rabbi feels "un-Jewish" to many Jews because it is perceived as discontinuous with a Jewish past that makes certain claims upon its present bearers. On question after question, the weight of tradition is thrown at women as an argument for keeping things the way they are.

It is because of the past's continuing power in the present that, when the rabbis profoundly transformed Jewish religious life after the destruction of the second Temple, they also reconstructed Jewish memory to see themselves in continuity with it. So deeply is the Jewish present rooted in Jewish history that changes wrought in Jewish reality continually have been read back into the past so that they could be read out of the past as a foundation for the present. Again and again in rabbinic interpretations, we find contemporary practice projected back into earlier periods so that the chain of tradition can remain unbroken. In Genesis, for example, Abraham greets his three angelic visitors by killing a calf and serving it to them with milk (Gen. 18:7–8), clearly a violation of the laws of kashrut which forbid eating milk and meat together. As later rabbinic sources read the passage, however, Abraham first served his visitors milk and only then meat, a practice permitted by rabbinic law.[14] Not only did Abraham and the other patriarchs observe the law given at Sinai; according to the rabbis, they actually founded rabbinic academies. *Genesis Rabbah* interprets Genesis 46:28, "And he sent Judah before him unto Joseph, *to teach* the way," to mean that he prepared an academy for the teaching of Torah.[15] The point is not that such readings were a conscious plot to strengthen rabbinic authority—though certainly they would have served that function—but that it was probably unimaginable to the sages that the values they lived by could not be taught through the Torah. The links between past and present were felt so passionately that any important change in the present had to entail a new understanding of history.

All this has an important moral for Jewish feminists. We too cannot redefine Judaism in the present without redefining our past, because our present grows out of our history. The Jewish need to reconstruct the past in the light of the present converges with the feminist need to recover women's history within Judaism. Knowing that women are active members of the Jewish community in the present, even though large sectors of the community continue to define themselves in male terms and to render women invisible,[16] we know that we were always part of the community—not simply as objects of male purposes but as subjects and shapers of tradition. To accept androcentric texts and contemporary androcentric histories as the whole of Jewish history is to enter into a secret collusion with those who would exclude us from full membership in the Jewish community. It is to accept the idea that men were the only significant agents in Jewish history when we would never accept this (still current) account of contemporary Jewish life. The Jewish community today is a community of women and men, and it has never been otherwise. It is time, therefore, to recover our history as the history of women and men, a task that will both restore our own history to women and provide a fuller Jewish history for the Jewish community as a whole.[17] Again to quote from Broner's Seder, "Mother, asks the clever daughter,/ who are our mothers?/ Who are our ancestors?/ What is our history?/ Give us our name. Name our genealogy."[18]

History, Historiography, and Torah

It is one thing to see the importance of recovering women's history, however, and another to accomplish this task in a meaningful way. First of all, qua historian, the Jewish feminist faces all the same problems as any feminist historian trying to recover women's experience. Both her sources and the historians who have gone before her record male activities and male deeds in accounts ordered by male values. What we know of women's past are those things men considered it significant to remember, seen and interpreted through a value system that places men at the center.[19] The Bible, for example, focuses on war, government, and the cult, all male spheres.[20] It describes women and their activities primarily as they aid or hinder the plans of men or, in rare cases, as they perform roles usually reserved for men.[21] The Talmud records the discussions of male rabbis in male academies, discussions that touch on women mainly as they pose some problem for male control.

But second, beyond these large issues, the Jewish feminist faces additional problems raised by working with religious sources. The primary Jewish sources available to her for historical reconstruction are not simply collections of historical materials but also Torah. As Torah, as sacred teaching, they are understood by the tradition to represent divine revelation, patterns of living adequate for all time. In trying to restore the history of Jewish women, the Jewish feminist historian is not only trying to revolutionize the writing of history but is also implicitly or explicitly acting as theologian, claiming to amplify Torah, and thus questioning the finality of the Torah we have. Indeed, to rewrite Jewish history to include women is to alter the boundaries of Torah and thus to transform it. It is important, therefore, in seeking to recover women's history in the context of a feminist Judaism to confront the view of Torah that this implies.

I understand Torah, both in the narrow sense of the five books of Moses and in the broader sense of Jewish teaching, to be the partial record of the "Godwrestling" of part of the Jewish people.[22] Again and again in the course of its existence, the Jewish people has felt itself called by and accountable to a power not of its own making, a power that seemed to direct its destiny and give meaning to its life. In both ordinary and extraordinary moments, it has found itself guided by a reality that both propelled and sustained it and to which gratitude and obedience seemed the only fitting response.

The term "Godwrestling" seems appropriate to me to describe the written residue of these experiences, for I do not imagine them à la Cecil B. deMille as the boomings of a clear (male) voice or the flashing of tongues of flame, publicly visible, publicly verifiable, needing only to be transcribed. I imagine them as moments of profound experience, sometimes of illumination but also of mystery, moments when some who had eyes to see understood the meaning of events that all had undergone. Such moments might be hard-won, or sudden experiences of clarity or presence that come unexpected as precious gifts. But they would need to be interpreted and applied, wrestled with and puzzled over, passed down and lived out before they came to us as the Torah of God.[23]

I call this record partial, for moments of intense religious experience cannot be pinned down and reproduced; they can only be suggested and pointed to so that readers or listeners may from time to time catch for themselves the deeper reality vibrating behind the text. Moreover, while moments of revelation may lead to abandonment of important presuppositions and openness to ideas and experiences that are genuinely new, they also occur within cultural frameworks that can never be escaped entirely, so that the more radical implications of a new understanding may not even be seen. I call Torah the record of part of the Jewish people because the experience and interpretation found there are for the most part those of men. The experience of being summoned and saved by a single power, the experience of human likeness to the creator God, the experiences of liberation and God's passion for justice were sustained within a patriarchal framework that the interpretation of divine revelation served to consolidate rather than to shatter.[24]

There is a strand in the tradition that acknowledges this partialness of Torah and that thus indirectly allows us to see what is at stake in the recovery of women's past. According to many ancient Jewish sources, the Torah preexisted the creation of the world. It was the first of God's works, identified with the divine wisdom in Proverbs 8. It was written with black fire on white fire and rested on the knee of God. It was the architectural plan God consulted in creating the universe.[25] For the Kabbalists, this preexistent or primordial Torah is God's wisdom and essence; it expresses the immensity of God's being and power. Our Torah of ink and parchment is only the "outer garments," a limited interpretation of what lies hidden, a document that the initiate must penetrate more and more deeply to gain momentary glimpses of what lies behind. A later development of the idea of a secret Torah asserted that each of the 600,000 souls that stood at Sinai had its own special portion of Torah that only that soul could understand.[26] Obviously, no account of revelatory experience by men or women can describe or exhaust the depths of divine reality. But this image of the relation between hidden and manifest Torah reminds us that half the souls of Israel have not left for us the Torah they have seen. Insofar as we can begin to recover women's experience of God, insofar as we can restore a part of their history and vision, we have more of the primordial Torah, the divine fullness, of which the present Torah of Israel is only a fragment and sign.[27]

What is the connection, however, between recovering Torah and recovering women's history? Retrieving primordial Torah is a large task to ask "history" to perform. And in fact, in the foregoing discussion, I have been slipping back and forth between different meanings and levels of the term "history." The rabbinic reconstruction of history, which I used as an example of rewriting Jewish history, by no means involved "doing history" in our modern sense. On the contrary, it was anachronistic and ahistorical. Taking for granted the historical factuality of the momentous events at Sinai and their essential congruence with their own religious perspective, the rabbis turned their attention to mining the eternal significance of these events. As they expanded Scripture to make it relevant to their own times, they clothed later traditions with authority and connected them to the original revelation. Reshaping Jewish memory did not involve discovering what "really happened," but projecting later developments back onto the eternal present of Sinai, and in this way augmenting and reworking Torah.[28]

Recovering women's history through modern historiography, that is, through a careful and critical sifting of sources, is a second meaning of history I have used implicitly. It is not just different from rabbinic modes of thinking but in many ways in conflict with them. Modern historiography assumes precisely that the original "revelation," at least as we have it, is not sufficient, that there are enormous gaps both in tradition and in the scriptural record, that to recapture women's experiences we need to go behind our records and *add* to them, acknowledging that that is what we are doing. As Yosef Yerushalmi points out in his book on Jewish history and Jewish memory, historiography stands in a radically different relation to the past from the kind of remembering rabbinic thought represents. Modern historical writing "brings to the fore texts, events, processes, that never really became part of Jewish group memory." It challenges and relativizes those memories that have survived.[29] It is not explicitly concerned with creating a living history for a particular people but rather with correcting memory to achieve a broader view of "what happened" in the past. While Yerushalmi's discussion of modern Jewish historiography takes no note of feminist history, it is especially the purpose of the feminist historian to challenge tradition in the way he describes. Surfacing forgotten processes and events, nameless persons and discarded sources, the feminist calls Jewish memory to the bar, accusing it of partiality and distortion, of defining Jewish women out of the Jewish past.

Insofar as feminists use the techniques of modern historiography, the tensions between feminist and traditional approaches to Jewish history are important and real, and the theological relevance of feminist history is not immediately obvious. And yet, like the rabbis, feminists too are not simply interested in acquiring more knowledge about the past but in uncovering what has been revealed—this time, to women. We want to incorporate women's history as part of the living memory of the Jewish people, and thus create a history that functions as Torah. Information about women's past may be instructive and even stirring, but it is not transformative until it becomes part of the community's collective memory, part of what Jews call to mind in remembering Jewish history. Historiographical research is crucial to a new understanding of Torah because it both helps recover women's religious experiences and relativizes the Torah we have, freeing our imaginations to consider religious possibilities neglected or erased by traditional sources. Historiography is not sufficient, however, to create a living memory. The Jewish feminist reshaping of Jewish history must proceed on several levels at once. Feminist historiography can open new questions to be brought to the past and can offer a broader picture of Jewish religious experience. It must be combined, however, with feminist midrash and feminist liturgy before it can shape the Jewish relationship to God and the world and thus contribute to the transformation of Torah.

Notes

1. Emil Fackenheim uses the term "root experience" in *God's Presence in History: Jewish Affirmations and Philosophical Reflections* (New York: New York University Press, 1970), 8–14.

2. Because of the importance of this story as a story, this is one of the places I consider the text as it has been received without regard to the historical problems it poses.

3. Judith Plaskow, "The Right Question Is Theological," in *On Being a Jewish Feminist: A Reader*, edited by Susannah Heschel (New York: Schocken Books, 1983), 231.

4. Rachel Adler, " 'I've Had Nothing Yet So I Can't Take More,' " *Moment* 8 (September 1983): 22f.

5. *Ibid.*, 23.

6. *Ibid.*, 22.

7. In the synagogue I belonged to in Wichita, Kansas, for example, the rabbi, after much discussion and argument, finally agreed to allow a woman to read the prayer for the congregation in English from below the *bimah* (elevated platform from which the Torah is read). When the *shammes* (synagogue beadle) threatened to have a heart attack, the rabbi withdrew the offer.

8. *Shabbat* 86a.

9. E. M. Broner, "Honor and Ceremony in Women's Rituals," *The Politics of Women's Spirituality: Essays on the Rise of Spiritual Power within the Feminist Movement*, edited by Charlene Spretnak (Garden City, NY: Anchor Press/Doubleday, 1982), 238.

10. *Ibid.*

11. Yosef Hayim Yerushalmi, *Zakhor: Jewish History and Jewish Memory* (Seattle: University of Washington Press, 1982), 9.

12. Martin Buber, *Israel and the World: Essays in a Time of Crisis* (New York: Schocken Books, 1963), 146.

13. Michael Walzer, *Exodus and Revolution* (New York: Basic Books, 1985); Esther Ticktin, "A Modest Beginning," *The Jewish Woman: New Perspectives*, edited by Elizabeth Koltun (New York: Schocken Books, 1976), 131.

14. Louis Ginsberg, *The Legends of the Jews*, 7 vols. (Philadelphia: Jewish Publication Society, 1909–1938), 5(1925): 235, note 140.

15. *Genesis Rabbah* 95: 3. Emphasis mine.

16. For example, in *The Body of Faith: Judaism as Corporeal Election* (Minneapolis: Winston Press, 1983), Michael Wyschograd talks about circumcision as a sign of the covenant as if Jewish women do not exist. See chapter 3, 83–84.

17. Elisabeth Schüssler Fiorenza, *In Memory of Her: A Feminist Theological Reconstruction of Christian Origins* (New York: Crossroad, 1983), xiv–xx. I am indebted to Schüssler Fiorenza for this whole paragraph and, indeed, much of my approach to the recovery of Jewish women's history.

18. Broner, "Honor and Ceremony," 238.

19. Gerder Lerner, *The Majority Finds Its Past: Placing Women in History* (New York: Oxford University Press, 1979), 160, 168f.

20. Phyllis Bird, "Images of Women in the Old Testament," in *Religion and Sexism: Images of Women in the Jewish and Christian Traditions*, edited by Rosemary Ruether (New York: Simon & Schuster, 1974), 41–42.

21. Just as Lerner says, *The Majority Finds Its Past*, 168.

22. The term "Godwrestling" comes from Arthur Waskow, *Godwrestling* (New York: Schocken Books, 1978).

23. H. Richard Niebuhr emphasizes the element of insight in revelation (*The Meaning of Revelation* [New York: The Macmillan Company, 1941], 101–2), while Martin Buber emphasizes the element of presence (*I and Thou*, translated by Walter Kaufmann [New York: Charles Scribner's Sons, 1970], 158–59). It seems to me these can be present to different degrees in different revelatory experiences.

24. See Norman K. Gottwald, *The Tribes of Yahweh* (Maryknoll, NY: Orbis Books, 1979), 685.

25. Ginsberg, *The Legends of the Jews*, 1(1906): 3–4.

26. Gershom G. Scholem, *On the Kabbalah and Its Symbolism* (New York, Schocken Books, 1965), 37–65.

27. Thanks to Martha Ackelsberg for calling my attention to the theme of the relation between primordial and manifest Torah.

28. Gershom Scholem, "Tradition and Commentary as Religious Categories in Judaism," *Judaism* 15 (Winter, 1966): 26.

29. Yerushalmi, *Zakhor*, 94.

23

A Jewish Theology of Jewish Relations to Other Peoples

ELLIOT N. DORFF

Judaism as an Evolving, Religious Civilization

The Jewish people is a complicated and complex phenomenon. Unlike most other peoples, the Jews cannot be defined by their occupancy of a particular piece of land. The name "Jews" comes from Judah, the part of modern Israel where they lived in ancient times, but for at least 2500 years the vast majority of Jews have not lived there, and even today the majority of the world's Jews live elsewhere. The Hebrew language is surely a defining element in Jewish identity, for it is the language of the Bible, Mishnah and prayer-book; but until the establishment of the modern State of Israel, Hebrew has not been the language Jews spoke on a daily basis since First Temple times (c. 950–586 BCE). The languages Jews have spoken, the foods they have eaten and the clothes they have worn have been determined instead by the particular places in which they found themselves— and that has been all over the world. All of the usual factors in defining a people, then, are skewed when it comes to the Jewish people.

One might then conclude that Jews are not a people, but a religion. Judaism is certainly a central element in the identity of Jews, but particularly in modern times there are many Jews who proudly affirm their Jewish identity but do not believe in the tenets of Judaism or obey its laws. Christians undoubtedly find this most peculiar, for one may be born into a Christian home and reared as a Christian, but one is only a Christian if one now believes that Jesus is the Christ. Adherence to the beliefs and practices of Judaism are not, in a similar way, a sine qua non for being part of the Jewish people.

Elliot N. Dorff, "A Jewish Theology of Jewish Relations to Other Peoples," in *People of God, Peoples of God: A Jewish-Christian Conversation in Asia,* Hans Ucko, ed. (Geneva, Switzerland: World Council of Churches, 1996), pp. 46–66. © World Council of Churches Publications, 1211 Geneva 2 Switzerland.

The Jewish people, then, can neither be reduced to adherents of the Jewish religion nor neatly characterized as a nation like all other nations. Whatever category we use for them, in fact, will be not quite right, for history has made the Jews a unique phenomenon. Mordecai M. Kaplan (1881–1983) suggested that Judaism be seen as a *civilization* since it includes all the elements of a civilization;[1] and that may be the best way to think of Jews. Thus, while the majority of the world's Jews have not lived in Israel since First Temple times, there have always been Jews there, and it has remained the land which Jews throughout the ages have seen as their homeland, for which they longed and prayed to return. Similarly, although Hebrew was not the first language of Jews for most of Jewish history, it was always their second language, primarily because it is the language of the prayerbook and the Bible. And while Jewish songs, dances, art, food and clothing have been heavily influenced by the lands in which Jews lived, all of these have ultimately flowed in recognizable ways from the sources of the Jewish tradition.

Kaplan, though, did not characterize Judaism only as a civilization; he defined it as an *evolving, religious* civilization. The Judaism of present times is not the same civilization as the Judaism of past centuries, for Judaism is a living, evolving civilization. That does not mean that there are no connections between the present forms of Judaism and the past; quite the contrary, part of what makes current forms of Judaism recognizably Jewish are the ties that Jews feel towards their past and the substantive ways in which their concepts and actions reflect those of Jews throughout history. Nor does the evolving character of Judaism mean that the new forms are necessarily better or will be longer lasting than the old ones; it is just that contemporary conditions demand new embodiments of the Jewish tradition which meet the needs of our time.

One of the ways in which civilizations differ from each other is in the factors that become central to their identity as against those that are more peripheral. Religion is central to the Jewish civilization, as Kaplan noted by defining it as an evolving, *religious* civilization. Thus, for example, the reason why Israel is the Jewish land is not because most Jews have lived there for most of their history, but because God promised it to Abraham and his descendants. The reason why Hebrew is the Jewish language is because it is the language of Jewish religious texts. Jews may adopt many kinds of cuisine, but they are Jewish only if they follow the dietary (*kosher*) laws of the Jewish religion.

Even if many contemporary Jews identify themselves as such primarily through other elements of the Jewish civilization, it is to the Jewish religion that we must turn to understand the identity of the Jewish people. And the Jewish religion is rooted in the covenant of the Jewish people with God.

A People Apart, Formed by a Covenant with God

The Hebrew Bible describes the historical roots of the Jewish people in substantial detail, from Abraham and Sarah, to Moses and the Exodus from Egypt, to the eventual conquest of the Promised Land. For the Bible, though, it is not these historical events that constitute the raison d'être of the Jewish people; rather, it is the theological phenomenon that the Jews are called by God to enter into a covenant with him, with mutual promises and responsibilities. The history is not irrelevant; it is the stage on which the covenant is first made and on which it is to be carried out for all time. This is very much a covenant *within history*.[2] But it is the relationship with God that makes the historical events matter.[3]

According to the terms of the covenant, the Jews are obligated to be loyal to God and to love him, expressing that love primarily through obedience of God's commandments. These commandments demand that Jews live out God's will in the thick of life, not only in a cloistered environment like a synagogue or monastery, and that they teach them to their children and "recite them when you stay at home and when you are away, when you lie down and when you get up" (Deuteronomy 6:7). They are, in other words, to pervade one's life.

In return for such love and loyalty, God is to reward the love and obedience of the Jews with continued existence through progeny as numerous as the stars in the heaven, ownership of the land of Israel, material well-being and, probably the most important of all, a continued, special relationship to God. By contrast, failure to abide by the covenant will, the Bible assures us, produce the reverse: physical debilitations, loss of the Promised Land and detachment from God. But out of respect for the covenant, even if the people sin grievously, God will not abandon them forever but will rather forgive them and return them to the Promised Land and to the blessings of progeny and well-being. That is part of God's promise. God will do this also because God by nature is not only just, but loving and merciful.[4]

God's patience, though, is also a function of his own interest in preserving the covenant, for the people Israel were to be God's great experiment with humankind—God's "Chosen People" to be "a light of the nations," a model for all other peoples of what God really wants in his human creatures (cf. Exodus 19:5–6; Deuteronomy 7:6; 32:9; Isaiah 42:1–4, 49:6; 51:4). Consequently, God has a vested interest in having Israel as a Chosen People: apparently convinced that he cannot demand model behaviour from everybody, God nevertheless wants a group of people who can exemplify what living a godly way of life is all about. Israel is, as it were, the "honours class" in the school of humanity.

God's choice of Israel for this task is not based on any rational grounds; indeed, the Bible specifies that it is not because of Israel's greatness that God chose Israel for this task; on the contrary, Israel was among the smallest of peoples (Deuteronomy 7:7). Nor is it because of Israel's goodness. Shortly after making the covenant, the people abandon God for the molten calf (Exodus 32–34; cf. Deuteronomy 9:5ff.). They sin again in not trusting God to take them into the Promised Land after ten of the twelve spies report the difficulty of the task ahead (Numbers 13–14). In both cases, God seriously considers destroying the people forthwith and starting over again with Moses leading some other people, but Moses, using a series of lawyerly arguments, prevails on God to retain his ties with Israel. Thus size and trustworthiness are not the reasons for God's choice of Israel; it is rather because God loved Abraham, Isaac and Jacob and made promises to them that he agrees to continue his relationship with their descendants, no matter what.

Conversely, the people Israel also do not engage in this relationship for thought-out, rational reasons. They agree to the covenant amidst thunder and lightning at Mount Sinai— hardly an opportunity for free, coolly reasoned, informed consent (Exodus 19–24, esp. 24:7; Deuteronomy 5, esp. v. 24). The rabbis later tell two stories about this process. According to one, God went to all the other peoples of the world and offered them his covenant and they each refused when they found out some of its demands. Finally, as a last resort, God went to the insignificant people Israel, and they agreed to it without ever hearing its terms.[5] That is consent, but certainly not informed. The other story picks up on the biblical description of the awesome setting of Mount Sinai and says that God actually held the mountain over their heads and said, "Either accept the covenant, or this will be your burial place!"[6] On this account, Israel's consent to be God's covenanted people was both uninformed and coerced.

Clearly, then, it was irrational love on both sides that brought God and Israel into this special relationship. But it was to be a wedding with no possibility of divorce. God complains bitterly thoughout the Bible of Israel's unfaithfulness; and, especially after the pogroms of the Middle Ages and the Holocaust in our own century, Jews have complained just as bitterly about God's failure to live up to his promise of protection and continuity. Some Jews, faced with these realities, have even converted to Islam or Christianity or, more recently, rejected Judaism for secularism or adopted an Oriental religion like Buddhism. The majority of Jews, however, continue in this relationship with God, however troubled it may be, and we believe that God continues with us as well.

Classical Judaism, in fact, does not grant Jews the option of leaving the covenant. Once a person is born to a Jewish mother or is converted to Judaism at age 13 or older, he or she is Jewish for life. A Jew who converts to another religion loses all privileges of being a Jew, such as marriage, burial and community honours, but retains all responsibilities of Jewish identity. "A Jew, even if he has sinned, is still a Jew," the Talmud says.[7]

This is because Jewish identity has never been defined by religious affirmations, although Judaism certainly has them; rather, being Jewish has historically been a function of being part of the Jewish people. Given the theological underpinnings of the covenant that called the people Israel into being, this might seem surprising, but it has been this way for at least two thousand years, if not from the time of the patriarchs. Since the Enlightenment, people in the West have been accustomed to thinking of nations as voluntary associations of individuals that anyone can choose to leave at any time, but Jewish peoplehood antedates such notions and has never accepted them. Instead, for Judaism all Jews, whether born or converted, are part of the Jewish people whether they like it or not, no matter what parts of the religion they affirm or deny and no matter how much of Jewish law they obey, Jewish identity, in other words, is a corporate identity of peoplehood that is as inescapable as one's body or eye colour. Some Jews may try to hide their Jewish identity, but it is still theirs.[8]

While some Jews may see this inextricable bond to the Jewish people as a burdensome trap, most Jews experience it as a great gift. No Jew need ever feel alone. Hillel, a first-century Jewish sage, said, "When I am here, everyone [of the Jewish people] is here."[9] That is not just a statement of ego on his part; it is a reflection of the strong bond all Jews feel towards each other. This is perhaps most dramatically felt at weddings and funerals, which Jews are commanded to attend to help the parties involved rejoice or mourn, but it is much more pervasive than that. Jews are supposed to pray, if at all possible, in the company of a quorum of ten Jews (a *minyan*); and Jewish law spells out a number of obligations that each Jew has to the local Jewish community and to the Jewish community worldwide. At times of persecution, that has involved massive, expensive and sometimes dangerous efforts to ransom captives and to relocate refugees to safe havens. But such duties to the community are not limited to emergencies; they pervade daily life. In other words, from the point of view of Judaism, one's very identity as an individual is a function of one's membership in the Jewish people. Early in the morning liturgy for each day, in fact, a Jew blesses God for having made him or her a Jew.

One is a Jew, then, on genealogical grounds, whether through physical birth to a Jewish woman or through rebirth as a Jew through conversion. But the substance of Jewish identity is not merely national or ethnic; on the contrary, it is highly theological and moral.

Jews must retain their Jewish identity because of the awesome seriousness of their covenant with God and its goal, namely, modelling what a human society can and should be. Even in contemporary times, when a significant percentage of Jews does not consider itself religious, the sense of a unique role to play in making this a better world persists as a critical factor in Jewish self-understanding.[10]

This aspiration for the moral has evoked mixed reactions among other peoples. While some have admired Jews for the moral commitment born out of their covenantal relationship with God, most have resented the Jews for this, for it implicitly puts them in a lower status and makes them feel guilty.

This makes it imperative to point out the "normality" of the people Israel. With all other peoples of the world Jews share the usual goals of simply living life as it comes, hoping for some achievements and joys and carrying on the traditions of their ancestors. Especially after the Holocaust, Richard Rubenstein has emphasized, we Jews must remind other people of this, for, he maintains, the mediaeval pogroms and the Holocaust were caused at least in part by the fact that Christians forgot that we are normal and turned our chosenness inside out, making us not people struggling to be more godly but the very embodiment of Satan.[11] Consequently, we must state openly that the people Israel is, after all, a normal group, with the usual human needs, desires and foibles. But despite the Holocaust and despite modern secularism, the covenant idea is so deeply engrained in the Jewish tradition that it permeates the consciousness of most Jews, even those who do not consider themselves religious. Whether consciously or subconsciously, whether in its original theological form or in a new secular form, the covenant makes Jews strive to extend what human beings can *morally* and *humanly* achieve, thus making the Jewish people, as the Bible says, "a kingdom of priests and a holy nation" (Exodus 19:5–6). In so doing, it becomes, for better and for worse, what the Moabite seer Balaam described as "a people that dwells apart, not reckoned among the nations" (Numbers 23:9; Deuteronomy 32:12; 33:28; Jeremiah 49:31; Micah 7:14).

Nationalism and Universalism

The national character of the covenant is clear-cut in both biblical and rabbinic literature. The covenant is specifically between God and the Jewish people; its terms do not apply to others:

> Now therefore, if you obey my voice and keep my covenant, you shall be my treasured possession out of all the peoples. Indeed, the whole earth is mine, but you shall be for me a priestly kingdom and a holy nation (Exodus 19:5–6).
>
> I the Lord am your God; I have separated you from the peoples. . . You shall be holy to me, for I the Lord am holy, and I have separated you from the other peoples to be mine (Leviticus 20:24,26; cf. Exodus 34:10; Leviticus 25:39–46; Deuteronomy 7:1–11; 10:12–22; 33:4; Jeremiah 11:1–13).

The rabbis continued this theme. Probably the best indication of this is what is said about the sabbath, which is the symbol of the ongoing covenant between God and Israel and thus, according to the rabbis, the equivalent of all the other commandments.[12] The Bible says: "The Israelites shall keep the sabbath, observing the sabbath throughout their generations as a perpetual covenant. It is a sign forever between me and the people of

Israel. . ." (Exodus 31:16–17). On this the rabbis comment: "It [the sabbath] is a sign between me and you" (Exodus 31:17): that is, not between Me and the other nations of the world" (*Mekhilta*, Ki Tissa).

This was not simply a matter of ideology: it had a pervasive effect on practice as well. Like any other legal system, Jewish law assumes that its rights and obligations apply fully only to the members of the national group. The rabbis make this explicit by asserting that non-Jews are subject to only the seven commandments given to the children of Noah—prohibitions against murder, idolatry, incest, eating a lamb torn from a living animal, blasphemy and theft and the requirement to establish laws and courts.[13] Non-Jews were given certain protections and privileges in Jewish law, as aliens often are in legal systems, but they were not required to take on "the yoke of the commandments" (a rabbinic expression) because that was exclusively a feature of God's covenantal relationship to the Jews.[14]

That part of the Jewish covenantal notion is fairly easy for Christians to understand because Christianity also conceives itself as the prime way of relating to God—indeed, as the "new covenant." What is more difficult to communicate is that for the Jewish tradition this did not mean (as it did for much of Christianity) that it was the only way for people to fulfill God's will for humankind and be "saved" (which has a very different meaning in Judaism from that in Christianity). Jews are required to obey the law because they are part of God's covenant with Israel at Sinai;[15] non-Jews were never part of the Sinai covenant and therefore they are not obligated under it. But this does not mean that they are excluded from God's concern or prevented from enjoying God's favour; on the contrary, if they abide by the seven commandments given to Noah and seek to be righteous, they have done all that God wants of them. "The pious and virtuous of all nations participate in eternal bliss," the rabbis said[16]—a sharp contrast to the eternal damnation inherited by those who reject Jesus according to some versions of Christianity. Even at the prime moment of nationalistic triumph, the Exodus from Egypt, the rabbis picture God rebuking the angels who are singing songs of praise over the destruction of the Egyptians in the Red Sea: "My children lie drowned in the sea and you sing hymns of triumph?"[17] Thus covenant does not entail exclusivity or triumphalism in Judaism.

But it is not easy to balance a sense of appreciation and pride in being God's covenanted people who follow God's preferred way with the firm belief that all people as God's creatures are the objects of his concern and eligible for his favour. Depending on historical circumstances, it is inevitable that sometimes one of these tenets has been emphasized to the exclusion of the other. During the persecutions under the Roman emperor Hadrian, expressions of extreme antipathy could be heard, such as the remark of Simeon bar Yohai that "the best of Gentiles should be killed." On the other hand, during the more friendly atmosphere of early Sassanid Babylon, Samuel claimed that God makes no distinction between Israel and the nations on the Day of Judgment.[18] In other times and places, the balance that Judaism affirms reasserted itself.

Both the tensions and the balance are probably best illustrated in the Jewish notion of Messianism. The ultimate aim, as Isaiah declared, is that all people worship God, so that there will be universal peace among people and in nature, even to the extent that the lion will lie down with the lamb (Isaiah 2:2–4; 11–12). But Israel has a special role to play as "a light of the nations" (Isaiah 49:1–6; 51:4); and, as several biblical prophets asserted, it is Israel's God that all people will ultimately worship and Israel's Torah that they will practise (Isaiah 2:2–4; 19:23–24; Zephaniah 2:11; 3:8–9; Zechariah 14:9). Moreover, according to the rabbis, in Messianic times Jews will be rewarded for their efforts to make

God's will known by the reunion of the tribes of Israel in the land of Israel, the rebuilding of Jerusalem, the restoration of Jewish political autonomy and general prosperity—to the extent that non-Jews will seek to convert to Judaism to take advantage of the Jews' new status but will not be allowed to do so because their motive is not disinterested:

> "You brought a vine out of Egypt" (Psalm 80:8). As the vine is the lowliest of trees and yet rules over all the trees, so Israel is made to appear lowly in this world but will in the hereafter inherit the world from end to end. As the vine is at first trodden under the foot but is afterwards brought upon the table of kings, so Israel is made to appear contemptible in this world. . . but in the hereafter the Lord will set Israel on high, as it is said, "Kings shall be your nursing fathers" (Isaiah 49:23) (*Leviticus Rabbah* 36:2).
>
> In the hereafter the Gentile peoples will come to be made proselytes but will not be accepted (*B. Avodah Zarah* 3b).

Thus those who are part of God's covenant with Israel are to enjoy special privileges for the added covenantal responsibilities they have borne, but ultimately all people are to participate in the human fulfillment of Messianic times and the hereafter.

The tension between national pride and universalist convictions evident in the biblical and rabbinic doctrine of the covenant is also manifest in modern treatments of the subject. For example, Franz Rosenzweig and Martin Buber affirm the two elements of the balance: Rosenzweig emphasizes the special character of Israel, Buber the universal aspirations of the covenant. In that sense the former is a "nationalist" and the latter a "universalist." A third resolution of this tension is the theory of Mordecai Kaplan that Jews ought to think of themselves not as *chosen*, which carries with it too many negative connotations about how they view non-Jews, but as having a specific *vocation* to carry out their own history and traditions, just as every other civilization does.[19] This preserves the national character of the Jewish people while enabling Jews to recognize in theory and in fact the unique character and special contributions of many nations and civilizations.

Idolaters and Monotheists

The universalist tendencies within the Jewish tradition are especially remarkable in light of the beliefs and practices of the other peoples whom the biblical authors and the talmudic rabbis had in mind. Whether Canaanites or Romans, they were by and large not monotheists but idolaters. The Hebrew Bible is relentless in its campaign against idolatry, enshrining the prohibition against it within the Decalogue itself announced on Mount Sinai (Exodus 20:3–6; Deuteronomy 5:7–10). Moreover, according to the Torah, the reason why God wants the Israelites to occupy the Land of Israel and displace the seven nations there is because of their idolatry and consequent immortality (Genesis 15:16; Deuteronomy 9:4–5). Similarly, the rabbis devoted an entire tractate of the Mishnah and Talmud, *Avodah Zarah*, to ensuring that Jews would not get close enough to idolatry or idolaters even to be tempted by it. Some passages make fun of idolatry, and the rabbis wrote liturgies thanking God for enabling Jews to be among those who spend their time in studying and practising the Jewish tradition rather than wasting away their lives following the emptiness and immorality of idolatry.[20]

Why the Jewish tradition objects so strongly to idolatry is open to interpretation. The descriptions of idolatry in biblical and rabbinic sources make it clear that part of the reason is the grossly immoral practices—including adultery, incest and child sacrifice—that characterized the cultic life of idolatrous peoples of the ancient world and often carried over to their general lives as well (see Leviticus 18; 2 Kings 21:3–7; 23:4–12; Jeremiah 7:30–31). But there was undoubtedly a theological reason as well: worshipping the sun, moon and stars amounts to making part of reality the whole of it, taking one of God's creatures as God himself; the error is even more egregious if one makes an idol of a human artifact. Thus idolatry involved both theological and moral errors that made it impossible even to recognize, let alone properly to worship, God.

Nevertheless, it is precisely the idolaters of ancient times about whom the rabbis also said that the righteous among them shall inherit a place in the world to come. This of course has direct implications for the relationships of Judaism to truly idolatrous faiths in our time, like Hinduism. Judaism would never embrace their polytheism as a vision of the truth or their idolatry as appropriate worship, but there are elements within Jewish literature and theology that would demand respect for those who practise such religions as creatures of God and even acknowledge that there are undoubtedly righteous people among them.

If this is true for polytheists, how much more for monotheists. Consequently, mediaeval Jewish sources, recognizing the strict monotheism of Islam, did not apply the laws against idolatry to Muslims. Because of the doctrine of the Trinity and the practice among some Christians of bowing before holy relics and statues of saints, mediaeval Jewish sources were less sanguine about Christianity; but some, especially Rabbi Menahem Meiri (1249–1316), understood Christianity as monotheistic as well.[21] Clearly, Christian persecution of Jews in many times and places did little to encourage such positive evaluations of Christianity, but even within that context some rabbis understood the monotheism at the heart of Christianity, and modern rabbis have done so with increasing regularity.

Jews' Relations to Other Religions: The Groundwork

With these classical understandings of the nature and mission of the Jewish people, how should contemporary Jews relate to people of other faiths? The primary issue here is not such generally human concerns as matters of justice in commerce, for in these areas what governs for Jews are Jewish conceptions of God as the creator of us all and Jewish laws insisting that all peoples be treated fairly. Later Jewish law went further: to establish good relations with non-Jews, Jews must help the poor and the sick of all peoples and aid in burying their dead and in comforting the mourners.[22] Such humanitarianism is not characteristic of many interactions among peoples in the modern world. Moreover, the ways in which Christians and others persecuted Jews throughout history make this high standard of civility in traditional Judaism remarkable: Jewish theology, unlike some forms of Christian and Muslim theology, did not blind Jews to the human necessity of being honest, fair and caring towards those who believed differently.

The deeper question is a theological one: how do Jews understand the truth-status of other religions? Are other peoples simply deluded, or might their religions contain truths from which Jews can themselves learn? But if other religions do contain truth, why (apart from family and historical considerations) should Jews remain Jewish?

The same question of course arises *within* the Jewish community, for pluralism there, too, requires justification.[23] After all, if I think I know the truth about what is and what ought to be, why should I tolerate, let alone appreciate, the mistakes of others, whether they be members of my people or not? Answering that question clearly and convincingly is absolutely critical if we are ever to move beyond persecuting or merely tolerating others to the point of actually understanding and appreciating them.

It seems to me that there are historical, philosophical and theological grounds for such pluralism in relations between Jews and people of other faiths:

1. *History.* Historically, Christianity has been subject to at least as much change and redefinition as Judaism, if not more. Even within the same denomination, creeds created centuries ago are continually changed, sometimes through outright amendment and sometimes through new interpretations, emphases or applications. This constantly evolving nature of both Judaism and Christianity makes some of the faithful uneasy; they long for certainty and stability. But each religion retains its relevance and dynamism only by opening itself to change.

In any case, like it or not, the historical fact is that both religions *have* changed and continue to change. Today's certainties, *even within the boundaries of one's own faith*, are not necessarily tomorrow's convictions. One need only think of the many ways in which one's beliefs or practices differ from those of one's ancestors to see this evolutionary point. The same holds true for one's understandings of others. The Second Vatican Council's repudiation of blaming Jews then or now for the death of Jesus and the recent rejection by the largest Lutheran denomination in North America of Luther's many antisemitic writings are relevant cases in point.

At the same time, history does not undermine one's ability to take a strong stand on what one believes, and it certainly does not prevent a community from drawing boundaries. For example, even though the contemporary Jewish community is much exercised over the question of who is a Jew, it has uniformly and authoritatively determined that groups like Jews for Jesus are decidedly *not* Jews. The historically evolutionary nature of both faiths should, however, help contemporary Jews and Christians get beyond the feeling that the present articulation of their faith is the only one possible for a decent person to have; on the contrary, history should teach us that people of intelligence, morality and sensitivity exist in other faiths too.

Awareness of Asian faiths should, if anything, make this point all the more compelling. Because Eastern faiths are not our own and have not had a long history of conflict with us, we can probably see all the more clearly the historical evolution of their ideas and practices and the influences from outside that have affected them through the ages. That may help us to recognize the same process of development in our own religions, for which we too have taken a little from here and a little from there in shaping what has come down to us as our particular form of Judaism or Christianity. That should convince us not to be so certain that the present articulation of our convictions must inevitably be—or even empirically will be—the only possible way for people of intelligence and moral sensitivity.

2. *Philosophy.* This realization is reinforced when one turns to philosophical considerations. All human beings, whatever their background or creed, operate within the same limitations on human knowledge. For many of us, our sacred texts and traditions reveal the nature and will of God (or, in the case of non-theological traditions, ultimate reality) as clearly and fully as we think possible. But when we recognize that other peoples make the same claim, we must either resort to vacuous and inconclusive debates about whose tradition is right or confront the inability of any of us to know God's nature or will with absolute certainty.

At the same time, philosophical factors do not—any more than historical considera-tions—make a specific faith impossible or inadvisable. We may think our particular un-derstanding of God is the correct one for all people, *as far as we can tell*, and we may advance arguments to convince others of this, even though we know ahead of time that no human argument on these matters can be conclusive.

Alternatively, we may take a more "live and let live" approach, recognizing that part of the persuasiveness for me of the arguments for my faith is that it is *my* faith and that of my family and my people. Such a position does not necessarily deny cognitive mean-ing to religion, as A.J. Ayer, R.B. Braithwaite and others did in the middle of this cen-tury;[24] it need only be a humble recognition that none of us is an objective observer, that we all view the world from a vantage point, and that our autobiographical background in-evitably plays—and perhaps should play—a role in which viewpoint is ours.

One could be, in Van Harvey's terminology, a "soft perspectivist" rather than a "hard perspectivist" or "non-perspectivist." In other words, one can say, against "non-perspec-tivism," that all of us do have a point of view which influences how we think and act; we do not look at the world through epistemologically transparent spectacles. At the same time, one may add, against "hard perspectivism," that our point of view need not blind us to other perspectives; indeed, we can possibly learn from the views of others.[25]

The latter approach would make for a much stronger foundation for mutually respect-ful Jewish-Christian relations, but even the former view, with its open recognition of the limits on what anyone can know of God, holds promise. That is because both views come out of a philosophically accurate assessment of our knowledge of God: we can and do say some things about God and act on our convictions, and our beliefs and actions can be justified by reasons that can be shared and appreciated by others; but other, equally rational, moral and sensitive people might differ with us and might also have good rea-sons for what they say and do. This is only to be expected in an area in which our knowl-edge is, by the very nature of the knower and the subject to be known, incomplete.

Asian faiths underscore this point, for by and large they have not been nearly as ex-clusive as the Western faiths have historically been. They have rather stated their con-victions and practices and left it to individuals to adhere to them or to other faiths as they choose. Westerners accustomed to an "either-or" approach to truth in both philosophy and religion feel decidedly uncomfortable with such a "both-and" approach. The epistemo-logical humility for which I am arguing, however, and which I see as the only philo-sophically responsible position to take, should goad us to learn an important lesson from our Asian brothers and sisters.

3. *Theology.* In addition to these historical and philosophical considerations, some im-portant Jewish theological tenets can be used to lay the groundwork for a genuinely plu-ralistic appreciation of others.

The Mishnah, the central collection of rabbinic law from the first and second centuries, asks why God initiated the human species by creating only one man (Adam). One rea-son, the Mishnah suggests, is to impress upon us the greatness of the Holy One, blessed be he, for when human beings mint coins, they all come out the same, but God made one mold (Adam) and yet no human being looks exactly like another. This physical pluralism is matched by an intellectual pluralism for which, the rabbis say, God is to be blessed: "When one sees a crowd of people, one is to say, 'Blessed is the Master of mysteries', for just as their faces are not alike, so are their thoughts not alike."

The Midrash, the written record of rabbinic lore, supports this further. It says that when Moses was about to die, he said to the Lord: "Master of the universe, you know the opinions of everyone and that there are no two among your children who think alike. I beg of you that after I die, when you appoint a leader for them, appoint one who will bear with [accept, *sovel*] each one of them as he thinks [on his own terms, *lefi da'ato*]." We know that Moses said this, the rabbis claim, because Moses describes God as "God of the *ruhot* [spirits, in the plural] of all flesh" (Numbers 24:16).[26] Thus God *wants* pluralism so that people will constantly be reminded of his grandeur.

Moreover, according to the rabbis, God intentionally reveals only a part of his truth in the Torah and the rest must come from study and debate.[27] Even with study there is a limit to human knowledge, for as the mediaeval Jewish philosopher Joseph Albo said, "If I knew Him, I would be He."[28]

God as understood in the Jewish tradition thus wants pluralism not only to demonstrate his grandeur in creating humanity with diversity, but also to force human beings to realize their epistemological creatureliness, the limits of human knowledge in comparison to that of God. From the standpoint of piety, pluralism emerges not from relativism, but from a deeply held and aptly humble monotheism.

There are some limitations to this line of reasoning as the basis for Jewish relations to other faiths. It may be the case that God wants us to think independently, but ultimately the biblical prophets assert that the Torah is God's true teaching, the one that all nations will ultimately learn. Micah, for example, a younger contemporary of Isaiah, copies the latter's messianic vision but then adds a line of his own that effectively changes it: "Though all the peoples walk each in the names of its gods, we will walk in the name of the Lord our God forever and ever" (Micah 4:5; compare Micah 4:1–3 with Isaiah 2:2–4). This is a decidedly pluralistic vision of Messianic times: every people shall continue to follow its own god. Even so, Micah added this line *after* quoting Isaiah's vision that "many peoples shall come and say: 'Come, let us go up to the mountain of the Lord, to the house of the God of Jacob, that he may teach us his ways and that we may walk in his paths'. For out of Zion shall go forth instruction, and the word of the Lord from Jerusalem" (Isaiah 2:3; Micah 4:2). Thus even for Micah, apparently, other gods and other visions of the good life might exist, but it is only Israel that has the true understanding of God's will.

In sum, God may indeed want multiple conceptions of the divine, but traditional sources assign non-Jewish views to a clearly secondary status. God may like variety among his creatures and he may even hold the people responsible only for what they could be expected to know (the seven Noahide laws); but ultimately only the Jews know what is objectively correct. This is liberal toleration—and it should be appreciated as such—but it certainly is not a validation of others' views. In that sense, it falls short of what Simon Greenberg, a contemporary Conservative rabbi, suggests as a criterion for genuine pluralism: that "your ideas are spiritually and ethically as valid—that is, as capable of being justified, supported and defended—as mine."[29] Indeed, Greenberg himself may not have wanted to extend his thesis beyond disagreements among Jews.

I would take a somewhat broader view. It is only natural that Jewish sources cited earlier should reflect a tension between nationalism and universalism. God is, according to Jewish belief, the God of all creatures, but, at the same time, he chose the Jews to exemplify the standards he really wants for human life. This is how *Jews* understand God's will, the reason why they commit all their energies and indeed their very lives to Jewish belief and practice.

Despite this nationalistic side of the Jewish tradition, however, what ultimately rings through it are the rabbis' assertions that non-Jews fully meet God's expectations by abiding by the seven Noahide laws and that "the pious and virtuous of all nations participate in eternal bliss." Thus Jewish sources that speak about God wanting plural approaches to him within the Jewish community can apparently also be applied, without too much tampering, to inter-communal relations. Of course, the same segments of the Jewish community that have difficulty with the former would undoubtedly have difficulty with the latter, and even some pluralists within the Jewish community would need to stretch their understanding and sensitivity to apply Jewish theology in this way. Nevertheless, a firm basis for this kind of theology exists within the Jewish tradition.

A Realistic but Open Model of the Covenant for Our Times

If Jews are to stretch in this way, they justifiably can expect Christians and others to do likewise. I personally have no doubt that Christians and others *can* find the requisite sources within their own tradition to do this *if they choose to do so*. Indeed, we must all develop the strands in each of our traditions that recognize that people with opinions differing from our own may be moral and intelligent and even have something to teach us about the true and the good. Recognition of the historical development of each of our traditions should help us to see that our contemporary understanding of things may not be ultimately correct, and attention to the philosophical limits of our knowledge should disabuse us even further of our claims to certainty. Within Judaism as well as many other faiths, theological concerns would also support such a move towards openness to others and the lessons they have to teach us.

In other words, universalism in our own day involves the recognition that God can and does relate to all people. The particular way in which God does this may vary, and it is inevitable that people will feel that their own approach is best, but this should not produce the conclusion that other paths to God are necessarily bad, ineffective or unauthentic. It may well be that God wisely entered into different forms of relationship with different peoples to fit the traditions, talents and sensitivities of each group. It may also be that God has planned different roles for each group. Franz Rosenzweig suggested that the divine task of Jews is to model what God wants and the divinely ordained task of Christians is to carry the message to the Gentiles; the respective numbers of the Jewish and Christian communities and their respective policies on missionizing seem to support such a view. As Seymour Siegel has said:

> If this suggestion were to be accepted by Jew and Christian, it would be possible to open a new era of dialogue and mutual enlightenment. Christians would not denigrate Judaism by viewing it as a vestige, an anachronism of ancient times. They would cease their missionizing activities vis-a-vis Jews. For Jews there would be a new recognition of the importance of Christianity, of its spiritual dimension and its task to bring the world of God to the far islands.[30]

In any case, the ultimate goal in speaking to one another is not to synthesize all the traditions of the world into one or to ignore the real differences among them. It is to make those differences the source of genuine understanding of and learning from one another, rather than of the wars and persecutions that have all too often plagued us.

In this process, Jews will remain a people apart, committed to their mission of being a light to the nations, modelling our own understanding of God's will. In doing this, we will be carrying out the duties of our own covenant with God. As the Psalmist says:

> O offspring of his servant Abraham,
> children of Jacob, his chosen ones.
> He is the Lord our God;
> his judgments are in all the earth.
> He is mindful of his covenant forever,
> of the world that he commanded, for a thousand generations,
> the covenant that he made with Abraham,
> his sworn promise to Isaac,
> which he confirmed to Jacob as a statute,
> to Israel as an everlasting covenant (Psalms 105:6–10).

Notes

The following common notations are used in the citations of the classical rabbinic texts: M. = Mishnah (ed. c. 220 C.E.); T = Tosefta (ed. about the same time); J. = Jerusalem (or Palestinian) Talmud (ed. approximately 400 C.E.); B. = Babylonian Talmud (ed. c. 500 C.E.); M.T. = *Mishneh Torah*, a code of Jewish law by Maimonides (1177 C.E.); S.A. = *Shulhan Arukh*, a code of Jewish law by Joseph Karo (1565 C.E.) with notes by Moses Isserles.

1. Mordecai M. Kaplan, *Judaism as a Civilization*, New York, Reconstructionist Press, 1934; cf. *The Religion of Ethical Nationhood*, New York, Macmillan, 1970.
2. For a mediaeval view of the importance of historicity see Judah Halevi, *Kuzari*, I, 11–43, tr. in *Three Jewish Philosophers*, Philadelphia, Jewish Publication Society, 1960, III, pp. 33–37; for a contemporary interpretation, Emil Fackenheim, *God's Presence in History: Jewish Affirmations and Philosophical Reflections*, New York, New York U.P., 1970; and *The Jewish Return into History: Reflections in the Age of Auschwitz and a New Jerusalem*, New York, Schocken, 1978.
3. On the theological and legal implications of the covenant idea for contemporary Jewish self-understanding, see my articles "Judaism as a Religious Legal System", *Hasting's Law Journal*, vol. 29, July 1978, pp. 1331–60; "The Meaning of Covenant: A Contemporary Understanding", in Helga Croner and Leon Klenicki, eds, *Issues in the Jewish-Christian Dialogue*, New York, Paulist Press, 1979, pp. 38–61; "The Covenant: The Transcendent Thrust in Jewish Law", *The Jewish Law Annual*, vol. 7, 1988, pp. 68–96; on efforts by two modern Jewish theologians to reshape the covenant idea to account for past and present relations with non-Jews, see "The Covenant: How Jews Understand Themselves and Others", *Anglican Theological Review*, vol. 64, no. 4, October, 1982, pp. 481–501.
4. These themes occur often in the Bible. For the promises see Gen. 15; 17; 26:1–5, 23–24; 28:13–15; 35:9–12; repeated, along with the curses for not fulfilling the terms of the covenant, in, e.g., Lev. 26; Deut. 6–7; 11:13–25, 28. That God will punish disobedience not only with physical deprivation and affliction but also with his absence is most clear in the prophetic writings, e.g., Isa. 29:10; Jer. 7:1–15; Ezek. 7:23–27; Amos 8:11–12; Hosea 3:4; 5:6; Micah 3:6–7; Lam. 2:9.
5. *Sifre Deuteronomy*, par. 343; *Numbers Rabbah* 14:10.
6. B. *Shabbat* 88a; B. *Avodah Zarah* 2b.
7. B. *Sanhedrin* 44a.

8. Milton R. Konvitz has explicated this well; see *Judaism and the American Idea*, New York, Schocken, 1978, pp. 139–59. See also my article, "Training Rabbis in the Land of the Free", in Nina Beth Cardin and David Wolf Silverman, eds, *The Seminary at 100,* New York, The Rabbinical Assembly and the Jewish Theological Seminary of America, 1987, pp. 11–28.

9. B. *Sukkah* 53a.

10. In the USA, a 1988 *Los Angeles Times* national survey showed that more than half of Jews considered commitment to social equality as the quality most important to their sense of Jewish identity, whereas only 17 percent cited religious observance. Jewish lawyers make up a hugely disproportionate number of those who do *pro bono* work for the indigent: cf. Donna Arzt, "The People's Lawyers", *Judaism*, vol. 35, no. 1, 1986, pp. 47–62; Jerold S. Auerbach and Donna Arzt, "Profits or Prophets: An Exchange", *ibid.*, vol. 36, no. 3, 1987, pp. 360–367; and the percentage of Jews who contribute to charity and the percentage of income contributed far exceeds the US norm; cf. Edward S. Shapiro, "Jews With Money", *ibid.* vol. 36, no. 1, 1987, pp. 1–16; Gerald Krefatz, *Jews and Money: The Myths and the Reality*, New Haven, Conn., Ticknor and Fields, 1982, ch. 11.

11. Richard Rubenstein, *After Auschwitz*, Indianapolis, Bobbs-Merrill, 1966, chs. 1–3, esp. pp. 58, 69–71. For a radical rethinking of the nature of the covenant after the Holocaust by an Orthodox rabbi, see Irving Greenberg, *The Jewish Way*, New York, Simon & Schuster, 1988, ch. 3, esp. pp. 87–93.

12. Cf. J. *Nedarim*, 38b; *Exodus Rabbah* 25:12.

13. T. *Avodah Zarah* 8:4; B. *Sanhedrin* 56a, 60a.

14. These privileges and protections included giving charity to the non-Jewish poor and personal obligations like burying their dead, attending their funerals, eulogizing their deceased and consoling their bereaved; cf. M. *Gittin* 5:8; T. *Gittin* 5:4–5; and my article, "Jewish Perspectives on the Poor", in *The Poor Among Us: Jewish Tradition and Social Policy*, New York, American Jewish Committee, 1986, pp. 21–55.

15. See, e.g., Deuteronomy 7:9–11; *The Haggadah of Passover*, ed. Philip Birnbaum, New York, Hebrew Publishing Company, 1953, p. 95.

16. *Sifra* on Leviticus 19:18.

17. B. *Megillah* 10b.

18. Simeon bar Yohai in J. *Kiddushin* 4:11 (66c); Samuel in J. *Rosh Hashanah* 1:3 (57a). Cf. Daniel Sperber and Theodore Friedman, "Gentile," *Encyclopedia Judaica*, vol. 7, pp. 410–14, which points out that the Jew's attitude towards the Gentile was largely conditioned by the Gentile's attitude toward him (see, e.g., *Esther Rabbah* 2:3). Moreover, to the extent that there was Jewish antipathy towards Gentiles, it was never based upon racial prejudice, but rather motivated by Gentiles' idolatry, moral laxity, cruelty to Jews and rejection of the Torah.

19. On Rosenzweig and Buber, see my article, "The Covenant: How Jews Understand Themselves and Others", *loc. cit.*, esp. pp. 484–93; on Kaplan, see my article, "The Meaning of Covenant: A Contemporary Understanding", *loc. cit.*, pp. 40–46.

20. Cf. B. *Avodah Zarah* 2ff.; J. *Berakhot* 7d.

21. The Tosafists say outright that "we are certain that the Christians do not worship idols" (Tos. to B. *Avodah Zarah* 2a, s.v. *asur*), but due to their trinitarianism they do not see them as full monotheists and classify them instead as Noahides who are not enjoined against trinitarian belief (Tos. to B. *Sanhedrin* 63b, s.v. *asur*; Tos. to B. *Berkhorot* 2b, s.v. *Shema*). R. Menahem Meiri sees Christians as monotheists: *Beit Ha-Behirah* to B. *Bava Kamma* 113b and to B. *Avodah Zarah* 20a. Maimonides, on the other end of the spectrum, applies all the strictures against idolatry to Christians: M.T. *Laws of Idolatry* 9:4 (deleted by censors in the ordinary editions). A good summary of this can be found in the article, "Gentile", *Encyclopedia Judaica*, vol. 7, pp. 410–14.

22. According to the Talmud, the commandment to love the stranger and not to wrong him occurs 36 times in the Torah (see B. *Baba Metzia* 59b; e.g., Exodus 22:20; 23:9; Deuteronomy 9:19;

and, perhaps most explicitly, Leviticus 19:33–34). Furthermore, "There shall be one law for the citizen and for the stranger who dwells among you" appears often in the Torah (e.g., Exodus 12:49; Leviticus 24:22; Numbers, 15:15–16). These principles, together with the need to avoid the enmity of non-Jews, made Jews treat non-Jews with the same principles of justice that they used for themselves and even to bury the non-Jewish dead and to provide for the basic needs of the non-Jewish poor. On obligations to non-Jews see B. *Gittin* 61a; M.T. *Laws of Gifts to the Poor* 7:7; *Laws of Idolatry* 10:5; *Laws of Mourning* 14:12; *Laws of Kings* 10:12; S.A. *Yoreh De'ah* 335:9, 367:1.

23. Elliot N. Dorff, "Pluralism", in Steven T. Katz, ed., *Frontiers of Jewish Thought*, Washington, B'nai Brith Books, 1992, pp. 213–33.

24. A.J. Ayer, *Language, Truth, and Logic,* London, Dover, 1936, pp. 114–120; R.B. Braithwaite, "An Empiricist's View of the Nature of Religious Belief", reprinted in Ian T. Ramsey, ed., *Christian Ethics and Contemporary Philosophy*, New York, Macmillan, 1966, pp. 53–73.

25. Cf. Van A. Harvey, *The Historian and the Believer*, New York, Macmillan, 1966, pp. 205–30; see also James W. McClendon Jr and James M. Smith, *Understanding Religious Convictions,* Notre Dame, Indiana, Univ. of Notre Dame Press, 1975, pp. 6–8.

26. The Mishnah cited is M. *Sanhedrin* 4:5; the blessing cited is in B. *Berakhot* 58a; and the Midrash cited is in *Midrash Tanhuma* on Numbers 24:16.

27. J. *Sanhedrin* 22a; *Midrash Tanhuma*, ed. Buber, Devarim, 1a; *Numbers Rabbah* 19:6.

28. Joseph Albo, *Sefer Ha-Ikkarim*, part II, ch. 30, tr. Isaac Husik, Philadelphia, Jewish Publication Society of America, 1946, vol. II. p. 206.

29. Simon Greenberg, "Pluralism and Jewish Education", *Religious Education*, vol. 81, 1986, p. 23; cf. p. 27, where Greenberg links pluralism to the absence of violence in transforming another person's opinion.

30. Seymour Siegel, "Covenants—Old and New", *Jewish Heritage*, spring 1967, pp. 54–59. Rosenzweig's suggestion appears in *The Star of Redemption*, tr. William W. Hallo, New York, Holt Rinehart & Winston, 1971, Part III, Books I and II; cf. esp. p. 166.

SECTION F.
LAW

24

Halakhic Man

JOSEPH SOLOVEITCHIK

Halakhic man is a man who longs to create, to bring into being something new, something original. The study of Torah, by definition, means gleaning new, creative insights from the Torah (*ḥiddushei Torah*). "The Holy One, blessed be He, rejoices in the dialectics of Torah" [a popular folk saying]. Read not here 'dialectics' (*pilpul*) but 'creative interpretation' (*ḥiddush*). This notion of *ḥiddush*, of creative interpretation, is not limited solely to the theoretical domain but extends as well into the practical domain, into the real world. The most fervent desire of halakhic man is to behold the replenishment of the deficiency in creation, when the real world will conform to the ideal world and the most exalted and glorious of creations, the ideal Halakhah, will be actualized in its midst. The dream of creation is the central idea in the halakhic consciousness—the idea of the importance of man as a partner of the Almighty in the act of creation, man as creator of worlds. This longing for creation and the renewal of the cosmos is embodied in all of Judaism's goals. And if at times we raise the question of the ultimate aim of Judaism, of the telos of the Halakhah in all its multifold aspects and manifestations, we must not disregard the fact that this wondrous spectacle of the creation of worlds is the Jewish people's eschatological vision, the realization of all its hopes.

The Halakhah sees the entire Torah as consisting of basic laws and halakhic principles. Even the Scriptural narratives serve the purpose of determining everlasting law. "The mere conversations of the servants of the fathers are more important than the laws [Torah] of the sons. The chapter dealing with Eliezer covers two or three columns [in the Torah scroll], and [his conversation] is not only recorded but repeated. Whereas [the uncleanliness of] a reptile is a basic principle of Torah law [*gufei Torah*], yet it is only from an extending particle in the Scriptures that we know that its blood defiles as flesh" (Gen. Rabbah 60:11). Our Torah does not contain even one superfluous word or phrase. Each

Joseph Soloveitchik, *Halakhic Man*, trans. Lawrence Kaplan (Philadelphia: Jewish Publication Society, 1983), pp. 99–128. © Jewish Publication Society, Philadelphia, PA 19103.

letter alludes to basic principles of Torah law, each word to "well-fastened," authoritative, everlasting halakhot. From beginning to end it is replete with statutes and judgments, commandments and laws. The mystics discern in our Torah divine mysteries, esoteric teachings, the secrets of creation, and the *Merkabah* [the chariot of Ezekiel's prophecy]; the halakhic sages discern in it basic halakhot, practical principles, laws, directives, and statutes. "The deeds of the fathers are a sign for the sons" [cf. Nahmanides, *Commentary on the Torah*, Gen. 12:6]. And this sign—i.e., the vision of the future—constitutes a clear-cut halakhah. Halakhic man discerns in every divine pledge man's obligation to bring about its fulfillment, in every promise a specific norm, in every eschatological vision an everlasting commandment (the commandment to participate in the realization of the prophecy). The conversations of the servants, the trials of the fathers, the fate of the tribes, all teach the sons Torah and commandments. The conversations of the servants of the fathers are, in truth, the Torah of the sons. The only difference between the conversation of Eliezer and the Scriptural portion concerning the reptile is that the former extends over two or three columns while the latter is but a brief passage.

Therefore, if the Torah spoke at length about the creation of the world and related to us the story of the making of heaven and earth and all their host, it did so not in order to reveal cosmogonic secrets and metaphysical mysteries but rather in order to teach *practical* Halakhah. The Scriptural portion of the creation narrative is a legal portion, in which are to be found basic, everlasting halakhic principles, just like the portion of *Kedoshim* (Lev. 19) or *Mishpatim* (Exod. 21). If the Torah then chose to relate to man the tale of creation, we may clearly derive one law from this manner of procedure—viz., that man is obliged to engage in creation and the renewal of the cosmos.[1]

Not for naught is Judaism acquainted with a Book of Creation, the mastery of which enables one both to create and destroy worlds. "Raba said: If the righteous desired it, they could be creators of worlds, as it is written, 'But your iniquities have separated between you and your God' (Isa. 59:2). (Rashi explains: We may infer from this that if they would not have any iniquities, there would be no distinction [between man and God, in the matter of creation]). Raba created a man. . . . R. Hanina and R. Oshia spent every Sabbath eve in studying the Book of Creation and created a third-grown calf" (Sanhedrin 65b).

The peak of religious ethical perfection to which Judaism aspires is man as creator.

When God created the world, He provided an opportunity for the work of His hands—man—to participate in His creation. The Creator, as it were, impaired reality in order that mortal man could repair its flaws and perfect it. God gave the Book of Creation—that repository of the mysteries of creation—to man, not simply for the sake of theoretical study but in order that man might continue the act of creation. "As soon as Abraham had understood, fashioned, engraved, attached and created, inquired and clearly grasped [the secret of creation], the Lord of the universe revealed Himself to him, called him His friend, and made a covenant with him between the ten fingers of his hand. . . ."[2] Man's task is to "fashion, engrave, attach, and create," and transform the emptiness in being into a perfect and holy existence, bearing the imprint of the divine name.

"The earth was chaos and void, and darkness was upon the face of the deep. . . . And God said: 'Let there be light'; and there was light. . . . God divided the light from the darkness. God called the light Day and the darkness He called Night. . . . Let there be a firmament in the midst of the waters, and let it divide the waters from the waters. . . . Let the waters under the heavens be gathered together unto one place, and let the dry land appear. . . . God called the dry land Earth, and the gathering of the waters He called Seas, etc." (Gen. 1:2–10).

When God engraved and carved out the world, he did not entirely eradicate the chaos and the void, the deep, the darkness, from the domain of His creation. Rather, he separated the complete, perfect existence from the forces of negation, confusion, and turmoil and set up cosmic boundaries, eternal laws to keep them apart. Now Judaism affirms the principle of creation out of absolute nothingness. Therefore, the chaos and the void, the deep, the darkness, and relative nothingness must all have been fashioned by the Almighty before the creation of the orderly, majestic, beautiful world. "A philosopher once said to Rabban Gamliel: Your God is a great artist, but He found good materials which helped Him: chaos and the void, the deep, the wind [*ruah*], water and darkness. He replied: Let the bones of that person [who so averred] be blasted! For the Scripture affirms that all these things were created. With regard to chaos and the void it is written: "I [God] make peace, and create evil' (Isa. 45:7); with regard to darkness it is written: 'I form the light and create darkness' (Isa. 45:7); with regard to the wind [*ruah*] it is written: 'He formeth the mountains, and createth the wind [*ruah*]' (Amos 4:13); with regard to the deep it is written: 'Out of nothing I carved out the deep' (Prov. 8:24)" [Gen. Rabbah 1:12]. All of these "primordial" materials were created in order that they subsist and be located in the world itself. Not for naught did He create them. He created them in order that they may dwell within the cosmos!

However, the forces of relative nothingness at times exceed their bounds. They wish to burst forth out of the chains of obedience that the Almighty imposed upon them and seek to plunge the earth back into chaos and the void. It is only the law that holds them back and bars the path before them. Now the Hebrew term for law, *hok*, comes from the root *h-k-k* (which means "to carve, engrave"). Thus the law carves out a boundary, sets up markers, establishes special domains, all for the purpose of separating existence from "nothingness," the ordered cosmos from the void, and creation from the naught. "When He carved [*hok*] a circle [*hug*] upon the face of the deep" (Prov. 8:27)—*hok*, the carving, the engraving, the law = *hug*, the circle = an all-encompassing boundary. The perfect and complete ontic being extends until this divinely carved-out boundary; beyond that border is the deep, chaos and the void, darkness, and the "nothingness," devoid of image and form.

However, this relative "nothingness" is plotting evil, the deep is devising iniquity, and the chaos and void lie in wait in the dark alleyways of reality and seek to undermine the absolute being, to profane the lustrous image of creation. "Thou didst cover it with the deep as with a vesture; the waters stood above the mountains. At Thy rebuke they fled, at the sound of Thy thunder they hastened away. . . . Thou didst set a bound which they should not pass over, that they might return to cover the earth" (Ps. 104:6–9). "When he assigned to the sea its limit, so that the waters might not transgress His command, when He carved out the foundations of the earth" (Prov. 8:29). The deep wishes to cast off the yoke of the law (*hok*), to pass beyond the boundary (*hug*) and limit that the Creator set up and carved out and inundate the world and the fullness thereof. However, at the rebuke of the Almighty, it flees in retreat. From the sound of His thunder it is driven back and hastens to its "lair"—the lair of nothingness. The sight of a tempestuous sea, of whirling, raging waves that beat upon the shore there to break, symbolizes to the Judaic consciousness the struggle of the chaos and void with creation, the quarrel of the deep with the principles of order and the battle of confusion with the law. The mysterious power of the delineated law and the limiting boundary which the Almighty implanted in existence presented itself in all its awesomeness and majesty to King David, the sweet singer of Israel, as reflected in the natural phenomenon of the orderly ebb and flow of the sea (caused by the gravitational force of the sun and the moon and the rotation of the earth). The sea at high tide and the sea at low tide appeared in their whirl of colors as a symbolic elemental process, as a bewitching spectacle of an eternal clash of forces. It is as though the sea at high tide, rushing to meet the shore, desires to destroy the boundary and the law, as though the disorder of the primordial forces, of chaos and confusion, desires to cleave asunder the perfect and exquisitely chiseled creation and lay it waste. Only the mighty strength of the law of the Almighty bars the path before them [the waves] and shatters them. "Thou rulest the proud swelling of the sea; when the waves thereof arise, Thou dost shatter them" (Ps. 89:10).

"R. Johanan said: When David dug the pits, the deep arose and threatened to submerge the world. . . . David thereupon inscribed the ineffable name upon a sherd, cast it into the deep, and it subsided."[4] When David began to dig the foundations of the Temple, he dug 15 cubits and did not reach the deep. Finally he found one potsherd and sought to lift it up. Said [the potsherd] unto him: You may not. Said [David] unto it: And why not? Said [the potsherd] unto David: Because it is I who am restraining the deep. Said [David] unto it: And for how long have you been here? Said [the potsherd] unto him: Since the Almighty proclaimed on Mount Sinai 'I am the Lord thy God' (Exod. 20:2). At that moment the earth trembled and began to sink and I was placed here to restrain the deep. David, nevertheless, did not listen to it. As soon as he lifted it, the waters of the deep arose and sought to inundate the world."[5] Thus the deep desires to burst out of the enclosures of the law and shatter the realms of orderly creation, the cosmic process, the regular course of the world, and plunge them all back into "nothingness," into desolation and ontic emptiness. However, it is held firm in the grip of the mighty law and its principles.[6]

All of kabbalistic literature is imbued with this idea. The "other side," the "husks," the "mighty deep," the "angels of destruction," the "offspring of chaos," etc., all symbolize the realm of emptiness and the void, the domain of "nothingness," devoid of any image or stature,[7] that does battle with the glorious existence enveloped by the luster of the image of the Divine Presence.

However, this view, which threads its way through the entire course of Jewish thought, is not just a mysterious theoretical notion but a practical principle, a fundamental ethico-halakhic postulate.

When man, the crowning glory of the cosmos, approaches the world, he finds his task at hand—the task of creation. He must stand on guard over the pure, clear existence, repair the defects in the cosmos, and replenish the "privation" in being. Man, the creature, is commanded to become a partner with the Creator in the renewal of the cosmos; complete and ultimate creation—this is the deepest desire of the Jewish people.

The Scriptural text "And the heaven and the earth were finished, and all the host of them" (Gen. 2:1)—the Targum, the Aramaic translation of the Pentateuch, translates *va-yekhulu,* "were finished," as *ve-ishtakhlelu,* "were perfected"—is both a profound expression of the soul of the people and the most fervent desire of the man of God. This lofty, ontological idea illumines the path of the eternal people. When a Jew on the Sabbath eve recites [this passage as part of] the *kiddush,* the sanctification over the wine, he testifies not only to the existence of a Creator but also to man's obligation to become a partner with the Almighty in the continuation and perfection of His creation. Just as the Almighty constantly refined and improved the realm of existence during the six days of creation, so must man complete that creation and transform the domain of chaos and void into a perfect and beautiful reality.

When a Jew goes outside and beholds the pale moon casting its delicate strands of light into the empty reaches of the world, he recites a blessing. The natural, orderly, cosmic phenomenon precipitates in his religious consciousness both melancholy thoughts and bright hopes. He contemplates this spectacle of the lawful cycle of the waxing and waning of the moon and sees in it a symbol of defectiveness and renewal. Just as the moon is "defective" and then "renewed," so creation is "defective" and will be "renewed," "replenished." To be sure, God "with His word created the heavens. [He] gave them a fixed time so that they should not alter their appointed charges" [from the blessing over the new moon]. We are not speaking here about any mythological notions, heaven forbid, but about the cognition of the natural law governing the courses of the heavenly hosts based upon clear, precise astronomical knowledge. However, the law itself, the orderly movement itself, symbolizes a wondrous mystery. The very court which would make its astronomical calculations "in the same manner as the astronomers, who discern positions and motions of stars, engage in calculations,"[8] would go outside and recite a blessing over the new moon. The Jewish people see in the orderly and lawful motion of the moon in its orbit a process of defectiveness and renewal, the defectiveness of the creation and its renewal, its replenishment. They, therefore, whisper a strange silent prayer: "May it be Thy will . . . to replenish the defect of the moon so that there be in it no diminution. And let the light of the moon be like the light of the sun, like the light of creation, like it was before it was diminished. As it is said: 'And God made the two great lights'" (Gen. 1:16) [from the prayer following the blessing over the new moon]. The Jewish people, by means of this prayer, give allegorical expression to their hope for the perfection of creation and the repairing of the defects in the cosmos, to their hope for the realization of that great and awesome symbolic eschatological vision: "The light of the moon shall be as the light of the sun" (Isa. 30:26).[9]

Examining matters from this esoteric vantage point, the Jewish people see their own fate as bound up with the fate of existence as a whole, that existence which is impaired and cleft asunder by the forces of negation and "nothingness." Physical reality and spiritual-historical existence—both have suffered greatly on account of the dominion of the abyss, of chaos and the void, and their fates parallel one another. When the historical process of the Jewish people reaches its consummation and attains the heights of perfection, then (in an allegorical sense) the flaws of creation as a whole will also be repaired. "He bade the moon renew itself for those who were burdened from birth, who like her will be renewed and will extol their Creator on account of the name of His glorious kingdom" [from the blessing over the new moon].

Man is obliged to perfect what his Creator "impaired." "Resh Lakish said: Why is the new-moon goat offering different, in that [the phrase] 'a sin offering unto the Lord' (Num. 28:15) is used in connection with it [whereas ordinarily the phrase 'a sin offering' is used without the additional 'unto the Lord']? Because the Holy One, blessed be He, said: This goat shall be an atonement for My diminishing the moon [i.e., it is as if the sin offering is not 'unto the Lord' but 'on behalf of the Lord']."[10] The Jewish people bring a sacrifice to atone, as it were, for the Holy One, blessed be He, for not having completed the work of creation.[11] The Creator of the world diminished the image and stature of creation in order to leave something for man, the work of His hands, to do, in order to adorn man with the crown of creator and maker.[12]

The perfection of creation, according to the view of halakhic man, is expressed in the actualization of the ideal Halakhah in the real world. And once again we see revealed before us the divergent approaches of the Halakhah and mysticism. While mysticism repairs the flaws of creation by "raising it on high," by returning it back to the source of pure, clear existence, the Halakhah fills the "deficiency" by drawing the *Shekhinah*, the Divine Presence, downward into the lowly world, by "contracting" transcendence within our flawed world.

A new aspect of the idea of holiness arises here. We have already emphasized that, while the universal *homo religiosus* understands the concept of holiness as a rebellion against this world, as a daring attempt to scale the very heights of transcendence, Judaism explains the concept of holiness from the perspective of the secret of "contraction." Holiness is the descent of divinity into the midst of our concrete world—"For the Lord thy God walketh in the midst of the camp . . . therefore shall thy camp be holy" (Deut. 23:15)—it is the "contraction" of infinity within a finitude bound by laws, measures, and standards, the appearance of transcendence within empirical reality, and the act of objectification and quantification of that religious subjectivity that flows from hidden sources. Now, however, in the light of the idea of creation stored up in the treasure-house of Halakhah, this outlook on holiness takes on additional dimensions. The dream of creation finds its resolution in the actualization of the principle of holiness. Creation means the realization of the ideal of holiness. The nothingness and naught, the privation and the void are rooted in the realm of the profane; the harmonious existence, the perfected being are grounded in the realm of the holy. If a man wishes to attain the rank of holiness, he must become a creator of worlds. If a man never creates, never brings into being anything new, anything original, then he cannot be holy unto his God. That passive type who is derelict in fulfilling his task of creation cannot become holy. Creation is the lowering of transcendence into the midst of our turbid, coarse, material world; and this lowering can take place only through the implementation of the ideal Halakhah in the core of reality (the realization of the Halakhah = contraction = holiness = creation).

• • •

The experience of halakhic man is not circumscribed by his own individual past but transcends this limited realm and enters the domain of eternity. The Jewish people's all-embracing collective consciousness of time—the sages of the tradition, the Second Temple era, the age of classical prophecy, the revelation on Mount Sinai, the Exodus from Egypt, the lives of the patriarchs, the creation itself—is an integral part of the "I" awareness of halakhic man. His time is measured by the standard of our Torah, which begins with the creation of heaven and earth. Similarly, halakhic man's future does not terminate with the end of his own individual future at the moment of death but extends into the future of the people as a whole, the people who yearn for the coming of the Messiah and the kingdom of God. The splendor of antiquity and the brilliance of the eschaton envelop halakhic man's time consciousness. We have here a blurring of the boundaries dividing time from eternity, temporal life from everlasting life. Spinoza, in order to introduce the idea of eternity (*sub quadam aeternitatis specie*) into the highest conception of the world afforded by knowledge, divested being of the attribute of time and ascribed to it only the attribute of space, extension. Judaism declares: There can be no eternity without time. On the contrary, everlasting life only reveals itself through the medium of the experience of time—the hour is transformed into infinity, the moment into eternity. Man can glimpse eternity only through the consciousness of time. The whole thrust of the various commandments of remembrance set forth in the Torah—for example, the remembrance of the Exodus, the remembrance (according to Nahmanides) of the revelation at Mount Sinai [see Nachmanides's critical glosses on Maimonides, *Book of Commandments*, "Negative commandments not included by Maimonides: No. 2"], the remembrance of the Sabbath day (through the recitation of the *kiddush*), the remembrance of Amalek—is directed toward the integration of these ancient events into man's time consciousness. The Exodus from Egypt, the divine revelation on Mount Sinai, the creation of the world, all are transformed into an integral part of the content of man's present consciousness, into a powerful, direct experience. The commandment to relate the story of the Exodus carries with it a unique halakhah: "In every generation a man must regard himself as if he came forth out of Egypt" [Pesahim 10:5; cf. Maimonides, *Laws of Hametz and Matzah* 7:6]. But how can a person regard himself as one of those who left Egypt, as a companion of Moses and Aaron in the remote dawn of our history, if not by including himself in this ancient past and in the process of redemption that occurred then? But these remembrances are not just tied up with the past; they also point the way to the infinite future. The redemption from Egypt is linked to the future redemption. This connection is drawn in the blessings of *emet ve-yatziv* and *emet ve-emunah* immediately following the morning and evening *Shema*, respectively. Similarly, we conclude the *seder* on Passover night by reciting *Hallel*, the great *Hallel*, and *Nishmat*, all of which speak of the Scriptural vision of the eschaton. The revelation on Mount Sinai foreshadows the perfection of the world under the kingdom of the Almighty, when His glory will be revealed unto all. The text of the blessing *Shofarot* [Rams' horns] in the Musaf prayer of Rosh Ha-Shanah bears witness to this connection. The blessing begins with verses describing the revelation of the Torah on Mount Sinai and concludes with verses depicting the sounding of the *shofar* of the Messiah and the future redemption of Israel. The remembrance of Amalek symbolizes Israel's battle against the hosts of wickedness and the arrogant kingdom until the coming of the Messiah. "This day, on which was the beginning of Thy work, is a memorial for the first day." This is the prayer of the Jewish people on Rosh Ha-Shanah [from the blessing *Zikhronot* (Remembrances) in the Musaf prayer of Rosh Ha-Shanah]. They celebrate the anniversary of the creation of the world. This metaphysical act is still embedded in the nation's consciousness, as they pray on that very day for the renewal of the cosmos. The infinite past enters into the present moment. The fleeting, evanescent moment is transformed into eternity. But the covenantal community, daughter Zion, continues thus her supplications before the King sitting in judgment: "Our God and God of our fathers, reign over the whole universe in Thy glory, be exalted over all the earth in Thy grandeur" [from the blessing *Malkhuyot* (Kingships) in the Musaf prayer of Rosh Ha-Shanah]. Not only the infinite past but also the infinite future, that future in which there gleams the reflection of the image of eternity, also the splendor of the eschatological vision, arise out of the present moment, fleeting as a dream. Temporal life is adorned with the crown of everlasting life.

"Moses received the Torah from Sinai, and transmitted it to Joshua," etc. [Avot 1:1]. This is the motto of the Halakhah. The *masorah*, the process of transmission, symbolizes the Jewish people's outlook regarding the beautiful and resplendent phenomenon of time.

The chain of tradition, begun millennia ago, will continue until the end of all time. Time, in this conception, is not destructive, all-consuming, and it does not simply consist of fleeting, imperceptible moments. This wondrous chain, which originated on that bright morning of the day of revelation and which stretches forward into the eschaton, represents the manner in which the Jewish people experience their own history, a history that floats upon the stormy waters of time. The consciousness of halakhic man, that master of the received tradition, embraces the entire company of the sages of the *masorah*. He lives in their midst, discusses and argues questions of Halakhah with them, delves into and analyzes fundamental halakhic principles in their company. All of them merge into one time experience. He walks alongside Maimonides, listens to R. Akiva, senses the presence of Abaye and Raba. He rejoices with them and shares in their sorrow. "David, king of Israel, yet lives and endures" [Rosh Ha-Shanah 25a]; "Our father Jacob did not die" [Ta'anit 5b; cf. Gen. Rabbah 96:4]; "Moses, our teacher, did not die" [Zohar I, 37b]. There can be no death and expiration among the company of the sages of tradition. Eternity and immortality reign here in unbounded fashion. Both past and future become, in such circumstances, ever-present realities.

In truth, the dualism bound up with the concept of time has been well known since Bergson. The distinction between the concept of mathematical time, frozen in geometrical space and entirely quantifiable, and the perception of time as pure, qualitative duration, forming the very essence and content of consciousness and streaming ever onward (and only the act of memory can enable one somehow to grasp hold of this rushing stream), was largely responsible for the rebellion of the human sciences (*geisteswissenschaften*) against the methodology of the mathematical, natural sciences. Nowadays, philosophy operates with a dual conception of time: (1) mathematical-physical time; (2) historical time. The former is being quantified in ever-increasing measure (its quantitative nature has been emphasized most strikingly by the union of space and time in the theories of Minkowski and Einstein), while the latter, from day to day, is apprehended more and more as pure quality. All of the investigations of the phenomenological school into the nature of time have as their aim elucidating its qualitative character. Similarly, the special nature of causality in the realm of the spirit (psychic-historical causality) occupies an important place in modern philosophy.

The Halakhah, however, is not particularly concerned with the metaphysics of time. Moreover, it is not inclined to transform time into pure, flowing, evanescent quality. Judaism disapproves of too much subjectivity, of an undue emphasis on quality. Therefore, it does not view time from the perspective of the *geisteswissenschaften*. The fact that the concept of time in the Halakhah is bound up with measurable time periods—days, weeks, months, years, sabbatical and jubilee cycles—demonstrates that Judaism does not desire a flowing stream of time but rather wishes to establish a time that is fixed and determined.[13]

The fundamental principle of the halakhic outlook on time is practical and ethical in nature.

We have already emphasized earlier that man is given the choice of deciding between two perceptions of time—evanescence and eternity—and ordering his life accordingly.

There is a kind of person who seeks refuge in the shadow of a fragmented, shattered time. He frequents a present that has cut itself off from the past and the future and finds itself in the narrow four cubits of the fleeting moment. The antimony contained in the idea of time—"The past already gone by, the future not yet nigh, the present, the blink of an eye" [a popular medieval adage]—appears here in all its terror. Yesterday has already passed, tomorrow is yet to come, and today rapidly descends into the abyss of oblivion. Such a man is subject to the general scientific law of causality—the cause rooted in the past determines the image of the future. His existence does not enjoy the blessings of liberty and free will. The yesterday creates both the now and the tomorrow, and all three deride and mock him. Actions long since gone precipitate deeds yet to come. Life is out of his control. He can create neither himself nor his future. There is no psychic continuity here, only an existence completely out of joint. Continuity, by definition, means the future imprinting its stamp upon the past. However, when today and tomorrow are dominated and controlled by yesterday, that spiritual constancy whose content is a never-ending process of self-creation simply disappears. Such a life the sages called *ḥayyei sha'ah*, temporal life.

But there is a kind of man who abides under the shadow of a complete and resplendent time. His soul, grounded "in days past" (Deut. 4:32), in the early history of his people, is devoted to the eschatological ideal. He looks behind him and sees a hylic matter that awaits the reception of its form from the creative future. He looks ahead of him and confronts a creative, shaping force that can delineate the content of the past and mold the image of the "before." He participates in the unfolding of the causal sequence and the ongoing act of creation. He views existence from the perspective of eternity and enjoys the splendor of creation. His consciousness embraces the entire historical existence of the Jewish people. Such a time consciousness, whose beginning and end is everlasting life, is the aim of Halakhah and is termed creation—the realization of the eternal Halakhah in the very midst of the temporal, fleeting world, the "contraction" of the glory of the infinite God in the very core of concrete reality, the descent of an everlasting existence into a reality circumscribed by the moment. Not for naught does Judaism speak of (1) the world as a finite entity; (2) the world under the aspect of eternity and infinity. A coincidence of opposites? Nevertheless! In the midst of finitude there appear traces of infinity; in the midst of the fleeting moment an ever-enduring eternity. The symbol of this outlook is the idea of repentance, which is identical with true creation.[14]

The old problem of the status of the individual, which had its roots in the philosophy of Aristotle and which, for a long time, engaged the attention of the Christian and Arab scholastics, found both its clearest expression and its most profound and original solution in the philosophy of Maimonides. Obviously, the view of Averroës, that only the universal active intellect is immortal and not the individual passive intellect, contradicts the very foundations of Judaism. Maimonides disagreed with this view, as did Albertus Magnus and Thomas Aquinas after him.[15] Nevertheless, the whole question of the immortality of the soul, particularly as it relates to the individual passive intellect (the hylic or potential intellect), is a very difficult and important one, and here Maimonides appears in his full intellectual and ethical splendor as he resolves this problem in a brilliant and striking fashion.

On the one hand, Maimonides subscribed to the view of Aristotle (and Plato)[16] that true, authentic existence is to be found only in the realm of the forms—the universal ideas—while the realm of particularity, rooted in matter (as an individuating principle) does not attain the level of complete being but exists only as an image of the universal. On the other hand, the Halakhah has always insisted upon the principle of individual immortality. How can these two apparently contradictory positions be maintained?

This same problem reappears in the discussion surrounding the issue of providence. For certainly the belief in individual providence is a cornerstone of Judaism, both from the perspective of the Halakhah and from the perspective of philosophical inquiry. It is the tenth of Maimonides's thirteen fundamentals of faith.[17] The protagonist of the religious drama, according to Judaism, is the individual, responsible for his actions and deeds, and there can be no responsibility or accountability without providence. Therefore, Maimonides placed man in a special category by himself, distinct from that of all other creatures, and proclaimed that man's own particular existence as an individual is of significance, both with reference to the principle of immortality and the principle of individual providence. "As for my own belief with regard to this fundamental principle, the meaning of divine providence, it is as I shall set it forth to you. In the belief that I shall set forth, I am . . . relying upon what has clearly appeared as the intention of the book of God and of the books of our prophets. . . . For I believe that in this lowly world—I mean that which is beneath the sphere of the moon—divine providence watches only over the individuals belonging to the human species and that in this species all the circumstances of the individuals and the good and evil that befall them are consequent upon their deserts, just as it says: 'For all His ways are justice' (Deut. 32:4). But regarding all the other animals and, all the more, the plants and other things, my opinion is that of Aristotle. . . . For all these texts [asserting that there is providence over animals] refer to providence watching over the species and not to individual providence. . . . It does not follow for me that by virtue of this opinion one may pose to me the following question—namely: Why does He watch over the human individuals and not watch in the same way over the individuals belonging to the other species of animals? For he who propounds this question ought to ask himself: Why did He give intellect to man and not to the other species of animals? The answer to this last question is: He willed it so."[18]

The gist of Maimonides's view is that man occupies a unique position in the kingdom of existence and differs in his ontological nature from all other creatures. With reference to all other creatures, only the universal, not the particular, has a true, continuous existence; with respect to man, however, it is an everlasting principle that his individual existence also attains the heights of true, eternal being. Indeed, the primary mode of man's existence is the particular existence of the individual, who is both liable and responsible for his acts. Therefore, it is the individual who is worthy of divine providence and eternal life. Man, in one respect, is a mere random example of the biological species—species man—an image of the universal, a shadow of true existence. In another respect he is a man of God, possessor of an individual existence. The difference between a man who is a mere random example of the biological species and a man of God is that the former is characterized by passivity, the latter by activity and creation. The man who belongs solely to the realm of the universal is passive to an extreme—he creates nothing. The man who has a particular existence of his own is not merely a passive, receptive creature but acts and creates. Action and creation are the true distinguishing marks of authentic existence.

However, this ontological privilege, which is the peculiar possession of the man who has a particular existence of his own, a privilege that distinguishes him from all other creatures and endows him with individual immortality, is dependent upon man himself. The choice is his. He may, like the individual of all the other species, exist in the realm of the images and shadows, or he may exist as an individual who is not a part of the universal and who proves worthy of a fixed, established existence in the world of the "forms" and "intellects separate from matter" [Maimonides, *Laws of the Foundations of the Torah* 4:9]. Species man or man of God, this is the alternative which the Almighty placed before man. If he proves worthy, then he becomes a man of God in all the splendor of his individual existence that cleaves to absolute infinity and the glorious "divine overflow." If he proves unworthy, then he ends up as one more random example of the biological species, a turbid and blurred image of universal existence.[19] "According to me, as I consider the matter, divine providence is consequent upon the divine overflow and the species with which this intellectual overflow is united. . . . But I believe that providence is consequent upon the intellect and attached to it. For providence can only come from an intelligent being, from one who is an intellect perfect with a supreme perfection. . . . Accordingly, everyone with whom something of this overflow is united will be reached by providence to the extent to which he is reached by the intellect. . . . When any individual has obtained, because of the disposition of his matter and his training, a greater portion of this overflow than others, providence will of necessity watch more carefully over him than over others—if, that is to say, providence is, as I have mentioned, consequent upon the intellect. Accordingly, divine providence does not watch in an equal manner over all the individuals of the human species, but providence is graded as their human perfection is graded. . . . It follows necessarily that His providence, may He be exalted, that watches over the prophets is very great and proportionate to their degree in prophecy and that His providence that watches over excellent and righteous men is proportionate to their excellence and righteousness. For it is this measure of the overflow of the divine intellect that makes the prophets speak, guides the actions of the righteous men, and perfects the knowledge of the excellent men with regard to what they know. As for the ignorant and disobedient, their state is despicable proportionately according to their lack of this overflow, and they have been relegated to the ranks of the individuals of all the other species of animals: 'He is like the beasts that speak not' (Ps. 49:13, 21)."[20]

Man, at times, exists solely by virtue of the species, by virtue of the fact that he was born a member of that species, and its general form is engraved upon him. He exists solely on account of his participation in the idea of the universal. He is just a member of the species "man," an image of the universal. He is just one more example of the species image in its ongoing morphological process (in the Aristotelian sense of the term). He himself, however, has never done anything that could serve to legitimate his existence as an individual. His soul, his spirit, his entire being, all are grounded in the realm of the universal. His roots lie deep in the soil of faceless mediocrity; his growth takes place solely within the public domain. He has no stature of his own, no original, individual, personal profile. He has never created anything, never brought into being anything new, never accomplished anything. He is receptive, passive, a spiritual parasite. He is wholly under the influence of other people and their views. Never has he sought to render an accounting, either of himself or of the world; never has he examined himself, his relationship to God and his fellow man. He lives unnoticed and dies unmourned. Like a fleeting cloud, a shadow, he passes through life and is gone. He bequeaths nothing to future generations, but dies without leaving a trace of his having lived. Empty-handed he goes to the grave, bereft of *mitzvah* performances, good deeds, and meritorious acts, for while living he lacked any sense of historical responsibility and was totally wanting in any ethical passion. He was born involuntarily, and it is for this reason and this reason alone that he, involuntarily, lives out his life (a life which, paradoxically, he has "chosen"!) until he dies involuntarily. This is man as the random example of the biological species.

But there is another man, one who does not require the assistance of others, who does not need the support of the species to legitimate his existence. Such a man is no longer a prisoner of time but is his own master. He exists not by virtue of the species, but solely on account of his own individual worth. His life is replete with creation and renewal, cognition and profound understanding. He lives not on account of his having been born but for the sake of life itself and so that he may merit thereby the life in the world to come. He recognizes the destiny that is his, his obligation and task in life. He understands full well the dualism running through his being and that choice which has been entrusted to him. He knows that there are two paths before him and that whichever he shall choose, there must he go. He is not passive but active. His personality is not characterized by receptivity but by spontaneity. He does not simply abandon himself to the rule of the species but blazes his own individual trail. Moreover, he, as an individual, influences the many. His whole existence, like some enchanted stream, rushes ever onward to distant magical regions. He is dynamic, not static, does not remain at rest but moves forward in an ever-ascending climb. For, indeed, it is the living God for whom he pines and longs. This is the man of God.

The fundamental of providence is here transformed into a concrete commandment, an obligation incumbent upon man. Man is obliged to broaden the scope and strengthen the intensity of the individual providence that watches over him. Everything is dependent on him; it is all in his hands. When a person creates himself, ceases to be a mere species man, and becomes a man of God, then he has fulfilled that commandment which is implicit in the principle of providence.

Notes

1. Consider the statement of R. Isaac [as cited by Rashi in his commentary on Gen. 1:1]: "The Torah should have begun with the verse 'This month shall be unto you the beginning of months' (Exod. 12:2), for that is the first commandment with which Israel was commanded. What is the reason, then, that it begins with [the story of] the beginning? Because [through beginning with the account of creation] 'He hath declared to His people the power of His works [in order] to give them the heritage of the nations' (Ps. 111:6). For if the nations of the world should say to Israel, 'You are robbers, for you conquered the lands of the seven nations,' they [Israel] could reply: 'The entire world belongs to the Holy One, blessed be He; He created it and He gave it to them [to the seven nations] and of His own will He took it from them and gave it to us.'" This gives expression to the idea [of the normative significance of creation] in a somewhat different form. The thrust of this statement is that we are in need of the account of creation insofar as it functions as normative guide to halakhic practice. Cf. Nahmanides, ad loc.
2. *Sefer Ha-Yetzirah*, in fine.
3. Cf. Haggigah 12a.
4. Sukkah 53a–b; Makkot 11a.
5. P. T. Sanhedrin 10:2 [29a].
6. The question as to whether the negative side of being has been in existence from the time of creation itself or whether it was precipitated by man's sin is a different problem and has no bearing upon the issue with which we are concerned. See Eruvin 18b. Cf. Gen. Rabbah 2:1–5: "'Now the earth was chaos and void, and darkness was upon the face of the deep' (Gen. 1:2). R. Berekiah cited [the verse]: 'Even a child is known by his doings, whether his work be pure and whether it be right' (Prov. 20:11). R. Berekiah said: While she [the earth] was as yet immature, she produced thorns; and so the prophet was one day destined to prophesy of her, 'I

beheld the earth, and, lo, it was chaos and void' (Jer. 4:23). . . . R. Tanhuma said: The earth foresaw that she was destined to meet her doom at the hand of man, as it is written, 'Cursed is the ground for thy sake' (Gen. 3:17). Therefore, the earth was *tohu* and *bohu* [i.e., bewildered and astonished]. R. Judah b. R. Simon interpreted the text ['Now the earth was chaos and void'] as referring to the generations. 'Chaos' refers to Adam who was reduced to chaos; 'and void' refers to Cain, who desired to turn the world back to void. . . . Resh Lakish applied the verse to the [various] exiles [to which Israel was subjected]. 'And the earth was chaos' refers to the Babylonian exile. . . . 'upon the face of the deep' refers to the exile [imposed by] the wicked kingdom [i.e., Rome]. . . . R. Abbahu said: 'Now the earth was chaos and void.' This alludes to the deeds of the wicked." The concept "offspring of chaos"—referrring to the Amalekites [alluded to in Gen. 6:13 according to the statement in the Zohar cited below], *gibborim* (cf. Gen. 6:4), *nefilim* (cf. Gen. 6:4; Num. 13:33), *refaim* (cf. Deut. 2:11, and *anakim* (cf. Num. 13:28, 33; Deut. 1:28, 2:11)—occupies a prominent place in the Kabbalah. Cf. Haggigah 13b–14a (Rashi, ad loc., s.v. *kodem she-bara ha-olam* and Tosafot, ad loc., s.v. *ve-tardan*); Zohar I, 24b–25b (on Gen. 2:4); Rabbis Isaac Nissenbaum, "*Toldin de-tohu*" [Offspring of chaos], [pp. 23–27], and "*Erev rav*" [Mixed multitude], [pp. 150–157], in *Kinyanei kedem* [Warsaw, 1931].

7. See Zohar I. 39B (on Gen. 1:2). "The first dwelling place starting from below: there is no knowledge there at all, for there is no form there at all in the imprint, etc."
8. To cite Maimonides's phrase, *Laws of the Sanctification of the New Moon* 1:6.
9. See *Guide* II, 29.
10. Shavu'ot 9a.
11. Of extreme interest is the talmudic passage (Sanhedrin 42a); "It was taught in the school of R. Ishmael: It would have sufficed had Israel merited no other privilege than to greet the presence of their Father in heaven once a month. Abaye said: Therefore we must recite it [the blessing] standing."
12. See Y. L. Peretz, *Rayze bilder: a yingl* [in Y. L. Peretz, *Bilder un shitzn* (Vilna, n.d.), pp. 43–47; trans. Helena Frank, "Travel Pictures: A Little Boy" in *Stories and Pictures* (Philadelphia, 1906), pp. 256–259]:

> "The innkeeper's appealing little boy with his jerky movements and his curls, full of feathers, still haunts me. Now he stands before my eyes with a scallion in hand and he wails, he wants another; or I hear him at evening prayer saying the *kaddish* in such a childlike, plaintively earnest manner that it pierces my very heart. . .
> "Hopping on one little foot he stretches his face upward to the moon; he sighs.
> "Has he seen a star fall?
> "No.
> "'Oh,' he says. 'How I wish the Messiah would come!'
> "What?
> "'I want the moon to become bigger already. It's such a pity on her. True, she sinned, but to suffer so much . . . we are already living in the sixth millennium.'
> "Altogether two requests: From his father on earth, another scallion, and from his father in heaven, that the moon become bigger.
> "A wild impulse seized me to tell him, 'Enough! Your father, down here, will soon get married again, soon you will have a stepmother, you will become a stepchild, and will have to wail for a piece of bread. Forgo the scallion; forget about the moon.'"

Those downtrodden and often externally unappealing *shtetl* personalities—the itinerant peddler hawking his needles, threads, and thimbles in the villages of the Pale; the plain, often coarse innkeeper; the fleshy villagers—were all nevertheless imbued with an inner bewitching attractiveness. An ember of holiness still smoldered in the hearts of these figures, who were drowning in almost overwhelming soul-crushing worries, pressures, troubles. A wondrous flame, burning in the depths of their being, lit up their desolate and oppressed spirits. On the one hand, it seemed as if all they were concerned with were the few miserable pennies and bare physical necessities they had to struggle to obtain, like that abandoned, lonely orphan boy (soon to be the object of a step-mother's wrath) who so longed for that second scallion. On the other hand, they yearned for the reign of cosmic righteousness (they were not satisfied with human righteousness alone) and its implementation in creation as a whole, again like this orphan boy who prayed that the diminution of the moon be replenished, that the Messiah should come—not on account of his own individual worries, not in order to be redeemed from his bleak existence, from the unbearable burdens weighing down upon him, but on account of his yearnings for the redemption of creation, for the perfection of the cosmos. "I want the moon to become bigger already. It's such a pity on her. True she sinned, but to suffer so much . . . we are already living in the sixth millennium." The orphan forgets that his father will soon take for himself a new wife, a stepmother, and that he will become a stepchild who will cry for a piece of bread; he prays for the suffering moon, pining away on account of her sin, and he sees in her torments a cosmic injustice. Is not the image of the Jewish people reflected in such yearnings? Bitter exile and cosmic righteousness, the bleak life of the ghetto and the dream about the replenishment of the new moon, the yearnings for the perfection of creation and ugly poverty—can there be a greater coincidence of opposites?

13. To be sure, even in other religions a tendency toward the quantification of time can be discerned, but certainly not to the extent prevalent in Judaism.

14. See Scheler, "Repentance and Rebirth"; William Douglas Chamberlain, *The Meaning of Repentance* (Philadelphia, 1943).

15. Maimonides's view regarding the question of the immortality of the nutritive and the vital souls differs, however, from that of Albertus and Thomas, and resembles somewhat the view of Aristotle, this despite the fact that Maimonides disagreed with Aristotle regarding the issue of will. However, this is not the place to elaborate. See Maimonides, *Laws of the Foundations of the Torah* 4:8.

16. This is not the place to analyze the nature of Maimonides's realism regarding the question of universals. However, his view regarding this issue drew upon both the philosophy of Plato and that of Aristotle, and many of the scholastics followed his approach to this problem.

17. Maimonides, *Commentary on the Mishnah*, introduction to Ḥelek.

18. *Guide* III, 17.

19. To be sure, even the wicked person (*rasha*) and the fool (*sakhal*) are not to be entirely identified with the man who is merely a random example of the biological species, for the former two are in possession of some good deeds and meritorious acts. See Maimonides, *Laws of Repentance* 8:1. "The good stored up for the righteous is life in the world to come, and it is the life unaccompanied by death and the good unaccompanied by evil. . . . The reward of the righteous is that they will attain this bliss and abide in this [state of] good; the punishment of the wicked is that they will not attain this life but will be cut off and die. He who does not attain this life is the one who is dead, who will never live but is cut off in his wickedness and has perished like the beasts. And this is the excision referred to in the Torah, as it is said, 'That soul shall be utterly cut off [*hikaret tikaret*], his iniquity shall be upon him' (Num. 15:31), which has been traditionally interpreted (Sanhedrin 62b): 'cut off' [*hikaret*] in this world, 'utterly cut off' [*tikaret*] from the world to come—i.e., that that soul which has separated from its body in this world does not attain life in the world to come but is also cut off from the world to come." And see Nahmanides's discussion of this Maimonidean statement in *Sha'ar ha-gemul* [The gate of reward] [in *Kol Kitvei Ha-Ramban*, ed. C. B. Chavel (Jerusalem, 1963), pp. 291–292].

25

Some Criteria for Modern Jewish Observance

JAKOB J. PETUCHOWSKI

Jewish tradition speaks about the "613 Commandments" of the Torah. But Rabbi Simlai, having been first to mention this number,[1] did not then proceed to enumerate them. As a result, later scholars differed among themselves about the best way to arrive at that number. For if only the commandments of the written Torah were counted, the figure would be less than 613. If, however, the commandments of the oral Torah were to be added to those of the Bible, the number would far exceed 613. A whole branch of medieval rabbinic literature is devoted to the task of "enumerating the Commandments." Various authors argued on behalf of their own counts. However, gradually the enumeration of Maimonides, in his *Sepher Hamitzvot* ("The Book of the Commandments"), achieved the greatest popularity; and it is generally his enumeration to which modern writings refer in their discussion of the 613 Commandments.

This discussion of the 613 Commandments continues vigorously, even though no modern Jew—the most pious included—observes all of them or could observe them even if he so desired. Numerous commandments have application to the Jerusalem Temple and the sacrificial cult. Others refer to the regulations governing the purity of priests and Levites, a subject which, again, is related to the Jerusalem Temple cult. Still others apply only to the reign of a Jewish king. In other words, the 613 Commandments—whatever they might be, and whatever enumeration of them we might choose to follow—were never meant to be observed by every Jew. Nevertheless, the concept of the 613 Commandments has become a slogan in modern Jewish life. The claim is frequently made that Orthodox Jews observe the 613 Commandments, while Reform Jews reject them.

Jakob J. Petuchowski, "Some Criteria for Modern Jewish Observance," in Alfred Jospe, ed., *Tradition and Contemporary Experience* (New York: Schocken/B'nai B'rith, 1970), pp. 239–48. © B'nai Brith Book Service, Washington, D.C. 20036.

That this claim cannot possibly be true of any Orthodox Jew we have already seen. But it is also not true that the Reform Jew *rejects* the 613 Commandments as a whole. If a Reform Jew loves his neighbor, he is observing one of the commandments (by everybody's method of enumerating them). If he refrains from murder, adultery, or theft, he is observing a second, a third, and a fourth commandment. If he pays his employees on time, returns a lost article to its owner, and honors his father and mother, he is observing a fifth, sixth, and seventh traditional commandment. There is no need to keep count of all the commandments that a Reform Jew does observe. If he leads a reasonably moral and ethical life, his style of life will not be bereft of a goodly number of the 613 Commandments. For they are not limited to the so-called ritual and ceremonial observances. The love of one's neighbor is no less a part of the commandments than is the practice not to mix meat and milk dishes. Thus, neither the Orthodox nor the Reform Jew can be described as either totally observing or totally rejecting the 613 Commandments. Both are *partial* observers. It should be added that the observance of the ethical commandments is obviously not a monopoly of the Reform Jew. Nor can it be said that even the most radical Reform Jew has completely divested himself of all so-called ceremonial observances.

It is, however, true that in matters of ritual and ceremonial observance the Reform Jew maintains less of the traditional heritage than does the Orthodox Jew. In the nineteenth century, Reform Judaism gave up many traditional Jewish observances because, as was said at that time, they were "too Oriental" or no longer "spoke to modern man." There was also an attempt to side with the "prophets" against the "priests," to regard the moral law alone as "divine," and to view the "ceremonial law" as something of purely human origin, which could either be modified or totally abolished.

This was indeed a break with Jewish tradition—a tradition which knew only of *mitzvot*, divine commandments, without distinguishing between moral and ritual commandments, to the detriment of the latter. Ritual and ceremony are not authentic Jewish concepts. Moreover, recent biblical scholarship no longer takes it for granted that the prophets invariably and inevitably took an antagonistic position toward the cult. It is, therefore, easy to criticize much of the position of nineteenth-century Reform Judaism from the perspective of the twentieth century.

Nevertheless, the position adopted in the last century contained an important insight to which the twentieth century must not close its eyes. In its most radical form, this insight was expressed by Samuel Holdheim (1806–1860). The ancient rabbis had already made a distinction between the *mitzvot* which are obligatory only in the land of Israel and those which retain their validity beyond the borders of the land of Israel.[2] The Jew of the Diaspora is obligated to fulfil the latter only. Holdheim went one step further. The Torah, he argued, has a twofold content. It contains a strictly religious element, which is eternally valid. But it also contains the legal constitution of the ancient Israelite theocracy; and that constitution is time-conditioned. Since God Himself abolished the theocracy by permitting Temple and State to be destroyed in the year 70 C.E., the constitution of that theocracy has likewise been abolished.[3]

Holdheim drew several radical conclusions from this distinction. He asserted, for example, that, while the weekly day of rest was an eternally binding religious commandment, the particular day of the week on which it is to be observed was determined by the constitution of the state, not by religion. In ancient Israel it happened to be Saturday; in Prussia it was Sunday. Altogether, Holdheim had a tendency to make life easy for himself by relegating all the commandments he did not particularly care for to the constitution of the ancient Israelite theocracy, thus depriving them of their binding character.

Holdheim went too far. Nevertheless, he was right in his view of the Torah and its twofold content. The Jew who, in the period of the Emancipation, voluntarily accepted his Judaism, did so in terms of a commitment to *religion*, not to the legal constitution of an ancient state. The commandments he observed were indeed—to use Franz Rosenzweig's terminology—"commandments," not "legislation." Behind the "commandment" there is only God, not the constitution of a state.

In the final analysis, the decision of the individual Jew to observe many, few, or no "commandments" depends on the seriousness with which he tries to hear the word of God in the Jewish tradition, and on how many of the old "laws" address him personally as "commandments." This applies no less to the western type of Orthodoxy than it does to Reform Judaism. Orthodox Judaism in western Europe and America has tacitly managed to ignore quite a few paragraphs of the Shulhan Arukh, while a man like Franz Rosenzweig, on the basis of a liberal approach, was able to accept as "commandments" addressed to him a maximum number of traditional observances.

But Reform Judaism committed two serious errors in the nineteenth century. The nonobservance of the *mitzvot* was made to look like one of the demands of Reform Judaism. One of the "planks" of the famous Pittsburgh Platform of 1885 stated with regard to the Mosaic legislation that "we accept as binding only its moral laws, and maintain only such ceremonies as elevate and sanctify our lives, but reject all such as are not adapted to the views and habits of modern civilization."[4] This, of course, was quite in Holdheim's spirit. Only the moral commandments are binding. The individual is not given an opportunity to hear—as Franz Rosenzweig did—"commandments" also among the "ritual" laws.

Such a categorical rejection of a large body of the *mitzvot* contains no less dogmatism than does an uncritical acceptance of the totality of the Shulhan Arukh. If Reform Judaism is truly meant to be liberal, it must be left to the individual to decide which of the commandments he accepts as binding for himself. However, in order to be able to make his decision, the Reform Jew must know and understand the material from which the choice is to be made. This, in turn, necessitates an intensive study of the Jewish tradition. Only the educated Jew who is well acquainted with his tradition can come to terms with it and make his own selection from the plethora of traditional ordinances. Yet, in this respect, a second error was committed in the last century. Once it had been agreed that only the moral commandments were binding, it was no longer felt to be necessary to burden religious instruction with the study of the "ritual" *mitzvot*. Jewish education was largely reduced to talk about ethical monotheism and a few chapters of biblical history. While there was a stress on the Reform Jew's freedom of choice, he was not familiarized with the material from which that choice was to be made.

The student of Jewish history can understand the reasons and conditions that led to this state of affairs. He can, on occasion, even find excuses. Nevertheless, the problems of the twentieth century are of an altogether different kind. We no longer believe that the European Jew becomes a better European, or the American Jew a better American, by shedding his Jewish particularism. Moreover, our knowledge of psychology has also made us somewhat more circumspect in our evaluation of "ritual" and of the "nonrational." If it was the task of Judaism in the nineteenth century to "adapt" itself to "the views and habits of modern civilization," we are today more critical of that "modern civilization."

If the nineteenth century felt it necessary to tell the Jew what he no longer had to observe in order to be like all other men, the twentieth century faces the task of leading the Jew back to the sources of Judaism in order to make him aware of the distinctiveness of his Jewish tradition and outlook.

These sources—Bible and Talmud, Midrash and philosophy, Kabbalah and Codes, poetry and the classics of the scientific study of Judaism—are the property of all Jews. In the obligation to study these sources there is no difference between the Orthodox and the Liberals, the Conservatives and the Reformers. It is a *mitzvah* which even the most radical of the Reformers cannot afford to ignore without calling into question his good faith and the seriousness of his conviction. That is why tradition said that "the study of the Torah surpasses the other commandments in importance."[5]

Only if the Reform Jew acts out of a full knowledge can there be talk of Reform Judaism at all. An ignoramus is only—an ignoramus. It is, of course, possible and even likely that, under certain circumstances, the Reform orientation might lead to the nonobservance of several traditional laws. It is possible but not inevitable. The example of Franz Rosenzweig again comes to mind. Nevertheless, even if the Reform orientation should lead, in a number of cases, to the nonobservance of *mitzvot*, it would be a nonobservance based on careful evaluation and not on ignorance. A true Reform Judaism, therefore, and one worthy of its name, would have to cultivate the study of the totality of our tradition, applying to it a set of criteria to guide the modern Jew in making his selections from it.

What, then, are those criteria?

I would suggest four criteria. First, *What has been the main thrust of the millennial Jewish tradition in a given case?* In examining the traditional material, we must not remain satisfied with first impressions, especially so because, in a tradition which spans four thousand years, the meaning of a given observance has not always been uniformly understood and interpreted.

A modern Jew might, for example, be under the impression that the prohibition of work on the Sabbath was simply directed against strenuous physical labor. He may assume that the Sabbath, throughout the centuries, has been a day of physical rest and relaxation. Moreover, we know that it was difficult in ancient days to make a fire by rubbing two sticks or stones together. Hence, the prohibition to cook or bake on the Sabbath was quite understandable. These activities involved hard work. But can this part of our tradition not be discarded today when it is no longer hard work to make a fire?

This conclusion is frequently drawn. Yet is it not warranted. A study of the Jewish sources will soon lead to the discovery that far more is involved in the Jewish Sabbath than the mere abstention from exhausting physical labor. The Sabbath is the day on which man, who works and creates throughout the week, shows himself to be but a creature. God alone is recognized as the Creator. On the Sabbath, the Jew refrains from interfering in the processes of nature. It is a day on which he is to leave nature unchanged, in recognition of the fact that his own powers over nature are limited. Consequently, if the purpose of the Sabbath is to express the notion that God, and not man, is the real Creator, the abstention from work, commanded in the Torah, aims at something over and above man's relaxation and physical recuperation.

The Sabbath law, with all its commandments and prohibitions, contains and implies far more than we have been able to hint at in connection with the prohibition of work. However, it illustrates what we mean by demanding, as one of the criteria for a modern Jewish observance, that, in any given case, an investigation be made into the main thrust of our millennial tradition. This examination is, of course, an objective and detached process. It does not yet commit us to anything.

What we are to do with the findings of our investigation is determined by our second criterion: *the manner in which I can best realize the traditional teaching in my life and in the situation in which I find myself.*

If the first criterion was purely scientific and objective, this second criterion already contains a conscious application of the Reform principle. Orthodox Judaism is, for example, objectively quite correct in deducing the prohibition of the use of cars and electricity on the Sabbath from the biblical prohibition of work—with "work" defined according to rabbinic categories. Tradition may indeed be so construed.

But as a Reform Jew, I must go beyond these considerations. I live in the here and now, and it is in this context that I must ask myself in which way I can observe the Sabbath best. Do I observe the Sabbath better if, on account of the distances involved, I refrain from going to the synagogue on the Sabbath, or from visiting friends, the bereaved, or the sick? Or is it not just the use of my car which helps me in my observance of the Sabbath in my particular situation? Does the true observance of the Sabbath compel me to keep my house cold and dark? Or is it not just the use of electricity which helps me to make the Sabbath the "day of light and joy" it was meant to be?

In other words, the Reform Jew is far more concerned with the Sabbath itself than with the letter of the Sabbath legislation, which testifies to the reality of the Sabbath as experienced by *past* generations. He wants to observe the Sabbath in the here and now. That is why factors come into play with which the legalists of earlier generations did not have to reckon.

A third criterion is *the voice of my own conscience.* This criterion, even more than the second one, reveals the liberalism of the Reform Jew and the influence of the Emancipation. The Reform Jew, in the words of Leo Baeck, is characterized by the "piety of the individual," and not, as was the Jew of the ghetto, by the "piety of the environment." As an individual, he is no longer subject to religious compulsion or the dictates of any ecclesiastical authority. As an individual, he is free to participate or not to participate in religious observance. Even if others believe that they have found the key to the proper observance of the law in the here and now, his conscience still has to assent.

Consider, for example, the law which states, in connection with Passover, that "there shall be no leaven seen with thee in all thy borders seven days" (Deut. 16:4). The main thrust of the tradition with regard to this law seems clear. Anything remotely subject to the suspicion that it may contain "leaven" ingredients not only must not be "seen" in the Jew's home during Passover, it must not even be in his possession. The application of this law, as interpreted by the rabbis, could thus lead to the wholesale destruction of food in the Jew's house just before Passover, were it not for the fact that the same rabbis who elaborated the stringencies of that law also evolved a legal fiction by means of which the full force of the law could be evaded. By "selling" the food to a non-Jew, with a minimum down payment and with the understanding that the Jew can buy it back after the festival, the food not only need not be destroyed but can remain on the Jew's premises, provided it is suitably locked up.

There is nothing wrong with legal fictions as such. No legal system can function without them. Indeed, one can appreciate the inventiveness of the ancient rabbis which enabled them to keep their legal system within humane dimensions. But it is one thing to appreciate the phenomenon historically, and quite another to accept it for myself, especially if I do not view my relation to God primarily in terms of a legal system. Thus, while it would be quite possible for the Reform Jew to solve his "leaven" problem along the lines indicated by the rabbis, possible even with his own "here and now," it is quite conceivable that he might also say, "Yes, it is possible to do it this way; *but my conscience speaks against it!* I shall refrain from eating leaven during Passover. I shall keep all leaven out of sight in my home. But I feel no need for the legal fiction of 'selling' my leaven. This would add nothing to my Passover observance. On the contrary, I would not feel intellectually honest were I to engage in this legal fiction. My conscience rebels against it."

In terms of the criterion we have outlined here, the Reform Jew would be justified in using such an argument. But he would also have to add that his fellow Jew has an equal right to listen to the voice of *his* conscience—even if his conscience makes him "sell" his leaven for Passover. Both are "Reform Jews," and the one cannot resent the other's selling of the leaven any more than the latter is able to regard the former's noncompliance with this practice as a sin.

The last-named criterion may well carry within itself the seeds of religious anarchy. The fourth criterion helps to maintain the balance. It is *the feeling of responsibility toward the covenant community*.

Judaism cannot be abstracted from the faith-community within which Judaism is lived—the faith-community with which God made a covenant at Sinai and which remained loyal to Him throughout the millennia. This covenant people, Israel, not only has a historical significance; its significance extends to the realm of redemptive history. Everything, therefore, that contributes to the survival and to the unity of the covenant community of Israel must be regarded as a religious commandment. On the other hand, everything that hurts the covenant community must be avoided.

In accordance with this perspective, the Reform Jew will observe a number of *mitzvot* toward which he might feel no personal obligation if his religion were a matter of the individual only, and not also of the community as a whole. Into this category belong the specific seventh day on which the Jewish Sabbath is to be kept, and all Jewish festivals, which have to be observed according to the Jewish calendar. In theory, it is conceivable that one could celebrate the ideal of freedom on some evening other than the eve of the fifteenth of Nisan. But the Seder, as the *Jewish* festival for freedom, can only be celebrated then. The same consideration governs the use of Hebrew in the Jewish worship service. Important as it is to find room for the vernacular in the synagogue, it is nevertheless true that the worshiping community of Israel knows itself as such particularly during moments of Hebrew prayer.

These illustrations do not reflect purely theoretical issues. They are based on questions which, at one time or another, were raised within Reform Judaism, and to which some radical answers were proposed in the last century. The twentieth century has largely turned away from radical solutions. And the feeling of responsibility toward the covenant community has played a not insignificant role in the change of orientation which has taken place in Reform Judaism.

It may not often occur that the four criteria that we have mentioned will be in complete accord. They are more likely to be in a constant state of tension. Moreover, one Jew may rate one criterion higher than does another Jew. Yet all will have to reckon with all the criteria all the time.

The four criteria, in their aggregate, represent the yardstick that the modern Jew must apply to his inherited tradition. Yet a yardstick is only—a yardstick. It cannot be the total content of one's religious faith and life. The latter requires more than a yardstick. It needs the material itself, the material of the millennial tradition. There are no shortcuts to the acquisition of that material. Two thousand years ago, when the tradition was still in its youth, Hillel stated that "the ignorant man cannot be truly religious."[6] What was true then is all the more true today. Only an intensified Jewish education—of child, youth, and adult—can make the application of the criteria meaningful. But only an application of the criteria can make tradition itself live.

Notes

A German version of the main contents of this essay appeared in the Swiss journal *Tradition und Erneureung*, November 1967.

1. *B. Makkot*, 23b.
2. *Mishnah Kiddushin*, 1:9; Sifre R'eh, para. 59 (ed. Friedman, p. 87a).
3. Cf. Samuel Holdheim, *Ueber die Autonomie der Rabbinen* (Schwerin, 1843), pp. 15–17.
4. Cf. David Philipson, *The Reform Movement in Judaism* (New York, 1907), p. 491.
5. *Shabbat* 127a.
6. *Avot* 2:5.

26

Dynamics of Judaism

ROBERT GORDIS

Ethics and Ritual in Judaism

As a result of the centrality of law in Judaism, the charge has been leveled for centuries, from the days of Paul to our own, that Jewish tradition is primarily legalistic; that is, preoccupied with the law rather than with ethics, with observance rather than with faith. Judaism has therefore been attacked as *external*, devoted to the letter rather than to the spirit; ritualistic, obsessed with minutiae of practice rather than with the presence of God; and legalistic, more concerned with adding to the sum of one's merits in the heavenly account book than with establishing a warm personal relationship with God and one's fellow beings.

Undoubtedly, these charges point to some genuine perils confronting the religious life, to which the biblical Prophets were sensitive. In the words of Isaiah:

> The Lord said, "Because this people draw near with their mouth
> and honor Me with their lips,
> While their hearts are far from Me,
> and their reverence for Me
> is a commandment of men learned by rote;
> Therefore, behold, I will again astonish this people
> with wonders and marvels;
> The wisdom of its wise men shall perish,
> and the prudence of its prudent men shall be destroyed."
>
> [29:13–14]

People have found it easier to reach for the shadow rather than to grasp the substance of religion; ritual observance all too easily degenerates into the be-all and end-all of piety.

Robert Gordis, *Dynamics of Judaism* (Bloomington, IN: Indiana University Press, 1990), pp. 63–68, 86–99, 105–7, 210–11. © Indiana University Press, Bloomington, IN 47404.

Bluntly put, observance of ritual is less expensive than obedience to moral imperatives, both psychologically and financially.

Traditional Judaism in every stage of its history has been acutely conscious of the peril of soulless conformity to ritual usurping the role of ethical sensitivity and moral concern. It emphasizes the overriding importance of right conduct, but it continues to regard both ritual and ethics, "the commandments between man and God" as well as those "between man and man," as embodiments of the divine will and hence binding upon the Jew.

But what of the relative importance of ritual and ethics in Judaism? Is it possible to discern any hierarchy of values in the tradition? Where a choice must be made between them, which is to be preferred? Here the evidence in both the Bible and the Talmud, though often overlooked, is extensive and unequivocal—ritual is important but ethics is paramount.

A comprehensive statement of the fundamentals of Judaism is recorded in the Talmud (B. *Makkot* 23b–24a) in the name of Rabbi Simlai:

> Six hundred thirteen commandments were given to Moses, 365 negative ones, equal to the number of days of the year, and 248 positive ones, corresponding to the number of organs in the human body.
>
> Then David came and reduced them to eleven:
>
> "Lord, who shall sojourn in your tent?
> Who shall dwell on your holy mountain?
> He who walks uprightly and does the right,
> and speaks the truth in his heart.
> He who does not slander with his tongue
> nor does evil to his friend,
> nor takes up a reproach against his neighbor;
> He, in whose eyes a reprobate is despised,
> but who honors those who fear the Lord;
> who swears to his own hurt and does not change;
> who does not put out his money at interest,
> and takes no bribe against the innocent.
> He who does these things shall never be moved."
>> [Psalm 15]
>
> Then came Isaiah and reduced them to six: "He who walks righteously and speaks uprightly, who despises the gain of oppression, who shakes his hands free from holding a bribe, stops his ears from hearing of bloodshed and shuts his eyes from looking upon evil" [Isa. 33:15].
>
> Then came Micah and reduced them to three: "He has told you, O man, what is good; and what does the Lord require of you, Only to do justice, and to love kindness, and to walk humbly with your God" [Mic. 6:8].
>
> Then Isaiah came again and reduced them to two: "Keep judgment and do righteousness" [Isa. 56:1].
>
> Finally Amos came and reduced them to one: "Seek Me and live" [Amos 5:4].
>
> So did Habakkuk, who said: "The righteous shall live by his faithfulness" [Hab. 2:4].

The most familiar lapidary summation of the essence of Judaism is that of Hillel. When a proselyte came to him demanding to learn the entire Torah while he stood on one foot,

Hillel's answer was brief, "What is hateful to you, do not do to your neighbor—that is the essence. Everything else is commentary. Go and study" (B. *Shabbat* 31a). Unfortunately, the final injunction in Hillel's utterance, "study," is all too often overlooked! Incidentally, this uncompromising ethical summation of the Jewish tradition occurs in a Talmudic tractate concerned with the observance of sabbath prohibitions with all their minutiae.

Two centuries later, the famous sages Akiba and Ben Azzai debated the question "Which is the most important verse in the Torah?" Rabbi Akiba cited the Golden Rule: "You shall love your neighbor as yourself" (Lev. 19:18). Ben Azzai, instead, proposed another verse: "This is the book of the generations of man; in the day that God created man, in the image of God did He make him" (Gen. 5:1). Instead of relying on the emotion of love to govern human conduct, Ben Azzai preferred to base human behavior on two fundamental principles: the unity of the entire race; and, consequently, the inalienable dignity of all its members, who have been created in the image of God.

While some voices have argued that the enterprise is futile, the quest for the *essence of Judaism* has had a long and respectable history. We may hazard one more attempt in this direction. In the Middle Ages, the *Zohar* declared, "God, Israel, and Torah are one," the classic statement of the organic relationship uniting religion, culture, and peoplehood in Judaism. Which of the three is *primus inter pares*? Parenthetically, it has been suggested that the three principal trends in contemporary Judaism—Orthodoxy, Conservatism, and Reform—have each made one of the triad paramount: Reform stressing religion, Conservatism (and its offshoot, Reconstructionism) peoplehood, and Orthodoxy Torah. Be this as it may, it is possible to demonstrate the centrality of the Torah through Talmudic reasoning, using two other passages in rabbinic literature. One, already cited in another connection, attributes to God the statement "Would that men forsook Me, but kept my Torah" (P. *Hagigah* 1:7). The other emanates from Saadia, the tenth-century gaon, who declared, "Our people is a people only by virtue of the Torah." If we juxtapose the two passages, we arrive at the conclusion that the Torah is the most important member of the triad.

To be sure, the organic relationship of these three basic elements is more important than their relative position on a theoretical scale. Without God there would be no Israel; without Israel there would be no Torah; without the Torah mankind would be ignorant of the will of God.

That ritual is a means to an end is explicitly stated in the observation of Rab, one of the creators of the Babylonian Talmud: "The ritual *mitzvot* were given only for the purpose of refining human nature."[1]

The passages thus far cited to demonstrate the *primacy of ethics* are drawn from the Aggadah, the nonlegal portions of rabbinic literature. But the testimony of the Halakhah is equally conclusive. It emerges from again juxtaposing two passages in the Talmud. One passage teaches that the saving of one's life takes precedence over all other commandments of the Torah, including even the sabbath (B. *Ketubbot* 5a). The other is concerned with the basic principles of Judaism for which a person must be ready to undergo martyrdom. It stipulates that the three sins of idolatry, sexual immorality, and murder are forbidden even at the risk of death. One of the sages, Rabbi Ishmael, goes further and declares that a person may even practice idolatry in order to save his life, except when the act is performed in public, where it may influence others to do likewise (B. *Sanhedrin* 7b). Thus only murder and sexual immorality are forbidden under all circumstances. It follows that in the hierarchy of rabbinic values, ethical conduct rates higher than saving human life, which in turn takes precedence over the sabbath, the most exalted and fundamental of Jewish ritual *mitzvot*.

This conclusion is codified in a classical passage in the Mishnah:

> Sincere repentance on the Day of Atonement has the power to bring forgiveness for the sins which a person has committed against God. As for the sins committed against his fellow men, they cannot be forgiven by the Day of Atonement until one makes restitution to the victim [M. *Yoma* 8:9].

Clearly infractions of the ethical law are more severe than violations of ritual law. Clearly justice is the ultimate value to which God's will must conform.

In the nineteenth century, the Danish theologian Soren Kierkegaard enunciated his famous doctrine of the "teleological suspension of the ethical," according to which the highest rung of faith is reached at times by suspending ethical law. Kierkegaard offers as proof of his thesis the willingness of Abraham, "the knight of faith," to sacrifice his son Isaac, a manifestly immoral act, in obedience to the divine command. This idea has proved attractive to some twentieth-century theologians in Christianity and even in Judaism.

We have demonstrated elsewhere that this approach fails to reckon with the background of the episode, which has led to a total misunderstanding of biblical teaching. That God could command an immoral act is a notion completely unacceptable to Judaism.

In the elaborate liturgy of the Day of Atonement, the central feature, which is repeated eight times during the day, is the "Great Confession" (*ʿal ḥet*): "For the sin that we have committed before You." No fewer than 40 offenses are then listed; all are ethical sins, not one a ritual transgression—a fact that, unbelievably, has generally been overlooked.

Finally, there is no iron curtain between the Halakhah and the Aggadah; the same spirit underlies them both. The Aggadah, "The Telling," utilizes the characters and the events in the Bible to teach the fundamentals of faith and ethics. The Halakhah, "The Way," takes the laws of the Torah as its point of departure in order to develop its system of laws, practices, and institutions in the area of men's relationship both to God and to one's fellows.

Thus the Babylonian Talmud reports the incident of a learned wine merchant whose hired workers by their carelessness permitted the casks they were carrying to be broken, with a total loss of the contents. When the aggrieved employer hailed his workers before the rabbinical court, all his arguments proved in vain, and it was ruled that he could not collect any damages. As the merchant was leaving in high dudgeon, he was called back by the judge and ordered to pay the workers for their day's labor. "Where is it written?" he asked indignantly. "In the Torah," was the judge's answer, "in the Book of Deuteronomy. 'Ye shall do what is just and right in the eyes of the Lord'" [6:18]. Obviously the judge was not quoting a legal citation, but invoking a normative ethical principle, *lifnim mishurat hadin*, "beyond the strict letter of the law.[2]

The history of Jewish law, as will be indicated below, demonstrates how the ethical insight of one generation became the legal requirement of the next. The Halakhah is the prose of Judaism, the Aggadah its poetry. The Halakhah represents the bottom line below which no one may descend; the Aggadah the upper reaches to which everyone should aspire. The content of the Halakhah and the Aggadah and their interaction produce the Jewish tradition.

It is to be hoped that the threadbare charges of "ritualism" and "legalism" will finally be consigned to the dustbin of history and that it will increasingly be recognized that in Jewish tradition and law the ethical is the highest rung on the ladder of faith.

This entire discussion of the primacy of ethics has concentrated on specific injunctions, positive or negative, and their relative position in the hierarchy of values. In this regard we have been true to the spirit of the great formative sources of Judaism, the Bible and rabbinic literature, which were rarely speculative and generally avoided abstractions. The Western theological tradition, on the other hand, following in the footsteps of the Greek philosophers, has developed a penchant for the theoretic approach toward ethics. The problem has been set forth lucidly by Jonathan Harrison:

> There are three ways in which God's command could be relevant to man's duties. The fact that God commands us to perform a certain kind of action might be what makes this kind of action right. On the other hand, it might be the fact that an action is right that causes God to command us to perform it. Finally, it might be the case that the fact that an action is right, and the fact that God commands it are one and the same fact; it might be that all we meant when we said that an action was right was that it was commanded by God.[3]

The debate between the advocates of a heteronomous ethics and an autonomous ethics is one of the long-standing issues in Western philosophy. It finds no echo in Jewish classical thought. In Genesis, when God informs Abraham of His decision to destroy the sinful cities of Sodom and Gommorah, Abraham counters, "Shall the Judge of all the earth not act justly?" (18:25). Clearly justice is the ultimate value to which God's will must conform; any dichotomy between them is unthinkable. The demand of ethics and the command of God are one.[4]

. . .

The Halakhic Process

The liberal and the conservative are both essential to any vital legal system, and the Halakhah is no exception. It is highly significant, however, that the outstanding exemplars of the Halakhah are creative and innovative figures. They represent the genius of Judaism at its highest, with careers that span twelve hundred years, from the Persian era to the early Middle Ages. They placed their stamp on the character of Jewish law and made it a viable system under radically changing social, economic, and political conditions. Their creative legal and intellectual activity enabled Judaism to function in the Hellenistic-Roman world, in the medieval Christian church-state, in the Islamic polity, and in the European feudal system. The Halakhah continued to operate in the early laissez-faire capitalist order and during the emergence of capitalist democracy, in the welfare state, and after the establishment of the state of Israel. Even Communist tyranny has not succeeded in obliterating loyalty to Jewish law. A vital Halakhah will have a significant role in the social and political order of the future.[5]

The Methods of Midrash and Mishnah

The origins of the Oral Law are to be found in the biblical period, for obviously no written law can operate without an oral tradition at its side to spell out its details and implications. The Halakhah became the basic spiritual enterprise in Judaism with Ezra (fifth century B.C.E.). His seminal influence is clear from the Talmudic statement "Ezra was worthy of having the Torah given through him, had not Moses preceded him" (B. *Sanhedrin* 21b). With Ezra's successors, the Sopherim (fifth to second century B.C.E.), the Pharisees (second century B.C.E. to first century C.E.), and the Tannaitic rabbis (first to third century C.E.), the two basic techniques of the Halakhah came into being.

One method, that of the Midrash, literally, "searching the scripture," is deductive; the other, that of the Mishnah, literally, "study," or the Halakhah, "the way," is inductive. The Midrashic method takes its point of departure from a painstaking study of the biblical text. Every passage, word, and letter is searched out and analyzed in order to deduce implications for contemporary life. The method of the Mishnah, on the other hand, originates in a life situation. When a problem or a controversy arises, the accepted authorities reach a decision on the basis of their religious and ethical perceptions. They may then seek to relate their ruling to a biblical text, which becomes its formal source and validation. Very often, the scriptual basis for the decision is left unexpressed.

While there is no iron curtain separating the two procedures, and the same scholars utilized both methods, two distinct types of literature emerged. The deductive method is embodied principally in the Halakhic Midrashim, the *Mekhilta, Sifra, Sifre*, which reached their present form early in the third century C.E. The inductive method is embodied in the Mishnah, compiled by Rabbi Judah Hanasi at about the same time.

After the third century, the fortunes of the two techniques diverged radically. The method of Halakhic Midrash was virtually exhausted by the end of the Tannaitic age, and no significant Halakhic Midrashim emerged thereafter. The reason is not far to seek. While the Torah is, indeed, "longer than the earth in measure and broader than the sea," the legal passages in the Torah total only a few hundred verses. No matter how fruitful the text and how ingenious the interpreter, there are limits to the interpretations afforded by the text. On the other hand, changing conditions and new insights may need to go beyond the biblical text, even when it is homiletically expounded.

The inductive method of the Mishnah, on the other hand, is as unlimited as life itself, with each day creating new configurations. Hence, the Mishnah of Rabbi Judah Hanasi included only a portion, albeit the most significant one, of the material available to the redactor. Even the second compilation of Tannaitic material, the *Tosefta*, attributed to his contemporary Rabbi Hiyya, did not exhaust this material. Hundreds of *baraitot*, "external traditions," survived outside both collections as *disjecta membra* and have been preserved only because they were later cited in the Gemara.

The entire later development of the Halakhah followed the method of the Mishnah rather than that of the Midrash. Predominantly, the Halakhah began with life, which it sought to relate to the body of accumulated tradition. This is true of the Gemara of both Palestine and Babylonia.

The availability of this technique of the Mishnah, deriving its impetus from life, created the potential for a Halakhah that would be appropriate to all times and conditions. This potential was actualized because in each generation there were scholars of courage and insight who adapted the received Halakhah to the needs of the age—Ezra, Hillel,

Rabban Johanan ben Zakkai, Rabban Gamaliel, Rabbi Akiba, Rabbi Judah the Patriarch, Rab, and Samuel, to cite only a few.

After it was consigned to writing, the Mishnah in turn became the subject of detailed analysis and extensive interpretation in the Gemara ("study") carried on by the *amoraim*, "expounders," in Palestine and in Babylonia.

After the sixth century the Mishnah and the Gemara, now constituting the Talmud, became a "canonical," or normative, Halakhah so that its text could not henceforth be altered. That all three terms—Mishnah, Gemara, and Talmud—literally mean "study" points to the importance that Judaism assigns to the study of the sacred texts as a cardinal commandment.

The Talmud, in turn, became the basis of minute analysis by later scholars, as had been the case with the Bible and the Mishnah centuries earlier. The interpretation of the hallowed text of the Talmud now became the activity of the Saboraim (sixth and seventh centuries C.E.) and the Geonim, the heads of the great Babylonian academies (seventh to eleventh century C.E.).

After the decline of Babylonia, a multiplicity of Jewish settlements arose in North Africa, Spain, Provence, Italy, Germany, and Poland. They created new literary forms in which the Halakhah continued to grow—legal treatises, commentaries, all-inclusive codes of law, and *responsa* by individual scholars on specific issues. *Responsa* have continued to augment the content of the Halakhah and show no signs of diminution even today, fifteen hundred years later. Every *Responsum* has two sections, the *she'elah*, "question," and the *teshuvah*, "answer." The question always arises out of a concrete situation encountered by the inquirer; the answer reflects the respondent's learning and sensitivity to the prevailing conditions.

Post-Talmudic Legislation

In theory, the Mishnah and the Gemara were the final authority, not to be added to or subtracted from. They were, however, subject to wide-ranging interpretation, and this process generally sufficed to meet most problems of Jewish life. But at times new important issues emerged that required different treatment. Rabbinic law made provisions for such radical steps, permitting the enactment by competent authorities of *taqqanot* "positive regulations" and *gezerot*, "negative ordinances." These legislative acts, which went beyond the bounds of the previously accepted Halakhah, were generally enacted for a fixed period and for a restricted territory.

Among the exceptions to these limitations was the *taqqanah* prohibiting polygamy. It was enacted by Rabbi Gershom of Mainz and his synod in the tenth century for the communities of what now constitute Germany, France, and Italy, to be valid for a period of one thousand years. Neither the time limit which has now expired nor the original territorial restriction has been invoked to abolish the ruling, which is permanent and universally observed by Jewry today. The same rabbinical synod enacted other significant *taqqanot*, including a major extension of the rights of women in divorce and the protection of the privacy of letters, which were generally sent by messengers.

The two techniques of *gezerah* and *taqqanah* are utilized infrequently in later periods, but they are still available as a last resort when the Halakhah is confronted by intractable problems.

Another far-reaching procedure used by rabbinic authorities has not been adequately noticed. When rabbinic leaders in medieval Jewry were confronted by a Halakhah they felt to be inappropriate to their situation, they sometimes adopted a strategy that can only be described as "tacit noncompliance." The problematic provision of the law was not rescinded, reinterpreted, or modified; it was simply ignored in practice and, where possible, passed over in silence in the literature. When the provision of the law could be reinterpreted, that was naturally preferred; if not, it was to all intents and purposes set aside for good and sufficient reasons.

Two major motivations were at work here. The first was the overriding desire to guarantee the physical survival of the Jewish people in the face of constant danger. The second was the wish to preserve traditional standards of family morality, for which, they believed, the subordinate position of women was essential. The following are a few instances of this practice:

1. A key element in biblical domestic law decreed that a father had the authority to give his daughter into marriage or sell her into slavery at will (Exod. 21:7). This absolute power was considerably abridged in the Mishnah by a process of interpretation. The Hebrew term *n*^c*arah*, "girl," which is used in several biblical texts, was given a technical meaning and was limited to females between twelve and twelve and a half years old. Before this period of "girlhood," the daughter was a *ketannah*, "a minor." During this period the father's right to marry her off was limited (B. *Ketubbot* 43b). The Babylonian sage Rab went further and declared, "A man is morally forbidden to marry off his daughter while she is a *ketannah*" (B. *Kiddushin* 41a). After the age of twelve and a half, the girl assumed the status of a *bogeret*, "mature person," and her father no longer had legal authority over her. Thus in theory, the *patria potestas* was reduced to a six-month period. In practice, however, during medieval and even modern days, parents continued to marry off their daughters as they chose at almost any age, betrothals (*tenaim*) often taking place in the early teen years.

2. The early rabbinic schools of the house of Hillel and the house of Shammai were in agreement that the commandment "Be fruitful and multiply" was fulfilled by the birth of two children. The schools differed only as to whether two sons were required, as Shammai held, or whether a son and a daughter would suffice, as Hillel maintained. Both views were disregarded in practice. Ultratraditional Jewish couples continue to propagate large numbers of children to the present day.

3. A Tannaitic statement quoted six times in the Talmud discusses the use of an absorbent by three categories of women—a minor, a pregnant woman, and a nursing mother—in order to prevent conception. Classical interpreters differ as to whether these women are permitted (and other women are not) or whether they are required to practice birth control (and other women are permitted). That these three categories *must* and other women *may* practice contraception is the prevalent interpretation among the commentators.[6]

Obviously widespread family limitation would drastically affect the biological survival of Jews threatened by man-made perils like expulsion and massacre, as well as the "natural" dangers of disease and malnutrition. Here, two strategies were adopted. First, the statement was interpreted, at variance with well-known and common linguistic usage, to forbid the practice of contraception to all three classes of women.[7] Second, virtually none of the medieval law codes, not even the *Mishneh Torah* of Maimonides and the *Shulhan*

Arukh of Rabbi Joseph Karo, make any reference to the subject, thus the possibility of discussing the option of practicing birth control is completely eliminated.[8]

4. The Talmud cites two Tannaitic Sages on the subject of educating women in the Torah. The conservative Rabbi Eliezer ben Hyrcanus declares that teaching the Torah to women is tantamount to teaching obscenity (M. *Sotah* 3:4) and forbids it. He is contradicted by Ben Azzai, who makes teaching the Torah to women obligatory. As is noted at several points in the present volume, the law is rarely decided in accordance with Rabbi Eliezer's opinion. Nonetheless, during the greater portion of Diaspora history, his negative view on the education of women prevailed. The teaching of the Torah to women has been almost nonexistent in traditional Jewish communities until the present.

5. In the sixteenth century Rabbi Joseph Karo codified the practice of Sephardic communities in a work entitled *Shulhan Arukh*, "The Prepared Table," to which Rabbi Moses Isserles added his *Mappah*, "Tablecloth," setting down the Ashkenazic practice in vogue among German and Polish Jews. This supplement, which is always printed as part of the central text, was indispensable in making the *Shulhan Arukh* normative for all traditional Jews.

On the subject of honors at the Torah reading, a statement in the *Shulhan Arukh*, based on a ruling in the *Tosefta*, reads:

> All persons may be included in the number of *aliyot* [the seven honors at the sabbath Torah reading], but the Sages declared, "A woman should not read [i.e., receive an *aliyah*] because of the honor of the congregation [since it would suggest that the males are unlearned].[9]

At this point, Rabbi Moses Isserles adds the crucial supplement: "What is meant is that women and minors may be added to other honorees at the Torah reading, but that not all the honors should be given to women or minors."[10] Clearly, this sixteenth-century ruling permits women to be called to the Torah, but it remained a dead letter until the middle of the twentieth century.

Obviously, every legal system must have a mechanism for deciding controversial issues, and the Halakhah is no exception. Interpreting the last three words of Exodus 23:2, *aḥarei rabbim lehattot*, to mean "one must follow after the many," the Rabbis established the principle that the majority view should prevail (B. *Hullin* 11a), though there were many exceptions—because of the eminence of a particular scholar or for some other special reason. An ancient Mishnah then asks the pertinent question, Why record the views of scholars that are not adopted? The answer is highly significant: future authorities might discover grounds for finding the minority view more appropriate (M. *Eduyot* 1:4–6), thus laying the groundwork for a possible revision and even a reversal of the law under changed circumstances.

This open-mindedness toward nonauthoritative views derived not only from the pragmatic considerations already indicated, but from a profound theological conviction that all the views expressed in the Halakhah are "the words of the living God."

The fourth-century Palestinian scholar Ulla declared:

> When the sages in Palestine adopted a restrictive enactment, they would not reveal the reason for twelve months, lest there be someone who would find the reasoning unconvincing and would therefore disregard the prohibition [B. *Abodah Zarah* 35a].

A well-known modern historian of the Halakhah finds a progressive principle in this apparently conservative procedure:

But why did they announce the reason for their enactment after a year? So that coming generations, if they found that the reason was no longer operative, would be able to set aside the enactment.[11]

The Decline of the Creative Impulse

As the Middle Ages progressed, a tragic anomaly revealed itself—later generations proved less creative and courageous than their predecessors. The so-called Dark Ages—the earlier part of the medieval period, until the eleventh century—were by and large marked by favorable conditions for Jewish life. Jews enjoyed friendly relations with their Christian neighbors and were relatively free from persecution. On the other hand, the later Middle Ages, which saw expanding horizons for Christian Europe as a result of the Crusades, the Renaissance, the Reformation, and the voyages of discovery of the New World, was a period of constantly worsening conditions for Jews. The massacres of Jewish communities perpetrated by the Crusaders; the establishment of the ghetto as a universal phenomenon; the Black Death; the successive expulsions of the Jews from England, France, Spain, and Portugal; the ravages wrought by the Thirty Years War in Germany; the Chmielnicki massacres in Poland; and the tragic debacle of the false Messiah, Shabbetai Zevi, represented body blows to the vitality of Judaism and its creative élan. As cultural horizons were narrowed and fears for the future were intensified, the urge to hold fast to the old with ever-increasing fervor became the dominant mood in Jewish traditional life. During the previous three centuries, both the taste and the capacity for creative activity had been drastically reduced, precisely at a time when the need for creativity was greatest.

Biblical law, the foundations of which were laid in the periods of seminomadism and early rural and urban cultures, was successfully applied to the more advanced agricultural and commercial conditions of the Greco-Roman era through the creative activity of the Rabbis. This corpus of the Halakhah was then put into operation during the feudal system, the age of the Industrial Revolution, and the various stages of capitalism. It continues to function in the world-girding conflict between democracy and communism in our day.

But in the last two hundred years traditional Judaism has faced massive and traumatic challenges, far greater than any of the past, perhaps less violent, but far more perilous. Only the Holocaust stands as a horrible "exception" that all but succeeded in destroying both Jews and Judaism. The political and civic Emancipation of the Jews, launched by the French Revolution, granted Jews as individuals political citizenship, economic opportunity, cultural equality, and a substantial measure of social integration. In return, the Emancipation in western and central Europe swept away the age-old structure of the Jewish community, with its power to tax and thus to govern its members. The parallel process of the Enlightenment, with its cargo of new philosophic and scientific ideas, undermined the authority of Jewish tradition and the validity of the Halakhah. In the last 150 years, the Emancipation and the Enlightenment moved inexorably from western and central Europe to the great mass settlements of East European Jewry. In the United States, Canada, and Latin America, no political emancipation was necessary, since Jews had never had a special status of inferiority. But neither was there a deeply entrenched tradition to withstand the onslaught of modernism. As wholesale defection from tradition became the rule, many observers were convinced that both Judaism and the Jewish people were in grave jeopardy in the modern age.

The natural reaction of the traditional rabbinate was to hold on to the old and reject the new. They intensified the demand for total adherence to the hallowed traditions and practices of the past, major or minor, appropriate or not, and gave no quarter to modern life and thought. The famous Hungarian rabbinic authority, the Hatam Sofer, borrowed a Talmudic dictum and coined a slogan designed to erect a dike against the floodwaters of the new age: *ḥadash asur min hatorah*, "Anything new is forbidden by the Torah." That this pronouncement has proved counterproductive is clear from the wholesale defection of the vast majority of modern Jews from the Halakhah.

Suspicion of the contemporary world became the hallmark of Orthodoxy, and this suspicion turned to bitter hostility and scorn for modern ideas and ideals. This attitude, compounded of meticulous observance of all Halakhic minutiae and total rejection of the gentile world, is all too comprehensive. It produced the phenomenon of the *baᶜalei teshuvah*, "penitents" or "returnees," who react violently to all manifestations of modern life and culture except for its economic opportunities. However understandable their position may be, it will prove less and less viable with the passing days. Its weakness lies in trying to turn the clock back to the sixteenth and seventeenth centuries. It is naive to imagine that a Western megalopolis can be transformed into an East European *shtetl*, which they regard as the only true model for the Jewish community.

As a minority within a minority in Western society, they cannot force the Jewish or the general majority to conform to their pattern. In increasing measure, therefore, they create their own enclaves in the larger cities or in independent suburban communities of their own. Their total self-assurance and fervent piety give more moderate elements in contemporary Orthodoxy a deep sense of inferiority and drive them inexorably to the right. Thus we have the paradox that the revival of Orthodoxy is an effective brake on Halakhic progress precisely when it is most needed.

Though creative Halakhic activity has been reduced, it never ceased completely because the pressures and demands of contemporary life cannot be ignored. Particularly in the state of Israel, where the Halakhah was declared operative in the areas of marriage, divorce, and personal status, new issues demanded solution. In all wings of modern Judaism scholars and thinkers are wrestling with the problems and working to restore the vital functioning of Jewish law in an age of rapid and dizzying change.

The long and fruitful history of Jewish law did not take place in isolation. Contrary to widespread impressions in some quarters today, the medieval ghetto and the modern *shtetl*, both of which were largely insulated from the world about them, represent only part of the varied Jewish experience through history. The ghetto and the *shtetl* possessed many positive qualities, but neither is a universal pattern or an ideal setting for a flourishing and creative Judaism. Nor do they offer a paradigm for a Jewish community in a free society. By and large, Jewish law, like all phases of Jewish culture, grew and developed most significantly in communities that existed in open societies and thus were able to respond without constraint to events in the world at large.

The process of reinterpretation and adjustment is only partially mirrored in the traditional Halakhic literature of the past two centuries. Much of the change in Jewish religious practice has taken place outside the limits set by the letter of the law. The formal content of the Halakhah has been the subject of passionate, indeed bitter, controversy; and the process of growth and adjustment has been neither easy nor systematic. Nevertheless, Jewish law has survived in the Diaspora in a variety of formulations. In the state of Israel, primarily for practical reasons, Jewish law has begun to undergo a renaissance, handicapped, to be sure, by the intellectual and ethical limitations of its official guardians in the present religious establishment.

Undoubtedly, the unyielding adherence to the letter of the law by its conservative partisans has played an important role in its preservation; but its vitality and its relevance to new conditions and problems are due to its protean capacity for adjustment upheld by its more liberal expounders.

The Dynamics of the Halakhah

Jewish tradition is best compared to a flowing river that possesses a mainstream, but also side currents and even crosscurrents that affect its flow significantly. To be sure, it is not always easy to determine at any given point which is the dominant and which is the secondary stream. At the time that the issues were being debated, the rabbinic Sages were sure that the Sadducees were not in the mainstream of the tradition. But they had no such certainty at the time with regard to the controversies of Hillel and Shammai, Rabbi Akiba and Rabbi Ishmael, Rab and Samuel, Raba and Abaye. Even with the benefit of hindsight, we require considerable knowledge, insight, and intellectual integrity to recognize the difference between the normative tradition and aberrant groups in Judaism and to do justice to the contributions of both.

When the tradition is alive and well, there is a complex process of interaction between the past and the present. Each age receives a body of doctrine and law from the preceding period. As it comes into contact with contemporary conditions, problems, and insights, the spiritual and intellectual leadership in Judaism is called upon to evaluate these new elements, which are struggling to be admitted into the sanctuary of the tradition. The leadership will recognize some aspects as dangerous and ill-advised and will reject them in toto. Others it will deem ethically sound, religiously true, and pragmatically valuable, and these will be incorporated. Many, if not most, new phenomena will be judged to contain both positive and negative elements. The former will be accepted in greater or lesser degree, often after being modified so as to bring them into greater conformity with the spirit and form of the tradition. To utilize the familiar but useful terminology of Hegel, past tradition constitutes the thesis, contemporary life is the antithesis, and the resultant of these two factors becomes the new synthesis. The synthesis of one age then becomes the thesis of the next; the newly formulated content of tradition becomes the point of departure for the next stage.

This is not to suggest even remotely that tradition is bound to surrender to "the spirit of the age." It is always free, indeed commanded, to examine the demands and insights of each generation and to accept, modify, or reject them as it sees fit. But when the tradition is healthy or, more concretely, when its exemplars are true to their function, they will be sensitive to the age and respond to it. Often there will be sharp divergences of view as to the validity of these new factors and how the tradition should respond to them. Indeed, the issue may remain *in suspenso* for some time. Ultimately, however, life is the determining factor, and from its decision there is no appeal.

This dialectic process, which has operated throughout the history of Judaism and is the secret of its capacity to survive, can be documented in all areas—ritual, civil and criminal law, marriage, and divorce. It is most evident in the great creative eras of rabbinic Judaism—the Tannaitic and the Amoraic periods, which saw the creation of the Mishnah and the Talmud. This capacity never ceased, but it was weakened in the Middle Ages. The rabbinic leadership now brought about an ever-increasing ghettoization of the spirit and made Jewish group survival, rather than the needs, interests, and desires of the individual, their basic concern. The strength of their influence on the present state of the Halakhah can scarcely be exaggerated, since, for the bulk of East European Jewry, the Middle Ages continued until the twentieth century.

From this paradigm of the dynamic of the Halakhah, an important theoretical and pragmatic conclusion emerges: The Halakhah is not to be seen locked in mortal combat with the contemporary age, the demands of which are, therefore, to be resisted with every means at its disposal. The Halakhah itself comprises both elements in the dialectic; continuity with the past and growth induced by the present. History is neither inimical nor irrelevant to the Halakhah. It is the soil from which the Halakhah springs. Cut off from history, the arena in which men and women live and struggle, the Halakhah is doomed to sterility and death. Nor are the Halakhah and sociology mortal foes. Sociology supplies the data that the Halakhah must examine in order to determine how to deal with a new situation.

A statement about the United States Constitution by Chief Justice John Marshall in 1819 applies equally to the divine constitution of the Jewish people, which is the Torah and its embodiment in Jewish law: "The constitution is intended to endure for ages to come, and consequently, to be adapted to the various crises of human affairs." Described in these impersonal terms, the Halakhic process would seem to be a smooth, peaceful movement from one stage to another, but this is far from the truth. The agents of the process are human beings, with their individual attitudes, passions, prejudices, and interests, all of which come into play in evaluating contemporary conditions and the need to deal with them. The 3,000 pages of the Talmud are a monument to controversy, recording the debates by hundreds of rabbis, their arguments testifying to the vitality and creativity of the tradition.

A few instances of the struggles involved in reaching decisions will make the Halakhic process come alive. Parenthetically, these may help to reconcile the reader to some of the less attractive features of current conflicts in rabbinic circles.

The Talmud reports that the school of Hillel and the school of Shammai were engaged in bitter controversy for many years. According to one report, physical violence broke out between them. Finally a heavenly voice proclaimed, "Both these and the others are the words of the Living God" (B. *Erubin* 13b), and the members of the two schools continued to intermarry, their differences notwithstanding (M. *Eduyot* 4:8).

Another far-reaching instance of the Halakhic struggle occurred in the year 70 C.E., when Jerusalem was being besieged by the Romans. Rabban Johanan ben Zakkai[12] saw that the imminent destruction of the Temple and the liquidation of the Sanhedrin, the supreme Jewish religious authority, would threaten the decimated and dispirited survivors with fragmentation, lack of leadership, and ultimate annihilation. He decided to transfer many of the functions of the Holy City of Jerusalem to the village of Jabneh. He set up his colleagues in his academy as a substitute Sanhedrin, with authority for the whole range of religious law, including civil and criminal jurisprudence. He also ordained younger scholars to serve as judges in the courts. Since the unity of the scattered Jewish people depended on their observing festivals on the same days, he arranged for the witnesses of the new moon to bring their testimony to Jabneh, as they had previously done with the High Court in Jerusalem. To build morale among the people, Rabban Johanan taught that even the destruction of the sacrificial system in the Temple, which had been the center-piece of the Jewish religion, was not fatal to Judaism, because prayer and deeds of loving kindness were equally acceptable to God.

Most dramatic of all was the procedure he established with regard to the blowing of the shofar on the sabbath. Before the destruction of the Temple, when Rosh Hashanah fell on the sabbath the shofar was blown only in the Temple and in the Holy City. After the destruction of the Temple, Rabban Johanan boldly transferred this special prerogative of the Temple to the academy of Jabneh as part of his unremitting effort to endow it with central authority. When he proposed this radical break with tradition, conservative members of his court, the Bnei Bathyra, said, "Let us discuss the question." Johanan replied: "Let us blow the shofar and then we'll discuss the question." After the shofar was blown, they said to him: "Now let us discuss it." He responded, "We already have heard the shofar in Jabneh and the act cannot be withdrawn" (B. *Rosh Hashanah* 29b).

Undoubtedly, the heroic mass suicide of Jewish warriors and their families at Masada was more dramatic than the slow, patient labors of Johanan ben Zakkai at Jabneh. But it was Jabneh, not Masada, that preserved both Judaism and the Jewish people.

For many centuries, including our own, Judaism has been calumniated as primitive and cruel because of the famous passage in Exodus "An eye for an eye, a tooth for a tooth" (21:24). The history of ancient society demonstrates that *lex talionis*, the law of retaliation, is itself an ethical advance over the more primitive doctrine that permitted any injury to be avenged without limit. Ancient societies regarded it as legitimate, indeed praiseworthy and heroic, to take a life for an injury. The biblical law restricts the punishment to the dimensions of the offense. The Talmud clearly recognized this in its comment "An eye for an eye," not "a life and an eye for an eye" (B. *Ketubbot* 38a).

Nevertheless, even this limitation came to be regarded as morally indefensible in the Mishnaic period, if not earlier. No scholar was more honored for his piety and learning than Rabbi Eliezer ben Hyrcanus, the archconservative of his time, who was committed to the strict construction of the text. Accordingly, he maintained that "an eye for an eye" was to be taken literally (B. *Baba Kamma* 84a). Rabbi Eliezer's view was duly recorded, but it was his opponents, who held that the verse meant "monetary compensation," who prevailed. Their views proved both normative and decisive for the spirit of Jewish law.

Legal philosophers have long known that discovering the law is often indistinguishable from creating the law. As Morris Raphael Cohen pointed out, "The process of lawmaking is called finding the law." He argues forcefully against regarding the process as "spurious interpretation," while noting that "it would be absurd to maintain that [legislators] are in no wise bound, and can make any law they please."

The United States Constitution possesses a quasi-sacred character in the American ethos; thus an analogy between the American and the Jewish systems of law may be fairly drawn. A proposal to establish a monarchy in the United States would contradict the "clear intent" of the fathers of the Constitution and would be unacceptable. On the other hand, the call sounded in some circles today for returning to "the original intent" of the Constitution is often disingenuous, usually unattainable, and generally counterproductive. First of all, we lack access to the mental processes of the original writers of the document. Second, various divergent views were reconciled in compromises and are reflected in the final text adopted. Third, the American people is not governed solely by the Constitution. In the past 200 years thousands of laws and regulations adopted by local, state, and federal legislative bodies and administrative agencies have defined the contours of American life. In the process they have modified and reinterpreted the Constitution. They have made it possible for a document created in a largely rural society in the early stages of industrialization to serve as the basic law of a technically advanced civilization.

The entire economic life of the nation would come to a virtual halt if the "original intent" of the Fourteenth Amendment were taken to be normative. When the statement "Nor shall any state deprive any person of life, liberty and property without due process of law" was ratified in 1868, its purpose was to safeguard the rights of the newly enfranchised slaves. Subsequently the word "person" was applied to the business corporation, which was defined as a "legal person," and our entire economic structure now relies upon this concept. There is no word in the Constitution about a presidential cabinet or political parties or judicial review; yet without them the governmental structure would crumble. The secret lies in finding the path between literalism and lawlessness.

A recent study of the late Chief Justice Earl Warren points out that he was in fact an ethicist who saw his craft as "discovering ethical imperatives in a maze of confusion." According to his biographer, Warren believed that "the rightness of results" was more important than "the doctrinal integrity of reasoning," but that "his results were not arbitrary." He believed that the Constitution of the United States embodied an ethical structure, and his job was to apply those standards. *Mutandis mutatis*, this was the role adopted by the Rabbis.

The function of the Rabbis in determining the growth of the Halakhah was clearly visible in every period. There was, however, another agent at work, unofficial and unacknowledged, which played a significant role in the development of Jewish tradition. In Judaism, the voice of the people is not the voice of God, but neither is it without influence.

• • •

The Rise and Growth of Custom

The power of the popular will, as distinct from the official Halakhah, is exemplified in the famous dictum "Custom sets the law aside" (P. *Yebamot* 12:1; B. *Baba Mezia* 7:1; B. *Sopherim*, 14).[13] Actually, as Alexander Guttmann has pointed out, the principle was not as far-reaching as it would appear to be on the surface.[14] It is cited only twice in the Palestinian Talmud and never in the Babylonian, though it was undoubtedly operative in both countries. In the Talmudic period, the doctrine was invoked when there was a difference of opinion among scholars regarding a law or when a set of exceptional circumstances prevailed.

Thus in connection with a borderline case of sabbath observance, the Talmud declares, "Let Israel alone [i.e., let them do as they please], for if they are not Prophets, they are the descendants of Prophets" (B. *Pesahim* 66b). Even more frequently, the Babylonian and the Palestinian Talmud invoked the principle "Go out and see how the people are acting" in order to determine the law (B. *Berakhot* 45a; B. *Erubin* 14b; B. *Pesahim* 24a; B. *Menahot* 38b; P. *Peah* 7:5; B. *Yebamot* 7:2).

When the scholars contemplated adding a new prohibition, a limited veto was accorded the people by the established rule "No prohibition is to be adopted if the majority of the community [*robh zibbur*] are unable to observe it."[15] Clearly, the sages of the Talmud were very sensitive to the needs, the desires, and the capacities of the people they were called upon to lead.

Only at widely separated points in history were there instances of overt rebellion against rabbinical authority that took on the dimensions of a movement. The first took place in the eighth century, in Babylonia, where there arose a varied group of opponents of the Talmud called Karaites, "devotees of the scripture," who called for a return to scripture as the sole authority in Judaism. For several centuries Karaism was both a fructifying influence and a significant threat to rabbinism in Egypt, Palestine, and Babylonia. Ultimately Karaism lost its power; it has remained a tiny sect within the Jewish people.[16]

After the final redaction of the Babylonian and the Palestinian Talmuds, which was a consequence of the decline of the Babylonian and Palestinian centers, new Jewish settlements developed along the coast of North Africa and throughout southern Europe. Living under Christian and Muslim rule, these communities were exposed to varying cultural, economic, and political conditions. This far-flung and varied Diaspora accepted the authority of Talmudic law, which served as the bond of unity among them.

At the same time there grew up a substantial amount of variation in liturgy and ritual observance. Often the variation in custom extended to an entire culture sphere or country. The traditional prayer book, the basic form of which had been established in the period of the Mishnah, now underwent an elaborate development. Different *nushaot*, or prayer rites, came into being, the Sephardic (or Spanish-Portuguese) and the Ashkenazic (or German-Polish), as well as lesser variants like the Italian and the Provençal. Local holidays or fast days were observed to mark crises successfully surmounted or disasters averted.

In the Middle Ages, hundreds of new poems were added to the traditional liturgy, particularly for the High Holy days and the three Pilgrimage festivals. These additions to the body of accepted prayers were made without disturbing what was hallowed from the past, and thus they aroused relatively little opposition. Nonetheless, these *piyyutim*, "liturgical poems," were frequently complicated, obscure, and even ungrammatical. They evoked the objections of such radically different figures as the medieval grammarian and commentator Rabbi Abraham Ibn Ezra (1092–1167) and the Halakhic authority Rabbi Elijah, the Gaon of Vilna (1720–97).

The scholars often quoted chapter and verse against some innovations, but the popular will frequently overrode their objections, and official leaders proved powerless to prevent adoption of certain practices.

The many differences in local background and experience, coupled with the beliefs and desires of the common people, produced the phenomenon of *minhag*, "custom," as distinct from *din*, "law." These *minhagim* reflected every conceivable level of content and outlook and were marked by considerable power and persistence.

While most of the customs dealt with ritual practices, some manifested a fine ethical sensitivity. Many of them were expressions of folk belief, at times influenced by those of non-Jewish neighbors. Many *minhagim* had a brief life span, others lasted for centuries, and some became permanent elements in Judaism.

In general, *minhag* evoked radically different reactions from the rabbinate. On the one hand, it was maintained that *minhag mebhattel halakhah*, "custom sets the law aside" (P. *Yebamot* 12:1; B. *Baba Mezia* 7:1; B. *Sopherim* 14), a principle that frequently prevailed in practice. On the other hand, it was noted that a transposition of the consonants of *minhag* produces the vocable *gehinnom*, "Hell."[17]

Each custom might be praised or condemned, depending on its nature and on the personality and outlook of a particular rabbi. The ubiquity and the persistence of *minhag* testify to the power of the popular will in determining many elements in the practice and theory of the Halakhah. The impact of local *minhag* is far from spent, even in America today, as will be demonstrated below.

To appreciate the full significance of custom, two widespread misconceptions regarding medieval Jewry must be laid to rest. First, though the tempo of development in Jewish law was reduced after the periods of the Mishnah and the Talmud, medieval Judaism was by no means bereft of creativity and innovative vigor, as the activity of Rabbi Gershom of Mainz, "the Light of the Exile," and later scholars abundantly attest. But the achievements of the elitist leadership were far exceeded by the proliferation of *minhag* in all areas of life, largely as the expression of the people.

Second, the segregation of Jews and Christians in the Middle Ages was much less complete than is commonly believed, and personal contacts were not infrequent. Influences, spiritual and intellectual, percolated from one community to the other. It is hardly an accident that early German pietism was contemporaneous with Rabbi Judah the Saint of Regensburg, the author of the *Sefer Hasidim*, and his circle; or that the upheaval in seventeenth-century world Jewry caused by the pseudo-Messiah, Shabbetai Zevi, was contemporaneous with millenarian movements in seventeenth-century Christian Europe. Other examples might also be cited. Though the precise channels of transmission may elude us, it seems clear that some Christian beliefs and practices penetrated the Jewish community, though they were thoroughly Judaized in the process.

Generally, the popular will had a democratic thrust. It expressed itself in a pressure for greater participation in religious life by all the elements in the Jewish people, not merely its upper echelons. Since custom was often an expression of the religiosity of the masses, it did not always reflect the highest intellectual level. But because it rose from the depths of the human soul, it survived.

• • •

Afterword

This [essay] has reached its end, but the process it has sought to delineate and analyze has not. The Jewish tradition, which has been contemporaneous with virtually the entire significant history of the human race, proved adequate to serve the needs of the Jewish people through all the vicissitudes of its history. Jewish law will survive into the future on precisely the same terms—and the task has become incomparably more challenging today because of the vastly enlarged possibilities and the massive problems of the nuclear age.

From the biblical era to the present, the process of growth and development in Jewish tradition and law, though varying in extent and creativity in differing epochs, remains clear. The prophetic insistence that righteousness, individual and collective, is the categorical imperative for humankind dominated all succeeding stages in the history of Judaism and imbued the Jewish people with a strong ethical consciousness, which played a decisive role in the later formulations of Jewish law. Succeeding generations, inheriting an extensive body of Jewish lore and law, found that the blend of idealistic aspiration and realistic understanding made the tradition effective and relevant, so that most of it could be maintained virtually intact from generation to generation.

Stability was one of the pillars on which Judaism rested; the other was its dynamism, its capacity to grow and develop with time. When confronted by changed social, economic, and political conditions, on the one hand, and by new ethical attitudes and insights on the other, its leaders reacted with insight and resilience to undertake the necessary accommodations between past and future to ensure a viable future.

Particularly during the earlier period, that of the Mishnah and the Talmud, when the Halakhah was actively in the making, the task of adjustment was undertaken by the recognized rabbinic authorities of the age. When the survival of their people was threatened, the Jewish leaders took steps to counter the danger, even if they called for a radical break with earlier, accepted attitudes. In later periods, particularly in the Middle Ages, the new patterns were sometimes felt more keenly by the masses of the people. While the Sages and scholars might not subscribe to the formula *Vox populi vox Dei*, they were astute enough to reckon with the popular will and adjust the law to conform with the people's *minhag* when the custom served to strengthen loyalty to Judaism. All these factors will continue to operate in the future with even greater strength than in the past, since the tempo of change is far greater in our century than in the preceding 2,000 years.

I have refrained from discussing problems created by the scientific and technological revolution of the twentieth century. New questions of great complexity for both the individual and society have emerged in many fields, from the exploration of outer space to research in subatomic physics, from bio-genetics to electronics. The definitions of life and death have become increasingly complicated and controversial, challenging the traditional concepts of the past. The ethical issues cannot be logically addressed since there is no unanimity, often not even consensus, on many scientific questions resulting from new discoveries. The widely differing responses of ethicists and theologians bear witness to the tentative and inconclusive nature of current thinking.

What is more, the traditional sources contemporary thinkers cite are all too often interpreted in a literalistic and uncritical spirit, with no recognition of the role that new insights and unprecedented conditions must play in finding proper solutions to our problems. It is no wonder, therefore, that religious tradition is frequently invoked to hamper progress rather than to advance it, thus bringing the wisdom of the past into disrepute among intelligent and sensitive people.

If the Halakhah is to remain alive and meaningful, and the Jewish people is not to become what Toynbee called it, "a fossilized relic of Syriac society," its scholars, thinkers, and leaders must demonstrate the three attributes of loyalty to traditional standards, moral sensitivity, and common sense.

The intellectual and spiritual enterprise of restoring a creative and relevant Halakhah is only the first element in building the Jewish future. A people needs a law, but the law needs a people. All the resources of education and persuasion must be used to attract modern Jews to a deeper personal attachment to the pattern of Jewish living in accordance with the tradition. Many other elements, such as literature, scholarship, folkways, music, and art, all contribute to the richness of the Jewish experience and need to be cultivated with energy and zest. But the Jewish people cannot survive for long without religion at its center. A vital Judaism requires a living Halakhah. Growth is the law of life, and the Law is the life of Judaism.

Notes

1. Midrash, Genesis Rabbah 44.
2. The incident is reported in both the Palestinian and the Babylonian Talmuds with some variations (P. *Baba Mezia* 6:8, B. *Baba Mezia* 83a). They have been given a "close reading" and the significance of the divergences has been acutely pointed out in Daniel H. Gordis, "Scripture and Halakhah in Parallel Aggadot," *Prooftexts* 5 (1985):183–90.
3. *The Encyclopedia of Philosophy* (New York and London, 1967), vol. 3, p. 73.
4. A noteworthy exception to the harmony between the Halakhah and ethics that the Rabbis found particularly difficult to contemplate was the permanent exclusion of a *mamzer* (illegitimate child) from the community, derived from Deut. 23:2. "No bastard shall enter the assembly of the Lord; even to the tenth generation, none of his descendants shall enter the assembly of the Lord."

   This subject is by no means of purely scholastic interest today. Aside from clear instances of adultery in our society, the horrors of the Holocaust have produced heartrending instances of women, informed that their husbands were dead, who in all innocence remarried and bore children who are technically illegitimate. In the state of Israel, where the religious Establishment is the ultimate authority in the area of personal status, the reactions have run the gamut from total indifference toward the plight of the principals to the use of various legal technicalities to resolve the situation.

   It should be added that some Halakhic scholars, sensitive to the ethical issues and the human suffering involved, believe that resources may be found within the traditional Halakhah for solving or at least alleviating the problem. The question deserves a fresh scholarly and legal investigation in our time.
5. Comprehensive treatments of the history of Jewish law are presented in I. H. Weiss, *Dor Dor Vedorshav*, 5 vols. (Vienna, 1871–91); Ch. Tchernowitz, *Toledot Ha Halakhah*, 4 vols. (New York, 1935–50); and Tchernowitz, *Toledot Haposkim*, 3 vols. (New York, 1946–47). Weiss's work was subjected to detailed criticism by I. Halevy, *Dorot Rishonim*, 6 vols. (1897–1939), but Weiss's basic positions remain essentially valid.

   Important later studies are L. Finkelstein, *The Pharisees*, 2 vols. (Philadelphia, 1st ed., 1938; 2d ed., with significant changes in emphasis, 1966); Finkelstein, *Akiba* (Philadelphia, 1936); J. Z. Lauterbach, *Rabbinic Essays* (Cincinnati, 1951); A. Guttmann, *Rabbinic Judaism in the Making* (Detroit, 1974); S. Zeitlin, *The Rise and Fall of the Judean State* (New York, 1968); and many papers in *Jewish Quarterly Review*.

   The significance of economic and political factors in the development of rabbinic law is underscored in L. Ginzberg, *Of Jewish Law and Lore* (Philadelphia, 1955), which includes his epoch-making essay, "The Role of Halakhah in Jewish Scholarship." A work intended for the general reader and undeservedly forgotten is S. Zucrow, *The Adjustment of Law to Life in Rabbinic Literature* (Boston, 1928). Several works in this area have recently appeared. Joel Roth, *The Halakhic Process: A Systemic Analysis* (New York, 1986), discusses legal principles adopted by the Halakhah itself for arriving at decisions in view of the multiplicity of views expressed in the literature. Elliot Dorff and Arthur Rosett, *A Living Tree: The Roots and Growth of Jewish Law* (New York, 1988) traces the stages in the history of Jewish law and compares it with current American jurisprudence.
6. The passages are B. *Yebamot* 12b, 100b; B. *Ketubbot* 39a; B. *Nedarim* 35a, 45b; B. *Niddah* 45a; T. *Nedarim* 2:6. The Hebrew participle *meshammeshot* simply means "practice," "use." It is given permissive force, "may use," by Rashi (on B. *Yebamot* 100b) and compulsive force, "must use," by Rabbenu Jacob Tam (*Tosafot* on B. *Ketubbot* 39a), Asheri, and Rabbenu Nissim (on *Nedarim* 35b). Both interpretations are grammatically sound.
7. For a discussion of the obviously strained meaning assigned to the passage in the desire to limit

its application, see R. Gordis, *Love and Sex: A Modern Jewish Perspective* (New York, 1978), chap. 8, esp. Note 12.

8. It is also omitted in the *Sefer Mitzvot Gadol, Tur, Beth Josef*, and several lesser codes.

9. See *Shulhan Arukh, Orah Hayyim* 282, 3.

10. He bases his comment on earlier authorities, Rabbi Isaac ben Sheshet and Rabenu Nissim.

11. See I. H. Weiss, *Dor Dor Vedorshav*, vol. 2, pp. 49–65.

12. This view of the career and activity of Rabban Johanan follows W. Bacher, *Die Haggadah der Tannaiten* I (Berlin, 1884–90), p. 74; and J. Dérenbourg, *Essai sur l'histoire et la géographie de la Palestine* (Paris, 1867), pp. 306ff. The mass of traditions recorded about Rabban Johanan ben Zakkai have been subjected to a radical critique by J. Neusner, *Development of a Legend: Studies in the Traditions Concerning Johanan ben Zakkai* (Leiden, 1970). The Israeli historian G. Alon has offered a revisionist interpretation of Rabban Johanan's ideas and activities in *The Jews and Their Land in the Talmudic Age*, edited and translated by Gershon Levi (Jerusalem, 1984), vol. 1, pp. 86–118. His view was criticized by E. Urbach, "Class Status and Leadership in the World of Palestinian Sages," *Proceedings of the Israel Academy of Sciences and Humanities*, 1966.

I find both the revisionist views and those opposed to them not much removed from those of Bacher and Dérenbourg. Alon points out that Rabban Johanan was not a member of the extreme anti-Roman party during the rebellion against Rome and was thus *persona grata* to the Romans. He believes that Rabban Johanan "did not ask for Jabneh and its sages" but was sent by the Romans to this half-gentile village during the hostilities. Alon makes the reasonable suggestion that Johanan's act was disapproved of by some members of the Jewish community, especially by the priests and the scholars, who saw his departure from Jerusalem as a desertion of the Holy City during its final agonies.

Alon suggests further that the priests' hostility to Johanan evoked a negative attitude on his part toward their desire for authority; and that there were scholars who regarded his attempts to give Jabneh a central position an unwarranted assertion of authority. These views seem very plausible.

13. See Alexander Guttmann, "Participation of the Common People in Pharisaic and Rabbinic Legislative Processes," in *Jewish Law Association Studies* I (Touro Conference Volume), edited by B. S. Jackson (Chico, CA, 1985), pp. 41–52.

14. Ibid., pp. 42–43.

15. As, e.g., B. *Baba Kamma* 79b; B. *Baba Batra* 60b; P. *Shebiᶜit* 4:2 (35b).

16. A comprehensive survey of the Karaites is presented by the leading contemporary authority on the subject, Leon Nemoy, in *Encyclopedia Judaica*, vol. 10, col. 761–85. It registers the progress in research on Karaism in this century since Abraham Harkavy's classic article in *Jewish Encyclopedia*, vol. VII, pp. 438a–446b (with an addendum by K. Kohler). See Leon Nemoy, *Karaite Anthology* (New Haven, 1952), for a selection of Karaite literature. A socioeconomic interpretation of the sect is given by R. Mahler, *Haqaraim* (Jerusalem, 1949).

17. The saying is quoted by Rabbi Ben-Zion Uziel, a former Sephardic Chief Rabbi of Israel, in *Mishpetei Uziel, Even Haᶜezer* (Jerusalem, 1964), pp. 431–32. He declares, "Whenever the original form and intent of a *minhag* is changed, it changes into the gates of Gehinnom."

27

Engendering Judaism

RACHEL ADLER

For most of Jewish history, the lives of Jewish women have been controlled by a legal system whose categories and concerns they have not helped to shape and from whose authority structure they have been excluded. The rulings of classical Jewish law, halakhah, made women a subordinate group within Judaism. One of the first understandings of modern feminist Jewish theology was that it must delineate a feminist perspective from which to confront halakhah. Some scholars proposed ways to fix halakhah, alleviating its worst injustices toward women.[1] Others saw it as unfixable, an intrinsically oppressive structure.[2] The only attempt that has not yet been made is to exercise our own covenantal authority to redefine and refashion halakhah fundamentally so that contemporary Jewish women and men can live it out with integrity.[3] Yet, if we define halakhah not as a closed system of obsolete and unjust rules, but as a way for communities of Jews to generate and embody their Jewish moral visions, that is exactly what we would do.

Halakhah comes from the root HLKh, to walk or to go. Halakhah is the act of going forward, of making one's way. A halakhah, a path-making, translates the stories and values of Judaism into ongoing action. That makes it an integral component not merely of Orthodoxy, but of any kind of Judaism. Such a definition of halakhah breaks the traditionalist monopoly on the word halakhah but risks some confusion about which system and ground rules I am discussing. In this chapter, therefore, I use the term "classical halakhah" when referring to the traditional system and "a halakhah" when hypothesizing about potential legal systems through which Judaism could be lived out.

Rachel Adler, "Here Comes Skotsl: Renewing Halakhah," in *Engendering Judaism* (Philadelphia: Jewish Publication Society, 1997), pp. 21–23, 34–41, 51–59. © Jewish Publication Society, Philadelphia, PA 19103.

Orienting Ourselves Through Stories

In this chapter, I would like to point us toward a potential halakhah. To determine where we ought to go, we must reflect on where we have been. We do this best by storytelling. As individuals, we continually rework and relate our life stories to ourselves and to others and project ourselves into possible futures through dreams and fantasies. We also lay claim as members of groups to the collective memories of the group. Transmitted from generation to generation, they help to constitute our sense of who we are and to shape our future actions.[4] The ethicist Alasdair MacIntyre says, "I can only answer the question, 'What am I to do?' if I can answer the prior question, 'Of what story or stories do I find myself a part?' "[5] Commitments emerge out of stories and are refashioned in stories.[6] I would like to begin, then, by retelling a Yiddish folktale in which some women act upon their dissatisfaction with halakhah in the version of the Jewish story they inhabit.[7]

Here Comes Skotsl

> Once upon a time, women began to resent that men seemed to own the world. Men got to read from the Torah and had all the interesting mitzvot and all the privileges. The women decided to present their grievance directly to God. They appointed Skotsl, a clever woman and a good speaker, as their representative. But how was the messenger to be dispatched? They decided to make a human tower. Skotsl was to scale the tower and then pull herself into heaven.
>
> They scrambled up on one another's shoulders, and Skotsl began to climb. But somebody shrugged or shifted, and women tumbled every which way. When the commotion died down, Skotsl had disappeared. Men went on ruling the world, and nothing changed. But still, the women are hopeful, and that is why, when a woman walks into a house, the other women say, "Look, here comes Skotsl." And someday, it might really be she.

"Here Comes Skotsl" plays ironically upon several traditional motifs, but I am going to read it specifically as a story about women's relationship with the law. In this story, women reject the halakhah as it stands and search for a way to recreate it. The ironies in the story reflect both the inadequacies of the tradition for addressing women as participants and the women's own feelings of inadequacy in confronting the law and its guardians.

The name Skotsl reflects these ambivalences. The ironic greeting *skotsl kumt* is reserved for women.[8] People roll their eyes and mutter "*skotsl kumt*" when a kvetch or a gossip arrives. But is the joke in this tale on the kvetches or on the tradition that gave them something to kvetch about? In the upside-down world of the story, the loquacity that makes "Skotsl" a social disaster marks her as leadership material, in fact, as a prospective savior. Traditionally, heaven promises earth a messiah, because, from the divine point of view, the world has a problem, but in this story the messiah is dispatched from earth to heaven because the divine point of view *is* the problem.

The storyteller slyly implies that it will be easier to climb into heaven and talk to God than to try to get a hearing from the tradition's human representatives. Hence, the rebels decide to negotiate with the Boss. To reach the inaccessible top of The authority structure, they construct themselves into a parody of the tower of Babel. The tower, like its prototype, topples in confusion, but the builders remain optimistic. The story is left open-ended, awaiting Skotsl's return.

The World That Was

The world Skotsl departed is now dead. Enlightenment thought, prizing objectivity, rationality, and universalism, estranged thinking Jews from their tradition and attenuated their links with the sacred stories that shape Jewish identity. Emancipation dismantled the Jewish community as a corporate sociopolitical entity. The Holocaust delivered the coup de grâce to the remnants of shtetl culture. The Judaism in which Skotsl and her peers sought new standing is itself a lot less steady on its legs.

What is supposed to happen when Skotsl comes? Will Jewish women simply obtain what Jewish men have? Or will the mitzvot we do and the Torah we learn be themselves transformed when women become fully visible and fully audible in Judaism? In non-Orthodox Judaisms, women have been given equal access, at least theoretically. But equal access to what? If Skotsl came today, she would confront fragmented Jewish communities in which only the merest threads of a communal praxis have survived. The Jewish discourse in which God and God's law really matter has become difficult and unconvincing, Arnold Eisen suggests, because of "the loss of sustaining experiences" that would give these words referents in a lived reality.[9] Will Skotsl arrive just in time to endow Jewish women with one-half of nothing?

Modernity has punched holes in the thought and practice of Judaism, and its practitioners have had to improvise to stanch the resultant hemorrhage of Jewish meaning. The effectiveness of these improvisations varies. Some relieve and restore us while others compound our unease. It is this discomfort that fertilizes Jewish theology. The more seriously Jews think about their Judaisms, the more likely they are to find them wanting. If Skotsl came today she might be astonished to discover that it is *men's* dissatisfactions with Judaism that dominate the field known as "modern Jewish thought." The problems Judaism presents for and about women are all too frequently ghettoized as "women's issues" and exiled from general discussion.[10]

One of the major philosophical projects of Jewish feminism has been to relocate Skotsl's problem within the context of pervasive modern Jewish discomfort. What the Yiddish folktale poses as a "women's problem" feminist theologians reframe as *the* paradigmatic Jewish problem, the exemplar par excellence that exposes the failures of all the branches and varieties of Judaism to engender a Jewish tradition for modernity.[11] The problem of Jewish women calls into question the operation of all the processes by which Judaism is reinterpreted and renewed.

Engendering Judaism

There is a double sense in which one can say that Judaism needs to be engendered. Progressive Jews understand Judaism as an evolving system, constantly reshaped and renewed through its relations with its changing historical contexts. Consequently, they would agree that a truly progressive Judaism must be one that consciously and continuously reengenders itself. In the second sense, however, Judaism has hardly begun to be engendered.

The progressive branches of Judaism have hardly begun to reflect and to address the questions, understandings, and obligations of both Jewish women and Jewish men. They are not yet fully attentive to the impact of gender on the texts and lived experiences of the people Israel. Until progressive Judaisms engender themselves in this second sense, they cannot engender adequate Judaisms in the first sense. That attempt has already been made, and it has failed.

Riv-Ellen Prell, an anthropologist of religion, describes how classical Reformers used the universalist, Enlightenment model of their host culture to eradicate the special status assigned women in Orthodoxy.[12] Because "all men are created equal," Reform Judaism included women by categorizing them as "honorary men." But making women honorary men made them deviant men. It required viewing their differences from men as defects in their masculinity. As Prell demonstrates, this definition of equality not only hid discrimination that blocked women's full participation: it barred women from articulating experiences and concerns that men did not share. To enforce equality, it abolished the few women's mitzvot prescribed by Orthodoxy, making women even less visible than before. The experience of classical Reform illustrates a defect that feminist legal critiques have identified in the universalist understanding of equality. An equality predicated on ignoring the differences that constitute distinctive selves both conceals and legitimates injustice.[13] An institution or enterprise is fully inclusive only if it includes people as the kind of people they really are.

Legal and philosophical critiques, not only by feminists, but by communitarians, both progressive and conservative, civil libertarians, and poststructuralists of every sort, ask us to reevaluate the Enlightenment universalist values of equality, autonomy, rights, and justice, values in which progressive Judaisms have invested heavily. These critiques suggest that universalist values that fail to recognize crucial differences among people create inadequate understandings of what it means to be human and, consequently, make poor guides for how human beings may live in community.[14]

When we reassess the impact of these values on modern Judaism, Skotsl's problem emerges as the prime indicator of a larger problem caused by inadequacies in the very modernity progressive Judaisms embraced so fervently. The problem of Jewish women, then, cannot be ghettoized so that women can discuss and solve "their" problem unilaterally. As a key to the problems of modern Judaisms themselves, this issue affects all of us, women and men. Engendering Judaism, like other kinds of human engendering, requires women and men to act cooperatively.

If Judaism cannot be engendered without solving the problem of women, it is equally true that it cannot be engendered without solving the problem of halakhah. Without a means through which the stories and the values of Judaism can be embodied in communal praxis, how are they to be sustained by experiences? Values and stories are empty and meaningless if we lack ways to act upon them. Without concrete, sensuous, substantial experiences that bind us to live out our Judaisms together, there is nothing real to engender.

The difficulty about proposing a halakhah to progressive Jews is their presumption that the term, its definition, and its practice belong to Orthodoxy. We urgently need to reclaim this term because it is the authentic Jewish language for articulating the system of obligations that constitute the content of the covenant.

Halakhah belongs to liberal Jews no less than to Orthodox Jews because the stories of Judaism belong to us all. A halakhah is a communal praxis grounded in Jewish stories.[15]

Ethicists, theologians, and lawyers who stress the centrality of narrative would argue that all normative systems rest upon stories. Whether the story is the Exodus from Egypt or the crucifixion and resurrection of Jesus or the forging of American independence, if we claim it as our own, we commit ourselves to be the kind of people that story demands, to translate its norms and values into a living praxis.[16]

A praxis is more than the sum of the various practices that constitute it. *A praxis is a holistic embodiment in action at a particular time of the values and commitments inherent to a particular story.*[17] Orthodoxy cannot have a monopoly on halakhah, because no form of Judaism can endure without one; there would be no way to live it out.

What happened to Judaism in modernity was that its praxis became both impoverished and fragmented. Some communal practices were taken over by the secular state. Other practices were jettisoned by congregations because they appeared foreign and "Oriental."[18] Still others were abandoned by individuals because they had come to see themselves as "private citizens" with minimal obligations to other private citizens. It became impossible to imagine a unified way to live as a human being, a citizen, and a Jew.

A contemporary Jewish praxis would reduce our sense of fragmentation. If we had a praxis rather than a grab bag of practices, we would experience making love, making *kiddush,* recycling paper used at our workplace, cooking a pot of soup for a person with AIDS, dancing at a wedding, and making medical treatment decisions for a dying loved one as integrated parts of the same project: the holy transformation of our everyday reality. Furthermore, we would experience ourselves less as fragmented enactors of divergent roles in disparate spheres—public/private, ritual/ethical, religious/secular, duty/pleasure— and more as coherent Jewish personalities.

We cannot simply resurrect the old premodern praxis, because it no longer fits us in the world we now inhabit. Some of its elements are fundamentally incompatible with participation in postindustrial, democratic societies.[19] The old praxis can be preserved intact only if we schizophrenically split off our religious lives from our secular lives and live two separate existences with two different sets of values and commitments. But the obligation to be truthful and the yearning to be whole are what made us progressive Jews in the first place. To be faithful to the covenant requires that we infuse the whole of our existence with our religious commitments. How is that to be done in our specific situation?

The secular values of equal respect, inclusivity, diversity, and pluralism obligate citizens to recognize and protect one another's integrity and well-being. Jews have obvious cause to espouse these values. At the same time, classical halakhah is committed to the subordination and exclusion of women in communal life. The inability of classical halakhah to resolve this dissonance is the paradigmatic example of its inadequacy as a praxis for Jews in modernity and leads inexorably toward challenges from Skotsl's modern incarnations.

What Authority? Whose Halakhah?

Yet, as its proponents are quick to acknowledge, the formulation of a progressive halakhah presents complex difficulties. What are to be its sources? What is its authority? For fundamentalist Orthodoxy, halakhah originates in the Written Law of the Pentateuch and in the Oral Law preserved in the Talmud. Both are believed to have been communicated directly by God to Moses. Both are regarded as infallible and immutable. All subsequent halakhic developments, such as codes and responsa, are viewed as implicit in these divine revelations. It is not that the law does not change in different situations, but that the change has already been decreed in a single atemporal revelatory event. "Whatever a disciple of the wise may propound by way of explaining a law in the most distant future was already revealed to Moses on Mount Sinai."[20]

The crucial difference between traditional halakhists and modernists is that modernists accept the premises of modern historiography: that societies are human constructions that exist in time and change over time, that ideas and institutions inhabit specific historical and cultural contexts, and that they cannot be adequately understood without reference to context.[21] These premises are incompatible with the belief that halakhah was divinely revealed in a single event and reflects an eternal and immutable divine will. Rejecting the supernatural account of halakhah in favor of historical and naturalistic explanations raises fundamental theological questions about the place of halakhah in Judaism. If halakhah evolved historically and reflects the cultures through which it passed, then what makes it holy? Why should it be obeyed? And what makes its rules and categories appropriate for contexts so different from those for which they were formulated?

When the response to these questions is to discard halakhah entirely, the ability of individuals and communities to live out their Judaism is dealt a crippling blow. The early history of Reform Judaism is a testimonial to how quickly and how devastatingly the deconstruction of halakhah can disembody everyday Judaism. Painfully conscious of the vulnerability of a halakhah unfortified by traditional absolutes, liberal halakhists are understandably protective of their fragile enterprise and apprehensive of the withering force of the theological questions raised by their own premises.[22] Rather than facing these questions head-on, then, liberal halakhists tend to evade or disarm them through formalist or positivist legal strategies. These strategies make it impossible for the core questions of feminist critique to be articulated. By translating the critique into terms classical halakhah has in its conceptual vocabulary, liberal halakhists distort the questions. The system's own terms and categories are taken as a given. The feminist critique of them is restated as "women's desire for equal access or equal obligation" and pasted onto a basically intact halakhic system, like a Band-Aid covering a superficial cut.

The Feminist Critique of Halakhah

The problems actually raised in the feminist critique, however, are *systemic* wounds too deep for liberal Band-Aids. As one of the originators of this critique, I have contended that members of a Jewish male elite constructed the categories and method of classical halakhah to reflect their own perspectives and social goals and have held a monopoly on their application.[23] Borrowing a term from the post-Christian theologian Mary Daly, I have called classical halakhah a methodolatrous system.[24] The method becomes a kind of false god. It determines the choice of questions, rather than the questions determining the choice of method. Questions that do not conform to the system's method and categories are simply reclassified as non-data and dumped out.

Jacob Neusner shows how, in Mishnah, one of the foundational documents of classical halakhah, the presumptions regarding the status and function of women determine the selection principles.[25] What is important to the framers of the Mishnah about women is the orderly transfer of women and property from one patriarchal domain to another.[26]

As Judith Wegner demonstrates, women's sexuality is a legal commodity, and, in cases where it is at issue, women are treated not as persons but as chattel.[27] Moreover, women are themselves ineligible to be normative members of the community. Their role is to be "a focus of the sacred" rather than to be active participants in the processes of sanctification.[28] Halakhic data about women favors those questions about women that are of interest to the rabbinic elite. Hence, there is much information on questions of marital status, women's tasks and obligations vis-à-vis husbands and fathers, the disposition of property women brought into marriage or subsequently acquired. Regarding women's activity in the masculine realms of Torah study, juridical activity, and public prayer, however, the Talmud's characteristic question is "How do we know that they are excluded?"[29]

The presumptions select the questions. The categories shape them. Adjudication creates precedents that reinforce the form future questions must take. By this means, Torah, Mishnah, Gemara, codes, and responsa amass huge bodies of data on their favored topics, whereas other issues are condemned to haunt the outer darkness. Hence, when women advance topics that do not affect preestablished legal concerns, the system either rejects them because it has no information on them or attempts to restate them in distortive androcentric terms that would allow it to apply its own categories and advance its own goals. At worst, it attempts to limit discourse to the topics on which it has the most information: the status problems of marriage, divorce, and desertion, and the participation problems of witnessing, judging, and liturgical performance—problems the system and its presumptions created.

The critique I have outlined here is not confined to Orthodox legal processes. Indeed, its implications are far more powerful for non-Orthodox revisions of halakhah because it suggests that liberal halakhists have failed to pursue the implications of their positions. If the source-texts of halakhah are not timeless or absolute but shaped within social contexts, if its categories must exclude much of our gendered modern life experiences as nondata, and if its authority structure is neither democratic nor inclusive, then adapting its content to modernity is an inadequate solution. To argue that the system requires no systemic critique, a liberal halakhist must ignore or discount that halakhic rules, categories, and precedents were constructed and applied without the participation of women, that they reflect perceptions of women as a commodified subclass, and that they are often inadequate or inimical to concerns that women themselves possibly would raise if they were legal subjects rather than legal objects.[30]

Liberal halakhah, then, requires a separate critique to illuminate how it has attempted to adjust halakhah to modernity while evading more searching questions about its authority and structure. The two philosophies of jurisprudence liberal halakhists have adopted as theoretical grounding for this project are legal formalism and legal realism.

Legal formalism asserts that what is definitive about law is its form. A legal outcome is valid if the system's rules and categories are correctly applied. Because the rules and categories that constitute the law's form are taken as givens about which there can be no argument, a formalist approach makes an end-run around questions about the sociohistorical contexts these forms may reflect. The only possible arguments concern whether the formal applications are valid or invalid. Although legal formalism can result in extremely repressive decision making, it can also open up tremendous freedom for new and ingenious applications of legal categories, because any application, however unprecedented, can be proposed, as long as it is formally defensible.

Legal realism, a theory of jurisprudence influential during the first half of the twentieth century, maintains that law is determined not by the language of legal texts and enactments but rather by the discretionary power of judges. This power, the legal realists have argued, is appropriately employed to shape social policy. The judge's decisions are "realistic" because they adapt the law to address social realities. The problem with legal realism is its tendency to reinforce the power of the already powerful. If the wording or intent of legal texts or the existence of legal precedents does not present curbs or boundaries for judicial decisions, the discretionary power of judges will be unrestrained. Given that decisors are chosen by the dominant group, who is likely to be selected to wield power, and whose social investments do such persons protect?[31]

Versions of liberal halakhah attempt to synthesize these apparently antithetical theories, one radically atemporal and the other radically context-dependent, because both are essential to the liberal project. What the theories have in common is that each offers a means of overriding the component of jurisprudence that is most resistant to change: the power of precedent.[32] In tandem, the two theories serve to authorize and to derive changes that run counter to all legal precedent. Legal realism allows the decisor to predetermine the outcomes he or she deems most appropriate to the time and place. Legal formalism provides the means to validate those outcomes as long as the categories are tenably applied.

Each theory supplements some lack in the other. Legal formalism has no intrinsic impetus toward legal change. As long as legal outcomes are formally valid, it is satisfied. Legal realism is predicated upon the necessity that law continually adjust to changing social contexts, but lacks any formal criteria for validity. Its sole criterion, the discretion of the individual judge, is nakedly subjective and potentially unlimited. The combination of the two maximizes the impetus for legal change while specifying and objectifying the criteria by which change is justified.[33] In this way, the contextualized power of the decisor is reinforced with the atemporal validity of the system's formal reasoning process.

A Feminist's Gallery of Liberal Halakhists

Both for formalism and for legal realism, an ultimate question remains. What is the source of their authority? In the case of legal formalism, what claim has halakhah's formal structure upon our obedience? The only liberal halakhist for whom the question presents no problem is Eliezer Berkovits, whose legal liberalism is undergirded by an Orthodox theology affirming the Torah as the revealed word of God.[34] This theology does not lead to legal fundamentalism for Berkovits, however. Implicit within Torah, according to Berkovits, is a set of ethical values that did not have to be divinely revealed. They are independently knowable through divinely endowed human reason and human social experience. These values ought to guide the interpretation of texts and the application of formal halakhic mechanisms.[35]

Louis Jacobs, the theorist who emphasizes most heavily the role of historical context in shaping Jewish law, forthrightly acknowledges the liberal problem.[36] If the Torah is an historically evolved composite document and not a verbatim record of what God told Moses on Mount Sinai, what obligates Jews to obey, and how are they to sort out what they are to do? "The ultimate authority for determining which practices are binding upon the faithful Jew," Jacobs declares, "is the historical experience of the people Israel."[37]

However, Jacobs rejects as "ancestor worship" the Kaplanian answer that the people Israel itself is the source of commandment.[38] He would maintain that the will of a transcendent Deity is revealed in the historical adaptations of the halakhah. This view is a variant of the Progressive Jewish doctrine of "continuing revelation." In Jacobs' account, halakhah's evolution, its creativity in adapting to historical context, is a history of progress.

This approach has certain pitfalls. It tends to underemphasize the extent to which the struggles of rival factions for dominance and power determine the establishment or suppression of halakhic positions, nor does it take into consideration that the evolution of halakhah may not correspond to what we think of as progress. A diligent historian can unearth any number of embarrassing and objectionable developments in the various stages of halakhah. For example, S. M. Passamaneck traces a trend in medieval halakhah not merely to arrest on reasonable cause but to punish, even by flogging, on reasonable cause without conclusive proof of guilt.[39]

Another great danger in the doctrine of revelation through history is that history itself will be sacralized. If we made history its own ethical arbiter, injustices of the past, like slavery or the subordination of women, could not be condemned, because within their historical contexts, they were not viewed as wrong. At its most conservative, sacralizing history begets a kind of moral conventionalism that makes moral initiative superfluous, because, "whatever is, is right."[40] Attributing change to the invisible hand of history would relieve us of responsibility for consciously and reflectively shaping the future of Judaism. We could simply wait for history to drag us in its wake. Conventionalism is a perversion of the doctrine of revelation through history, but it suggests a cautionary lesson: God may speak to us through history, but what God is saying may be less than obvious.

One way to sidestep the challenge of history to the authority of halakhah is to make the system formally self-sufficient. The Conservative halakhist Joel Roth borrows from secular legal formalism the concept of a *grundnorm*, a presumption that grounds the legal system proceeding from it.[41] Roth offers two versions of this *grundnorm*.

> The document called the Torah embodies the word and will of God, which it behooves man to obey, as mediated through the agency of J E, P, and D, and is, therefore, authoritative. An alternative possible formulation might be: The document called the Torah embodies the constitution promulgated by J, E, P, and D, which it behooves man to obey, and is therefore authoritative.[42]

Theoretically, the *grundnorm* could justify all of classical halakhah's exclusions and subjugations of women, but Roth employs it instead in attempting to remedy inequities. Roth takes the authority invested in the *grundnorm* and confers it upon the halakhic principle *ein lo ladayyan ella mah she-einav ro'ot*, "a judge can only rely on what his own eyes see." Judicial discretion becomes the fundamental means by which halakhic inequities toward women are to be amended.[43] Obligations from which they were previously excluded could be conferred upon women, and their disadvantages in marriage and divorce law alleviated. Judicial discretion, in other words, could enable halakhic authorities to redefine women as honorary men.[44]

The *grundnorm* is not an unmixed blessing for feminists. It poses uncomfortable theological problems. Do the passages concerning the trial by ordeal of the suspected adulteress or the characterization of homosexuality as an abomination and a capital crime really embody the word and will of God? Alternatively, if we leave God out of it and attribute the documents solely to J, E, P, and D, we are still left with texts whose androcentrism and patriarchal bias disadvantage and peripheralize one-half of the people Israel. What makes J, E, P, and D deserving of our unconditional obedience?

Moreover, what is the *grundnorm* for? Does it have any behavioral consequences of its own, or does it merely legitimate the judicial discretion that really drives the system? "As the sole normative interpreters of the meaning of the Torah," Roth declares, "Torah means whatever the rabbis say it means."[45] As David Ellenson points out, "Given the principle of [judicial discretion] and the assent to the *grundnorm* . . . it is almost logically impossible to imagine what might be an infringement of principle in the halakhic system."[46] If judges can remake the law at will, the *grundnorm* is legally irrelevant.

Leaving aside the question of how such unrestricted authority could be ethically justified, what would qualify a decisor to wield it? In Roth's adaptation of traditional criteria, the prerequisites would be a rabbinic education and ordination and a theological loyalty oath affirming the divine origin of the *grundnorm* and the authority of the sages as its sole, legitimate interpreters.[47] In other words, those who currently hold a monopoly on the halakhic process would also monopolize both the admission process and the interpretive process. Adherence to Roth's *grundnorm* would preclude a metacritique of the halakhic system. Formulating such a critique would automatically disqualify an entrant. Critique from outside the ranks is illegitimate by definition and can be ignored, since only the rabbis are legitimate interpreters. Skotsl and her peers would be immediately escorted to the door.

Halakhic authority, as Roth envisions it, is a closed system with benevolent intentions. Hence, women rabbis could also become authorities—as long as they committed themselves not only to the traditional halakhic process but to the stipulated theological underpinnings. These would implicitly require women rabbis to reject the feminist critique and to sign on as honorary men. In the absence of the feminist critique, however, there would be no reason to engender new halakhah addressing women's distinctive experiences, much less any conceptual vocabulary to articulate such concerns.

Redefining the Game: Toward A Proactive Halakhah

The presumption liberal halakhists share is that modern halakhah must be a version of traditional halakhah adapted for a modern context by bringing formalist or positivist legal strategies to bear upon traditional texts. Decision making would remain in the hands of a rabbinical elite whose prescriptions are to be handed down to hypothetically obedient communities. The goal of liberal halakhah is to repair inadequacies of classical halakhah exposed by modernity while leaving the system basically intact.

Liberal halakhah believes itself to be modern because it is reactive to classical halakhah. To be truly progressive, however, a halakhah would have to be *proactive*. The place to begin is not with the principles we need to preserve or the content we may need to adapt but with what we mean by halakhah altogether. An understanding of law that lends itself to such a project can be found in the work of an American legal theorist, Robert Cover. Using Cover's understanding of what is meant by law, it is possible to explain how the feminist project qualifies as a lawmaking enterprise. Cover's account of the constitution and transformation of legal meanings could provide sufficient common ground to enable representatives of classical and liberal versions of halakhah and their feminist critics to enter into conversation. It offers a basis upon which feminist hermeneutics, praxis, and commitments can make defensible claims to authenticity.

Law is not reducible to formal lawmaking, Cover maintains, because it is generated by a *nomos*, a universe of meanings, values, and rules, embedded in stories. A *nomos* is not a body of data to master and adapt, but a world to inhabit. Knowing how to live in a nomic world means being able to envision the possibilities implicit in its stories and norms and being willing to live some of them out in praxis.[48]

Cover characterizes the genesis and the maintenance of law as two distinct elements in legal development. He calls these the *paidaic* or worldcreating mode and the *imperial* or world-maintaining mode. Paidaic activity effects *jurisgenesis*, the creation of a *nomos*, a universe of meaning, out of a shared body of precepts and narratives that individuals in community commit themselves to learn and to interpret. This generative mode is unstable and impermanent, but without its creative and revitalizing force, societies could not sustain the sense of meaning and shared purpose essential to social survival.

The paidaic mode can create worlds, but it cannot maintain them. Inevitably, the single unified vision that all social actors share in a paidaic period splinters into multiple nomic worlds holding differing interpretations. To coordinate and maintain these diverse worlds within a coexistent whole, there is a need to enforce standard social practices among them. The imperial mode universalizes the norms created by jurisgenesis and empowers institutions to reinforce them by coercion, if necessary. However, institutionalization and coercion are not the only means by which the imperial mode maintains the stability of law. Because the imperial world view does not strive for unanimity, but harmonious coordination of its differing parts, it can admit as an adaptive mechanism some tolerance for pluralism, a value foreign to the paidaic ethos.[49] Cover imagines these two legal moments, the paidaic and the imperial, coexisting in dynamic equilibrium.

Our modern problem with halakhah is reflected in the failure of this equilibrium, in the unmediated gap between the impoverished imperial world we inhabit and the richer and more vital worlds that could be. It is into this "paidaic vacuum" that Skotsl and her mission vanished. By means of feminist jurisgenesis, we can bridge that gap and regenerate a *nomos*, a world of legal meaning in which the stories, dreams and revelations of Jewish women and men are fully and complexly integrated.

Cover offers the image of the bridge to express the dynamism of the meaning-making component that both constitutes and propels law. Law-as-bridge is a tension system strung between "reality," our present world of norms and behavioral responses to norms, and "alternity," the other normative worlds we may choose to imagine. In other words, the bridge is what connects maintenance-law to jurisgenerative potentiality. Law is neither reality nor alternity but what bridges the gap between them: "the committed social behavior which constitutes the way a group of people will attempt to get from here to there."[50] Ultimately, law is maintained or remade not by orthodoxies or visions but by commitments of communities either to obey the law as it stands or to resist and reject it in order to live out some alternative legal vision.

Cover's image of the bridge built of committed praxis grounded in story reinforces the necessity of a halakhah, for only by means of halakhah can Judaism embody its sacred stories and values in communal praxis. At the same time, Cover's bridge image makes it possible to think freshly about halakhah, because it counters precisely those features that progressive Jews, and progressive feminists in particular, find repressive in halakhah's traditional formulations. It is dynamic rather than static, visionary rather than conservative, open to the outside rather than closed, arising communally, cooperatively, covenantally, rather than being externally imposed and passively obeyed. The metaphor of the bridge also expresses what it is like to inhabit a modern *nomos*. Bridges are generally open rather than enclosed. They span gaps and connect disparate entities, functions that reflect the needs of open, democratic societies populated by diverse groups of highly individuated modern selves.[51]

I have said that Cover's image of law as a bridge offers progressive Jews a representation of halakhah harmonious with their dynamic understanding of Judaism. Now juxtapose to Cover's image the classic metaphor of protective confinement that R. Hiyyah bar Abba attributes to his teacher Ulla: "From the time that the Temple was destroyed, the Holy One has had nothing in His world but the four cubits of the halakhah" (B. Berakhot 8a). This metaphor eloquently expresses the constriction of God's earthly holdings from the grandeur of the Temple to this austere and narrow cell that is both prison and refuge.

The walls of the Diaspora cubicle are, at the same time, externally imposed barriers and internally established boundaries protecting it from engulfment by rival systems of meaning. The metaphor recalls Peter Berger's description of how structures of religious meaning in premodern times made sense of the world and fought off the chaotic emptiness of unmediated reality. Berger depicts these constructed universes of meaning as rickety, jerry-built fortresses reinforced by "plausibility structures" whose function is to wall out the howling wilderness of meaninglessness all around.[52] The metaphor of the cube is static as well as closed. It lacks a means of extending itself toward alternity.

Like Cover's bridge builders, Skotsl and her cohorts also build toward an envisioned alternity: a way out of halakhah-as-cube. But the only way they can imagine effecting change is vertically, rather than horizontally. They offer themselves as a ladder so that one gifted individual may climb outside the human realm to request a recreated Torah from the very top of the hierarchy and bring it back down to the bottom. Implicit in this image is the women's assumption of their profound powerlessness to grasp, appropriate, and refashion the law. Their sense of impotence and subjugation is reminiscent of Kafka's parable "The Problem of Our Laws":

> Our laws are not generally known; they are kept secret by the small group of nobles who rule us. We are convinced that these ancient laws are scrupulously administered; nevertheless, it is an extremely painful thing to be ruled by laws that one does not know. I am not thinking of possible discrepancies that may arise in the interpretation of the laws, or of the disadvantages involved when only a few and not the whole people are allowed to have a say in their interpretation. These disadvantages are perhaps of no great importance. For the laws are very ancient . . . and though there is still a possible freedom of interpretation left, it has now become very restricted. Moreover, the nobles have obviously no cause to be influenced in their interpretation by personal interests inimical to us, for the laws were made to the advantage of the nobles from the very beginning, they themselves stand above the laws, and that seems to be why the laws were entrusted exclusively into their hands.[53]

Like Kafka's narrator, the women in the folktale perceive authority as remote and inaccessible. Rather than seeing themselves as sharers in the covenantal authority through which the people Israel translate the Torah into communal praxis, they are so desperately estranged from the sources of justice that they attempt a feat Scripture has already declared unnecessary:

It is not in the heavens, that you should say, "Who among us can go up to the heavens and get it for us and impart it to us, so that we may observe it? . . . No, the thing is very close to you in your mouth and in your heart to observe it" (Deut. 30:12,14).[54]

Because the Torah is no longer in heaven, mistakes cannot be rectified by building a tower from history into eternity. Instead, we must discover within ourselves the competence and good faith through which to repair and renew the Torah within time. We must *extend* Torah as we extend ourselves by reaching ahead. The aptest metaphor for that constructive task is that of the bridge we build from the present to possible futures.

Down to Work: The Tools for Bridge Building

A bridge needs to be built, and Jewish women and men will have to build it together. The task requires us to look afresh at our sacred texts, at other revelatory stories about Jewish lives, and at the moral imperatives in our own lives that impel us to constitute a new interpretive community. What are the special resources feminists can contribute to building the bridge? What have we learned in articulating feminist questions and feminist methodologies that will transform the world of Jewish meaning?

One crucial contribution will be the methodologies feminists have developed for understanding and using narrative. Narrative will be central to any Jewish nomic project because Jewish tradition is itself a sedimentation of stories and stories about stories. But not all methods of interpreting and augmenting the stories of tradition include women, whether as readers, storytellers, or interpreters. Feminist scholars of law and philosophy have pioneered in using narrative both as a method of vision and as a tool of legal and philosophical critique.[55] As a method of vision, feminist narratives draw upon fantasies and desires, prophecies and prayers to imagine possible worlds in which both women and men could flourish. As a tool of critique, narrative can expose within abstract theories assumptions about the nature and experience of being human, what people know, how they live, what they want, and what they fear.

These assumptions inform the highly particular stories with which universalizing theories are pregnant. Bringing out the story within the abstraction allows us to see which human characteristics, experiences, desires, and fears a theory has chosen to address and how it has understood them. For example, as Seyla Benhabib points out, in the social contract theory of Thomas Hobbes, the denizens of the state of nature are adult males who have sprung up "like mushrooms." The story excises the primal experiences of dependency and nurturing, childhood and motherhood from its account of the human condition.[56] Once its story is exposed, a defective theory can be challenged with counternarratives embodying previously excluded experiences and perspectives.

A related tool feminists can bring to nomic bridge building is an awareness of the importance of context in evaluating human understandings, obligations, and intentions.[57] A foundational principle of all progressive feminisms is that women's roles are not biologically determined and unchanging.[58] They are consequences of social structures and social experiences that differ significantly from one time and place to another. Human lives and human understanding are shaped within contexts, but human beings also possess the ability to reshape and restructure those contexts. Because narratives testify so powerfully to the impact of context, they are capable of reflecting the context-bound nature of human existence more accurately than abstract theories that claim to express truths unrestricted by time and place.

Contexts narrow the range of possibilities in narratives and provide boundaries for both history and fiction. At the same time, because contexts are conditional rather than inevitable, there is always a possibility of bursting their boundaries, of breaking and remaking contexts. The mutability of contexts is related to the capacity for change in human beings themselves. Human beings in their contexts create the need and the potential for structural transformations.

Another characteristic of contexts that makes them important for the renewal of law is their particularity. Because law requires applying general categories to specific situations, it can be hostile to particularities, regarding them as irrelevant details that, if stripped away, would reveal the situation's conformance to an existing legal category. But some particularities are not irrelevant. They may be the features that give settings and situations their distinguishing character. Removing them from consideration may distort the meaning of a situation and lead to injustice. Injustice is even more apt to result if categories reflecting one group's understanding of which particularities are important are then imposed on differing groups. Feminist legal scholars are expanding the concept of legal relevance in American law by insisting that more richly particularized contexts with wider temporal boundaries be considered as evidence.[59]

Understanding people as legal subjects requires more than an understanding of contexts, however. We need richer language in which to describe human desires and human motivations. One source for this language is the conceptual vocabulary of modern psychological theory. Secular feminist jurisprudence has begun to explore its potential for providing richer and more complex accounts of motivation in legal stories.[60] Psychological theories can delineate the impact upon human development of gender, of kinship and other social relationships, and of the larger social environment and its possibilities. Psychological theories can account not only for rational human calculation but for what is irrational or arational in human beings. They can express ambivalences, ambiguities, and subtle gradations in states of mind. The ability of psychological theories to provide accounts of gendered human identity and action that are both deeply contextualized and deeply individualized renders them powerful and convincing as components of feminist analysis and critique. Jean Bethke Elshtain identifies this use of psychoanalytic language for feminist ends as a major desideratum of feminist discourse. She explains:

> The feminist ends I have in mind include the articulation of a philosophy of mind which replaces the old dualism with which we are still saddled in favor of an account which unites mind and body, reason and passion, into a compelling account of human subjectivity and identity, and the creation of a feminist theory of action that complicatedly invokes both inner and outer realities. A third feminist end to which psychoanalysis could [contribute] is the amplification of a theory of language as meaning . . . to articulate an interpretive story of female experience.[61]

The Jewish worlds we create, like all nomic worlds, will be shaped by our understanding of what is entailed in being human. The range of human possibilities depends upon the depth and complexity of this philosophical anthropology. What it means to be human in a world of meaning determines that world's conception of justice, for notions of justice are predicated upon understandings of the needs and duties of humankind, and particular visions of human flourishing. For the task of formulating an enriched Jewish conception of human nature, then, psychological language alone will not be adequate. New understandings of Jewish narratives and Jewish values will be needed.

With its profusion and variety of narratives, codes, and prophecies, Judaism has resources for subtle and multifaceted conceptions of human nature. However, the conceptions of human nature that predominate in Jewish thought, as in Western philosophy and law, are unitary. Feminist legal theorists and philosophers have shown how this conception of a single human nature is inadequate and distortive. It sets up as a norm one particular variant of male human nature from whom all others are regarded as deviant. Instead, human nature needs to be understood as a spectrum of meaningful human differences.

In addition, difference itself needs to be redefined as *variation*, rather than *deviation*. The constitutional scholar Martha Minow observes, "For both legal difference and difference in general, a difference 'discovered' is more aptly a statement of a relationship expressing one person's deviation from an unstated norm assumed by the other."[62] To remove the stigma from gender difference, we would have to identify unstated standards that assume that maleness is normative and replace them with norms that reflect gendered existences. Narratives of women's subjective experiences will be useful sources for such new norms. They can help to delineate experiences differing from men's or those not experienced by men at all.[63]

How can we make law reflect the human differences that condition people's choices and decisions without unfairly favoring particular differences? Minow argues that a single strategy for the legal treatment of difference is inadequate, because injustice can result either from noticing difference or from ignoring it.[64] Just as singling others out negatively constructs their difference as deviance, so does refusal to acknowledge and accommodate difference in a world tailored to the specifications of some groups and not others. Sometimes it is the recognition of difference and sometimes the refusal to recognize difference that enables people to be included in the larger community.

• • •

Talking Our Way In

We now find ourselves in the ironic position of having fought mightily to justify our attempts to converse with a tradition that has not, as yet, evinced a desire to converse with us. Like the women who built themselves into a human tower, having worked so hard to arrange the conversation, we now have to figure out how to begin it. What should Skotsl say when she pulls herself into heaven? Perhaps the folktale leaves her at the point when she is pulling herself in because that is the part of the story the storytellers cannot yet imagine. But if we are to extend the story, we will have to imagine it, and in order to do so we will once more draw upon the legal hermeneutics of Robert Cover. His advice to Skotsl would be to tell stories about law.

The task requires a skillful speaker, but it is by no means impossible. However primitive their attempts and however incomplete their story, Skotsl and her peers have a sense of legal purpose. Skotsl does not go up to heaven empty and helpless. She has been sent with a message. Implicit in the message is a different vision of what halakhah should be. If, as Cover contends, this implicit vision must be made explicit in narrative, then, ironically, Skotsl will have to do in heaven exactly what she would have had to do on earth: delineate and defend her vision by telling stories.

As the messiah dispatched from earth, she must bring revelations to heaven, disclosing stories unknown to the tradition, the stories of its female claimants. It is equally important, however, that Skotsl tell the tradition its own stories in a new way. The alternative tradition she presents must assert its authenticity by grounding itself in narratives the tradition believes it owns and understands. Out of the multipotentiality of those narratives, she must draw meanings that contest the tradition's legal meanings. She must make the law her accomplice in its own destabilization.

The subversive potential in law's foundational narratives renders it vulnerable at its root. "Every legal order," Cover observes, "must conceive of itself as emerging out of that which is itself unlawful."[65] An obvious example is the American legal system, which is grounded in a colonial rebellion against the authority of the British crown. The narratives of transgression upon which legal systems are founded, Cover argues, remain potentially lawless because they are precedents both for law and for the transgression of law. Consequently, there is always the threat that they may burst their restraints and challenge the very systems they authorize.[66] A feminist could note how many of these foundational transgressions are violations of patriarchal sexual boundaries. Tamar tricks her father-in-law Judah to free herself from a levirate limbo. David's son born from his tainted relationship with Bathsheba is his chosen heir. Hosea's God, violating all legal precedent, promises to reconcile with His promiscuous mate. A Skotsl challenging traditional halakhah's attitudes regarding sexuality and relationship could argue that its code, applied to the narratives that ground it, would delegitimate the people Israel and abrogate their covenant.

Even without reference to foundational stories, law can be made to abet its own critique, Cover argues, because its dependence upon narrative as a component inherently divides law against itself. The alliance binding legal precepts designed to control to uncontrollable narratives upon which their legitimation depends is inherently unstable:

> There is a radical dichotomy between the social organization of law as power and the organization of law as meaning. . . . The uncontrolled character of meaning exercises a destabilizing influence upon power. Precepts must "have meaning," but they must necessarily borrow it from materials created by social activity that is not subject to the strictures of provenance that characterize what we call formal lawmaking.[67]

Raw coercion is insufficient to authorize law. It must claim legitimating moral qualities, which it locates in its constitutive narratives. But narratives are generated within the bounds of space, time, and culture. Their resonances echo within these social contexts, always unstable, always open to the possibility of transformation.[68] This circumstance alone destabilizes the meanings upon which law relies. In addition, the multiple layers of meaning, the ambiguities and contradictions of sacred narratives, cannot be contained by systems of precept. Consequently, it is always possible that the meaning-component upon which law depends will rise to accuse it, and that the thickness[69] of its narratives will enable interpretations that will call into question its favored interpretations.

If law is constitutionally vulnerable to re-vision and reinterpretation because it depends on narrative, the obvious next step for potential revisors is to examine just how narratives can upset the legal enterprises within which they are enshrined. Cover refers to "sacred narratives of jurisdiction that . . . ground judicial commitments."[70] By the same token, however, some narratives may ground critiques and re-visions of judicial commitments. By retelling these narratives, we can destabilize the accepted meanings of law. Skotsl's gambit could be to retell and reinterpret stories like these.

Two good candidates for Skotsl's purposes are provocative narratives about the woman the rabbis love to hate, Yalta, the wife of R. Nahman, the aristocratic and wealthy daughter of the Exilarch R. Huna.[71] Let us see how a feminist Jew could read these as destabilizing narratives concerning women and the making of halakhah and use them to claim an alternative hermeneutic for reading the tradition's texts.

> Ulla once happened to be a guest at R. Nahman's house. He ate a meal, led the grace after meals, and passed the cup of blessing to R. Nahman. R. Nahman said to him, "Please pass the cup of blessing [*kasa d'virkhata*] to Yalta, sir." He replied, "This is what R. Yohanan said: 'The issue of a woman's belly [*bitna*] is blessed only through the issue of a man's belly [*bitno*],' as the Bible says, 'He will bless the issue of your [masc. sing.] belly [*p'ri bitnkha*]' (Deut 7:13). It does not say 'her belly' but 'your belly.'"
>
> So too a *baraita* [an earlier Tannaitic text] teaches: R. Natan said: "Where is the prooftext in Scripture that the issue of a woman's belly is blessed only through the issue of a man's belly? As the Bible says, 'He will bless the issue of your [masc. sing.] belly [*p'ri bitnkha*].' It does not say 'her belly' but 'your belly.'"
>
> When Yalta heard this, she got up in venomous anger [*zihara*], went to the wine storeroom and smashed four hundred jars of wine. R. Nahman said to Ulla, "Please send her another cup." He sent [it to her with the message]: "All of this is a goblet of blessing [*navga d'virkhata*]." She sent [in reply]: "From travelers come tall tales and from ragpickers lice."[72]

At first glance, the story is bewildering. What is the meaning of the scene at the table? What is the point of Ulla's prooftexts, and why is Yalta so offended? Traditional interpreters read this as a story about a man who insults his host by refusing to follow the custom of the household, incurring the enmity of his spoiled and arrogant hostess.[73]

This story occurs in a chapter of Talmud concerned with the collective recitation of grace after meals. If three or more have eaten together, one calls the others to prayer and leads the blessing. Women's participation is a controversial issue. It is quickly established that women may not be counted in the quorum of three. But may they call other women or slaves to a collective grace? How may they participate if they are at the table with men?

Our text follows a talmudic discussion enumerating ten rules about the cup of blessing over which the master of the house or an honored guest recites the grace after meals. The tenth rule directs, "He sends it around to the members of his household as a gift, so that his household will be blessed." Juxtaposed to this teaching is this story in which Ulla withholds the cup from his hostess.

The exegeses Ulla quotes, first from his teacher, Yohanan b. Nappaha, and then from an earlier tannaitic source, appear at first to be theological rather than legal. They do not mention the cup of blessing, much less conclude that it may not be passed to women. But when the legal scholar Ulla cites them to justify his act, they acquire a practical legal application. Ulla uses his sources to argue that women may be excluded solely on the basis of biological inferiority, even in a case where the law has not specifically mandated their exclusion.

What is at issue, according to Ulla, is what the cup of blessing means. He produces a biblical prooftext that seems implicitly to define blessing as fertility. The recipient of blessing in this prooftext is a masculine singular "you." Hence, Ulla maintains, the Bible itself asserts that fertility belongs exclusively to men:

> He will favor you [masc. sing.] and bless you [masc. sing.] and multiply you [masc. sing.]: He will bless the issue of your [masc. sing.] womb [*p'ri bitnkha*] and the produce of your [masc. sing.] soil, your [masc. sing] new grain and wine and oil; the calving of your [masc. sing.] herd and the lambing of your [masc. sing.] flock in the land He swore to your fathers to assign to you. (Deut. 7:13)

Ulla and his rabbinic sources use this prooftext to assert that the primary actor in human fertility is the male, whereas the woman's role is only secondary and derivative.[74] If men are the ultimate source of the blessing of fertility, then the cup of blessing may be said to rest exclusively in their domain, and women can have only indirect access to it. In Ulla's biological metaphor, male potency is conflated both with spiritual blessing and with social dominance. By analogy, just as women cannot be fertile through any act of their own, so too they cannot be blessed through any act of their own but only through the agency of men acting for and upon them.

Ulla's biological interpretation strips the cup of its nuances. For in the original ten rules text, the cup's blessing is linked to a variety of spiritual and material blessings. Ulla reduces the meaning of blessing to fertility alone, just as he reduces the multivocal symbolism of the cup to a single symbolic representation: the womb, the human receptacle into which a sanctifiable liquid is poured, resulting in the blessing of fertility. Similarly, Ulla narrows the meaning of the ceremony of passing of the cup. The inclusive version of the ceremony affirms that everyone present at the table is a recipient of God's bounty and a petitioner for future blessings. In Ulla's ritual, however, women may only watch while men pass the blessing to other men. Ulla's reformulation symbolically enacts not the universal sharing of God's abundance but the transferral of ownership over wombs from patriarch to patriarch.[75]

Clearly Ulla's custom is unknown to R. Nahman. Since a version of the custom exists that does not exclude women, we may wonder why Ulla insists upon imposing his own custom at his host's table and why he defends it at such length. Why, in other words, is he bent upon reducing his hostess to a womb? Perhaps he is compensating for other disparities. Yalta, daughter of the fabulously wealthy leader of the Jews of Babylonia, is Ulla's superior both in affluence and in lineage. The only thing Ulla has that Yalta does not is that appendage around which he and his sources have been creating a justificatory structure. Small wonder that Yalta heads for the wine storage to preempt Ulla four hundred times, shattering the containers and spilling out the sanctifiable liquid whose blessing Ulla has reserved for men alone.

In the final incident of the story, Ulla, urged by R. Nahman, sends Yalta another cup with the message, "All this is a goblet [*navga*] of blessing," which Rashi paraphrases: "all the wine in the pitcher is like a cup of blessing; drink from it." Yalta, daughter of a scholarly family, recognizes this as chicanery. Ulla betrays the lesser holiness of this cup by terminology that is never used in any other context to signify the cup of blessing, an Aramaic word not cognate with the Hebrew *kos*. A *navga* of blessing bears the same resemblance to a *kasa* of blessing as a "holy cabinet" does to a "holy ark." It is the same object with the mystery of sanctity removed from it.

Decoding this manipulation just as she had decoded the original insult, Yalta mocks its perpetrator: Ulla, the traveler between the Palestinian and Babylonian academies, must be telling her a traveler's tall tale! She flings his insult back in his face, declaring that it is Ulla himself who is disgusting. His offer of wine from the unsanctified pitcher is like a beggar offering his lice, a worthless and repulsive gift from a giver with nothing to give.

For the engenderer of law, this is a story about law as power. Ulla, a traveling rabbi unremarkable for wealth or ancestry, is able to humiliate an affluent and clever aristocrat because he is a member of the exclusively male group that shapes and enforces laws, a group Yalta is ineligible to join. This single advantage trumps all Yalta's advantages of birth, wealth, learning, and wit. Without it, she may as well be a verminous beggar. Even in her own house, she can be placed at the mercy of Ulla's (and her husband's) dubious alms.

But, while Yalta cannot shape law-as-power, she can challenge law-as-meaning. As a destabilizer of law, she exposes its hidden meanings and debunks its mystifications. Rather than accept her exclusion quietly, she chooses to make the ceremony impossible for every-one. We are told what "blessing" means both for the writers of the ten rules text and for Ulla. We do not know what Yalta understands the blessing to be, because that was of no interest to the text's transmitters. But we know that she wanted to drink from the cup of blessing herself, and that she knew a phony cup of blessing when she saw one.

In the previous narrative, Yalta was the victim of legal chicanery; in another story from a different tractate, Yalta turns the tables on the rabbis. In this story, Yalta asks for a rab-binic decision about whether the vaginal secretion that has stained her garment is to be considered menstruous. The rabbi, using prescribed tests and descriptions, must rule whether or not the spot is uterine blood and consequently whether the woman from whom it came is pure or impure. If impure, she is subject to the restrictions upon conjugal sex and intimate contact incumbent upon menstruants.

> Yalta brought blood to Rabbah b. Bar Hana, and he ruled that it was impure. Then she turned around and brought it to R. Yitzhak b. R. Yehudah, and he ruled that it was pure. How could he do such a thing when a *baraita* [an earlier tannaitic text] teaches: "If a sage ruled it impure, his colleague is not permitted to rule it pure. If he ruled it forbidden, the colleague may not rule it permitted"? At first, [R. Yitzhak] ruled that it was impure. When she told him, "Every other time [Rabbah] has ruled for me that [blood] just like this was pure, and today he has a pain in his eye," R. Yitzhak then ruled it pure.[76]

The first unusual element in the story is that it presents the woman not merely as an object in a legal problem, but as a person with her own investment in the decision and its consequences. The story reveals to us her desire not to be declared a menstruant. The first judge renders a disappointing decision: Yalta's blood is ruled impure. Since rabbinic law lacks an appellate court, Yalta resourcefully sets up her own. She seeks out the second opinion, which the *baraita* wishes to forbid because it undermines the solidarity of the judges. In justification, she explains demurely that the first judge was temporarily in-competent to deliver an accurate opinion.

There are two ways of reading the narrative, one of which is considerably less desta-bilizing than the other. One could argue that Yalta is merely asking for accurate assess-ment of evidence and consistency in judgment; her evidence has been misassessed, be-cause of the judge's indisposition. Consequently, his ruling must be considered inconsistent with other rulings on the same evidence and therefore arbitrary and unjust. This reading affirms the system's rules and categories and the proper positions of judge and judged within them. It portrays Yalta's recourse to a second authority as an exceptional response to unusual circumstances and hence a poor basis for a precedent. This would be the tra-dition's preferred reading of the story.

But a darker, more ironic reading results if we assume that Yalta's account of Rabbah Bar Hana's judicial record and indisposition is a calculated attempt to manipulate the system and that her motivation for turning to a second judge is not an intellectual distaste for legal inconsistency but a desire to avoid the stigma of impurity. That is how we would read this story if we regarded it as "a folktale of justice"[77] and viewed Yalta as the trickster in the tale, the folkloric prankster who incarnates and unmasks what is arbitrary, chaotic, or unjust in our universe.[78]

Traditionally, tricksters are disreputable types. Zestfully pursuing their con games and dirty deals, they expose to public derision a world with its pants down, where authority is not really just, wisdom is not really wise, and there's no percentage in playing by the rules. In the trickster's laughter, then, there is an implicit social critique. When the pretensions of the powerful to justice and purity are deflated, the legitimacy of their human authority is called into question. At that moment, the rules are up for grabs.

As a distinctively rabbinic trickster, Yalta is a kind of legal guerrilla. She exposes the hidden relativity of the law and the hidden fallibility of its interpreters. The purportedly divine Torah must be translated into human authority. The *baraita* seeks to protect rabbinic authority and its appearance of objectivity through a policy of judicial solidarity. But as soon as Yalta can expose dissent beneath this solidarity, she demonstrates that authority is not infallible; two disagreeing authorities cannot both be right.

If authority is divisible, it is potentially manipulable. If it is fallible, it is open to critique. If authority is human, it is vulnerable; if the judge's human pain may distort his judgment, perhaps his particular human perspective may also skew his rulings. The authority passing judgment on women's blood, Yalta slyly suggests, has a pain in its eye, and that is why it mistakenly rules that blood impure.

Yalta's legal guerrilla tactics are predicated upon her skepticism that the authorities are dispensing justice. A legal realist could argue that the law is whatever a duly appointed authority says it is, and indeed, this appears to be the position of the *baraita*. A legal formalist could argue that whether the blood was declared pure or impure is immaterial. The decision is valid as long as the jurist used the system's processual rules and content categories in a defensible way. Yalta reminds us that what grounds authority is power, and power has social investments. Power can use authority to include and empower broadly. But power can also exercise authority to stigmatize, to subordinate, and to exclude. Yalta as legal guerrilla strips away the mask of justice, revealing the cruel face beneath.

Skotsl as legal guerrilla retells Yalta's stories. Applying her feminist hermeneutic, she finds a mirror within the story and holds this mirror up to the tradition's face. The purpose of a feminist Jewish hermeneutic is not to reject either text or law but to seek ways of claiming them and living them out with integrity. It keeps faith with texts by refusing to absolve them of moral responsibility. It honors halakhah by affirming its inexhaustible capacity to be created anew.

By renewing halakhah we bridge the gap between the impoverished world of meaning we currently inhabit and the richer and more vital worlds that might be. Our mission, like Skotsl's, is to make connections where there has been a rift, to make conversation where there has been silence, to engender a new world.

Engendering Judaism, like other kinds of human engendering, is a project that women and men must undertake together. We must converse, tell stories, play, and know one another if we are finally to inhabit a single *nomos* as partners and friends.[79] Together we can regenerate a world of legal meaning that fully, complexly, and inclusively integrates the stories and revelations, the duties and commitments of Jewish women and men. Then, when Skotsl returns, we can welcome her together. "Come on," we'll tell her, "we have a bridge we want to show you."

Notes

1. Some representative positions are: Rachel Adler, "The Jew Who Wasn't There: Halakha and the Jewish Woman," *Davka* (summer 1971), reprinted in *On Being a Jewish Feminist*, ed. Susannah Heschel (New York: Schocken, 1983), 12–18; Blu Greenberg, "Judaism and Feminism," in *The Jewish Woman*, ed. Elizabeth Koltun (New York: Schocken, 1976), 179–192; Cynthia Ozick, "Notes Toward Finding the Right Question," in *On Being a Jewish Feminist*, 120–151; Rachel Adler, "I've Had Nothing Yet, So I Can't Take More," *Moment* 8 (September 1983): 22–26.
2. Judith Plaskow, "The Right Question Is Theological," in *On Being a Jewish Feminist*, 223–233.
3. One essay written after this chapter was completed that raises these issues is Tikva Frymer-Kensky, "Toward a Liberal Theory of Halakha," *Tikkun* 10 (July/August 1995): 42–48, 77.
4. On the distinction between memory and history, see Yosef Hayim Yerushalmi, *Zakhor: Jewish History and Jewish Memory* (New York: Schocken, 1989), 8–22, 94–96, 108–110.
5. Alasdair MacIntyre, *After Virtue*, 2nd ed. (Notre Dame, IN: University of Notre Dame Press, 1984), 216.
6. Narrative ethicists would argue that even nonstoried principles such as Kant's categorical imperative or Mill's utilitarianism implicitly contain the germ of an unarticulated story. For an illustration, see my discussion of Seyla Benhabib later in this chapter.
7. Beatrice Weinreich, ed., *Yiddish Folktales*, trans. Leonard Wolf (New York: Pantheon with YIVO, 1986), 103. 1 thank Rabbi Lynn Gottlieb, who first called this story to my attention.
8. B. Weinreich suggests that Skotsl is a contraction of *dos ketzl*, the little cat. Uriel Weinreich, *Modern English-Yiddish Yiddish-English Dictionary* (New York, McGraw-Hill with YIVO, 1968), simply lists the expression, glossing "Well, look who's here! Welcome." Alexander Harkavy, *Yiddish-English Dictionary*, 22nd ed. (New York: Hebrew Publishing Company, 1928), lists the expression under *kotsl* and suggests that it is a contraction of *Gotts vill*, "God's will," as in the traditional morning blessing for women: "Blessed are you who made me according to your will." Professor Mikhl (Marvin) Herzog observes, "The phrase is probably derived from something like MHG *bis gote (unde mir) willekommen* 'be welcome to God (and me).' Whenever it occurs it is associated with someone's arrival, but rarely does it retain the implication of welcome and nowhere one of blessing. Initial *s* is generally interpreted as the brief form of the neuter definite article *dos* and consequently *kocl* is taken to be a designation for the visitor (generally one who visits infrequently); thus 'the *kocl* is coming.'" Marvin Herzog, *The Yiddish Language in Northern Poland: Its Geography and History*, IJAL Publication No. 37 (Bloomington: Indiana University Press, and The Hague: Mouton, 1965), 66–67. Professor Chana Kronfeld has suggested to me that a *skots* is a tale, but I have been unable to document this. Most authorities concur that the greeting is usually ironic and usually addressed to a woman.
9. Arnold M. Eisen, *The Chosen People in America: A Study in Jewish Religious Ideology* (Bloomington: Indiana University Press, 1983).
10. Thumbing through a popular Judaica catalogue recently, I noticed that Howard Eilberg-Schwartz's book *God's Phallus* was listed under Modern Jewish Thought, whereas Judith Plaskow's *Standing Again at Sinai* (San Francisco: Harper and Row, 1979) was listed under Women's Issues. Both works deal with the theology of gender. "Gender and Judaism," dealing with the depiction of masculine and feminine roles in Jewish history and texts, is still rather an avant-garde category.

11. Heschel, "Introduction," in *On Being a Jewish Feminist*, xxiii.

12. Riv-Ellen Prell, "The Vision of Woman in Classical Reform Judaism," *Journal of the American Academy of Religion* 50 (1983): 575–589.

13. Martha Minow, "The Supreme Court 1986 Term: Forward: Justice Engendered," *Harvard Law Review* 101 (1987): esp. 31–70.

14. See, for example, MacIntyre, *After Virtue*; Michael Sandel, *Liberalism and the Limits of Justice* (Cambridge: Cambridge University Press, 1982); Martha Minow, *Making All the Difference: Inclusion, Exclusion and American Law* (Ithaca, NY: Cornell University Press, 1990).

15. For an account of the relationship between stories and praxis in law, see Robert Cover, "The Supreme Court 1986 Term: Forward: *Nomos* and Narrative," *Harvard Law Review* 97, no. 4 (1983):4–68.

16. Michael Goldberg, *Jews and Christians: Getting Our Stories Straight* (Nashville: Abingdon Press, 1985), 13–19. Michael Goldberg, "The Story of the Moral: Gifts or Bribes in Deuteronomy?" *Interpretation* 38 (January 1984):15–25, demonstrates how an underlying story may be detected in a specific law.

17. My use of the term "praxis" has obvious kinships with the Marxian use of the term "revolutionary praxis," on which see Anthony Giddens, *Capitalism and Modern Social Theory* (Cambridge: Cambridge University Press, 1971), 6–8, 20; with the notion of Christian liberation praxis, on which see Gustave Gutierrez, *A Theology of Liberation*, trans. and ed. Sr. Caridad Inda and John Eagleson (Maryknoll, NY: Orbis, 1973), 6–18; and with the reappropriation of Aristotelian *phronesis*, practical wisdom, by narrative ethicists. See, for example, Alisdair MacIntyre, *After Virtue*, chap. 15.

18. Michael Meyer, *Response to Modernity: A History of the Reform Movement in Judaism* (New York: Oxford University Press, 1988), 16–27, 210–211. See also the practices of Abraham Geiger and Samuel Holdheim in David Rudavsky, *Modern Jewish Religious Movements: A History of Emancipation and Adjustment* (New York: Behrman House, 1967), 177–183, as well as his account of the Pittsburgh Platform, 298–302.

19. A daunting catalogue of such dissonant elements is provided by John D. Rayner, "Between Antinomianism and Conservatism," in *Dynamic Jewish Law: Progressive Halakha: Essence and Application*, ed. Walter Jacob and Moshe Zemer (Tel Aviv: Rodef Shalom Press, 1991), 126–127. He says, "Considering that whole, vast areas of its contents relate to sacrifices and priesthood, and ritual purity and male superiority and polygamy and yibum and halitzah and mamzerut and corporal punishment and capital punishment . . . for Progressive Jews to affirm such a system, subject only to a few cosmetic changes, is so bizarre that I can only understand it as either self-deception for the sake of the emotional comfort or else propaganda for the sake of the political advantage to be gained from a traditionalist posture."

20. *The Talmud of the Land of Israel: A Preliminary Translation and Explanation*, vol. 2, *Pe'ah*, trans. Roger Brooks (Chicago: University of Chicago Press, 1990), 128.

21. Yosef Hayim Yerushalmi, *Zakhor*, 81–103 discusses the problems Jewish historiography poses for Judaism as a religious commitment.

22. The following are examples of eminent liberal halakhists and their works: Eliezer Berkovits, *Not in Heaven: The Nature and Function of Halakha* (New York: Ktav, 1983); Elliot N. Dorff and Arthur Rosett, *A Living Tree: The Roots and Growth of Jewish Law* (Albany: State University of New York Press, 1988); Louis Jacobs, *A Tree of Life: Diversity, Flexibility and Creativity in Jewish Law* (Oxford: Oxford University Press for the Littman Library, 1984); Joel Roth, *The Halakhic Process: A Systemic Analysis* (New York: Jewish Theological Seminary of America, 1986). An excellent book, which I discovered too late to include in my discussion, is Moshe Zemer, *Halakha Shefuya* (Israel: D'vir, 1993).

23. The following discussion summarizes my article, "I've Had Nothing Yet, So I Can't Take More," *Moment* 8 (September 1983): 22–26. See also Plaskow, "The Right Question Is Theological," 223–233.

24. Mary Daly, *Beyond God the Father* (Boston: Beacon, 1973), 11–12.

25. Jacob Neusner, "The System as a Whole," in *The Mishnaic System of Women*, part 5: *A History of the Mishnaic Law of Women*, 5 vols. (Leiden: E. J. Brill, 1980), 13–42. This point is made particularly on 14.

26. Ibid., 13–21.

27. Judith Wegner, *Woman in the Mishnah: Person or Chattel* (New York: Oxford University Press, 1988), 186–191.

28. Neusner, "The System As a Whole," 16.

29. Adler, "I've Had Nothing Yet, So I Can't Take More," 24.

30. For an introduction to new ritual concerns expressed by women, see Rebecca Alpert, "Our Lives Are the Text: Exploring Jewish Women's Rituals," *Bridges* 2 (spring 1991): 66–80. For a simplified account of a feminist Jewish hermeneutics, see Rachel Adler, "Talking Our Way In" *Sh'ma* 23 (Nov. 13, 1992): 5–6; and William Cutter, "What the Teacher Learns—and Ponders," *Sh'ma* 23 (Nov. 13, 1992): 6–8.

31. Such analyses are ultimately indebted to the postmodern philosopher Michel Foucault. See in particular his *Power/Knowledge: Selected Interviews and Other Writings, 1972–1977* (New York: Pantheon Books, 1980).

32. Mark Washofsky, "The Search for Liberal Halakhah," in *Dynamic Jewish Law*, 27–51. Washofsky criticizes both Berkovits and Roth for underestimating legal consensus as a systemic principle. However, his own recommendation that liberal halakhists directly confront the halakhic consensus by demonstrating poor reasoning or the existence of equally valid alternatives is itself a formalist solution that undermines the power of consensus.

33. In Judaism, legal formalism can be made to undergird legal realism. The classical system enunciates a legal principle from which judicial discretion can plausibly be derived: *ein lo ladayyan ella mah she-einav ro'ot*, "a judge can only rely on what his own eyes see." This principle is invoked by Eliezer Berkovits as a rational principle, which is necessarily applied contextually, 53–57, and by Joel Roth, who elevates it to a "quasi-ultimate systemic principle," 86–113.

34. Eliezer Berkovits, *Not in Heaven*, 1–2, 47–48, 71–73.

35. Ibid., 19–22. Eliezer Berkovits, *Crisis and Faith* (New York: Sanhedrin, 1976), 97–121. Berkovits makes this argument on Maimonidean grounds.

36. Jacobs, 236–247.

37. Ibid., 245.

38. Ibid., 246.

39. S. M. Passamaneck, "Reflections of Reasonable Cause in Halakhah," in *Jewish Law Association Studies VI: The Jerusalem 1990 Conference Volume*, ed. B. S. Jackson and S. M. Passamaneck (Atlanta: Scholars Press, 1992). In the case of the *moser* informer, medieval responsa permit even execution without talmudic standards of proof. Shoshanna Gershenzen, "When Jews Kill Jews: Communal Integrity vs. Judicial Ethics in Medieval Jewish Responsa" [unpublished paper].

40. Alexander Pope, "An Essay on Man," in *Eighteenth Century Poetry and Prose*, 2nd ed., ed. Louis I. Bredvold, Alan D. McKillop, and Lois Whitney (New York: Ronald Press, 1956), 370–384, esp. line 294.

41. Roth, *The Halakhic Process*, 10.

42. Ibid.

43. Ibid., 81–113.

44. Joel Roth, "On the Ordination of Women As Rabbis," in *The Ordination of Women As Rabbis. Studies and Responsa*, Moreshet Series vol. 9, ed. Simon Greenberg (New York: Jewish Theological Seminary, 1988).

45. Roth, *The Halakhic Process*, 81–113.

46. David Ellenson, "The Challenges of Halakhah," *Judaism* 38 (summer 1989): 362.

47. Roth, *The Halakhic Process*, 151. Although Roth gives both theistic and nontheistic bases for the *grundnorm*, rabbis must subscribe to the theistic version.

48. This paragraph summarizes Robert Cover, "*Nomos* and Narrative," 4–18.

49. Ibid. 13n.

50. Robert Cover, "The Folktales of Justice: Tales of Jurisdiction" *Capital University Law Review* 14 (1985): 181.

51. For the most precise description of the modern self, its nature, its moral sources, and its historical context, see Charles Taylor, *Sources of the Self: The Making of Modern Identity* (Cambridge, MA: Harvard University Press, 1989), esp. 3–107.

52. Peter L. Berger, *The Sacred Canopy* (New York: Anchor, 1969).

53. Franz Kafka, "The Problem of Our Laws," in *Parables and Paradoxes* (New York: Schocken, 1961), 155.

54. A major defense of rabbinic authority turns upon this very prooftext. It is related in a dramatic midrash (B. Baba Metzia 59b) how a Tannaitic majority rules against the minority opinion of the powerful and influential Eliezer ben Hyrcanus, refusing to be swayed by the miracles he performs or even the heavenly voice that proclaims his opinion correct. Once Torah has entered history, the midrash seems to argue, authority is transferred irrevocably from its divine giver to its human receivers. They must make sense of it for themselves and determine how it must be practiced, even though, from the transcendent perspective, some of their decisions may be wrong. The addenda to the narrative of the rabbinic confrontation render its interpretation even more ambiguous. In one addendum, the prophet Elijah relates to Rabbi Natan how God laughed and exclaimed, "My children have defeated Me!" In another, the subsequent excommunication of Eliezer ben Hyrcanus is sympathetically described. The making and remaking of Torah are experienced simultaneously as occasion for divine laughter and for human tragedy. Law's tragedies arise out of the inevitable conflicts between the coercive force by means of which law is stabilized and standardized in communal praxis and the conscientious resistance of differing individuals. On this point, see Robert Cover; "Violence and the Word," *Yale Law Journal* 95 (1986): 1601–1629.

55. Feminists are not the only scholars to have rediscovered narrative. We have already seen its importance in the work of Robert Cover. Ethicists and theologians who use it extensively include Alasdair MacIntyre, Stanley Hauerwas, and Michael Goldberg.

56. Seyla Benhabib, "The Generalized and Concrete Other: The Kohlberg-Gilligan Controversy and Moral Theory," in *Women and Moral Theory*, ed. Eva Feder Kittay and Diana T. Meyers (Totowa, NJ: Rowman and Littlefield, 1987), 154–177. Another version of this essay can be found in Seyla Benhabib, *Situating the Self: Gender, Community and Postmodernism in Contemporary Ethics* (New York: Routledge, 1992), 148–177, but I will cite the version in *Women and Moral Theory*.

57. Narrative and contextuality are also distinguishing themes of critical legal studies. This account of context is indebted to Roberto Mangabeira Unger, *Passion: An Essay on Personality* (New York: Free Press, 1984), 5–15.

58. For a lucid explanation of the distinctions among essentialist, social constructivist, and poststructural feminisms, see Linda Alcoff, "Cultural Feminism Versus Post-Structuralism: The Identity Crisis in Feminist Theory," *Signs* 13 (spring 1988): 405–436.

59. Kenneth Karst, "Woman's Constitution," *Duke Law Journal*, no. 3 (1984): 447–508, esp. 499–500.

60. See in particular Robin J. West, "Jurisprudence and Gender," *University of Chicago Law Review* 55:1 (winter 1988): 1–71; and Robin J. West, "Authority, Autonomy and Choice: The Role of Consent in the Moral and Political Visions of Franz Kafka and Richard Posner," *Harvard Law Review* 99 (December, 1985): 384–428. In the latter, West concludes, "It may be true, as Bentham thought, that 'all men calculate.' It is not true as Posner blithely assumes that all men calculate all of the time" (425).

61. Jean Bethke Elshtain, "Feminist Discourse and Its Discontents: Language, Power, and

Meaning," in *Feminist Theory. A Critique of Ideology*, ed. Nannerl O. Keohane, Michelle A. Rosaldo and Barbara Gelpi (Chicago: University of Chicago Press, 1982), 127–145.

62. Minow, "Engendering Justice," 35–36.

63. Robin J. West, "The Difference in Women's Hedonic Lives: A Phenomenological Critique of Feminist Legal Theory," in *At the Boundaries of Law: Feminism and Legal Theory*, ed. Martha Albertson Fineman and Nancy Sweet Thomadsen (New York: Routledge, 1991), 115–134.

64. Minow, "Engendering Justice," 11–14.

65. Robert Cover, "*Nomos* and Narrative," 23.

66. Ibid., 19–25.

67. Ibid., 18.

68. For a discussion of the instability of context, see Roberto Mangabeira Unger, *Passion: An Essay on Personality*, 5–15.

69. The term "thickness" refers to multiple layers of meaning that an act or story may possess. The term was popularized by Clifford Geertz, "Thick Description: Toward an Interpretive Theory of Culture," in *The Interpretation of Cultures* (New York: Basic Books, 1973), 3–30.

70. Robert Cover, "Folktales of Justice," 183. See also David Schulman, "AIDS Discrimination: Its Nature, Meaning and Function," *Nova Law Review* 12 (spring 1988):1117–1119, for an example of the way in which a re/revisioning of civil rights can account for a place in society for people with AIDS. Schulman refers to law's re-membering those who are dismembered from society because of the stigma of their status.

71. Read, for example, the disapproving thumbnail biography of Yalta in Adin Steinsaltz's commentary on B. Berakhot 51b.

72. Berakhot 51b. My translation.

73. See, for example, Maharsha and Ein Yaakov commentaries to Berakhot 51b. Yaakov bar Shlomo N. Haviv, *Ein Yaakov*, vol. 1 (New York: Avraham Yitzhak Friedman, n.d.), 158.

74. Certain ancient metaphysical biologies propound such views. Aristotle claims that only fathers are true parents, and mothers, themselves deformed beings, contribute not form but only passive matter toward the creation of a child: Aristotle, *Generation of Animals*, 2; 2.735A1–10. David Feldman, *Marital Relations, Birth Control and Abortion in Jewish Law* (New York: Schocken, 1974), argues that "the talmudic commentators" espoused a popular variation of Aristotelian biology in which "a foetus is formed from female blood and male seed prevailed," 133–134. A brillant feminist analysis of Aristotle's "motherless metaphysics of the monstrous female" can be found in Catherine Keller, *From a Broken Web: Separation, Sexism and the Self* (Boston: Beacon, 1986), 48–50.

75. On the thesis that the sexual and procreative capacities of women are regarded as patriarchal property, see Judith Wegner, *Woman in the Mishnah: Person or Chattel*, 168–181.

76. B. Niddah 20b. My translation.

77. Cover, "The Folktales of Justice."

78. "Trickster," *Funk and Wagnalls Standard Dictionary of Folklore, Mythology and Legend*, vol. 2 (New York: Funk and Wagnalls, 1950), 1123–1125. For application to biblical narrative, see Susan Niditch, *Underdogs and Tricksters* (San Francisco: Harper and Row, 1987).

79. Hebrew speakers will note that in biblical and Tannaitic Hebrew, all these verbs of communication and relation sometimes serve as euphemisms for sexual intercourse. What I envision is a world in which "intercourse," in its literal sense of "interaction," is truly communicative.

Part IV

Two Pivotal Experiences in the Twentieth Century

Much of the Jewish religious thought of the last four decades of the twentieth century has focused on the topics that have occupied Jewish thinkers over the ages, topics such as creation, revelation, redemption, chosenness, covenant, law, faith, and prayer. Even with regard to those subjects, however, the modern contexts of political freedom for Jews in the Western world, rooted in Enlightenment ideology, and the fresh ways of thinking pioneered by non-Jewish and Jewish thinkers in the last two centuries and especially the last forty years, have prompted new ways of thinking about those themes, as we discussed in Part III.

Having explored contemporary thought on those perennial issues, it is fitting that we consider what are arguably two completely new topics in our time—namely, the Holocaust and the establishment of the State of Israel. Previous thought about the problem of evil, the role of God in history, and redemption surely have paved the way for recent Holocaust and Zionist thought; in fact, one of the issues that must be addressed is whether these events pose distinctly new questions or whether they are merely instances—albeit dramatic ones—of theological issues that have been around for a very long time. Either way, considerable effort during the last four decades of the twentieth century has been spent on trying to understand the impact of the Holocaust and the State of Israel for Jewish existence and belief.

The Holocaust in the Context of the Problem of Evil

From one perspective, the Holocaust is simply an instance of the long-standing problem of evil—that is, how can an omniscient, benevolent God allow unjustified evil to occur? The Holocaust is surely a particularly egregious example of that problem, given the number of people who suffered and the intentional and sustained cruelty involved; but for some thinkers the theological issues raised by the Holocaust are none other than those already familiar to us from previous manifestations of evil. We shall therefore first examine the nature of that problem and the types of responses that have been offered over the centuries. We shall then describe the efforts of contemporary thinkers to determine whether the theological problems raised by the Holocaust are the same as those raised in the past, and are therefore amenable to past resolutions, or if they are distinctly new ones, requiring a completely different response.

The classical problem of evil emerges out of the combination of four beliefs: (1) God is all-powerful (omnipotent); (2) God is all-knowing (omniscient); (3) God is good; and (4) there is unjustified suffering in the world. If any of these premises is denied, there is no inconsistency in holding the remainder. After all, if (1) God is not omnipotent, God may well know that there is undeserved suffering and may wish that it were otherwise; God just cannot do anything about it. If (2) God is not omniscient, God may be able and willing to remove undeserved suffering from the world; God just does not know that it exists. If (3) God is not good, God may know that there is undeserved suffering and have the ability to remove it; God just does not care—or, worse, sadistically wants innocent people to suffer. And finally, if (4) there is no undeserved evil in the first place, then God can consistently be omnipotent, omniscient, and good; that, though, seems to require that we close our eyes to what is manifestly part of our experience—namely, that good people suffer and bad people prosper.

The Rabbis of the Talmud and Midrash responded to this problem in many ways, not worrying, in a manner typical of them, of inconsistencies in their responses. Sometimes they maintained, in the manner of Job's friends, that, for example, there is no sickness without sin, that, more generally, there is indeed a correlation between goodness and reward (and between evil and punishment), even if we cannot perceive it.[1] In other words, some Rabbis took refuge in our human ignorance, thus softening tenet (4), if not denying it altogether: despite appearances, all suffering is a deserved result of God's justice, not a product of his alleged impotence, ignorance, capriciousness, or malice.

Other Rabbis invoked human ignorance in the exact opposite way—namely, by claiming, like God of the whirlwind in the Book of Job (Chapters 38–42), that human beings should not presume to know God's ways and that God's role in the world is ultimately inscrutable to us. God decrees whatever He does, and we have no standing to question those divine decisions.[2]

Still other sections of rabbinic literature suggest that we are wrong to expect reward for good deeds and punishment for bad ones in the first place, that, like a Kantian, principled ethic, one should do the right thing simply because it is the right thing, not for the sake of, nor even with any expectation of, correlative consequences. Thus the Mishnah maintains that "the reward of fulfilling a divine commandment is the opportunity (and perhaps the moral and psychological readiness) to do another one, and the punishment for sinning is that one finds another opportunity (and the moral and psychological readiness) to sin again."[3] This approach saves God's power and knowledge by maintaining that our lot in life has nothing to do with the moral quality of our actions, thus denying or softening either God's benevolence (if one thinks that a good God should be just) and/or the existence of undeserved evil (since, by hypothesis, there is no linkage between goodness and deserts).

By far the most prevalent rabbinic response to the problem of evil, though, was the doctrine of the world to come: although in this world good people suffer and evil ones prosper, God, who is just and good, will rectify the moral accounts of each one of us, as it were, in a life after death. The Rabbis (Pharisees) were so insistent that God's justice demanded a world to come that they maintained that anyone who denies it—or even anyone who denies that the Torah promises it—loses his or her place in the world to come.[4]

During the Middle Ages, Jews devised yet other approaches to the problem of evil. Maimonides, following Augustine, maintained that there is no undeserved evil in the world because evil is only the absence of good. God's presence is wholly good, but God could not fill the world with His presence because that infinite divine goodness would burst the bounds of all the finite creatures on earth. God is all-powerful, but God's omnipotence does not extend to the logically impossible.[5] Thus Maimonides resolves the problem of evil by both emptying evil of its content (that is, by denying or softening tenet 4) and by restricting God's omnipotence (tenet 1).

Another approach popular during the Middle Ages—and adopted by Maimonides as well[6]—was "the free will defense." That is, most evils that human beings experience are the product either of other people's bad use of their free will or, more commonly, of their own bad choices. God could intervene each time individuals are about to harm themselves or others, but that would effectively eliminate human free will. We would become machines, programed to do what God wants of us. God surely could have created us that way and thereby prevented much harm, but then God would Himself have been diminished in stature, for to fashion creatures with free will and then to convince them to act properly is a much greater feat than to program machines. Evil occurs in the world, then, primarily because God benignly wants to insure the conative essence of our humanity.

How do these explanations fare when called upon to justify faith in God despite the Holocaust? For some Jews—and indeed, for some Jewish thinkers—they do just fine. Some Jews believe that Hitler and his cohorts will get their just punishment in a life after death. Others, primarily in the ultra-Orthodox community, believe that the Holocaust was a just punishment for Jewish secularism and all the divine commandments that were violated in practicing that life style, exactly the quid pro quo theology of Deuteronomy. The fact that it was specifically the pious Jews of Eastern Europe who suffered in the Holocaust in far greater numbers and percentages than their secular cousins in the West does not seem to bother those who hold this view, which others find to be a blasphemy against both God and the Holocaust's victims. Still others believe that the Holocaust is a frightening reminder that God's will is inscrutable, but we must follow God's laws nevertheless.

The manifest role of Hitler and of the many people who acted in complicity with him—either actively promoting his program or passively letting it happen—makes the free will defense especially attractive for many Jews. Some, pointing to the avowedly secular nature of both Hitler's Germany and Stalin's Russia, maintain that the Holocaust proves once and for all that human beings cannot be trusted to be moral on their own, that only a God-centered society has a chance (even if not a guarantee) of acting morally in the face of evil.[7]

Eliezer Berkovits is a good example of those who retain a traditional Jewish faith despite the Holocaust. He does so by invoking the biblical image of God "hiding His face." God may punish us or may show indifference to us for a time (He may "hide His face"), but He still remains God in the full sense of the biblical image of God. Berkovits combines this with a version of the free-will defense, maintaining that "he who demands justice of God must give up man [with free will]; he who asks for God's love and mercy beyond justice must accept suffering." Berkovits also suggests, though, that Israel's history exists in the realm of the Ought, a completely different plane from that of the Is, where the history of the other nations is played out. We may not understand God's actions as they relate to the realm of the Is, but that does not, for Berkovits, undermine the authority of the divine realm of the Ought, even if the faith history embodied in the realm of the Ought "holds on to reality . . . by the skin of its teeth." The establishment of the State of Israel so soon after the Holocaust, though, testifies that the People Israel's witness to the divine realm of the Ought is not for naught, that traditional Jewish faith still makes sense.

God's Role in History

Others, though, respond in the polar opposite way, claiming that if God did not intervene in an evil program as massive and demonic as the Holocaust, then God can never be expected to intervene in human history. This, of course, denies a foundational tenet of Jewish belief highlighted by the central Jewish story of the Exodus from Egypt—namely, that God can and does act in history. The failure of God to intercede in the Holocaust thus prompts some Jews to be atheists, while others, like Richard Rubenstein, revise their conception of God to exclude the expectation that God will act in history. God instead becomes the awesome, amoral, indeed threatening forces of nature, before which we cower.

Why not invoke the traditional defenses to justify God and still retain belief in a God of history? Rubenstein maintains that while that may have worked for Jews in the past, the Holocaust makes that theological strategy untenable. Not only is the Holocaust much more massive in its destructiveness than previous military defeats, inquisitions, and pogroms were; the Holocaust was perpetrated by the most advanced civilization in history, Germany. That gives the lie to the rational, progressive notions of the nineteenth and early twentieth centuries, according to which human beings are on a trajectory of ever greater humanization as we learn more and more, and it also, for Rubenstein, undermines all credibility of the doctrine of God acting in history. The uniqueness of the Holocaust, that which requires a radical change in the Jewish conception of humanity and of God, is both the unparalleled immensity of its death and destruction and the supposedly advanced culture of the peoples who perpetrated it.

Others, like Emil Fackenheim, see the Holocaust instead as a new revelation, a 614th commandment, prohibiting us from giving Hitler a posthumous victory. We must instead be motivated by our memory of the Holocaust to attack all forms of indecency and to fight for the continued existence of Judaism and of Jews. Ironically, for Fackenheim the Holocaust opens up the possibility for Jews of all forms of religious belief, including atheism, to hear God's command. That very revelation, though, creates a radical disjunction between everything that preceded it and the time thereafter. The only way that we, who live after the Holocaust, can maintain a linkage with the Judaism of those who lived before it is by relying on the models of those who lived through the Holocaust and nevertheless maintained their faith and hope. Judging from the outside, these survivors, and we who follow their example, may seem irrational and even inappropriate in maintaining Jewish faith, but the empirical fact that those whose very lives were threatened by the Holocaust nevertheless persisted in their faith must, according to Fackenheim, outweigh all such considerations of rationality and propriety.

Finally, for Irving Greenberg, the Holocaust is "radical counter-testimony to Judaism and Christianity," for it denied the infinite and absolute value that both religions attribute to each human being. It challenges Christianity also in the complicity of Christians and Christian institutions in fomenting murder, and it undermines secular culture's promises of universalism and humanitarianism. As Greenberg poignantly puts it, "No statement, theological or otherwise, should be made that would not be credible in the presence of the burning children." The life of faith is lived in-between the extremes of the horror of the Holocaust and the dignity of the redemption of the Exodus, graphically demonstrated in our own times by the establishment of the State of Israel. To deny either is to deny the Jewish experience in contemporary history. He thus advocates dialectical faith, or "moment faiths," for there will always be moments when faith in God, the Redeemer, is possible for an individual and moments when it is not. "The difference between the skeptic and the believer is [then] the frequency of faith, and not the certitude of position." The central religious testimony after the Holocaust becomes "the reaffirmation of meaningfulness, worth, and life—through acts of love and life-giving. The act of creating a life or enhancing its dignity is the counter-testimony to the Holocaust." Indeed, during the Holocaust and in its aftermath, the secular/religious dichotomy has been dissolved; only the moral quality of one's response to evil counts.

The State of Israel

If the problem of evil has many roots in biblical and rabbinic thought, the special place of Israel does as well. One of the blessings God promises Abraham, Isaac, and Jacob is the land of Israel, and God takes the Israelites out of Egypt specifically to receive the Torah at Sinai and to live its message in the Promised Land. So much was Israel to be the land of the Israelites that the Torah prohibits a return to Egypt (Exodus 14:13; Deuteronomy 17:16; 28:68). Conversely, the ultimate punishment for the Israelites was that God removed His presence from them, using the Babylonians as his tool to destroy the Temple, "the place of His dwelling," and to force them into exile.

The Rabbis of Mishnaic times were equally committed to living in the land of Israel, categorizing that as a positive commandment (*yishuv eretz yisrael*). Those living elsewhere were to see themselves as under the obligation to try to emigrate to Israel (that is, go on *aliyah*, literally, going up to the land), for Israel was not only the homeland and the historical cradle of the Jewish People, but the holy land promised by God. Moreover, the Temple could be only there, and most of the Torah's agricultural laws could be observed only there. Ultimately, the Messiah would appear there and bring all Jews living in exile back to the land as one of the signs of the arrival of the Messianic era.

Despite these Israel-centered sentiments, from the destruction of the Second Temple (and with it, the Second Commonwealth) in 70 C.E. to the founding of the modern State of Israel in 1948, the vast majority of the world's Jews lived elsewhere. Amid multiple praises for the land of Israel, the Babylonian Talmud (200–500 C.E.) nevertheless records the view that "whoever lives in Babylonia [modern-day Iraq] is accounted merit as though he lived in the land of Israel" (B. *Ketubbot* 111a), for that is where the preeminent academies of Jewish learning were. Moreover, the Babylonian rabbis already noted in their time that the Jewish head of their community (the Exilarch) had real political power granted by the Persians, while in Palestine, the President of the Sanhedrin, operating under Roman rule, could make decisions only narrowly within Jewish law (B. *Horayot* 11b). Saadia Gaon (882–942) later fought a major battle with the Jews of his time living in Palestine so that the *geonim*, the leaders of the Babylonian academies from the eighth to the eleventh centuries, would retain power over determining the calendar and, with it, the holy days of the Jewish year.

While the political power of Jews to rule themselves under the domain of non-Jewish rulers waxed and waned throughout history, the centers of Jewish population and culture for most of Jewish history were definitely outside of Israel, located in Babylonia from approximately the third to eleventh centuries, then in Europe and North Africa from the eleventh to the twentieth centuries, and now in North America as well as in the modern State of

Israel. The Jewish population of the United States has exceeded that of the State of Israel throughout its history, although some demographers predict that that may change in the second or third decade of the twenty-first century. In any case, the historical fact has been that most Jews have lived outside of the land of Israel for the vast majority of Jewish history.

While Jews have expressed a longing to return to Zion three times daily in their prayers, the ideal of Zion in some nineteenth- and early twentieth-century thinkers was no longer tied to the land of Israel, but rather to an ideal Jerusalem. Some theorists, like Hermann Cohen and Franz Rosenzweig, thought that it was counterproductive to encourage Jews to return to the land of Israel. In Cohen's case, Jews were to spread the messianic ideal among the nations, and they could not do that if they were cooped up, as it were, on one small piece of land. For Rosenzweig, devotion to retaking the land would lead to Jews spilling their blood for it, thus draining the eternal character from the Jewish people and transforming it into a nation like all others. The early Reform movement in America objected to Zionism as a narrow nationalism. The Reform rabbinate therefore included this plank in its Pittsburgh Platform in 1885:

> We recognize, in the modern era of universal culture of heart and intellect, the approaching of the realization of Israel's great messianic hope for the establishment of the kingdom of truth, justice, and peace among all men. We consider ourselves no longer a nation, but a religious community, and therefore expect neither a return to Palestine, nor a sacrificial worship under the sons of Aaron, nor the restoration of any of the laws concerning the Jewish state.[8]

Orthodox leaders by and large objected to the Zionist agenda for yet another religious reason: only the Messiah was to establish the new Jewish homeland in Israel. For Jews to do that on their own initiative would be an act of human hubris, taking away God's prerogative, and therefore doomed to failure.

Secular Zionists, though, under the leadership of Theodore Herzl, convened the First Zionist Congress in Basel, Switzerland, in 1897, and they began settling the land. Some religious Zionists (the Mizrahi movement) participated in this effort, and the Conservative Movement, under the leadership of Solomon Schechter, was heavily involved in Zionist efforts from Schechter's first speech on the subject in 1906. Mordecai Kaplan's emphasis on the role of the land of Israel and the Hebrew language in Jewish identity also played a major role in Conservative Jewry's support for Zionism. The vast majority of those who established the modern Jewish community in Israel, though, were secularists.

Consequently, it is not surprising that secular Zionist ideologies developed over time in order to explain and motivate Zionist activity. Theodore Herzl's own book, *The Jewish State*, articulated a political Zionism. Ahad Ha'am (pen name for Asher Ginsberg) developed cultural Zionism. Aaron David Gordon, Beryl Katznelson, and others developed theories of Zionism as a labor movement, a theory that led to the establishment of cooperative communities (*kibbutzim*) in Israel and that ultimately would convince the Soviet Union and its Communist allies to support the establishment of what they thought would be a socialist state there during the November, 1947 debate of the United Nations about whether a Jewish state should be established in Palestine.

As of this writing, as the state of Israel has just celebrated its fiftieth birthday, five decades of living as a Jewish state, albeit all under siege, have led to new visions of Zionism. They have also produced new understandings of the relationship between the

State of Israel and the Diaspora. Much of this thought is still in the making, but we have included a few readings here to indicate its issues and breadth.

A. B. Yehoshua, a leading Israeli novelist and essayist, challenges diaspora Jewry to reconsider its relationship to the *golah* (diaspora existence) and to the State of Israel. He avers that diaspora Jewry has lived for centuries in a state of profound neurosis, proclaiming their love for and commitment to the land of Israel and yet avoiding at all costs the concrete steps necessary to return to that homeland. The biblical sources themselves, he argues, already exhibit this ambivalence toward the Land of Israel, and the history of the Jewish people has reflected this hypocrisy. The Jewish people, Yehoshua argues, is suffering from a collective illness. But what are its causes and, more importantly, where does a cure lie?

For Yehoshua, the root of the problem lies in the perennial conflict between the two elements of Jewish identity, the religious and the national. The former directs Jews toward spiritual ends, while the latter directs Jews toward the building of a sovereign national life in its own territory. So long as Jews remain in the Diaspora, they need not face the conflict between their religious values and their national goals, for they do not live in a totally Jewish environment in which there is even the possibility of actualizing their religious goals in their national life. Making *aliyah*, however, would bring that centuries-old conflict out into the open and so force Jews to reconcile this tension at the heart of their identity. Rather than doing so, Yehoshua postulates, Jews choose life in the Diaspora. It is time, he suggests, for Israeli leaders to challenge diaspora Jews to overcome this fear and confront the hard choices, for these are the questions at the very heart of Jewish existence. Only then will diaspora Jews come to recognize the inherent superiority of Jewish life in a Jewish state and make the choice to abandon their neurotic existence in the *golah*.

Yeshayahu Leibowitz, a prominent but unconventional Israeli scientist and Orthodox philosopher, believes that the sense of alienation between Jews and non-Jews in Western societies has vanished, and so Zionism cannot be based on anti-Semitism. Indeed, Israel cannot be the answer to Jewish feelings of insecurity, for "nowhere is Jewish existence so threatened as it is in the state of Israel"—presumably by its constant state of war with its neighbors and by the avowed secularism of some 85% of its citizens. Neither can Zionism be defined as the quest to be a model society, for every nation in the world seeks to be that. Israel's secularism also mitigates against basing Zionism on a prophetic or messianic vision. Instead of all these, for Leibowitz, Zionism is simply the political expression of Jews who no longer wanted to be ruled by non-Jews (*Goyim*); "Zionism is best defined as the program for the attainment of political and national independence . . . [and] the effort to maintain this independence." It has no religious significance at all, for living in Israel and being committed to the idea of a Jewish state have no relationship with the essential religious sense of the obligation to observe Torah and Mitzvot (the commandments). "The values people wish to realize, whether general humanistic ones like the idea of a 'model society,' or specifically Jewish [ones] such as the 'prophetic vision and the messianic promises,' or, more authentically, a condition in which 'the earth shall be full of the knowledge of the Lord,' are not the affair of the state." They are, however, the goals of particular groups *within* the state, for the state's coercive apparatus is not appropriate to the implementation of such values and, in any case, "the realization of Zionism affords no guarantee of the actualization of these values." The special sanctity of the land of Israel, for Leibowitz, refers exclusively to the fact that some commandments can be done only there, such as the Torah's agricultural laws that were limited to Israel; there is no holiness inherent in that piece of land.

This is clearly a principled view of Judaism that owes much to Kant, as Leibowitz himself admits. Its appeal lies in making Judaism simple: it consists exclusively in following God's commandments. Its faults, though, derive from that very simplicity, for Jews have not historically been identified exclusively by their religious commitment, as central as that may have been; they have also been defined by their shared literature, language (Hebrew), history, and aspirations—including the return to Zion. To denude Israel of its religious importance as Leibowitz does, then, is to ignore the breadth of meaning that Jewish identity as a whole, and Israel in particular, has had for most Jews in times past and continues to have to this day.

David Hartman, in contrast to both Yehoshua and Leibowitz, ascribes religious significance to the State of Israel. He specifically does not see Israel as the product of God's will or design, for that would lead to the dilemma of why God did not act to prevent the Holocaust. Hartman instead attributes religious significance to Israel because of its possible influence on the religious life of Jews. "If an event in history can be a catalyst for a new perception of the scope of Torah, if it widens the range of halakhic [Jewish legal] action and responsibility, if it provides greater opportunities for hearing God's *mitzvot*, then this already suffices to endow the event with religious significance, for it intensifies and widens the way God can be present in the daily life of the individual and the community." Because "Israel expands the possible range of halakhic involvement in human affairs beyond the circumscribed borders of home and synagogue to the public domain," it holds out the promise for an increased level of holiness, for realization of "the full scope of the covenantal spirit of Judaism." But the land "must always be perceived as an instrumental and never as an absolute value," thus undermining "the idolatry of state power." Messianic categories might be applied to the State of Israel, according to Hartman, not in the sense of God participating in the creation or activities of the State, nor in the sense that Israel has achieved a divine reality, but rather in the sense that Israel *aspires* to greater openness and love of God's commandments on the part of the total Jewish community. In doing this, it is thrust into the dilemma of how to balance Western democratic values of individual conscience and pluralism with traditional Jewish ideas of a single, communal standard, with all else being categorized as idolatry; but that is part of the challenge of creating a messianic state worthy of the name.

Hartman's view is decidedly religious, for what makes Israel special for him is the religious potential that Israel promises. His is a liberal form of traditional Judaism, though, as manifested by his insistence that Israel be the homeland for all Jews, regardless of their religious proclivities, and that Israel's policies reflect that goal. One should appreciate that compassion and openness, but the question still remains as to whether most Jews—indeed, most Israelis—would share his religious understanding of, and goals for, Israel.

Moreover, as Hartman himself states, the ultimate definitional problem that Israel must face is the conflict between its identity as a Jewish state and its identity as a democracy. Israel, of course, is not alone in this kind of problem: France, Ireland, Italy, and other countries are struggling with a parallel situation in trying to determine the extent to which, and the ways in which, they are Catholic countries. Israel, though, has the unenviable task of addressing this problem as the only Jewish state in the world, with no other nation's experience to use as a guide. The issue is not only theoretical: the way it is resolved now has, and will continue to have, major implications for political, social, and religious policies in Israel.

Finally, for Marc Ellis, "When today we speak of the formative events of Holocaust and Israel, Jews need to add the experience of the Palestinian people as a formative event for the Jewish people as well." To maintain that the Holocaust is historically unique is, according to Ellis, to marginalize and trivialize it. Instead, the Holocaust must stand as the symbol for the need of all human beings to fight against those people and conditions that cause human suffering. When seen that way, the Holocaust requires Jews, negatively, to oppose Israeli repression of Palestinians and, positively, to seek to build a respectful and harmonious community with the Palestinians despite past wrongs. In this effort, Jews can and should learn from contemporary Christian theologians who have confronted the question of how Christians can remain committed to their faith despite Christian complicity with the perpetrators of the Holocaust—namely, through a search for a coalition of messianic trust (Metz), a realization that the massacres of the innocent continue in our own time (Gutierrez), revolutionary forgiveness (Heyward), and the prophetic hope that we can reach a stage "when one person is not another's evil, one people's redemption is not another people's damnation" (Ruether).

"First and foremost, this new configuration suggests that deabsolutization of Israel is crucial to Jewish politics and theology. Jews are essentially a diaspora people who choose to live among the peoples of the world. . . . It may be that at this point a state organization of the Jewish community of Israel is important, but that hardly means forever." Thinking in this way "liberates Israel from the throes of redemption, a function it cannot fulfill." The State of Israel, then, is, for Ellis, not a theological goal in and of itself; it is rather a political arrangement that some Jews desire now. That may be understandable, given the horrific experience of the Holocaust and the aspiration to create new forms of Jewish expression in its wake. Such motivations to create a state of their own, though, do not relieve Israelis from the moral obligations of any other state, let alone from the lessons of the Holocaust that the Jews, of all people, should have learned—namely, that Palestinians may not be oppressed as a means toward that end.

Needless to say, Ellis' view of both the theological status of Israel and the policies it should adopt is not embraced by most Jewish writers, especially religious ones. The policies of Prime Ministers Rabin and Peres in the mid-1990s, though, moved in the direction Ellis recommends, and secular Israeli Jews, and many American Jews as well, may indeed think in terms close to his theory—even if they are reticent to voice their views. In any case, he certainly challenges not only the innocent enthusiasm that many Jews have for Israel, but also the serious, theological assertions embedded in the Jewish tradition and in the minds of many contemporary Jews that the renewed State of Israel is "the beginning of the flowering of our redemption."

After nineteen centuries of wandering the world without a homeland, Jews greet the existence of the State of Israel in our time with joy and with hope. Its relationship to Jewish theological claims, if any, its character as a Jewish and yet a democratic state, and its relationship to the Jews of the Diaspora, though, are all very much matters of theoretical, as well as practical, discussion.

Notes

1. God rewards the obedient and faithful, and He punishes the disobedient: Leviticus 26; Deuteronomy 28; etc. The specific application of that to illness: Leviticus 26:14–16; Deuteronomy 28:22, 27, 58–61. The Rabbis' assertion that because of the linkage of sickness with sin, illness cannot be healed until all one's sins are forgiven: B. *Nedarim* 41a.
2. E.g., B. *Menahot* 29b.
3. M. *Avot (Ethics of the Fathers)* 4:2.
4. M. *Sanhedrin* 10:1.
5. Maimonides, *Guide for the Perplexed*, Part III, Chapters 8–24, especially Chs. 10, 12, 15.
6. *Ibid.*, Part III, Ch. 12.
7. See, for example, Robert Gordis, *A Faith for Moderns* (New York: Bloch, 1960), pp. 35, 115, 216.
8. This has been printed in many books on the history of Reform Judaism in America. See, for example, Eugene B. Borowitz, *Reform Judaism Today* (New York: Behrman House, 1983), p. 193 (in the Supplement, following the numbered pages of the book). Alternatively, see "Pittsburgh Platform," *Encyclopedia Judaica* 16 vols. (Jerusalem: Keter, 1971), 13:571.

28

Faith after the Holocaust

ELIEZER BERKOVITS

The Hiding of the Face

The problem thus raised by the prophets and the teachers of the Talmud is of course the age-old problem of the theodicy. The manner of its formulation testifies to the fact that there was a full realization in biblical and Talmudic times that there is indeed undeserved suffering in history.[1] This, of course, requires a modification of the concept of *Mipnei Hataeinu*, "Because of our sins." No doubt it does demand great strength of character of an individual—and how much more of an entire people—to acknowledge that one's misfortunes are due to one's own failings and to accept responsibility for them.[2] At the same time, looking at the entire course of Jewish history, the idea that all this has befallen us because of our sins is an utterly unwarranted exaggeration. There is suffering because of sins; but that all suffering is due to it is simply not true. The idea that the Jewish martyrology through the ages can be explained as divine judgment is obscene. Nor do we for a single moment entertain the thought that what happened to European Jewry in our generation was divine punishment for sins committed by them. It was injustice absolute, injustice countenanced by God.

In biblical terminology, we speak of *Hester Panim*, the Hiding of the Face, God's hiding of his countenance from the sufferer. Man seeks God in his tribulation but cannot find him. It is, however, seldom realized that "the Hiding of the Face" has two meanings in the Bible, which are in no way related to each other. It is generally assumed that the expression signifies divine judgment and punishment. We find it indicated, for instance, in Deuteronomy, 31:17–18, in the words:

> Then My anger shall be kindled against them in that day, and I will forsake them, and I will hide My face from them, and they shall be devoured, and many evils and

Eliezer Berkovits, *Faith after the Holocaust* (New York: Ktav, 1973), pp. 94–113, 128–37. © Ktav Publishing House, Hoboken, NJ. 07030.

troubles shall come upon them; . . . , And I will surely hide My face in that day for all
the evil which they shall have wrought, in that they are turned unto other gods.

But the Bible also speaks of the Hiding of the Face when human suffering results,
not from divine judgment, but from the evil perpetrated by man. Even the innocent may
feel himself forsaken because of the Hiding of the Face. A moving example of this
form of *Hester Panim* is the Forty-Fourth Psalm, from which we have already quoted
a short passage. One should study the entire psalm: we shall recall here only its closing verses:

> All this is come upon us; yet have we not forgotten Thee,
> Neither have we been false to Thy covenant.
> Our heart is not turned back,
> Neither have our steps declined from Thy path;
> Though Thou hast crushed us into a place of jackals,
> And covered us with the shadow of death.
> If we had forgotten the name of our God,
> Or spread forth our hands to a strange god;
> Would not God search this out?
> For he knoweth the secrets of the heart.
> Nay, but for Thy sake are we killed all the day;
> We are accounted as sheep for the slaughter.
>
> Awake, why sleepest Thou, O Lord?
> Arouse Thyself, cast not off for ever.
> Wherefore hidest Thou Thy face,
> And forgettest our affliction and our oppression?
> For our soul is bowed down to the dust;
> Our belly cleaveth to the earth.
> Arise for our help,
> And redeem us for Thy mercy's sake.

The Hiding of the Face about which the psalmist complains is altogether different from
its meaning in Deuteronomy. There it is a manifestation of divine anger and judgment
over the wicked; here it is indifference—God seems to be unconcernedly asleep during
the tribulations inflicted by man on his fellow. Of the first kind of *Hester Panim* one might
say that it is due to *Mipnei Hataeinu*, that it is judgment because of sins committed, but
not of the second kind. It is God hiding himself mysteriously from the cry of the innocent. It is the divine silence of which the rabbis spoke in the Talmud.

The Affirmation

Not only had the problem already been raised in all seriousness and full intellectual honesty in biblical and Talmudic times, it was also fully realized that at stake was God's presence in history. There was full awareness that the seriousness of the problem was apt to
lead many a Jew to what is today called radical theology or the rejection of divine concern with human destiny. Ezekiel reported about the reaction of some people to the catastrophe of the destruction of the Temple and the loss of independence. He quotes their
words: " . . . The Lord seeth us not, the Lord hath forsaken the land."[3] Like Ivan
Karamazov, they too maintained that since God has absented himself, all was permissi-

ble. These were the early radical theologians in ancient Israel. The prophet Malachi, too, knew them. It is to them that he lets the words of God be addressed:

Your words have been all too strong against Me,
Saith the Lord.
Yet ye say: "Wherein have we spoken against Thee?"
Ye have said: "It is vain to serve God;
And what profit is it that we have kept His charge,
And that we have walked mournfully
Because of the Lord of hosts?
And now we call the proud happy;
Yea, they that work wickedness are built up;
Yea, they try God, and are delivered.[4]

"To walk mournfully because of the Lord" is not to walk like Ivan Karamazov, not to consider everything permissible, but to live obeying the laws of God. It is, however, useless to do so. God is not really concerned or, perhaps, he cannot do much about it anyway. For do not the wicked prosper and are not the proud happy? Is not evil successful? How may it be reconciled with God's providential presence?

Such were the radical theologians of old Israel. There is at least one outstanding figure known to us in talmudic times who belongs in the same category. He was Elisha ben Abuyah, at one time the teacher of the great Rabbi Meir. He lost his faith because he could find no solution to the problem of the theodicy. In view of the suffering of the innocent, he questioned God's justice and providence. He found no answer and became *Aher*, a changed person. According to one opinion he witnessed the accidental death of a young boy who was engaged in a work by which he was fulfilling a biblical commandment and also obeying the will of his father, thus honoring him as also required by the Bible. According to another version, he saw how the tongue of the martyred Hutspith, the Interpreter, was dragged along by a pig. He exclaimed at the sight: "The mouth from which issued wisdom like pearls should lick the dirt!" At that, "he went out and sinned."[5] There were others like him, less distinguished. Inevitably, in the course of Jewish history, the quest and the questioning continued. We even have a prayer for the radical theologian on record. According to one interpretation, in the abridged form of the *Amidah* we pray "For those who in this long exile are critical of God, believing that He has forsaken them. May they experience God's providential care, His mercy and grace."[6]

If Judaism rejected its radical theologians through the ages, it was not because of lack of sensitivity to the seriousness of the problem that they raised. The men of faith in Israel knew very well of the problem. They experienced it in their own lives on their own bodies. How often did they cry out in their agony over the terrible experience of God's absence! The Psalms, for example, are replete with the experience and the cry. Who could have felt the absence of God more crushingly than the man who exclaimed:

Awake, why sleepest Thou, O Lord?
Arouse Thyself, cast not off forever.
Wherefore hidest Thou Thy face,
Arouse Thyself, cast not off forever.
And forgettest our affliction and our oppression?
For our soul is bowed down to the dust;
Our belly cleaveth unto the earth.

Arise for our help,
And redeem us for Thy mercy's sake!

It was the excruciating experience of divine indifference that caused the psalmist to plead:

How long, O Lord, wilt Thou forget me for ever?
How long wilt Thou hide Thy face from me?[8]

The intensity of the experience comes to most moving expression in the phrase: "wilt Thou forget me for ever?" No one ever has an everlasting experience. The phrase tells of the long wait for divine help that was all in vain; it conveys the idea of utter hopelessness, of radical abandonment by God. The words would not have been inadequate for the agony of the death camps.

It is because of the apparent divine unconcern that the psalmist has to cry out:

Arise, O Lord: O God, lift up Thy hand;
Forget not the humble.
Wherefore doth the wicked contemn God,
And say in his heart: "Thou wilt not require?"[9]

Such passages, and numerous others of the same kind, give expression to the struggles of men of faith against the demonic in history. They are the questioning, searching, yes! even the accusing cry of faith induced by God's silence in the face of evil. It is also the lament of Isaiah, when he declares:

But Zion said: "The Lord hath forsaken me,
And the Lord hath forgotten me."[10]

Obviously, to feel that one is forgotten by God is not a realization that one is being punished for one's sins. Whom God punishes is not forgotten by God. Zion's plight of being abandoned and forgotten is the experience of divine unconcern of God's indifference toward human destiny. Through the ages, men of faith knew that human suffering was not to be explained by divine punishment alone, as expiation for guilt and divine justice done. They knew well that the poor and the weak were the victims, that wickedness and evil often held the upper hand, that God was often silent in history.

The experience of God's "absence" is not new: each generation had its Auschwitz problem. Neither is the negative response of resulting disbelief new in the history of Jewish spiritual struggle: each generation had its radical theology. Yet, the men of faith in Israel, each facing his own Auschwitz, in the midst of their radical abandonment by God, did not hesitate to reject the negative resolution of the problem. Notwithstanding the fact that so much in their experience tended to lead to the conclusion that there is "neither judgment nor a Judge," they insisted: "Still there is judgment and there is a Judge." Significantly, the formulation is Rabbi Akiba's, himself—as we saw—the saintly giant of Jewish martyrdom.[11]

However, if the problem was seen so clearly, how was it met? Needless to say, what we have called the simplistic theory of history that wishes to explain it all by the principle of "Because of our sins," the idea that if a man does the will of God and lives uprightly all will be well with him and that if he suffers his very suffering testifies against him, was indeed rejected. But the rabbis spoke of the silence of God as a historical fact, not of his absence. The one who is silent may be so called only because he is present.

Somehow they are able to hold on to both ends of the dilemma. It is not an either-or proposition for them. Indeed the same may be said of the nature of the problem as it is originally raised in the Bible. The same Jeremiah who contends with God because the way of the wicked prosper, also refers to God as "the righteous judge who examines the reins and the heart."[12] He predicts the destruction of Jerusalem because of the sins of her people. Habakkuk, too, in the very same context in which he complains about God's standing by as the wicked swallows up the righteous also speaks of the scourge of the Chaldeans, "that bitter and impetuous nation" that is sent out by God "for a judgment and established for a correction."[13] In the same breath, he holds on to the theory of God's worldwide historic providence of justice as well as to the facts of history which seem to contradict it. This dramatic grasping at once both horns of the dilemma finds its most moving expression in Job, when he exclaims:

> Though he slay me, yet will I trust in Him;
> But I will argue my ways before Him.[14]

There is trust in God to the end; yet there is contest with him, because the facts of human experience seem to assail that trust. How was it possible for these men to retain their faith in the God of history, in his justice and providence, notwithstanding the fact that their own historical experience seemed to contradict the faith and the trust?

Much more astounding, however, is the fact that even though the Jewish people were fully aware of the conflict between history and teaching, yet they staked their very existence on the original biblical proposition that life and the moral good were identical, as were death and evil; on the view that all history was ultimately under divine control, that all depended on doing the will of God, on living in accordance with his Torah. Flying in the face of all historical experience, they organized their own existence in history on the proposition that "the Eternal is nigh unto all of them that call upon Him, to all that call upon Him in truth."[15] Nor did they do it naively, childishly, not realizing the full implication of their undertaking. After Jeremiah, Habakkuk, Job, and the divine silence actually experienced in their history, how could they affirm three times daily in their prayers that "the Eternal is good to all and His tender mercies are over all His works."[16] without a great deal of sophistication! A quality of this sophistication I find in a midrash that deals with our subject. It is a comment on the words of the psalmist, "The Eternal preserveth the faithful."[17] Playing on the Hebrew *emumin* (faithful) and its association *amen* (an exclamatory affirmation) and *emunah* (faith, trust), it is maintained in the typical midrashic style: "The faithful," these are those who answer with *Amen* in complete trust (*emunah*). What does this mean? They say: "Blessed be the One who quickens the dead." It has not yet come about, nevertheless they believe in God, that he does quicken the dead. They say: "Blessed be the Redeemer of Israel." But he has not redeemed them, except for a very short period, after which they became once more oppressed; yet, they believe that I shall redeem them. . . . O for the faithful whom God preserves.[18] One can almost see the sad smile on the faces of the rabbis who left us with this comment. "God preserves the faithful?" God the Redeemer, the Resurrector? Indeed? Yes, indeed. Nevertheless, and in spite of it all, it is so. We adorn God with a great many attributes which mean to describe his actions in history even though they are contradicted by the facts of history. Fully aware of the facts, with open eyes, we contradict our experience with our affirmations. Yes, all these attributes of God in history are true; for if they were not true now, they will yet be true.

The Explanation

It would seem to us that what the just-quoted midrash wishes to convey is the idea that God is what Judaism believes him to be. True enough, many of His attributes are not manifest in history, but they will yet be revealed. On what grounds could such a statement have been made?

We have discussed earlier the two different forms of *Hester Pamin*, of the "Hiding of the Face": one as judgment, the other as apparent divine indifference toward the plight of man. We may glean a hint of the theological significance of such apparent divine indifference from a passage in Isaiah. The prophet says of God:

> Verily Thou art a God that hidest Thyself,
> O God of Israel, the Saviour.[19]

In this passage God's self-hiding is not a reaction to human behavior, when the Hiding of the Face represents God's turning away from man as a punishment. For Isaiah, God's self-hiding is an attribute of divine nature. Such is God. He is a God who hides himself. Man may seek him and he will not be found; man may call to him and he may not answer. God's hiding his face in this case is not a response to man, but a quality of being assumed by God on his own initiative. But neither is it due to divine indifference toward the destiny of man. God's hiding himself is an attribute of the God of Israel, who is the Savior. In some mysterious way, the God who hides himself is the God who saves. Thus, Isaiah could also say:

> And I will wait for the Lord that hideth His face from the house of Jacob and I will hope for Him.[20]

One may well wait and hope for the God who hides his face, if the God who hides himself is the Savior. But how may the Hiding of the Face assume this second meaning and become a divine attribute in such close association with God's self-revelation as the Savior? An analysis of a talmudic passage may lead us to an appreciation of this second— and more fundamental—meaning of the concept of the Hiding of the Face. It is no mere coincidence that it happens to be a discussion between Rabbi Meir and his quondam teacher Elisha ben Abuyah, who—as we have seen—became Aher, "another," because of the problem of evil on earth. It is said that after Aher had turned into the "path of licentiousness," he asked Rabbi Meir: "What is the meaning of the saying that 'God hath also made the one over against the other?' "[21] Answered the former disciple: "Whatever the Holy one, blessed be He, created in his world, he also created its opposite. He created mountains and he created hills; he created oceans and he created rivers." To which Aher countered: "Not like this spoke your master Rabbi Akiba. But said he: God created the righteous and he created the wicked; he created Gan Eden (Paradise) and he created Gehenna. . . . "[22]

The dating of the discussion as having taken place "after Aher had turned into the path of licentiousness" is an indication that the subject of the discussion has some bearing on Aher's problem and heresy. What is it they are discussing? It would seem to us that the subject of their discussion is the dialectical principle, which is seen as a principle of creation, incorporated in the functioning of the universe. Rabbi Meir expresses it in general terms. Whatever God created, he also created its opposite. It could not be otherwise. There could be no mountains without valleys. A thing is defined by its limits. It is recognizable for what it is by contrast to its opposite. A is A because it is limited by non-A; it has self-hood because it is encumbered, because it is denied by non-A. Rabbi Akiba seems to express the same dialectical principle, but he gives it a limited ethical application. The dialectics of creation is responsible for the opposites: the righteous and the wicked, good and evil. Without good, no evil; without evil, no good! Why then did Aher oppose the general formula of the dialectical principle, holding on to the manner of its specifically ethical application by Rabbi Akiba? There is a vast distinction between Rabbi Meir's grasp of the dialectics of creation and the way Aher wants it to be understood. The example in the case, on which Aher insists, is adequate to illustrate the dialectics. However, it must have been noted that Rabbi Meir's example is somewhat gauche. The dialectical contrast would have to be between mountains and valleys, oceans and continents, not between mountains and hills nor between oceans and rivers. Yet, in his opening comment, Rabbi Meir invokes the dialectics of creation. It would seem to us that in Rabbi Meir's opinion the dialectics in creation does not represent pure opposites. The contrast is not absolute but relative. There is no absolute valley as there is no absolute mountain; the highest mountain is only a high hill and the lowest valley is really a bit of a hill. So too with the opposites of water and land. Neither the oceans nor the continents are absolutely alien to each other. The difference is only a relative one, like the one between oceans and rivers, like that between more and less. There is neither absolute depth to which to sink, nor absolute heights to which to rise. Aher cannot accept it, for the former disciple really discusses the problem and case of his sometime master. If the opposites of creation are absolutes, then good and evil too are absolutes; the creator is then directly responsible for both. He is then really beyond good and evil, for he is equally involved in both or, as one might also say, he is indifferent to ethical considerations. If so, Aher is right; there is neither judgment nor a Judge. It is for this reason that he insists on citing Rabbi Akiba whose formulation seems to suggest this kind of divine irresponsibility or indifference. The opposites, according to this version are the *Sadiq* (Righteous) and the *Rasha* (Wicked). God himself created both, is Aher's interpretation of Rabbi Akiba's statement. The *Sadiq* is what he is and the *Rasha* is what he is; the one is not to be praised, the other, not to be condemned. God himself created them that way. They are part of a universe that has no partiality for either of them. And once again, Aher himself is vindicated. It is exactly this kind of interpretation that Rabbi Meir wishes to obviate by his "bad" example of the dialectics. The opposites are not absolutes, which means they are not categories of creation. Rabbi Meir is not in disagreement with Rabbi Akiba. It is Aher who insists on an interpretation of Rabbi Akiba's statement that was never intended by its author. Rabbi Akiba never meant to say that God actually creates the *Sadiq* and the *Rasha*, that good and evil are indifferently incorporated in the universe. His whole life contradicts this kind of a teaching. Nor is it likely that Aher was unaware of it. It is with tongue in cheek that he reminds his former disciple: "Not like this did your master Rabbi Akiba explain it. . . . " Rabbi Meir spoke in general terms; he did not expatiate on the dialectics of good and evil, of the righteous and the wicked. Out of tact and consideration for the feelings of his former teacher, he did not pursue the implications for ethics and morality of a dialetics that does not recognize absolutes as ontological categories of creation. Aher understood him well. One imagines the impishly appreciative smile in his face as he was saying: "Not like this did your master explain it. . . . " Indeed, not like this; yet, exactly like this.

Rabbi Akiba expresses in ethical terms the significance of the dialectics of Rabbi Meir. God does not determine in advance that one person be a *Sadiq*, and another a *Rasha*. But unless the possibility existed for a man to be a *Rasha*, if he so desires, one could not only [not] be a *Rasha*, one could not be a *Sadiq* either. For one can only be a *Sadiq* as a result of responsible choices made in the freedom of available alternatives. Where the choice is nonexistent, where the possibility of becoming a *Rasha* is not open to man, the possibility of becoming a *Sadiq* too has been excluded. The ethical significance of Rabbi Meir's "bad" dialectics is that being a *Sadiq* is conditioned by man's freedom to choose the way of wickedness, just as being a *Rasha* presupposes his freedom to turn into the path of righteousness. The *Sadiq* is defined by the *Rasha* as the *Rasha* is defined by the *Sadiq*. That which is good is so because of the possibility of evil and vice versa. If, now, the dialectical principle is at work in the universe yet the opposites are not to be understood as absolute categories of creation and being, then God's creating the *Sadiq* and the *Rasha* means that God created both possibilities for man, to be a *Sadiq* or to be a *Rasha*. We have quoted Isaiah's statement earlier that God forms the light and creates darkness, makes peace and creates evil. Isaiah of course did not mean to say that God actually does evil. Rejecting Manichean dualism, the prophet maintains that God alone is the Creator. He created evil by creating the possibility for evil; He made peace by creating the possibility for it.[23] He had to create the possibility for evil, if He was to create the possibility for its opposite, peace, goodness, love.

In a sense, God can be neither good nor bad. In terms of his own nature He is incapable of evil. He is the only one who *is* goodness. But since, because of his very essence, he can do no evil, he can do no good either. God, being incapable of the unethical is not an ethical being. Goodness for him is neither an ideal, nor a value; it is existence, it is absolutely realized being. Justice, love, peace, mercy, are ideals for man only. They are values that may be realized by man alone. God is perfection. Yet because of his very perfection, he is lacking—as it were—one type of value; the one which is the result of striving for value. He is all light; on just that account, he is lacking the light that comes out of the darkness. One might also say that with man the good is axiology; with God, ontology. Man alone can strive and struggle for the good; God is Good. Man alone can create value; God is Value. But if man alone is the creator of values, one who strives for the realization of ideals, then he must have freedom of choice and freedom of decision. And his freedom must be respected by God himself. God cannot as a rule intervene whenever man's use of freedom displeases him. It is true, if he did so the perpetration of evil would be rendered impossible, but so would the possibility for good also disappear. Man can be frightened; but he cannot be bludgeoned into goodness. If God did not respect man's freedom to choose his course in personal responsibility, not only would the moral good and evil be abolished from the earth, but man himself would go with them. For freedom and responsibility are of the very essence of man. Without them man is not human. If there is to be man, he must be allowed to make his choices in freedom. If he has such freedom, he will use it. Using it, he will often use it wrongly; he will decide for the wrong alternative. As he does so, there will be suffering for the innocent.

The question therefore is not: Why is there undeserved suffering? But, why is there man? He who asks the question about injustice in history really asks: Why a world? Why creation? To understand this is of course far from being an answer to our problem. But to see a problem in its true dimension makes it easier for us to make peace with the circumstances from which it arises. It is not very profitable to argue with God as to why He created this world. He obviously decided to take his chance with man; he decided for this world. Given man, God himself could eliminate moral evil and the suffering caused by it only by eliminating man, by recalling the world of man into nothingness.

These theological concepts have found their more intimate expression in the language of religious affirmation. We are familiar with biblical passages that speak of God's mercy with the sinner. We readily appreciate pronouncements like the one in Ezekiel that declares:

> As I live, saith the Lord God, I have no pleasure in the death of the Wicked, but that the wicked turn from his way and live. . . . [24]

In keeping with deep-rooted biblical tradition, the rabbis in a homily interpreted the plural form of the Hebrew expression that describes God as "long-suffering" as meaning that God is long-suffering in numerous ways. He is long-suffering with the wicked as well as with the righteous. We have great understanding for the fact that God is merciful and forgiving, that he does not judge man harshly and is willing to have patience with him. God is waiting for the sinner to find his way to him. This is how we like to see God. This is how we are only too glad to acknowledge him. But we never seem to realize that while God is long-suffering, the wicked are going about their dark business on earth and the result is ample suffering for the innocent. While God waits for the sinner to turn to him, there is oppression and persecution and violence among men. Yet, there seems to be no alternative. If man is to be, God must be long-suffering with him; he must suffer man. This is the inescapable paradox of divine providence. While God tolerates the sinner, he must abandon the victim; while he shows forebearance with the wicked, he must turn a deaf ear to the anguished cries of the violated. This is the ultimate tragedy of existence: God's very mercy and forebearance, his very love for man, necessitates the abandonment of some men to a fate that they may well experience as divine indifference to justice and human suffering. It is the tragic paradox of faith that God's direct concern for the wrongdoer should be directly responsible for so much pain and sorrow on earth.

We conclude then: he who demands justice of God must give up man; he who asks for God's love and mercy beyond justice must accept suffering.

One may call it the divine dilemma that God's *Erek Apayim*, his patiently waiting countenance to some is, of necessity, identical with his *Hester Panim*, his hiding of the countenance, to others. However, the dilemma does find a resolution in history. If man is to be, God himself must respect his freedom of decision. If man is to act on his own responsibility, without being continually overawed by divine supremacy, God must absent himself from history. But man left to his freedom is capable of greatness in both—in creative goodness and destructive evil. Though man cannot be man without freedom, his performance in history gives little reassurance that he can survive in freedom. God took a risk with man and he cannot divest himself of responsibility for man. If man is not to perish at the hand of man, if the ultimate destiny of man is not to be left to the chance that man will never make the fatal decision, God must not withdraw his providence from his creation. He must be present in history. That man may be, God must absent himself; that man may not perish in the tragic absurdity of his own making, God must remain present. The God of history must be absent and present concurrently. He hides his presence. He is present without being indubitably manifest; he is absent without being hopelessly inaccessible. Thus, many find him even in his "absence"; many miss him even in his presence. Because of the necessity of his absence, there is the "Hiding of the Face" and suffering of the innocent; because of the necessity of his presence, evil will not ultimately triumph; because of it, there is hope for man.

Mighty and Awesome

In other words, God's presence in history must remain—mostly—unconvincing. But, perhaps, this is a mere theory, unsupported by experience? After all, how can one prove an unconvincing presence convincingly? There is another passage in the Talmud that leads us to a deeper grasp of our problem and its possible solution. Ezra, the great rejuvenator of Judaism at the time of the return from Babylon, and his associates in his endeavors were known as the "Men of the Great Assembly." The Talmud discusses the question of this honorific title. How did they deserve it? The answer is given. They were so called because they restored the old glory of the divine crown. The "crown" was described by Moses when he called God: "the great God, the mighty and the awful."[25] But Jeremiah, in the light of the experiences of his generation, could not accept this description. He was perplexed. Strangers mock him in his sanctuary! Where is his awesomeness? No longer did he say of God, as did Moses, that he was "awful." Then came Daniel. His charge was: Strangers subjugate his children! Where are his mighty deeds? He stopped saying of God that he was mighty. But then came Ezra and his assembly and they explained: "That indeed is his mightiness, that he subdues his inclination and grants long-suffering to the wicked. And this in itself is a proof of his awesomeness; for were it not for the fear of him, how could one people (i.e., Israel) survive among the nations."[26] One might say that as a challenge to faith the problems of Jeremiah and Daniel were not different in essence from the problem of the present post-Auschwitz generation of Jews. The vulgarity that God might have died did not enter the mind of Jeremiah or Daniel. But they were perplexed by their God. How was he to be understood? What were his attributes in view of the manner of his functioning in history? If God's enemies feared him, they would not dare mock him. If God were mighty, he would use his might to protect his people.

Most noteworthy in this discussion of our problem is the complete antithesis in the position of the side that raises the question and the one that offers the solution. The question as to God's presence in history is raised on the assumption that the fear of God ought to subdue the enemies of God and the power of God ought to protect God's people. The answer is based on a radical redefinition of the concepts of the fear and the might of God. The mightiness of God is shown in his tolerance of the mocking of his enemies; it is revealed in his long-suffering. This is in keeping with the interpretation of the words of the psalmist that we quoted earlier: "Who is like unto you among the mighty?"—enduring insults and remaining silent. The awesomeness of God is revealed in the survival of Israel. The meaning of the redefinition of the concept of the divine power is twofold. First of all, it means that it is impossible for God to be present in history by using his physical omnipotence. If God had meant to rule the world of man by material might, he might well have given up the thought at its very conception. Man can only exist because God renounces the use of his power on him. This, of course, means that God cannot be present in history through manifest material power. Such presence would destroy history. History is the arena for human responsibility and its product. When God intervenes in the affairs of men by physical might as, for instance, in the story of Exodus, we speak of a miracle. But the miracle is outside of history; in it history is at a standstill. However, beyond that we are introduced to a concept of divine mightiness that consists in self-restraint. For the omnipotent God to act powerfully would indeed be a small matter. The rabbis in the Talmud saw the mightiness of the Almighty in that he controls his inclination to judge and to punish and behaves in history as if he were powerless. To curb the use of power where infinite power is at hand, to endure the mocking of one's enemies when one could easily eliminate them, that is true strength. Such is the mightiness of God. God is mighty, for he shackles his omnipotence and becomes "powerless" so that history may be possible. In spite of his infinite power, he does not frighten man but lets him find his own way, extending to him his long-suffering. God is mighty in the renunciation of his might in order to bear with man.

Yet he is present in history. He reveals his presence in the survival of his people Israel. Therein lies his awesomeness. God renders himself powerless, as it were, through forebearance and long-suffering, yet he guides. How else could his powerless people have survived! He protects, without manifest power. Because of that, Israel could endure God's long silences without denying him. Because of the survival of Israel the prophets could question God's justice and yet believe in him. The theology of a God unconvincingly present in history alone might not have sufficed. The dilemma cannot be resolved on the intellectual level alone. And, indeed, neither Jeremiah, nor Habakkuk, nor even Job, were given an intellectually valid answer. The talmudic conclusion was correctly reached: God was silent. Yet, the dilemma was resolved, not in theory, but strangely enough, in history itself. Now, historical facts that conflict with a philosophy of history *eo ipso* refute that philosophy. But historical facts, however numerous, cannot refute another historical fact, however irregular and solitary. It is indeed true, as was seen by Jeremiah, Habakkuk, and others, that a great deal of the historical experience contradicts some essential Judaic propositions of a just and benevolent providence; the way of the wicked often succeeds, God is much too often silent. But it is even more true that seen in the light of the generally observed facts and processes of history, the very idea of a people of God, of constituting a people on the basis of a commitment to do the will of God and to the belief that life and death are determined by the ethical categories of good and evil, was a fantastic proposition. All history advised against it. From the very beginning, all the powers and processes that determine the course of history were poised to render its materialization impossible. Indeed, had it all been only an idea, a theology or philosophy, the testimony of the facts of history would have rendered the concept of a people of God and the propositions on which it was to be based ridiculously absurd. However, this fantastic concept became itself a fact of history. The people of God did come into being; it entered history, it became itself a historical reality, exercising great historical influence and demonstrating mysterious survival power. It has all been quite irregular. It is all in conflict with the rest of historical experience, yet itself a fact of history.

There is this difference between a fact and an idea. The more irregular an idea is, i.e., the less it is in harmony with the generally prevailing principles relevant to it, the less the likelihood that it is valid and true. The same may be said of a philosophy of history: the more it is contradicted by historical experience, the less tenable it is. But a fact obeys the opposite rule. The more irregular it is, the more unique it is, the less in keeping with what is generally observed and experienced, the greater is its significance. The more intensely a unique historical reality is disavowed and challenged by the overwhelming force of a universal historical experience, and yet it is able to maintain itself and to survive all conflicts and all challenges, has by its very staying power proved its unique vitality as well as the validity of the principle which it proclaims. Such a unique and absurdly irregular historic fact has been the people of God. But because it is a historic fact of inexplicable surviving power, the more it is challenged by the facts of universal history, the more is it confirmed in the unique stands which it takes, simply because it does take that stand

and survives in spite of it all. Jeremiah could face with complete intellectual honesty the unpleasant fact that the way of the wicked does prosper, without embracing it as an ultimate truth in history upon which to base a Machiavellian type of philosophy. He could do that because the reality of Israel, notwithstanding all its contemporary misery, pointed as a fact in the opposite direction. The rabbis of the Talmud could speak of the silence of God at the time of the destruction of the Temple and the state and yet remain true to His word, because notwithstanding the *hurban* Israel survived, remained historically viable, full of future expectation.

This, however, means that a Jewish philosophy of history is not to be based on the teachings alone. The teaching, as such, is contradicted by a great deal of historical experience. But neither should Jews allow such conflicting evidence to sway them in determining their outlook on history, for such evidence itself is contradicted by their own existence, by the historic reality of Israel, by the place of the Jewish people in history, by the survival of the people of God; yes, by the fact that once again this people of God is back in its ancient homeland, in Zion and Jerusalem.

It would seem to us that there are two histories: one, that of the nations and the other, that of Israel. The history of the nations is self-explanatory. It is naturalistic history, explainable in terms of power and economics. It is exactly on those terms that the history of Israel remains a sealed secret: it defies that kind of interpretation. The history of Israel alone is not self-explanatory; it testifies to a supra-natural dimension jutting into history. Now, if the two could have been neatly divided and separated from each other, things might have worked out quite nicely. There would not have been either antisemitism or pogroms, either ghettos or crematoria. But unavoidably, both histories take place in the same time dimension and occupy the same space; together they form the history of mankind. Of necessity, the two histories interpenetrate. Thus, in the naturalistic realm occasionally the Voice is heard and a glimpse is gained of the presence of the supra-natural in this world. On the other hand, the wild unbridled forces of the naturalistic realm ever so often invade—and wreak havoc in—the this-worldly domain in which sustenance of meaning and purpose is drawn from the super-natural dimension.

Jews are confused in our times because they imagine that the problem of Jewish faith arises from the conflict between Jewish teaching and Jewish or general historical experience. In fact, the conflict takes place between two histories. There are two realms: the realm of the Is and that of the Ought. The history of the nations is enacted mainly in the realm of the Is. It is naturalistic history, essentially power history. The history of Israel belongs chiefly in the realm of the Ought; it is faith history, faith that what ought to be, what ought to determine and guide human life, should be and will be. Faith history is at cross-purposes with power history, but history it is. As long as Israel lives, the Ought holds on to reality be it only by the skin of its teeth. As long as this is the case, the Ought has proved its vitality as a this-worldly possibility; it has found admittance into the realm of the Is. As long as Israel is, the Ought to, is; the Supernatural has acquired a footing in the Natural. As long as this is so there is hope for both—for there is hope for the ultimate merger of the two realms, when the Ought will be fully real and the real will be convincingly identified as the life which is the Good. In the meantime the conflict obtains, not between ideas and philosophies, which is easily bearable, but between fact and fact; between the powerful reality of the Is and the meaningful and mysterious reality of the Ought. Since it is a conflict between fact and fact, history and history, reality and reality, the conflict is clash, a battle accompanied by untold human suffering.

Why has it been so arranged by the God of history? We may not find an explanation. Decisive is, however, the realization that no matter what our solution may be to our specific problems, it must not abandon the truth to which the reality of Israel testifies. No matter how silent God may every so often be, we have heard his voice and because of that we know his word; no matter how empty of God vast tracts of the waste lands of history may appear to be, we know of his presence as we stand astounded contemplating our own existence. True, these are contradictory experiences which present the mind with a serious dilemma. But no matter how serious the dilemma, it cannot erase the fact of the enduring reality of Israel. Even if no answers could be found we would still be left with the only alternative with which Job too was left, i.e., of contending with God while trusting in him, of questioning while believing, inquiring with our minds yet knowing in our hearts! And even as we search for the answer, we praise Him as the rabbis of old did: who is like you our God, mighty in silence!

• • •

The Witness After the Holocaust

Does all this justify God's silence during the European holocaust of the Jewish people or does it even explain it? As we have already stated, it is not our intention to explain it, and certainly not to justify it. We have tried to show what is implied in Judaism's faith in the God of history independently of our contemporary experience. The question is, of course, well-grounded: Can such faith still be maintained in the face of the destruction of European Jewry? People of our day are often apt to give quick and mainly emotional answers to the question. This is understandable. We have been too close to the catastrophe, too deeply and personally involved. However, notwithstanding our deep emotional involvement, it is essential first of all to gain a clear intellectual grasp of the problem.

The Jewish, radical theologian of our day—and the numerous less sophisticated people whose preoccupation with the problem of Auschwitz does not let them reach any other solution but the negative one—do not understand the true nature of the quandary of faith that confronts us. The problem of faith here is a problem of theology in the broadest sense of the word. What becomes questionable is the manner in which God relates himself to the world and to man. Strictly speaking, the questioning of God's justice in his relation to history has little to do with the quantity of undeserved suffering. The enormity of the number of martyrs of our generation—six million—is not essential to the doubt. As far as our faith in an absolutely just and merciful God is concerned, the suffering of a single innocent child poses no less a problem to faith than the undeserved suffering of millions. As far as one's faith in a personal God is concerned, there is no difference between six, five, four million victims or one million. Nahmanides expressed the thought clearly in his *Sha'ar Ha'gmul* in the following words: "Our quest [regarding theodicy] is a specific one, about [the plight of] this particular man. . . . This problem is not reduced if those who fall are few in number; nor does it become more serious if their number increases. For we are not discussing [the ways of] man. . . . Our arguments concern the Rock, whose work is perfect and all His ways just; there is nothing perverse or crooked in them."[27] Nothing is easier than to miss, for emotional reasons, the decisive importance of such a statement. How can one compare the suffering of a few to that of a multitude? How dare one raise the problem over the death of one innocent child as one must over that of a million and a half innocent Jewish children slaughtered by the Germans! One cannot and one dare not—as long as one judges man. There is a vast difference between less injustice and more injustice, between less human suffering and more. One human tragedy is not as heartbreaking as the same tragedy multiplied a millionfold. A man who murders one person is not as guilty as a mass murderer. The German crime of the ghettos and concentration camps stands out in all human history as the most abominable, the most sickening, and the most inhuman. But justice and injustice, guilt and innocence are matters of degree only for man. When one questions the acts of an Absolute God, whose every attribute, too, is absolute by definition, the innocent suffering of a single person is as incomprehensible as that of millions, not because the sufferings of millions matter as little as those of one human being, but because with Him the suffering of the one ought to be as scandalous as that of multitudes. An absolutely just God cannot be a tiny bit unjust. The least injustice in the Absolute is absolute injustice. An infinitely merciful God cannot be just a little bit unconcerned about innocent suffering. The least amount of indifference in the Infinite is infinite indifference. With Elisha ben Abuyah to have witnessed one case of undeserved suffering of the innocent was sufficient to raise the problem and cause him to lose faith. Such was also the insight of Camus. One compares the two sermons of the priest in *The Plague*. The first is a fire-and-brimstone preachment about the divine judgment that descended upon the sinful city; the second one is the mild acknowledgment of an impenetrable mystery. What happened between the two preachings? The priest had to witness the agony of a single child dying of the plague. One case was sufficient to change the man, who ultimately dies of the sickness of the incomprehensible.

Once the problem of evil is understood in its valid dimensions, the specific case of the holocaust is not seen to be essentially different from the old problem of theodicy.

It is still the old problem of Epicurus that confronts us. If God desires to prevent evil but is unable, he is not omnipotent. If he is able to prevent evil, but does not desire to do so, he is malevolent. If he is able and desires to prevent it, whence evil? The problem has been discussed by all thinking and believing people through the ages. It is one of the themes in Plato's *Statesman*. Already in those days there were those who from the presence of evil in the world concluded that God must be absent from history. He had to be far removed from the earthly scene; he could have no knowledge of man. If he did, how could he tolerate the evil that was done under the sun! This consideration was also one of the reasons for the assertion in later Aristotelianism that God had no knowledge of "singulars" and thus, divine providence was in no way concerned with the plight of the individual being or creature. These were the early forms of what in our days likes to call itself radical theology.

Once the questioning of God over the holocaust is motivated by the vastness of the catastrophe, the questioning itself becomes ethically questionable. It is of course more human to query God about the suffering of the many rather than the few, but it is certainly not more humane. On the contrary, it is more ethical, and intellectually more honest and to the point, to question God about the life and happiness of which even a single soul is being cheated on this earth than to base one's doubts and quest on the sacrificial abandonment of millions. With God the quantity of injustice must be immaterial. To think otherwise is itself a sign of callous indifference toward injustice and human suffering. To suggest that one could put up with less evil and less injustice, but not with so much, is cruelly unethical. Indeed, the holocaust was only possible because mankind was quite willing to tolerate less than the holocaust. This was the decisive aspect in the guilt of man in our times. It is important to understand the true nature of the problem if one involves God in it, questioning his ways with man and the world. It is the precondition for developing the attitude that may enable us to live meaningfully with the problem, even though its ultimate solution may forever escape us. Understood in its vastest intellectual dimension and its radical ethical relevance, the question is not why the holocaust, but why a world in which any amount of undeserved suffering is extant. This, of course, means that the question is tantamount to, why man? why a world of man? For, indeed, if man is to be as a being striving for value-realization, God must tolerate and endure him as a failure and an accusation.

How long is he to be tolerated as a failure, how long to be endured by God as an accusation of God? Who is to say! In order to answer the question, one ought to know the heart of God. How long God is willing to endure his creation even as a failure is the secret of creation itself. God's dominion over the world is not a dominion of justice.[28] In terms of justice, he is guilty. He is guilty of creation. But is he guilty of indifference or is he guilty of too much long-suffering? How vast is the infinitude of his mercy, his patience with man? When is it the moment for his justice to intervene and to call a halt to misused human freedom? Can we gauge the reach of his love even for the wicked, be they even those of his creatures who choose to become his failures? According to midrashic teaching, at the time of the drowning of the hosts of Pharaoh in the Red Sea the angels in heaven, as is their wont, were preparing to chant the daily hymn in praise of the Almighty. But God silenced them with the words: "The works of my hands are drowning in the sea and you sing my praises!"[29] It is not an easy matter for God to execute judgment over the guilty. Even "his failures" are the works of his hands.

The question after the holocaust ought not to be, how could God tolerate so much evil? The proper question is whether, after Auschwitz, the Jewish people may still be witnesses to God's elusive presence in history as we understand the concept. What of the nemesis of history and what of Jewish survival?

The Nazi crime of the German people attempted to eradicate the last vestiges of a possible innate sense of humanity, it sought the conscious extirpation from human nature of the last reminder of the fear of God in any form. It was the ultimate rebellion of nihilism against all moral emotion and all ethical values. However, this up to now mightiest and most morbid manifestation of human hubris too was overtaken by its complete and inescapable nemesis. In every field the very opposite of its goals has been accomplished. "Das Tausendjährige Reich," the empire for a millenium, was in ashes after twelve terrible years. Instead of the much heralded "Gross Deutschland" there is a divided Germany with greatly reduced frontiers. The nemesis is not limited to Nazi Germany alone, it has overtaken Western civilization itself. The holocaust is not exclusively the guilt of Germany; the entire West has a goodly share in it. One of the most tragic aspects of the world catastrophe of Nazism is to be seen in the fact that it was able to assume its vast dimensions of calamity mainly because of the tolerance and "understanding" that it enjoyed in the world community of nations for many years. During the period of favorable international climate nazified Germany was able to create one of the most powerful war machines in all history, to poison the minds of vast sections of the world's population, and to corrupt governments and public officials in many lands. This was possible partly because, with the help of the antisemitic heritage of the West, Nazi Germany was able to bring about the moral disintegration of many peoples with diabolical efficiency and speed and partly—and not altogether independently of it—because of the cynical calculations of worldwide power politics. Germany was meant to become the bulwark of the West against the threat of Russian communism. To this end many were willing to ignore the German-Nazi challenge to elementary justice and humanity. After all, its worst venom was directed against the Jews only. Even after the Second World War had already pursued its horrifying course in Europe for several years, there were still influential forces in the high seats of power, and even on the throne of so-called "spiritual grandeur," that hoped for a rapprochement between Nazi Germany and the Western powers. They thought it politically wise to go slow on Nazi-German criminality, piously hoping to bring off the brotherly alliance that would enable them to launch the greatest of all crusades, that against Soviet communism. Thus they became accomplices in the criminality of Auschwitz and the gas chambers. Nothing of what they had hoped for has been achieved. Instead of a curbing of communism, for which Germany and her sympathizers hoped, communism has reached its widest penetration the world over. This is not stated with any partiality for communism, but solely from the point of view of an observer who tries to detect the functioning of nemesis in history. Nazi Germany could have been stopped early in its track had there been less indifference toward the plight of the Jews and a better understanding of the demoralizing power of antisemitism. But antisemitism had long been a respectable trait in Western civilization. Thus, the Second World War became inevitable, as a result of which all the formerly great powers of Europe had been reduced to second and third rank. And even Russia and the United States who came out of the war as superpowers dwarfing all others, what have they gained if, as a result of their overwhelming might, they render each other's future, as well as that of all mankind, rather questionable? It is no mere coincidence that having countenanced the Final Solution to the Jewish problem, partly with glee and partly with equanimity, the world is now confronted with the serious possibility of a Final Solution to the entire problematic existence of man on this planet. Every one of the ambitions that the forces of power history have been pursuing have been weighed and found wanting. Had the nations and their churches not been silent and indifferent to what was recognizably afoot in the early days of nazism, world history would have taken an entirely different course and mankind would not now be balancing on the very edge of the thermonuclear abyss. This post-holocaust era is charged with the nemesis of history. This is the ignoble twilight hour of a disintegrating civilization.

It is true that Jewish people had to pay a terrible price for the crimes of mankind and today, too, as part of mankind, they are themselves deeply involved in the crisis of the human race, yet the Final Solution intended for it is far from being final. Though truncated, Israel survived this vilest of all degradations of the human race. Not only has it survived, but rising from one of its most calamitous defeats, it has emerged to new dignity and historic vindication in the state of Israel.

The most significant aspect of the establishment of the state of Israel is the fact that Jews through the ages knew that it was to come. They were waiting for it during their wanderings for long and dark centuries. There was little rational basis for their faith in the eventual return to the land of their fathers. Yet they knew that one day the faith would be translated into historical reality. They lived with that faith in the sure knowledge of divine concern. For the Jew, for whom Jewish history neither begins with Auschwitz nor ends with it, Jewish survival through the ages and the ingathering of the exiles into the land of their fathers after the holocaust proclaim God's holy presence at the very heart of his inscrutable hiddenness. We recognized in it the hand of divine providence because it was exactly what, after the holocaust, the Jewish people needed in order to survive. Broken and shattered in spirit even more than in body, we could not have been able to continue on our Jewish way through history without some vindication of our faith that the "Guardian of Israel neither slumbers nor sleeps." The state of Israel came at a moment in history when nothing else could have saved Israel from extinction through hopelessness. It is our lifeline to the future.

Confronting the holocaust, the relevant consideration is the full realization that it does not preempt the entire course of Jewish history. One dare not struggle with the problem of faith as if the holocaust were all we knew about the Jew and his relation to God. There is a pre-holocaust past, a post-holocaust present, and there is also a future, which is, to a large extent, Israel's own responsibility. Auschwitz does not contain the entire history of Israel; it is not the all-comprehensive Jewish experience. As to the past, we should also bear in mind that the Jew, who has known so much of the "Hiding of the Face," has also seen the divine countenance revealed to him. Notwithstanding Auschwitz, the life of the patriarchs is still with him; the Exodus did not turn into a mirage; Sinai has not come tumbling down; the prophets have not become charlatans; the return from Babylon has not proved to be a fairy tale. It is, of course, possible for people to secularize the history of Israel and deny the manifestation of a divine presence in it. However, such secularization is independent of the holocaust. It is not very meaningful to interpret the entire course of Jewish history exclusively on the basis of the death-camp experience of European Jewry. If the believer's faith in Israel's "encounters" with God in history is false, it must be so not on account of Auschwitz, but because the "encounters" just did not happen. On the other hand, if these manifestations of the divine presence did occur, then they are true events and will not become lies because of the holocaust.

For the person who does not recognize the presence of God in the Exodus, at Sinai, in the words of the prophets, in innumerable events of Jewish history, Auschwitz presents no problem of faith. For him God is forever absent. Only the Jew who has known of the presence of God is baffled and confounded by Auschwitz. What conclusions is he to draw from this terrifying absence of divine concern? Is God indifferent to human destiny? But the Jew knows otherwise. He knows of the most intimate divine concern. Has God, perhaps, died? Is it possible that once upon a time there was a God who was not indifferent toward Israel, but that now something has happened to him, he has gone away, he is no longer? This is plain silly. It is possible for a human being to lose faith in God. But it is not possible for God to die. He either is and therefore, will ever be; or he is not and, therefore never was. But if God who was, is, and will ever be, is it possible that at Auschwitz he rejected Israel, he turned away from Israel as a punishment for its sins? To believe this would be a desecration of the Divine Name. No matter what the sins of European Jewry might have been, they were human failings. If the holocaust was a punishment, it was a thousandfold inhuman. The only crime of man for which such punishment might be conceivable would be the Nazi crime of Germany, and even there, one would hesitate to impose it.

The Jew of faith is thus left with the perplexing duality of his knowledge of God. He knows of the numerous revelations of the divine presence as he knows of the overlong phases of God's absence. Auschwitz does not stand by itself. Notwithstanding its unique position as perhaps the most horrifying manifestation of divine silence, it has its place in

Jewish history beside the other silences of God together with the utterances of his concern. The Jew was called into being by the revelation of the divine in history. It is because God allowed his countenance to shine upon man that he is what he is. Only because of that does he know of the absence of God. But thanks to that, he also knows that God's absence, even at Auschwitz, is not absolute. Because of that it was possible for many to know God even along the path to the gas chambers. There were many who found him even in his hiding. Because of the knowledge of God's presence, the Jew can find God even in his absence.

No, the holocaust is not all of Jewish history, nor is it its final chapter. That it did not become the Final Solution as was planned by the powers of darkness enables the Jew who has known of the divine presence to discern intimations of familiar divine concern in the very midst of his abandonment. This, too, is essentially an old Jewish insight.

Yet all this does not exonerate God for all the suffering of the innocent in history. God is responsible for having created a world in which man is free to make history. There must be a dimension beyond history in which all suffering finds its redemption through God. This is essential to the faith of a Jew. The Jew does not doubt God's presence, though he is unable to set limits to the duration and intensity of his absence. This is no justification for the ways of providence, but its acceptance. It is not a willingness to forgive the unheard cries of millions, but a trust that in God the tragedy of man may find its transformation. Within time and history that cry is unforgivable. One of the teachers of the Talmud notes that when God asks Abraham to offer him his son Isaac as a sacrifice, the exact rendering of the biblical words reads: "Take, I pray thee, thy son."[30] In the view of this teacher the "binding of Isaac" was not a command of God, but a request that Abraham take upon himself this most exacting of all God's impositions. In a sense, we see in this a recognition that the sacrificial way of the innocent through history is not to be vindicated or justified! It remains unforgivable. God himself has to ask an Abraham to favor him by accepting the imposition of such a sacrifice. The divine request accompanies all those through history who suffer for the only reason that God created man, whom God himself has to endure. Within time and history God remains indebted to his people; he may be long-suffering only at their expense. It was hardly ever true as in our own days, after the holocaust. Is it perhaps what God desires—a people, to whom he owes so much, who yet acknowledge him? Children, who have every reason to condemn his creation, yet accept the creator in the faith that in the fullness of time the divine indebtedness will be redeemed and the divine adventure with man will be approved even by its martyred victims?

Notes

1. This is true, notwithstanding the attempt by some talmudic teachers to interpret the phenomenon as an appropriate balancing of justice between this world and the world to come. See, for instance, *Talmud Babli, Kiddushin*, 39 b. Medieval Jewish philosophers often follow the same inadequate argument.
2. Not to be confused with the Christian interpretation of Jewish history, mentioned earlier in the text. The Jew says: Because of our sins. The Christian maintains: Because of your sins. The one is critical self-judgment; the other, hypocritical judging of others.
3. Ezekiel 8: 12.
4. Malachi 3: 13–15.
5. Talmud Babli, *Kiddushin*, 39 b.

6. According to Rabbenu Yona, quoted in *Kesef Mishne*, Maimonides, *Hilkhot Tefilla*, 2, 2.
7. Psalms 44: 24–27.
8. Ibid., 13: 2.
9. Ibid., 10: 12.
10. Isaiah 49: 14.
11. *Bereshit Rabba*, 29, 14.
12. Jeremiah 11: 20.
13. Habakkuk 1: 12.
14. Job 13: 15.
15. Psalms 145: 18.
16. Ibid., 145: 9.
17. Ibid., 31: 24.
18. *Midrash T'hillim*, 31.
19. Isaiah 45: 15.
20. Ibid., 8, 17.
21. Ecclesiastes 7: 14. More in keeping with the Hebrew original, and in conformity with the manner in which the verse was understood by the rabbis in the Talmud, we depart somewhat from the rendering of the verse in the R. V.
22. *Talmud Babli, Hagiga*, 15 a.
23. See our discussion of the quotation from Isaiah and the concept of creation connected with it in our book, *God, Man and History*, ch. 9.
24. Ezekiel 33: 11.
25. Deuteronomy, 10, 17.
26. *Talmud Babli*, Yoma, 69 a. For the references to Jeremiah, Daniel, Ezra, cf. *Jeremiah*, 32, 18; *Daniel*, 9, 4; *Nehemiah*, 9, 32.
27. *Shaar Ha'gmul* in *Hiddushei Ha'Ramban*, Part I., p. 193, ed. B'nei Brak, 5719 A.M.
28. We are not unaware of the biblical verse that assets that "all His ways are justice." (Deut. 32: 4) Obviously, the midrashic statement we have quoted in our text about the creation of the world by mercy and justice is not in keeping with such a reading. However, the Hebrew Bible does not have: "all His ways are justice." But, "all His ways are *Mishpat*." I have shown in a recent work how misleading it is to translate the biblical *Mishpat* as "justice" in the sense of Western civilization. See the chapter, "The Biblical Meaning of Justice," in my *Man and God, Studies in Biblical Theology*, Detroit: Wayne State University Press, 1969.
29. *Talmud Babli, Sanhedrin*, 39 b.
30. Ibid., 89 b.

29

After Auschwitz

RICHARD RUBENSTEIN

Traditonal Religious Thought and the Holocaust

The question of God and the Holocaust has been of far greater interest to religious thinkers than to philosophers. Elsewhere I have argued that a principal function of theology is to foster dissonance reduction where significant items of information are perceived to be inconsistent with established beliefs, values, and collectively sanctioned modes of behavior.[1] At first glance, the Holocaust would appear to be such an item of information and one that would naturally concern religious thinkers. Nevertheless, as we shall see, many important Jewish religious authorities have emphatically rejected the idea that the occurrence of the Holocaust is in any way inconsistent with the traditional Jewish conception of divinity. In spite of the fact that the *Shoah* has been characterized by Rabbi Yitzhak (Irving) Greenberg, a leading Jewish Holocaust theologian, as "the most radical countertestimony to religious faith, both Jewish and Christian," some of the most faithful and observant Jewish religious leaders have offered a contrary opinion.[2] These leaders have asserted that their faith in God has been confirmed by the catastrophe. The views of Rabbi Elchonon Wassermann of Baranovitch (1875–1941) are representative of Orthodox Jewish thought during the Holocaust years.[3] Writing between *Kristallnacht* and the beginning of the war, Wassermann interpreted the Nazi onslaught as due to three Jewish "evils": secular nationalism; assimilation, especially through Reform Judaism; and the alleged contempt for the Torah in the scientific study of Judaism. For Wassermann, the Nazi assault was ultimately God's appropriate response against those who had proven unfaithful to His Torah. Wassermann also saw the promise of redemp-

Richard Rubenstein, "Covenant and Divinity: The Holocaust and the Problematics of Religious Faith," in *After Auschwitz*, second edition (Baltimore: Johns Hopkins University Press, 1994), pp. 159–63, 171–76, 197, 200. © Johns Hopkins University Press, Baltimore, MD 21218.

tion in the misfortunes. Indeed, he argued that the more intense the suffering of the people, the closer the advent of the Messiah, a theme that has been taken up once again in contemporary Israel.[4]

Wassermann's life was fully consistent with his faith. When taken to be killed by four Latvian murderers in July 1941, he spoke of his own death, as well as the death of others like him, as a *korban*, a sacrificial offering, for the Jewish people: "Let us go with raised heads. God forbid that any thought should enter the mind of anybody to make the sacrifice (*korban*) unfit. We now carry out the greatest Mitzvah, *Kiddush Hashem* (sanctification of God's name). The fire which will burn our bodies is the fire which will resurrect the Jewish people."[5] Wassermann's response to the Holocaust was typical of that of the Orthodox rabbinate of the period in both eastern Europe and North America. Far from being a "radical countertestimony to religious faith," the events were widely regarded as confirming the tradition and the fulfillment of God's plan.

The opinions of Rabbi Joseph Isaac Schneersohn, the late Lubavitcher Rebbe, were another example of the same tendency. According to Schneersohn, Hitler is but God's instrument for chastising the Jews, who had abandoned the ways of Torah; Nazism is divine punishment visited upon the Jews for rejecting the Torah and choosing assimilation.[6]

The Orthodox interpretation of the Holocaust as divinely inflicted punishment or the sacrificial precondition for the coming of the Messiah rests upon the biblical doctrines of covenant and election. As we have noted, whenever Israel experienced *radical communal misfortune*, her religious teachers almost always interpreted the event as did Wassermann and Schneersohn, that is, as divine punishment. This was the case in 586 B.C.E., when Jeremiah prophesied concerning the impending fate of Jerusalem, which was then threatened by Nebuchadnezzar, King of Babylon:

> These are the words of the Lord to Jeremiah: I am the Lord, the God of all flesh; is anything impossible for me? Therefore these are the words of the Lord: I will deliver this city into the hands of the Chaldeans and of Nebuchadnezzar, king of Babylon, and he shall take it. The Chaldeans who are fighting against this city will enter it, set it on fire and burn it down, with the houses on whose roofs sacrifices have been burnt to Baal and drink-offerings poured out to the other gods, by which I was provoked to anger. From their earliest days Israel and Judah have been doing what is wrong in my eyes, provoking me to anger by their actions, says the Lord (Jer. 32:26–30).

Given Jeremiah's belief in the election of Israel, it was impossible for him to view the Fall of Jerusalem as an event devoid of profound religious significance. The prophet understood that divine election placed an awesome responsibility on Israel. Undoubtedly, he was mindful of the terrible warning the prophet Amos had pronounced upon his own people: "Listen, Israelites, to these words that the Lord addresses to you, to the nation that he brought up from Egypt: *For you alone have I cared among all the nations of the world; therefore will I punish you for all your iniquities*" (Amos 3:1–2, italics added).

Jerusalem fell yet again at the end of the Judeo-Roman War of 66–70 C.E. At the time, the rabbis, who had succeeded the prophets and the priests as the religious authorities within Judaism, interpreted their people's misfortunes as had their predecessors. A characteristic example of the rabbinic response is to be found in the liturgy for the Holy Days and Festivals still used by traditional Jews: "Thou hast chosen us from among all peoples; thou hast loved us and taken pleasure in us, and hast exalted us above all tongues; thou hast hallowed us by thy commandments, and brought us near unto thy service, O our

King, and thou has called us by thy great and holy Name. . . . *But on account of our sins we were exiled from our land and removed far from our country.*"[7]

To the extent that Judaism and Christianity affirm the election of Israel, both traditions must consider the Holocaust as more than a random occurrence. Indeed, contemporary Orthodox Jews in Israel affiliated with Gush Emunim (the Bloc of the Faithful) consider the Holocaust to be an indispensable event in God's redemptive plan for human history. Unable to accept the Holocaust as a purely punitive event, they tend to interpret it as the catastrophic precondition for the final messianic redemption of Jewish and world history, the "birth pangs of the Messiah." For almost two thousand years traditional Judaism sought to restrain the messianic impulse within the Jewish people. In the aftermath of the Holocaust and the wars of the State of Israel, a highly influential segment of contemporary Orthodoxy has become overtly messianic.[8]

Historians have long debated the question of the uniqueness of the Holocaust. They have noted similarities between it and the massacre of the Armenians in World War I, Stalin's mass destruction of classes and groups he regarded as objectively antagonistic, and the Pol Pot regime's genocide of Kampuchea's urban population.[9] As noted above, there is one aspect of the Holocaust which is absolutely different from all other programs of extermination and mass destruction in the modern period: *The fate of the Jews is a matter of decisive religiomythic significance in both Judaism and Christianity.* No example of mass murder other than the Holocaust has raised so directly or so insistently the question of whether it was an expression of *Heilsgeschichte*, that is, God's providential involvement in history.

An important example of the mythic importance of Jewish misfortune, in this case as proof of Christian truth, is to be found in Martin Luther's "On the Jews and Their Lies": "Well, let the Jews regard our Lord Jesus as they will. We behold the fulfillment of the words spoken by him in Luke 21:20,22f.: 'But when you see Jerusalem surrounded by armies, then know that its desolation has come near . . . for these are days of vengeance. For great distress shall be upon the earth and wrath upon this people.'"[10]

I have also noted that R. Johanan ben Zakkai also regarded the Fall of Jerusalem as a consequence of God's chastisement of a sinful Israel.[11] The terrible curses enunciated in Deuteronomy are part of the theological and religious basis for R. Johanan's interpretation of Jewish suffering. I cannot cite the entire text in this context; nevertheless, the following verses capture its spirit and intent: "If you do not observe and fulfill all the law written down in this book . . . then the Lord will strike you and your descendants with unimaginable plagues, malignant and persistent. . . . Just as the Lord took delight in you . . . so now it will be his delight to destroy and exterminate you. . . . The Lord will scatter you among all peoples from one end of the earth to the other" (Deut. 28:58–64).[12]

As noted, Jewish and Christian authorities had no disagreement concerning the belief that God is the ultimate Author of Israel's misfortunes. They disagreed only in identifying the nature of Israel's sin.

Given the classical theological positions of both Judaism and Christianity, the fundamental question posed by the Holocaust is not whether the existence of a just, omnipotent God can be reconciled with radical evil. That is a philosophical question. The religious question is the following:

Did God use Adolf Hitler and the Nazis as his agents to inflict terrible sufferings and death upon six million Jews, including more than one million children?

Even if God is seen as the ultimate Author of the death camps, it does not follow that His actions at Auschwitz were necessarily punitive. Both Judaism and Christianity allow for the possibility that the innocent may be called upon to suffer sacrificially for the guilty. Neither the Hebrew Bible nor the Christian Scriptures interpret *every* misfortune as divine punishment. For example, in the Book of Job the protagonist is depicted as having experienced the worst misfortunes without having offended God. Similarly, the "Suffering Servant" of Isaiah 53 appears to have been an innocent victim. As we shall see, an important theological interpretation of the Holocaust depicts the victims as sacrificial offerings. As we have noted, the Holocaust has also been interpreted as the "birth pangs of the Messiah."

Nevertheless, until the 1967 war, whenever Israel experienced *radical communal misfortune*, her traditional religious teachers almost always interpreted the event as divine punishment. Of all the misfortunes experienced by the Jewish people, only three can be reckoned as major communal disasters that irrevocably altered the character of the Jewish world: Nebuchadnezzar's defeat of Judea in 586 B.C.E., the Fall of Jerusalem to the Romans in 70 C.E., and the *Shoah*. Not since 70 C.E. had world Jewry experienced a catastrophe remotely like what was endured between 1939 and 1945. In reality, never before in history had Jews experienced so overwhelming a disaster.

• • •

I expressed these new convictions [about the challenge of the Holocaust to traditional Jewish theology] in March 1966 in the symposium, "The State of Jewish Belief," published in *Commentary* and included them in the first edition of *After Auschwitz*:

> I believe the greatest single challenge to modern Judaism arises out of the question of God and the death camps. I am amazed at the silence of contemporary Jewish theologians on this most crucial and agonizing of all Jewish issues. How can Jews believe in an omnipotent, beneficent God after Auschwitz? Traditional Jewish theology maintains that God is the ultimate, omnipotent actor in the historical drama. It has interpreted every major catastrophe in Jewish history as God's punishment of a sinful Israel. I fail to see how this position can be maintained without regarding Hitler and the SS as instruments of God's will. The agony of European Jewry cannot be likened to the testing of Job. To see any purpose in the death camps, the traditional believer is forced to regard the most demonic, antihuman explosion of all history as a meaningful expression of God's purposes.[13]

This statement has been interpreted as an expression of atheism. On the contrary, it contains no denial of the existence of God, although it rejects the biblical image of the God who elected Israel. After my encounter with Dean Grüber, I became convinced that Jews were confronted by an inescapable either/or: *One can either affirm the innocence of Israel or the justice of God at Auschwitz.*

Today, I understand that there can be other alternatives. We can, for example, say with Maybaum that the Holocaust victims died a sacrificial death for the sake of the coming of the messianic era *precisely because they were innocent*. We can affirm with Jewish messianists that the Holocaust was an indispensable aspect of the "birthpangs of the Messiah"; we can also affirm with American premillennial dispensationalists that the Holocaust was part of the divine timetable leading up to Christ's Second Coming, the Rapture, Armageddon, and the Millennium. Nevertheless, Jewish messianists must face the fact that millions of innocent victims died horribly for the sake of the Lord's plan. For Christian dispensationalists there is no problem of the victims' innocence since those who perished were not faithful Christians. Apart from the question of whether any utopia is worth the bloody price of a Holocaust, the messianic views justify the real death of millions for the sake of an imaginary glorious future.

Those of us who prefer to wait until the arrival of the glorious messianic future before taking it into account have yet to find a credible alternative to the dilemma mentioned above: we can either affirm the innocence of Israel or the justice of God but not both. If the innocence of Israel at Auschwitz is affirmed, whatever God may be, He/She is not distinctively and uniquely the sovereign Lord of covenant and election. If one wishes to avoid any suggestion, however remote, that at Auschwitz Israel was with justice the object of divine punishment, one must reject any view of God to which such an idea can plausibly be ascribed. Although not an atheist, I did assert that "we live in the time of the death of God." The meaning of that statement is summarized in the following passage:

> No man can really say that God is dead. How can we know that? Nevertheless, I am compelled to say that we live in the time of the "death of God." *This is more a statement about man and his culture than about God.* The death of God is a cultural fact. . . . Buber felt this. He spoke of the eclipse of God. I can understand his reluctance to use the more explicitly Christian terminology. I am compelled to use it because of my conviction that the time which Nietzsche's madman said was too far off has come upon us. There is no way around Nietzsche. Had I lived in another time or another culture, I might have found some other vocabulary to express my meanings. . . . When I say we live in the time of the death of God, I mean that the thread uniting God and man, heaven and earth, has been broken. We stand in a cold, silent, unfeeling cosmos unaided by any purposeful power beyond our own resources. After Auschwitz, what else can a Jew say about God? (Italics added.)[14]

Today, I no longer regard the cosmos as "cold, silent, unfeeling." At the very least, insofar as man is a part of the cosmos and is capable of love as well as hate, the cosmos cannot be said to be entirely cold and silent. My earlier position can be seen as the expression of an assimilated Jew who had returned to Judaism because of the *Shoah*, devoted a quarter of a century to Jewish learning, committed himself to the defense of his people and its inherited religious traditions, and then found that he could no longer believe in the God of that tradition or in the crucial doctrines of covenant and election *without regarding Auschwitz as divine punishment*. Given both the loss of faith this entailed and the events of World War II which brought it about, my view of the divine-human relationship was, at the time, understandably bleak. Today, I would balance the elements of creation and love in the cosmos more evenly with those of destruction and hate than was possible in 1966. What has not changed is a view of God quite different from the biblical and rabbinic mainstream, as well as an unqualified rejection of the notion that the Jews are in any sense a people either chosen or rejected by God. On the contrary, Jews are a people like any other whose religion and culture were shaped so as to make it possible for them to cope with their very distinctive history and location among the peoples of the world. Put differently, I have consistently rejected the idea that the existence of the Jewish people has any superordinate significance whatsoever.

Rejection of the biblical God and the doctrine of the Chosen People was a step of extraordinary seriousness for a rabbi and Jewish theologian. These views understandably elicited the question whether anyone who accepted such views had any reason for remaining Jewish. For millennia the literature and the liturgy of normative Judaism have been saturated with the idea that God had chosen Israel and that the obligation to obey the laws and traditions of the Torah was divinely legitimated. Why, it was asked, should anyone keep the Sabbath, circumcise male offspring, marry within the Jewish community, or obey the dietary laws if the God of the Bible did not exist?

From one point of view there is considerable merit to these questions. From another there is none. Without a credible affirmation of the existence of the God of the prophets and the rabbis, Judaism becomes a matter of personal preference, a preference some may be tempted to abandon. Immediately after World War II the argument was advanced that racism prevents any escape from Jewish identity. In reality, inter-marriage provides an escape route for the grandchildren, if not the children, of mixed marriages. Those who desire to abandon Jewish identity can begin the process even if they cannot complete it. Nevertheless, a knowledge of the negative consequences of unbelief does nothing to enhance the credibility of a belief system.

In the 1960s and 1970s, I responded to the question of whether Judaism can be maintained without traditional faith by arguing that the demise of theological legitimations did not entail an end to the psychological or sociological functions fulfilled by Judaism. Save for the case of conversion, entrance into Judaism is a matter of birth rather than choice. Even conversion to Christianity does not entirely cancel Jewish identity. There is an ethnic component to Jewish identity, intensified by recent historical experience, which persists long after the loss of faith. Every Jew says of the *Shoah*, "It happened to us." For non-Jews, the *Shoah* is something that happened to another people. Just as no Armenian can ever forget the Armenian genocide during World War I, Holocaust consciousness has become an ineradicable component of the Jewish psyche.[15] Religion is more than a system of beliefs; it is also a system of shared rituals, customs, and historical memories by which members of a community cope with or celebrate the moments of crisis in their own lives and the life of their inherited community.

Religion is not so much dependent upon belief as upon practices related to the life cycle and a sense of shared historical experience. No matter how tenuous the faith of average Jews or Christians, they normally find their inherited tradition the most suitable vehicle for consecrating such events as the birth of a child or a marriage. In a crisis such as the death or a parent or child, the need to turn to the rituals of an inherited tradition is even more urgent.

Although in 1966 I had become convinced that there is a void where once God's presence had been experienced, it did not follow that Judaism had lost its meaning or power or that a theistic God of covenant and election is necessary for Jewish religious life, at least for the first and second post-Holocaust generations. Dietrich Bonhoeffer had written that our problem is how to speak of God in an age of no religion. I saw the problem as how to speak of religion in an age of the absence of God. Judaism can be understood as the way Jews share the decisive times and crises of life through the traditions of their inherited community. The need for that sharing is not diminished in the time of the death of God. If it is no longer possible to believe in the God who has the power to annul the tragedies of existence, the need religiously to share that existence remains. In place of the biblical image of God as transcending the world he has created, I came to believe that a view of God which gives priority to immanence may be more credible in our era.

In mysticism and dialectic pantheism I found a view of God I could affirm after Auschwitz. Ironically, by virtue of His, or perhaps Its, all-encompassing nature, the God who is the Source and Ground of Being is as much a God-who-acts-in-history as the transcendent Creator God of the Bible, as any reader of Hegel would understand. What the dialectical-mystical interpretation excludes is the distinctive ascription of guilt to Israel and the category of divinely inflicted punishment to the Holocaust. *Creative destruction and even destruction transcending the categories of good and evil may be inherent in the life of Divinity, but not punitive destruction.*

The dialectical-mystical elements in my thinking have endured; the pagan element has proven less durable. In the aftermath of the *Shoah*, with the rebirth of an independent Jewish state for the first time since the Judeo-Roman wars, there was a certain plausibility to the argument that a people that is at home lives a very different kind of life than a band of wandering strangers. During the whole period of their wanderings, the vast majority of the Jewish people prayed that they might be restored to the land of their origin. Wherever they dwelt in the Diaspora their lives and their safety were wholly dependent upon the tolerance of others. During the two thousand years of the Diaspora, Jewish history always had a goal, namely, return to the homeland. That goal was given expression in prayers originally written in the aftermath of the Judeo-Roman Wars and still recited three times daily in the traditional liturgy.[16]

If Jewish history has as its goal return to the land of Israel, Jewish history appeared to have, at least in principle, come to an end when that goal was attained in 1948 with the establishment of the State of Israel. It may have made sense to worship a God of history while Jewish history was unfulfilled, that is, while Jews still envisioned the goal of their history as a return to Israel in the distant future. The Jewish situation changed radically when that goal appeared to have been attained. Not only did Jewish history seem to have come to an end, but after Auschwitz the God of History was no longer credible. In the biblical period, whenever the people had felt at home in the land, they turned to the earth gods of Canaan. Biblical monotheism had effectively defeated polytheism but not necessarily nature paganism. After Auschwitz and the return to Israel, the God of Nature, or more precisely the God who manifests Himself, so to speak, in and through nature was the God to whom the Jews would turn in place of the God of History, especially in Israel. This is consistent with the view that religion is essentially the way we share the crisis moments, that is, the turning points, of both the life cycle and the calendar. My rejection of the biblical God of History led me to a modified form of nature paganism.

With the passing of time, however, the pagan spirit that predominated in *After Auschwitz* receded into the background. That paganism was inextricably linked to the idea that a significant portion of the Jewish people was "at home" in the land of Israel. However, most of the world's Jews were not "at home" in Israel. Even those domiciled within its borders were ever mindful that the fragile state and its people could be annihilated were Israel's neighbors ever to win a single decisive military victory. Moreover, the majority of the Jews of the Diaspora had no desire to settle there. Clearly, the "goal" of Jewish history had not been reached and Jewish history was not at an end. On the contrary, having returned, the people of Israel may be faced with the prospect of an unending, non-negotiable life-and-death struggle against an implacable league of enemies. There may be intermittent periods of relative peace, but the historical model governing the Arab view of Israel remains that of the Crusades.

• • •

The Survival of Faith in the Traditional God

Does that mean that the ancient and hallowed faith in the biblical God of covenant and election has no future among religious Jews? On the contrary, it is probably the one theological option most likely to have a future. Whatever doubts secularized Jews may currently entertain, that belief has been the allowed, authoritative faith of the community of Israel from time immemorial until the modern period. It has given the Jewish people the supremely important gifts of meaning and hope. Instead of viewing their experiences as a series of unfortunate and essentially meaningless happenings, biblical-rabbinic faith has enabled the Jewish people to see their history as a meaningful expression of their relations with God. Moreover, no matter how desperate their situation became, their faith enabled them to hope that, sooner or later, "Those who sow in tears will reap in joy." The old biblical-rabbinic view that God is the ultimate Actor in history and that the Jewish people are bound to him by an eternal covenant remains the most coherent, logically consistent way of understanding Jewish experience and history which is acceptable to the Jewish people. In my own theological writings I have pointed out the bitter, yet inescapable, consequences of affirming that faith after Auschwitz. Nevertheless, no credible theological alternative has emerged which does not deny the very foundations of normative Judaism.

I have also become convinced that most religious Jews will eventually affirm faith in the God of covenant and election, even if such an affirmation entails regarding Auschwitz as divine punishment. Faith in covenant and election appear to be indispensable to the Jewish religious mainstream. One does not have to be a Jew to be a monotheist. What distinguishes Judaism is the faith that God has chosen the Jewish people to serve and obey Him by fulfilling his commandments as revealed in Scripture and authoritatively interpreted by the rabbis. Only a Judaism that is firmly rooted in the divine revelation at Sinai can defend the community from anomy. The liberal compromises that have flourished since the Enlightenment detach Jewish life and practice from all intellectual and theological moorings. In the long run, the liberal compromises offer little more than institutionalized alienation in which functional legitimations, supported by nostalgia and the guilt the living feel toward the dead, act as surrogates for lost theological legitimations.

In the past, traditional Judaism enabled most Jews to cope with their very difficult life situation as strangers in the Christian and Moslem worlds. However, the world's largest Jewish community, the American Jewish community, is diminishing in numbers as a result of an historically unprecedented intermarriage rate. One can ask whether large-scale intermarriage may be a delayed demographic response to the Holocaust on the part of those who no longer believe, as Jews once did, that Judaism is worth dying for. If this is the case, it is very likely that outside of Israel the Jewish religious mainstream will eventually consist primarily of a relatively small remnant who continue to affirm faith in the God of history and the election of Israel. Without traditional faith, there may simply be no reason for Jews to remain eternal strangers in a predominantly Christian world.[17]

Moreover, most Christian religious authorities expect Jews either to affirm faith in the biblical God of covenant and election or to accept Christ as their Savior. From an evangelical perspective, the Jews are the chosen people to whom God sent His Son as humanity's Redeemer. In the Christian view, the Jews have, of course, failed to recognize the true nature of Jesus Christ. Hence, God's election passed from the Israel "according to the flesh" to the Israel "according to the spirit," which consists of all those who have recognized Christ's true nature. Nevertheless, believing Christians have no doubt that, sooner or later, at least a "saving remnant" of Israel will finally see the light.[18] Like Judaism, Christianity cannot abandon the doctrines of covenant and election.

Moreover, Christian influence on Jews and Judaism is far greater than is often recognized, especially in the United States. By virtue of the fact that both Christians and Jews regard the Bible as a divine inspiration, Christians give Jews a context of plausibility for their most deeply held beliefs. If Jews lived in a culture in which the majority accorded the Bible no greater respect than the Greek myths, Jews might still hold fast to their beliefs, but they would receive no cognitive reinforcement. Even the fact that Jews and Christians disagree about the true nature of Jesus reinforces the context of plausibility, for the disagreement is about the true meaning of the Book both regard as divinely inspired.

The profound influence of American Christianity on American Judaism, even Orthodox Judaism, ought not to be underestimated. The world's largest Jewish community lives in and is ultimately dependent for its security and the security of the State of Israel on the world's largest Christian community. The State of Israel's strongest American Christian supporters are Fundamentalists, especially Protestant premillennial dispensationalists, who believe in the inerrancy of Scriptural revelation and who also believe that the return of the Children of Israel to the Promised Land is an indispensable element in God's plan for humanity's salvation in Christ. As conservative Christian influence continues to grow within the United States, it will encourage Jews to affirm a faith rooted in biblical revelation.

Thus, both external and internal influences foster a renewed Jewish affirmation of covenant and election. Even those Jews whose reasons for remaining in the Synagogue are primarily ethnic rather than religious are likely to convince themselves that the principal beliefs of the Jewish mainstream are true. To do otherwise would be to create too great a dissonance between belief and practice. If the survival of the Jews as a group outside of Israel is perceived to depend upon religious affiliation and some measure of Jewish religious practice, which in turn are thought to be legitimated by faith in the God of covenant and election, even those whose basic commitment is ethnic are likely to find some way to affirm *the only system of religious belief that legitimates Jewish survival.* The alternative is to abandon Jewish identification altogether. That alternative is actually being taken by the unprecedented number of young Jews who marry non-Jews and whose children or grandchildren are raised as Christian. While this is not the context in which to discuss the widespread phenomenon of intermarriage among contemporary Jews, that phenomenon must be seen as a powerful response to the Holocaust on the part of those Jews who have asked themselves Fackenheim's question concerning the morality of exposing distant descendants to anti-Semitic indignities by bringing children up as Jews. Those Jews who believe that in preserving Judaism they are fulfilling God's will have no difficulty in exposing their descendants to the potential hazards of a future catastrophe. Those who have lost that faith have no reason for so exposing their descendants. Religious belief and practice will remain in tension as long as the traditional legitimations of Jewish religious practice cannot be affirmed. Traditionally, the entire body of Jewish religious practice was founded upon the belief in God's revelations to Moses, the patriarchs, and prophets. As long as this fundamental belief is not affirmed, there will be a painful dissonance between Jewish religious practice and belief. As the horror of the Holocaust recedes in time, religious Jews, although greatly diminished in number, may once again find themselves reducing the dissonance by declaring with the traditional Prayer Book that "because of our sins all this has come upon us." That time has not yet come, but it may very well be on its way.

Of necessity, those Jews will reject the interpretation of Divinity I have set forth in these pages. That is to be expected. It is by no means certain that Judaism can survive without faith in the God of Israel as traditionally understood. I can only hope that those who affirm the traditional interpretation of God are motivated by honest belief rather than the conviction that, true or false, such a credo must be given verbal assent for the sake of Jewish survival, often hoping that their children will be able to believe what they cannot. A proud and glorious tradition deserves more than a self-deceiving exercise in bad faith.

For those of us who lived through the terrible years, whether in safety or as victims, the *Shoah* conditions the way we encounter all things sacred and profane. Nothing in our experience is untouched by that absolutely decisive event. Because of the *Shoah*, some of us enter the synagogue to partake of our sacred times and seasons with those to whom we are bound in shared memory, pain, fate, and hope; yet, once inside, we are struck dumb by words we can no longer honestly utter. All that we can offer is our reverent and attentive silence before the Divine.

Notes

1. Richard L. Rubenstein, *The Age of Triage* (Boston: Beacon Press, 1983), p. 132.
2. The phrase is from Irving Greenberg, "Cloud of Smoke, Pillar of Fire: Judaism, Christianity, and Modernity after the Holocaust," in *Auschwitz: Beginning of a New Era?* ed. Eva Fleischner (New York: Ktav, 1977), pp. 9–13; reprinted in this volume.
3. Elchonon Wassermann, *Ma'amar Ikvossoh Demeshicho Vema'mamar Al Ha'emunah* (Treatise on the Footsteps of the Messiah and on Faith) (New York: 1939, in Yiddish), cited by Gershon Greenberg, "Orthodox Theological Responses to Kristallnacht: Chayyim Ozer Grodzensky ("Achiezer") and Elchonon Wassermann," paper presented at the Eighteenth Annual Scholars Conference on the Church Struggle and the Holocaust, Washington, D.C., 1988. I am indebted to Professor Greenberg for having made this paper available to me, as well as several others dealing with Orthodox responses to the Holocaust.
4. Ibid., p. 40.
5. Efraim Oshry, *Churban Litta* (New York: 1951, in Yiddish), pp. 48–50, cited and translated by Gershon Greenberg, "Orthodox Theological Responses to Kristallnacht."
6. Joseph Isaac Schneershon, "Redemption Now," *Netzach Yisroel* III (1948) 6–7 [Hebrew], cited by Gershon Greenberg, "Reflections upon the Holocaust within American Orthodoxy, 1945–1948," unpublished paper, 1988.
7. Joseph H. Hertz, ed., *The Authorised Daily Prayer Book* (New York, 1948), pp. 820–21. See also Richard L. Rubenstein, *The Religious Imagination* (Indianapolis: Bobbs-Merrill, 1968), pp. 127–30.
8. For an overview of this development, see Ian Lustick, *For the Land and the Lord: Jewish Fundamentalism in Israel* (New York: Council on Foreign Relations, 1988); see also Michael Berenbaum, *After Tragedy and Triumph: Modern Jewish Thought and the American Experience* (Cambridge: Cambridge University Press, 1990), pp. 134–55.
9. I have dealt with the elements of continuity and singularity of the Holocaust as a state-sponsored program of population elimination in *The Age of Triage*.
10. Martin Luther, "On the Jews and Their Lies," trans. Martin Bertram, in *Luther's Works*, ed.

Franklin T. Sherman and Helmut T. Lehman (Philadelphia: Fortress Press, 1971), vol. 47, p. 139.

11. In a well-known tradition, Yohanan is depicted as having seen a famine-stricken Jewish girl on the road to Emmaus after the Fall of Jerusalem in 70 C.E. Out of desperation for something to eat, the girl extracted undigested barleycorn from the excrement dropped by an Arab's horse. Yohanan commented to his disciples on what he had seen, citing Deuteronomy 28:47–48: "Because you did not serve the Lord your God when you had plenty, therefore you shall serve your enemy in hunger and thirst. Because you did not serve the Lord . . . by reason of the abundance of all things, therefore you shall serve your enemy in want of all things." "Mekhilta Bahodesh," in Jacob Z. Lauterbach, ed. and trans., *Mekhilta de Rabbi Ishmael* (Philadelphia: Jewish Publication Society, 1948), vol. 2, pp. 193–94.

12. To this day the classical rabbinic response to the Fall of Jerusalem determines the character of the traditional liturgy. For example, the Musaf service for the Holy Days and Festivals includes the following prayer: "Thou has chosen us from among all peoples; thou hast loved us and taken pleasure in us, and hast exalted us above all tongues; thou has hallowed us by thy commandments, and brought us near unto thy service, O our King, and thou has called us by thy great and holy Name. . . . *But on account of our sins we were exiled from our land and removed far from our country*" (italics added). Hertz, *Daily Prayer Book*, pp. 820–21. See also Rubenstein, *Religious Imagination*, pp. 127–30.

13. "The State of Jewish Belief: A Symposium," *Commentary*, August 1966; reprinted in *After Auschwitz*, 1st ed., p. 153.

14. Rubenstein, *After Auschwitz*, 1st ed., pp. 151–52.

15. On the Armenian genocide as cultural and psychic inheritance, see Michael Arlen, *Passage to Ararat* (New York: Farrar, Straus and Giroux, 1975).

16. Among the typical prayers of this genre, we find:

> Sound the great shofar for our freedom; raise the ensign to gather our exiles, and gather us from the four corners of the earth. Blessed art thou, O Lord, who gatherest the dispersed of thy people. . . .
> And to Jerusalem, thy city, return in mercy, and dwell therein as thou has spoken; rebuild it soon in our days as an everlasting building, and speedily set up therein the throne of David. Blessed art thou, O Lord, who rebuildest Jerusalem.

(Hertz, *Daily Prayer Book*, pp. 146–47).

17. See Rubenstein, "Naming the Unnameable; Thinking the Unthinkable (A Review Essay on Arthur Cohen's *The Tremendum*)," *Journal of Reform Judaism*, Spring 1984, pp. 43–54.

18. For the New Testament source of these ideas, see Romans 9–11.

30

The Jewish Return into History

EMIL FACKENHEIM

Our topic has two presuppositions which, I take it, we are not going to question but will simply take for granted. First, there is a unique and unprecedented crisis in this period of Jewish history which needs to be faced by all Jews, from the Orthodox at one extreme to the secularists at the other. (Thus we are not going to discuss the various forms of Judaism and Jewishness as though nothing had happened.) Second, whatever our response to the present crisis, it will be, in any case, a stubborn persistence in our Jewishness, not an attempt to abandon it or escape from it. (Thus we shall leave dialogues with Jews who do not want to be Jews for another day.)

How shall we understand the crisis of this period in Jewish history? We shall, I believe, be misled if we think in the style of the social sciences which try to grasp the particular in terms of the universal. We shall then, at best, understand the present Jewish crisis only in terms of the universal Western or human crisis, thus failing to grasp its uniqueness; at worst we shall abuse such an understanding as a means of escaping into the condition of contemporary-man-in-general. Instead of relying on the sociological mind, we must rely on the historical mind, which moves from the particular to the universal. But the historical mind, too, has its limitations. Thus no contemporary Jewish historian at the time of the destruction of the First or the Second Temple could have fully understood the world-historical significance of that event, if only because, in the midst of the crisis, he was not yet on the other side of it. We, too, are in the midst of the contemporary crisis, and hence unable fully to understand it. As for our attitude toward the future, this cannot be one of understanding or prediction, but only one of commitment and, possibly, faith.

How shall we achieve such fragmentary understanding of our present crisis as is possible while we are still in the midst of it? A crisis as yet unended can only be understood

Emil Fackenheim, *The Jewish Return into History* (New York: Schocken, 1978), pp. 19–24, and *To Mend the World* (New York: Schocken, 1982), pp. 294–302, 308–13.

in terms of contradictions as yet unresolved. Jewish existence today is permeated by three main contradictions:

1. The American Jew of today is a "universalist," if only because he has come closer to the full achievement of equal status in society than any other Jew in the history of the Diaspora; yet this development coincides with the resurrection of Jewish "particularism" in the rebirth of a Jewish nation.

2. The Jew of today is committed to modern "secularism," as the source of his emancipation; yet his future survival as Jew depends on past religious resources. Hence even the most Orthodox Jew of today is a secularist insofar as, and to the extent that, he participates in the political and social processes of society. And even the most secularist Jew is religious insofar as, and to the extent that, he must fall back on the religious past in his struggle for a Jewish future.

3. Finally—and this is by far the most radical contradiction, and one which threatens to engulf the other two—the Jew in two of the three main present centers of Jewry, America and Israel, is at home in the modern world, for he has found a freedom and autonomy impossible in the premodern world. Yet he is but twenty-five years removed from a catastrophe unequaled in all of Jewish history—a catastrophe that in its distinctive characterizations is modern in nature.

These are the three main contradictions. Merely to state them is to show how false it would be for us to see our present Jewish crisis as nothing more than an illustration of the general Western or human crisis. I will add to the general point nothing more than the mere listing of two specific examples. First, we may have a problem with "secularity," like our Christian neighbors. But our problem is not theirs, if only because for us—who have "celebrated" the secular city since the French Revolution—the time for such celebrating is past since the Holocaust. Second, while we have our problems with academically inspired atheism and agnosticism, they are central at best only for Jews who want to be men-in-general. For the authentic Jew who faces up to his singled-out Jewish condition—even for the authentic agnostic or atheistic Jew—a merely academically inspired doubt in God must seem sophomoric when he, after Auschwitz, must grapple with despair.

We must, then, take care lest we move perversely in responding to our present crisis. We must first face up and respond to our Jewish singled-out condition. Only thus and then can we hope to enter authentically into an understanding of and relation with other manifestations of a present crisis which is doubtless universal.

In groping for authentic responses to our present Jewish crisis, we do well to begin with responses which have already occurred. I believe that there are two such responses: first, a commitment to Jewish survival; and second, a commitment to Jewish unity.

I confess I used to be highly critical of Jewish philosophies which seemed to advocate no more than survival for survival's sake. I have changed my mind. I now believe that, in this present, unbelievable age, even a mere collective commitment to Jewish group-survival for its own sake is a momentous response, with the greatest implications. I am convinced that future historians will understand it, not, as our present detractors would have it, as the tribal response-mechanism of a fossil, but rather as a profound, albeit as yet fragmentary, act of faith, in an age of crisis to which the response might well have been either flight in total disarray or complete despair.

The second response we have already found is a commitment to Jewish unity. This, to be sure, is incomplete and must probably remain incomplete. Yet it is nonetheless real. Thus, the American Council for Judaism is an anachronism, as is, I venture to say an Israeli nationalism which would cut off all ties with the Diaspora. No less anachronistic is a Jewish secularism so blind in its worship of the modern secular world as wholly to spurn the religious resources of the Jewish past; likewise, an Orthodoxy so untouched by the modern secular world as to have remained in a premodern ghetto.

Such, then, are the responses to the present crisis in Jewish history which we have already found in principle, however inadequately in practice. And their implications are even now altogether momentous. Whether aware of what we have decided or not, we have made the collective decision to endure the contradictions of present Jewish existence. We have collectively rejected the option, either of "checking out" of Jewish existence altogether or of so avoiding the present contradictions as to shatter Jewish existence into fragments.

But the question now is whether we can go beyond so fragmentary a commitment. In the present situation, this question becomes: can we confront the Holocaust, and yet not despair? Not accidentally has it taken twenty years for us to face this question, and it is not certain that we can face it yet. The contradiction is too staggering, and every authentic escape is barred. *For we are forbidden to turn present and future life into death, as the price of remembering death at Auschwitz. And we are equally forbidden to affirm present and future life, at the price of forgetting Auschwitz.*

We have lived in this contradiction for twenty years without being able to face it. Unless I am mistaken, we are now beginning to face it, however fragmentarily and inconclusively. And from this beginning confrontation there emerges what I will boldly term a 614th commandment: *the authentic Jew of today is forbidden to hand Hitler yet another, posthumous victory.* (This formulation is terribly inadequate, yet I am forced to use it until one more adequate is found. First, although no anti-Orthodox implication is intended, as though the 613 commandments stood necessarily in need of change, we must face the fact that something radically new has happened. Second, although the commandment should be positive rather than negative, we must face the fact that Hitler did win at least one victory—the murder of six million Jews. Third, although the very name of Hitler should be erased rather than remembered, we cannot disguise the uniqueness of his evil under a comfortable generality, such as persecution-in-general, tyranny-in-general, or even the demonic-in-general.)

I think the authentic Jew of today is beginning to hear the 614th commandment. And he hears it whether, as agnostic, he hears no more, or whether, as believer, he hears the voice of the *metzaveh* (the commander) in the *mitzvah* (the commandment). Moreover, it may well be the case that the authentic Jewish agnostic and the authentic Jewish believer are closer today than at any previous time.

To be sure, the agnostic hears no more than the *mitzvah*. Yet if he is Jewishly authentic, he cannot but face the fragmentariness of his hearing. He cannot, like agnostics and atheists all around him, regard this *mitzvah* as the product of self-sufficient human reason, realizing itself in an ever-advancing history of autonomous human enlightenment. The 614th commandment must be, to him, an abrupt and absolute *given*, revealed in the midst of total catastrophe.

On the other hand, the believer, who hears the voice of the *metzaveh* in the *mitzvah*, can hardly hear anything more than the *mitzvah*. The reasons that made Martin Buber speak of an eclipse of God are still compelling. And if, nevertheless, a bond between Israel and the God of Israel can be experienced in the abyss, this can hardly be more than the *mitzvah* itself.

The implications of even so slender a bond are momentous. If the 614th commandment is binding upon the authentic Jew, then we are, first, commanded to survive as Jews, lest the Jewish people perish. We are commanded, second, to remember in our very guts and bones the martyrs of the Holocaust, lest their memory perish. We are forbidden, thirdly, to deny or despair of God, however much we may have to contend with him or with belief in him, lest Judaism perish. We are forbidden, finally, to despair of the world as the place which is to become the kingdom of God, lest we help make it a meaningless place in which God is dead or irrelevant and everything is permitted. To abandon any of these imperatives, in response to Hitler's victory at Auschwitz, would be to hand him yet other, posthumous victories.

How can we possibly obey these imperatives? To do so requires the endurance of intolerable contradictions. Such endurance cannot but bespeak an as yet unutterable faith. If we are capable of this endurance, then the faith implicit in it may well be of historic consequence. At least twice before—at the time of the destruction of the First and of the Second Temples—Jewish endurance in the midst of catastrophe helped transform the world. We cannot know the future, if only because the present is without precedent. But this ignorance on our part can have no effect on our present action. The uncertainty of what will be may not shake our certainty of what we must do. ❧

To Mend the World

What is a Jew? Who is a Jew? These questions have troubled Jews, ever since the Emancipation rendered problematic all the old answers—those of Gentiles and those given by Jews themselves. Today, however, these same old questions, when asked by Jews, bespeak a hidden dread. It is true that the old post-Emancipation answers are still with us: a "religious denomination," a "nationality," a "nation like other nations," or, currently most fashionably in North America, an "ethnic group." Also, the much older Halakhic answer—"a child born of a Jewish mother or a convert to Judaism"—has gained a new lease on life; and, whether it is admitted or not, this is very largely thanks to the existence of the State of Israel. Finally, the fact of Israel itself, a modern state in the modern world, has shaken and confused all the old answers, i.e., the old post-Emancipation ones and the still older Halakhic ones, lending the question of Jewish identity a new kind of urgency. (The state exists. It *is* a state. It has problems that brook no postponement.) All this is true. Not true, however, is that all the above definitions, whether taken separately or together, today either exhaust the depth of the question or even so much as touch a dimension that is now in it. As for conferences on Jewish identity conducted in such terms alone, in these the hidden dread is shut out.

A Jew today is one who, except for an historical accident—Hitler's loss of the war— would have either been murdered or never been born. One makes this statement at a conference on Jewish identity. There is an awkward silence. And then the conference proceeds as if nothing had happened.

Yet the truth of the statement is undeniable. To be sure, the heroism and sacrifices of millions of men and women made the Nazi defeat no mere accident. But victory was not inevitable. Thus without as brief a diversion as the Yugoslav campaign Russia might have been conquered. Thus, too, Hitler might have won the war had he not attacked Russia at all when he did—a gratuitous, suicidal lapse into a two-front war that is surrounded by mystery to this day.

No mystery, however, surrounds the condition of a world following a Nazi victory— the "New Order," as it already was called, or the "Free New Order," as in due course it might have been called. (As it was, the Auschwitz gate already bore the legend *Albeit macht Frei*.) Such are the names and the propaganda. The reality would have resembled a vast, worldwide concentration camp, ruled by a *Herrenvolk* assisted by dupes, opportunists, and scoundrels, and served by nations conditioned to slavery. We say "worldwide," although a few semi-independent satellite states, modelled, perhaps, after Vichy France, might have been tolerated at the fringes. Of these the United States would surely have been the most prominent.

Such is the outer shape of a worldwide Nazi "New Order." Its inner essence would have been a murder camp for Jews, for without Jews to degrade, torture, and "exterminate," the rulers could have spiritually conditioned neither themselves to mastery nor the world to slavery. (Had Julius Streicher not said: "Who fights the Jew, fights the devil; who masters the devil, conquers heaven"?) However, with all, or almost all, Jews long murdered, the New Order would have had to invent ever-new Jews for the necessary treatment. (Had not Hitler himself once remarked that, if there were no Jews, it would be necessary to invent them?) Or alternatively, in case such an inventing were impossible—who except *real* Jews are the devil?—one would have had to maintain the fiction that Jews long dead were still alive, a mortal threat to the world. (Had not Goebbels declared in the Berlin *Sportpalast* that Jews alone of all peoples had not suffered in the war but only profited from it—this in 1944, when most Jews of Europe were dead?) We speak advisedly of *all*, or almost all, Jews being dead. A worldwide Nazi New Order that permits semi-independent satellite states at its fringes is conceivable; Jews permitted refuge in them are not. (Had not Professor Johann von Leers argued that, by the principle of hot pursuit, the Third Reich had the legal right and the moral duty to invade surrounding countries, for the purpose of "exterminating" the "Jewish vermin"?) And if nevertheless only *almost* all Jews were dead, if a *few* still survived, this would be due to the help of some Gentiles whose ingenuity, endurance, and righteousness will always pass understanding.

Such would be our world today if, by ill fortune, Hitler had won the war. But by good fortune he lost the war; then why, for the sake of a future Jewish identity, conjure up the spectre of his victory? The answer is simple. One survivor, a poet, rightly laments that, except for a few missing persons, the world has not changed. Another, this one a philosopher, charges just as rightly that the world refuses to change, that it views the reminding presence of such as himself as a malfunctioning of the machinery. Long before either Jewish plaint—long before the *Ereignis* itself—the Christian Sören Kierkegaard had spelled out the abstract principle—that a single catastrophic event of monumental import is enough to call all things into question ever after. We have cited such witnesses against others. As we now turn to our native realm of Jewish self-understanding, we can do no other than cite them against ourselves.

Even to do so only tentatively—preliminarily, as it were by way of experiment—is to discover, quite independently from all the previous complicated reflections and simply by looking at the facts, that to minimize, ignore, "overcome," "go beyond" the dark past for the sake of a happy and healthy future Jewish self-understanding is impossible. Empirically, to be sure, all this *is* possible: the phenomenon exists on every side. But morally, religiously, philosophically, humanly it is an impossibility. Shall we trust in God because we—though not they—were spared? Shall we trust in man because here and now—though not then and there—he bears traces of humanity? Shall we trust in ourselves—that we, unlike them, would resist being made into *Muselmänner*, the living dead, with the divine spark within us destroyed?

We can do none of these things; they are all insults, one hopes unwitting, to the dead. And beyond these unintended insults lies the attempt to repress the hidden dread, to deny the rupture that is a fact. Above we asserted that philosophy and Christian theology can each find its respective salvation not by avoiding the great rupture, but only by confronting it. We must now turn this assertion against ourselves.

The move from non-Jewish to Jewish post-Holocaust thought is not a step but a veritable leap. This is so by dint of a single fact the implications of which brook no evasion. "Aryan" victims of the Third Reich, though robbed, enslaved, subjected to humiliation, torture, and murder, were not *singled out* unless they *chose* to *single themselves* out; Jews, in contrast, were *being* singled out *without choice of their own*. We have already considered this difference as it was manifest during the Holocaust itself. We must now consider its implications for today.

There are two such implications. First, whereas much of the post-Holocaust world is ruptured, the post-Holocaust *Jewish* world is *doubly* ruptured, divorced by an abyss not only from its own past tradition but also—except for such as Huber and Lichtenberg who, even then, bridged the gulf from the non-Jewish side—from the Gentile world. Second, whereas post-Holocaust philosophical and Christian thought finds a *Tikkun* in such as Huber and Lichtenberg, post-Holocaust Jewish thought finds itself situated after a world which spared no effort to make a *Jewish* Huber or Lichtenberg systematically impossible. For "Aryans," "crime," then as always, was a *doing*, so that in their case the Nazi tyranny, like other tyrannies, *created* the possibilities of heroism and martyrdom. For "non-Aryans," however, the crime was *being itself*, so that in *their* case—a *novum* in history, all previous tyrannies included—every effort was made to *destroy* the very possibility of both heroism and martyrdom, to make all such choosing, actions, and suffering into an irrelevancy and a joke, if indeed not altogether impossible. The Jewish thinking considers the choiceless children; their helpless mothers; and finally—the achievement most revelatory of the essence of the whole Nazi world—the *Muselmänner*, these latter once free persons, and then dead while still alive: and he is filled not only with human grief but also with a metaphysical, religious, theological terror. Ever since Abraham, the Jewish people were singled out, for life unto themselves, and for a blessing unto the nations. And again and again throughout a long history, this people, however weary, responded to this singling-out act with the most profound freedom. (No response is as profoundly free as that to a singling-

out of God.) Ever since 1933, this people was singled out for death, and no effort or ingenuity was spared to make it into a curse to all those befriending it, while at the same
time robbing it of the most elementary, most animal freedom. (No freedom is either more
elementary or more animal than to relieve the bowels at the time of need.) The Reich had
a research institute on the "Jewish question." Its work included serious, scholarly, profes-
sional studies. These can have had no higher aim than to discover the deepest roots of
Jewish existence and, after four thousand years of uninterrupted life, destroy them. The
Jewish thinker is forced to ask: Was the effort successful?

*It is unthinkable that the twofold rupture should win out. It is unthinkable that the age-
old fidelity of the religious Jews, having persisted through countless persecutions and
against impossible odds—Yehuda Halevi expressed it best—should be destroyed forever.
It is unthinkable that the far less ancient, no less noble fidelity of the secular Jew—he
holds fast, not to God, but to the "divine spark in man"—should be smashed beyond repair. It is unthinkable that the gulf between Jews and Gentiles, created and legislated
since 1933, should be unbridgeable from the Jewish side so that the few but heroic, saintly
attempts to bridge it from the Gentile side—we shall never forget such as Lichtenberg
and Huber—should come to naught.* It is this unthinkability that caused in my own mind,
on first confronting it, the perception of a "614th commandment," or a "commanding
Voice of Auschwitz," forbidding the post-Holocaust Jew to give Hitler posthumous victories. (This is the only statement of mine that ever widely caught on, articulating, as one
reviewer aptly put it, "the sentiments . . . of Jewish shoe salesmen, accountants, police-
men, cab-drivers, secretaries.")

But we must now face the fact—and here my thinking is forced to move decisively
beyond the earlier perception just mentioned—that the unthinkable has been real in our
time, hence has ceased to be unthinkable; and that therefore the "614th commandment"
or "commanding Voice of Auschwitz" may well be a moral and religious necessity, but
also, and at the same time, an ontological impossibility. In his time, as sober a thinker as
Immanuel Kant could argue that since moral freedom, while undemonstrable, is at any
rate also irrefutable, we all *can* do that which we *ought* to do. On our part and in our time,
we need but visualize ourselves as victims of the Nazi logic of destruction in order to see
this brave doctrine dissolve into the desperate cry, "I cannot be obligated to do what I no
longer can do!" Indeed, such may well have been the last silent cry of many, just before,
made into the living dead, they were no longer capable of crying even in silence. Nor are
we rescued in this extremity by the Jewish symbol of *Tikkun* in any of its pre-Holocaust
uses, even when, as in the most radical of them, a rupture is admitted and confronted. We
have seen that during the Holocaust the Nazi logic of destruction murdered kabbalistic no
less than nonkabbalistic Jews—and their *Tikkun* with them. A would-be kabbalistic *Tikkun*
of *our own* post-Holocaust rupture would inevitably be a flight from *that* rupture, and
hence from our post-Holocaust situation as a whole, into an eternity that could only be
spurious.

We are thus driven back to insights gained earlier in the present work: the moral necessity of the "614th commandment" or "commanding Voice of Auschwitz" must be "root-
less and groundless" (*bodenlos*) unless it is an "ontological" possibility; and it *can* be such
a possibility only if it rests on an "ontic" reality. With this conclusion all our Jewish thinking and seeking either come to a dead halt or else find a *novum* that gives it a new point
of departure.

The Tikkun *which for the post-Holocaust Jew is a moral necessity is a possibility because during the Holocaust itself a Jewish* Tikkun *was already actual*. This simple but enormous, nay, world-historical truth is the rock on which rests any authentic Jewish future, and any authentic future Jewish identity. (As is gradually emerging, it is also the pivotal point of the developing argument of this work.) We have already seen that the singled-out Jewish resistance *in extremis* to the singling-out assault in its own extremity is ontologically ultimate. As we now turn from the Jewish past to a prospective Jewish future we perceive that this ontological Ultimate—a *novum* of inexhaustible wonder, just as the Holocaust itself is a *novum* of inexhaustible horror—is the sole basis, now and henceforth, of a Jewish existence, whether religious or secular, that is not permanently sick with the fear that, were it then and there rather than here and now, *everything*—God and man, commandments and promises, hopes and fears, joys and sorrows, life itself, and even a human way of dying—would be *indiscriminately* prey to the Nazi logic of destruction. The witnesses cited earlier all crowd back into the mind. We recall those we named. We also think of many we did not name and, above all, of the countless ones whose memory can only be nameless. As we ponder—ever reponder—their testimony, we freely concede that we, or others before us, may have romanticized it. We also concede that, yielding to all sorts of delusions, they may have done much romanticizing themselves. (Both errors are human.) But such concessions reveal only the more clearly that the astounding fact is not that many succumbed to the Nazi logic of destruction but rather that there were *some* who did *not* succumb. Indeed, even one would suffice to warrant a unique astonishment—and deny the evil logic its total victory.

We have reached this conclusion before. Our task now is to consider its implications for an authentic Jewish future. Above we repudiated the belief—an outworn idealism then, a case of humanistic twaddle now—that there is a core of human goodness that is indestructible. Now we must repudiate the belief—an outworn theology then, a case of Jewish twaddle now—that there is a Jewish substance that cannot be destroyed. Rather than in any such terms, the Jewish resistance to the singling-out Holocaust assault must be thought of as a life-and-death, day-and-night struggle, forever threatened with collapse and in fear of it, and saved from actual collapse—if at all—only by acts the source of whose strength will never cease to be astonishing. Their resistance, in short, was the *Tikkun* of a rupture. *This* Tikkun *is the* ultimate *ground of our own*.

• • •

What is a Jew? Who is a Jew? After *this* catastrophe, what is a Jew's relation to the Jewish past? We resume our original question as we turn from one rupture in post-Holocaust Jewish existence—of the bond with the Gentile world—to the other—of the bond with his own past history, past tradition, past God.

After all previous catastrophes ever since biblical times, a Jew could understand himself as part of a holy remnant. Not that the generation itself was holy, a presumptuous view, and one devoid of any real meaning. The generation was rather *heir* to holy ones—not to the many who had fallen away but rather to the few that, whether in life or the death of martyrdom, had stayed in fidelity at their singled-out Jewish post. Was there ever a self-definition by a flesh-and-blood people that staked so much—staked *all*—on fidelity? It is the deepest definition of Jewish identity in all Jewish history.

It cannot, however, be the self-definition of this Jewish generation for, except for an accident, we, the Jews of today, would either have been murdered or never born. *We are not a holy remnant. We are an accidental remnant.* However we may wish to evade the grim fact, this is the core definition of Jewish identity today.

The result is that we, on our part, cannot consider ourselves heir to the few alone. (For the religious among us, the martyrs and their prayers; for the secularists, the heroes and their battles.) We are obliged to consider ourselves heir to the whole murdered people. We think of those made into *Muselmänner* by dint of neither virtue nor vice but some "banal incident." We think of the children; their mothers; of the countless saints, sinners, and ordinary folk who, unsuspecting to the end, were gassed in the twinkling of an eye. And what reaches us is nothing so much as *the cry of an innocence that shakes heaven and earth; that can never be stilled; that overwhelms our hopes, our prayers, our thought.* Maimonides is said to have ruled that any Jew murdered for no reason other than being a Jew is to be considered holy. Folk tradition, already existing, cites Maimonides to this effect and views *all* the Jewish victims of the Holocaust as *kedoshim*—as holy ones. Only in this and no other sense are we, the accidental remnant, also a holy remnant. *In this sense, however, our holiness is ineluctable and brooks no honest escape or refusal.*

This circumstance places us into a hermeneutical situation that, after all that has been said about a post-Holocaust *Tikkun*, is new and unique still. Indeed, the dilemma in which we are placed is so extreme, so unprecedented, so full of anguish as to seem to tear us in two; and as to cause us to wonder whether, at the decisive point where all comes to a head, a post-Holocaust *Tikkun* of any kind is not seen, after all, to be impossible.

The dilemma is as follows. If (as we must) we hold fast to the children, the mothers, the *Muselmänner*, to the whole murdered people and its innocence, then we must surely despair of any possible *Tikkun*; but then we neglect or ignore the few and select—those with the opportunity to resist, the will and strength to resist, deriving the will and strength we know not whence—whose *Tikkun* (as we have seen) precedes and makes mandatory our own. And if (as also we must) we hold fast to just these select and their *Tikkun*, then *our Tikkun*, made possible by *theirs*, neglects and ignores all those who performed no heroic or saintly deeds such as to merit holiness and who yet, murdered as they were in utter innocence, must be considered holy. Not accidentally, "Holocaust theology" has been moving toward two extremes—a "God-is-dead" kind of despair, and a faith for which, having been "with God in hell," either nothing has happened or all is mended. However, post-Holocaust thought—it includes theological concerns but is not confined to them—must dwell, however painfully and precariously, between the extremes, and seek a *Tikkun* as it endures the tension.

The *Tikkun* emerging from this tension is composed of three elements: (a) a recovery of Jewish tradition—a "going back into possibilities of [Jewish] *Dasein* that once was *da*," (b) a recovery in the quite different sense of recuperation from an illness; and (c) a fragmentariness attaching to these two recoveries that makes them both ever-incomplete and ever-laden with risk. Without a recovered Jewish tradition—for the religious Jew, the Word of God; for the secular Jew, the word of man and his "divine spark"—there is no Jewish future. Without a recuperation from the illness, the tradition (and hence the Jewish future) must either flee from the Holocaust or be destroyed by it. And without the stern acceptance of both the fragmentariness and the risk, in both aspects of the recovery, our Jewish *Tikkun* lapses into unauthenticity by letting *theirs*, having "done its job," lapse into the irrelevant past.

To hold fast to the last of these three elements is hardest but also most essential. Once Schelling and Hegel spoke scathingly about theological contemporaries who were momentarily awakened from their dogmatic slumber by the Kantian philosophy but soon used that philosophy as a soporific: every old dogma, bar none, could become a "postulate of practical reason." Jewish thought today is in a similar danger. We remember the Holocaust; we are inspired by the martyrdom and the resistance: and then the inspiration quickly degenerates into this, that every dogma, religious or secular, is restored as if nothing had happened. However, the unredeemed anguish of Auschwitz must be ever-present with us, even as it is past *for* us. *Yom Ha-Shoah cannot now, or ever after, be assimilated to the ninth of Av.*

The attempt, to be sure, is widely made; but it is impossible. The age-old day of mourning is for catastrophes that are punishment for Jewish sins, vicarious atonement for the sins of others, or in any case meaningful, if inscrutable, divine decrees. The new day of mourning cannot be so understood, for it is for the children, the mothers, the *Muselmänner*—the whole murdered people in its utter innocence. Nor has the *Yom Ha-Shoah* ceremonial any such content, for it commemorates not Jewish sin but innocent Jewish suffering; not sins of others vicariously atoned but such as are incapable of atonement; not an inscrutable decree to be borne with patience but one resisted then, and to be resisted ever after. As for attempts to find a ninth-of-Av meaning in the Holocaust—punishment for the sins of Zionism; or of anti-Zionism; or a moral stimulus to the world—their very perversity confirms a conclusion reached earlier in the present work: *Galut* Judaism, albeit most assuredly not *Galut* itself, has come to an end.

Even so the attempt to assimilate *Yom Ha-Shoah* to the ninth of Av must be viewed with a certain sympathy. The cycle of the Jewish liturgical year—Rosenzweig described it sublimely—is an experience anticipating redemption. The ninth of Av, though a note of discord, fits into this cycle: but does *Yom Ha-Shoah*? The ninth of Av does not touch the Yom Kippur—the Jewish "experience" of the "end" not through "dying" but living. *Yom Ha-Shoah* cannot but touch it; indeed it threatens to overwhelm the Yom Kippur. Martin Buber has asked his post-Holocaust Jewish question—not whether one can still "believe" in God but whether one can still "speak" to Him. Can the Jew still speak to God on Yom Kippur? If not, how can he speak to Him at all? The Jewish fear of *Yom Ha-Shoah*—the wish to assimilate it to the ninth of Av—is a fear, in behalf not only of *Galut* Judaism but also of Judaism itself.

"Judaism and the Holocaust" must be the last, climactic question not only of the present exploration but also of this whole work. Meanwhile we ask what ways of Jewish *Tikkun* there could be even if the climactic question had to be indefinitely suspended. These ways are many; their scope is universal. (The task is *Tikkun Olam*, to mend the world.) Yet they would all become insubstantial without one *Tikkun* that is a collective, particular Jewish response to history. This *Tikkun* may be said to have begun when the first Jewish "DP" gave a radical response to what he had experienced. Non-Jewish DPs, displaced though they were, had a home to which to return. This Jewish DP did not—and even so was barred by bayonets and laws from the land that had been home once, and that Jewish labor was making into home once again. Understandably, many of his comrades accepted these facts with a shrug of centuries, and waited for someone's charity that would give them the blessings of refuge, peace, and oblivion. (They waited in camps, often the very places of their suffering—and for years.) This Jewish DP took his destiny in his own hands, disregarded the legal niceties of a world that still classified him as Pole or German, still without Jewish rights, and made his way to the one place where there would be neither peace nor oblivion but which would be, without ifs and buts, home.

The *Tikkun* that is Israel is fragmentary. This fact need not be stressed, for it is reported almost daily in the newspapers. The power of the State is small, as is the State itself. It can offer a home to captive Jews but cannot force captors to set them free. Limited abroad, it is limited at home as well. It cannot prevent strife. It cannot even guarantee its Jewish citizens a culture or a strong Jewish identify. *Galut* Judaism may have ended; but there is no end to *Galut* itself, inside as well as outside the State of Israel.

If the *Tikkun* is fragmentary, the whole enterprise is laden with risk. (This too the papers report assiduously.) Within, *Yerida*—emigration of Israelis—threatens to rival or overtake *Aliyah*, the Ingathering. Without, for all the talk of a comprehensive peace, implacable enemies remain; and while enemies elsewhere seek to destroy a regime, or at most conquer a state, *these* enemies seek destruction of a state—and renewed exile for its Jewish inhabitants.

What then is the *Tikkun*? It is Israel itself. It is a state founded, maintained, defended by a people who—so it was once thought—had lost the arts of statecraft and self-defense forever. It is the replanting and reforestation of a land that—so it once seemed—was unredeemable swamps and desert. It is a people gathered from all four corners of the earth on a territory with—so the experts once said—not room enough left to swing a cat. It is a living language that—so even friends once feared—was dead beyond revival. It is a City rebuilt that—so once the consensus of mankind had it—was destined to remain holy ruins. And it is in and through all this, on behalf of the accidental remnant, after unprecedented death, a unique celebration of life.

It is true—so fragmentary and precarious is the great *Tikkun*—that many want no share of it, deny it, distort it, slander it. But slanders and denials have no power over those who are astonished—ever again astonished—by the fact that in this of all ages the Jewish people have returned—*have been* returned?—to Jerusalem. Their strength, when failing, is renewed by the faith that despite all, because of all, the "impulse from below" will call forth an "impulse from above."

31

Cloud of Smoke, Pillar of Fire: Judaism, Christianity, and Modernity after the Holocaust

IRVING GREENBERG

Judaism and Christianity: Religions of Redemption and the Challenge of History

Both Judaism and Christianity are religions of redemption. Both religions come to this affirmation about human fate out of central events in history. For Jews, the basic orientating experience has been the Exodus. Out of the overwhelming experience of God's deliverance of His people came the judgment that the ultimate truth is not the fact that most humans live nameless and burdened lives and die in poverty and oppression. Rather, the decisive truth is that man is of infinite value and will be redeemed. Every act of life is to be lived by that realization.

For Christians, the great paradigm of this meaning is the life, death, and resurrection of Jesus Christ. By its implications, all of life is lived.

The central events of both religions occur and affect humans in history. The shocking contrast of the event of salvation come and the cruel realities of actual historical existence have tempted Christians to cut loose from earthly time. Yet both religions ultimately have stood by the claim that redemption will be realized in actual human history. This view has had enormous impact on the general Western and modern view that human liberation can and will be realized in the here and now.

Implicit in both religions is the realization that events happen in history which change our perception of human fate, events from which we draw the fundamental norms by

Irving Greenberg, "Cloud of Smoke, Pillar of Fire," in *Auschwitz: Beginning of a New Era? Reflections on the Holocaust*, Eva Fleischner, ed. (New York: Ktav, 1977), pp. 7–9, 11–14, 15, 17–18, 19, 27–30, 31–33, 41–42, 44–52, 54–55. © Ktav Publishing House, Hoboken, NJ 07030.

which we act and interpret what happens to us. One such event is the Holocaust—the destruction of European Jewry from 1933 to 1945.

The Challenge of the Holocaust

Both religions have always sought to isolate their central events—Exodus and Easter—from further revelations or from the challenge of the demonic counter-experience of evil in history. By and large, both religions have continued since 1945 as if nothing had happened to change their central understanding. It is increasingly obvious that this is impossible, that the Holocaust cannot be ignored.

By its very nature, the Holocaust is obviously central for Jews. The destruction cut so deeply that it is a question whether the community can recover from it. When Adolf Eichmann went into hiding in 1945, he told his accomplice, Dieter Wisliceny, that if caught, he would leap into his grave laughing. He believed that although he had not completed the total destruction of Jewry, he had accomplished his basic goal—because the Jews could never recover from this devastation of their life center. Indeed, Eichmann had destroyed 90 percent of East European Jewry, the spiritual and biological vital center of prewar world Jewry. Six million Jews were killed—some 30 percent of the Jewish people in 1939; but among the dead were over 80 percent of the Jewish scholars, rabbis, full-time students and teachers of Torah alive in 1939.[1] Since there can be no covenant without the covenant people, the fundamental existence of Jews and Judaism is thrown into question by this genocide. For this reason alone, the trauma of the Holocaust cannot be overcome without some basic reorientation in light of it by the surviving Jewish community. Recent studies of Prof. Simon Herman, an Israeli social psychologist, have indicated that the perception of this event and its implications for the Jews' own fate has become a most widespread and powerful factor in individual Jewish consciousness and identity.[2]

The Holocaust as Radical Counter-Testimony to Judaism and Christianity

For Christians, it is easier to continue living as if the event did not make any difference, as if the crime belongs to the history of another people and faith. But such a conclusion would be and is sheer self-deception. The magnitude of suffering and the manifest worthlessness of human life radically contradict the fundamental statements of human value and divine concern in both religions. Failure to confront and account for this evil, then, would turn both religions into empty, Pollyanna assertions, credible only because believers ignore the realities of human history. It would be comparable to preaching that this is the best of all possible worlds to a well-fed, smug congregation, while next door little children starve slowly to death.

Judaism and Christianity do not merely tell of God's love for man, but stand or fall on their fundamental claim that the human being is, therefore, of ultimate and absolute value. ("He who saves one life it is as if he saved an entire world"—B. T. Sanhedrin 37a; "God so loved the world that He gave His only begotten son"—John 3:16.) It is the contradiction of this intrinsic value and the reality of human suffering that validates the absolute centrality and necessity of redemption, of the Messianic hope.

• • •

In short, the Holocaust poses the most radical counter-testimony to both Judaism and Christianity. Elie Wiesel has stated it most profoundly:

> Never shall I forget the little faces of the children, whose bodies I saw turned into wreaths of smoke beneath a silent blue sky.
> Never shall I forget those flames which consumed my faith forever.
> Never shall I forget that nocturnal silence which deprived me, for all eternity, of the desire to live.
> Never shall I forget those moments which murdered my God and my soul and turned my dreams to dust.
> Never shall I forget these things, even if I am condemned to live as long as God Himself. Never.[3]

The cruelty and the killing raise the question whether even those who believe after such an event dare talk about God who loves and cares without making a mockery of those who suffered.

Further Challenge of the Holocaust to Christianity

THE MORAL FAILURE AND COMPLICITY OF ANTI-SEMITISM. Unfortunately, however, the Holocaust poses a yet more devastating question to Christianity: What did Christianity contribute to make the Holocaust possible? The work of Jules Isaac, Norman Cohn, Raul Hilberg, Roy Eckardt, and others poses this question in a number of different ways. In 1942, the Nietra Rebbe went to Archbishop Kametko of Nietra to plead for Catholic intervention against the deportation of the Slovakian Jews. Tiso, the head of the Slovakian government, had been Kametko's secretary for many years, and the rebbe hoped that Kametko could persuade Tiso not to allow the deportations. Since the rebbe did not yet know of the gas chambers, he stressed the dangers of hunger and disease, especially for women, old people, and children. The archbishop replied: "It is not just a matter of deportation. You will not die there of hunger and disease. They will slaughter all of you there, old and young alike, women and children, at once—it is the punishment that you deserve for the death of our Lord and Redeemer, Jesus Christ—you have only one solution. Come over to our religion and I will work to annul this decree."[4]

There are literally hundreds of similar anti-Semitic statements by individual people reported in the Holocaust literature. As late as March 1941—admittedly still before the full destruction was unleashed—Archbishop Grober (Germany), in a pastoral letter, blamed the Jews for the death of Christ and added that "the self-imposed curse of the Jews, 'His blood be upon us and upon our children' had come true terribly, until the present time, until today."[5] Similarly the Vatican responded to an inquiry from the Vichy government about the law of June 2, 1941, which isolated and deprived Jews of rights: "In principle, there is nothing in these measures which the Holy See would find to criticize."[6]

In general, there is an inverse ratio between the presence of a fundamentalist Christianity and the survival of Jews during the Holocaust period. This is particularly damning because the attitude of the local population toward the Nazi assault on the Jews seems to be a critical variable in Jewish survival. (If the local population disapproved of the genocide or sympathized with the Jews, they were more likely to hide or help Jews, resist or condemn the Nazis, which weakened the effectiveness of the killing process or the killer's will to carry it out.) We must allow for the other factors which operated against the Jews in the countries with a fundamentalist Christianity. These factors include Poland and the Baltic nations' lack of modernity (modernity = tolerance, ideological disapproval of mass murder, presence of Jews who can pass, etc.); the isolation and concentration of Jews in these countries, which made them easy to identify and destroy; the Nazis considered Slavs inferior and more freely used the death penalty for any help extended to Jews; the Nazis concentrated more of the governing power in their own hands in these countries. Yet even when all these allowances are made, it is clear that anti-Semitism played a role in the decision not to shield Jews—or to actually turn them in. If the Teaching of Contempt furnished an occasion—or presented stereotypes which brought the Nazis to focus on the Jews as the scapegoat in the first place; or created a residue of anti-Semitism in Europe which affected the local populations' attitudes toward Jews; or enabled some Christians to feel they were doing God's duty in helping kill Jews or in not stopping it—then Christianity may be hopelessly and fatally compromised. The fact is that during the Holocaust the church's protests were primarily on behalf of converted Jews. At the end of the war, the Vatican and circles close to it helped thousands of war criminals to escape, including Franz Stangl, the commandant of the most murderous of all the extermination camps, Treblinka, and the other men of his ilk. Finally in 1948, the German Evangelical Conference in Darmstadt, meeting in the country which had only recently carried out this genocide, proclaimed that the terrible Jewish suffering in the Holocaust was a divine visitation and a call to the Jews to cease their rejection and ongoing crucifixion of Christ. May one morally be a Christian after this?[7]

EVEN SOME CHRISTIANS WHO RESISTED HITLER FAILED ON THE JEWISH QUESTION. Even the great Christians—who recognized the danger of idolatry, and resisted the Nazi government's takeover of the German Evangelical Church at great personal sacrifice and risk—did not speak out on the Jewish question.[8] All this suggests that something in Christian teaching supported or created a positive context for anti-Semitism, and even murder. Is not the faith of a gospel of love, then, fatally tainted with collaboration with genocide—conscious or unconscious? To put it another way: if the Holocaust challenges the fundamental religious claims of Christianity (and Judaism), then the penumbra of Christian complicity may challenge the credibility of Christianity to make these claims.

IS THE WAGER OF CHRISTIAN FAITH LOST? There is yet a third way in which this problem may be stated. In its origins, Christianity grew out of a wager of faith. Growing in the bosom of Judaism and its Messianic hope, Jesus (like others), could be seen either as a false Messiah or as a new unfolding of God's love, and a revelation of love and salvation for mankind. Those who followed Jesus as the Christ, in effect, staked their lives that the new orientation was neither an illusion nor an evil, but yet another stage in salvation and a vehicle of love for mankind. "The acceptance . . . of Jesus as the Messiah means beholding him as one who transforms and will transform the world."[9] As is the case with every vehicle, divine and human, the spiritual record of this wager has been mixed—comprising great inspiration for love given and great evils caused. The hope is that the good outweighs the evil. But the throwing into the scales of so massive a weight of evil and guilt raises the question whether the balance might now be broken, whether one must not decide that it were better that Jesus had not come, rather than that such scenes be enacted six million times over—and more. Has the wager of faith in Jesus been lost?

The Challenge to Modern Culture

The same kinds of questions must be posed to modern culture as well. For the world, too, the Holocaust is an event which changes fundamental perceptions. Limits were broken, restraints shattered, that will never be recovered, and henceforth mankind must live with the dread of a world in which models for unlimited evil exist.

. . .

No assessment of modern culture can ignore the fact that science and technology—the accepted flower and glory of modernity—now climaxed in the factories of death; the awareness that the unlimited, value-free use of knowledge and science, which we perceive as the great force for improving the human condition, had paved the way for the bureaucratic and scientific death campaign. There is the shock of recognition that the humanistic revolt, celebrated as the liberation of humankind in freeing man from centuries of dependence upon God and nature, is now revealed—at the very heart of the enterprise—to sustain a capacity for death and demonic evil.

. . .

One of the most striking things about the Einsatzgruppen leadership makeup is the prevalence of educated people, professionals, especially lawyers, Ph.D.'s, and yes, even a clergyman.[10] How naive the nineteenth-century polemic with religion appears to be in retrospect; how simple Feuerbach, Nietzsche, and many others. The entire structure of autonomous logic and sovereign human reason now takes on a sinister character.

. . .

As Toynbee put it, "a Western nation, which for good or evil, has played so central a part in Western history . . . could hardly have committed these flagrant crimes had they not been festering foully beneath the surface of life in the Western world's non-German provinces. . . . If a twentieth-century German was a monster, then, by the same token a twentieth-century Western civilization was a Frankenstein guilty of having been the author of this German monster's being."[11] This responsibility must be shared not only by Christianity, but by the Enlightenment[12] and democratic cultures as well. Their apathy and encouragement strengthened the will and capacity of the murderers to carry out the genocide, even as moral resistance and condemnation weakened that capacity.

The Moral Failure and Complicity of Universalism

Would that liberalism, democracy, and internationalism had emerged looking morally better. But, in fact, the democracies closed their doors to millions of victims who could have been saved. America's record is one of a fumbling and feeble interest in the victims which allowed anti-Semites and provincial economic and patriotic concerns to rule the admission—or rather the nonadmission—of the refugees. Indeed, the ideology of universal human values did not even provide sufficient motivation to bomb the rail lines and the gas chambers of Auschwitz when these were operating at fullest capacity, and when disruption could have saved ten thousand lives a day. Thus the synthetic rubber factory at Buna in the Auschwitz complex was bombed, but the death factory did not merit such attention.[13] The ideology of universalism did have operational effects. It blocked specifying Jews as victims of Nazi atrocities, as in the Allied declaration of January 1942, when the Nazis were warned they would be held responsible for their cruel war on civilians. In this warning, the Jews were not mentioned by name on the grounds that they were after all humans, not Jews, and citizens of the countries in which they lived. The denial of Jewish particularity—in the face of the very specific Nazi war on the Jews—led to decisions to bomb industrial targets to win the war for democracy, but to exclude death factories— lest this be interpreted as a *Jewish* war! The very exclusion of specifying Jews from warnings and military objectives was interpreted by the Nazis as a signal that Jews were expendable. They may have read the signal correctly. In any event, liberalism and internationalism became cover beliefs—designed to weaken the victims' perception that they were threatened and to block the kind of action needed to save their lives.[14]

• • •

Especially disastrous was the victims' faith in universalism and modern humanitarian values. It disarmed them.

> The basic factor in the Ghetto's lack of preparation for armed resistance was psychological; we did not at first believe the Resettlement Operation to be what in fact it was, systematic slaughter of the entire Jewish population. For generations East European Jews had looked to Berlin as the symbol of law, order, and culture. We could not now believe that the Third Reich was a government of gangsters embarked on a program of genocide "to solve the Jewish problem in Europe." We fell victim to our faith in mankind, our belief that humanity had set limits to the degradation and persecution of one's fellow man.[15]

• • •

Jewish Theological Responses to the Holocaust

Dialectical Faith, or "Moment Faiths"

Faith is living life in the presence of the Redeemer, even when the world is unredeemed. After Auschwitz, faith means there are times when faith is overcome. Buber has spoken of "moment gods": God is known only at the moment when Presence and awareness are fused in vital life. This knowledge is interspersed with moments when only natural, self-contained, routine existence is present. We now have to speak of "moment faiths," moments when Redeemer and vision of redemption are present, interspersed with times when the flames and smoke of the burning children blot out faith—though it flickers again. Such a moment is described in an extraordinary passage of *Night*, as the young boy sentenced to death but too light to hang struggles slowly on the rope. Eliezer finally responds to the man asking, "Where is God now?" by saying, "Here He is—He is hanging here on this gallows . . . "[16]

This ends the easy dichotomy of atheist/theist, the confusion of faith with doctrine or demonstration. It makes clear that faith is a life response of the whole person to the

Presence in life and history. Like life, this response ebbs and flows. The difference between the skeptic and the believer is frequency of faith, and not certitude of position. The rejection of the unbeliever by the believer is literally the denial or attempted suppression of what is within oneself. The ability to live with moment faith is the ability to live with pluralism and without the self-flattering, ethnocentric solutions which warp religion, or make it a source of hatred for the other.

Why Dialectical Faith Is Still Possible

THE PERSISTENCE OF EXODUS. Of course, the question may still be asked: Why is it not a permanent destruction of faith to be in the presence of the murdered children?

One reason is that there are still moments when the reality of the Exodus is reenacted and present. There are moments when a member of the community of Israel shares the reality of the child who was to have been bricked into the wall but instead experienced the liberation and dignity of Exodus. (The reference here is to the rabbinic legend that in Egypt, Jewish children were bricked into a wall if their parents did not meet their daily quota of bricklaying.) This happens even to those who have both literally and figuratively lived through the Holocaust. Wiesel describes this moment for us in *The Gates of the Forest*, when Gregor "recites the Kaddish, the solemn affirmation . . . by which man returns to God his crown and his scepter."[17] Neither Exodus nor Easter wins out or is totally blotted out by Buchenwald, but we encounter both polar experiences; the life of faith is lived between them. And this dialectic opens new models of response to God, as we shall show below.

THE BREAKDOWN OF THE SECULAR ABSOLUTE. A second reason is that we do not stand in a vacuum when faith encounters the crematoria. In a real sense, we are always choosing between alternative faiths when we make a decision about ultimate meaning. In this culture the primary alternative to religion is secular man in a world closed off from any transcendence, or divine incursion. This world grows out of the intellectual framework of science, philosophy, and social science, of rationalism and human liberation, which created the enterprise of modernity. This value system was—and is—the major alternative faith which Jews and Christians joined in large numbers in the last two centuries, transferring allegiance from the Lord of History and Revelation to the Lord of Science and Humanism. In so many ways, the Holocaust is the direct fruit and will of this alternative. Modernity fostered the excessive rationalism and utilitarian relations which created the need for and susceptibility to totalitarian mass movements and the surrender of moral judgment. The secular city sustained the emphasis on value-free sciences and objectivity, which created unparalleled power but weakened its moral limits. (Surely it is no accident that so many members of the Einsatzgruppen were professionals.) Mass communication and universalization of values weakened resistance to centralized power, and served as a cover to deny the unique danger posed to particular, i.e. Jewish, existence.

In the light of Auschwitz, secular twentieth-century civilization is not worthy of this transfer of our ultimate loyalty. The victims ask that we not jump to a conclusion that retrospectively makes the covenant they lived an illusion and their death a gigantic travesty—a product of their illusions and Gentile jealousy of those pathetically mistaken claims.[18] It is not that emotional sympathy decides the validity or invalidity of philosophic positions. The truth is sometimes very unpleasant, and may contradict cherished beliefs or moral preferences. But the credibility of systems does rise or fall in the light of events which enhance or reduce the credibility of their claims.[19] A system associated with creating a framework for mass murder must be very persuasive before gaining intellectual assent. The burden of the proofs should be unquestionable. Nothing in the record of secular culture on the Holocaust justifies its authority claims. The victims ask us, above all, not to allow the creation of another matrix of values that might sustain another attempt of genocide. The absence of strong alternative value systems gives a moral monopoly to the wielders of power and authority. Secular authority unchecked becomes absolute. Relative values thus become the seedbed of absolute claims, and this is idolatry. This vacuum was a major factor in the Nazi ability to concentrate power and carry out the destruction without protest or resistance. (The primary sources of resistance were systems of absolute alternative values—the Barmen Conference in the Confessional Church, Jehovah's Witnesses, etc.)[20] After the Holocaust it is all the more urgent to resist this absolutization of the secular. As Emil Fackenheim has pointed out, the all-out celebration of the secular city by Harvey Cox reflected the assimilation of Christian values to a secular civilization given absolute status.[21] It is potential idolatry, an idolatry to which we more easily succumb if we have failed to look at the Holocaust.

If nothing else sufficed to undercut this absolute claim of nonaccessibility of the divine, it is the knowledge that the absence of limits or belief in a judge, and the belief that persons could therefore become God, underlay the structure of *l'univers concentrationnaire*. Mengele and other selectors of Auschwitz openly joked about this. I will argue below that the need to deny God leads directly to the assumption of omnipotent power over life and death. The desire to control people leads directly to crushing the image of God within them, so that the jailer becomes God. Then one cannot easily surrender to the temptation of being cut off from the transcendence, and must explore the alternatives. Surely it is no accident that in the past forty years language analysts like Wittgenstein, critics of value-free science and social sciences, existentialists, evangelical and counter-culture movements alike, have fought to set limits to the absolute claims of scientific knowledge and of reason, and to ensure the freedom for renewed encounter with the transcendental.

THE LOGIC OF POST-HOLOCAUST AND, THEREFORE, POST-MODERN FAITH. A third reason to resist abandoning the divine is the moral urgency that grows out of the Holocaust and fights for the presence of the Lord of History. Emil Fackenheim has articulated this position in terms of not handing Hitler posthumous victories. I prefer an even more traditional category, and would argue that the moral necessity of a world to come, and even of resurrection, arises powerfully out of the encounter with the Holocaust. Against this, Rubenstein and others would maintain that the wish is not always father to the fact, and that such an illusion may endanger even more lives. To this last point I would reply that the proper belief will save, not cost, lives (see below). It is true that moral appropriateness is not always a good guide to philosophic sufficiency; but the Holocaust experience insists that we best err on the side of moral necessity. To put it more rationally, sometimes we see the narrower logic of a specific argument rather than the deeper logic of the historical moment or setting. This could make the narrower logical grounds formally consistent and persuasive, yet utterly misleading, since they may start from and finish with the wrong assumptions.

Moral necessity validates the search for religious experience rather than surrender to the immediate logic of nonbelief. Thus, if the Holocaust strikes at the credibility of faith, especially unreconstructed faith, dialectically it also erodes the persuasiveness of the secular option. If someone is told that a line of argument leads to the conclusion that he should not exist, not surprisingly the victim may argue that there must be alternative philosophical frameworks. Insofar as the Holocaust grows out of Western civilization, then, at least for Jews, it is a powerful incentive to guard against being overimpressed by this culture's intellectual assumptions and to seek other philosophical and historical frameworks.

• • •

The moral light shed by the Holocaust on the nature of Western culture validates skepticism toward contemporary claims—even before philosophic critiques emerge to justify the skepticism. It is enough that this civilization is the locus of the Holocaust. The Holocaust calls on Jews, Christians, and others to absolutely resist the total authority of this cultural moment. The experience frees them to respond to their own claim, which comes from outside the framework of this civilization, to relate to a divine other, who sets limits and judges the absolute claims of contemporary philosophic and scientific and human political systems. To follow this orientation is to be opened again to the possibilities of Exodus and immortality.

This is a crucial point. The Holocaust comes after two centuries of Emancipation's steadily growing domination of Judaism and the Jews. Rubenstein's self-perception as a radical breaking from the Jewish past is, I think, misleading. A more correct view would argue that he is repeating the repudiation of the God of History and the Chosen that was emphasized by the modernizing schools, such as Reconstructionism. This position had become the stuff of the values and views of the majority of Jews. "Being right with modernity" (defined by each group differently) has been the dominant value norm of a growing number of Jews since 1750, as well as Christians. Despite the rear-guard action of Orthodox Judaism and Roman Catholicism (until the 1960s) and of fundamentalist groups, the modern tide has steadily risen higher. The capacity to resist, criticize, or break away from these models is one of the litmus tests of the Holocaust as the new orienting experience of Jews, and an indication that a new era of Jewish civilization is under way. This new era will not turn its back on many aspects of modernity, but clearly it will be freer to reject some of its elements, and to take from the past (and future) much more fully.

THE REVELATION IN THE REDEMPTION OF ISRAEL. I have saved for last the most important reason why the moment of despair and disbelief in redemption cannot be final, at least in this generation's community of Israel. Another event has taken place in our lifetime which also has extraordinary scope and normative impact—the rebirth of the State of Israel. As difficult to absorb in its own way and, like the Holocaust, a scandal for many traditional Jewish and Christian categories, it is an inescapable part of the Jewish historical experience in our time. And while it is a continuation and outgrowth of certain responses to the Holocaust, it is at the same time a dialectical contradiction to many of its implications. If the experience of Auschwitz symbolizes that we are cut off from God and hope, and that the covenant may be destroyed, then the experience of Jerusalem symbolizes that God's promises are faithful and His people live on. Burning children speak of the absence of all value—human and divine; the rehabilitation of one-half million Holocaust survivors in Israel speaks of the reclamation of tremendous human dignity and value. If Treblinka makes human hope an illusion, then the Western Wall asserts that human dreams are more real than force and facts. Israel's faith in the God of History demands that an unprecedented event of destruction be matched by an unprecedented act of redemption, and this has happened.[22]

This is not simply a question of the memories of Exodus versus the experience of Auschwitz. If it were a question of Exodus only, then those Jews already cut off from Exodus by the encounter with modern culture would be excluded and only "religious" Jews could still be believers.

But almost all Jews acknowledge this pheonomenon—the event of redemption and the event of catastrophe and their dialectical interrelationship—and it touches their lives. Studies show that the number of those who affirm this phenomenon as central (even if in nontheological categories) has grown from year to year; that its impact is now almost universal among those who will acknowledge themselves as Jews, and that its force has overthrown some hierarchies of values that grew as modernity came to dominate Jewish life.[23] In fact, the religious situation is explosive and fermenting on a deeper level than anyone wishes to acknowledge at this point. The whole Jewish people is caught between immersion in nihilism and immersion in redemption—both are present in immediate experience, and not just historical memory. To deny either pole in our time is to be cut off from historical Jewish experience. In the incredible dialectical tension between the two we are fated to live. Biblical theology already suggested that the time would come when consciousness of God out of the restoration of Israel would outweigh consciousness of God out of the Exodus. In the words of Jeremiah: "The days will come, says the Lord, when it shall no longer be said: 'as God lives who brought up the children of Israel out of the land of Egypt' but 'as God lives who brought up the children of Israel from the land of the north and from all the countries whither He had driven them,' and I will bring them back into their land that I gave to their fathers" (Jer. 16:14–15).

DESPITE REDEMPTION, FAITH REMAINS DIALECTICAL. But if Israel is so redeeming, why then must faith be "moment faith," and why should the experience of nothingness ever dominate?

The answer is that faith is living in the presence of the Redeemer, and in the moment of utter chaos, of genocide, one does not live in His presence. One must be faithful to the reality of the nothingness. Faith is a moment truth, but there are moments when it is not true. This is certainly demonstrable in dialectical truths, when invoking the truth at the wrong moment is a lie. To let Auschwitz overwhelm Jerusalem is to lie (i.e., to speak a truth out of its appropriate moment); and to let Jerusalem deny Auschwitz is to lie for the same reason.

The biblical witness is that a permanent repudiation of the covenant would also have been a lie. "Behold, they say: our bones are dried up and our hope is lost; we are cut off entirely" (Ezek. 37:11). There were many who chose this answer, but their logic led to dissolution in the pagan world around them. After losing hope in the Lord of History, they were absorbed into idolatry—the faith of the gods of that moment. In the resolution the crisis of biblical faith, those who abandoned hope ceased to testify. However persuasive the reaction may have been at that time, every such decision in Israel's history—until Auschwitz—has been premature, and even wrong. Yet in a striking talmudic interpretation, the rabbis say that Daniel and Jeremiah refused to speak of the Temple.[24] The line between the repudiation of the God of the covenant and the Daniel-Jeremiah reaction is so thin that repudiation must be seen as an authentic reaction even if we reject it. There is a faithfulness in the rejection; serious theism must be troubled after such an event.

• • •

The Central Religious Testimony After the Holocaust

Recreating Human Life

In the silence of God and of theology, there is one fundamental testimony that can still be given—the testimony of human life itself. This was always the basic evidence, but after Auschwitz its import is incredibly heightened. In fact, it is the only testimony that can still be heard.

The vast number of dead and morally destroyed is the phenomenology of absurdity and radical evil, the continuing statement of human worthlessness and meaninglessness that shouts down all talk of God and human worth. The Holocaust is even model and pedagogy for future generations that genocide can be carried out with impunity—one need fear neither God nor man. There is one response to such overwhelming tragedy: the reaffirmation of meaningfulness, worth, and life—through acts of love and life-giving. The act of creating a life or enhancing its dignity is the counter-testimony of Auschwitz. To talk of love and of a God who cares in the presence of the burning children is obscene and incredible; to leap in and pull a child out of a pit, to clean its face and heal its body, is to make the most powerful statement—the only statement that counts.

In the first moment after the Flood, with its testimony of absurd and mass human death, Noah is given two instructions—the only two that can testify after such an event. "Be fruitful and multiply and replenish the earth" (Gen. 9:1–7), and "but your life blood I will hold you responsible for"—"who sheds man's blood, shall his blood be shed; for in the image of God made He man" (Gen. 9:5–6). Each act of creating a life, each act of enhancing or holding people responsible for human life, becomes multiplied in its resonance because it contradicts the mass graves of biblical Shinar—or Treblinka.

Recreating the Image of God

This becomes the critical religious act. Only a million or billion such acts can begin to right the balance of testimony so drastically shifted by the mass weight of six million dead. In an age when one is ashamed or embarrassed to talk about God in the presence of the burning children, the image of God, which points beyond itself to transcendence, is the only statement about God that one can make. And it is human life itself that makes the statement—words will not help.

Put it another way: the overwhelming testimony of the six million is so strong that it all but irretrievably closes out religious language. Therefore the religious enterprise after this event must see itself as a desperate attempt to create, save, and heal the image of God wherever it still exists—lest further evidence of meaninglessness finally tilt the scale irreversibly. Before this calling, all other "religious" activity is dwarfed.

But where does one find the strength to have a child after Auschwitz? Why bring a child into a world where Auschwitz is possible? Why expose it to such a risk again? The perspective of Auschwitz sheds new light on the nature of childrearing and faith. It takes enormous faith in ultimate redemption and meaningfulness to choose to create or even enhance life again. In fact, faith is revealed by this not to be a belief or even an emotion, but an ontological life-force that reaffirms creation and life in the teeth of overwhelming death. One must silently assume redemption in order to have the child—and having the child makes the statement of redemption.

• • •

The Context of an Image of God

In a world of overpopulation and mass starvation and of zero population growth, something further must be said. I, for one, believe that in the light of the crematoria, the Jewish people are called to re-create life. Nor is such testimony easily given. One knows the risk to the children.

But it is not only the act of creating life that speaks. To bring a child into a world in which it will be hungry and diseased and neglected, is to torment and debase the image of God. We also face the challenge to create the conditions under which human beings will grow as an image of God; to build a world in which wealth and resources are created and distributed to provide the matrix for existence as an image of God.

We also face the urgent call to eliminate every stereotype discrimination that reduces—and denies—this image in the other. It was the ability to distinguish some people as human and others as not that enabled the Nazis to segregate and then destroy the "subhumans" (Jews, Gypsies, Slavs). The ability to differentiate the foreign Jews from Frenchborn Jews paved the way for the deportation first of foreign-born, then of native, French Jews. This differentiation stilled conscience, stilled the church, stilled even some French Jews. The indivisibility of human dignity and equality becomes an essential bulwark against the repetition of another Holocaust. It is the command rising out of Auschwitz.

This means a vigorous self-criticism, and review of every cultural or religious framework that may sustain some devaluation or denial of the absolute and equal dignity of the other. This is the overriding command and the essential criterion for religious existence, to whoever walks by the light of the flames. Without this testimony and the creation of facts that give it persuasiveness, the act of the religious enterprise simply lacks credibility. To the extent that religion may extend or justify the evils of dignity denied, it becomes the devil's testimony. Whoever joins in the work of creation and rehabilitation of the image of God is, therefore, participating in"restoring to God his scepter and crown." Whoever does not support—or opposes—this process is seeking to complete the attack on God's presence in the world. These must be seen as the central religious acts. They shed a pitiless light on popes who deny birth control to starving millions because of a need to uphold the religious authority of the magisterium; or on rabbis who deny women's dignity out of loyalty to divinely given traditions.

Religious and Secular after the Holocaust

THE END OF THE SECULAR-RELIGIOUS DICHOTOMY. This argument makes manifest an underlying thrust in this interpretation. The Holocaust has destroyed the meaning of the categories of "secular" and "religious." Illuminated by the light of the crematoria, these categories are dissolved and not infrequently turned inside out.

We must remember the many "religious" people who carried out the Holocaust. There were killers and murderers who continued to practice organized religion, including Christianity. There were many "good Christians," millions of respectable people, who turned in, rounded up, and transported millions of Jews. Some sympathized with or were apathetic to the murder process, while perceiving themselves as religiously observant and faithful—including those who did an extra measure of Jew-hunting or betrayal because they perceived it as an appropriate expression of Christian theology. Vast numbers of people practiced religion in this period, but saw no need to stand up to or resist the destruction process.

. . .

IF "ALL IS PERMITTED," WHAT IS THE "FEAR OF GOD"? The Holocaust is overwhelming witness that "all is permitted." It showed that there are no limits of sacredness or dignity to stop the death process. There were no thunderbolts or divine curses to check mass murder or torture. The Holocaust also showed that one can literally get away with murder. After the war a handful of killers were punished, but the vast majority were not. Catholic priests supplied disguises and passports for mass murderers to help them escape punishment. German and Austrian officials cleared them of guilt—or imposed a few years of prison for killing tens of thousands. Men in charge of legally ostracizing Jews and clearing them for destruction became secretaries to cabinet ministers. Men who owned gas-producing companies, those who had built crematoria, were restored to their full ownership rights and wealth. Thirty years later, an anti-Nazi woman was imprisoned for seeking to kidnap and deliver for extradition a mass murderer, while he went free. Austrian juries acquitted the architects of the Auschwitz gas chambers. If all is permitted, why should anyone hold back from getting away with whatever one can? The prudential argument, that it is utilitarian not to do so, surely is outweighed by the reality that one can get away with so much. And the example of millions continually testifies against any sense of reverence or dignity to check potential evil.

I would propose that there is an explanation; a biblical category applies here. Whoever consistently holds back from murder or human exploitation when he could perpetrate it with immunity—or any person who unswervingly devotes himself to reverence, care, and protection of the divine image which is man, beyond that respect which can be coerced—reveals the presence within of a primordial awe—"fear of God"—which alone evokes such a response.

The biblical category suggests that fear of God is present where people simply cannot do certain things. It is, as it were, a field of force that prevents certain actions. The midwives feared God (Exod. 1:21), and therefore they simply could not kill newborn babies. When fear of God is not present, then there are no limits. Amalek could attack the weak and those who lagged behind because Amalek did not "fear God" (Deut. 25:18). A man can be killed in order to be robbed of his fair wife in a place where there is no fear of God (Gen. 20:11). We posit that this presence is a shield. This is why people cannot kill human beings in the "image of God"—they must first take them outside the pale of unique-ness and value before they can unleash murder. They must first be convinced that there is no divine limit. In the glare of the fires, by their piercing rays, we now can see clearly who has this fear of God and who does not.

It makes no difference whether the person admits the presence of God. From the bib-lical perspective, the power of the limit reveals that the divine presence's force is oper-ating. (This is the meaning of Rabbi Akiva's statement in the Talmud, that in the moment that the thief steals, he is an atheist. Otherwise, how could he disobey the divine voice that says: Thou shalt not steal.)

RELIGIOUS AND SECULAR SELF-DEFINITION IN LIGHT OF AUSCHWITZ. Nor can we take self-definitions seriously. During the Holocaust, many (most?) of the church's protests were on behalf of Jews converted to Christianity. Consider what this means. It is not im-portant to protest the murder of Jews; only if a person believes in Jesus Christ as Lord and Savior is there a moral need to protest his fate.[25] Can we take such self-definitions of religious people as reflection of belief in God?

When, in May and June 1967, it appeared that another Holocaust loomed, men of God remained silent. Pope Paul VI, moved by all sorts of legitimate or normal considerations (concern for Christian Arabs, concern for holy places, theological hang-ups about secu-lar Israel) remained silent. A self-avowed atheist, root source of much of modern athe-ism, Jean-Paul Sartre, spoke out against potential genocide—even though he had to break with his own deepest political alliances and self-image in his links to Arabs and Third World figures to do so. He knew that there is one command: Never another Holocaust. Which is the man of God, which the atheist? By biblical perspective? By Auschwitz per-spective? Are title, self-definition, official dress, public opinion—even sincere personal profession—more significant than action?

If someone were to begin to strangle you, all the while protesting loudly and sincerely: "I love you!" at what point would the perception of that person's sincerity change? At what point would you say, "Actions speak louder than words"? As you turn blue, you say, "Uh . . . pardon me, are you sure that I am the person you had in mind . . . when you said, 'I love you'?"

One must fully respect the atheist's right to his own self-definition. But from the reli-gious perspective, the action speaks for itself. The denial of faith has to be seen as the action of one determined to be a secret servant, giving up the advantages of acknowl-edged faith, because at such a time such advantages are blasphemous. Perhaps it reveals a deeper religious consciousness that knows there must be a silence about God—if faith in Him is not to be fatally destroyed in light of the Holocaust and of the abuse of faith in God expressed by a Himmler. Thus, the atheist who consistently shows reverence for the image of God, but denies that he does so because he is a believer in God, is revealed by the flames to be one of the thirty-six righteous—the hidden righteous, whom Jewish tra-dition asserts to be the most righteous, those for whose sake the world exists. Their faith is totally inward and they renounce the prerequisites of overt faith; and for their sake the world of evil is borne by God.[26]

THE STATE OF ISRAEL: A STUDY IN SECULARITY AND RELIGION AFTER AUSCHWITZ. By this standard, the "secular" State of Israel is revealed for the deeply religious state that it is. Both its officially nonreligious majority as well as its official and established religious minority are irrelevant to this judgment. The real point is that after Auschwitz, the existence of the Jew is a great affirmation and an act of faith. The re-creation of the body of the people, Israel, is renewed testimony to Exodus as ultimate reality, to God's continuing presence in history proven by the fact that his people, despite the attempt to annihilate them, still exist.

Moreover, who show that they know that God's covenant must be upheld by re-creating his people? Who heard this overriding claim and set aside personal comfort, cut personal living standards drastically, gave life, health, energy to the rehabilitation of the remnants of the covenant people? Who give their own lives repeatedly in war and/or guard duty to protect the remnant? Surely the secular Jews of Israel as much as, or more than, the religious Jew, or non-Jews anywhere.

The religious-secular paradox goes deeper still. Instead of choosing to flee at all costs from the terrible fate of exposure to genocide, instead of spending all their energy and money to hide and disappear, Jews all over the world—secular Jews included—renewed and intensified their Jewish existence and continued to have and raise Jewish children. Knowing of the fate to which this choice exposes them (a fate especially dramatically clear in Israel, where year after year the Arabs have preached extermination); aware of how little the world really cared, or cares, and that the first time is always the hardest—what is one to make of the faith of those who made this decision and who live it every day, especially in Israel? The answer has been given most clearly by Emil Fackenheim. To raise a Jewish child today is to bind the child and the child's child on the altar, even as father Abraham bound Isaac. Only, those who do so today know that there is no angel to stop the process and no ram to substitute for more than one and one-half million Jewish children in this lifetime. Such an act then, can only come out of resources of faith, of ultimate meaningfulness—of Exodus trust—on a par with, or superior to, father Abraham at the peak of his life as God's loved and covenanted follower. Before such faith, who shall categorize in easy categories the secular and the devout Israeli or Jew?

A classic revelation of the deeper levels can be found in the "Who is a Jew" controversy, and in the Israeli "Law of Return," which guarantees every Jew automatic admittance into Israel. This law has been used against Israel, in slogans of "racism," by those who say that if Israel only de-Zionizes and gives up this law she would have peace from her Arab neighbors, and by Christians and other non-Jews who then assess Israel as religiously discriminatory. All these judgments cost the secular Israelis a great deal—not least because any weakening of public support means a heightened prospect of genocide for themselves and their children. In turn, the secular Israeli is bitterly criticized by observant Jews for not simply following the traditional definition of who is a Jew. In 1974 this issue even disrupted attempts to form a government, at a time when life-and-death negotiations hung in the balance. Why, then, has the law been stubbornly upheld by the vast majority of secular Israelis?

It reveals the deepest recesses of their souls. They refuse to formally secularize the definition of "Israeli" and thereby cut the link between the covenant people of history and the political body of present Israel—despite their own inability to affirm, or even their vigorous denial of, the covenant! They see Auschwitz as revelatory and commanding, normative as great events in covenant history are, and they are determined to guarantee automatic admission to every Jew—knowing full well he is always exposed (by covenantal existence) to the possibility of another Holocaust with no place to flee. The lesson of

Auschwitz is that no human being should lack a guaranteed place to flee again, just as the lesson of the Exodus was that no runaway slave should be turned back to his master (Deut. 23:16). (Needless to say, there is self-interest involved also—more Jews in Israel strengthen the security of Israel. But the admixture of self-interest is part of the reality in which religious imperatives are acted upon by all human beings.)

In light of this, Zionism, criticized by some devout Jews as secular revolt against religion and by other observant Jews for its failures to create a state that fully observes Jewish tradition, is carrying out the central religious actions of the Jewish people after Auschwitz. Irony piles upon irony! The re-creation of the state is the strongest suggestion that God's promises are still valid and reliable. Thus the secularist pheonomenon gives the central religious testimony of the Jewish people today. In the Holocaust many rabbis ruled that every Jew killed for being Jewish has died for the sanctification of the name of God. In death as in life, the religious-secular dichotomy is essentially ended.

Dialectical Reflections on the End
of the Secular-Religious Difficulty

CONTRA HUMANISM. Once we establish the centrality of the reverence for the image of God and the erosion of the secular-religious dichotomy after Auschwitz, then the dialectic of the Holocaust becomes visible. Such views could easily become embodied in a simple humanism or a new universalist liberation that is totally absorbed in the current secular option. To collapse into this option would be to set up the possibility of another idolatry. True, it would be more likely a Stalinist rather than a fascist idolatry; but it reopens the possibility of the concentration of power and legitimacy which could carry out another Holocaust. We are bidden to resist this temptation. Indeed, there is a general principle at work here. Every solution that is totally at ease with a dominant option is to be seen as an attempt to escape from the dialectical torment of living with the Holocaust. If you do escape, you open up the option that the Holocaust may recur. A radical self-critical humanism springing out of the Holocaust says no to the demons of Auschwitz; a celebration of the death of God or of secular man is collaboration with these demons.

CONTRA PROTEAN MAN. The fury of the Holocaust also undercuts the persuasiveness of another modern emphasis—the sense of option and choice of existence. This sense of widespread freedom to choose identity and of the weakening of biological or inherited status is among the most pervasive values of contemporary culture. It clearly grows out of the quantum leap in human power and control through medicine and technology, backed by the development of democratic and universalist norms. It has generated a revolt against inherited disadvantage, and even genetic or biological limitations. The freedom of being almost protean is perceived as positive—the source of liberation and human dignity. In light of the Holocaust, we must grapple with the question anew. Is the breaking of organic relationships and deracination itself the source of the pathology which erupted at the heart of modernity? Erich Fromm has raised the issue in *Escape from Freedom*. Otto Ohlendorf—the head of D Einsatzgruppe, and one of the very few war criminals willing to admit frankly what he did and why—stressed the search for restored authority and rootedness (e.g., the failure to conserve the given as well as the freely chosen in modern culture) as a major factor in the scope and irrationality of the Nazis' murderous enterprise.

Since the attack started against the people of Israel, but planned to go on to Slavs and other groups, it poses a fundamental question to the credibility of modern culture itself. There has not been enough testing and study of this possibility in the evidence of the Holocaust yet, but it warrants a serious study and an immediate reconsideration of the persuasiveness of the "freedom-of-being" option in modernity. The concept is profoundly challenged by the Jewish experience in the Holocaust.[27] For the demonic assault on the people of Israel recognized no such choice. Unlike the situation that prevailed in medieval persecutions, one could not cease to be a Jew through conversion. In retrospect, liberation turned out to be an illusion that weakened the victims' capacity to recognize their coming fate or the fact that the world would not save them—because they were Jews.

CONTRA THE SUPERIORITY OF THE SPIRIT OVER THE FLESH. This insight also reverses the historical, easy Christian polemic concerning the "Israel of the flesh" versus "Israel of the spirit." After all, is not Israel of the spirit a more universal and more committed category, a more spiritually meaningful state, than the status conferred by accident of birth? Yet the Holocaust teaches the reverse. When absolute power arose and claimed to be God, then Israel's existence was antithetical to its own. Israel of the flesh by its mere existence gives testimony, and therefore was "objectively" an enemy of the totalitarian state. By the same token neither commitment to secularism, atheism, or any other faith— nor even joining Christianity—could remove the intrinsic status of being Jewish, and being forced to stand and testify. Fackenheim, Berkovits, Rubenstein, and others have spoken of the denial of significance to the individual Jew by the fact that his fate was decided by his birth—whatever his personal preference. But classical Jewish commentators had a different interpretation. The mere fact that the Jew's existence denies the absolute claims of others means that the Jew is testifying. The act of living speaks louder than the denial of intention to testify, as I have suggested in my comments on fear of God above. During the Holocaust, rabbis began to quote a purported ruling by Maimonides that a Jew killed by bandits—who presumably feel freer to kill him because he is a Jew—has died for the sanctification of the Name, whether or not he was pressured before death to deny his Judaism and his God.[28] This testimony, voluntarily given or not, turns out to be the secret significance of "Israel of the flesh." A Jew's life is on the line and therefore every kind of Jew gives testimony at all times.

Israel of the spirit testifies against the same idolatry and evil. Indeed, there were sincere Christians who stood up for their principles, were recognized as threats, and sent to concentration camps. However, Israel of the spirit only has the choice of being silent; with this measure of collaboration, it can live safely and at ease. Not surprisingly, the vast majority chose to be safe. As Franklin Littell put it, when paganism is persecuting, Christians "can homogenize and become mere gentiles again; while the Jews, believing or secularized, remain representatives of another history, another providence."[29] It suggests that from now on one of the great keys to testimony in the face of the enormously powerful forces available to evil, will be to have given hostages, to be on the line because one is inextricably bound to this fate. The creation of a forced option should be one of the goals of moral pedagogy after the Holocaust. It is the meaning of chosenness in Jewish faith. The Christian analogy of this experience would be a surrender of the often self-deceiving universalist rhetoric of the church and a conception of itself as people of God—a distant community of faith with some identification—that must testify to the world.

• • •

Living with the Dialectic

The dialectic I have outlined is incredibly difficult to live by. How can we reconcile such extraordinary human and moral tensions? The classical traditions of Judaism and Christianity suggest: by reenacting constantly the event which is normative and revelatory. Only those who experience the normative event in their bones—through the community of the faith—will live by it.[30] I would suggest, then, that in the decades and centuries to come, Jews and others who seek to orient themselves by the Holocaust will unfold another sacral round. Men and women will gather to eat the putrid bread of Auschwitz, the potato-peelings of Bergen-Belsen. They will tell of the children who went, the starvation and hunger of the ghettoes, the darkening of the light in the Mussulmen's eyes. To enable people to reenact and relive Auschwitz there are records, pictures, even films—some taken by the murderers, some by the victims. That this pain will be incorporated in the round of life we regret; yet we may hope that it will not destroy hope but rather strengthen responsibility, will, and faith.

After Auschwitz, one must beware of easy hope. Israel is a perfect symbol for this. On the one hand, it validates the right to hope and speak of life renewed after destruction. On the other hand, it has been threatened with genocide all along. At the moment it is at a low point—yet prospects for a peace also suddenly emerge. Any hope must be sober, and built on the sands of despair, free from illusions. Yet Jewish history affirms hope.

I dare to use another biblical image. The cloud of smoke of the bodies by day and the pillar of fire of the crematoria by night may yet guide humanity to a goal and a day when human beings are attached to each other; and have so much shared each other's pain, and have so purified and criticized themselves, that *never again will a Holocaust be possible.* Perhaps we can pray that out of the welter of blood and pain will come a chastened mankind and faith that may take some tentative and mutual steps toward redemption. Then truly will the Messiah be here among us. Perhaps then the silence will be broken. At the prospect of such hope, however, certainly in our time, it is more appropriate to fall silent.

Notes

1. Dieter Wisliceny, affidavit dated November 29, 1945, printed in *Nazi Conspiracy and Aggression* (Washington: Government Printing Office, 1946), 8:610; he quotes Eichmann as follows: "I laugh when I jump into the grave because of the feeling I have killed 5,000,000 Jews. That gives me great satisfaction and gratification." Rudolf Hoess, the head of Auschwitz, reports Eichmann's joy grew out of his conviction that he had landed a fatal blow by devastating Jewry's life center. In Hoess's responses to Dr. Jan Sehn, the examining judge, printed as appendix 3 in Hoess's autobiography, *Commandant of Auschwitz* (London: Weidenfeld & Nicolson, 1959), p. 215. The estimate of Jewish scholars, rabbis, and full-time students killed is by Rabbi M. J. Itamar (Wohlgelernter), formerly secretary-general of the Chief Rabbinate of Israel. Heydrich, the original head of the Final Solution project and its driving force until his

death by assassination, instructed the Einsatzgruppen that in killing the Jews of Eastern Europe, they would be killing the "intellectual reservoir of the Jews."

2. Simon Herman, *Israelis and Jews: A Study in the Continuity of an Identity* (New York: Random House, 1970), pp. 78–80, 175, 186, 191, 203–4, 211–13; idem, lecture given at the annual meeting of the Memorial Foundation for Jewish Culture in Geneva, July 9, 1974, published in 1975 *Proceedings of the Memorial Foundation for Jewish Culture*; idem, "Ethnic Identity and Historical Time Perspective: An Illustrated Case Study; the Impact of the Holocaust (Destruction of European Jewry) on Jewish Identity," mimeographed (Jerusalem, 1972); idem, research in progress.

3. Elie Wiesel, *Night* (New York: Hill & Wang, 1960), pp. 43–44.

4. Michael Dov Weissmandl, *Min Hametzar* (1960; reprint ed., Jerusalem, n.d.) p. 24. See also Weissmandl's report of his conversation with the papal nuncio in 1944. He quotes the nuncio as saying: "There is no innocent blood of Jewish children in the world. All Jewish blood is guilty. You have to die. This is the punishment that has been awaiting you because of that sin [deicide]." Dr. Livia Rotkirchen of Yad Vashem has called my attention to the fact that the papal nuncio tried to help save Jews and used his influence to do so. Weissmandl's quote appears to be incompatible with that image. Dr. Rotkirchen speculates that Weissmandl, in retrospect, attributed the statement to the wrong person. In any event, this judgment that the Jews deserved their fate as punishment for deicide or rejecting Christ is a strong and recurrent phenomenon. On the papal nuncio's work, see Livia Rotkirchen, "Vatican Policy and the Jewish 'Independent' Slovakia (1939–1945)," *Yad Vashem Studies* 6 (1967): 25–54.

5. Pastoral letter of March 25, 1941, A. B. Freiburg, no. 9, March 27, 1941, p. 388; quoted in Günter Lewy, *The Catholic Church and Nazi Germany* (New York: McGraw-Hill, 1964), p. 294.

6. Saul Friedlander, *Pius XII and the Third Reich: A Documentation* (New York: Knopf, 1966), p. 97. Cf. the whole discussion of the decrees by the Vatican, ibid., pp. 92–99.

7. "Ein Wort zur Judenfrage, der Reichsbruderrat der Evangelischen Kirche in Deutschland," issued on April 8, 1948 in Dietrich Goldschmidt and Hans-Joachim Kraus, eds., *Der Ungekundigte Bund: Neue Begegnung von Juden und christlicher* (Stuttgart, 1962), pp. 251–54. The extent to which Vatican circles helped Nazi war criminals escape is only now becoming evident. See on this Gitta Sereny, *Into That Darkness* (London: Andre Deutsch, 1974), pp. 289–323. See also Ladislav Farago, *Aftermath: Martin Bormann and the Fourth Reich* (New York: Simon & Schuster, 1974).

8. Cf. memorandum submitted to Chancellor Hitler, June 4, 1936, in Arthur C. Cochrane, *The Church's Confession Under Hitler* (Philadelphia: Westminster Press, 1962), pp. 268–79; J. S. Conway, *The Nazi Persecution of the Churches* (London: Weidenfeld & Nicolson, 1968), pp. xx, xxiii, 84–85, 261–65.

9. A. Roy Eckardt, *Elder and Younger Brothers* (New York: Scribner's, 1967), p. 107.

10. The trial record of the Einsatzgruppen leaders shows that of twenty-four defendants, Herren Schubert (p. 97), Lindow (p. 99), Schulz (p. 135), Blume (p. 139), Braune (p. 214), Sandberger (p. 532), Haensch (p. 547), Strauch (p. 563), and Klingelhoefer (p. 564) were lawyers. Other professionals included architect Blobel (p. 211), economist Sieberg (p. 536), professor Six (p. 555), banker Noske (p. 570), secondary-school instructor Steimle (p. 578), economist Ohlendorf (p. 224), dentist Fendler (p. 570), and last but not least, clergyman Biberstein (p. 542).

11. Arnold Toynbee, *A Study of History*, vol. 60, p. 433, quoted in Eliezer Berkovits, *Faith After the Holocaust* (New York: KTAV, 1973), p. 18.

12. Arthur Herzberg, *The French Enlightenment and the Jews* (New York: Columbia University Press, 1968); Uriel Tal, *Yahadut V'Natzrut BaReich HaSheni* [Jews and Christians in the Second Reich], *1870–1914* (Jerusalem: Magnes Press, 1969); and Eleanore Sterling, *Er Ist Wie Du: Fruh Geschichte des Anti Semitismus in Deutschland, 1815–1850* (Munich: Chr. Kaiser, 1956). One should also note Elie Wiesel's biting words on the moral collapse in the camps of "the in-

tellectuals, the liberals, the humanists, the professors of sociology and the like." Elie Wiesel, "Talking and Writing and Keeping Silent," in Franklin H. Littell and Hubert G. Locke, *The German Church Struggle and the Holocaust* (Detroit: Wayne State University Press, 1974), p. 273. It could be that relativism and tolerance, in themselves good or neutral moral qualities, combine with excessive rationalism and functionalism to weaken the capacity to take absolute stands against evil: they rationalize that everything is relative and there is no need to say no! at all costs.

13. Henry Feingold, *The Politics of Rescue* (New Brunswick: Rutgers University Press, 1970), passim and summary, pp. 295–307; David Wyman, *Paper Walls* (Amherst: University of Massachusetts Press, 1968).

14. *Punishment for War Crimes: The Inter-Allied Declaration Signed at St. James's Palace, London on 13th January, 1942 and Relative Documents* (New York: United Nations Information Office, [1943], pp. 5–6. See also U.S. Department of State, *Foreign Relations of the United States: Diplomatic Papers, 1942* (Washington: Government Printing Office, 1960), vol. 1, p. 45, and *Foreign Relations of the United States: Diplomatic Papers, 1941* (Washington, Government Printing Office, 1958), vol. 1, p. 447.

15. Alexander Donat, *The Holocaust Kingdom: A Memoir* (New York: Rinehart, 1965), p. 103.

16. Wiesel, *Night*, p. 71.

17. Wiesel, *The Gates of the Forest*, p. 225–26.

18. Rubenstein, *After Auschwitz*, pp. 9–101.

19. Anthony Flew and Alistair MacIntyre, *New Essays in Philosophical Theology* (London: SCM Press, 1958), pp. 103–5, 109–30.

20. Cf. Hoess, *Commandant of Auschwitz*, pp. 88–91; Saul Friedlander, *Counterfeit Nazi: The Ambiguity of Good*, (London: Weidenfeld & Nicolson, 1969); p. 21–22, 36, 59, 64.

21. Emil Fackenheim, "On the Self-Exposure of Faith to the Modern Secular World," reprinted in *Quest for Past and Future* (Boston: Beacon Press, 1968), pp. 289 ff.

22. Cf. I. Greenberg, *The Rebirth of Israel: Event and Interpretation* (forthcoming).

23. Compare and contrast Marshall Sklare (with Joseph Greenblum), *Jewish Identity on the Suburban Frontier* (New York: Basic Books, 1967), especially pp. 214–49, 322–26, with T. I. Lenn and Associates, *Rabbi and Synagogue in Reform Judaism* (Hartford: Lenn and Associates, 1972), especially chap. 13, pp. 234–52. Note especially the younger age shift on p. 242. Cf. also how low Israel rates in the "essential" category of being a good Jew, in respondents in Sklare, p. 322.

24. Cf. B. T. Yoma 68b.

25. J. S. Conway, *The Nazi Persecution of the Churches*, pp. 261–65; Saul Friedlander, *Counterfeit Nazi*, pp. 37, 38, 145–49; Falconi, *Silence of Pius XII*, p. 87; Friedlander, *Pius XII and the Third Reich*, pp. 92–102, but see also pp. 114 ff.; Gitta Sereny, *Into That Darkness*, pp. 276 ff., 292–303. See also Weissmandl, *Min Hametzar*, pp. 21–22, 23–24. Cf. also Karl Barth's mea culpa on the Jewish Issue in a letter to Eberhard Bethge quoted in E. Bethge, "Troubled Self-Interpretation and Uncertain Response in the Church Struggle," in Littell and Locke, *German Church Struggle*, p. 167.

26. Cf. Irving Greenberg, "A Hymn to Secularists" (Dialogue of Irving Greenberg and Leonard Fein at the General Assembly in Chicago, November 15, 1974, [cassette distributed by Council of Jewish Federations and Welfare Funds, New York, 1975]).

27. Cf. Erich Fromm, *The Fear of Freedom* (American title, *Escape from Freedom*), 1st ed. (London; Routledge & Kegan Paul, 1942). See George Stein, *The Waffen SS* (Ithaca: Cornell University Press, 1970); for Ohlendorf's testimony, see *Trials of War Criminals Before the Nuremberg Military Tribunals Under Control Council Law No. 10, October 1946–April 1949* (Washington: Government Printing Office, 1952), vol. 4; *United States of America v. Otto Ohlendorf et al.*, case No. 9, pp. 384–91.

28. The purported Maimonides ruling is quoted in Rabbi Simon Huberband's essay on Kiddush

Hashem (Santification of God's name), found in the collection of his Holocaust writings printed under the title *Kiddush Hashem* (Tel Aviv: Zachor 1969), p. 23. Rabbi Menachem Ziemba, the great rabbinical scholar of Warsaw, is quoted as citing the same Maimonides ruling in Hillel Seidman, *Yoman Ghetto Varsha* (New York: Jewish Book, 1959), p. 221. An exhaustive search of Maimonides' work (including consultation with Dr. Haym Soloveichik, who has edited a mimeographed collection of Maimonides' writings on Kiddush Hashem for the Hebrew University) makes clear that there is no such ruling in Maimonides. The acceptance during the Holocaust of the view that Maimonides issued such a ruling—even by scholars of Maimonides such as Ziemba—only shows the urgency of the need for such a ruling. The rabbis instinctively recognized that every Jew was making a statement when killed in the Holocaust—the very statement that the Nazis were so frantically trying to silence by killing all the Jews. This is contra Richard Rubenstein's comments in "Some Perspectives on Religious Faith After Auschwitz," in Littell and Locke, *German Church Struggle*, p. 263.

29. Franklin H. Littell, *The German Phoenix: Men and Movements in the Church in Germany* (Garden City, N.Y., 1960), p. 217.
30. Haggadah of Pesach; Exod. 12:13, 20:1–14, 22:21; Lev. 11, esp. v. 45, 19:33–36, 23:42–43, 25:34–55; Deut. 4:30–45, 5:6–18, 15:12–18, 16:1–12, 26:1–11; Josh. 24; Judg. 2:1–5, 11–12; Jer. 2:1–9, 7:22–27, 11:1–8, 16:14–15, 22:7–8, 31:3–33, 32:16–22, 34:8–22; Ezek. 20; Neh. 9.

32

Exile as a Neurotic Solution

A. B. YEHOSHUA

The Jews and the *Golah*

The demographic balance of the past year shows that in the State of Israel there are 3,300,000 Jews and 570,000 Arabs. The population growth among the Arabs is astounding (when the State was established the Arabs numbered only 120,000). They increased fivefold in 30 years, without immigration, in spite of a small but steady emigration of intellectuals and others. The natural growth of the Jews last year was about 50,000. There were also 21,000 new immigrants, and 17,000 people left the country. Thus the Jewish population increase through *aliyah*, was a net of 4,000. This is our demographic condition, at a time of peace talks, when the government wishes to incorporate an additional 1,250,000 Arabs from the West Bank and Gaza Strip, and when the refusal of the Jewish people to come and settle in Israel is becoming more adamant. One ought to publish these figures as part of a chart, noting the proportion of the world's Jews living in Israel and abroad. In fact, it would be worthwhile to make a slide of such a chart, screening it from time to time on television, before or after the news, or as a backdrop for rabbis, with or without army rank, politicians, professors steeped in the sources, or impassioned authors making their routinely inflammatory speeches about "the eternal, deep, and wondrous bonds which tie the Jewish people to the Land of Israel."

I begin with these few concrete facts because people shy away from abstract questions irrelevant to their immediate situation. Yet, the question of the *golah* [Jews living outside Israel] lies at the root of a great many practical questions. The *golah* and our attitude to it constitutes the most Jewish of questions because it clearly and reliably defines the essence of the Jew. When people talk about Jewish values, I do not know what they mean. When pressed they usually say: to have Jewish values means to love the Land of Israel and the Jewish people. This is like saying, to have Danish values means to love Denmark

---

A. B. Yehoshua, "Exile as a Neurotic Solution," in *Diaspora: Exile and the Contemporary Jewish Condition*, Etan Levine, ed. (New York: Steimatzky Publishing, 1986), pp. 15–35. © A. B. Yehoshua.

and the Danish people. But when I talk about the *golah* I know that I am talking about something totally Jewish, something specifically Jewish. I am touching on the heart of the problem.

In the past 15 years, discussion of questions about the *golah* has been of a descriptive character. The central problems were how to enhance the affinity between Israel and the *golah*, what was the situation with regard to assimilation there, and so forth. But the primary issue that has always been at the root of the intramural struggle of Zionism among the people is still why have a diaspora at all? It is as though people are now ashamed to ask this question.

There are two attitudes toward the *golah*. One regards the *golah* as a kind of accident that befell the Jewish people, a tragedy wrought upon the Jews by the nations of the world. According to this view the *golah*, although it has lasted for a long time, is essentially transient, and the nation yearns for redemption. It simply awaits more favorable conditions that will enable its return. All roads lead either to Israel or to assimilation. When peace comes, and with it some respite, then the *golah* will gradually disintegrate and the nation will stream to Israel. This conception ignores the basic fact that the dispersion was not forced upon us; it was, rather, something we forced upon ourselves. It should not be viewed as an accident or a tragedy, but rather as a distortion—a basic deviant trait in our national makeup—and that is why any solution must be different from what is commonly imagined.

The other attitude views the *golah* as a permanent, almost natural state. If one accepts this view, it is remarkable that other nations do not also maintain diasporas worthy of the name, scattered throughout many countries. People with this attitude sense the depth of Jewish people's need for the *golah*, how closely woven the *golah* is to essence of the Jew, and they try to see exile as a legitimate and normal state. As a consequence of this attitude the question sometimes arises: why bother to have a state? And even when the necessity for an independent national center is not rejected, there is a duality in which the *golah* and the center are seen as equal in value. This framework of ideas ignores the simple fact that the *golah* was the source of the most terrible disasters to befall the Jewish people; that because of the *golah* the nation was almost completely wiped out in our generation; that in spite of the existence of the State of Israel, the *golah* constitutes a threat to a large community of Jews in the Soviet Union and is likely to pose a grave threat to the Jews of South America; and that the *golah* is the root cause for that infamous Jewish fate which is a given in any discussion on Jewish questions. I shall try to synthesize these concepts. To that end I shall divide my remarks into three parts.

Historical Facts

I shall begin by noting some simple and well-known historical facts, the juxtaposition of which is intriguing and sometimes even astounding (Gen. 12:1 et seq.). Abraham, the founder of the nation, was born outside *Eretz Yisrael*. He left his native land and went to Israel as the most distinguished of new immigrants, and it was he who received the promise which bound the land and the nation together. It transpires that the first new *oleh* was also the first *yored* (emigrant from Israel) for as soon as economic conditions in the land began to deteriorate, Abraham went down to Egypt. It is strange to think that this man, who gave up so much in leaving his father's house, having finally reached the Promised Land, could leave it so easily and choose to go into exile.

Jacob died in exile. He followed his sons to Egypt, although he did ask to be reburied in *Eretz Yisrael*. Could it be that herein lies the hidden purpose of the land—to be a burial ground for Jewish bones? Or is it also the land of the living? Abraham and Jacob were founding fathers, and they brought forth a new nation. Yet the attitude of these patriarchs, which ought to have served as an example to the generations to come, was already ambivalent. The nation was created in the *golah*. Have we grasped the full significance of this? The Jewish people was neither created nor born in its land. Thus, the elementary association between nation and land is not natural for the Jews.

Then came the 40 years of wandering in the desert. Where was the law given to us if not in the wilderness? This is another fact of which the implications are not always fully understood. The Law—the system of values which were to define our identity and establish our goal—was not given to us in the Land of Israel. That special bond forged between the people and God was not established in the Land of Israel, but in the desert, in that no-man's land between the *golah* and *Eretz Yisrael*. We shall see how throughout its history the Jewish people seeks that no-man's land time and again, especially when it seeks spiritual renewal.

In the desert we are both alive and dead. The wilderness is a place of death, and in this place of death the new nation was born. The wilderness is also a sterile, untouched, pure place. It is there that the people prepares itself before entering the land. But there is always a fear of *aliyah*, for this act of *aliyah* is highly significant. It is not simply conquest of any country by a nomadic people, but a conquest with a spiritual significance.

The promise of the land to the people is accompanied by stringent conditions. Force alone will not ensure continued possession of the land. The people will remain in possession of their land only if they heed the word of the Lord, and obey His commandments. If they do not, they will suffer grave penalties, of which the most severe will be expulsion and exile. In the earliest of the scriptures, this basic principle is laid down: the people takes precedence over the land in every sense. Remaining in the land and retaining possession of it is conditional, but there are no conditions attached to the survival of the people as people. The people can commit the most terrible sins, but its continued existence is never in question. It may be punished, but never exterminated. It is true that the *golah* will emerge, but that is not the end of the matter; it is possible to survive there, and it is possible to return.

The books of Numbers and Deuteronomy are worth reading. The people had not yet realized its independence for a single moment. It had not yet set foot in the Promised Land. Yet it is already being told about exile and the return therefrom. There are already clear signs that it is possible for the nation to exist without *Eretz Yisrael*, without a country.

All the important national–religious festivals that we celebrate—Sukkot, Pesach, Shavuot (as distinct from the purely religious holidays such as Rosh Hashana and Yom Kippur)—are concerned with the experiences of the people in the wilderness rather than in the Land of Israel. The people arrives, conquers the land, and establishes its kingdom. After some time the kingdom is split in two. Hundreds of years pass, the Kingdom of Israel is destroyed, and its ten tribes are exiled and vanish. That part of the nation which apparently always behaved in a more natural and normal fashion than the more Jewish part in Judea, also behaved normally when it was exiled. It lost its identity and nationality. It behaved as other nations do.

When the kingdom of Judah was destroyed and the people went into exile in Babylon, it survived. It preserved its identity and behaved according to the precepts laid down in the book of Deuteronomy. It proved that the people comes before the land and that it possesses a formula for survival as a nation without a country. It demonstrated the tenacity and power of the spirit and the imagination. Following the decree of Emperor Cyrus in 537 B.C.E. (Ezra I:iff. and Nehemiah I:iff.), part of the people came home to build the Second Commonwealth and gradually reestablished its independence. Part of the nation did not return, preferring to remain of its own volition in the first *golah*. That part of the people that did not return belonged to the upper strata, dignitaries who maintained their Jewish affinity. Nevertheless, they did not join those returning home, preferring to remain in exile. Perhaps it was convenient for them that part of the nation was returning and setting up a national home which could serve as a haven for them in time of need. Or perhaps they already perceived the possibility that the national center might be destroyed again. If that were to be the case, they may have felt that it would perhaps be better to keep the land as a dream, a hope, and a mission rather than to see it once more as a disappointing reality.

On the eve of the destruction of the Second Temple, one-third of the people was already abroad. They left of their own choice and settled in various parts of the Roman Empire, and outside it. This *golah* had a deep affinity for the Land of Israel, supported it financially and politically, and, to a degree, even encouraged a rebellion against the Romans. This insane and hopeless uprising, which had not the slightest chance of success and brought nothing but disaster (the sack of Jerusalem accompanied by the most fearful slaughter), this pointless and unnecessary rebellion was actually encouraged to a certain extent by the Jews of the *golah*. These Jews, living in a totally non-Jewish ambience, surrounded by idolatry and abominations, in the midst of defilement itself, who voluntarily gave up any vestige of Jewish national life, actually encouraged the extremists and the zealots in Jerusalem to demand full political independence—something that not one people in the Roman Empire had been granted.

Rabban Yohanan Ben-Zakkai's departure from Jerusalem on the eve of the destruction—to establish the School of Yavneh—was already informed with the perception that the Jews would have to give up their country. His purpose was to create an alternative Jewish way of life for the *golah*, and to prepare the people for survival there. Ben-Zakkai was carried out of the city in a coffin, in the guise of a corpse; this legend is vividly symbolic of Jewish life in the *golah*. The Jewish people must disguise itself—this is the key to understanding the diaspora. Whoever assumes the guise of a corpse remains very much alive in his inner being, for he has to devise the most sophisticated means of looking like a dead man. The new doctrine which was created was, in effect, a return to a Sinaitic situation. That is to say, the people that had twice been found wanting had to prepare once again for the test. This time, however, it would be a serious preparation, perhaps even an infinite, eternal preparation, for the test had also become most serious—complete redemption, the culmination of history, the end of days. After such a test, a man has no more need of anything.

Thus began two thousand years of exile, and I do not think I err if I claim that in 1,800 years—from the destruction of the Second Temple until the birth of Zionism—the Jewish people did not make one serious or significant effort to return to *Eretz Yisrael* and restore its lost independence. This people, with the resourcefulness, flexibility, and cunning to reach almost every point on the face of the earth—from the Atlas Mountains to the Indian Desert, from Tierra del Fuego to the Siberian steppes—did not make one real effort to come back and settle in *Eretz Yisrael*. Further, the Jews settled in masses in every country around the Mediterranean basin, except *Eretz Yisrael*. In their wanderings the Jews circled around and about the Land, drawn to it yet fearing it. It is depressing to hear ideologues telling us with pride how many Jews there were in *Eretz Yisrael* throughout the generations, or to hear tribute paid to the one family of Peki'in (who reputedly never left the country at all, remaining in the land since the destruction of the Second Temple), and to hear praise of every rabbi who made *aliyah* with his flock of disciples. Had the Jews become as attached to *Eretz Yisrael* as they became to Poland, for example, or Babylon, or had the Jews fought for their right to live in *Eretz Yisrael* as they fought for that right in an England from which they were, in any case, later expelled, this need to prove that Jews did live in *Eretz Yisrael* or to recount the story of Rabbi Yehuda Halevi being smitten with such yearning that he went to Israel in spite of everything would not be necessary. It is true that Jews were sometimes forbidden to come and live in Israel, and that there were many harsh edicts. But in what country was the habitation of Jews not subjected to constraints, expulsions, and prohibitions? And just as the Jews succeeded in finding loopholes in the barriers erected against them in so many countries, they could have done the same in *Eretz Yisrael*, in which the regime changed hands no less than six times after the destruction.

Zionism

Zionism was born at the end of the last century, not out of a new yearning for *Eretz Yisrael*, nor out of a sudden hatred of the *golah*, but from fear of the *golah*. It suddenly became clear just how dangerous and terrible the *golah* could be. Zionism was a movement with only a few isolated adherents, and they were violently opposed by the Orthodox, the Socialist *Bund*, and the assimilationists. The mass of the people did not believe in Zionism and did not want it. When the Balfour Declaration was issued in 1917, and a powerful nation like Great Britain gave its blessing to the possibility of establishing a Jewish state in *Eretz Yisrael*, the Jews *still* did not come to Israel en masse. No sharp-witted sophistry can evade this decisive fact, the consequences of which have been so disastrous. We could have established a Jewish state in *Eretz Yisrael* in the 1920s. While hundreds of thousands of Jews were emigrating from Eastern Europe to the West in the years from 1917 to 1921, only 30,000 Jews came to Israel, and this was *after* the Balfour Declaration. At that time the Jewish people numbered 15 million. Had but one-tenth of them come to Israel, we could have established a Jewish state before the Holocaust. One-and-a-half-million Jews living in *Eretz Yisrael* at that time would have established that state as a decisive fact in a Middle East which was then only awakening from its long slumber. And if we had had a state before the Second World War, the Holocaust would never have attained such appalling proportions. Thus, indirectly, the Jewish people itself was responsible for its own terrible fate in this century.

However, if anyone needs final and absolute proof of the dubious attitude of the Jewish people toward *Eretz Yisrael*, of the fact that it made no serious attempt to return to the land, of its fear of the return to the land, of its attachment to the *golah*, he has only to look to the first 30 years of the existence of the Jewish state. The gates are open, the possibilities are many, but the immigrants do not come. Most of the waves of immigration consisted of people fleeing persecution in the *golah*: survivors of the Holocaust, Jews from Arab countries, refugees from the Communist countries. Only a small minority came here of its own free will, and this minority is dwindling still further.

Ambivalence toward Israel and the *Golah*

What are the common denominators that deter Jews of such varying social background from going to Israel? These must be the same common factors which deterred Jews from coming for hundreds of years. Russian Jews who risk their lives to get out of the Soviet Union would rather live in a German city, on charity from a Jewish or even a Christian organization, than come to Israel, which offers them better conditions if only from an economic point of view. The Jews of Lebanon prefer to live a hundred yards from the headquarters of the Popular Front for the Liberation of Palestine, close to the centers of anti-Israel hatred and propaganda, beside the vipers' lair, in a city marked by hostility and strife and subject to attacks by the Israeli Air Force—all this rather than come to Israel. The Jews of Argentina prefer life in a fascist country whose economy is crumbling, where anti-Semitism is on the upsurge, rather than come to Israel. And now Iran.

There are endless examples: the Jews of Syria up until 1967; the Jews of Morocco and Algeria. Each community ostensibly had its own explanation for not coming to Israel. Some cite economic grounds, some the security situation in Israel. Others say it is hard for them to leave the country in which they were born. Some give reasons of a religious nature. But it is precisely because the reasons given for staying are so varied and sometimes contradictory, and because of the fact that the face of Israel and her attractions have altered so radically in the past 30 years (from a cooperative pioneering society to a capitalist state, from a state with a secular character to one with a national–religious emphasis) that an underlying, basic reason must be found for this determination: to remain in the *golah*. It is inconceivable that such a variety of deterrents could so consistently produce the same result.

I sometimes stand amazed at those who try to explain the Jews remaining in the *golah* on economic grounds, as if the most important thing to the Jews were the fleshpots, as though Marx were right when he said Mammon is the god of the Jews.[1] This argument, sometimes adopted by serious people, is not only insulting in that it accepts the basest anti-Semitic theories; it is also fundamentally invalid. This concept presents the Jews throughout history as rich merchants.

Others would have the reasons for the lack of emigration to Israel as being fear of the security situation. But this theory, too, explains the excuse rather than the essence. One has only to see how Jews flock to Israel when it is threatened, and the way that Jewish students fight to get on planes to take them straight to war, to realize that this theory is not true either. And, of course, there are Jewish communities that live in far greater physical danger than does Israel.

Faced with the diversity of phenomena of 2,500 years of *golah* and with many Jewish communities so different from each other, one cannot settle for explanations valid for a particular time or place. One must seek the underlying causes. Such a common denominator is called for because of the decisive fact that in all its prayers and other spiritual expressions, the Jewish people rejected permanent existence in the *golah*. Normative Judaism never legitimized the *golah*. On the contrary, the diaspora was always regarded as a national disaster, a temporary situation, a *fall*, and the roof of all evil. Even the *Shekhinah*— the Divine Presence—was considered to be in exile. The world, it was felt, would not be right until the *golah* disappeared. That is to say (and I put this briefly and in general terms in order to get to the essence), hatred and total rejection of the *golah* situation is coupled with an intense compulsion to preserve it and live in it. The few attempts to legitimize the diaspora failed. For example, in the 19th Century, reform Jewry in the United States attempted to build a legitimate system of diaspora existence and to place the link with *Eretz Yisrael* in the same light as the religious ties of the Catholics with the Vatican. Reform Jews changed their minds after the Second World War, and today they can, without hesitation, be described as part of the Zionist movement.

When such a fundamental and difficult question as this ambivalence is examined, what emerges is behavior of a palpably neurotic nature. (I am using a clinical term to describe collective behavior, *façon de parler*, for lack of appropriate terms to describe collective neuroses and pathologies.) The nation hates the *golah* and dreams of *Eretz Yisrael*. At all levels of its authentic spiritual activity, the nation rejects the *golah*; on the other hand, throughout its historical activity it has been preoccupied with the one problem of how to survive in the *golah*, how to go on maintaining that hated existence.

Suppose, for example, that we had an unmarried friend who hated and suffered from his unmarried status, proclaimed that he believed in family life, and avidly sought it; this man wanted children as a continuance of himself. Suppose that despite this he spoiled—almost intentionally—all possibilities of marriage, that every time we arranged a union between him and any woman, he did everything to get out of it, not because he did not like the woman or was incapable of love, but out of fear of marriage, in which he so fervently believed. Would it not be our duty to this friend to try to find out, by therapeutic or other means, the underlying motives for his profound neurotic conflict? The Jewish people are in need of just such therapy; and the first step in any course of treatment is diagnosis—in this case insight.

Thus the basic question is, why? What is the reason for this neurotic, painful, and compulsive choice of the *golah*? Why does the entire people fear sovereign, normal life in *Eretz Yisrael*? That, in my view, is the ultimate question for the Jewish people, and it is appropriate that we devote all our intellectual and spiritual powers to its clarification. In this framework, I shall try to postulate two answers, albeit speculative, as working hypotheses.

The *Golah*

The Solution to the Conflict of Religion and Nationality

The Jewish people is a most interesting and original compound of nationality and religious groups, of a natural system (family, tribe, people) with a value system. The national system is very open and flexible. The very ancient definition of a Jew as one born of a Jewish mother stretches the limits of nationality very far indeed. The fact that the Jew belongs to the people does not by definition obligate him—and this is very important—to inhabit a particular territory, to speak a particular language, or to adopt particular cultural and spiritual values. His biological attachment in itself is sufficient to identify him as a Jew. On the other hand, the value system is clear, well-defined, and distinguished by thousands of precise details. At one time, of course, the two systems were bound up with each other, but not to such a degree that it was impossible to perceive the two distinct elements that made up the identity and way of life of the people.

It was precisely because the religious identity was so specific that the national identity could be so blurred. For example, because the distinctive qualities of Yom Kippur are common to all Jews, those observing it could be far from each other, scattered, speaking different languages, living in different landscapes and in varying community situations. The religious basis made it possible to have a very indistinct national existence. Nationality, however, limited the religion. That means that the religious message and content did not hold good for the entire world, but only for the Jewish people, which was defined by a national criterion (born of a Jewish mother) and not a religious criterion. In other words, Judaism as a religion endows the identity of the Jew with legitimacy, even if he does not maintain any connection with it. The religion provides legitimacy for even the most tenuous identity. The Jew can be a complete assimilationist (even an apostate), lacking any connection with the Jewish people from a national point of view. Yet the religious system will still identify him as a Jew with a religious potential, or, in other words, as a permanent candidate for repentance. Were the Jewish people to identify itself exclusively as a national entity, it would never be able to live with such a loose definition.

Between the national and religious systems there exists a constant tension, arising out of the permanent contradiction between their aims. On the one hand, there is a normal national system functioning in accordance with the basic needs of national existence in a territory, and, on the other hand, there is the religious system, which sets spiritual goals for the people and tries to subordinate the people's existence to religious and spiritual demands.

As we examine our history, we shall see how the contradiction between these two systems gives constant rise to bitter conflicts—for example, the conflict between Moses and the people in the wilderness, the conflicts between priest and king, and the conflicts between prophet and king. At first Samuel refused to anoint a king over Israel, seeing it as a betrayal of himself (I Sam. 8:4ff.). Like him, the prophets in their sermons were constantly chastising kings, for they were incapable of accepting the fact of monarchy as a natural, national dynamic. They saw it as a tragedy, as a betrayal and a disavowal of the mission of the commonwealth of priests, of a holy people. One could say that there has been conflict in all nations between the spiritual and the temporal powers, and that this was not uniquely Jewish. This is true. However, with the Jewish people the phenomenon assumed a particularly grave aspect because the theater of conflict was confined to the Jewish people alone. The other great monotheistic religions broke out of national confines, finding other outlets for the energies fueling the conflict. Unable to force themselves on national regimes, these religions set out to spread their message among other peoples. The victory of the state over the church at the close of the Middle Ages led the Christian church to embark upon a campaign of missionary conquest. Among nations other than the Jews, the religious system always found available detours for the ideological struggle. The universal option of Christianity and Islam released them from the need to enter into an overt struggle over power in a particular nation. In contrast, the Jewish religion has no universal aims. It is intended solely for the Jewish people and has no stake in other peoples. It cannot, therefore, forego its authority over the Jewish people. Its success or failure can be tested only in the Jewish context. Consequently, the intervention of religion in polity is unavoidable.

This endless friction between the religious and national systems ignited constant controversy, and threatened to split the nation. All the other conflicts—spiritual, class, and power struggles—are pale beside this one. The solution lay in the *golah*, because life in the *golah* is not a total Jewish existence requiring an unequivocal resolution of this dichotomy. The Jewish framework in the *golah* is essentially voluntary. The Jew is, in essence, free to direct the fervor of his Judaism in any way he desires. The power of coercion is limited. A Jew is expected to observe the commandments, but he cannot be forced to do so. He can be ostracized, even excommunicated, by the Jewish community, but he cannot be put to death.

Thus, the struggle was directed outward rather than inward. Since the constant attack on the Jews was from outside, it was desperately important to survive and preserve the identity of the people as such; all parties rallied around this cause. Disputes over the content of Jewish identity were of secondary importance. That is, of course, a broad generalization. There were internal conflicts over the components of Jewish identity: for example, the controversy between the Hasidic movement and its opponenets, the *Mitnagdim*, and other controversies between religious world views. But these were theoretical controversies, not struggles for real control over assets and political centers of power. In all other nations, real civil wars were fought because the objectives in the conflict were tangible. Among the Jews, the parties to the dispute were always at the mercy of a third party, foreign and essentially hostile, which was recognized as the genuine threat.

The *golah* freed the national and religious systems from the need to disavow each other. It blunted and restrained the conflict. For example, the Lubavitcher Rabbi who lives in New York can only ask the Jews of New York to refrain from traveling on the Sabbath, to send their children to Jewish schools, and to eat only kosher food. But if the Lubavitcher Rabbi were to come to Israel, he would in principle be able to compel the Jews to refrain from traveling on the Sabbath, to study Judaism, and to eat only kosher food, and it would be his religious duty to do so. The holistic national–religious framework makes coercion obligatory. In the *golah* one can preach, cajole, educate, or persuade, but in a totally Jewish ambience there comes a moment of truth, and at that moment the choice must be either religious or secular. Life in the *golah* postpones that moment of truth. It is as if the people senses how dangerous is its conflict with itself and therefore tries to put off the condition of full sovereign life which can exist in *Eretz Yisrael*. There the conflict must break out into the open. A religious Jew is ready to put up with desecration of the Sabbath in the *golah*, but desecration of the Sabbath in *Eretz Yisrael* outrages him. He prefers not to come to *Eretz Yisrael* where he will be unable to avoid seeing this desecration with his own eyes, for if he does see it, and if he does nothing about it, he risks becoming responsible for it. Any other value system would fare exactly like religion. For example, a Jew who believes in a decent progressive society and wishes to define Judaism as the value system of a just society, will always nurture his dream of progressive Judaism abroad rather than come to Israel where he would have to see to what extent the historical reality of Jewish sovereignty contradicted his dream. When he lives in Paris or Buenos Aires he cannot engage in a real conflict of values with other Jews because that conflict would not take place in a total Jewish reality. He can only endeavor, ask, persuade, or educate Jews to be pacifists, socialists, or humanists. When the system under which Jews live as Jews is not total but partial, the central questions are not theirs to decide. They do not have to confront tangible realistic decisions, but only theoretical ones.

The Solution for the Need to be Different: A Chosen People

Among the elemental atoms that constitute our identity lies the need to be different, unique, special, set apart from the entire family of nations. This need stems from our inherently diasporic nature. Because Jewish national identity was often blurred and the land in which one was born was perceived as being alien, there was a compulsion to be different. The religious system sanctified isolation and otherness with the phrase: "Thou hast chosen us,"[2] which runs like a leitmotif throughout the spiritual levels of the national–religious activity. It is a people that shall dwell alone, a different people. The House of Israel shall not be like all the nations. "To be like all the nations" carries a negative connotation in Judaism.

However, is it not basically impossible to be different from all the nations? Indeed, is the concept "all the nations" real at all? Cast in individual terms we would immediately discern the absurdity of wanting to be different from all other people. When anyone says that he is different from all other people, we agree. We are all different in a different sense. On the individual level this desire to be chosen and different from all other people appears to be absurd, but it is astonishing to see how far we are prepared to adopt this concept and aspiration on the national level. Such pretentiousness places the billions of people throughout the world in one category—the category of "behaving like all men"—and places Jews in a separate category, different from everyone else. Time and time again I have been unable to believe my ears when people of varying positions expressed the view: "we must not be like the other nations."

Can all the variations of nationality be placed in one category? Can it be said that all the tribes and peoples in the proliferation of their behavior, religion, and culture are like all the nations, and that only the Jewish people stands apart from them? Over the years, Professor Yishayahu Leibowitz has reiterated that the Jews eat, dress, and copulate differently from other peoples—as though the Japanese, Indians, Nepalese, or Eskimos do not eat, dress, or copulate differently from other peoples. All nations share this relative difference, but the Jewish people is told in unequivocal terms that it should be different from all the nations. Vast quantities of commentary have been written on the question of otherness. The Jewish people groans under this burden, which it was unable to live up to when living a normal sovereign existence in its own country. The only way to put it into practice was to go into exile. When you are in the *golah* you are indeed different from other peoples.

Imagine an artist's palette. Each color is equally distinguishable from the others, but none is more different than any other. If I wish to make the red more different without altering its essence, I must change its situation. If I take the red, break it up, and splatter it like drops onto the other colors, it will indeed be different from the other colors—but not in its essence. That is the Jewish *golah* solution—it creates differences between us and other peoples. Since it is apparently impossible to make ourselves different in essence, we make ourselves different in a technical sense, as it were, and this technical differentiation generates a substantive state, which we may not like, and which causes us physical and spiritual suffering, but which also constitutes a solution—albeit a neurotic one—to an impossible aspiration.

I have offered two hypotheses to explain the basic nature of the attraction which exile holds for the Jew. I am sure these two hypotheses will arouse resistance because they are so abstract. Yet is it conceivable that Jews came to *Eretz Yisrael* from any number of countries, from a variety of circumstances, for just such spiritual or intellectual—which is to say abstract—reasons? I venture to answer yes. The answer to this question must be sought in intrinsic causes since all the extrinsic ones do not explain anything. One cannot describe Jewish history as a unique case of dedication on the part of a people to spiritual and religious principles, and in the same breath claim that the fleshpot was of paramount importance to that same people. If we strip away layers of time and place—the particulars of historical situations throughout the generations—we find certain transcending structures, myths, and basic concepts that motivate all of us; we all line up according to a few basic patterns. The backdrops may change constantly, the actors may change, and the style may be different, but the text, in its essence, repeats itself. If we wish to grapple with the exiled essence within us, we shall have to change some of the fundamental Jewish concepts. The fate of the Third Jewish Commonwealth will be like that of the other two unless we deal with the root of the problem. In the early days of Zionism, some experiments in long-range intellectual reexamination of certain basic concepts were begun. To people with insight, simple continuity seemed dangerous and futile. Atavistic survivalistic tendencies of the Jewish people were considered to be too powerful for Zionism to ignore, but the physical struggle for the establishment of the state drained all the spiritual and intellectual energies that ought to have been expended in a fundamental examination of the basic questions. And the Holocaust created the illusion that the great debate with the forces of the *golah* had been unequivocally settled by a cruel history.

The most astonishing aspect of the *golah* condition is that the Holocaust, while destroying a third of our people, did not destroy the *golah* in the collective Jewish mind, and with astonishing rapidity, the people went back to the old ways. Zionism thought that at long last history had provided final and absolute proof of the terrible dangers of the diaspora, but an overwhelming majority of the people thought otherwise. It viewed the Holocaust as merely another station along the bitter path guided by the meaninglessness of Jewish destiny.

The Jewish people is a permanent remnant of itself. The *golah* now, once again, grows steadily stronger, though not in absolute terms, since the process of assimilation continues. Still the *golah* is growing stronger, relative to Israel. Consequently, the *golah*, which is regarded as the champion of Israel, is at the same time a threat to her. The not inconsiderable group of Israeli Jews who staked their identity on the survival of the State of Israel has to maintain itself in the face of the *golah* which threatens to undermine the sovereign existence won at the cost of so much effort. The great debate about *aliyah* to Israel which Ben-Gurion tried to arouse on an emotional and instrumental plane should be renewed and pursued in even greater depth.

The *golah* condition is authentic and lies at the basis of our history. It is the womb from which the Jewish people emerged. To put it in psychoanalytic terms, the people have an urge to return to the womb, particularly when it has to face up to the imperatives of national sovereignty, when reality begins to weigh heavily. There is no way of knowing ontologically what came first, but it is almost certain that all components–a religio–nationality, the sense of chosenness, and the *golah*—merged.

The Exile—an abnormal reality—was found to be an efficient reality from the viewpoint of Jewish existence. It posits suffering but prevents an explosion of a more serious kind, forestalling a crisis which the people cannot handle. As with every neurotic solution, this one, too, cannot bring happiness and should not be regarded as permanent. Better a known and manageable neurosis with which the people can live than a dark unknown where it would have to stand exposed and alone before a jealous and demanding God, and prove that it is a people chosen above all others, a priestly and holy people. The people fears that its emptiness and impotence will be exposed; or perhaps it is the other way around, and it fears an exposure of the emptiness and insignificance of God. However, in this century the pathology of the neurotic solution suddenly became apparent. It became manifest as a source of suffering which was too great and which detracted from our ability to cope with reality. At the end of the 19th Century, in the countries of secular, modern Europe, Jews began to sense the first unpleasant signs of modern anti-Semitism. The Holocaust revealed the true depth of the abyss on whose edge the Jews had been walking (where they had intended to continue walking until the end of time). This mortal conflict with the external environment appeared much more terrifying than the internal conflicts in the Jewish people, including those conflicts which the people had always tried to avoid or postpone.

Zionism is a process of self-liberation from the fears of independence, and its method is mainly to demonstrate that the alternative to independence is worse. At its most profound and at its best, Zionism was a beginning of a process of self-consciousness, a process of breaking the vicious cycle of diaspora to being a chosen people, to national religion in which the people was trapped. The vitality of Zionism stemmed from the plight of the people. The *golah* could be a viable alternative only for an unnatural life. The spectacular success of Zionism is due first and foremost to the help it derived from the objective situation—the suffering of the Jews. Strangely, the peoples of the world, too, helped the Zionist cause. They had their reasons; they understood how abnormal Jewish existence in their midst was, and they were afraid of the murderous confrontation into which the existence of the Jews was likely to drag them. The decisive step was taken. A total Jewish reality was reestablished. Independence was renewed. But a mere thirty years after the establishment of the State of Israel, there are already disturbing signs of the revival of the *golah*. The most flexible people in the world has already learned the laws of the new, modern reality, and is adjusting the *golah* condition to it. The existence of a center frees people to strike deeper roots in the *golah*, for it now has an insurance policy. In Israel this arouses strange, almost heretical reflections. As it constitutes an ongoing presence, many young people are suddenly becoming aware that the *golah* posits a real alternative to life in Israel. What are we to do to prevent the collapse of the Third Jewish Commonwealth? How can we ensure that the 20 percent of the Jewish people living in a state of national independence can be assured of the continuity of their way of life and of a long-term future of this round of the return to Zion?

Underlying Concepts

In my article "In Praise of Normality,"[3] I tried to establish the urgent need for stressing normality as a value, and to conduct an intramural Jewish struggle against the concept of chosenness. We must see ourselves as an integral part of humanity, neither superior nor inferior. We must adopt this position as an unequivocal value, without evasions or sophisticated interpretations. Declaring that we are better has three adverse effects: (1) it causes people to suspect us; (2) it imposes upon us criteria which we ourselves cannot live up to; and (3) it causes us, consequently, frustration and self-recrimination. The State of Israel has a basic right to exist, even if it has organized crime, corruption, and social injustice. We wish to improve the quality of our existence, not because we have to prove our moral superiority, nor to justify our existence to someone, but simply because we want to improve ourselves. Once and for all we must get rid of the slave mentality, which turned an inferiority complex into a sense of mission, superiority, and elitism. The more conscious we are of the negative instincts which underlie our sense of superiority, the more chance we have of uprooting it.

The Religious Question

Secular Zionists always sensed that the religious question was one of the most dangerous traps lying in wait for them, so they always preferred to bind the sleeping tiger in the fetters of political coalition agreements. The status quo is, however, a highly explosive concept. The potential for conflict is frightening because the emotions pent up on both the secular and religious sides are immensely powerful. These tensions have to be placated and shored up in agreements, for the slightest breach in the dam could lead to a deluge. Perhaps in the early days of statehood there was a misguided notion that the days of religion were numbered, and its sting could be blunted by means of agreements and the status quo, and by the legitimacy with which the secular system would endow it; subsequently, religion would become institutionalized and gradually lose its vitality until it died a quiet death; or alternately perhaps it was felt that it would be better to erect a network of agreements precisely because a religious revival was in the offing and it threatened to be so uncontrollable as to sweep away the entire system. Whatever the reason, the purpose of the status quo was in one way or another to suspend the struggle between religion and state. The status quo in Israel was intended to replace the *golah* experience as the salient factor which had muted the eternal conflict in the total Jewish system of life. The difficult security situation always served as a convenient excuse for preserving the status quo. However, there was always an unspoken assumption among Israelis that when peace came, the wars of the Jews would break out over the religious question. Historically the most violent clashes between the citizen and the authorities, or between rival groups of citizens, were always over religious questions.

I have no wish at present to go into the complex questions aroused by the conflict between religion and state. I shall only say that this conflict always induces an escape to the *golah*. If we really want to eliminate the *golah* as a viable possibility—at least for the Jews now living in Israel—we must consider changing the religion from within. What is needed is a religious reform. Some of the basic values of the religion must be questioned, the national horizon of the religion must be made more flexible, and above all, new and separate sources of authority must be created inside the religion. We are in need of some new and genuine religious reformers. We need a Jewish Luther. These reformers could come from the margins of Orthodoxy and could receive powerful support from the Reform and Conservative movements, which, for their part, will have to undergo a process of "Israelization." To put it bluntly, religion is too important to be left to the religious. Secular Jews, or those who are known as secular, must become involved in religious affairs, not as romantic penitents, but as daring reformers.

It is astonishing to see what a cool reception the secular element in Israel's leadership gave movements of religious reform and how totally insignificant was the help it extended to them. There were two particular reasons for this: (1) The subject was highly sensitive for the religious parties. They were ready to make concessions on many issues, provided their exclusive authority in the field of religion went unchallenged. (2) The American coloration of these movements appeared artificial and lacking in authenticity to Israel's leaders, who grew up on notions of authenticity delimited by the Eastern European Jewish experience. Had Ben-Gurion at the height of his power, intellectual influence, and enormous authority gone to pray on Yom Kippur in an Israeli-style Reform synagogue instead of shutting himself up in his house for the day to pore over Spinoza or Aristotle, he would have endowed reformist thought with a decisive measure of legitimacy. In addition, reformist thought would have undergone a radical process of Israelization. It is only now that some time has elapsed—since Begin came to power—that one of the profound differences has emerged between the present administration and the previous one: that is, namely, the inner attitude toward religion. The leaders of the Labor movement had been much more secular than the average Israeli of today.

There can be no realistic hope for a normalization of the Jewish people without a radical approach to the religious questions. If we want to see any significant change in the next 100 years, we shall have to start rethinking the religious question right now. A total war against religion will be meaningless because the Jewish people has a profound collective psychological need for religion, although this impulse is governed by a cyclical pattern of ebb and flow. The only reform that secular Jews want is the kind that will make things easier by granting them freedom *from* religion. This way of thinking is basically misguided. The problem is not to make the commandments less burdensome, but to expose them to the complexity of life and to fulfill them while changing them. It is astounding to see to what extent the Jewish religion has managed to resist change and to survive without changing its essence even in *Eretz Yisrael* under Jewish sovereignty. Since Jewish orthodoxy is not capable of changing and does not want to, the change will come only through the creation of additional centers of authority.

In summary, in order to get right to the source of the *golah* virus within us, there is a need for profound thought, involvement, and courage on our part. Brenner once said: "That is the question. In order that our character may be changed as far as possible, we must have an environment of our own. Yet in order that we may create that environment with our own hands—our character has to change completely." We already possess the environment. We do not wish to change our character merely for the sake of changing it, but in the clear context of the unending war against the *golah* potential lurking inside each one of us.

A Program for the Immediate Future

A number of practical conclusions emerge as courses for action in the immediate future. If Israel's Prime Minister were to appear at the opening conference of the Bond drive in the United States and, instead of speaking once again about Israel, the territories, and relations with the United States, he were to announce ceremonially that this year the State of Israel refused to accept money from the *golah* out of anger over the fact that only the money immigrates to Israel, not the Jews; if Israel's Prime Minister or her senior representatives were, by a dramatic and demonstrative act, to condemn the *golah* for the absence of *aliyah* and were to announce that the money was being sent back to the *golah* for the sole purpose of boosting *aliyah*; if the State of Israel were to stop sending teachers, educators, and community emissaries to a Jewish community that does not fulfill even minimal *aliyah* quotas; perhaps some impression would be made, and perhaps the question of the *golah* would be placed at the center of things. I do not claim that millions, or even hundreds of thousands would come, but even if only a few extra thousands came, it would be sufficient. That in itself would constitute a revolution.

At present approximately 2,000 American Jews per year immigrate to Israel. Even if the number increased to 20,000, not even a half of 1 percent of American Jewry would be represented. But from the point of view of Zionist fervor, it would be a drastic change. On the one hand, such an *aliyah* would put a stop to the catastrophe of Jews leaving Israel, and on the other, an additional 100,000 Jews would be bound in the *golah* to Israel through family connections and friendships. From a scientific and cultural point of view, it would bring about a most important occurrence. But can it be done? One can at least begin intending to do it. One can try to believe that it is possible.

Recently Israel has become a too-familiar presence in the *golah*, especially in the United States. Paradoxically, it is no longer necessary to immigrate to Israel to live in Israel, and it is possible to acquire scraps of significant Israeli reality in the *golah* itself. The aura of distance and mystery surrounding Israel has become blurred, if it has not vanished altogether. The media contributed to this, but they are not the only ones to blame. The constant deepening of relations between the *golah* and Israel has obscured the dividing line between them. Perhaps it was thought that in this way people's hearts would be prepared for *aliyah*, but the reverse is true. What has been created is a legitimate reality of substitutes for *aliyah*—of quasi-*aliyah*. We must at all costs reestablish a certain feeling of alienation between the *golah* and Israel—a controlled disengagement, as it were.

A not inconsiderable group of Jews abroad has forged a network of very intimate relations with the leadership of the State of Israel. This group is party to more of Israel's state secrets than are parallel groups of Israelis. At the cost of a 5 percent contribution to the national budget, the *golah* has become a recognized intermediary in our relations with foreign governments—a service we rightly chose to do without in the early years of statehood. The mutual dependence of Israel and the *golah* has greatly increased. Spiritually the *golah* needs Israel. Our political conflicts, our economical problems, and, in a certain sense, Israeli culture provide the spiritual nourishment for Jewish identity in the *golah*. These have replaced the Talmud, the Kabbalah, and the Responsa. Hence the *golah* will not abandon Israel at the moment when it initiates an ideological conflict over *aliyah*. Of course a few such attempts will be made, but that part of the Jewish people (which for the sake of convenience we shall call Jewish People A), which accounts for 3 million out of the 11 million Jews in the *golah*, which nurses a very profound affinity to Israel and Judaism, and which supplies Jewish services to the other 5 or 6 million (Jewish People B), can never sever its link. It is now in our power (Jewish People B), before it is too late, to cause group A a certain shock, and to demand that it make a choice to end the eternal schizophrenia from which it suffers. At present the *golah* and Israel tightly clasp each other's hands. But if we were to upset the inertia of this stability by quickly withdrawing our hands from group A's grasp, the resulting imbalance would pull them sharply towards us. A state of peace could free us from our dependence on the *golah*, and would restore our upright stance. But even before full peace comes, we must begin to develop a different attitude and posture with regard to the *golah*. Instead of engaging in Jewish education in the *golah*, we must engage exclusively in the promotion of *aliyah*. Too much Jewish education obscures the need to come to Israel. Instead of trying to tempt and induce Jews to come here, we must coldly expose the pathology, immorality, and hypocrisy of the *golah*. We must start a quarrel with the most warmhearted of Jews, the Jews who are most loyal to Israel, for they are our public. It is true that this will be a quarrel among brothers, but it seems to me that this would be preferable to the condition of peace that exists at present.

According to the most optimistic studies, in the year 2000, only about 50 percent of the population in the borders of greater Israel will be Jewish and this assumes an *aliyah* of 25,000 a year, with only a small *yeridah*. There is the very real danger that in another 50 years we will lose our majority even inside the Green Line (pre-1967 Israel). With peace, of course, there will be the opportunity and the hope for large-scale *aliyah*. But let us not forget that there is also a possibility of emigration and the scattering of the Jews throughout the region. In conditions of economic prosperity, and in a world in which distances are becoming less significant, Jews could live in the *golah*—in Tunis, for example—and teach their children Judaism by means of Israeli television programs.

The virus of the *golah* is in our blood. Let us not forget that. We are descendants of those Jews of whom, at the time of the Second Temple, and in the difficult conditions of the ancient world, the famous Greek geographer Strabo wrote: "It is hard to find a place in the entire world in which this people does not live." Gershom Scholem once said that it is as if Israel by its very existence had absorbed the sparks of the redemption imprisoned in the *golah*, and as if it thereby freed the *golah* from the need for redemption and from the guilt of nonredemption. It is up to us to do everything in our power in order not to exculpate the *golah* from the guilt of nonredemption. (The absolute criterion in our relationships with the *golah* must be guided by what increases *aliyah* and what limits it.) It goes without saying that *yordim* are to be condemned and should on no account be given jobs in Israeli institutions abroad; however, there is no moral validity in condemning the *yordim* without condemning life in the *golah* in general.

Do we really need another internecine quarrel? Will it do any good? My answer is yes. The conflict with the *golah* will uncover what we in Israel have in common, as distinct from those living abroad. It will show once again what the cardinal things are—the things for which we are fighting: freedom and independence. Instead of fighting with each other tooth and nail over the issue of an acre more or an acre less territory, we shall see that the real issues lie elsewhere. The essence of our life in Israel is different from that of *golah* life, and the differences should not be obscured. Spiritual life in the *golah* is like that of a man who has built his house on the water's edge, is preoccupied with the question of whether the water will inundate his home, and is engaged in endless efforts to keep it out. We in Israel, on the other hand, are like a man who has removed his house far from the erosive powers of the waves. The problem of the water no longer preoccupies him. He is able to build his house, cultivate his land, and create something new.

I believe that deep inside every man lies a desire for redemption, and each man possesses a latent vitality. I shall never forget a wonderful story from the time of the "illegal" *aliyah* from Morocco. It happened early in the 1960s, when ships were collecting Jews from Morocco, which was already completely under Moslem control. One day a ship arrived in one of the ports to pick up some Jews from a remote village. For various reasons the expected immigrants did not arrive and the ship could not wait. The Jewish agency representatives on the ship went to the nearest Jewish community, knocked on the doors and said: "Are you prepared to leave for Israel, right now, without further ado? Take whatever you can. Take your chance." And, in fact, quite a number of Jews got up and left, then and there. This impulsive component can be found in every one of us.

I am always astounded to rediscover in conversations with Jews abroad—intellectuals and others well-established in their jobs and their business—that they do not rule out the possibility that one day they might come to Israel. It is not just talk aimed at making an impression on others; "the redemption gland" exists in every Jew. A thousand obstacles, personal and collective, lie in the path of anyone who wishes to make *aliyah*; yet the decisive fact is that there is a minority that has done so of its own free will.

One of the most compelling reasons for peace has not been heard: namely that peace is likely to increase *aliyah* and to reallocate resources for *aliyah*. Peace is likely to release Soviet Jews from their prison. Our historical responsibility is not toward land. It lies first and foremost with people. History will never forgive us if, because of our attachment to the ideal of settlement in all parts of *Eretz Yisrael*, we abandon a huge Jewish community in the Soviet Union to anti-Semitism and assimilation.

For thousands of years the Jews have said: "Next year in Jerusalem," meaning it, yet not meaning it. The same is true today; however, in the past generation a new group has emerged that cannot say "next year in Jerusalem," because it is already living in the real down-to-earth Jerusalem. This group will never again be satisfied with the abstract concept of celestial Jerusalem (a Christian concept that first appears in the New Testament: Galatians 4:25, Revelations 3:12 and 21:2).

The great debate between Israel and the *golah* must be resumed at once, without hypocrisy, with all its fierceness and honesty.

Notes

1. D. Runes (Ed.), *A World Without Jews.* New York: Philosophical Press, 1959.
2. I. Singer, *Standard Prayer Book.* New York: Block Publishing Co., 1943.
3. A. B. Yehoshua, *Between Right and Right.* New York: Doubleday, 1981.

33

The Third Jewish Commonwealth

DAVID HARTMAN

The rebirth of Israel and the ingathering of many Jews from the four corners of the globe has awakened new biblical religious passions within the Jewish community. Jerusalem is no longer a dream, an anticipation, a prayer for the future, but a living, vibrant reality. The Six-Day War further encouraged the belief that Israel is moving toward the fulfillment of the biblical promise. A deep sense of messianic grandeur fills the hearts of many young enthusiasts who feel called upon to settle in every corner of the biblical boundaries of the land of Israel in order to realize the prophetic promise of redemption.

It is not my concern in this chapter to deal with the moral and political difficulties that this messianic fervor generates. I wish rather to consider (1) how the rebirth of Israel can be given religious significance without having to make the bold theological claim that it is a manifestation of God's final redemptive action in history; (2) how the Maimonidean perspective on messianism can provide new normative directions for Israeli society; and (3) how the challenges that Israeli society must face create a new moral and spiritual agenda for Jews throughout the world.

The Religious Significance of Israel

Most Jewish religious responses to the rebirth of the state of Israel do see in it God's providential hand.[1] Two major halakhic thinkers who have taken such a view are Rabbis Kook and Soloveitchik. Kook, the first Ashkenazi chief rabbi of Israel in the Mandate period, viewed the Zionist revolution as part of God's redemptive scheme in history. He attributed profound religious significance to the Zionist revolution—despite its antireligious origins and manifestations—with the help of a dialectical perspective on history: Judaism's

David Hartman, "The Third Jewish Commonwealth," in *A Living Covenant* (New York: Free Press, 1985), pp. 278–99. © Simon & Schuster, New York, NY 10019.

development in exile had caused the repression of vital spiritual forces in the Jewish people, and only by the overthrow of much of traditional Judaism would new, healthy forces and energies within the Jewish people be released. The Zionist activist concern for restoring the Jewish people to its homeland would unleash new messianic redemptive forces.[2] It was Kook's deepest conviction that ultimately the new energies brought forth by the revolution would be integrated with the covenantal Torah spirit in a higher religious synthesis. He looked forward to a new unity between the larger prophetic passion for history found in the Bible and the sober concern for details that characterizes talmudic Judaism.[3] Most religious Zionist youths in Israel are taught to perceive the state from this messianic perspective.

Soloveitchik, too, embraces the state of Israel, but without a messianic dialectic. In *Reflections of the Rav*, Soloveitchik characterizes the period of the Holocaust as the state of *hester panim*, a "hiding of the divine face," a state when God turned His back, as it were, chaos ruled, and human beings had no sense of the divine presence in the world. Israel's rebirth represents *middat ha-din*, the "attribute of God's judgment," which gives human life a sense that there is some divine order, justice, and structure in the world, that the world is not entirely under the sway of barbaric chaotic forces.

> We cannot explain the Holocaust but we can, at least, classify it theologically, characterize it, even if we have no answer to the question, "why?" The unbounded horrors represented the *tohu vavohu* anarchy of the pre-*yetzirah* state. This is how the world appears when God's moderating surveillance is suspended. The State of Israel, however, reflects God's return to active providence, the termination of *Hester Panim*.
>
> That Israel is being subjected to severe trials in its formative years does not negate the miraculous manifestations of Divine favor which have been showered upon the State. Clearly, this is *Middat Hadin*, not *Hester Panim*. (p. 37)

In his essay "Kol dodi dofek" ("The voice of my beloved knocks"),[4] Soloveitchik utilizes the Purim story, in which natural events are appreciated as expressions of God's providential design, for understanding the theological significance of contemporary events. Just as the tradition understood that God worked His redemption for Israel through the actions of King Ahasuerus, so too we can sense God acting once again in history through the United Nations decision on the partition of Mandatory Palestine. Soloveitchik once again hears the voice of his beloved God in the events of contemporary Jewish history that have changed the social and political condition of the Jewish people. For Soloveitchik, the State of Israel has made Jews less vulnerable to physical persecution. It has also aroused a new sense of Jewish identity among Jews who were being carried along on a strong current of assimilation. The rebirth of the state of Israel has shattered the Christian theological claim of God's rejection of the Jewish people as witnessed by their endless suffering and wandering. These and other factors are strong indications for Soloveitchik of God's providential involvement in contemporary Jewish history. Solovietchik pleads with the community to see in the rebirth of Israel an invitation by God to a new and deeper relationship of love. We must "open the door" to go out to meet our Beloved. We begin to demonstrate our responsiveness to God's invitation to renew the love affair between Israel and God by settling the land and by becoming responsible for the political and economic development of the Jewish state.

For Soloveitchik, the shared suffering and common historical fate of the Jewish people represent what he calls *brit goral*, a covenant of destiny, which is the foundation for the important *halakhic* category of collective responsibility (*kol Yisrael arevim zeh la-zeh*).[5] Care for others, feelings of empathy, and a sense of solidarity are not secular categories in Soloveitchik's appreciation of halakhic Judaism. Indeed, the covenant of Sinai requires that the covenantal community have a deep sense of solidarity. Political action that seeks to achieve a secure home for the Jews, thereby giving dignity and new vitality to Jewish communal life and identity, thus acquires religious significance and can be understood as mirroring God's providential love for Israel. Soloveitchik's hope is that the community in Israel will find the way to move from a shared covenant of destiny to a shared covenant of meaning, *brit ye'ud*, based on the halakhic framework of Torah.

Soloveitchik and Kook have provided conceptual frameworks within which religious Jews can attribute religious significance to the rebirth of Israel initiated by people in revolt against their tradition. Soloveitchik's framework assumes the halakhic significance of a shared covenant of destiny and adopts the model of Purim in which God can manifest Himself through the natural unfolding of historical events. Kook's offers a dialectic messianic understanding of Jewish history and of Zionism.

As I have already stated, I do not interpret current events in nature and history as direct expressions of God's will or design. I look exclusively to the Torah and *mitzvot* as mediators of the personal God of the covenant. That, however, does not mean that I must adopt Leibowitz's position and ascribe no religious significance to the rebirth of Israel.[6] From my perspective, the religious meaning one gives to events relates not to their divine origin but to their possible influence on the life of Torah. If an event in history can be a catalyst for a new perception of the scope of Torah, if it widens the range of halakhic action and responsibility, if it provides greater opportunities for hearing God's *mitzvot*, then this already suffices to endow the event with religious significance, for it intensifies and widens the way God can be present in the daily life of the individual and the community. One can religiously embrace modern Israel not through a judgment about God's actions in history but through an understanding of the centrality of Israel for the fullest actualization of the world of *mitzvot*. This covenantal appreciation of history dispenses with the impossible task of reconciling God's loving redemptive actions in the rebirth of Israel with His total withdrawal from and indifference to our tragic suffering in Auschwitz. Soloveitchik's conceptual distinction between *hester panim* (hiding of the divine face) and *middat ha-din* (attribute of God's judgment) only underlines the impossibility of that task, since we are left paralyzed by the prospect that the loving personal God of *middat hadin* can withdraw into *hester panim* and allow the triumph of such demonic evil in the Holocaust.

My position regarding the centrality of modern Israel for the full realization of the Torah as a way of life is in sharp opposition to those religious trends in Judaism which regard the Zionist quest for normalcy as a revolt against the Torah. For certain schools within Judaism, the paradigm of Jewish spirituality is God's miraculous providential guidance in the desert. Freedom from the normal burden of natural existence is perceived by them as a necessary condition for the full appreciation and realization of the Torah.[7] This view is reflected in the talmudic tradition by Rabbi Simeon ben Yohai,[8] for whom the Torah can be adequately studied only by those in a condition of total grace as symbolized by the manna in the desert or under messianic utopian conditions where the Jewish community will not have to be responsible for its economic well-being.

> Rabbi Simeon ben Yohai used to say: "Only to those who have manna to eat is it given to study the Torah. For behold, how can a man be sitting and studying when he does

not know where his food and drink will come from, nor where he can get his clothes and coverings? Hence, only to those who have manna to eat is it given to study the Torah." (*Mekhilta de-Rabbi Ishmael, va-yassa* 3)

Our rabbis taught: " 'And you shall gather in your corn' [Deut. 11:14]. What is to be learnt from these words? Since it says, 'This book of the law shall not depart out of your mouth' [Josh. 1:8], I might think that this injunction is to be taken literally. Therefore it says, 'And you shall gather in your corn,' which implies that you are to combine the study of Torah with a worldly occupation." This is the view of Rabbi Ishmael. But Rabbi Simeon ben Yohai says: "Is that possible? If a man plows in the plowing season, and sows in the sowing season, and reaps in the reaping season, and threshes in the threshing season, and winnows in the season of wind, what is to become of the Torah? No; but when Israel perform the will of the Omnipresent, their work is performed by others, as it says, 'And strangers shall stand and feed your flocks, etc.' [Isa. 61:5], and when Israel do not perform the will of the Omnipresent their work is carried out by themselves, as it says, 'And you shall gather in your corn.' " (*Berakhot* 35b)

For Rabbi Simeon ben Yohai, the political conditions under which the Torah can reach its fullness are met only when Jews do not have to participate in the normal functioning of everyday society. The passion for learning cannot be realized if the community is preoccupied with the normal, everyday problems of survival. God could not have demanded that the community be so wholly engaged in studying the Torah and yet burden us with those problems.

From this perspective, the covenant was made in the desert to teach that only under conditions of total supernatural grace can the Torah be fully actualized within the life of the community of Israel. For me, however, the separation of learning from the normal concerns of daily life is a distortion and abrogation of the covenantal spirit of Judaism. I give preference to *midrashim* that imply that the covenant was made in the desert to teach the community that Judaism as a way of life was not exclusively a function of political sovereignty.[9] We were born as a people within the desert in order to understand that the land must always be perceived as an instrumental and never as an absolute value. The memory that the covenant was made in the desert prevents us from falling victim to the idolatry of state power. The desert, however, was not meant to serve as a paradigm for the life of *mitzvot*. The desert is the founding moment of covenantal consciousness, but never the controlling feature of its development. It was a prelude pointing to the land, where the covenantal challenge received at Sinai was meant to be realized. The centrality of the land in Judaism teaches us that *mitzvah* must not remain an aspiration, a utopian hope to be realized in messianic conditions of history, but must be tested and concretized within the normal, everyday conditions of human existence. Whereas the desert is a moment of withdrawal and concentration, what is received in that moment has to be transformed into a way of life. The land exposes the Jewish people and the Torah to the test of reality.

The Jewish society that we build in Israel has to validate the claim made in the Jewish tradition regarding how a Torah way of life creates a holy community, "a kingdom of priests and a holy nation" (Exod. 19:6). If the Torah is truly capable of sanctifying every aspect of human reality, if it is capable of giving new moral and spiritual dimensions to politics, if "its ways are ways of pleasantness and all its paths are peace" (Prov. 3:17), if the Torah scholar is a paradigm of the builder of peace, this must be seen and confirmed through the way we live our daily lives and not only proclaimed in our prayers.

A community that defines itself by learning and prayer is liable to be deceived by the richness of its powers of linguistic expression when evaluating its own moral and religious integrity. The existence of the state of Israel prevents Judaism from being defined exclusively as a culture of learning and prayer. Here Judaism must draw its pathos also from the exigencies of the concrete needs of life. "Not the learning is essential but the doing" then becomes constitutive of Torah study. Learning that excuses one from responsibility for the physical well-being of a nation, that provides a conceptual framework with its own inner coherence but whose correspondence to what actually takes place in reality is never tested, may have compelling logical vigor and be intellectually fascinating, but it has lost the sanctity of Torah, since it has become irrelevant to life itself.

If the desert is an instrument, a preparation, but never a substitute for what living is all about, then the land of Israel represents the intrusion of the normal into the desert covenantal consciousness. When the nation enters the land of Israel, the manna ceases to be the source of their economic sustenance.[10] In the land of Israel, the community must face the challenge of planting trees and harvesting crops, of exposure to economic hardships, of building a national political reality in a world that does not necessarily share or appreciate God's "dream" that Israel become a holy nation. The Torah was not given at Sinai for a messianic society; it was meant to be implemented and developed within an unredeemed world.[11] The dangers and seductions of pagan culture did not disappear when the Israelites entered the land of Israel. The concrete concern with military security did not stop with the conquests of Joshua. The need to build institutional frameworks of power and yet retain the covenantal ideal of a holy nation accompanied the community throughout the building of the first Jewish commonwealth. The same unredeemed world was the context for the renewal of the covenant by Ezra and Nehemiah in the second commonwealth and must be faced with courage by Jews as we build the third commonwealth under similar nonmessianic historical conditions.[12]

The normalization of Jewish consciousness that comes from living in the land of Israel is therefore not antithetical to covenantal consciousness, but is a necessary condition for its full realization. The land of Israel is holy from the covenantal perspective because it invites *greater* responsibility and initiative on the part of the community. It is the framework in which ways must be found to make the Torah a viable way of life for a community.

A radically different view of the centrality of the land of Israel for Judaism is taken by Nachmanides, commenting on Leviticus 18:25ff. For Nachmanides the land of Israel is holy because of its unique ontological relationship to God.

> But the Land of Israel, which is in the middle of the inhabited earth, is the inheritance of the Lord, designated to His Name. He has placed none of the angels as chief, observer, or ruler over it, since He gave it as a heritage to His people who declare the unity of His Name.

The land of Israel vomits out its sinful inhabitants (Lev. 18:28), continued Nachmanides, because only in this land does one live under God's direct providence. Since there is this unique ontological relationship between God and the land, Jews in the diaspora live as if they have no direct relationship to God and perform *mitzvot* only in preparation for their return to the land of Israel.[13]

In contrast to Nachmanides and in the spirit of Maimonides, I regard the land of Israel as central to the *mitzvot* because it invites greater initiative and gives the community a wider range to express its normative consciousness.[14] The land of Israel represents the freeing of Jews from the direct and total dependence on grace experienced in the desert and signifies the movement toward human initiative and responsibility as the defining feature of the covenantal community. Whereas Nachmanides believed that greater self-reliance undermines the full flowering of the covenant, my claim is that God is present in the land of Israel because there Jews are not frightened to be independent and responsible for a total society.

I view the Zionist revolution as a rejection of the view of Rabbi Simeon ben Yohai regarding the utopian conditions required for Israel to fulfill its covenantal destiny in history. I understand Zionism as a rejection of the theological claim that a unique providential relationship to Israel frees the Jews from having to be concerned with the ways in which nations seek to ensure their survival. In its profoundest sense, Zionism is the total demythologization of that Jewish historical covenantal consciousness which is represented by the spirit of Nachmanides.[15] As my covenantal anthropology has sought to demonstrate, we can build a new Jewish society within the framework of a tradition that places *mitzvah* at the center of its perception of the meaning of Jewish existence. By infusing Torah with the original Zionist passion for Jewish responsibility, we can renew the Sinai covenant once again in the conditions of modern Israel.

Although one can understand the Zionist quest for normalcy within covenantal categories, it is nevertheless true that the major trend of secular Zionism sought to replace the covenantal identity of the Jew with a secular political national identity. Though distinctive elements of Zionism indicate its continuity with traditional Judaism, such as the centrality of peoplehood, identification with biblical history, and, most important, the significance of the land of Israel for the political rebirth of the Jewish people, nevertheless Zionism is generally regarded as a departure from the covenantal tradition. Not only did its adherents repudiate the traditional posture of waiting for the messianic redemption and of avoiding active intervention in the political arena of history, but Zionists often viewed traditional Judaism as an obstacle in the path of Jewish national political rebirth.

For many centuries before Zionism, Judaic religious consciousness had been characterized by the sense that the everyday world was a preparation for a future messianic reality. It was felt that the temporal world does not reflect the full power of God as Creator and Lord of History, nor can it contain the reward promised to the community for allegiance to the covenant. Jewish teachings about the immortality of the soul and the resurrection of the dead and Jewish utopian messianism reflected this deep Judaic belief in a future world that would be in harmony with our most cherished aspirations.

For traditional religious Jews, the instruments for affecting history were prayer, observance of the *mitzvot*, and Torah study. The covenantal community was not to sully its hands with the uncertainties and political and moral ambiguities of modern nationalism. Judaism was secure if it was able to build healthy families, if it could have vibrant schools and synagogues. The Jewish covenantal community could leave responsibility for a total social and political order to the nations of the world, while it lived in anticipation of the ultimate triumph of Judaism in the messianic reality.

Scholem was correct in a certain sense in his observation that there is a conservative instinct within the halakhic temperament. Halakhic Jews were afraid to expose their dreams of history to the test of reality. The fate of the first and second commonwealths, Bar Kochba's abortive revolt against Rome, and the tragic failures of all messianic movements in Jewish history created in religious Jews a prudent, conservative instinct not to hope for too much in terms of their national political existence. The central significance attached to the land of Israel, Jerusalem, and the ingathering of the exiles was expressed with passion daily in the life of prayer, but was to be realized only in a messianic kingdom. History had taught the Jews not to attempt to translate those prayers into a program of action.

Jewish hope was nurtured by the belief that the third Jewish commonwealth would not in any way share the vulnerabilities of the previous attempts to build a Jewish society in the Holy Land. Rabbinic *midrashim* taught that the third commonwealth would last forever.[16] It would be free of all the tragic features of human history. It would usher in a historical period in which humanity would be liberated from sin, and suffering would be abolished from human life. In that time, the community would no longer be burdened by the haunting and problematic features of freedom, contingency, and the human propensity for evil.

As long as the Judaic hope for the third commonwealth reflected such a longing for certainty, Zionism could not emerge as an effective political movement. Zionism had therefore to define itself as a movement seeking to overthrow the traditional religious sensibility. If the community was to learn to act effectively in history, Jewish historical consciousness had to be radically transformed. And indeed, the quest for normalcy, initiative, and responsibility was in fact pursued through a revolt against Judaic covenantal faith. The house of learning and the synagogue were deemed enemies of the revolution. Prayer was perceived as escapism and as bad faith. Only by a complete overthrow of everything the tradition cherished could the revolution succeed. The pious student of Torah had to be derided, rejected, and replaced by the pioneer. Secular Zionism ushered in a passionate yearning for new anthropological models that celebrated the dignity of human physical power. Jewish historical figures who demonstrated heroism in battle were held in high esteem. The new leadership of the community were those whose eyes were anchored to the everyday and who sought pragmatic solutions to the pressing problems of the third commonwealth.

For many Jews, Israel has become the new substitute for traditional Judaism. Israel is possibly the last haven in the world for Jewish secularism. Israeli "normalcy" enables many to assimilate and be like all the nations of the world without feeling guilty for having abandoned their ancestors. With all the risks that Israel poses to the future of covenantal Judaism, I am nonetheless prepared to build my hopes for Judaism's future on this new reality. For, as the tradition teaches, where there is a potential for desecration, there is also a potential for sanctification.

I live with the guarded hope that out of this complex and vibrant new Jewish reality will emerge new spiritual directions for the way Judaism will be lived in the modern world. Israel expands the possible range of halakhic involvement in human affairs beyond the circumscribed borders of home and synagogue to the public domain. Jews in Israel are given the opportunity to bring economic, social, and political issues into the center of their religious consciousness. The moral quality of the army, social and economic disparities and deprivations, the exercise of power moderated by moral sensitivity—all these are realms that may engage halakhic responsibility. From this perspective, the fact that Israel enables us to make the whole of life the carrier of the covenant is in itself sufficient to ascribe profound religious significance to the secular revolt that led to Israel's rebirth. I celebrate Israel's Independence Day with the recitation of the Hallel psalms, thus expressing gratitude to God for having been given the opportunity to renew the full scope of the covenantal spirit of Judaism. My religious celebration is not a judgment on God's activity, but only on the opportunity that Israel makes possible. The opportunity may be missed. But that does not in any way detract from the religious possibilities created by the event. The recitation of psalms of thanksgiving on Independence Day does not entail any divine guarantee regarding the successful realization of those opportunities.[17]

A Messianic Appreciation of Israel

Although, as I have shown, the vitality of Judaism does not depend on belief in the messianic resolution of history, and although I do not require the messianic notion to give religious significance to the rebirth of Israel, I am nonetheless prepared to consider how Israel's rebirth can be appreciated within messianic categories. For some time, I have had an ambivalent attitude toward the messianic vision of history. On the one hand, whenever Jews sought to act on the basis of their messianic hope, the result was invariably catastrophic. Furthermore, when messianism gains dominance, the community may find the gap between the imperfect present and their messianic vision so great that contemporary reality is considered an unsuitable arena for the larger normative vision contained in the Torah. When this happens, messianism may lead the Jew into a posture of passive anticipation.

On the other hand, if the messianic vision is abandoned, the resultant anchorage exclusively in the world of immediacy and everyday concerns may lead to cynicism or despair regarding the possibility of achieving anything radical in human history and may discourage responsible action by the halakhic community. A present that is not open to some larger vision of the future may turn sour and be drained of vitality. Wherever one turns, either toward or away from the messianic idea, there are dangerous risks, but presumably also new spiritual opportunities. I am prepared to take the risks of messianism because of the influence messianism can possibly have on moving the community toward a different appreciation of Israel and Judaism.[18]

Moreover, it seems to be the case that the majority of the religious Zionist community in Israel perceives Israel within a messianic redemptive scheme of history. To ignore or argue against messianism in this context would be to isolate oneself from effective discussion with this community regarding the spiritual and political direction of Israeli society. It is, I believe, politically essential to develop a shared language between Jews who look forward to the unfolding of a redemptive process in Jewish history and those whose religious response to Israel is grounded in the concern with the renewal of the covenant of Sinai.[19] I believe that Maimonides' portrayal of messianism can serve as the basis for such a shared language.

I have shown that one's religious interpretation of events does not presuppose knowledge of how God acts in history. Furthermore we have seen that messianic hope is fully compatible with the principle of *olam ke-minhago noheg*, "the world pursues its normal course." In light of Maimonides' understanding of messianism, I believe that it is possible to have a messianic appreciation of Israel without making factual claims that this or that event in the history of Israel is a providential redemptive divine act. Messianism can instead be understood as a *normative category* by which we evaluate the quality of life in the present reality of Israel. For religious Zionists who in their prayers refer to Israel as the beginning of redemption, *hathalta de-geulah*, messianism must make a difference in the way we conduct our economic, social, and political affairs. The commitment to

Israel as initiating the process of redemption requires of Jews a significant reorientation in the way Judaism is understood and practiced. It would be short-sighted to manifest the messianic spirit only in the reclaiming and the rebuilding of the land. Any messianic appreciation of Israel worthy of the name must seek to discern the fulfillment of the biblical promise in the widening of the Jewish people's capacity for love. It is in a changed people and not only in a changed landscape that one must channel the messianic passion for the rebirth of Israel.

The longing for a messianic reality, in Maimonidean terms, expresses the community's love for and commitment to *mitzvah*. As I understand this, one who longs for the day when the full scope of the Torah can be reinstituted regards *mitzvah* as a joyful expression of living before God as a responsible normative agent in history. Messianism in this spirit reflects a triumph over any Pauline critique of *halakhah*. It regards *mitzvah* as a source not of guilt but of joy. A normative existence is not antithetical to human freedom, spontaneity, and passion, nor need the *mitzvot* and their materialization in *halakhah* be an oppressive force estranging us from our own individuality. *Halakhah* can be an expressive educational system, reflective of the richness of the individual's and the community's longing for God.[20]

Messianism not only expresses the love for and joy in *mitzvah* but equally gives us direction for the way halakhic jurists must apply *halakhah* to society. An essential feature of messianism is the ingathering of the exiles and the return of the entire community to its biblical homeland. The messianic emphasis upon the ingathering should direct contemporary halakhic jurists to develop Jewish law in ways that would reflect the spirit of the Kantian categorical imperative: shape Jewish law in a way that makes it a viable option for the *whole* Jewish community gathered together as an independent polity in the present era. Such an orientation toward the halakhic system would be guided by the aspiration to allow all Jews to share in the appreciation of *mitzvah*. In that situation, one does not render halakhic decisions that require that there be nonobservant Jews in the community in order for the society to function. Given this perspective, it would be counter to the very spirit of the Torah to bring about legislation in the Knesset excusing religious women from army service out of a concern to protect their modesty and their loyalty to Judaism, while ignoring the needs of women who come from nonreligious families. Nor would Sabbath regulations be developed that rely on there being nonobservant Jews in the community. One has to envision what is needed for a police force, fire patrol, army, foreign service, and international communication network to function within a society loyal to the Torah.[21] Contemporary halakhic thinking needs to be infused with the messianic spirit of responsibility and love for the *total* community. If one thinks of halakhic norms in terms of the survival and advantage of a particular religious group, one's thinking is antimessianic and reflects the sectarianism of an exilic perspective on Judaism.[22]

The spirit of Judaism in exile reflects the concern of a community living in a hostile environment to survive and not be swallowed up by its alien surroundings. Not surprisingly, then, the religious consciousness of exilic Judaism puts great emphasis on the *mitzvot* that separate Jews from their alien environment. Under such circumstances, the holy often becomes defined by what separates Israel from the nations. For that reason, Sabbath observance in the home, *kashrut* laws, and similar *mitzvot* that set Jews apart from their environment became the focus of the covenantal passion. However, when Judaism becomes a total way of life of a reborn nation, the covenantal passion cannot be poured only into those *mitzvot* which separate Israel from the rest of humanity. When Jews live in their own environment and are responsible for the unfolding of the spirit of Judaism in a total society, they must also link their covenantal religious identity to the *mitzvot* through which they share in the universal struggle to uphold human dignity. The normalization of the Jewish people brought about by Zionism makes possible a new appreciation of the *mitzvot*, whereby the social, ethical, and political attain their full covenantal place.

In the messianic society, a total way of life and the society's entire social and economic structure have to mirror God's covenantal judgment. When that is so, the social, moral, and political status of the society becomes a religious issue. The Sabbath in a messianic society is not only the Sabbath of the seven-day week but also the Sabbatical and Jubilee years. The egalitarian spirit of the laws of those years should move the society and its political leaders to a concern with greater degrees of social and economic equality. How the laws of the Sabbatical and Jubilee years can be expressed in a modern economic system is a serious halakhic question that many have tried to answer in different ways. One thing, however, is clear. Something radical will happen to Judaism when we are challenged to have our economic and social order mirror the Sabbath's celebration of the world as a creation and of human beings as creatures and not absolute masters over nature or other human beings.[23]

A Maimonidean messianic consciousness does not seek to build a Jewish state that compensates for past exilic powerlessness, deprivation, and abuse.

> The sages and prophets did not long for the days of the Messiah that Israel might exercise dominion over the world, or rule over the heathens, or be exalted by the nations, or that it might eat and drink and rejoice. Their aspiration was that Israel be free to devote itself to the law and its wisdom, with no one to oppress or disturb it, and thus be worthy of life in the world to come. (MT *Hilkhot Melakhim* 12:4)

Messianism for Maimonides is a liberation from and a complete victory over a triumphalist power-seeking nationalism. A messianic society's guiding principle is to seek to expand the powers of knowledge, wisdom, and love. Exilic religious consciousness has been dominated by fear, estrangement, and questions of communal survival. The psychology of religious persons in a premessianic reality is often the psychology of alienated persons who do not trust the world and therefore cannot open themselves fully to it. One whose self-identity is dominated by this sense of estrangement and fear cannot become a lover of God. Love becomes a potent possibility in our spiritual life when the problems of physical survival do not dominate our existence and when the political reality is not seen as oppressive or as harboring the dangers of aggression, war, and violence. The passion of love can begin to emerge when we derive from our polis the ability to feel at home in the universe. The more fear and estrangement are overcome, the more God and the Torah can be percieved in terms of love, and the more one can liberate oneself from seeing God in terms of reward and punishment or a nationalist triumphalist vision.

I am fully aware of the extreme difficulty of bringing this messianic appreciation of the third Jewish commonwealth to the social and political reality of Israel. We are still very worried about national survival. The atmosphere of war is not conducive to the creation of conditions that encourage the expansion of powers of love. The Zionist revolution has been enacted in a vulnerable reality in which there is no telling when wars will end and suffering will cease. There is therefore an understandable fear of the stranger in the land. Nevertheless, in spite of the imperfect conditions of Israel, and in spite of the enormous energies that have to be expended on survival, I believe that there is a heroic spirit in this society that is capable of accepting messianism as a normative challenge. The courageous covenantal spirit of the new Israeli Jew, which was revealed to me with immense power and tenderness by my son-in-law, Aharon Katz, of blessed memory, has led me to believe that there may be tremendous spiritual forces within Israeli society that have not yet been fully tapped.

We have developed a new heroic type capable of enormous sacrifice and dedication to the security of our society. Given our long exilic history, it is truly remarkable that we have developed a new human type that has given up fear. Its heroism, which has been abundantly demonstrated on the field of battle and in the rebuilding of the land, can equally be channeled to give expression to other features of the heroic ideal in Judaism.

Maimonides taught that *kiddush ha-shem*, sanctification of the name of God, is manifested on three levels. The first is the courage to stand in opposition to religious oppression, the willlingness to die to defend one's loyalty to Torah and *mitzvot*. That is the heroism of the martyr who is prepared to give up life for what is seen to be the essential spiritual vision of the nation. However, Maimonides believes that Jewish spiritual heroism not only is the willingness to die, but also shows itself in a second form when one is able to overcome the motives of fear and reward as a ground for worship.

> Whoever abstains from a transgression or fulfills a commandment not from any personal motive nor induced thereto by fear and apprehension or by the desire for honor but solely for the sake of the Creator, blessed be He, sanctifies the name of God. (MT *Hilkhot Yesodei ha-Torah* 5:10)

Heroism is not only shown in the courage to transcend the normal instinct of self-preservation, but is also reflected in the ability to transcend the motives of self-interest in one's appreciation of Judaism. To be directed by the passion of love is for Maimonides to live a heroic existence.

But there is also a third heroic ideal. It is the actions of the *hasid*, of the pious individual whose behavior is a compelling example encouraging people to take the Torah and God seriously. The *hasid*'s example makes God's name beloved and sought after; it opens the hearts and souls of others to the living waters of the Torah. This kind of heroism is not only heroism in opposition to an alien environment, but also a demonstration of the strength and integrity of Judaism as a total way of life.

> And if a man has been scrupulous in his conduct, gentle in his conversation, pleasant toward his fellow creatures, affable in manner when receiving them, not retorting even when affronted, but showing courtesy to all, even to those who treat him with disdain, conducting his commercial affairs with integrity . . . and doing more than his duty in all things, such a man . . . has sanctified God and concerning him scripture says: "And he said to me, 'You are my servant, O Israel, in whom I will be glorified' [Isa. 49:3]." (Ibid., 5:11)

The task of covenantal Jews now is to show that we can build a Judaic society not by resorting to dogmatism and legal coercion, but, like the *hasid*, by means of the compelling example of the way we live our daily lives. We must avail ourselves of the opportunities given to us through education and must not deceive ourselves that religious legislation can in any significant way alter the character structure of a people. If we learn to appreciate the power of love and personal example, we may be able to walk in the covenantal path of Abraham, who made God beloved through the compelling power of his own actions.[24]

Israel and the New Jewish Agenda

So far I have described, from a covenantal perspective, the new opportunities provided by the rebirth of Israel. It is hardly less necessary, however, to be aware of the new risks that have arisen simultaneously. Opportunities and risks alike owe their origin to the fact that the creation of the third Jewish commonwealth confronts Judaism and the Jewish people with a new moral and political agenda, whose implications go beyond the strict geographical confines of the Jewish state. For a long time in history, we did not have to deal with questions that touch upon the relationship between *halakhah* and political power, since we were a powerless community. Especially from the emancipation period onward, Judaism was not involved with the public domain of power and politics. Judaism gave meaning to the individual. It taught Jews how to conduct their family life. It provided frameworks for the celebration of the holy. It provided a structure that kept alive the major historical moments that shaped the community's spiritual self-understanding. Judaism, however, did not have to deal with those agonizing moral questions that confront a nation that has military and political power. In the political sphere, our activity was limited to the fight for minority rights, religious tolerance, and freedom of conscience in countries where we were an oppressed or vulnerable minority. As a result of the rebirth of Israel, our political situation has dramatically changed. In Israel, religious and nonreligious Jews have a new sense of power and belonging that they have rarely felt throughout their long sojourn in the diaspora.

Israel, however, not only allows us to give expression to what is most noble in the Jewish tradition, but it also readily exposes moral and spiritual inadequacies in that tradition. Israel therefore provides unique conditions for a serious critique of Judaism as it is practiced by committed halakhic Jews. In Israel there is no external non-Jewish world to inhibit the tradition's full self-expression. Moral attitudes that one never expected to characterize Jewish behavior can surface in this uninhibited, passionate, and complex Jewish reality. Triumphalist nationalism, lack of tolerance for other faith communities, indifference, and often an open disregard for the liberal values of freedom of the individual, human dignity, and freedom of conscience can be found articulated by would-be religious leaders in Israeli society. A mature appreciation of our liberation struggle requires that we recognize the mixed blessings that freedom and power bring to Jewish living.

Although Israel resulted from a profound revolt against the tradition, this revolution was materialized in a land that makes Jews aware of being attached to the three-thousand-year drama of their people. The Zionists did not leave their historical family when they undertook to revolt against the tradition. I would compare the Zionist revolt to a young person who loses patience with his parents, announces he is leaving home, goes to the door, slams it in great anger, but fails to leave the house.[25] The Zionists' radical revolution, after all, was realized in a land that forces a confrontation with different aspirations that have been part of the Jewish historical tradition. In deliberately choosing to materialize the Zionist revolution in the land of the covenant, secular Zionists make the claim that they have truly fulfilled the Jewish aspirations in history. Their claim invites severe criticism from other groups in the Jewish world who do not perceive the secular Zionist revolution as much of a fulfillment of the prophetic tradition. Mystics and sober *halakhists* who believe that the political task of the Jewish people is to wait patiently for God's final redemptive action in history, messianic religious activists who understand the Zionist revolution as the way God has utilized the secular forces in history for the sake of the realization of Torah—these people will never sit by idly and allow the secular Zionist dream of normalization to take root in the biblical land of Israel. Each one claims the whole field. The very fact that the revolution is realized in the land of Jewish historical aspiration forces a confrontation with all who claim to be the authentic carriers of Jewish tradition.

In Israel, intense ideological passions surface daily and confront one another in the public arena of our shared communal life. Major governmental decisions are influenced by the different Jewish dreams that inspired our national rebirth. Messianic religious visions collide with a socialist secular understanding of the significance of the Jewish state. This is what results from Jews feeling at home. Each group believes this is its own home. This feeling is often translated into a paternalistic attempt to have everyone share one's appreciation of how a Jewish national home should look. In Israel, therefore, religious and secular Jews try to influence the public domain so that it might mirror their understanding of how Jews should live. Paradoxically, Israel, which unites Jews from the four corners of the world, is the most vivid demonstration of how divided and estranged from one another we are. We prayed to be reunited with our scattered brethern—without realizing how different we had become from one another. Our sense of unity currently results more from the enemies who seek to destroy us than from an internal consensus as to how we believe the Jewish people should live in the modern world.

How do you build a Jewish society when there is no significant consensus as to what is normative in Jewish history nor any agreement about the sources out of which to build new norms? Can *halakhah* accommodate itself to the modern values of tolerance and freedom of conscience? Is there a way of sustaining the intense passion for Judaism and monotheism and yet appreciating the important modern value of religious pluralism? Does liberalism, with its concern for freedom of conscience, undermine the *halakhah*'s uncompromising rejection of idolatry? Should secular Zionism, which makes perpetuation of the nation the ultimate value of the Jewish people, be identified as a modern form of idolatry? The question of tolerance and pluralism refers not only to Judaism's relationship to other faith communities but above all to how Jews live among themselves. *Halakhic* thinkers must grapple with the fact that many Jews do not perceive *halakhah* and the talmudic tradition as normatively binding. There are many Israelis who are prepared to study Torah but will resist to the end the imposition of halakhic practices that clash with their own sense of personal freedom and conscience. What are the limits of tolerance for other Jews that could be acceptable to a halakhic community? What happens when religious Jews seek the legislative power of the state to impose halakhic practices on the community? Does this not invite the same corruption that has characterized the fate of other religions when they used political power to promote their vision of life? It is morally disastrous and religiously arrogant to claim that we have nothing to learn from the mistakes of other religions regarding the use of political power for the implementation of religious values.

It is not a simple task to translate a biblical perception of reality into the conditions of a modern democratic society. The way Joshua entered the land is hardly a paradigm for learning how to tolerate different faith communities and for allowing different groups the freedom to express their own particularity.[26] The separation of church and state and the American appreciation for pluralism are not yet firmly established in the Israeli political imagination. In contrast to the Western Jewish diaspora, Israel does not provide for a neutral or secular political public arena in which to orchestrate the different competing ideologies present in contemporary Jewish living. The diaspora allows different religious groupings to form their own synagogues. Each can have its own "four cubits of the law" in a way that does not impinge upon the life of the total Jewish community. In the diaspora, Jews live their public life under the protective umbrella of the larger non-Jewish political order and express their personal Jewish identity within their respective schools, synagogues, and community centers. The diaspora, in contrast to Israel, does not force the confrontation between religious and secular Jews or between the different ideological branches of Judaism to develop into overt conflict. Pluralism, therefore, does not surface as an urgent issue in the diaspora.

A long and arduous path must be traveled before we can create a healthy bridge between the needs of a modern democratic liberal society and the biblical and talmudic understanding of Jewish politics. On the one hand, Judaism is a repudiation of any spiritual vision that is related exclusively to the private and intimate domains of the personal life. Yet, on the other hand, if Judaism seeks expression in the communal political domain, does it not expose itself to the very corruptions that have characterized theocratic states in history? It will not be easy, therefore, to bring John Stuart Mill's advocacy of civil liberty and Isaiah Berlin's appreciation of pluralism into a serious and fruitful discussion with Maimonides and the talmudic tradition's understanding of how a halakhic polity should conduct its daily life.[27] What makes for the spiritual vitality of our third Jewish commonwealth is the fact that we cannot ignore these new fundamental issues.

The Zionist quest for normalcy should free the Jewish people of any myth about the unique moral and spiritual powers of the Jewish soul. In taking upon ourselves responsibility for a total society, we must allow ourselves to be judged by the same standards as we have judged others.[28] The Torah challenges us to become a holy people. It does not tell us that we are immune from the moral weaknesses and failures that affect every human being. The Jewish nation is not free from the same potential corruptions that affect any human community that has taken upon itself the bold challenge of living with power. Our newly gained sense of belonging and power enables us to look critically and honestly both at ourselves and at the halakhic tradition without the apologetic stance so characteristic of a community that saw itself as a persecuted and vulnerable minority. A community that feels dignified and secure in its identity and place in the world can allow itself the mature activity of honest critical self-appraisal.

To the degree that we can look at ourselves in a nonapologetic light, to that degree will we demonstrate our liberation from an exilic consciousness that is fundamentally timid, frightened, and outer-directed. We are free now to ask what we think of ourselves without being overly concerned with the way others will listen and respond to our agonizing self-appraisal. Because of our "role" as the suffering stranger in history, many have perceived the Jew as the moral conscience and critic of social and political injustice.[29] In building the third Jewish commonwealth, our role must shift from moral criticism of others to self-judgment. In coming home, the task before us is to clean up our own house.

If a moral message will emanate from Jerusalem, it will result not from what we say but from what we do. For the covenant to be renewed in its full power and vitality, Jews must be willing to face the serious moral and religious problems that arise when they seek to participate fully in modern society. This challenge faces Jews in both Israel and the diaspora, but it arises in its most acute and total form in Israel. The quality of life that we build in Israel will accordingly be paradigmatic for and influence the manner in which

Judaism develops everywhere in the modern world. For wherever Jews live, they must bring the passion of their faith commitment to the moral and political concerns of their society. Torah is not, as Spinoza claimed, merely the political constitution of a nation with its own political sovereignty. Torah is a way of life not circumscribed by geographic boundaries. The rabbis taught in the Talmud that the *mitzvot* must be observed wherever a Jew is called upon to do battle against the false gods of history (*Kiddushin* 37a). It is the destiny of Jews wherever they may be to say no to all modern forms of idolatry.[30]

The significance of the rebirth of Israel cannot be circumscribed to those who live in Israel. The endless Zionist discussions regarding the relationship of Israel to the diaspora are usually futile. I reject the radical Zionist claim that a vibrant Jewish life is impossible in the diaspora. It is a total evasion of our larger responsibility to the Jewish people if we offer the diaspora only one message: "Come to Israel in order to safeguard your grandchildren from assimilation." Israel should not be understood merely as a haven for the persecuted and the wandering Jew or as a guarantee against assimilation. It is shortsighted to use the Holocaust as a justification for the need for a Jewish national home. Israel from my perspective provides a new direction for Judaism's confrontation with modernity. It opens up the possibility of renewing the covenantal drama of Sinai in a vital new way. The rebirth of Israel marks the repudiation of the halakhic ghetto as the means for guarding Jewish survival in history. Israel not only argues against the ghettoization of Judaism, but is also a rejection of the mistaken universalism that characterized the assimilationist tendencies that affected many Jews as a result of the breakdown of the ghetto. The birth of the third Jewish commonwealth teaches all of Jewry that being rooted in a particular history and tradition need not be antithetical to involvement and concern with the larger issues affecting the human world.

It would have been understandable if in response to the tragic suffering of the Jewish people in this century, and their profound disillusionment with Western values, Jews would have restricted their visibility in and concern for history. However, the covenant of Sinai teaches the Jew to trust and be open to the world again. The Sinai covenant does not allow Jews to adopt a spiritual orientation that gives up on history and emphasizes the inner life of the soul. To be a covenantal Jew is to share in Moses' understanding of God's dream for Israel and history. Moses is the paradigm of the way a Jew is to hear the significance of *mitzvah* in his or her life. Moses knew that he must leave the contemplative spiritual bliss that he discovered on the peak of Mount Sinai and enter into the struggle of history down below. Moses demonstrated that love of God must be found within the context of community. The heavy responsibility of implementing the Sinai covenant in the third Jewish commonwealth can be borne with dignity and joy because Judaism has always taught that in the eyes of God the doors of renewal are never closed.

Ben-Gurion and many Zionists believed that to build a healthy third commonwealth, it was necessary to leap back beyond the talmudic period, go back to the Bible, and reject much that exilic Jewish history gave to the Jewish world. I believe that they were mistaken. Estrangement from the postbiblical history of Judaism deprives the community of the important perspectives and values initiated by Ezra and Nehemiah and developed by rabbinic teachers in the talmudic tradition. Jeremiah and Ezekiel offered the community a utopian vision, but Ezra and Nehemiah rebuilt the community within imperfect historical conditions. They taught the Jewish people that the Sinai covenant could be renewed in spite of the gap between prophetic hope and reality. The rabbinic traditon has taught us to say grace over an incomplete meal. Rabbinic Jews can find spiritual meaning even though all their deepest hungers and longings are not fully gratified. It is to the rabbinic tradition that we must turn to learn how the prosaic details of daily life can be made the carriers of the larger covenantal prophetic vision of history. The third Jewish commonwealth can be enriched by the passionate sobriety of the covenantal tradition that places the hearing of *mitzvah* at the center of its conception of God and the world.

> The Lord spoke to you out of the fire; you heard the sound of words but perceived no shape—nothing but a voice. (Deut. 4:12)

Notes

1. Even anti-Zionist Satmar Hasidim and the Netorei Karta community of Meah Shearim view the state of Israel as God's providential act, though as a great and supreme trial rather than as a blessing. The rebirth of Israel, they claim, tests the community's loyalty to Torah and *mitzvah* by challenging it to await God's redemption *despite* the deceptive promises and successes of Zionism. Many more Jews, of course, see Israel's rebirth not as a trial but as a blessing bestowed by God upon the Jewish people. Belief in a personal God who acts in history can lead one to recite special prayers of joyful thanksgiving on Israel's Independence Day or to mourn the fact that the majority of Jews have succumbed to the seductions of a Zionist state that threatens the covenantal identity of the Jewish people. The attempt to understand the actions of a personal God in history is thus not an unambiguous enterprise.

    See Aviezer Ravitzky, "Ha-zafui ve-ha-reshut ha-netunah," in Aluf Har-Even ed., *Yisrael li-kerat ha-meah ha-21* (Jerusalem: Van Leer Foundation, 1984), pp. 135–197, especially pp. 140–146, noting a strong necessitarian perception of history of religious Zionists and anti-Zionists alike.

2. See A.I. Kook, *The Lights of Penitence* . . . (New York: Paulist Press, 1978), pp. 256–269, 282–302. Also S. Avineri, *The Making of Modern Zionism* (London: Weidenfeld and Nicholson, 1981), chap. 16.

3. Kook, *The Light of Penitence* . . . , pp. 196–199 and 253–255.

4. "Kol dodi dofek," pp. 77–82.

5. *Rosh ha-Shanah* 29a and *Shavuot* 39a.

6. See Y. Leibowitz, "Jewish Identity and Jewish Silence." in Ehud Ben Ezer, ed., *Unease in Zion* (New York: Quadrangle, 1974), pp. 177–200. Also his *Emunah, historiyah va-arakhim*, pp. 112–134.

7. Maimonides takes strong exception to this view: *Commentary to the Mishnah on Pirkei Avot* 4:7, MT *Hilkhot Talmud Torah* 3:1–11. The view is adopted, by contrast, in *Tur, Hilkhot Talmud Torah* 246.

8. See Urbach, *The Sages*, pp. 603–614.

9. E.g., *Mekhilta, ba-hodesh* 5:

    > Why was the Torah not given in the land of Israel? . . . To avoid causing dissension among the tribes. Else one might have said: "In my territory the Torah was given." And the other might have said: "In my territory the Torah was given." Therefore, the Torah was given in the desert, publicly and openly, in a place belonging to no one. To three things the Torah is likened: to the desert, to fire, and to water. This is to tell you that just as these three things are free to all who come into the world, so also are the words of the Torah free to all who come into the world.

    See also S. Talmon, "The 'Desert Motif' in the Bible and in Qumran Literature," in A. Altmann, ed., *Biblical Motifs* (Cambridge: Harvard University Press, 1966), pp. 31–63.

10. *Lev. Rab.* 25:5.

11. This is the basis of my serious disagreement with Steven Schwarzschild, who understands *ha-lakhah* and the Jewish people only within messianic categories. Israeli normalcy is for him therefore a paganization of the Jewish people. But Israeli normalcy need not mean, as in A. B. Yehoshua, *Between Right and Right* (New York: Doubleday, 1981), that whatever Jews do in Israel is by definition Jewish. I hold that living in Israel is not a substitute for the normative Jewish tradition, but a framework for its implementation.

12. See further my "Power and Responsibility," *Forum* 44 (Spring 1982), 53–58.

13. See also *Sifre* Deut. 43, quoted by Nachmanides in this context. Also Henoch, *Nachmanides*, pp. 141–159; D. Rapel, "Ha-Ramban al ha-galut ve-ha-geulah," in Y. Ben Sasson, ed., *Geulah u-medinah* (Jerusalem: Ministry of Education, 1979), pp. 79–109.

14. The holiness of the land of Israel consists in that certain *mitzvot* can be performed only there, according to MT *Hilkhot Beit ha-Behirah* 10:12-13 (following *Kelim* 1:6). See also the distinction between the holiness of Jerusalem, which derives from the divine presence, and that of the land of Israel, ibid. 6:14-16. Further, MT *Hilkhot Terumah* 1:2–6 (from 1:3 it would seem that the concept of the land is defined in juridical and political terms rather than in metaphysical or theological ones).

15. See N. Rotenstreich, "Dimensions of the Jewish Experience of Modernity," in *Essays on Zionism and the Contemporary Jewish Condition* (New York: Herzl Press, 1980), pp. 4–18, which brings out the shifts in historical consciousness that accompanied the emergence of Zionism. On the connection between messianism and Zionism, see J. Katz, "The Jewish National Movement," *Journal of World History* 11 (1968), 267–283.

16. Among many examples, see *Shevi'it* 6:1 and *Kiddushin* 1:8 in the Jerusalem Talmud; *Mekhilta, shirta* 1.

17. This is my answer to Leibowitz's criticism in his review of my *Joy and Responsibility* in *Petahim*. He claims that by my ascription of religious significance to the renewal of Jewish national independence, "Judaism is brought down to the level of the faith of the magicians in Egypt who saw the finger of God in particular events in human reality." As I have just pointed out, I make no judgment on God's activity but only on the new opportunities that Israel provides for living our Judaism. Regarding particular events, such as the Six-Day War, I claim only that they may influence individual Jews to feel greater commitment to the community and sensitize them to the historic dimension of Judaic spirituality that is fundamental for halakhic commitment.

My position is also unaffected by Leibowitz's claim that "the mass movement of Jews away from Judaism has not been halted, nor has it even been slowed, under the influence of the national Jewish rebirth." I am not making an empirical statement about the actual return of Jews to the worship of God, but am merely speaking of opportunities. Israel can be a profound instrument serving the renewal of Jewish spirituality because it forces individual Jews to become responsible for a total way of life in a land that anchors them to their biblical and talmudic historical roots. That the covenantal community has not yet been renewed does not vitiate my argument. What I claim is only that in Israel there are unprecedented living conditions that may renew Jewish spiritual sensibilities. Apart from expanding the possible range of *mitzvah*, those conditions also highlight the notion of collectivity and act against the loss of historical memory. Israel as a political entity focuses attention on the inescapable fact that Jews share a common historical destiny. And Israel as a land acts against the propensity of modern technological society to create individuals who, in their concern for novelty and progress, tend to regard the ideas and visions of the past as backward and inapplicable to their own times and lives.

My disagreement with Leibowitz regarding the place of events generally—and of the rebirth of Israel in particular—in the building of one's religious consciousness thus reflects our respective anthropologies. I claim that Jews serve God with their total personality, which is embedded in historical and communal contexts. Leibowitz's man of faith, by contrast, is nurtured by an act of will irrespective of the sociopolitical conditions of history. Under any conditions,

Leibowitz's halakhic individual is able to transcend his own human interest and the needs of the community in an Akedah-like act of unconditional surrender and affirm the dignity of religious worship. The absence in Leibowitz's philosophy of any relationship between *mitzvah* and the shaping of human character enables him to transcend the significance of historical contexts and events. Judaism as a total way of life for a whole society, however, cannot be built exclusively on an Akedah model of spirituality. The Zionist yearning for Jewish "normalcy" is a rejection of the Akedah consciousness as the definitive feature of Jewish spirituality.

18. Here I part ways completely with Leibowitz, for whom messianism is a menacing religious category that should be eliminated as totally and as quickly as possible. See his manner of understanding Maimonides on messianism in *Emunah, historiyah va-arakhim*, pp. 89–111.

19. I am grateful to the leadership of the Netivot Shalom movement for their role in bringing me to this realization.

20. It is a task for another work to spell out what it means to regard *halakhah* as both an educational and a legal system. Heschel's writings have made a beginning in this direction.
    Compare *Pesikta de-Rav Kahana* 12:25:

> "Moreover," said Rabbi Jose bar Rabbi Hanina, "the divine word spoke to each and every person according to his particular capacity. And do not wonder at this. For when manna came down for Israel, each and every person tasted it in keeping with his own capacity—infants in keeping with their capacity, young men in keeping with their capacity, and old men in keeping with their capacity. . . . Now if each and every person was enabled to taste the manna according to his particular capacity, how much more and more was each and every person enabled according to his particular capacity to hear the divine word. Thus David said: 'The voice of the Lord is in its strength' [Ps. 29:4]—not 'The voice of the Lord in His strength' but 'The voice of the Lord in its strength'—that is, in its strength to make itself heard and understood according to the capacity of each and every person who listens to the divine word."

This *midrash* indicates that *mitzvah* can be appropriated not merely as a formal duty but also as expressive of the particular individual's relationship to God. Accordingly, the statement that "He who is commanded and fulfills it is greater than he who fulfills it though not commanded" (*Kiddushin* 31a, etc.) does not oblige us to identify *halakhah* with acting out of a sense of duty. Compare, however, Rashi on *Rosh ha-Shanah* 28a: "They [the *mitzvot*] were not given to Israel for enjoyment, but as a yoke on their necks." Similarly, Rashi on *Berakhot* 33b.

21. Leibowitz was the first halakhic philosopher to realize, already in the late 1940s, that the creation of the state of Israel demands that the religious community face this fundamental challenge. As he expected no initiatives in this respect from the established halakhic jurists, he addressed his call directly to the religious community. His theory of halakhic change, which eliminates the necessity of precedent, sought to provide a basis for the community to accept the challenge. See Leibowitz, "Rashei perakim leva'ayat dat Yisrael bi-medinat Yisrael," pp. 85–87; "Yemei Zikkaron," pp. 95–97; "Dat u-medinah," pp. 105–107; also *Emunah, historiyah va-arakhim*, pp. 71–74.

22. Soloveitchik has frequently deprecated self-righteous sectarian tendencies of this kind in modern orthodoxy.

23. One of the forthcoming publications of the research fellows of the Shalom Hartman Institute will be a collection of essays devoted to this topic.

24. See *Yoma* 86a and Maimonides, *Sefer ha-Mitzvot*, positive commandment 3.

25. As Scholem remarked in Ehud ben Ezer, ed., *Unease in Zion*, p. 273: "Zionism has never really known itself completely—whether it is a movement of continuation and continuity, or a movement of rebellion." Also Scholem, "Reflections on Jewish Theology," pp. 290–297. See H. Fisch, *The Zionist Revolution* (London: Weidenfeld and Nicholson, 1978), for a discussion of the paradox (chap. 1–2) and for a very different covenantal understanding of Zionism.

26. Neither are MT *Hilkhot Avodah Zarah* 7:1, 10:1, and 5–6 or MT *Hilkhot Melakhim* 5:1–6, 6:1–6, and 8:10.

27. Contrast Maimonides' advocacy of coercion in MT *Hilkhot Gerushin* 2:20 with Berlin's defense of negative liberty in *Four Essays on Liberty* (Oxford: Oxford University Press, 1969), chap. 3. The work of M. J. Sandel has an important bearing on how Judaism needs to deal with the question of liberalism; see, e.g., his *Liberalism and the Limits of Justice* (Cambridge: Cambridge University Press, 1982).

28. According to *Sanhedrin* 21a, a king cannot be a member of a court because "if they may not be judged, how could they judge?"

29. Hermann Cohen was a notable example who has been followed by various contemporary Jewish theologians who have serious difficulty in coming to terms with the power embodied in the state of Israel.

30. "Why was he [Mordecai] called 'a Jew' [Esther 2:5]? Because he repudiated idolatry. For anyone who repudiates idolatry is called a Jew . . ." (*Megillah* 13a). See my *Joy and Responsibility*, pp. 145–149.

34

The Religious and Moral Significance of the Redemption of Israel

YESHAYAHU LEIBOWITZ

Let me object, at the outset, to any attempt to explain anyone's views by where he comes from or who he is. I object as well to any attempt to distinguish between those who come from a milieu shaped by Western culture and others whose cultural and spiritual origins lie in Eastern Europe. I, too, belong to the Western world although, geographically speaking, I come from the east. I spent my childhood in Russia, but am familiar with Western science, philosophy, literature, and society no less than are the "Westerners." I recall a public debate more than thirty years ago between myself and the late Dr. Isaac Breuer, one of the most interesting thinkers among religious Jews in the generation preceding ours, for whom I had great respect despite the considerable differences between our respective views. In that debate we drifted off to general philosophical problems, and although they were relevant to the issues that were close to our hearts, Judaism, Torah, and faith, they were fundamentally ontological and epistemological problems. Since Breuer argued persistently from the Jewish viewpoint, I said to him: "Dr. Breuer, why should we deceive ourselves? You know as well as I that in our treatment of philosophical questions both of us—who consider ourselves believing Jews, whose intention is to assume the yoke of the Kingdom of Heaven and the yoke of Torah and Mitzvoth—do not draw upon Jewish sources but upon the atheistic antisemite Kant. We cannot do otherwise!" Breuer conceded at once that it would be impossible—even he could not do it—to discuss philosophical problems without recourse to Kant. Today, too, it is not the lack of familiarity with various aspects of European culture that created the rift between us. We are all equally steeped in Western culture.

Yeshayahu Leibowitz, "The Religious and Moral Significance of the Redemption of Israel," in *Judaism, Human Values, and the Jewish State*, Eliezer Goldman, ed. (Cambridge: Harvard University Press, 1992), pp. 106–22. © Harvard University Press, Cambridge, MA 02138.

Severe criticism has been voiced against our attitude—the attitude of Judaism—to the Gentile world. Some accused us of attaching no human value to Gentiles, and of ignoring the image of God in *every* person. To this my reply is far more radical. A few days ago we concluded the Day of Atonement saying: "man has no preeminence over the beast: for all is vanity," and "You have distinguished man from the first and acknowledged him to stand before You." The question is not whether the Gentile is of value but whether *man* has any value, be he Jew or Gentile. About "God created man in His own image, in the image of God created He him," Rabbi Se'adiah Gaon said: "and in respect of this image everyone is equal, the righteous as well as the wicked, the one is a man and the other is a man."[1] Those who would ground morality on the image of God in man may remember that Adolf Hitler and Adolf Eichmann were created in God's image like you and me, and also every rapist and murderer, as well as the most righteous of men. The ultimate message of the Day of Atonement is that man, as such, has no intrinsic value; he acquires value insofar as he stands before God. In the last verse of Jonah, which is also read on the Day of Atonement, man and beast are on the same plane: "more than six score thousand persons . . . and also much cattle." Man—any man—is by nature beastlike; it is only the service of God that raises him from nullity to significance and confers value on him. "Let not the wise man glory in his wisdom, neither let the mighty man glory in his might, let not the rich man glory in his riches. But let him that glorifies glory in this, that he understands and knows Me" (Jer. 9:22–23). Neither the essence nor the nature of man, his attributes or peculiar capacities, not even his achievements are of inherent importance. In God's reply to Jonah there is no mention of the fact that the people of Nineveh repented. Why? Because even man's great attainment, repentance, can only lead to expiation, but does not change human nature. In this respect there is no difference between Jew and Gentile.

The expression "a light to the nations" as used by Ben-Gurion and others to indicate the vocation of the Jewish people departs considerably from its original biblical meaning. The expression is borrowed from the Book of Isaiah, where it refers expressly to the prophet himself, charged with the mission "to bring Jacob again" to God, and beyond that, to be a "light to the nations"—much as Jeremiah was ordained to be "a prophet unto the nations."[2] The idea that the people of Israel has been endowed with a capacity for instructing and guiding all of humanity has no basis in authentic Jewish sources, and played no role—at least no more than a marginal one—in the consciousness of generations of Jews who assumed the yoke of the Kingdom of Heaven in the form of the yoke of Torah and Mitzvoth. This idea was fabricated by the heretics—from the Apostle Paul to Ben-Gurion—who meant to cast off the yoke of Torah by substituting for it a faith in an abstract "vocation."

The Jewish people were not given a mission; it was rather charged with a task—the task of being servants of God ("A Kingdom of Priests and a holy nation"). To transform religion and religious faith from a task and obligation into an endowment and a destiny is to degrade them. In the Ne'ilah prayer, and in that most sublime of prayers, Alenu, we give thanks to God for the good fortune to be His servants, while the elevation of the world through the Kingdom of God is assigned to Him and not to us. Similarly, in the prayer of the Days of Awe, we beseech God to impose fear of Him on all His creatures so that they may unite for compliance with His will. No mention is made of any role which Israel is called upon to play in realizing this vision.

The obligation imposcd on the people of Israel was never met by the Jews, and they do not fulfill it today. The law-giver of Israel said on the day of his death: "behold while I am yet alive with you this day you have been rebellious against God and how much more after my death? . . . for I know that after my death you will surely be corrupted" (Deut. 31:27–29). More than three thousand years have elapsed since then—and the words of Moses remain true. It would seem that my predecessors in this debate have confused the vision of the prophets of Israel about the deeds of God with a vision of what the Jews will do, as if the God of Israel were a Jew like the God of the Christians.

The so-called messianic vision, the redemption of humanity and of the world, is depicted in the sources as the act of God, not as the enterprise of the people of Israel, which requires rehabilitation like all of mankind. In this respect there is no difference between Jews and other human beings. "The earth also was corrupt before God and the earth was filled with violence"—this holds for Jews and Gentiles alike. Furthermore the entire notion of the re-forming of the world and the redemption of humanity is peripheral, not central, to the religious thought, feeling, and faith of Judaism, not to mention its religious practice. Frequent repetition of the five verses opening the second chapter of Isaiah, while ignoring their location between chapter 1, which is read as the Haftarah of the Sabbath preceding the ninth of Av (the anniversary of the destruction of the Temple), and the strong exhortation following them, offers an escape from the severity of the demand made of man by the Bible. Were we to group together all the verses in the Bible which, literally or by interpretation, refer to the redemption of the world and the rehabilitation of mankind in days to come we would see how few they are by comparison to the main body of prophetic discourse, which conveys the austere demand to serve God *in the world as it is.*

My construal of biblical prophecy does not rest on the authority of philosophers or theologians, but rather on the Tossafist annotators, who seem remote from philosophy and theology, and who express a "simple" faith in God and His Torah.[3] In connection with a statement in the Talmud about prophecy, the Tossafists comment that "the prophet only prophesies *what ought to be.*"[4] Here we have presented to us in full force the pure faith as opposed to the faith in magic and oracles. If prophecy were a statement of what will happen, it would have no religious significance. What is the distinction between the meteorological forecast and a prophetic oracle about tomorrow's weather? Both of them oblige me to do nothing, they are irrelevant to the service of God. One of the Tanna'im already said " 'and the years draw near, when you shall say, I have no pleasure in them' (Eccles. 12:1)—those are the days of the Messiah, wherein there is no merit and no liability," which implies that there is no meaning and value in the religious sense, except in our world, where a deliberate effort ("pleasure") is required in the struggle to serve God. The conditions and circumstances in which man serves God are, in a religious sense, immaterial. Even if we extend the reference from the individual to the collective, to the larger Jewish collective, or even to all of humankind—it is all simply the world taking its natural course. Possibly this course of the world also includes the redemption at the end of days. Yet religious fulfillment does not attach specifically to this state of affairs, but rather to the service of God in *any* state of affairs. And so we return to the meaning of the end of Ne'ilah: "man has no preeminence over the beast: for all is vanity," on the one hand, and "you have distinguished man from the first and acknowledged him to stand before you" on the other. Man's standing before God is not contingent upon objective circumstances, whether these pertain to the world or to man. His faith is not affected by such circumstances, if the man is a true believer. Faith which is thus affected is not true faith.

The religious participants in this debate made ample use of the pronoun "we" when they spoke of "Judaism," "Jewish people," and "faith." I would like to ask: who are "we"? Does "we" mean all of the contemporary Jews? Some contrasted "us" with "the infidels." I presume there is no human group in which religious disbelief is as widespread today as among Jews. It is doubtful whether there is a human group in which the community of believers has dwindled as it has among Jews. This is hardly surprising, for the faith demanded in Judaism requires very great fortitude. Not in vain did the psalmist exclaim: "you mighty ones that do His bidding" (Ps. 103:20). What is surprising is not the prevailing lack of faith among Jews, but rather the dominance of faith among them for so many generations. It is in conflict with human nature. It requires of one to subdue his inclinations and even suppress his human sensibilities. Let me remind you of Abravanel's comment relating to the Aqedah: " 'And Abraham rose up early in the morning, and saddled his ass'—he overcame his materiality." To this he added a remark that is quite amazing if we recall that messianic redemption *in the future* is pivotal to Abravanel's thought, as the antithesis to Christian messianic redemption. He continues: "And that is the ass to be ridden by the Messiah—king." We may infer, then, that even for Abravanel the vision of messianic redemption is not simply the expectation of a future historical event, but chiefly the expectation that the faith of Abraham the Patriarch, of whom it was said that he believed in God, shall be the faith of the entire world. This is the very opinion of Maimonides on messianic redemption, which he expresses at the conclusion of his code with the verse: "for the earth shall be full of the knowledge of God as the waters cover the sea" (Isa. 12:9). As for the vision of messianic redemption as a future event in history—a belief that Maimonides enumerates as one of the fundamental articles of faith in the Jewish tradition—his real attitude is suggested to the discerning reader in his scathing comments on the aggadic redemption stories: "And never should one preoccupy oneself with the Aggadoth, nor should one dwell on the Midrashim that deal with these matters and their cognates, *and one should not make them principal*, for they do not lead to fear or to love." Consider the consequences for Judaism of every historical development in which messianic redemption became central to Jewish faith. Such situations brought forth Christianity, led to Sabbateanism and to Frankism, and in our day this focus has become a stumbling block to the disciples of Rabbi Kook, who were not intellectually equipped to understand his teaching.[5] Maimonides was aware of the danger of the ascendency of the messianic idea as a substitute for the authentic faith in God, which consists in assuming the obligation to observe Torah and Mitzvoth.

Of the two great distortions of Jewish faith, the first was the Kabbalah, which converted the obligation imposed upon the Jewish people into a vocation affecting the cosmos and God Himself. The Mitzvoth were interpreted as a method for mending disruptions in the world of divinity and rectifying the world's disorders. In that way man himself is elevated, as it were, to a divine level. This is the very opposite of the idea of Ne'ilah on the Day of Atonement. The Kabbalah transformed the Judaism of the service of God into a mythology about God, the world, humanity, and the Jewish people. The actual Jewish people, which under natural conditions is bound by Torah and practical Mitzvoth was identified with the mystical notion of Knesseth Israel (the "soul of the nation," in Rabbi Kook's words), which is identical with the Shekhinah, kabbalistically identified with the last Sefirah, that of Malkhuth (kingdom). Now, the Sephirah Malkhuth is related to the sixth Sephirah, Tifereth (splendor), which is represented by the Patriarch Jacob, who is Israel. Thence derives the pagan trinity of the Holy-Blessed-be-He, the Torah, and Israel. The contrast between regarding Torah and Mitzvoth as the service of God *for its own sake* and regarding them as magical means *for the sake of something else* (the redemption of Israel, the rehabilitation of the world, or for God's own need) is not confined to the medieval context; it is still meaningful in our days. The great dispute among Yemenite Jews between the Darda'im (the followers of Maimonides) and the Akashim (adherents of the *Zohar*) at the beginning of the twentieth (!) century is proof enough. This split in Jewish religious thought is interestingly documented by the articles and proclamations of Rabbi Yahieh Qafah of San'a and his colleagues ("Those Who Pray to a Long-Nosed Idol and to a Short-Nosed Idol," and "Those Who Believe in a Decemy"); it is countered by awkward, stammering reactions of the Jerusalem rabbis (including Rabbi Kook).[6]

I was never a follower of Rabbi Kook, and the dangers inherent in his doctrine impressed me more than its lofty aspects. I am cognizant of his greatness as a scholar and a man of faith and not only through his writing and published talks, for I had the great privilege of meeting him and speaking face to face. I shall always remember a long conversation, in the course of which he graciously answered my queries about Maimonides and the Kabbalah. It revealed his greatness,—but also his limitations.

It was a mark of his stature that he made no attempt whatsoever to bridge the enormous gulf separating what, in his view and deepest conviction, was *Torath Heʾemeth* (Doctrine of the Truth, meaning the Kabbalah), from the conceptual world of Maimonides—to Kook, as to any Jew versed in Torah but especially to a great scholar, "the Great Eagle," "the Right-Hand Pillar," "the Mighty Hammer" of the Halakhah, whose work has been basic for halakhic learning and ruling for seven hundred years.[7] The rift between Maimonides and the Kabbalah was for him a stern fact, which, unlike many other kabbalists, he made no attempt to blur. Some of them passed over this in embarrassed silence. Others reacted to it by fabricating the silly legend that toward the end of his life Maimonides studied the Kabbalah and accepted it. Still others, who realized and admitted the bitter truth, came to the point of maligning him, occasionally in a very harsh manner.[8] That was not the way of Rabbi Kook. No one knew better than he what Maimonides was to Judaism. In his conversation with me he insisted most emphatically on the validity of the Doctrine, which Maimonides did not know or at least did not acknowledge. Nevertheless he stated that it was Providence that gave Maimonides to the Jewish people to safeguard them against the danger of falling into idolatry, a danger particularly threatening to the adherent of the Doctrine of the Truth. Even as "the greater the person, the greater his evil inclination," the greater the measure of truth in one's faith, the greater is the danger of its distortion.[9] "Between paradise and hell there is a partition two fingers thick." Precisely the ardor of faith in God may cause those of feeble character or mind to stumble. The golden calf ("these be your gods O Israel") was made by the generation to which the Shekhinah revealed itself, and the evil inclination of idolatry capered among the Israelites all the while the Shekhinah was present in the Temple. The role of Maimonides in combating idolatry was like that of the prophets and of the men of the Great Assembly (who shaped rabbinic Judaism early in the second commonwealth.)

Maimonides did not introduce the "alien corn" of Greek wisdom into Judaism, as many naïve people believe. The extreme form of his doctrine of divine unity, which is the absolute denial of all the attributes to the point of ignoring or spurning the Doctrine of Truth, established a bulwark against the danger of gross anthropomorphism inherent in that doctrine, making of the service of God a worship of mediators.

At the time of my encounter with Rabbi Kook I was young and did not dare to tell the great old man to his face that even the enormous influence Maimonides had over believing Jews of all subsequent generations was incapable of saving many of them from being tripped by Kabbalah into Sabbateanism, Frankism, or apostasy; that he was incapable of preventing multitudes of genuine believers from lapsing into worshiping "divine names" and angels owing to Kabbalah. Today one can add that even the Doctrine of Truth of Rabbi Kook himself, which involves a confusion of the actual people of Israel with a mystical Israel, has become, in the hands of his disciples and their disciples, a deification of the nation and a fetishism of the land.

Reform Judaism is the second historical distortion of the Jewish religion. For the service of God through Torah and Mitzvoth as the end of religion, the Reform movement substitutes an end the Jewish people is destined to attain. And, paradoxically, in this respect Reform resembles the Kabbalah, except that the Kabbalah assigns to the Jewish people and Judaism a cosmic-metaphysical vocation, namely the rehabilitation of the world, the rectification, as it were, of a breach in the divine realm itself. Moreover, the Kabbalah endeavors to maintain the halakhic system as it is, ascribing to the practice of Mitzvoth a magical efficacy toward fulfilling this religious function. Reform, by contrast, assigns to Judaism a human-mundane vocation, "to be a light to the nations." Accordingly, it adapts the Mitzvoth in ways that seem most appropriate to this end, or even abrogates them when they seem superfluous or dysfunctional to that vocation. What is common to Kabbalah and Reform is the dissolution of faith *lishmah* [for its own sake], Torah *lishmah*, and worship *lishmah*, which are the very essence of the historical halakhic Judaism. These are then replaced by faith, Torah, and service for the sake of "redemption," the redemption of the Jewish people, of the world, of humanity. Reform Judaism empties Judaism of its religious content and reduces it to ethical humanism.

At this point some comments on Jewish Ethics cannot be avoided. There is no Hebrew word for "ethics," and the term "Mussar" in the sense of ethics is a neologism. In biblical Hebrew "Mussar" means teaching. Neither in Scripture nor in the language of the Sages is there a word for ethics, even as there is no biblical term for the concept "conscience." Indeed, only the ethical atheist follows his conscience, which is his inclination, whereas the believer who fears God is not guided by his heart or eyes.

Ethics is not a program of behavior. In itself an act is morally indifferent. A person loads and cocks a rifle and releases the safety catch; aims at someone and presses the trigger. In one instance, as a result of this action, the agent may be called an abominable murderer; in another instance, he may be regarded as a heroic soldier defending the fatherland. Clearly, it is not the act that is being judged but the intention. Moral judgment pertains to the intention of the actor. Ethics, then, is not the doctrine of correct behavior, but the doctrine of man's right intention. The intention does not guarantee the "goodness" of the action. The person may err, and the consequence of a good intention may be very bad. But moral judgment does not pertain to the result but to the intention.

Opinions differ, however, with respect to what is meant by "pure intention" and "the good." Western thought elaborated two major answers to this question, neither of Jewish origin.

The first maintains that man's moral judgment consists in the guidance of his will in accordance with apprehension of the truth about the world, not by his interests, feelings, drives, or passions. This is the great idea of Socrates, who believed in the Olympian gods.

According to the second, man's moral judgment consists in the guidance of his will, not by his inclinations or interests nor by knowledge and understanding of the world, but by recognition of his duty, a recognition which is imposed by conscience, by the self-awareness of a rational being. This is the great idea of Kant. But the text of Shema says: "And that you may not go astray after your own heart and after your own eyes." The prohibition of following "your own heart" is a negation of Kant's great principle; the prohibition of following "your own eyes" is the rejection of the great principle of Socrates. And the reason for the two negations is: "I am the Lord your God." The believing man is guided by his consciousness of his standing before God, not before man. His judgment is not moral. Morality is an atheistic category.

Some of my predecessors in this debate seem to enjoy the pleasant illusion that the establishment of the state of Israel and its existence enhance the prestige of Judaism in a religious sense, both among the Jews and among the nations. I have written and said much about the status of Judaism in the Israeli state. This time I shall confine myself to recounting a conversation I had with Ben-Gurion some twenty years ago. He then said to me: "I well understand why you demand so insistently the separation of religion and state. Your object is that the Jewish religion reinstate itself as an independent factor so the political authority will be compelled to deal with it. I will never agree to the separation of religion from the State. I want the state to hold religion in the palm of its hand." The status quo, which formally interweaves elements pretending to be religious with the secular executive and administrative system of the state—an integration which the representatives of "religious national" Judaism make every effort to perpetuate—reflects the cast of mind of a man who entertained a bitter hatred of Judaism. It was to this conversation with Ben-Gurion that I alluded when I once wrote: "The status of Jewish religion in the state of Israel is that of a kept mistress of the secular government—therefore it is contemptible." The state of Israel does not radiate the light of Judaism to the nations, not even to the Jews.

I vehemently oppose the view that Zionist theory and practice are necessarily or essentially connected with the idea of "light to the nations." It seems to me that those who find allusions to this idea in the works of Ahad Ha'am and Herzl are mistaken. But even if such allusions existed, they would not turn a wild misconception into the truth. I reject the attempts to adorn the state of Zionism with a religious aura. Rather than exalt Zionism and the state, these efforts devaluate religion, turning it from the service of God into the fulfillment of human needs and aspirations. As to the meaning of Zionism—here is an account of a conversation I had some time ago with an important non-Jewish foreign journalist. He asked: "What is the meaning of Zionism?" He had previously posed this question to several Israeli public figures and received various answers. One was that Zionism is an endeavor to build a model society. My reaction was that this is the goal of many people of all nations and cultures, Jews and non-Jews, and striving to achieve this end does not necessitate the existence of a separate Jewish nation and state. Another answer identified Zionism with freeing the Jews from their state of alienation among the nations that regard them as foreigners and do not permit them to integrate except in a formal-legal sense, so they lack a feeling of existential security. This reply was rejected by the journalist himself, who pointed out that in the post-Hitlerite generation the obstacles to full integration of Jews were removed in all Western societies. In these countries Jews were massively absorbed into the economy and into cultural life, business organizations, and the academies, and were active in science and literature and even in politics. The sense of alienation between Jews and Gentiles has vanished, and the rise of Jews to positions of influence does not evoke any resistance and does not draw the attention of the non-Jewish public. In the United States Jews have served as secretary of state, attorney general, and mayor of its largest city; in Austria a Jew was chancellor. Forty-seven British M.P.s were Jews, and the first woman ever to become a minister in France was Jewish. As for feelings of insecurity, nowhere is Jewish existence so threatened as it is in the state of Israel. Some of the journalist's interlocutors identified Zionism as a mystical phenomenon, as the fulfillment of the prophetic vision and the messianic promises. Given the utter secularization of the great majority of the Jewish people, this is absurd.

My own answer to that non-Jew was that Zionism is the expression of our being fed up with being ruled by *Goyim*. I am aware that this "we" does not extend to all Jews. Still, it is the motive shared by Zionist Jews who differ widely in their human values and in their conceptions of Judaism. Zionism is best defined as the program for the attainment of political and national independence. Now that this has been attained in the form of a sovereign state, Zionism consists in the effort to maintain this independence. This is the function the state of Israel performs for the Jewish people, in addition to inspiring "the fear of authority" as does every system of government to maintain peace and tranquillity. More than that should not be expected for any state. The values people wish to realize, whether general humanistic ones like the idea of a "model society," or specifically Jewish ones such as the "prophetic vision and the messianic promises," or, most authentically, a condition in which "the earth shall be full of the knowledge of the Lord," are not the affair of the state. Their realization is a proper object for the aspirations and striving of individuals and groups *within* the state. It is outside the sphere of action of the executive and administrative apparatus of state coercion, which can never be the suitable instrument for the implementation of these values.

Zionism is not defined or determined by social, moral, or religious values. Moreover, the realization of Zionism affords no guarantee of the actualization of these values. Similarly, there is no congruence between Zionism and the concern for the well-being and physical safety of the Jews. True enough, the first two generations of Zionists—those of Herzl and Weizmann—believed that Zionism was a historical necessity because Jews were denied assimilation among the nations. The early Zionists believed that Jews in exile were eternally doomed to be aliens, either as tolerated foreigners or as outcast and oppressed strangers. They could only be delivered from this tragic situation by setting up a national home in their own land. This conception does not fit the contemporary scene. We are witnessing the accelerated assimilation of Jews and their complete integration in their host societies. The only ones resisting this process are Jews who do not want it. Zionism today is therefore a matter of a voluntary, deliberate decision made by Jews—a minority of them. It has also become evident that Jewish independence affords no guarantee to the well-being and security of the Jewish people, who are threatened in their land more than anywhere else. It follows that, in this respect too, the Jew is required to make a decision to accept (for himself and his wife and children) the risk involved in living under conditions of Jewish national independence.

Zionism has no connection to Judaism in its essential religious sense of the obligation to observe Torah and Mitzvoth; this is an absolute obligation imposed upon us regardless of particular historical circumstances or existential conditions. Zionism has no bearing on it whatsoever, since this task is binding on us in our land as in exile, in freedom as in bondage, and the effort to fulfill it continues and will continue so long as there are Jews who recognize it. Zionism as an aspiration to political-national independence is a legitimate Jewish aspiration, and the state is dear to us as its fulfillment. But it must not be given a religious aura. Only what is done for the sake of Heaven has religious significance. The category of holiness is inapplicable to the state. I deny that the establishment of the state of Israel and its very existence signal a beginning of the realization of the values of Judaism. Sovereignty is essential to the state, along with an executive apparatus and the power and authority of coercion. The state fulfills an essential need of the individual and the national community, but it does not thereby acquire intrinsic value—except for a fascist who regards sovereignty, governmental authority, and power as the supreme values.

A state, as an instrument for satisfying certain needs, is not a vehicle for realizing values. Values are actualized only by human beings striving to that end, and not by an executive apparatus. Justice, equity, morality, or education, not to mention the religious values of fear of God, love of God, and the service of God, could never materialize with the mere attainment of sovereignty. Within the framework of the state men and women must fight for them. If Jews are not seen struggling for these values in the state of Israel, the state is not to blame. Equally, the great crisis of Judaism, "the hurt of my people," may not be attributed to the state as such. I do not expect our state to be a light to the nations. It is no light even to the people of Israel, who walk in darkness.

Some people contend that it is impossible to separate faith in God from moral-humanistic values. In God's words about Abraham, the "way of God" is defined as "righteousness and judgment," which is also the calling of his sons and their descendants. To this I reply that after God asserts that Abraham is a man of righteousness and judgment, and after He hearkens to Abraham on the issue of "doing right" to the men of Sodom, He still put Abraham to the test. To what end? What we learn about Abraham from the trial of the Aqedah that we did not know previously is the quality of Abraham's faith, what was meant when it was said of him that "he believed in God." Is it the kind of faith that is revealed in service of God for its own sake, or for the sake of such human desiderata as righteousness and judgment on earth? There are atheists and pagans who seek righteousness and judgment, and they instruct their children and household in their exercise. Even Avimelekh King of Gerar protested: "Will you slay also a righteous nation?" But Abraham is required to assume the service of God even when it is dissociated from all human needs, feelings, and values, even from the great historical ends which he was promised. For such service of God for His own sake reward or punishment are irrelevant. The Midrash already points out that Abraham could have presented forceful arguments: "Yesterday you said that through Isaac will be named your issue and today you tell me to bring him as an offering—yet he kept silent." Abraham (like Avimelekh) argues vigorously in his debate with God in His role of righteous judge, in analogy with a truthful human judge. But he refrains from all argument when God is revealed to him in His divinity. Contrary to what my predecessor in the debate said here, namely, that one cannot detach the service of God from human needs and values, the trial of the *Aqedah* conveys to us the essence of faith as man's ability to dissociate the consciousness of his standing before God from the problems of the individual, humanity, and the world. That is why Abraham is said to "fear God," and not because of his stand in the debate on justice, to which all those who wish to empty the Torah of its religious meaning and to reduce it to "moral" principles love to allude.

(*From the audience*: It is possible to say that God has no interest in man and his world?)

I have no knowledge of the divine intentions. How could I answer your question? I only know of the interest man has, or should have, in God; on this point I draw your attention to the Ne'ilah prayer and to the first clause in Maimonides' *Hilkhoth Yessodei Hatorah*.[10] As for God's interest in the world, let us invoke the prayerbook: He "was before creation's teeming birth," as He "was when his fiat all ordained." ("You were ere yet the world was created, and are the same since its creation.") The meaning of this may be gleaned from the third clause of the above-mentioned chapter in Maimonides' Code.[11]

(*From the audience*: "You have completely ignored the notions of Israel as the chosen people and of the holiness of Israel—"a holy nation."")

These attributes are functional rather than essential. They do not describe a property that the people already possess, but refer to what they ought to be. In other words, these terms apply by virtue of a demand put to the people of Israel, directing it to strive toward that goal. As the object of this demand its status is lofty and sublime. The terms do not refer to properties Jews actually possess. This is put clearly and unequivocally in the benediction "Who has chosen us from among all peoples and given us His Torah"; "Who has chosen us from all nations . . . and sanctified us with His Mitzvoth."[12] The Pentateuch pronouncements are, "You will be holy" (Lev. 15:2) and "That you may remember and do all my commandments and be holy to your God" (Num. 15:40). This contradicts Qorah, according to whom "all the congregation are holy, every one of them" (Num. 16:3). The difference between the conception of election and sanctity as an eternal task, and their conception as indigenous characteristics of the people of Israel since the days of the Patriarchs until now, is the difference between belief in God and belief in nature. In the natural and human sphere there is only potential holiness—the intention to serve God, which brings man closer to God. Whoever ascribes holiness *in actu* to man, to nation, to an object, or to a country elevates that thing to divine rank, though God alone is Holy. Such a person has stumbled into idolatry.

(*From the audience:* Rabbi Judah Halevi attributes holiness to the Jewish people.)

Rabbi Judah Halevi, the divine poet, expresses in the prayers, in the *Selihoth*, and in the *Yotzeroth*, the pure faith in God. But as author of the *Kuzari* he entangled himself in religious polemics and stumbled into racist-nationalist chauvinism. Maharal and Rabbi Kook follow in his footsteps. Maimonides, in his celebrated reply to Rabbi Obadiah the proselyte, inveighs with extreme severity against any concept of biological holiness which is putatively ingrained in the Jewish race and peculiar to it.[13]

(*From the audience*: What about "a treasured people" (*Am Segulah*)?)

The singularity of the Jewish people consists in the Torah that was given to the people and the service imposed upon it. Without these the Jews are like all the others. The greatest believer among the Jews, Maimonides, does not at all mention the Jewish people in the first four chapters of his great Code, in which he discusses man's knowledge of God and His unity as well as man's knowledge of the world and of himself. "Israel" appears with striking suddenness at the beginning of chapter 5: "the entire house of Israel is enjoined to sanctify the Great Name." The Gentiles are not thus enjoined. The acknowledgment of God is universal: the trait that is peculiar to Israel is the service of God by observance of the Torah and its Mitzvoth. Consequently, Maimonides does not regard prophecy as singularly Jewish. "It is fundamental to religion that the Deity inspires *men* with prophecy."[14] This, of course, is in sharp contrast to Rabbi Judah Halevi's view.

It should however be noted that when Judah Halevi portrays the Hassid (*Kuzari* article 3), he suceeds in extricating himself from the racial-national and national-territorial elements of his doctrine and presents a figure of a servant of God that resembles the figure portrayed by Maimonides in the final chapters of his *Guide*.

(*From the audience*: What of the sanctity of the land of Israel?)

This term, too, refers to the service of God, namely to the Mitzvoth which obtain only in the land of Israel. The country has no intrinsic holiness and the Mitzvoth do not derive from its holiness. Rather, it is the Mitzvoth, when observed, that confer sanctity upon the land. This is well brought out by the Mishnah in Tractate *Kelim*, which describes ten degrees of sanctity attaching to certain locations and ascribes each of them to certain Mitzvoth which are in force at the specific location.

Faith in the "holy God" ought to prevent man from ascribing intrinsic holiness to anything in the world. It ascribes holiness in the world only to the service of God. The appellation "God's estate" applied to the land of Israel does not refer to any special quality of this country, for "The earth is the Lord's and the fullness thereof, the world and they that dwell therein." And in respect of this relation to God, Paraguay and Cambodia and their peoples are equal to the land of Israel and its people. But there are special Mitzvoth in the service of God that are binding on the people of Israel only in their land, and it is these that confer its peculiar virtue upon this country. Possibly it was his concern lest the Torah be conceived as the Torah of the land of Israel that prevented Maimonides from including the settling of the land of Israel among the Mitzvoth.

I can find no statement more fitting to sum up my view on the nature of sanctity than the following words of Rabbi Meir Simhah Cohen of Dwinsk:

> The Torah and faith are the very principles of the Jewish nation, and all the sanctities—the Land of Israel, Jerusalem, etc.—derive from the Torah, and are sanctified by the holiness of the Torah . . . Don't imagine that the Temple or the Tabernacle are holy, in themselves, God forbid. The Exalted One "dwells" among his children, and if they desecreted the covenant, their sacredness is removed from the Temple and Tabernacle and they are like profane vessels . . . In sum, there is nothing holy in the world save the Exalted One in His necessary existence . . . All the sanctities derive from the imperative of the Creator to build Him a tabernacle in which to offer sacrifices for His sake alone . . . There is no holiness or divine matter whatsoever save the Being of the Creator, may His Name be exalted.[15]

Notes

Throughout these notes, "Ed." refers to Elizer Goldman, editor of *Judism, Human Values and the Jewish State*, (Cambridge: Harvard, 1992).

1. Rabbi Se'adiah ben Joseph (892–942) was a rabbinic scholar and head of the Yeshiva of Sura, philosopher, biblical exegete, grammarian, and poet—Ed.

2. The reference is to Isa. 49:6: "It is too slight a thing that you should be my servant to raise up the tribe of Jacob, and to restore the preserved of Israel. I will also give you for a light to the nations"—Ed.

3. The Tossafists were Ashkenazic scholars of the twelfth and thirteenth centuries. Many of their opinions were collected in the *Tossafoth*, or comments additional to Rashi's commentary on the Babylonian Talmud. These are printed in the standard editions of the Talmud alongside the text—Ed.

4. The statement occurs in a Tossafist comment to *Yevamoth* 50a and refers to the prophecy in 1 Kings 13:2 concerning the birth of Josiah. The Tossafist points out the contingency of this prophecy, which might have remained unfulfilled had not Hezekiah repented, been granted additional years of life, and subsequently begat Menasseh, Josiah's father. He answers that the prophet prophesized what ought to have happened had Hezekiah not sinned and been punished with illness—Ed.

5. The Frankists were a Sabbatean sect among Polish and Moravian Jews led by Jacob Frank (1726–1791). In the sixties of the eighteenth century many of them, including Frank himself, converted to Christianity, even as Sabbatai Zevi converted to Islam—Ed.

6. For several centuries Yemenite Jewry was strongly influenced by Maimonides. His halakhic rulings were generally accepted and his theological outlook dominated learned circles. The efflorescence of Palestinian Kabbalah in the sixteenth century left its mark on the practice and thought of Yemenite Jewry, as it did all over the Diaspora. Rabbi Yahieh Qafah led a religious movement in the early years of this century, which might be described as a return to Maimonides. The terms "long-nosed" and "short-nosed" are ultra-literal renditions of widespread appellations for two groups of *Sefiroth* (emanations). "Decemy," referring to the system of Sefiroth in its entirety, was intended to suggest a parallel to the Christian Trinity—Ed.

7. The epithets "great eagle" and others occur frequently in references to Maimonides in the rabbinic literature—Ed.

8. Kabbalists who reacted in this manner include Rabbi Joseph Karo, in *Maggid Mesharim,* R. Meir ibn Gabbai in *Avodath ha-Kodesh,* the Vilna Gaon, and others.

9. B. T. *Sukkah* 52a.

10. Maimonides, *Mishneh Torah: Book of Knowledge*, "Laws Concerning the Basic Principles of the Torah," I, 1.

11. The sentences in quotes are taken from passages recited before the morning prayer. The reference to Maimonides' Code is to the third clause of the opening chapter—Ed.

12. The quoted phrases are taken respectively from the benediction before reading or studying the Torah and from the Qiddush of the holidays—Ed.

13. Maimonides' responsa.

14. *Mishneh Torah: Book of Knowledge*, "Laws Concerning the Basic Principles of the Torah," VII.

15. R. Meir Simhah Cohen, *Meshekh Hokhmah* to Exodus 32:19.

35

Beyond Innocence and Redemption

MARC ELLIS

Just days after the beginning of the Palestinian uprising Thomas Friedman, a reporter for the *New York Times,* wrote a provocative article with the telling title, "How Long Can Israel Deny Its Civil War?" His thesis, backed by statistics from the West Bank Data Project, was that the new outbreak of hostilities was simply an escalation of a decade of violence. "There is a new trend in Palestinian resistance," Friedman quotes Meron Benvenisti, director of the West Bank Data Project. "Palestinian violence is largely out in broad daylight by individuals and groups who spontaneously express their feelings, undeterred by the consequences of their actions. The fact that there are more killings shows the rising frustration level of the occupiers and the occupied. Before, the Palestinians were afraid of the Israeli soldiers, but they are not anymore." As Friedman concludes his article, "Indeed, maybe the real lasting effect of the past two weeks of violence will be to force Israelis and Palestinians to realize that they have been talking about their conflict in obsolete language. Yes, it is still territorially based—but the territories in dispute are not the West Bank and Gaza strip, but all of Palestine." A year and a half later in June 1989, with over five hundred Palestinians dead and fifty thousand injured, the Israeli army chief of staff, Dan Shomron, was reported by the *Times* as saying that only harsher measures can halt the uprising. "People ask why we don't end the *intifada.* Whoever demands the wiping out of the *intifada* has to remember that there are only three ways to achieve it: transfer, starvation or physical extermination—that is, genocide."[1]

This, then, marks the distance traveled from the trial of Adolph Eichmann to Jerusalem. When Friedman writes of civil war and Shomron speaks of genocide, they are voicing a reality that remains unspoken: that the occupation is over, and now the options are narrowed to justice, expulsion, or annihilation. Described as a war of attrition, the best that

Marc Ellis, *Beyond Innocence and Redemption* (New York: Harper and Row, 1990), pp. 156–64, 177–90. © Harper Collins Publishers, New York, NY 10022.

can be claimed is that the uprising is "under control." These are the words of Defense Minister Yitzhak Rabin, who in December 1989 promised to continue the "confrontations, the hitting, the arresting, the introduction of the plastic bullet, the rubber bullet and the curfews on a large scale."[2]

With the narrowed choices before the Jewish community, what does Jewish theology have to say at this most critical time? As we have seen, Irving Greenberg has written at length, yet his analysis seems impotent before the need to make a fundamental choice rather than a corrective maneuver. The framework of Holocaust theology itself mitigates serious discussion and decision on the fundamental challenge before the Jewish people: to move beyond innocence and redemption and to realize the cost of Jewish empowerment. And what do other theologians who work in the shadow of Holocaust theologians, the progressive Jewish theologians like Arthur Waskow, have to contribute? Waskow's essential response to the uprising and the Israeli measures to repress it is that if one loves Israel, work for Jewish renewal in the United States. From other theologians, there is silence, or tired repetition of old arguments.[3]

Confronting State Power

The challenge to the Jewish community now is a critical retrieval of the tradition of dissent and the incorporation of Palestinian voices in the Jewish experience. What has been offered by theologians and commentators thus far lacks the empathy and ability to achieve this. The litmus test posed by David Biale, a symmetry of suffering and rights between Jews and Palestinians over the last forty years, is a false symmetry. The Palestinians have been done a great historical wrong by the Jewish people. The only way forward, it seems, is a solidarity with the Palestinian people that is at the same time confessional and political. Could we say that the task of Jewish theology is to lay the groundwork for solidarity with the Palestinian people and that any theology that does not pose that as the central question is a theology that legitimates torture and murder? To carry out this task means first of all that Jewish self-perception needs to be radically altered and the framework of discussion drastically reoriented. And if the tradition of dissent is to be politically efficacious before Shomron's options are invoked, that is, if Jews are serious about dissent and not simply demonstrating that Jews have in fact protested, then a new Jewish self-understanding needs to be created. Unfortunately, it is doubtful that mainstream theologians will be of help in this matter, for like Holocaust theologians they, at least in their theological writings, pretend Palestinians hardly exist. The works of Eugene Borowitz, Michael Wyschogrod, and David Hartman exemplify this neglect and this failing.[4]

The initial dilemma Jews face may be stated in the following way. For the first time in two thousand years Jews have a state of their own. Jewish dissenters inside and outside Israel have to confront a state power controlled by Jews with a theology that tells Jews that to confront Jewish state power is to delegitimate it and thus confrontation is an act that leads to suicide. Of course, this dilemma is complicated by the fact that 75 percent of the Jews in the world live outside Israel and thus confront that state's power outside its political framework. And finally, there is no way of confronting Israeli power without breaking through the myths of innocence and redemption that are used by Jews to legitimate the state. From these perspectives, with the testimony available, there is little choice but to commit the excommunicable sin—undermine the legitimacy of Israel. If this, however, is the option, many Jews would agree with Roberta Strauss Feuerlicht when she writes, "Zionists executed the psychological coup of the century by taking Palestine from the Arabs and then pretending Jews were Arab victims. Yet this wrong cannot be righted by another. Israel exists and must continue to exist; the alternative would mean another holocaust."[5]

But this is precisely the dead end of Jewish dissent, the place where the rough edges are unfolded and the litmus test invoked. There is no state in the world that can or does, in an ultimate sense, base its existence on moral right, despite rhetoric to the contrary. The recognition of a state, its basis, lies in its ability to govern a specific territory with enough consent, volunteered or coerced, to allow that governance. Israel, like the United States or the Soviet Union, India or Guatemala, exists as a state for better and for worse because it has the requisite power and consent to govern. To lose that ability to govern is to change political leadership; threats from the outside can be met with moral and po-litical suasion, but ultimately the military guarantees survival. Thus Israel exists because it exists, that is, because it is able to assert enough power and gain enough consent to sur-vive. This of course is true for a Palestinian state as well; it can be claimed as a right, it can be declared to exist, but it will come into being only when it is able to govern a ter-ritory with enough power and consent to make it viable.

So the argument is not about the existence of Israel but, rather, about the question of a Jewish state. At this point in history there is little doubt that to participate fully in Israeli society one has to be of Jewish descent, though beyond birth to Jewish parents there seems little demanded. What helps Jews rise in Israeli society is what helps people to rise in many societies: social and cultural background, class, and education. What then is the context of the term Jewish in the title Jewish state? This is the crux of the matter and why many Jews sense that normalization is hardly enough. And we are now aware that many of Israel's "normal" policies over the years—organized displacement and continuous ex-pansion, for example—are rejected, at least by the tradition of dissent, as unacceptable to Jewish history and struggle over the millennia. To frame this discussion in a prophetic-normalization dichotomy is to miss the significance and depth of the questions placed be-fore Jews by Jewish history and the inclusive liturgy of destruction.[6]

The term self-determination, that Jews deserve the ability to decide their own fate in their own country like all other peoples, and that the denial of that right is perforce a sign of anti-Jewishness is, like the term Holocaust, ambiguous and lacking in context. For most groups and individuals, historically and in the present, the ability to determine their own future is part of sometimes successful, other times unsuccessful struggles within com-munal and nation-state systems. Aside from the larger question of the meaning of self-determination, self-determination as regards Jews is also complex. Some measure of self-governance is found in Diaspora Orthodox Jewish communities, as it has been found throughout the last two thousand years, and the offer of participation in a pluralist arena of self-determination seems to achieve (not without its difficulties, of course) what most Jews appear to want: participation in the public realm with others of like and unlike mind. It would be hard to argue, for example, that the Jewish community does not participate in the American political process. On the contrary, everything points to the opposite con-clusion; that is, it participates and influences the process well beyond its small numbers in the American population.[7]

Pluralism is thus crucial to the discussion of self-determination. Dissenting groups, both Jewish and non-Jewish, in the United States are no further from state power than

dissenting groups in Israel. There is clearly a pluralism in Israel, found in different political parties, associations, and interest groups, that is similar to that in other countries, except that in this case the major and minor participants are Jewish. Yet, over 18 percent
of the Israeli population within the 1967 borders, and over 40 percent if the occupied territories are included, are, as Palestinians, removed from the normal acts of self-determination. This Palestinian population suggests a possibility of pluralism beyond that within
the Jewish community. The uprising points to a large population, pluralist in its own ways,
yearning to participate in the process of self-determination—yet forced to act outside the
legal processes of Israeli society.

Today Jews throughout the world participate in pluralist activities of self-determination, including in Israel. Yet the historical question remains of the need, in nineteenth-
and early twentieth-century Europe and during and after the Holocaust, for a self-gov-
erning Jewish community. In retrospect, a minority of Jews felt strongly about this need,
strong enough to leave their homes or, if refugees, to choose a more difficult life in
Palestine than was available in other countries. The quest for identity and for some of the
attachment of that identity with the ancient Jewish homeland is hard to deny; one would
not want to argue with it. The problem lies less in the desire than in the actuality, for self-
determination has a price for which another people pays dearly.

From the literature, however, self-determination had a twofold and sometimes contradictory raison d'être: the desire to be free to define oneself, and the renewal of Jewish
spirit and culture. This first purpose involved political independence, the government and
the army; the second cultural and spiritual regeneration, the land and the university. Self-
determination was seen as a means for the unencumbered development of Jewish life,
though priority, political or cultural, was crucial to how one saw that development and
what one was willing to do to achieve it.[8]

Ultimately the quest for self-determination was and remains a historical one. What is
the mission and witness of the Jewish people? What does it mean to be Jewish? Is
Jewishness achieved best within an almost totally Jewish framework or in an environment
with others accepted in the personal and public arena as equals? Substantive questions,
like these of course, are always found and worked through in a historical context. Judah
Magnes, for example, found it important for Jewish renewal in the first half of the twentieth century to have an enlarged Jewish community in Palestine. But he also placed limitations on the importance of Jewish return by refusing to displace another people in pursuit of that goal, as he also limited the definition of Jewish self-determination by arguing
for autonomy and integration with the Palestinian Arabs.

The question then and now, as Magnes, Buber, and Arendt saw it, is not whether Jews
should live in Palestine but how the community in Palestine is to be organized. A bina-
tional state with Jewish autonomy, integrated into a larger pluralistic structure was one
possibility. Another possibility was an exclusive Jewish state, which would create the consequent need for territory filled with Jews and free of Arabs. It is this latter choice that
underlies the continuing expulsion of Palestinian Arabs. Settlements are created; the West
Bank and Gaza are left economically underdeveloped; and the territories are de facto an-
nexed, leading to the expulsion of the population to Jordan and Lebanon. These actions
are components of a logical policy deriving from the choice of communal organization.
The Palestinians are therefore right: the choice to pursue a small or enlarged Jewish state
demands either subservience of the Arab population or, better yet, their disappearance into
neighboring countries. However, Palestinians were not alone in this understanding: dis-

senting Jewish Zionists felt that this policy would defeat the intent of Jewish renewal and instead create a cycle of violence and destruction in which Jews would be either master or victim, or both at the same time.[9]

Self-determination in an exclusively Jewish state, even when 18 or 40 percent of the people are non-Jewish, creates a further question relating to Jewish history: Are Jews essentially a ghetto people? The irony of the demand for self-determination today, especially for those who live in democratic pluralistic states, is that Israel can be seen in a ghetto framework, seen as an isolated, ingathered community unable to move freely in the area that surrounds it, in constant fear of annihilation, and dependent on others for moral, political, economic, and military support. In this way Israel can be seen as approaching a ghettolike reality in continuity with the ghettos of eastern Europe, albeit an empowered ghetto. The Zionist dream that all Jews will come to live in Israel by choice or through emigration forced by anti-Jewishness at a future time has undergone a painful reversal. As Feuerlicht comments: "Israelis should not be preparing to receive American Jews; American Jews should be preparing to receive Israelis."[10]

The ghetto quality of Jewish Israeli life is, with its concomitant choices, encouraged at least partly in Holocaust theology. Between the lines and sometimes directly within innocence and redemption is the foreboding image of a future holocaust. Wiesel's travel to Israel during the 1967 war was not undertaken in anticipation of sharing a victory toast but with a sense of defeat and annihilation. Anyone who reads Holocaust theology and who has spoken with Jewish Israelis realizes that one subtext of life in Israel is the prospect of annihilation or, because of Israel's power, a fight to the finish. The Masada complex, Jews choosing suicide rather than be conquered by the Romans, has been analyzed ad nauseam, yet the truth of that complex can only be seen as relational, in the context of innocence and redemption. Only then does the last stand of the Jewish people make sense. There is a feeling in Holocaust theology and in Israel, beneath Wiesel's tears and the *sabras'* toughness, that Israel is a dream that cannot last. This time, however, because of the power of Israel, others will perish as well. One might call innocence, redemption, and the last stand a dangerous and unholy trinity that threatens the Jewish people more gravely than the Christian Trinity ever had the power to do. Thus self-determination has traveled to the last stand of the Jewish people: Holocaust is past *and* future.[11]

Though the trinity that ends in the "last stand" is present in Holocaust theology, the operative trinity today is innocence and redemption coupled with expansion. This is the unspoken reality that Holocaust theology refuses to deal with. Arthur Hertzberg points this out in his letter to Wiesel: refusing to say no explicitly to expansion is to support it, because this has been and is the policy of the Israeli government. Even the Jewish voices in response to the uprising, which say no to occupation, hardly touch on this point of continuity in Israel's history. It is as if the policy of settlement and occupation that began in the 1890s is an aberration, a correctable mistake rather than a logical and consistent policy relating to the promotion of a Jewish state. The underlying ideology of state power, Likud and Labor, remains untouched, as do the first legs of the trinity, innocence and redemption. In short, to advocate the end of the occupation without discussing how the occupation is integral to the triumph of state power in Israel is to miss the significance and the possibility the uprising presents: to reappraise the entire venture. In the end the distance between Elie Wiesel and Michael Lerner, while important in the contemporary political arena, may not be as great as it at first glance seems.

Thus the task presented is to forge a new relationship to the state of Israel, rather than oppose it or dissociate oneself from it. The reality is that Jews are connected together, though in ways different than the command of state loyalty in the name of religion. That part of the literature of dissent that argues the sense of peoplehood as false, stressing primary loyalty to the state a Jew lives in—for example, the classical Reform dissent of Elmer Berger—is ultimately superficial as a way of opposing Zionism. Fackenheim is closer to the truth when he argues the commanding voice of Auschwitz as a voice speaking to the Jewish people, though his emphasis on survival almost as an end unto itself empties that voice of meaning as it is used to oppress another people.

Is there a path for the Jewish people that leads beyond American liberalism and Israeli expansionism, that is connected with the Jewish people but not so self-involved that it becomes a form of idolatry? One path might be what Orthodox Judaism once was, which is now found only among the "extreme" sects of Hasidic Judaism: a self-contained Jewish community that carries on its business wherever it is, fulfilling the law and awaiting the Messiah. The neoorthodox position of Arthur Waskow tries to combine orthodoxy and contemporary life, that is, innovative prayer and ritual with ancient tenets and beliefs, as well as a heightened political commitment from a perspective rooted in Judaism. It has found a willing audience among a minority of Jews searching for their roots. Yet its appearance of addressing the Jewish issues of our time along with American political issues is more a matter of feeling than substance. Holocaust theology quite rightly surfaces Holocaust and Israel as the central questions of our time, and neoorthodox reform movements skirt these issues with alacrity.[12]

One of the major problems that both Holocaust and neoorthodox theology share in different ways is a self-defeating self-involvement—a preoccupation, as it were, with being authentically Jewish. The United Jewish Appeal dinners and the weekend *hauvorot* of progressive Jews gathering to celebrate the Sabbath, all fine in their own right, can become engines of self-affirmation that emphasize return to land or return to self. Both represent a view of history that is oriented around Jewish experience and outlook. Both Holocaust theology and neoorthodox reform, though different in many respects, come to the same destination, Jewish affirmation.

Although Jewish affirmation is important, it is not enough. The Jewish people in Israel and America have overwhelmingly and consistently rejected religious language, the language of ritual and prayer, as the vehicle of Jewish affirmation and have for at least two decades accepted Israel in its place. However, once the presumed innocence and redemption is challenged, that affirmation has to change, and the Jewish people are left with difficult questions. Is there Jewish life beyond neoorthodox Judaism and the state of Israel? Is it possible to move beyond ancient archetypes of Yavneh, where rabbis gathered after the destruction of the Second Temple and began rabbinic Judaism, and Masada, where almost a thousand Jews committed suicide rather than be conquered by the Romans? Again Holocaust theology is instructive here. In his essay "To Be a Jew," Elie Wiesel writes: "Thus there would seem to be more than one way for the Jew to assume his condition. There is a time to question oneself and a time to act; there is a time to tell stories and a time to pray; there is a time to build and a time to rebuild. Whatever he chooses to do, the Jew becomes a spokesman for all Jews, dead and yet to be born, for all beings who live through him and inside him. His mission was never to make the world Jewish but, rather, to make it more human." And in his essay "Cloud of Smoke, Pillar of Fire," Irving Greenberg writes: "After the Holocaust no statement, theological or otherwise, should be made that would be not credible in the presence of the burning children," and, "The victims ask us above all not to allow the creation of another matrix of values that might sustain another attempt at genocide."[13]

The way forward is not to abandon the dialectic that Holocaust theology poses, or to skirt it, but to reassert and broaden it, to see Holocaust and empowerment as ways of connecting Jews to the world rather than isolating them from it. It is to see ourselves as Jews in history rather than simply creating a Jewish history. The question of survival and the assertion of Jewishness, as articulated by Wiesel and Greenberg, take second place to the quality of Jewish witness. In a sense this is to restate the obvious; as Jews we are in history with others, and Jewish particularity should be a sign of affirmation to ourselves and to others as well. The singled-out condition about which Fackenheim writes needs to be transformed as a calling into history for the sake of others, as a sign of fidelity and solidarity. Attempts to move beyond vulnerability to the self-assured strut of a people who know who they are and will defend that affirmation against everyone and everything to the end only create a people who hasten that end. If Jewish history teaches Jews that survival is fragile and must be guarded, it also tells us that survival without witness is ultimately meaningless.[14]

Today more than anything Jews need clarity of thought—freedom to think through relationships with the Holocaust and with Israel unencumbered by the threat of excommunication. The tradition of dissent provides one such avenue, as exemplified by Judah Magnes and Noam Chomsky. The liturgy of destruction provides another in the voice of the Palestinian people. Paradoxically the bridge between the tradition of dissent and the liturgy of destruction may be Christians, who now participate in both.

· · ·

A Coalition of Messianic Trust

Perhaps, paradoxically, it is in dialogue with our former enemies, Western Christians, and our present "enemies," Palestinians, that the possibility of Jewish renewal of the hidden tradition can take place. Such a dialogue addresses the two formative events of our time—Holocaust and Israel—and provides an avenue for healing and repentance so crucial to the emergence of critical thought. Only after healing and repentance can the commanding voice of Auschwitz be realized in its particularity with its universal implications and the liturgy of destruction expanded so that we can be honest with ourselves. It is in this framework that our relation to Holocaust and Israel may move beyond innocence and redemption, which have become for Jews and Palestinians burdensome and oppressive.

If Martin Buber led the way in the 1950s with a willingness to reach out to the German people, it is Johann Baptist Metz, a German Catholic theologian, and Gustavo Gutierrez, a Latin American liberation theologian, who provide glimpses of the difficult path from the Christian side, as well as the possibility of life for Jews beyond the Holocaust.

Metz's essay, "Christians and Jews After Auschwitz," is worth contemplating in this regard. He begins with a question to his fellow Christians: "Will we actually allow Auschwitz to be the end point, the disruption which it really was, the catastrophe of our history, out of which we can find a way only through a radical change of direction achieved via new standards of action? Or will we see it only as a monstrous accident within this history but not affecting history's course?" Metz answers his own question by asserting that the future of Christianity is dependent on an affirmative answer to the first question: a radical change of direction is demanded. However, this cannot be accomplished through abstract reflection on dogma or even on the complicity of the Church; it cannot be accomplished by personal Christian reflection or even institutional action alone. The change can occur only by embracing the suffering and the heirs of that suffering.[15]

According to Metz, Christians are from now on "assigned to the victims of Auschwitz—assigned, in fact, in an alliance belonging to the very heart of saving history." Thus Metz considers insulting and incomplete any attempts at Christian theology and language about meaning when they are initiated outside the Holocaust or try in some way to transcend it. Meaning, especially divine meaning, can be invoked only to the extent that such meaning was not abandoned in Auschwitz itself. This is why Metz responds to the question whether it is possible for a Christian to pray after Auschwitz in the affirmative: "We can pray after Auschwitz because people prayed *in* Auschwitz."[16]

Metz's understanding of history is dynamic, as a calling forth of memory and as a movement into the future. The alliance Metz projects within saving history, that is, within the particularity of being Jewish and Christian but also somehow affecting both together at the deepest level, is a call to the common task of resistance, that might include new suffering. This saving historical alliance would, in the first instance, mean the radical end of every persecution of Jews by Christians, surely an understandable goal of dialogue. But again, Metz moves beyond dialogue. If any persecution were to take place in the future, it could only be a persecution together, of Jews and Christians—*as it was in the beginning.* The reason for this common persecution in the beginning—the refusal to recognize the Roman emperor as God that called into question the foundations of Rome's political religion and thus branded Christians and Jews as atheists—is a call to political activity in the contemporary world. Still more, however, is the vision of embrace that arises from this analysis. Metz cautiously suggests that Jews and Christians could arrive one day at a "coalition of messianic trust in opposition to the apotheosis of banality and hatred present in our world." Thus the memory of suffering is a call beyond dialogue to an embrace that lies at the very root of the struggle to be faithful in a world of injustice and oppression.[17]

Metz calls Christians to carry the victims of their history with them into the future. Put more strongly, there is no future for Christianity unless the victims of Christian history are heard in the present. But can the victims of Christian history embrace their oppressors? Can the victims of Christian history, in this case the Jews, specifically in the contemporary manifestation of the Holocaust, enter this coalition of messianic trust by choice, open to the transformations that lie before them, including the possibility of persecution? Is the call of Auschwitz the same for Jews as it is for Christians? And if we know that only a minority of Christians has embarked on the road that Metz so hauntingly outlines, can we expect more than a minority of Jews to see such a road as possible after Auschwitz? And what does it mean if a minority of Jews and Christians affirms this coalition of messianic trust—not in the theological abstraction but in political action that may lead to suffering?

Though, for Gustavo Gutierrez, the answers are far from clear, the questions raised by the Holocaust are present in his own people. Queried whether, because of the suffering he witnesses, Gutierrez doubts the existence of God, he responds, "Existence no; God's presence everyday." Here Latin American theologians are quite close to Holocaust theologians. That is why Elie Wiesel can feel a camaraderie with Gutierrez, expressed in a greeting on the occasion of Gutierrez's sixtieth birthday.

> I feel very close to Gustavo Gutierrez, even though we have not met one another. We share a common passion for Job—whose situation intrigues and saddens us at the same time—and a need to believe that God has not abandoned creation. Some theologians would describe our approach as "liberative." And indeed, why not? I feel at home with the term "liberation." Because we are created in the image of God, we human beings ought to be free just as God is free. And, like God, we should want to be vehicles of freedom for others. Or, to put it another way, those persons are truly human who recognize themselves in the freedom of others, and who measure the extent of their own freedom by its relationship to that of their fellow human beings. It was in order that we might be free that God chose to create us. Persons who live in fear, in oppression, in hunger, in misery, are not free. What remains free, however, is their thirst for freedom, their desire to free themselves—the part of them that God, as only God can do, loves to enlighten in the fulfillment of hope.
>
> Yes, I feel very close to Gustavo Gutierrez. Along with him, I believe that God is not an abstraction but a living presence. To the prisoner, God represents memory, to the starving, a smile; and to the wandering exile, a companion on the way.
>
> The mystical tradition teaches us that even God is in exile. In the process of freeing the oppressed from their oppression, and the humiliated from their shame, we are likewise freeing God.[18]

Gustavo Gutierrez's recent meditation on the Book of Job is also important in this emerging solidarity of Christians and Jews. If for Metz the ability to pray continues for Christians after Auschwitz because some Jews continued to pray in Auschwitz, and if this connection allows a coalition of messianic trust in the future as once existed in the past, Gutierrez's thought allows Jews to see the possibility of God amid suffering as a call to commitment within the present.

Gutierrez's book, *On Job,* revolves around the question of how one can speak about God amid suffering, especially the suffering of the innocent. "How are we to talk about a God who is revealed as love in a situation characterized by poverty and oppression? How are we to proclaim the God of life to men and women who die prematurely and unjustly? How are we to acknowledge that God makes us a free gift of love and justice when we have before us the suffering of the innocent?"[19]

Gutierrez begins by differentiating between the questions that modernity poses, that is, how it is possible to believe in God in a world of technology, science, and affluence—questions posed to the Western Christian world—and the question that innocent suffering poses to those on the margins of society, that is, how it is possible to believe in God when your experience is one of abuse and injustice, as it too often is in the Third World. For Gutierrez, the distinction of these two situations is illustrated in the difference between Blaise Pascal, the great European philosopher, and Job:

> In Pascal's case, the wager has to do with the existence or nonexistence of God. The question Pascal asks is: "Which will you choose?" In Job the choice is between a religion based on the rights and obligations of human beings as moral agents, and a disinterested belief based on the gratuitousness of God's love. Pascal employs a crystal-clear, almost mathematical logic in responding to the questionings of the modern mind and the first manifestations of unbelief. In Job the challenges arising from the suffering of the innocent are met in a tortuous trial in which progress is made through a

series of violent jolts. Pascal warns that a choice must be made between unbelief and God, and points out that not to choose is to choose: "You must wager. There is no choice; you are already committed." In Job the choice is between a religion that sets conditions for the action of God and applies a calculus to it, and a faith that acknowledges the free initiative at work in God's love; to make no choice is to live in despair or cynicism.[20]

For Gutierrez, Pascal issues his wager to bourgeois nonbelievers; the wager in Job is issued in the world of the nonpersons. Pascal's wager is the first step to meet the challenge of modernity; the wager in Job starts on the garbage heap.[21]

According to Gutierrez, Job undergoes two transformations of viewpoint as he begins to reject the doctrine of retribution for the suffering of the innocent. The first occurs when he realizes that the suffering of the innocent is broader than his own individual suffering and that the real issue is the suffering and injustice that mark the lives of the poor: "Those who believe in God must therefore try to lighten the burden of the poor by helping them and practicing solidarity with them." The speeches of God to Job occasion the second shift, in which Job begins to understand that justice is found within a horizon of freedom formed by the gratuitousness of God's love. Thus the Book of Job for Gutierrez poses two types of language about God, the language of prophecy, which opposes at every turn the suffering of the innocent, and the language of contemplation, which within the commitment to justice allows a vision beyond the present and the actual. "In the Book of Job, to be a believer means sharing human suffering, especially that of the most destitute, enduring a spiritual struggle, and finally accepting the fact that God cannot be pigeonholed in human categories." In contemporary times this is what Luis Espinal, a priest murdered in Bolivia, was doing when he wrote: "Train us, Lord, to fling ourselves upon the impossible, for behind the impossible is your grace and your presence; we cannot fall into emptiness. The future is an enigma, our road is covered with mist, but we want to go on giving ourselves, because you continue hoping amid the night and weeping tears through a thousand human eyes." For Gutierrez, this is what Job did: "He flung himself into an enigmatic future. And in this effort he met the Lord."[22]

Thus the questions of Job are contemporary questions for the poor and suffering of Latin America. They are for Gutierrez similar questions to the ones faced in the Jewish Holocaust. Yet while the questions flowing from the Holocaust remain, the suffering has ended. For Latin Americans, however, the suffering increases daily. Gutierrez sees the Holocaust as an "inescapable challenge to the Christian conscience and an inexcusable reproach to the silence of many Christians" during the Nazi period, but for Latin Americans the question is not precisely "How are we to do theology after Auschwitz?"

> The reason is that in Latin America we are still experiencing every day the violation of human rights, murder, and the torture that we find so blameworthy in the Jewish Holocaust of World War II. Our task here is to find the words with which to talk about God in the midst of the starvation of millions, the humiliation of races regarded as inferior, discrimination against women, especially women who are poor, systematic social injustice, a persistent high rate of infant mortality, those who simply "disappear" or are deprived of their freedom, the sufferings of peoples who are struggling for their right to live, the exiles and the refugees, terrorism of every kind, and the corpse-filled common graves of Ayacucho. What we must deal with is not the past but, unfortunately, a cruel present and a dark tunnel with no apparent end.[23]

Therefore in Peru, as in all of Latin America, the question shifts: "How are we to do theology while Ayacucho lasts? How are we to speak of the God of life when cruel murder on a massive scale goes on in 'the corner of the dead'? How are we to preach the love of God amid such profound contempt for human life? How are we to proclaim the resurrection of the Lord where death reigns, and especially the death of children, women, the poor, indigenous, and the 'unimportant' members of our society?"[24]

If Metz and Gutierrez articulate the Jewish and Christian experience of suffering, as well as raise questions about God's presence amid that suffering, Carter Heyward, an Episcopal priest, continues the relation and moves it forward. In her first book, *The Redemption of God: A Theology of Mutual Relation,* Heyward attempts to rethink Christology through the ethical demands of justice and the suffering of the innocent. The Holocaust figures prominently in her analysis, and two chapters of her book deal with the questions of theodicy raised by Elie Wiesel. For Heyward, the questions posed remain; they suggest patterns of relation that bind us as human beings together and in so doing suggest a different way of addressing one another and God. The Holocaust and other human suffering, especially the suffering of women, call Christians to reevaluate their understanding of God and Christology itself. Jesus becomes neither Lord nor divine but rather brother and sister: "Jesus is to be remembered, not revered. Remembering Jesus does not warrant Jesusolatry or Christolatry, idolatry of a male God. Remembering Jesus does not warrant the worshipping of Jesus, but rather compels us to be open to the God of Jesus, the one whom Jesus called 'Abba': Daddy. Moreover, to remember Jesus does not mean that we 'imitate' Jesus, but rather that, like him, we seek to act with God in our own time, under the political, social, psychological, physical, and institutional conditions of our own place." Heyward's reimaging of God and Jesus are to some extent indebted to and remarkably close to the early Wiesel and Irving Greenberg as well.[25]

Heyward's passion for justice takes her deeper into feminist analysis and to many of the troubled areas of the Third World. In August 1984 she, along with other teachers and students of the Episcopal Divinity School in Cambridge, journeyed to Nicaragua to investigate the impact of American foreign policy on the Nicaraguan revolution and the call of Christian faith in response to these policies. For us, the important aspect of Heyward's sojourn among the Nicaraguan people is the discovery of what she terms *revolutionary forgiveness.* This forgiveness of those who have harmed the people, the former guards of Somoza, the contras, and those who arm the contras, the government of the United States, at first startled Heyward and her companions. Yet upon reflection its logic became clear. Revolutionary forgiveness had nothing to do with forgetting injustice but, rather, understanding and overcoming it. To begin with, an important distinction between persons and oppressive systems has to be made, and revolutionary forgiveness has as its corequisite that systems and structures of injustice be changed. Heyward writes:

> Those who forgive must be wise as serpents, and the act of forgiving must be as strategically potent as it is spiritually potent. Which is why, at this time, the Sandinistas cannot forgive the contras. People cannot simply "forgive"—invite back into their lives on a mutual basis—those who continue to do harm to them and their people. We do not believe that any of us can forgive those who continue to violate us. Otherwise "forgiveness" is an empty word. Forgiveness is possible only when the violence stops. Only then can those who have been violated even consider the possibility of actually loving those who once brutalized and battered them. Only then can the former victims

empower the victimizers by helping them to realize their own power to live as liberated liberators, people able to see in themselves and others a corporate capacity to shape the future.[26]

This is how Heyward interpreted Tomas Borge's forgiveness of his torturer: "His act of forgiveness was an invitation—in spite of what had happened—in which Borge was signaling his desire that this man come into right-relation with him and with the Nicaraguan revolutionary movement. To try to forget acts of violence which have been done to us is foolish, probably impossible. To base forgiveness on remembering what happened is to move toward the future in the belief that we will be stronger together than we would be apart. Borge may have determined also that after persons are forgiven they are at least as likely to join those who forgave them as to repeat their violent behavior. Forgiveness can also be a pragmatic political act."[27]

Thus, for Heyward, revolutionary forgiveness hardly sentimentalizes injustice or allows it to continue. Instead, it carries with it a knowledge of power that seeks to transform injustice, to remember as a way of creating a future beyond injustice, to confess in order to acknowledge wrong relations, to repent as a commitment to stop the injustice, and to provide solidarity with the victims of injustice.[28]

Heyward's understanding of revolutionary forgiveness as acts of reconciliation within the context of achieving justice brings us to consider again Rosemary Radford Ruether's description of false messianism as the use of a dream of a redeemed life to cover over lies and deception. False messianism is in opposition to revolutionary forgiveness and undermines the very possibility of breaking the cycle of injustice. We might say that false messianism deliberately makes revolutionary forgiveness impossible as it seeks to label those who see through it as traitors who endanger the existence of the community. Ruether contrasts false messianism with the prophetic hope, which seeks a "self-critical and transformative relationship to the divine call and future hope." Prophetic hope judges historical reality by its distance from the ideal rather than covering up this distance with deception. Thus prophetic hope calls the critic to reform reality, beginning with oneself, to bring self and society closer to the divine ideal. "It is by keeping human hopes and ideals as critical measuring rods to judge historical reality, rather than using them as ideological self-sacralization, that one keeps redemptive hopes from being turned into false messianism." The signs of prophetic hope are similar to the process of revolutionary forgiveness. "When one person is not another's evil, one people's redemption is not another people's damnation. Graced moments are moments of repentance that create reconciliation and overcome enmity."[29]

The importance of the analysis of Christian thought now comes into focus. Metz's search for a coalition of messianic trust, Gutierrez's realization that the massacres of the innocent continue in the corner of the dead, Heyward's revolutionary forgiveness, and Ruether's prophetic hope are all rooted to some extent in the Jewish Holocaust; each attempts to rethink Christian commitment in that light. That is, they have taken the challenge of Jewish history as a confrontation with their own and as a challenge to create a Christianity of justice and compassion. What is ironic is that the process of dialogue has shifted to become a newly thought-out Christian theology challenging Jewish theology and history. Could it be that the issues of trust and forgiveness, suffering in the present and prophetic hope, represent critical thought that cannot (at this point) be generated within the Jewish community? Could it be that the new dialogue partner for the revival of the

Jewish hidden tradition will be less modern secular thought than the critical Christianity being fashioned by such theologians as we have analyzed? In touch with the Jewish experience and searching for a Christianity beyond false piety and triumphalism, Metz, Gutierrez, Heyward, and Ruether may be where Arendt and Buber and the deepest inclinations of Wiesel and Greenberg find a connective challenge. But this can only happen if Christians offer and Jews receive critical solidarity, that is, a solidarity that moves beyond frightened silence or paternalistic embrace. Critical solidarity at this point in Jewish history means confronting Jewish theology and policies that legitimate oppression. Here, Ruether is the only one of these theologians to take this most important step. To take the Holocaust seriously without condemning the brutality of the Israeli occupation is no longer enough.[30]

A critical solidarity brought forth through our former enemies may presage a conversion favoring our present "enemies," the Palestinian people. If Metz is correct that Christians in the West can only move forward with the victims of Christianity, the Jewish people, it is also true that the Jewish people can only move forward with the victims of Jewish empowerment, the Palestinian people. In fact, the challenge of the Palestinians in their struggle for freedom and dignity is one that necessitates the revival of critical thought. The issues they raise in their rebellion against oppression are exactly those that are in need of reclamation: separation of religion and power, the use of Jewish history as a path of generosity rather than oppression, the renewal of Jewish life as a contribution to creative and pluralistic cultures rather than a univocal and thus stultifying imposition of one culture on another. As important is the recognition of Jewish history in the faces of the other: Palestinian suffering, diaspora, ghettoization, deportation, and murder. Emmanuel Levinas, the French Jewish philosopher, wrote that ethics arises out of the face of the other. One might expand this to say that critical thought about the systems of oppression and the theologies that legitimate them arise when we begin to be with and understand those who suffer from that oppression. Paradoxically, the critical thought and ethical possibility ensuing from such an encounter are also a bridge back to the deepest ethical impulses of the very community now betraying those values in oppression. If Jews represent the road back to the values of the Western Christian tradition, Palestinians represent a similar road back to the values of the Jewish tradition. Of course, intent in and of itself is hardly the issue; the Jewish struggle vis-à-vis Christians and the Palestinian struggle vis-à-vis the Jews is the challenge.

Yet beyond challenging others in their very being, Palestinians have also presented concrete avenues to begin the Jewish process of recovering ethics and values. The declaration of a Palestinian state on the West Bank and Gaza, recognition of the state of Israel, in effect nullifying the P.L.O. charter provision calling for the elimination of Israel—all are difficult steps that are practical, concrete invitations to Israel to settle historical grievances and begin anew. And if these seem too sweeping to begin with, other concrete proposals from within the occupied territories have surfaced as a basis for the start of negotiations. At a press conference in January 1988, a broad spectrum of West Bank and Gaza Palestinian leaders and representatives of nationalist institutions demanded that Israel,

> Abide by the 4th Geneva Convention pertaining to the protection of civilians, and declare the Emergency Regulations of the British Mandate null and void.
>
> Comply with Security Council Resolutions 605 and 607 [relating to recent deportations]. . . .

Release all prisoners arrested during the recent uprisings. . . . Rescind all proceedings against them. . . .

Cancel the policy of expulsion and allow all deported Palestinians . . . to return to their homes. . . . Release all administrative detainees. . . . Accept applications for family reunions. . . .

Lift the siege of all Palestinian refugee camps and withdraw the Israeli army from all population centers.

Conduct a formal inquiry into the behavior of soldiers and settlers, and take punitive measures against all those convicted. . . .

Cease all settlement activity and land confiscation and release lands already confiscated. . . . End the harrassment of the Arab population by settlers in the West Bank and Gaza and in the Old City of Jerusalem.

Cancel all restrictions on political freedoms including restrictions on freedom of assembly and association. Hold free municipal elections under the supervision of a neutral authority.

Remove restrictions on participation of Palestinians from the territories in the Palestine National Council . . . to ensure a direct input into the decision-making process of the Palestinian nation by the Palestinians under occupation.[31]

The steps suggested have now been complemented with a foundational approach that enjoins critical thought on both the Jewish and Palestinian sides. Naim Ateek's work, especially his challenge to Jews to admit that they have wronged the Palestinian people and to Palestinians to understand in a deeper way the European trauma through which Jews have recently passed, provide the foundational approach that, though not probing every issue of concern to either side, allows the themes enunciated earlier—trust, the continuation of suffering in the present, revolutionary forgiveness, and prophetic hope—to develop. Ateek's approach allows a process of insight and activity that moves beyond an ethic of retribution toward a future of mutual involvement, recognition, and ultimately integration. Thus he allows Jews to feel the birth of a Jewish state was necessary if they also admit that from the Palestinian perspective it was also wrong. Palestinians can continue to assert that in the process of building a Jewish state Palestinians were wronged, even as they try to understand the reasons some Jews had for such an undertaking. Ateek thus forces both sides to discard the ideological blinders that mask a false messianism: Jews are no longer innocent; Palestinians will not reclaim all of Palestine. In fact, ultimately the dreams of Jewish innocence or Palestinian restoration will give way to a desire to live in a creative environment of mutual trust that, after a long and bloody history, brings out the best in both peoples.[32]

The Revival of Critical Thought

The revival of the hidden tradition of Jewish life, that is, the resumption of a boundary position vis-à-vis political and religious power, is joined by those Western Christians and those Palestinians of Christian and Muslim background who seek a path beyond injustice and suffering. Thus, a new political and theological framework for the Jewish people is suggested as Western Christians and Palestinians similarly search out a framework requisite to the history within which they are living. It could be that the boundary position once located between the Jewish community and European civilization is now to be found at the intersection of the Jewish, Western Christian, and Palestinian communities. If we take as the task of theology the creation of a framework to nurture the questions a people needs to ask about the history it is creating, it is here in the intermingling of difficult and bloody histories that a future may be born.

First and foremost, this new configuration suggests that deabsolutization of Israel is crucial to Jewish politics and theology. Jews are essentially a diaspora people who choose to live among the peoples of the world. In essence, understanding this relativizes the geographic location of any particular Jewish community while appreciating the specific qualities of each; we begin for example to speak about the Jewish community in America and the Jewish community in Israel and Palestine. The communal organization of each community and its relation to its neighbors is less defining and more flexible, responding to the needs of the hour rather than defending an imposed order that no longer serves those needs. It may be that at this point a state organization of the Jewish community of Israel is important, but that hardly means forever. Realizing this frees Jewish theology from legitimating a state that is simply an organizational tool that furthers or hinders the essential hope of the community. In the case of the Jewish community, legitimating the state of Israel means also becoming court theologians in the United States in order to ensure its economic and military aid to Israel. As Christians found out long ago, and Jews are beginning to find out today, theologies that legitimate states tend to legitimate injustice. As I. F. Stone, a secular Jewish journalist, once remarked, "all governments are liars," and though it is startling to many Jews, Israel as a state is hardly exempt.[33]

Deabsolutizing the state of Israel means at the same time deabsolutizing the Holocaust. The effect is to rescue the Holocaust both from trivialization and a dramatization that ultimately sees the Holocaust as part of the Jewish future rather than its past. Placing the Holocaust in its historical framework also liberates Israel from the throes of redemption, a function it cannot fulfill. The Holocaust then regains its historical call to end the suffering of the Jewish people and all peoples, including and especially the Palestinian people. Thus the particular experience of suffering speaks to a world of suffering rather than simply to Jews. The call becomes one of solidarity and connectedness rather than to an affirmation characterized with anger and the experience of isolation. The dialectics of suffering and empowerment, innocence and redemption, specialness and normalization are confronted and transformed by this solidarity. As Jewish theology is freed from state building in Israel and state supporting in the United States, its vocation as an agent of critical reflection becomes possible again.

In this framework Israel becomes, at one level, a state like any other, capable of good and bad but unworthy of ultimate loyalty. Thus the framework of statehood is relativized even as the bonds between Jewish communities may grow stronger. What once evoked a theological commitment immune from criticism is now returned to its rightful place in the political arena, deserving of respect when functioning as an agent of justice, subject to criticism from the perspective of Jewish history and theology. A major element of this critical relationship to the state is helping the state bring the Jewish people into closer proximity to the Palestinian people. If the state succeeds in this task, then it paradoxically acts less like a state and more like an agent of Jewish ethics.

Jews have too often been confused on this point; to do what is necessary in Israel and Palestine means challenging a rhetoric that says that the state of Israel is completely different from other states. Solidarity with the Palestinian people means preparing for a transformation of the Jewish state into something else, perhaps a confederation or even a unified state with autonomous and integrated communities, much like the structures the early dissenters in Zion spoke of. All states are "liars"; all states seek perpetuation of their structure as a matter of course. However, the revival of critical thought may push the state of Israel to do what states are loath to do—act beyond their perceived and often enshrined interests.

The politics of Israel, even its military operations, assumes a different place in light of Jewish critical thought. Again, the challenge is whether these elements of Israel broaden the intersection of Jew and Palestinian, Jew and Arab, or narrow it. The myth of Israel's weakness is debunked by a concrete and critical evaluation of its power, and future conflicts are relegated to the business of statecraft, rather than the fear of another holocaust. The responsibility for preventing a military defeat is first and foremost a political venture to minimize the possibility of conflict. But where the interests of a state are served by exacerbating conflict then military victory or defeat can be looked at with a critical eye. At any rate, it is crucial to demythologize what every state at some point in its history experiences, military defeat. Israel's power in the Middle East is superior at this point, but in the last two wars, the Yom Kippur War in 1973 and the invasion of Lebanon in 1982, Israel, though not defeated, could hardly claim victory.[34]

It must be stated unequivocally that a military defeat of Israel would be from the Jewish Israeli side horrible, but in no way comparable to the Holocaust. Defeat would represent a political and military failure of a state organization with consequences for the Jewish community living in that state. It would represent a failure of an empowered community to come to grips with its environment. But it would not threaten the continuation of the Jewish people, as so often prophesied by Holocaust theologians. To consider military defeat is merely to prevent the kind of thinking that makes such defeat almost inevitable. The time for Israel to seek peace—which can only come with justice—is now, while the state has superior power. To see its success in war as redemptive or its failure in war as another holocaust is to take from the state of Israel responsibility for its primary role: to be a vehicle at this point in history in minimizing and then overcoming the division of Jew and Palestinian.

To shift perspectives on Holocaust and Israel is to refashion the current trends of Jewish identity, at least as defined by Jewish institutional leadership and Jewish theology. Rather than avoiding the perils of statecraft or responsibility, as Greenberg suggests, the framework for Jewish identity must question the process of normalizing that which was and ought today to be considered abnormal. Because Jews as a people are no longer innocent, and because Jews are in danger of becoming everything we loathed about our oppressors, Jews must use this experience to choose a new direction. The shift in Jewish identity occurs not by bypassing the formative events of Jewish history, the Holocaust and the state of Israel, but by reevaluating them in the light of Jewish experience with suffering and power. The task is not so much realizing the imperfections of exerting power but reorienting that power before it is too late. The stories of the broken clubs and Mengele are less exaggerations or aberrations than warnings that the entire history of Jewish suffering and struggle is in danger of being perverted, becoming in a strange twist that against which it protests. This warning also expresses intuitive connections with the Palestinian people. When today we speak of the formative events of Holocaust and Israel, Jews need to add the experience of the Palestinian people as a formative event for the Jewish people as well. To do so brings Jews beyond innocence and redemption to a posture of humility and confession. Could it be that underneath the expressions of Jewish pride and power lies the desire to be free of the limitations they impose? Could it be that Jews know they are wrong and are looking for a way beyond the oppression of others?

At the intersection of Jewish, Western Christian, and Palestinian thought and activity lies the revival of the hidden tradition of Jewish life. It is here that the most intimate and urgent questions are raised. And it is from this particular configuration that the future contribution of the Jewish people to the world will be made. That there is no theological movement of any consequence in Jewish life that promotes the revival of the hidden tradition, hence no Jewish theology that promotes critical thought, is a lamentable fact to be faced. The point where Jewish thought meets other traditions thus is often spoken of in secular terminology. The opportunity created by this meeting of traditions may give birth to a theology but is not a theology itself. Hence those who use overt theological language may mistake the revival of the hidden tradition for mere humanism, as if this itself were a critique, while mistaking its theological language for theological integrity. This is as typical of theological orthodoxy as it is of states: mistaking rhetoric for substance. Like the state of Israel, however, contemporary Jewish theology faces a test that portends its own transformation: that is, solidarity with the Palestinian people. This is where the realm of critical thought may join forces with overt religious language and move beyond the division of secular and religious. And here too lies the possibility of moving beyond innocence and redemption, beyond a false normalization, to the deepest impulses of the Jewish people.

Notes

1. Thomas L. Friedman, "How Long Can Israel Deny Its Civil War?" *New York Times,* 27 Dec. 1987, 3; quoted in Alan Cowell, "Three Palestinians Killed in Protests in the Gaza Strip," *New York Times,* 17 June 1989, 6. For Friedman's recent discussion of these issues, see his *From Beirut to Jerusalem* (New York: Farrar Straus Giroux, 1989).
2. Joel Brinkley, "Israel Defense Chief Sees Failure in Quelling Uprising," *New York Times,* 5 Dec. 1989. Also see Kenneth Kaplan, "Intifada 'Under control,'" *Jerusalem Post International,* 16 Dec. 1989.
3. For Arthur Waskow's analysis of the situation, see his "Peace and the Palestinians," *Genesis* 2 19 (Spring 1988): 8–12. Waskow essentially supports Michael Lerner's positions, though his mix of biblical imagery and contemporary politics distorts the reality of the situation.
4. See Eugene B. Borowitz, *Liberal Judaism* (New York: Union of American Hebrew Congregations, 1984); Michael Wyschogrod, *The Body of Faith: Judaism as Corporeal Election* (New York: Seabury, 1983); David Hartman, *A Living Covenant: The Innovative Spirit in Traditional Judaism* (New York: Macmillan, 1985). The challenge to see the Palestinians at the center of Jewish history and theology has been ignored. See Marc H. Ellis, *Toward a Jewish Theology of Liberation: The Uprising and the Future* (Maryknoll, NY: Orbis, 1989); idem., "Solidarity with the Palestinian People: A Jewish Theological Perspective," *New Outlook* 32 (Feb. 1989): 40–41. For Hartman's latest views, see "The Uprising: Israelis Address American Jews," *Tikkun* 3 (Mar./Apr. 1988): 19–20, and his comments in Shelley Kleiman, "On Moderate Ground: An Alternate Image of Judaism," *Jerusalem Post International,* December 1989. Analysis of these and other Jewish theologians will figure prominently in my next book on the future of Jewish theology.
5. Roberta Strauss Feuerlicht, *The Fate of the Jews: A People Torn Between Israeli Power and Jewish Ethics* (New York: Times Books, 1983), 284.
6. Of course, the other side of Jewish privilege is discrimination against Palestinian Arabs. Though

most of Jewish writing on the problems of Israel does not mention Palestinians, when they are mentioned it is in relation to the West Bank and Gaza. However, the challenge from the beginning has been Palestinians within Israel, now approximately 18 percent of the population. Essentially three policies have been applied to Palestinians within the Jewish state: expulsion, ghettoization, and second-class citizenship. For discussion of the forgotten ones, see Fouzi El-Asmar, *To Be an Arab in Israel* (Beirut, Lebanon: Institute for Palestine Studies, 1975), and Ian S. Lustick, *Arabs in the Jewish State: Israel's Control of a National Minority* (Austin TX: Univ. of Texas Press, 1980).

7. For two perspectives on Jewish influence on United States foreign policy, see Paul Findley, *They Dare to Speak Out: People and Institutions Confront Israel's Lobby* (Westport, CT: Lawrence, Hill, 1985), and Edward Tivnan, *The Lobby: Jewish Political Power and American Foreign Policy* (New York: Simon & Schuster, 1987).

8. It is interesting that despite the past and contemporary suffering in Jewish history, Jews have continually chosen to live among others in pluralist situations. This choice was reaffirmed after the Holocaust and is reaffirmed again today even with a Jewish state. Thus American Jews remain in America, and Russian Jews consistently prefer America to Israel, that is, the great majority of Jews seek the challenge of freedom and the creativity of pluralism. For an interesting discussion of these themes, see Jacob Neusner, *Stranger at Home: The Holocaust, Zionism, and American Judaism* (Chicago: Univ. of Chicago Press, 1981).

9. Simha Flapan's discovery of the continuity of policies of David Ben-Gurion and Menachem Begin in relation to Palestinians underlies the essential logic of a Jewish state. It needs to be spoken of in unequivocal terms: a Jewish state within the pre-1967 borders or encompassing the occupied territories demands the refusal of equal political, cultural, and economic rights to Palestinians. This discussion, present in the early dissenters in Zion, is largely absent among contemporary dissenters.

10. Feuerlicht, *Fate of the Jews,* 287.

11. In this regard, see an interview with Emil Fackenheim, "Western Jews' Attitude Disappoints Fackenheim," *Canadian Jewish News,* 3 Nov. 1988, 9. For Israel's ability to carry others with them, see Shai Feldman, *Israeli Nuclear Deterrence: A Strategy for the 1980s* (New York: Columbia Univ. Press, 1982), and Aaron S. Klieman, *Israel's Global Reach: Arms Sales as Diplomacy,* (Washington: Pergamon Brassey's, 1985). For the necessity of Israel's nuclear capability see Robert Harkavy, "Survival Imperatives," *Transaction: Social Science and Modern Society* 23 (January/February, 1986): 63–72.

12. Thus I would part company with those who argue the primacy of the American experience, or any national experience, for the Jewish people, including that of Israel. At this point in history Jews, like others, live within nation-state systems, but no state has an ultimate claim on our identity or loyalty. As Jews we live in America, France, or Israel, but our history existed long before and will (we hope) long after these particular forms of social organization disappear. A major task of the renewal of Jewish life is to relativize these forms of social organization, which also means that our links with state power must be questioned in Israel and the United States. Because I believe that Jewish empowerment is important and thus a return to Jewish orthodoxy (the synagogue) or an "advance" to Jewish liberalism or neoconservatism (state power) is impossible and/or a mistake, the content and means of empowerment is in need of a lengthy discussion. Suffice it to say here that this position takes issue with the positions represented by Elmer Berger, Arthur Waskow, Jacob Neusner, and Irving Greenberg. Though the content of the policy of the Jewish Committee on the Middle East is appealing, its foundational principle is not. See "Time to Dissociate from Israeli Policies," *Nation* 249 (3 Oct. 1988): 292.

13. Elie Wiesel, *A Jew Today* (New York: Vintage, 1979), 16: Irving Greenberg, "Cloud of Smoke, Pillar of Fire: Judaism, Christianity and Modernity After the Holocaust," in *Auschwitz: Beginning of a New Era?* ed. Eva Fleischner (New York: KTAV, 1977), 23, 29.

14. For a discussion of these themes of solidarity, see Marc H. Ellis, *Toward a Jewish Theology of Liberation: The Uprising and the Future* (Maryknoll, NY: Orbis, 1989), 79–84.

15. Johann Baptist Metz, *The Emergent Church: The Future of Christianity in a Postbourgeois World,* trans. Peter Mann (New York: Crossroad, 1981), 18, 19.

16. Ibid., 19.

17. Ibid., 20.

18. Elie Wiesel, "Greeting," in Marc H. Ellis and Otto Maduro, eds., *The Future of Liberation Theology: Essays in Honor of Gustavo Gutierrez* (Maryknoll, NY: Orbis, 1989), 40.

19. Gustavo Gutierrez, *On Job: God-Talk and the Suffering of the Innocent,* trans. Matthew J. O'Connell (Maryknoll, NY: Orbis, 1987), xiv.

20. Ibid., 15.

21. Ibid., 10.

22. Ibid., 92.

23. Ibid., 93.

24. Ibid. For a dialogue on Jewish theology and Latin American liberation theology see Otto Maduro, ed. *Jews, Christians and Liberation Theology* (Maryknoll, NY: Orbis, forthcoming).

25. Isabel Carter Heyward, *The Redemption of God: A Theology of Mutual Relation* (New York: Univ. Press of America, 1982), 199, 54–59.

26. Carter Heyward, Anne Gilson, et al., *Revolutionary Forgiveness: Feminist Reflections on Nicaragua* (Maryknoll, NY: Orbis, 1987), 108.

27. Ibid., 104.

28. Ibid., 103–10. Heyward concludes: "In Nicaragua, we began to see that forgiveness cannot happen unless people give up images of themselves as alone, set apart, or different and join in the struggle to build a social order in which every person and living creature is respected" (p. 110).

29. Rosemary Radford Ruether and Herman J. Ruether, *The Wrath of Jonah: The Crisis of Religious Nationalism in the Israeli-Palestinian Conflict* (San Francisco: Harper & Row, 1989), 238, 239.

30. For earlier reflections on solidarity between Jews and Christians in the struggle for liberation, see Ellis, *Jewish Theology,* 73–75. For difficulty with religious language in the face of oppression, see Joan Casanas, "The Task of Making God Exist," in *The Idols of Death and the God of Life: A Theology,* ed. Pablo Richard et al., trans. Barbara E. Campbell and Bonnie Shepard (Maryknoll, NY: Orbis, 1983), 113–49. To those who fear Christian interaction with Jewish theology in the present, a historical view is important. See Jacob Neusner, *Judaism in the Matrix of Christianity* (Philadelphia: Fortress, 1986).

31. "Palestinians Under Occupation Present Steps Toward Peace," *New York Times,* 15 Mar. 1988, 20.

32. Naim Ateek, *Justice and Only Justice: Toward a Palestinian Theology of Liberation* (Maryknoll, NY: Orbis, 1989), 168–173.

33. An example of this was the use of the American Jew John J. Pollard as a spy for Israel, which raised the question of dual loyalty for American Jews but, more substantially, the willingness of the Israeli government, like all governments, to deceive. See Fred Axelgard and Peretz Kidron, "Pollard: The Flak Flies in the U.S. and in Israel," *Middle East International,* 20 Mar. 1987, 2–6. Israel's involvement in the Iran-contra affair is another example of deception. See Jane Hunter, "The Iran-Contra Affair: Ollie's Off-the-Shelf Enterprise: Was Israel to Walk Away with It?" *Israeli Foreign Affairs* 3 (Aug. 1987): 1, 5. For a much earlier example of deception, this in relation to the Holocaust and high-level Israeli government officials in the 1950s, see Ben Hecht, *Perfidy* (New York: Julian Messner, 1961). His book is a meditation on the theme of how the conditions of state and the human condition in general are also found in the Jewish state and Jewish individuals.

34. Yehoshafat Harkabi makes a similar point when he cautions against Israel's feeling its army can overcome any adversary: "The problem is that, if Israel is so strong, it can allow itself to follow any policy perceived as being to its benefit, while ignoring possible reactions in the

world and among the Arabs. The emphasis on Israeli might is thus liable to be an impediment to rational thinking. The paradox here is that, in order to survive, Israelis must free themselves of the myth that their survival is guaranteed in all circumstances and conditions. . . . From this perspective, it may be that the Lebanon war has been an invaluable lesson." See Harkabi, *Israel's Fateful Hour,* trans. Lenn Schramm (New York: Harper & Row, 1988), 44.

Part V

Looking Toward the Future of Jewish Thought: A Symposium

The essays collected here testify to the fact that theological issues within the contemporary Jewish community are the subjects of considerable controversy. It seems only fitting, then, to conclude this anthology by presenting several contrasting perspectives on the theological enterprise and its prospects for the future.

Arthur Green's essay on "New Directions in Jewish Theology in America" serves as the point of departure for this symposium. For Green, Jewish theology is "a religious attempt to help the Jewish people understand the meaning of Jewish life and Jewish existence out of the store of texts, symbols and historical experiences that are the shared inheritance of all Jews." From this definition follow the tasks the theologian must undertake: to mine the Jewish textual tradition for insights, to interpret the historical experience of this people, and, above all, to draw from and contribute to the lived religious experience of Jews. For Green, working within a neo-hasidic tradition, this translates into a focus on God's immanence, the centrality of speech (both divine and human), and the need to locate all theological reflection in the context of religious devotion, especially prayer.

Drawing on Buber's dialogical thinking, Rebecca Alpert emphasizes relationship over immanence, diversity over unity, the resources available to the Jewish theologian from outside the tradition as much as those available from within. Thus she is prepared to embrace a Buddhist or Quaker emphasis on silence over (or alongside) a traditionally Jewish emphasis on language and speech. She also insists that Jewish theology attend to issues of justice in the social world as much as to issues of wholeness in our inner lives.

David Ellenson seeks to place contemporary Jewish theology into proper historical context. Jewish religious thought, he notes, emerges from the intersection of authentic elements within the tradition and distinctive characteristics of modern American life, including the value placed on individual experience and pluralism. Accordingly, the theological temperament of our time is necessarily "tentative and personal."

Finally, drawing on post-modern critiques of philosophy, Peter Ochs emphasizes that when theologians read Scriptural texts they enter into a process of integrating text and life. Revelation itself, for "textural reasoners" like Ochs, is not *in* the text, but in the interpretive activity of readers (both in the present and past) who reasoned with the texts and, in so doing, appropriated God's teaching for themselves. Accordingly, Ochs sees Jewish theology emerging less from "the individual's inner experiences of numinosity" or from the conceptual critique of traditional values and categories than from the intersubjective practices of a text-reasoning community.

Reading classical Jewish texts, reflecting on the experience of the Jewish people, and drawing from other intellectual and religious sources all contribute significantly to contemporary Jewish theology. Yet each thinker must determine for him or herself how to approach these tasks. Therein lies the challenge, and also the vitality, of Jewish theology. So it has always been; so it remains today and into the future.

36

New Directions in Jewish Theology in America

ARTHUR GREEN

Theology has not been the creative forte of the Jewish people throughout most of the twentieth century. We have been too busily engaged in the process of surviving to have had the energy to devote to sustained religious reflection. We have struggled to find our way as latecomers into modernity, to establish ourselves on new shores and amid unfamiliar cultural landscapes. We have survived an encounter with evil incarnate that cost us the lives of fully a third of the Jewish people, including an untold number of thinkers, teachers, and their students, hasidic masters and disciples, many of whom in better times might have helped us to figure out the puzzles of Jewish theology. For the past fifty years the Jewish people as a body politic has been fully and singlemindedly engaged in the task of reconstruction, in our case meaning above all building the State of Israel as a secure national home for the Jewish people and securing emigration rights for Jews who chose to go there. Besides these monumental undertakings, all else seemed to pale.

Nevertheless, we have hardly been bereft of theologians and religious thinkers. In recent memory there have been two bursts of theological creativity especially worthy of note. One began in the late 1960s, when such thinkers as Emil Fackenheim, Richard Rubenstein, Arthur Cohen, and others began to integrate the lessons of the Holocaust into Jewish religious parlance. The other has taken place over the course of the past two or three years and has more to do with both the recovery of religious language and the ways it may, must, or may not be updated in order to carry Jewry into the rather uncharted waters that lie ahead in what most seem to believe is a radically new era in the history of

Arthur Green, "New Directions in Jewish Theology in America," David W. Belin Lecture in American Jewish Affairs (Ann Arbor, MI: Jean and Samuel Frankel Center for Judaic Studies, University of Michigan, 1994), pp. 1–13. © Jean and Samuel Frankel Center for Judaic Studies, University of Michigan, Ann Arbor, MI 48109.

the Jewish people. Here the names of David Hartman, Irving Greenberg, Judith Plaskow, Arthur Waskow, Neil Gillman, and Eugene Borowitz all come to mind. Quite a rogues' gallery of thinkers for a people too busy to theologize!

But this latter crop of thinkers appears precisely—and hardly accidentally—at a time when I believe the Jewish people is ready for theology and, indeed, needs it urgently. I breathe deeply, add a *barukh ha-shem* [Blessed be God], and note that nowhere in the world in 5754 are there persecuted Jews who need our help. With the possible exceptions of small communities in Syria and Iran, whose condition will change as a result of progress on other fronts, there is no one through whom North American Jews can live a vicarious Jewish life or for whose sake they can postpone thinking about the nature of their own Jewishness "because there are more urgent things to do."

Indeed thinking about our own Jewishness is precisely what we Jews need most to do. We need to define our goals for the continuity of Jewish life. What do we mean by a Jewish future in America? How much of Judaism, what sort of religious life, what kind of community can we imagine existing several generations into the future? How much of assimilation can we tolerate and still survive as a distinct culture? How will we believe in our Judaism, and what will be the important Jewish experiences we will share with our children? We need to create a vision of a contemporary Judaism that will attract the coming generations and articulate a meaning deep and powerful enough to help us withstand the tremendous assimilatory powers by which we are surrounded. If there is to be a future for Jewish life on this continent, I believe that the theologian will now have a great deal to do with it.

The following remarks are offered from a particular theological point of view. I do not present them as an objective description of a historical phenomenon called Jewish Theology. They are, if you will, a theologian's rather than a historican's definition of the Jewish theologian's task. I see myself as a theologian in the tradition of an East European school of Jewish mystical theology, itself the heir of the kabbalistic and hasidic traditions. The chief figures in this school (here identified as such for the first time) in the twentieth century were Judah Loeb Alter of Ger, author of the *Sefat Emet*; Abraham Isaac Kook, chief rabbi of Palestine during the British mandate; Hillel Zeitlin, teacher and martyr of the Warsaw ghetto; and my own teacher, Abraham Joshua Heschel.

This school is defined by a sense that the starting point of theological reflection is the cultivation of inwardness and the opening of the soul to God's presence throughout the world. The members of this group may all be characterized as experientialist mystics. Each of them celebrates inward religious experience, his own as well as that provided by literary or historic example, as the primary datum with which the theologian has to work. Each in one way or another also points toward an ultimately unitive view of religious truth, a unity that transcends the borders of particularisms. They are all engaged in a search for Jewish expression of transcendent oneness, such as might "broaden the bounds of the holy" to overcome even such seemingly intimate distinctions as those between the holy and the profane or between the divine, the natural or worldly, and the human realms.

This group of thinkers also has some other key elements in common. All are awed by the constantly renewing presence of God within the natural world; they may in this sense be said to share a "Creation-centered" theological perspective. Their perspective is deeply immanentist: God is to be known by seeing existence through its "innermost point," by attaining an inward vision, or by addressing the questions of "depth theology." A certain crucial veil needs to be lifted in order to enable the mind to acheive a more profound (and essentially intuitive) view of reality. Their religion is in this sense universalistic, relating in the first instance to a divine reality that is not limited to the particular Jewish setting. Within the group there is an evolution to be traced on this question, from the *Sefat Emet*, still living within the hasidic/mythical universe which sees only the Jewish soul as potentially aware of divinity, to the much greater universalism of a Heschel, a full respecter of the spiritual legitimacy of non-Jewish religious life.

These East European spiritual teachers are all thoroughly comfortable with their Judaism, a garment that is completely natural to them. None of them is primarily a "defender" of the tradition, nor is any of them interested in proving his own orthodoxy to others. They all see *halakhah* as a natural part of the way Jews live, but they do not turn primarily to halakhic texts as their source of spiritual nurturance. In this way they are to be distinguished from another group of East European religious figures, the pan-halakhists of the Lithuanian school, who proclaim *halakhah* itself to be the only authentic expression of Judaism.

This group of Jewish mystical or experientialist theologians is also to be distinguished in the broadest terms from the German-Jewish theological developments of the nineteenth and twentieth centuries. The East Europeans published chiefly in Hebrew, secondarily in Yiddish, until Heschel brought their insights to America in expanded English translation. The German-Jewish theological enterprise was conducted entirely in the German language. The difference, perhaps seemingly a superficial one, is related to two very major divergences:

1. The East Europeans wrote for people who knew Judaism deeply from within. There was no need here to explain basic Jewish terms, beliefs, attitudes. Even kabbalistic ideas, presented in a new way by Kook or Zeitlin, would fall on well-attuned ears.

The German Jewish enterprise was a highly self-conscious one, always seeking to discover and describe the "essence" or "true spirit" of Judaism and explain it to an audience of non-Jewish as well as uninformed Jewish readers.

2. To do so convincingly (and there is much of apologetics in the air of German-Jewish thought) Judaism must be described and defended in terms set by the canon of German philosophical thought in the period, primarily Immanuel Kant and G. F. W. Hegel. Even Martin Buber and Franz Rosenzweig, who were in open existential rebellion against the over-domination of systematic philosophy, had their agendas largely set by the needs of that rebellion, by being over/against Kant, as personified by Hermann Cohen, or Hegel, the subject of young Rosenzweig's doctoral dissertation and the address of the first portion of his *Star of Redemption*.

The East Europeans, by contrast, were steeped deeply in the pre-modern Jewish religious sources and their classical idiom. When they did turn to such modern thinkers as Nietzsche or Bergson, they did so out of a sensed affinity between these writers and their own Jewish sources.

I begin my remarks with this excursus on spiritual lineage partly because I want to make it clear that I see theology as a significant undertaking only in a devotionalist context, i.e., a context where prayer (in the broadest sense), a cultivation of interiority, and awareness of divine presence in all of life are given primacy. As this may be considered a somewhat odd or off-beat position among contemporary Jews, I begin by emphasizing its historic roots. In a broader sense, the views I articulate may be called neo-hasidic. I believe that postmodern Jews' recovery of the kabbalistic-hasidic tradition is a decisive event in our ongoing spiritual history, one that should have a great impact upon the future of Jewish theology.

Bearing this legacy in mind, I shall attempt that which the tradition in its wisdom so thoroughly avoids: a definition of Jewish theology and its task. *Each Jewish theology is a religious attempt to help the Jewish people understand the meaning of Jewish life and Jewish existence out of the store of texts, symbols, and historical experiences that are the shared inheritance of all Jews.*

This definition seeks to emphasize several key points. It begins by understanding theology as a "religious" undertaking. This point is far from obvious, especially in a world where theology too often dresses itself in academic garb and seeks a borrowed legitimacy from philosophy or social science. By "religious" in this context, I mean to say that theology emerges from living participation in the life of the faith-community. It seeks to give expression in the language of that community to the essentially ineffable experience of divinity and to articulate a series of beliefs around the relationships of God, world, and person. (In the case of Judaism, there is added to this universal triad a second specifically Jewish three: God, Torah, and the Jewish people.)

In order to do this, theology must have recourse to language. Herein lies the first of many tensions that characterize the theological enterprise. The mystic knows God mostly in silence. Surely the deep well of inner awareness in which the divine is to be found reaches far beyond the grasp of words or concepts. Both personal experience and kabbalistic tradition confirm this. Knowing full well the inadequacy of words and the mental constructs they embody, the theologian has no choice but to become articulate. In this we are heirs to both the prophet and the mystical teacher who rail against their inability to refrain from speaking. We continue to rail—and continue to speak.

Our speaking is saved from *utter* inadequacy by our tradition of sacred speech. God speaks the world into being, according to our Torah, an act that is repeated each day, or perhaps even each moment, in the ongoing renewal of creation. We know that such divine speech is not in our human language, nor is the cosmic speech-act anything quite like our own. Nevertheless, the claim that the God we worship is a God of words is of value as we seek to use language to speak about the sacred. Our prayerbook introduces each day's verbal worship by blessing God "who spoke and the world came to be." Prayer is the bridge between the abstract notion of divine speech and the use of human words to speak of God. Let us say it in the language of grammar: the divine first person use of speech—God's own "I am"—is usually inaccessible to us, except in rare moments. Our third person voice in theologizing—"God is"—rings hollow and inadequate. These are brought closer by our willingness to use speech in the second person—the saying of "You" in prayer, our response to the divine "you" we feel addressed to us—which redeems speech for us and brings the divine into the world of language.

This clearly means that theology is dependent upon prayer. Prayer is a primary religious activity, a moment of opening the heart either to be filled with God's presence or to cry out at divine absence. Theology comes later, the mind's attempt to articulate and understand something that the heart already knows. In defining theology as a "religious" activity, I mean to say that it grows out of a rich and textured life of prayer. The theologian's prayer-life, which may be as filled with questioning, doubt, and challenge as it is with submission and praise, is the essential nurturer of religious thinking.

In Jewish terms, theologizing is part of the *mitsvah* of knowing God, listed by Maimonides as first among the commandments. Knowledge of God is the basis of both worship and ethics, according to many of the Jewish sages. The term *da'at*, or knowledge, bears within it a particularly rich legacy of meaning. It is best translated "awareness," the intimate and consciousness-transforming knowledge that all of being, including the human soul, is infused with the presence of the One. This *da'at*, sometimes compared in the sources to the knowledge with which Adam "knew" his wife Eve, is far more than credence to a set of intellectual propositions. It is a knowing whose roots extend back in the Tree of Life, not just to the Tree of Knowledge. We know God out of a thirst that fills our whole being. Religious knowledge, not at all the same as "information about religion," never comes in response to mere intellectual curiosity.

But the language the Jewish theologian speaks is not one of words alone. The traditions of Israel are filled with speech-acts of a trans-verbal sort. These are epitomized by the sounding of the *shofar*, described by some sources as a wordless cry that reaches to those places (in the heavens? within the self? in the Self?) where words cannot penetrate. The same may be said of all the sacred and mysterious silent acts of worship: the binding of *tefillin*, the waving of the *lulav*, the eating of *matsot*. All of these belong to the silent heart of the Jewish theological vocabulary. Each *mitsvah*, say the kabbalists, is a half-hidden way of pronouncing God's name. All this is part, indeed the very heart, of language.

In defining Jewish theology as an "attempt to help the Jewish people," I mean to say that the theologian has an active and committed relationship to the community. A Jewish theologian is a theologian who works with the Jewish people, not just with the symbolic vocabulary of the Jewish tradition. There is no Judaism without Jews, and that is no mere tautology. To be a Jewish theologian, especially in an age when the very future of our existence is threatened, is to accept the value of Jewish continuity and to direct one's efforts toward the building of a Jewish future. This does not mean that theology is to become the handmaiden of survivalism or that particular theological ideas are to be judged on their value for Jewish survival. The prophets hardly limited themselves in this way, nor should we. But it does mean that the theologian speaks out of the midst of a living community and addresses himself or herself in the primary sense to that community of Jews. If there are other masters to be served, as there always are (I think of such masters as pluralism, consistency, scholarly objectivity, political correctness, and so forth), let us remember that the Jewish people and its needs should come near the head of the line.

Here again I must refer to the particular tradition out of which I speak. In this tradition, Jewish theology has passed only in the last two generations from the hands of *rebbes* to those of their less-defined modern successors. The legacy of the hasidic master is not yet forgotten here. He may be characterized as a latter-day descendent of the Platonic philosopher-king. Drawn by his own inclination to dwell exclusively in the upper realms of mystical devotion, he is forced by communal responsibilities to dwell "below," amid his people, and concern himself with their welfare. Cleaving fast to both realms at once, he thus becomes a pole or channel between heaven and earth. While the contemporary theologian should stay far from the pretense and pomposity that often result from such exaggerated claims of self-importance, he or she would do well to imitate the grave sense of communal as well as spiritual responsibility, and the link between these two, that went with the mantle of those who "said Torah." We too are saying Torah, that is bringing Torah into being, in a certain sense.

Jewish theology seeks to understand "the meaning of human life and Jewish existence." The questions faced by theology are universal. It exists in order to address itself to the essential human quest for meaning; while nurtured from the wellsprings of tradition, it grows most vigorously in the soil of personal religious quest. It wants to address issues of life and death, our origins in Creation, and the purpose of existence itself. Its answers will come in Jewish language, to be sure, and hopefully in rich and undiluted Jewish language. But it takes its place as a part of the human theological enterprise and is healthily nourished today as in all ages by contact with the best in philosophical, religious, and scientific thinking throughout the world. The American Jewish theologian who understood *this* best was Mordecai M. Kaplan. He developed a theology in response to the finest western social thought of his day, much as his German-Jewish counterparts did so in response to idealist philosophy. A Jewish theology for today must stand in dialogue—mutual and unapologetic dialogue—with the best of theological understanding of religion, science, and the humanities in our own contemporary world.

Alongside its universal concerns, Jewish theology will also have to turn itself to the particular, seeking out the meaning of distinctive Jewish existence and the special contribution that the Jewish people has to offer. We have just lived through the most terrible age of martyrdom in Jewish history, and ours is a time when being a Jew can still mean the potential sacrificing of one's children's lives so that our people may live. At the same time, our community suffers terrible losses due to assimilation and indifference. In the face of this reality, the would-be theologian in our midst must offer us some reason why the continuation of our existence is religiously vital, even at such a terrible price. To do anything less would betray the trust we as a community place in the theologian. The Jewish theologian should have something to say to the large number of Jews, including many of our deepest seekers and most sensitive religious souls, who have turned away from Judaism and sought their spiritual nourishment elsewhere. To these Jews we should not offer condemnation—their souls are truly "babies captive among the heathen"—to use a halakhic phrase. Nor should we seek to "convince" them by vain arguments that Judaism is "better" or "more true" than other religions. Rather we should open to them an experiential path to return home. The Jewish theologian as one who articulates religious experience should not forget this audience.

"Texts, symbols, and historical experiences" are the quarry out of which a contemporary Jewish theology is hewn. We are a tradition and a community shaped by and devoted to a text. In the primary sense, text refers here to the written Torah, read and completed each year by Jews in an ever-renewing cycle of commitment. Whatever the origins of that text, the Jewish religious community has accepted it as holy. It may no longer stand as the authoritative word of a commanding God, but it remains the most essential sanctum of the Jewish people, a source of guidance, wisdom, and ancient truth. Our relationship to it may at times include protest and rebellion along with love and devotion. But it remains our Torah, and we remain its Jews. We can no more reject it and spiritually remain Jews than the fish can reject water, to use a classic image, or than the mature adult can reject his or her own legacy of memory, one that inevitably includes both joy and pain.

Many of our most important sources are written in the form of commentaries to this text. These the theologian must study, seeking to add his or her contemporary voice to this tradition. Here the aggadic strand is particularly important. Jewish theology in its most native form is narrative theology. It tells our story. The theologian was originally one who "told the tale"—that of Creation, of Exodus, of Abraham and Isaac, or of Ruth and

Naomi—and subtly put it into a distinctive theological framework. This method is ours to study and continue, as is amply demonstrated by the widespread renewal of midrashic writing in recent decades, a great sign of health within Jewish theological creativity. The contemporary Jewish theologian could do no better than to retell the tale or tell some new tales in his or her own way. Much of the best of Jewish theology in the twentieth century has been written by poets and novelists. I think of Paul Celan, Uri Zvi Greenberg, and Jacob Glatstein; of S. Y. Agnon, Franz Kafka, I. B. Singer, and Elie Wiesel; these offer significant humbling to those of us who call ourselves theologians.

Works of ancient *aggadah* were reshaped by the kabbalists within their own systematic framework to create a profound sort of mystic speech. Study of this aggadic-kabbalistic tradition and the search for ways to adapt it to contemporary usage is a key task of Jewish theology. The old aggadic-homiletic tradition is re-opened once again within Hasidism. Study of the creative use made of traditional sources by the hasidic masters will serve as another important paradigm for contemporary efforts. The vast literature of Hebrew theological and moral treatises, a genre almost completely neglected other than by historical research, should also be important to the theologian. These too should be part of "text" in its broadest sense, as should be the artistic and musical creations of many generations and varied Jewish communities throughout the ages. All of them belong to what I mean by "text."

I have already mentioned symbols as forms of silent religious speech. Here I would like to digress in order to add a reflection on the power of religious symbolism as constituted in the language of the *kabbalah*. The kabbalists taught of the ten *sefirot*, primal manifestations of the endless One that encompasses all of being. Each of these ten is represented in kabbalistic language by one or more conventional terms and by a host of symbolic images. A certain face of the divine reality, to take one example, is conventionally called *hesed*, or grace. But in kabbalistic writings it is often referred to by such symbol-terms as "morning," "milk," "Abraham," "the right hand," "the priest," "love," "south," "lion (on the divine throne)," "myrtle twig," and a host of other names. Each of these terms, when used in the kabbalists' symbolic reconstruction of the Hebrew language (for we are speaking of nothing less) has the same referent. What the kabbalist has in effect created is a series of symbolic clusters, and when any member of a cluster is invoked, all the others are brought to mind as well. I call this reconstruction, not deconstruction, of language. The clusters make for powerful new meanings of words and patterns of association. Meaning is thus greatly amplified and broadened, though within contours that remain quite clear to one who plays well at this symbolic keyboard. *Kabbalah* makes for an enrichment and amplification of meaning, not its breakdown.

It is particularly important that each of these clusters contains elements of both classically Jewish and natural symbols. The Bible saw the variety and splendor of creation as the great testament to God's handiwork. But nature was to a degree desacralized in later Judaism, which viewed study, religious practice, and reflection on Jewish sacred history as the chief areas where one should seek contact with God. The kabbalist greatly reinvigorates Jewish language by this symbolic resacralization of the natural world. Rivers, seas, seasons, trees, and heavenly bodies are all participants in the richly textured description or "mapping" of divinity, which is the kabbalist's chief task.

Jewish theology needs to find a way to repeat this process, to "redeem" the natural for our theology and to bring the religious appreciation of the natural world into central focus as an object of Jewish concern. We need to do this first and foremost for our own souls. We need to lead our religious parlance out of the ghetto that allows for the sacrality only of what is narrowly ours and allow ourselves to see again, to "lift up our eyes to the hills," to "raise our eyes to heaven and see who created these," opening ourselves anew to the profound sacred presence that fills all of being. We also need to do this as members of the human religious community, all of which is charged in our day with creating a religious language that will re-root us in our natural surroundings and hopefully lead to a deeper and richer appreciation—and therefore to less abuse and neglect—of our natural earthly heritage. In this area Jewish theology is lagging far behind the Jews, many of whom take leading roles in the movement for preservation of the planet but with little sense that Judaism has anything to offer to these efforts.

The Judaism of Kook, Zeitlin, and Heschel is one that had begun to undertake this task. All of them saw this world in its variety and splendor as nothing less than the multicolored garb of divine presence. For fifty years Judaism has, however, turned in other directions. Shaken to our root by the experience of the Holocaust, our religious language took the predictable route of self-preservation by turning inward, setting aside this universalist agenda as non-essential to our own survival. We needed in those postwar years to concentrate fully on our own condition, first in outcry and later in the rebuilding of our strength, especially through the creation of Israel and its cultural and religious life. Now that time has begun to work its inevitable healing on both mind and body, we find ourselves somewhat shocked and frightened by the rapid pace of this turn inward and the narrowing effect it has had on Jewish thought. In the face of these, we find ourselves turning back to the interrupted work of our nascent Jewish universalists and theologians of radical immanence, knowing that we need to resume their task.

The impact of these history-making decades is not lost, however. In adding "historical experiences" to the texts and symbols that comprise the sources of our Jewish learning, I mean to say that there has been a profound change wrought on the Jewish psyche by the events of this century. We are no longer able to ignore the lessons of our own historical situation, as Jews sought to do for so many years. Emancipation, Zionism, and persecution have all joined forces to drive us from that ahistorical plateau where the Jewish people once thought it dwelt in splendid isolation. We need a theology that knows how to learn from history, from our role among the nations, from our experiences both as victim and as conqueror. Without the ability to handle these real-life situations with moral integrity and strength, our Judaism of texts and symbols will become mere cant.

Finally, we need to insist in our definition that all these are "the shared inheritance of all Jews." Nothing in our tradition belongs to an exclusive group within the Jewish people. This includes groups defined by religious viewpoint, by national origin, by gender, and by all the rest. The legacy of Hasidism is too important to be left to the *hasidim* alone; Sephardic ballads and Yemenite dance no longer belong to the descendants of those groups alone. Words like *halakhah* or *yeshivah* should not be left to the Orthodox; they are the inheritance of all Israel. So are observances like dwelling in the *sukkah*, bathing in the *mikveh*, and dancing with the Torah. None of the legacy belongs exclusively to men, and none of it exclusively to women.

All of this should be sufficiently obvious not to need stating here, but that is unfortunately not the case. The theologian should be committed to the entirety of the Jewish people, more than to any sub-group or denomination within it. This will mean an ongoing devotion to the endless task of educating Jews—all kinds of Jews—and bringing them home to their roots in the people Israel. It is both a *mitsvah* and a privilege to participate in this task. For having a key role in it, the theologian should be grateful.

37

Another Perspective on Theological Directions for the Jewish Future

REBECCA T. ALPERT

Arthur Green offers a remarkably thorough and rich definition of Jewish theology that is surely a blueprint for future efforts at theologizing. Green suggests that Jewish theology must: be grounded in a living community of Jews, depend on words and symbols and therefore on prayer, seek to know God, adumbrate life's meaning in both universal and distinctly Jewish dimensions, be in dialogue with the insights of the contemporary world, focus on Torah expressed through midrash and symbols, be related to our current historical reality, and be shared by all Jews. This definition provides room to explore the necessary theological questions that will face us in the next generation. Everyone who takes up the enterprise of Jewish theology should be sure to use this framework as a checklist against which to measure his or her work.

Green begins his essay by describing the personal position which grounds his definition, which he describes as neo-hasidic or mystical theology. This theological stance is predicated on the cultivation of inwardness, in which the individual's religious experience is the primary source of data. Mystical theology has a view of religious truth that posits a divine reality of transcendent oneness that overcomes distinctions, while at the same time being creation-centered and therefore immanenist. The traditions of Judaism and halakhah are natural and comfortable parts of this perspective.

My personal theological stance differs significantly from Arthur Green's. Rather than cultivate inwardness, I have focused my quest for God based on a relational theology in the spirit of Martin Buber. That Buberian orientation has also led me to an "outwardness" that manifests itself in the political, in an ultimate interest in justice as the crown of relation. As a feminist, the possibility of a divine oneness is alien to me. Rather, I look for

---

Rebecca T. Alpert, "Another Perspective on Theological Directions for the Jewish Future," published in this volume for the first time.

God in the multiplicity of being, in the celebration of differences and distinctions, and in the quest not to hierarchialize those differences. And as an American Jew, whose heritage combines secular, Reform and Reconstructionist perspectives, my relationship to Jewish tradition and observance is neither natural nor comfortable, but something I come to consciously and thoughtfully.

I would like to contribute some nuances to Green's definition based on my very different perspective that may be helpful in moving Jewish theology into the twenty-first century. An outwardly oriented, feminist, conscious Judaism looks differently at the universal dimensions of the meaning of life, and our dialogue with the contemporary world. It suggests a different interpretation of the symbolic structure of Torah and reorients our understanding of how this theology is shared among Jews.

Green suggests that the theological pursuit to understand the meaning of human life is grounded in "personal religious quest" and "rich and undiluted Jewish language." This quest is then supported by dialogue with insights from outside. From my perspective, the search for meaning may not necessarily originate in personal quest nor be expressed exclusively in Jewish language. In fact, some of the insights from other religious and secular cultural traditions may both stimulate these questions and provide language to address them. When this is the case, the roles of traditional Judaism and insights from the contemporary world are reversed, and the dialogue between them begins with those outside insights which then enter into dialogue with Jewish tradition by raising questions about traditional Jewish perspectives.

The question of sexual identity is an obvious example. Part of my struggle to understand my own humanity derives from the questions I ask myself when I take cognizance of my erotic attraction to women. If my personal quest were to arise on Jewish soil, the answer to those questions would be profoundly alienating. Jewish traditional texts render lesbian desire invisible at best. Rather, my internal awareness of these feelings arises in "the soil" of feminism, gay liberation, and queer studies. These philosophies have the insights that then enable me to go into dialogue with Jewish tradition to explore the theological implications of my internal feelings. And I need to acknowledge that those internal feelings might have been repressed rather than experienced in contexts other than the one in which we live today. So I would argue that Green's position makes an a priori assumption that an inwardly oriented, Jewishly grounded worldview is where we start. As a Jew whose Judaism is both conscious and thoughtful, my theological questions will most likely originate in a different way and therefore change the nature of the dialogical process.

This observation also applies to those Jews who "have turned away from Judaism and sought their spiritual nourishment elsewhere." Green suggests that these people, who have presumably found their spiritual home in other religious traditions, should be brought back to Judaism. The work of theologians is to help these "deep seekers and sensitive religious souls" find spiritual nourishment on Jewish soil. But if we approach this consciously, we may discover that those religious seekers may have as much to offer Judaism as Judaism has to offer to them. We can, for example, take in to our Jewish lives the insights of Buddhist meditation and begin a dialogue that does not assume that there is a clearly Jewish way of achieving those insights, but rather finds a Jewish way of integrating them. This is how Jews have adapted to living in many societies throughout our history, although not always as consciously as we do today. While Green suggests that the mystic's insights begin in silence, he acknowledges that Judaizing them means giving them voice. Buddhist insight suggests a more powerful role for silence, in prayer and in action. This is not easy to maintain in Jewish settings; we often find silence awkward in the context of prayer. Individual prayer is loudly enunciated in traditional prayer settings, and the organ drowns out the silent prayer in Reform services. So while the mystics (and the ancient rabbis, and the reformers, and the women who prayed over their Shabbas candles) all appreciated silence, they did not know what to do with it. But the Buddhists (and Quakers and Catholic monastics) do know. And we can best be served, I believe, when we consciously appreciate their insights and bring pieces of what they have to offer into our prayer. Rather than claim credit for understanding the power of silence in worship, we should admit that Jewish worship is weak in this area, and borrow from other traditions' wisdom. To enable religious seekers to find their nourishment in Jewish settings, Jewish settings should be open to learning from those seekers what they have found elsewhere, and find ways of appreciating what is brought in.

I am deeply moved by Green's passionate description of the power of aggadah, of the telling of stories to illuminate our theological perspective. I am similarly interested in his digression to reflect on how religious symbols in kabbalah, specifically those related to the natural sphere, can become an important source for environmentalism. Stories and symbols are indeed powerful ways of making theology. But what is missing from Green's theological program, except in this one reflection, is an awareness of the need for theology to be about justice. This inwardly focused religious perspective does not create the opportunity for outward awareness except in this one instance and in his acknowledgement that Jewish theology must be contextualized in the external realities of history. But theology has to go farther. It has to be about issues of justice and human interrelatedness. We are obligated to examine, as the prophets did, what it is that God wants of us beyond a high level of communication and self-awareness. For surely it is our task to make this world a better place. Inside the Jewish community, we must deal with issues of relational ethics, of class and gender privilege, and of our role as American Jews in supporting Israeli governmental policies. But we must also go beyond the Jewish community to address issues such as poverty, racism, restrictions on reproduction freedom, corporate greed, and violence that are plaguing American society today. And we must understand our role in the global village: to stand up against war, hunger, and economic injustice around the world. The Jewish community has an important role to play in society; a theology for the future must make the imperative to pursue justice central, not peripheral, to its task. There is much wisdom in Jewish symbols and stories about justice, and we have an obligation to share it. This is our prophetic heritage as a Jewish people.

Finally, I could not agree more with Green's contention that all this is "the shared inheritance of the Jews." We must know each other's cultures—hasidic, new age, feminist, Sephardic. All of Judaism belongs to all of us. And that does require education and openness. But that process cannot be at the expense of our willingness to accept our differences and understand that those who claim a particular Jewish legacy are entitled to embracing it as their own. While I might appreciate halakhah or Sephardic ballads, to use Green's examples, they belong to me only in the broadest sense, as part of the heritage of the Jewish people.

But it is also necessary for us to respect the characteristics that distinguish us from one another, to love our particularities as Jews. As Jews we are one, but we are also many. Our passionate disagreements as a "quarrelsome people" will be alleviated only by appreciating our unity *and* our diversity. As Jewish feminist theologians have come to learn (through painful experience) over the last two decades, there are many feminisms and there are many Judaisms. We must understand our ultimate connections, but we must also respect our differences.

Although it seems like a small matter, the high value I place on Jewish diversity may be my greatest difference with Art Green's theological blueprint. I believe that the underlying assumption of Green's passionate defense of our shared heritage has as much to do with his mystical theological passion for "transcendant oneness that overcomes distinctions" as it does with trying to resolve the disagreements we have today among Jews. Accepting our cultural differences while maintaining that we are one is directly linked to accepting our theological differences.

Our theological differences are vast. Nonetheless, I want room in my Judaism for a great variety of theological perspectives. I want room to explore the meaning of ancient Hebrew Goddess worship; to let its existence seep into my contemporary struggles with a masculine God. I want room for those who are secular to work out their "theologies" without reference to God. And I also want room for those who absolutely believe that God gave Moses the Torah on Mt. Sinai. I do not need the Orthodox, or the mystics, or even Reform Jews for that matter, to believe as I do. But unity in diversity means remaining open to the different ways we express our Jewishness and our theological understandings.

As Jews we share more than an inheritance: we share life in a community and we share a future. To contribute to improving a world that is fragmented and unjust, we must learn to appreciate one another's differences, to work for justice, and remember that there is room to learn consciously from the insights of other traditions. This is what I would add to Arthur Green's theological reflections about the Jewish future.

38

The Nature and Direction of Modern Jewish Theology: Some Thoughts Occasioned by Arthur Green

DAVID ELLENSON

The writing of modern Jewish theology in North America, as in all the Western world, has been a difficult task. Like all Jewish communities in the West, the destruction of the semi-autonomous political framework of the medieval Jewish community, the rise of a modern historical consciousness that disenchanted formative religious myths and fragmented communal memory, and the attenuation of commitment to common religious practices and rituals informed by an allegiance to halakha have all combined to destroy the unitary sense of communal life that facilitates rigorous theological reflection. Modernity, by shattering the plausibility structure that informed and sustained traditional Jewish life and belief, has made the articulation of Jewish thought in the modern setting an arduous enterprise. It has surely destroyed the possibility of a univocal contemporary Jewish theology. This is why the writing of Jewish religious thought in the modern world has been such a scattered and highly pluralistic enterprise.

Yet, as Arthur Green correctly points out, ours has hardly been a community bereft of theologians and religious writers. Indeed, the years following the Holocaust bore witness to a renewed call for Jewish theology. Emil Fackenheim, Joseph Soloveitchik, and Abraham Joshua Heschel all played crucial roles in reviving serious theological reflection on this continent, and others such as Eugene Borowitz, Jakob Petuchowski, Milton Steinberg, Richard Rubenstein, Irving Greenberg, David Hartman, and Emanuel Rackman

David Ellenson, "The Nature and Direction of Modern Jewish Theology," published in this volume for the first time.

provided a range of depth and variety that marked the theological ferment and character of these post-war years.

These men did not write for a predominantly immigrant American Jewish community, and all went beyond the type of exhortative religious writing that marked the character of most Jewish religious works during the first half of the twentieth century. Their aim, unlike their predecessors on this continent, was to do more than draw haphazardly in loose conceptual patterns upon the storehouse of symbols and images contained in traditional Judaism to provide a desired fit between American culture and Judaism. Instead, these men, more secure and self-confident in their status as Jewish-Americans, authored more inward-directed works addressing the Jewish people about the distinctive elements of Jewish faith. Trained in European or American university settings, they were open to dialogue about matters of theological substance across denominational and interreligious lines.

In addition, all these men were informed in their compositions and portraits of Judaism by non-Jewish thinkers such as Kierkegaard, Barth, Tillich, and Niebuhr, as well as modern religious and philosophical trends such as existentialism and pragmatism. Removed from the unbridled confidence in Enlightenment thought and reason that had guided their own Western-Jewish theological predecessors, many of them adopted the biblical-rabbinic dialectic of Covenant as the central notion upon which to establish Jewish theological reflection. Furthermore, the tragedy of the Holocaust and the establishment of the State of Israel increasingly came to dominate the theological conversations of a number of these thinkers in the decades following the 1960s.

These men created a framework for the emergence, revival, and renewal of American Jewish theology during the 1990s, and one would be remiss in failing to acknowledge the crucial role these thinkers played in establishing the directions that mark the present and future state of modern American Jewish theology. At the same time, new roads have been built, and contemporary Jewish religious writings reflect the novel influences of recent years.

The thought of Arthur Green illustrates the influences of both the old and the new on current Jewish theology. On the one hand, Green defines himself as a theologian standing in the tradition of an east European school of Jewish theology, one championed on these shores by his own teacher, Abraham Joshua Heschel. As he points out in his major theological work, *Seek My Face, Speak My Name: A Contemporary Jewish Theology*, it is a school informed by a sense of divine immanence as well as interiority. Green asserts that the starting point for theological reflection is the cultivation of inwardness and the opening of the soul to God's presence throughout the world. At the same time, Green demands that the flow of divine energy which we experience as God's love needs to step outside itself. Love needs another. In articulating these sentiments, Green draws powerfully on themes commonly found in Lurianic Kabbalah.

On the other hand, the power and direction of his thought and the affinity that so many modern Jews feel when reading Green are not simply the results of an internal and insular Jewish tradition. They are also the products of a larger quest for spiritual renewal that marked so many Americans during the 1960s and 1970s, a time when Green and his generation came to maturity. The heritage of modern America, as much as the legacy of Eastern Europe, animates his thought. This demonstrates the ongoing openness of the Jewish theological enterprise to intellectual currents in the larger world. Simultaneously, his thought indicates that the events and concerns that were so central to his immediate

American theological predecessors are not necessarily his. The theme of Covenant does not figure prominently in his writings, and while he does not ignore epoch-making events such as the the Holocaust or the State of Israel in constructing his thought, neither appears to play a seminal role. Instead, Green can be said to focus on religious experience (both personal and communal), the texts of the tradition, and the power of community in hewing out a religious path for present-day Jews.

Judith Plaskow and Rachel Adler, our two most prominent feminist theologians, adopt an approach that bears much in common with the method advanced by Green. At first glance, this might seem surprising. After all, Green articulates an American vision of a venerable and rich Jewish mystical tradition, while Plaskow and Adler seek to rescue Jewish tradition from the reality of a silence, for the female voices they embody and the women's presence they demand were formerly absent from the tradition. Plaskow, in *Standing Again at Sinai*, and Adler, in *Engendering Judaism*, grant expression to the religious experiences of women, and each testifies to the power of community in fostering a novel theological vision for both Jewish men and women. In addition, neither woman abandons the textual tradition that is their rightful heritage. Each woman reveals herself to be an exegete par excellence of the Bible, and Adler draws upon the texts and concepts of rabbinic writings in novel and unprecedented ways.

In so doing, both Plaskow and Adler reveal a theological orientation that is identical to that of Green. All three value human religious experience as a source for Jewish theological reflection and insight. Each affirms the power of text and community as a ground for the emergence of Jewish religious thought, even as each recognizes in a postmodernist vein the futility of constructing arguments that would establish the objective authority of the theology each advocates.

Their writings do not exhaust the theological creativity of our day. Hartman and Borowitz continue to respond to the contingencies of the present. Dorff and Gillman have been important theological voices in recent years, and Emanuel Levinas has found a score of champions and interpreters who have brought his work to the forefront of contemporary Jewish theological reflection. Nor should one ignore the attention more popular Jewish religious authors such as David Wolpe or Lawrence Kushner have garnered. All testify to the ferment and interest in modern Jewish thought, and each deserves critical and extended discussion.

However, I have highlighted the recent theological writings of Green, Plaskow, and Adler in this brief response because their work captures the theological temperament of our time, and is representative of the characteristics that dominate Jewish religious thinking at present. The orientations that define their writings are illustrative of the emotive, yet tentative and personal tenor that informs so much Jewish theological work today. I suspect this trope will direct most Jewish theological works for the foreseeable future. Ours is unlikely to be an age that will provide a comprehensive and compelling answer to the challenges posed by Spinoza to the authority of the Tradition over three hundred years ago in his *Theological-Political Tractate*.

Some may lament the inability of our era to provide such theological certitude. However, by acknowledging that ours is an era that must accept the contingency of starting-points and, by recognizing that ours is a time that cannot experience what Nietzsche termed "metaphysical comfort," we are not unique, and we should not be puffed up with such post-modern hubris that we imagine that our generation alone has confronted such a problem. After all, seven decades ago Franz Rosenzweig faced the same dilemma, and he then observed that prior to the advent of the modern era no Jews would have squirmed on the needle point of theology and dogma—a "why" alone as he put it—in justifying their life and faith as Jews.

No great systematic Jewish theology in the tradition of a Steinhem or a Cohen will be forthcoming in our day. Furthermore, even if it were, many of us would doubt its claims for absolute certitude and veracity. Instead, our theological writings will be episodic and fragmentary. Some will condemn this as a shortcoming. Yet, for many of us, such finite reflection upon the texts, symbols, and experiences of Jewish life and tradition will be sufficient. We, like so many of our ancestors, will participate from our own personal and communal vantage-points in a conversation that stretches back over the millennia, and we will recognize that our conversation—guided and informed as it is by the literary elements and symbols as well as communal experiences that are the inheritance of the entire Household of Israel—possesses a transformative and transcendent power, a holiness, that is beyond our ability to adequately articulate and explain. We will, at such moments, hear the murmur of angels both as individuals and as a community, and we will feel the power of the divine. Our community, in the future as in the past, will engage in our search for God in a multiplicity of ways, and while we know that religion is not primordially a matter of reflection, our theologians, however haltingly, will be privileged to seek expression for the manifold understandings that will emerge from those engagements.

39

B'nei Ezra: An Introduction to Textual Reasoning

PETER OCHS

When the wall was rebuilt and I set up the doors, tasks were assigned to the gatekeepers, the singers, and the Levites.
(Neh 7:1)

In his elegant introduction to Jewish theology today, Arthur Green gives witness to our living after incomprehensible Destruction. The Destruction left us numb, he suggests. Once among the few survivors we staggered to our feet, we could utter words only as tools of survival: saving our bodies first, then rebuilding a refuge-polity in Israel. Here, in this diaspora-American-refuge, a few lent their bodies to the polity, but most of us lent our voices, instead, and money, and, by paying visits when needed, we fulfilled the *mitzvot* of *bikkur holim* (visiting the sick) or *kibud em v'av* (honoring parents). We have been Nehemiah's cousins from the old country.

> When the seventh month arrived . . . the Israelites being [settled] in their towns . . .
> the entire people assembled as one in the square before the Water Gate, and they asked
> Ezra the scribe to bring the scroll of the Teaching of Moses with which the Lord had
> charged Israel. (Neh. 8:1)

Once settled, at least physically, we turned to reconsider our moral and spiritual survival. Professor Green calls this our turn to thinking about our own Jewishness and declares, with Ezra, that *this* is a time when the Jewish people is ready for theology and, indeed, needs it urgently.

> Ezra the priest brought the Teaching before the congregation, men and women and all
> who could listen with understanding. (8.2)

Need we explain again—we do!—the inclusivess of this gathering? Men, women, and all who could listen with understanding. Green explains that theology is articulated by and for particular communities, living in certain historical contexts. He links his own theo-

---

Peter Ochs, "B'nei Ezra: An Introduction to Textual Reasoning," published in this volume for the first time.

logical community with the communities of Eastern European Jewry before the Shoah and with the less defined society of neo-hasidic thinkers that includes his teachers: Alter, Kook, Zeitlin, Heschel. Living before and after the Shoah, this list of mystical theologians forms a narrow theological bridge over the chasm that Arthur Cohen called a caesura in history. This side of the bridge, Green finds himself as mystic theologian in dialogue with thinkers in other, sometimes overlapping sub-communities: Hartman, Greenberg, Plaskow, Waskow, Gillman, and Borowitz. Green shares with them all, we may note, both the sense that now we start anew but out of one great and expanding Teaching, linked to us through many narrow bridges, and the insistence that, unlike many of our forebears, our communities include in their leadership men, women, and all who can understand. Like most of these thinkers, Green also lives in the persistent diaspora-American-refuge. Here, Ezra preaches to his cousins still in Babylonia, as well as those with him in Israel.

> Ezra opened the scroll in the sight of all the people, for he was above the people; as he opened it, the people stood up. Ezra blessed the Lord, the great God, and all the people answered, Amen, Amen, with hands upraised. Then they bowed their heads. . . . Jeshua, Bani . . . and the Levites explained the Teaching to the people, while the people stood in their places. They read from the scroll of the Teaching of God, translating it and giving the sense; so they understood the reading. (8:4–8).

One Teaching, one Ezra, many readers, many translators. My responses to Green's essay are offered from out of another sub-community of Jewish theologians, self-described most recently as a community of "textual reasoners." The sub-community is linked to Green's and his peers, but it looks to the past through its own choice of narrow bridges and receives in its own way the Teaching they deliver. Nonetheless, the two sub-communities appear to share several rules for receiving this Teaching:

1. The communities gather around activities of rebuilding after destruction, which includes the perceived destruction not only of the body and state, but also morality, spirit, and rationality. (The text-reasoning community emphasizes the latter more than Green's community.)

2. The subject of normative judgments in these communities is therefore plural: members of the group say "we believe thus and so," even though any individual member's characterization of the "we" may be contested by other members. I will, for example, make claims about the beliefs of textual reasoners; even though I know many of my peers will not exactly agree with many of my claims, I also know they will accept the differences among us as differences that belong within the community's discourse.

3. Community members recognize that the relative-nothingness out of which we recreate our world (I use the term "we" with the caveats just noted) is filled with relics of antecedent worlds, and we cannot usually pick and choose: some of the pieces are neutral, some useful, some very dangerous, as they may include active elements of the evils that destroyed those worlds. At times, however, we can seek to avoid some of the more obvious elements of this kind. Green, for example, avoids replaying what he considers the assimilationist practices of the German-Jewish philosophers, who sought to legitimate their theologies within the terms of the general German philosophies of the day. Textual reasoners, on the other hand, may avoid replaying other practices that Green preserves. One example is a neo-hasidic tendency to couch theological claims within the terms of some fairly sharp binary oppositions: for example, between beliefs that are in the group (Jewish) versus out of the group (Gentile), that come from within the heart or within our beings versus those that are derived from external behavior or rationality, and so on. Textual reasoners may claim that these oppositions themselves derive from the Jews' struggles to survive religiously in hostile environments; when the oppositions are relaxed, then Jewish theology may no longer be reducible to either one of these pairs.

4. Within limits set by what it seeks to avoid, each community begins its rebuilding by affirming the authority of a sacred Teaching it derives from the Jewish past. Both communities reject the Jewish Enlightenment practice of subsuming the teachings of Torah under purportedly universal canons of reasoning. They reject, in other words, the modern academic practice of evaluating Biblical and rabbinic literature according to predetermined standards of rationality: whether the standards are set by historians ("a document is rational if it refers clearly to some identifiable events") or naturalist philosophers ("a document is rational if it could conceivably follow from some universal premises or probable observations"). Enlightenment reasoners define the standards first, and read or listen second. Members of these two Jewish communities both respond, *"naaseh v' nishmah,"* we enact first, then we inquire. In the Babylonian Talmud, Tractate Shabbat, the midrash associates these words of the Israelites at Mt. Sinai with the words of angels who do God's bidding, accepting God's words before they evaluate them. For Emmanuel Levinas, the midrash remembers what Enlightenment thinkers forget: that we are born into an order of relationships that sets a limit to any autonomous thinking. One accepts the Torah before one knows it; the acceptance is not naive, however, but a sober enactment of one's responsibilities for others.[1]

Levinas' reading is often cited by textual reasoners to support the kind of move Green makes, placing academic rationality back in the service of inherited relationships and antecedent traditions. In this sense, the textual reasoners stand there among Ezra's congregation. Once having re-received the words of Torah, however, these reasoners do not bow their heads for too long. With Green's neo-hasidim, the textual reasoners are critics of tradition, as well as participants in it; they work in or near academia, and the words they retrieve from the sacred traditions do not speak by themselves. They speak by way of an oral Torah, *torah she b'al peh*, that has its prototype in classical rabbinic re-readings of Torah, but that remains incomplete until it is re-enacted in the contexts of contemporary life. Textual reasoners tend to retain more trust than do neo-hasidim in the role of disciplined rationality in this re-enactment.

> It has been taught: R. Yose said, Had Moses not preceded him, Ezra would have been worthy of receiving the Torah for Israel. Of Moses, it is written, "And Moses went up to God" (Ex. 19:3), and of Ezra it is written, "He, Ezra, went up from Babylon" (Ez. 7:6). *(Bab. Talmud, Tractate Sanhedrin)*

Enraged by the Israelites' sin of the golden calf, Moses broke the first tablets he brought down from Mt. Sinai (Ex 32:19); from then on, the Israelites were guided only by words brought down a second time. This seems to be a prototype for Jewish teaching ever since: where each teaching (from the root *l'shanot*) is a "second-ing" or "repetition" *(mishneh)*, inscribed after some experience of terrible loss, on stones carved by human hands (See Ex. 34:1). This time, it is the shattered tablets. Another time, it is Chorban, the Destruction of the First Temple, followed by Ezra's re-teaching from the raised platform. Later, it is another Chorban, of the Second Temple, followed by the Mishnah itself, the re-teaching that initiates the literature of Talmudic Judaism. What does this recurrent pattern say to us, today, in the shadow of our century's own horrible destruction? To respond to this question is to offer some portrait of the patterns of religious thinking that characterize textual reasoning as it emerges now alongside but also distinct from the practices of Green's neo-hasidism.

The Thickness of Revelation

The Talmudist David Weiss Halivni argues that, for a significant stream of Talmudic thinking, Ezra acquires a status near, or in ways equal to, that of Moses.[2] There is a tradition, for example, that the Torah texts transmitted by the priestly scribes to Ezra were imperfect, that Ezra instituted a process of restoring those texts, and the dots that appear over ten verses in the Torah (the *eser nekudot*) mark places where Ezra did not yet carry out the revision:

> Some give another reason why the dots are inserted. Ezra reasoned thus: If Elijah comes and asks "Why have you written these words" [why have you included these suspect passages?], I shall answer, "That is why I dotted these passages." And if he says to me, "You have done well in having written them," I shall erase the dots over them (*Bamidbar Rabbah* III.13).

The text implies that the Torah that was received by the scribal priests, by the Pharisees, and by the proto-rabbis in Second Temple days was not a self-sufficient record of God's spoken word but was so only through the mediation of an interpretive tradition eventually named the Oral Torah. As later recorded in the Mishnah, the rabbis received this Oral Torah from Moses by way of Ezra: "for Ezra had dedicated himself to seek [/interpret, *l'drosh*] the Torah of the Lord so as to observe it, and to teach laws and rules to Israel" (Ez. 7:10). In Halivni's words, Ezra was thus a principal architect of the oral law. The issue is not, first, a matter of historiography (who precisely was the one who received and revised which text?) nor of ideology (how did the rabbis read their method of inquiry into a received text tradition?), but of hermeneutical-behavioral practice: how do we in the scriptural tradition describe and enact our relationship to the God who is our ultimate teacher?

Our answer, Halivni implies, is that God speaks Torah, that Torah is received only through Israel's interpretive practices of God's word, as they are exemplified in the interpretive practices of the rabbinic sages and completed only when we enact them, as well, within our own communities of interpretation and practice. God's Teaching thus appears to us in the relationship that binds written Torah and oral practice.

Revelation as Reasoning

The scholar of Bible and midrash, Michael Fishbane, devotes his lengthiest book to studying how the Bible interprets itself: for example, how Deut. 4:16b–19 ("be careful . . . not to make for yourselves a sculptured image. . . : the form of a man or a woman, the form of any beast on earth . . .") reapplies the creation imagery of Gen. 1:14–27. Fishbane suggests that we can, per hypothesis, reconstruct the ways in which a passage (like Deut. 4) interprets another one (like Gen. 1). In this case, "the Deuteronomist offers a form of aggadic exegesis that establishes a distinct rhetorical nexus between the themes of creation and idolatry. . . , reinfor[cing] the Israelite theologoumenon [theological claim] that idolatry is a sin against the creator and his transcendence."[3] Fishbane's study suggests that almost every passage of written Torah can be re-read as interpretive commentary on other, hermeneutically antecedent passages.[4] The teachings of Torah, in other words, appear first as interpretive judgments about other teachings, rather than as judgments about the world-itself beyond the text. Noting that these judgments can be collected into groups of judgments, or types, Fishbane labels each type a rule of interpretive judgment, or logos. In these terms, we could recharacterize the written Torah as a collection of revealed logoi, or, to use the English term, revealed *reasonings*.

Does the community of textual reasoners gather itself around a tradition of revealed reasoning? This might sound odd to those who recall our critique of Enlightenment efforts to subsume the teachings of Torah under prior conceptual schemes. It might sound odd because certain prominent schools of postmodern criticism have equated any canon of disciplined rationality with an a priori scheme of this kind. The textual reasoners do not criticize reasoning, however, but only the absolutization of some single rule of reasoning, particularly one that allows interpreters to extend lessons learned from one context of interpretation over all other possible contexts: as if the key to understanding all texts lay, for example, in what we learn from historiography, or from semiotics, or from what happened in the Exodus. While reading comes before reasoning, the reading also gives rise to further reasoning. We call this "further" reasoning to indicate that "reading" and "reasoning" may mark different places on a continuum of interpretive behaviors. If Enlightenment or modern thinkers choose to segregate some activity of strict rationality from all other human activities, especially ones that entail relationship to others, this does not mean that the rest of us have to think this way. In our practices, reasoning refers to any reiterable pattern of response to one's perceptions or readings that can be diagrammed as a set of rule-informed behaviors. The issue is only which kind of reasoning is to be performed when and for what purpose.

The Particular Origins of a Reasoning, and Its More General Import

Textual reasoning names a particular family of reasonings that have emerged in the life of a particular community of Jewish thinkers; like any reasoning, however, this one displays general features that may also be of significance to other communities. The community numbers among its teachers Hermann Cohen, Martin Buber, and especially Franz Rosenzweig and Emmanuel Levinas. The great philosopher of Jewish Enlightenment, Cohen, came to argue that, by itself, philosophy grasps only the universal and cannot therefore examine the moral concepts which arise only in relation to individual lives. The prophets first comprehended these. While platonic science provides philosophy its method of moral inquiry, the Hebrew prophets, alone, introduce the object of this inquiry, humanity encountered in its suffering, and the purpose of knowledge, which is to end this suffering.

In his studies of rabbinic midrash, Fishbane offers a reading appropriate to Cohen's claim. He notes how the midrash in *Exodus Rabbah* (XXX.24) rereads Isa. 56:1, "Thus said the Lord: Observe what is right and do what is just; for soon my Salvation shall come *(ki qeroba yeshuati lavo)*."[5]

Scripture does not say your salvation but My salvation. . . . If you [Israel] do not have merit, I shall perform [the salvation] for, as it were, as long as you are in trouble, I am with you, as it says: I am with him (Israel) in trouble *(imo anokhi betzarah)* (Ps. 91:15).

God is with Israel sufferingly, in shared pathos. Re-reading the scriptural passage within its own literary context, the rabbinic midrash performs an act of what we may label "scriptural reasoning": reasoning stimulated by biblical (revealed) reading alone. The midrash is shaped by what Fishbane labels a rabbinic "mythos" of divine compassion for human pain, which mythic concept, we may add, is both "in" the scriptural text (it could not be articulated without the scriptural stimulus) and "out" of it (shaped only in the interpreting life of the rabbinic community). In more technical terms, we may say that the mythic concept of divine compassion functions as predicate of rabbinic judgments about the scriptural personae of God. For Cohen, this mythic concept is a "moral concept," which then functions as the predicate of his Jewish philosophic-scriptural reasonings about the relations among humans and God: God acts toward us with compassion, so should we act toward others; all claims of philosophical ethics follow from this primary claim. For textual reasoners, this move from scriptural to philosophical judgment constitutes what we may label a "theological" claim. Theology is an appropriate term for any act of scriptural or textual reasoning; once having noted that, we need not avoid the term "theology" (as do some who fear it belongs only to Enlightenment or to a strictly logocentric, Christian practice), nor add it to each claim that comes from scripture (theology is always already there, as they say, in the scriptural-textual reasoning). *Textual reasoning may now be defined, more strictly, as reasoning stimulated by reading scriptural reasoning* (rather than scripture itself). prototypically, by reading rabbinic midrash. Scriptural reasoning is more narrowly limited hermeneutically, as only one corpus gives rise to it, but also more widely varied, as the family of scriptural reasonings would include Jewish, Christian, and Muslim readings. Textual reasoning is more varied hermeneutically, as its sources are secondary to the Bible, but it shapes more narrow traditions of reading: rabbinic versus patristic and so on.

For textual reasoners, Buber extends the claims of his teacher, Cohen, in a crucial way. He argues that Cohen correctly derived philosophical ethics from the philosopher's prophetically-trained, compassionate response to suffering, but that Cohen failed to disclose the socio-linguistic context of that response. Suffering is not simply pain; it is what follows when others do not care for one's pain, which follows when they do not notice it, which follows when they lack the language to identify it. Language is a social affair. To attend to another's pain is to name the fact of that pain, which is to share in the modes of relation in which that pain can be identified: what, adapting Cohen's own terminology, Buber called "I–Thou" relations. I–Thou relations enable one to introduce new words that name new experiences that allow one to *see* pain in the other that one would not previously have seen and to identify new modes of action in response to that pain and thus new obligations to act.

Hu michadesh b'khol yom maaseh b'reshit: as it says in the morning liturgy, God renews each day the order of creation. For God to renew is to speak God's creative words again in new ways that are ever-responsive to the new pains and needs that may arise. In this sense, God reveals the divine name to Moses as *ehyeh imach*: I will be with you; as we have heard in the midrash, that is, "I will be with you in your suffering." Wherever you suffer, I am there, to learn to see anew and offer the new words that will capture your pain and guide others to heal it. For humans to enter into I–Thou relations is thus to enter into the modes of relation of which God alone is fully capable: to be able to ever-renew one's discourse to capture the other's pain.

Franz Rosenzweig, the other great student of Cohen's, has become the textual reasoner's most beloved teacher: first, because he showed how to transform post-Kantian philosophy and phenomenology into a form of scriptural reasoning; and second, because he showed how this reasoning enters into everyday practice. The second lesson came from Rosenzweig's study of halakhic Judaism: the rabbinic Judaism that shows how Israel's prophetic encounters with God are completed only in the ways we reform our concrete institutional practices. The first lesson came from Rosenzweig's seeking to transform the modern philosophy he inherited into an instrument, rather than an enemy, of this rabbinic Judaism. Western philosophy, he suggests, has lost its way because it has forgotten the ultimate source and purpose of its conceptual abstractions. These abstractions do not serve themselves, but arise, instead, as marks of the legitimate attempts of Western thinkers to reform oppressive institutions (institutions that cause suffering), and they have meaning only if they stimulate such reformation. Like the American pragmatists Charles Peirce, William James, and John Dewey—and anticipating the Jewish pragmatists Mordecai Kaplan and Max Kadushin—Rosenzweig argued that Western academicians have misplaced the guidebooks that explain what they are supposed to do with their abstractions. These are books that interpret the lessons of the Bible as concrete instructions about how to transform our personal and social institutions into instruments of relationship to the God who daily renews the orders of creation and through whom we may each day renew the orders of language that either bind us, or fail to bind us, to one another. In our terms, these are books of "scriptural reasoning," prototypically the Mishnah, Talmuds, and collections of classical rabbinic midrash; to interpret these books as instruments for renewing and reforming modern thought is to engage in "textual reasoning," as exemplified in Rosenzweig's writings.

For textual reasoners, Emmanuel Levinas is Rosenzweig's most significant disciple because, more than Rosenzweig was able to do himself, Levinas begins the concrete work of rereading the Talmudic corpus as resource for reforming modern academic inquiry. This means applying the wisdom of a particular tradition of scriptural reasoning to reforming the academic practices of folks who come from many different traditions. It remains for the contemporary community of textual reasoners to extend Levinas' own extension of Rosenzweig's work and to explain how this work actually transforms modern academic inquiry into an instrument of scriptural reasoning. The textual reasoners, we might say, receive the preachings of Rosenzweig, Levinas, and their peers and translate their words in different ways to different subcommunities.[6]

In closing, here are illustrations of how a sampling of these reasoners might extend or emend the exercise I have begun in this essay. For the sake of the essay, I have magnified the importance of a single aspect of textual reasoning—the response to suffering—as if it represented a central focus of this entire theological movement. In doing this, I emphasize the pragmatic dimension of textual reasoning, as illustrated in Max Kadushin's study of midrash[7] as a way of reforming, at once, potentially oppressive social practices and problematic practices of scriptural reasoning. Among other textual reasoners, Robert Gibbs tends to make comparable use of Levinas and Rosenzweig, noting, for example, that Rosenzweig introduces his New Thinking as a bridge between theology and a Western tradition of philosophy that lacked attentiveness to the sufferings of others. To regain this attentiveness is to redescribe philosophy as a study of speech-acts, characterized as the performances through which the other makes itself known to the listener, even before the listener "has" experiences *of* the other. To learn this attentiveness is to learn to love, which is to learn to hear the other's call for love, which as Rosenzweig argues in *The Star of Redemption*, is ultimately God's command to Israel and thus to humanity.[8] To love the other first is to care for the other as condition of knowing: a movement completed in Levinas' conception of substitution for the other, which, says Gibbs, becomes expiation for the other.[9] As Susan Handelman writes (articulating one of the sources of her many literary-philosophical studies in textual reasoning and neo-hasidism),

> For Levinas, the primary relation to the other is asymmetrical and modelled on the Jews' proclamation at Sinai, *na'aseh ve-nishmah*, "we will do, and we will hear". . . . I am first called by and bound over to the other; only after (and as a result) of that primary binding do I then become the "equal" of the other.[10]

Yudit Greenberg explains that, for Rosenzweig (as for Levinas), this turn to the other represents "a rejection of modern philosophical trends in general, as well as a departure from trends in modern Jewish philosophy."[11] It means that Jewish philosophy will now emerge, not from the individual thinker's reflections on experience, but from actual participation in Jewish communal life, with its particular myths, symbols, and rituals, and its elemental story of the love between God and person, which "love is the moment of the soul's awakening into authentic selfhood."[12] For Greenberg, this study introduces into Jewish philosophy the "mythic element" that is missing in modern philosophy but that reconnects postmodern Jewish thought to the narratives of Kabbalah and thus to narrative studies of scholars like Elliot Wolfson.[13] Through a series of detailed textual studies, Wolfson shows how kabbalistic hermeneutics contributes to textual reasoning: how, for example, a "hermeneutics of visionary experience" may be culled from the zoharic narratives. At the same time, he also notes how the Kabbalah's contribution to this reasoning may be limited by its gender and ethnic constructions.[14] In this way, Wolfson contributes both to textual reasoning's opening to mythic studies and to its persistently philosophical leaning: as if to remind Jewish philosophical theologians, first, that they reason only out of the narrative traditions of Torah but, then, that they *reason* rather than merely *read* to distinguish between what in those traditions is reparative and redemptive and what may be oppressive. Emerging after destruction, textual reasoners remember, in Steven Kepnes' paraphrase of Paul Ricoeur, the need both to retrieve and to reform what lay before.[15] They thus re-address the scriptural Text as Thou, and in so doing also draw it into dialogic relation with the human community that says I or We.

"tasks were assigned to the gatekeepers, singers, Levites" (Neh. 7)

Art Green's "neo-hasidic" community joins the community of textual reasoners in the task of rebuilding after this century's Destruction. There are overlapping memberships,[16] but there are also different tendencies between the communities. Both reason in response to scriptural reading; both emphasize the ethical dimension of scriptural reasoning; but text reasoners tend to draw their rules of interpretation from intersubjective or public practices rather than from the individual's inner experiences of numinosity *or* the individual's capacity to conceptualize "transcendental oneness." Textual reasonings are more influenced by (1) postmodern criticisms of the modern scholar's tendency to privilege historiography over other forms of inquiry, and of the modern theologian's practice of "onto-theology" (theology as study of the nature of "being itself"), and (2) a premodern affection for formal studies of textuality (logic, semiotics, and rhetoric) as vehicles for displaying a dimension of God's scriptural speech. It is best not to make too much of the differences, however, as the historical moment calls for both singers and gatekeepers and. . . .

Notes

1. See "The Temptation of Temptation," in E. Levinas, *Nine Talmudic Readings*, trans. Annette Aronowicz, Bloomington, IN: Indiana University Press, 1990.

2. David Weiss Halivni, *Peshat and Derash: Plain and Applied Meaning in Rabbinic Exegesis* (Oxford, UK: Oxford University Press, 1990). See also David Halivni, *Revelation Restored* (Boulder, CO: Westview Press, 1997).

3. Michael Fishbane, *Biblical Interpretation in Ancient Israel* (Oxford, UK: Oxford University Press, 1985) 322. To take another example from the Ezra narrative, Fishbane notes how Ezra is portrayed as law-interpreter as well as Torah-teacher. "Ezra was informed by his princes that 'the people of Israel, and the priests, and the Levites have not *nivdalu*, separated themselves from the people of the land whose abhorrent practices are like those of the Canaanites, . . . the Ammonites, the Moabites, the Egyptians, and the Amorites' (9:1)" (Fishbane, p. 114). In response, Ezra mourns (9:4) and then later agrees with his princes' proposal to expel all foreign wives and separate the Israelites from the peoples of the land (10:11). Fishbane notes that the proposal makes deliberate allusion to Deut. 7, "wherein the Israelites are prohibited to intermarry with the local population" (Fishbane, p. 116). It appears that the princes want both to associate their new commonwealth with the Israelites' first settlement of the land and also to add more recent enemies (Ammonites and Moabites) to the old Deuteronomic list. In this case, the Bible extends an earlier conception of national holiness to a new setting, while also revising the details of the older law. If Ezra reforms the Torah text, it appears he also extends and reforms Torah law.

4. In similar fashion, Tikvah Frymer-Kensky examines ways in which verses of the Five Books of Moses reinterpret other verses, for example, in which Moses himself restates (or misrepresents?) God's words. She suggests that the written Torah problematizes any notion that individual verses have the status of revealed text independent of their relation to the whole of the written Torah. See, for example, Frymer-Kensky, "Revelation Revealed," Proceedings of the 1997 International Conference on Textual Reasoning, Drew University (ms.; forthcoming).

5. Michael Fishbane, "Extra-Biblical Exegesis: The Sense of Not-Reading in Rabbinic Midrash," in P. Ochs, editor. *The Return to Scripture in Judaism and Christianity* (Mahwah, NJ: Paulist Press) 182ff.

6. Part of the challenge of textual reasoning is to build a communal environment for Jewish theological inquiry in academia. Toward this end, a Society for Textual Reasoning has been formed, co-chaired by David Novak and Peter Ochs, and an electronic *Journal of Textual Reasoning*, co-edited by Michael Zank, Aryeh Cohen, and Shaul Magid (Journal addresses are: mzank@bu.edu; tr@bu.edu). The Journal sponsors four annual issues as well as a daily chat network among its 300 members. Members of the Society meet for three annual meetings, integrating textual study and philosophical reflection.

7. According to Kadushin, to compose a midrash is to adopt some "value-concept" (his term for "primary word" or "virtue") as premise (and thus grammatical predicate) of one's interpretation of a scriptural text (as grammatical subject) on some particular occasion. See, inter alia,

Max Kadushin, *The Rabbinic Mind*, 2nd ed. (New York, NY: Blaisdell Pub., 1965); Peter Ochs, editor. *Understanding the Rabbinic Mind, Essays on the Hermeneutic of Max Kadushin* (Atlanta, GA: Scholar's Press, 1990).

8. See Robert Gibbs, *Correlations In Rosenzweig and Levinas*, (Princeton, NJ: Princeton University Press, 1992) 57ff, 98ff, passim.

9. Gibbs, pp. 219ff.

10. Susan Handelman, "Crossing and Recrossing the Void: A Letter to Gene," in P. Ochs, editor. *Reviewing the Covenant: Eugene Borowitz and the Postmodern Renewal of Theology* (Albany, NY: State Universty of New York Press, forthcoming).

11. Yudit Greenberg, *Better Than Wine: Love, Poetry and Prayer in the Thought of Franz Rosenzweig* (Atlanta, GA: Scholar's Press, 1996) 141.

12. Greenberg, p. 142.

13. Greenberg, p. 149.

14. Elliot Wolfson, *Through a Speculum That Shines: Vision and Imagination in Medieval Jewish Mysticism* (Princeton, NJ: Princeton University Press, 1994) 326–392.

15. In his studies of Buber's biblical hermeneutics, Kepnes examines the dual tendency of textual reasoners to resituate modern philosophy, historiography and literary studies within traditions of rabbinic reading and to respond to legitimate, modern criticisms of those traditions (see, e.g., his *The Text as Thou* [Bloomington, IN: Indiana University Press, 1992]). Textual reasoners tend to display their reformatory, or critical, concerns in either relatively rationalist or relatively narrativist ways. David Novak, Eugene Borowitz, Norbert Samuelson, and Almut Bruckstein, for example, tend to uphold the relatively rationalist trajectory. See, for example, Borowitz, *Renewing the Covenant: A Theology for the Postmodern Jew* (Philadelphia, PA: The Jewish Publication Society, 1991); and Novak, *The Election of Israel, The Idea of the Chosen People* (Cambridge: Cambridge University Press, 1995); and Samuelson, *Judaism and the Doctrine of Creation* (Cambridge: Cambridge University Press, 1994). Daniel Boyarin exemplifies the narrativist trajectory. Several of his books, for example, evaluate the capacity of rabbinic interpretation to reform oppressive institutions, illustrating its capacity to deconstruct and then critically reconstruct scriptural rules of interpretation (*Intertextuality and the Reading of Midrash* [Bloomington, IN: Indiana University Press, 1990]) or its failures to underwrite such reforms (see his forthcoming work on gender difference and rabbinic culture). Other varieties of Jewish textual and critical inquiry may be seen in the works of scholars who joined all the thinkers already mentioned in this essay in a recent international conference on Textual Reasoning: Tzvi Blanchard, Marc Bregman, Aryeh Cohen, Robert Eisen, Charlotte Fonrobert, Steven Fraade, Menachem Lorberbaum, Shaul Magid, Susan Shapiro, Michael Signer, and Edith Wyschogrod.

16. For example, Susan Handelman, one of the founders of the textual reasoning community, is also very active in the neo-hasidic community. On the other hand, Green numbers Eugene Borowitz among his theologian colleagues, and Borowitz is another textual reasoning founder.

Suggestions for Further Reading

We have organized this list of additional readings to follow the major sections of this reader. In many cases, the first good place to read more by a given author is in the remainder of the book from which our selection has been taken. As those books are listed in the Acknowledgments section, we have not repeated them here. We instead include here other books of interest by the authors represented in this volume, as well as works on related topics by authors not included in this reader. We have included only works in English and have not included any of the scholarly literature written about Jewish thought in general or about any individual thinkers. Finally, we have restricted this list to books, leaving aside the hundreds of individual articles on these topics, which have been published in journals and various anthologies. Even within these limitations, the following list is by no means exhaustive, but is intended to give the interested reader some guidance in pursuing the topics covered in this volume.

I. Classical Theologians in the Twentieth Century: Approaches to God

A selection of Hermann Cohen's Jewish writings, edited and translated by Eva Jospe, can be found in *Reason and Hope* (Norton, 1971).

Franz Rosenzweig's other major works include *On Jewish Learning*, edited by Nahum Glatzer (Schocken, 1965). Those interested in his views on Christianity will want to consult *Judaism Despite Christianity*, edited by Eugen Rosenstock-Huessy (University of Alabama, 1969). A fine collection of Rosenzweig's work can be found in Nahum Glatzer's edited volume *Franz Rosenzweig: His Life and Thought* (Schocken, 1961).

Among Martin Buber's other major works are: *Eclipse of God: Studies in the Relation between Religion and Philosophy* (Harper, 1952), *Israel and the World* (Schocken, 1948), *Good and Evil* (Scribner's, 1953), *Two Types of Faith* (Macmillan, 1951), *Hasidism and Modern Man, The Origin and Meaning of Hasidism*, both edited by Maurice Friedman (Horizon Press, 1966 and 1960), and *On Judaism*, edited by Nahum Glatzer (Schocken, 1967).

Abraham Isaac Kook's writings have not been widely translated into English. In addition to the volume from which our selection was taken, readers may wish to consult *Rav A. Y. Kook: Selected Letters,* translated and annotated by Tzvi Feldman (Ma'aliot Publications, 1986).

Mordecai Kaplan's magnum opus is his *Judaism as a Civilization* (Schocken, 1967). Other important books include *The Meaning of God in Modern Jewish Religion* (Reconstructionist Press, 1937), *Questions Jews Ask: Reconstructionist Answers* (Reconstructionist Press, 1956), *Judaism Without Supernaturalism* (Jewish Reconstructionist Foundation, 1958), *The Purpose and Meaning of Jewish Existence* (Jewish Publication Society, 1964), and *The Religion of Ethical Nationhood* (Macmillan, 1970).

Abraham Joshua Heschel's other important works include: *Man is Not Alone: A Philosophy of Religion* (Farrar, Straus and Giroux, 1951), *The Sabbath: Its Meaning for Modern Man* (Farrar, Straus and Young, 1951), *Israel: An Echo in Eternity* (Farrar, Straus and Giroux, 1951), *Man's Quest for God* (Scribner's, 1954, recently reprinted as *Quest for God), The Prophets* (Harper & Row, 1962), and T*he Insecurity of Freedom: Essays on Human Existence* (Schocken, 1975).

II. Contemporary Reflections on Traditional Themes

God: Louis Jacobs' thought is found in *A Jewish Theology* (Behrman House, 1973). See also Elliot Dorff's *Knowing God* (Jason Aronson, 1992), Jacob B. Agus, *The Jewish Quest* (Ktav, 1983), Michael Goldberg, *Jews and Christians: Getting Our Stories Straight* (Abingdon Press, 1985), Daniel Gordis, *God Was Not in the Fire* (Scribner, 1995), Robert Gordis, *A Faith for Moderns* (Bloch, 1960), Harold Schulweis, *For Those Who Can't Believe* (HarperCollins, 1994), Kenneth Seeskin, J*ewish Philosophy in a Secular Age* (State University of New York Press, 1990), Seymour Siegel and Elliot Gertel, eds., *God in the Teachings of Conservative Judaism* (Rabbinical Assembly, 1985), Arthur Waskow, *Godwrestling* (Schocken, 1978) and *Godwrestling—Round 2* (Jewish Lights, 1996), and Marcia Falk's *The Book of Blessings* (HarperSan Francisco, 1996).

Creation: Norbert Samuelson, *Judaism and the Doctrine of Creation* (Cambridge University Press, 1994) and *Creation and the End of Days: Judaism and Scientific Cosmology*, edited by David Novak and Norbert Samuelson (University Press of America, 1986). See also Daniel C. Matt, *God and the Big Bang* (Jewish Lights, 1996).

Revelation: Other works by Immanuel Levinas include *Difficult Freedom,* translated by Sean Hand (Johns Hopkins Press, 1990) and *Nine Talmudic Readings* translated by Annette Aronowicz (Indiana University Press, 1990). See also Barry S. Kogan, "Reason, Revelation and Authority in Judaism: A Reconstruction" in Norbert Samuelson, ed., *Studies in Jewish Philosophy* (University Press of America, 1987). For a description and analysis of representative Reform, Conservative, and Orthodox views of revelation, see Elliot N. Dorff, *Conservative Judaism: Our Ancestors to Our Descendants* (United Synagogue, 1996), pp. 96–149. See also chapters in a number of the books listed in the section above on God.

Redemption: Menachem Kellner has edited a collection of Steven Schwartzschild's writings, *The Pursuit of the Ideal* (State University of New York Press, 1990). See also Neil Gillman, *The Death of Death* (Jewish Lights, 1997).

Covenant/Chosenness: Other words relating to the Jewish covenant in relation to non-Jews include Eugene Borowitz, C*ontemporary Christologies: A Jewish Response* (Paulist Press, 1980), Richard Rubenstein, *My Brother Paul* (Harper and Row, 1975), and David Novak, *The Image of the Non-Jew in Judaism* (Edwin Mellen Press, 1983), and *Jewish-Christian Dialogue: A Jewish Justification* (Oxford University Press, 1989). See also Arnold M. Eisen, *The Chosen People in America* (Indiana, 1983). Many of the books listed above in the section on God also include chapters on covenant or chosenness.

Law: Joseph Soloveitchik's other important works include: *The Halakhic Mind: An Essay on Jewish Tradition and Modern Thought* (Free Press, 1986), and *Reflections of the Rav: Lessons in Jewish Thought,* ed., Abraham R. Besdin, (World Zionist Organization, 1979). Jakob Petuchowski's primary work of Jewish thought is *Ever Since Sinai* (Scribe Publishing, 1961). Other works that deal with the theology of Jewish law (as distinct from legal discussion per se include: David Novak, *Law and Theology in Judaism,* (Ktav, 1974 and 1976), Eliezer Berkovits, *Not in Heaven: The Nature and Function of Halakha* (Ktav, 1983), Eugene B. Borowitz, *Reform Judaism Today,* Parts I and II, (Behrman Houe, 1983), Louis Jacobs, *A Tree of Life* (Oxford, 1984), Emanuel Rackman, *One Man's Judaism* (Philosophical Library, 1970), Joel Roth, *The Halakhic Process, A Systematic Analysis* (Jewish Theological Seminary, 1986) and Seymour Siegel, ed., *Conservative Judaism and Jewish Law* (Rabbinical Assembly, 1977).

III. Two Pivotal Experiences in the Twentieth Century

Holocaust: Emil Fackenheim is the author of several works, many focused on the Holocaust and the State of Israel: *Encounters between Judaism and Modern Philosophy: A Preface to Future Jewish Thought* (Basic Books, 1973), *God's Presence in History: Jewish Affirmations and Philosophical Reflections* (Harper Torchbooks, 1970), and *Quest for Past and Future: Essays in Jewish Theology* (Beacon Press, 1968). Some of Elie Wiesel's essays are found in *Legends of Our Time,* (Holt, Rinehart and Winston, 1968) and *One Generation After* (Random House, 1970). See also, Marc Ellis, *Ending Auschwitz: The Future of Jewish and Christian Life* (John Knox Press, 1994), Michael Goldberg, *Why Should Jews Survive? Looking Past the Holocaust Toward a Jewish Future* (Oxford, 1995), Frederick S. Plotkin, *Judaism and Tragic Theology* (Schocken, 1973), John K. Roth and Michael Berenbaum, eds., *Holocaust: Religious and Philosophical Implications* (Paragon House, 1989), and Harold M. Schulweis, *In God's Mirror* (Ktav, 1990). Other works on the problem of evil in Judaism include: David Birnbaum, *God and Evil* (Ktav, 1989) and David Blumenthal, *Facing the Abusing God: A Theology of Protest* (Westminster/John Knox Press, 1993).

The State of Israel: Contemporary religious reflections on the State of Israel and on the Zionist movement can be found in Hillel Halkin, *Letter to an American Jewish Friend* (Jewish Publication Society, 1977), Ben Halpern, *The American Jew: A Zionist Analysis* (Theodore Herzl Foundation, 1956), Arthur Hertzberg, *Israel in America* (Schocken, 1979) and *Jewish Polemics* (Columbia University, 1992), Jacob Neusner, *Stranger at Home: The 'Holocaust,' Zionism and American Judaism* (University of Chicago, 1981) and *Israel in America—A Too Comfortable Exile?* (Beacon Press, 1985), Jakob Petuchowski, *Zion Reconsidered* (Twayne, 1966). Other essays on Israel by David Hartman can be found in his *Joy and Responsibility: Israel, Modernity and the Renewal of Judaism* (Ben-zvi Posner/Shalom Hartman Institute, 1978). See also Arnold Eisen, *Galut* (Indiana, 1986) and Benjamin J. Segal, *Returning* (World Zionist Organization, 1987).

Other, somewhat older works of interest include:
Will Herberg's *Judaism and Modern Man* (Farrar, Straus & Young, 1951) and *Protestant, Catholic, Jew* (Doubleday, 1955) and Milton Steinberg's *Anatomy of Faith,* ed. Arthur Cohen (Harcourt, Brace & Co., 1960) and *A Believing Jew,* ed. Maurice Samuel (Harcourt, Brace & Co., 1951).

Biographical Sketches

Editors

ELLIOT N. DORFF

Rector and Sol and Anne Dorff Professor of Philosophy at the University of Judaism in Los Angeles, Elliot N. Dorff has written seven books and over one hundred articles on issues in Jewish law, Jewish ethics, and Jewish theology. He currently serves as Vice-Chair of the Conservative Movement's Committee on Jewish Law and Standards. In spring 1993, he served on the Ethics Committee of President Clinton's Health Care Task Force. In spring 1998, his book on Jewish medical ethics, *Matters of Life and Death*, was published by The Jewish Publication Society. His own theology is articulated most fully in his *Knowing God: Jewish Journeys to the Unknowable* (1992) and, in part, in his *Conservative Judaism: Our Ancestors to Our Descendants* (1977, 1996).

LOUIS E. NEWMAN

Louis Newman is Professor of Religion and Director of the Program in Judaic Studies at Carleton College in Northfield, Minnesota. His research focuses primarily on issues in classical and modern Jewish ethics. He is the author of *Past Imperatives: Studies in the History and Theory of Jewish Ethics* (1998) and coedited, with Elliot Dorff, *Contemporary Jewish Ethics and Morality: A Reader* (1995). In 1994–95, he was Carleton's faculty representative to the Pew Charitable Trust's "Roundtable on Higher Education," which sponsors national forums on challenges facing institutions of higher education. His book, *An Introduction to Jewish Ethics,* will be published by Prentice-Hall in 2000.

Contributors

RACHEL ADLER

Rachel Adler teaches at Hebrew Union College–Los Angeles and the University of Southern California. She is the author of *Engendering Judaism: A New Theology and Ethics* (1997).

REBECCA T. ALPERT

Rebecca T. Alpert is codirector of Women's Studies and Assistant Professor of Religion at Temple University. She is coauthor of *Exploring Judaism: A Reconstructionist Approach* (1985) and author of *Like Bread on the Seder Plate: Jewish Lesbians and the Transformation of Tradition* (1997).

ELIEZER BERKOVITS (1908–1992)

Ordained at the Hildesheimer Rabbinical Seminary in Berlin, Eliezer Berkovits held several pulpits—in Germany until 1939, and subsequently in England, Australia, and, from 1950–1958, in Boston. From 1958 until he moved to Israel in 1975, he was Professor of Jewish Philosophy at Hebrew Theological College in Chicago. He articulated his own theology in *God, Man and History* (1959), *Faith after the Holocaust* (1973), *Crisis and Faith* (1976), and *Not in Heaven: The Nature and Function of Halakha* (1983).

EUGENE BOROWITZ

Eugene Borowitz is the Sigmund L. Falk Distinguished Professor of Education and Jewish Religious Thought at Hebrew Union College—Jewish Institute of Religion, New York. His latest book, *The Jewish Moral Virtues*, written with Francie Schwartz, will be published by the Jewish Publication Society.

MARTIN BUBER (1878–1965)

Born in Vienna, Buber joined the Zionist movement in 1898, rising to become editor of several of its journals and ultimately moving to Israel in 1938, where he espoused a cultural form of Zionism and openness to the Arab population there. He was significantly influenced in his own theology by his studies of Hasidism and by the existentialism he learned from Hermann Cohen and developed in dialogue with Franz Rosenzweig. His theology was controversial in many Jewish circles due to his insistence that Jewish law was not essential to Jewish spirituality and, at times, even antithetical to it. A prolific author on Hasidism, Zionism, and the Bible, the books that best articulate his own approach to Judaism are *I and Thou* (1938), *Eclipse of God* (1952), and *The Knowledge of Man* (1965).

ARTHUR A. COHEN (1928–1986)

Author of a number of novels and novellas in addition to works in Jewish theology, Arthur A. Cohen edited two books on Jewish theology, *Arguments and Doctrines: A Reader of Jewish Thinking in the Aftermath of the Holocaust* (1970) and, with Paul Mendes-Flohr, *Contemporary Jewish Religious Thought* (1987). He also wrote several books articulating his own Jewish commitments: *The Natural and the Supernatural Jew* (1963), *The Myth of the Judeo-Christian Tradition* (1969), and *The Tremendum: A Theological Interpretation of the Holocaust* (1981).

HERMANN COHEN (1842–1918)

Hermann Cohen taught philosophy at the University of Marburg from 1865 to 1912 and founded adult institutes of Jewish studies in Poland and Berlin thereafter, including the illustrious Hochschule für die Wissenschaft des Judentums. His most important contributions to Jewish thought came late in his life, when his new focus on the experience of the individual turned him from neo-Kantian idealism to his new, proto-existentialist theology, articulated in his *The Concept of Religion in the System of Philosophy* (1915) and in *The Religion of Reason out of the Sources of Judaism* (1918).

ELLIOT N. DORFF

See "Editors" section.

DAVID ELLENSON

David Ellenson is I. H. and Anna Grancell Professor of Jewish Religious Thought at Hebrew Union College-Jewish Institute of Religion, Los Angeles. During the 1997–98 academic year, he served as a Fellow at the Institute for Advanced Studies and a Lady Davis Visiting Professor of the Humanities in the Department of Jewish Thought at the Hebrew University of Jerusalem.

MARC ELLIS

Marc Ellis is Visiting Scholar at The Center for Middle Eastern Studies at Harvard University. He is the author, most recently of *Ending Auschwitz: The Future of Jewish and Christian Life* (1994) and *Unholy Alliance: Religion and Atrocity in Our Time* (1997).

EMIL FACKENHEIM

Born in Halle, Germany, Emil Fackenheim was ordained at the Hochschule für die Wissenschaft des Judentums in Berlin in 1939. He emigrated to Canada in 1940 and joined the philosophy department at the University of Toronto in 1948. Originally a Hegel scholar, most of his Jewish writing has been preoccupied with the challenges to Jewish faith of living in the aftermath of the Holocaust and in the age of a re-established Jewish state. He is author of *Quest for Past and Future* (1968), *Encounters between Judaism and Modern Philosophy* (1973), and *What is Judaism?* (1987), in addition to the books from which the selections in this volume were taken. He currently resides in Jerusalem.

MARCIA FALK

Marcia Falk is the author of *The Book of Blessings: New Jewish Prayers for Daily Life, the Sabbath, and the New Moon Festival* (1996), a bilingual (Hebrew-English) prayer book that re-visions and re-creates traditional Jewish liturgy from a non-heirarchical, feminist perspective.

NEIL GILLMAN

Neil Gillman is Professor of Jewish Philosophy at the Jewish Theological Seminary of America. His *The Death of Death: Resurrection and Immortality in Jewish Thought* was published by Jewish Lights Publishing (1997).

ROBERT GORDIS (1908–1992)

Professor of Bible at the Jewish Theological Seminary of America, congregational rabbi, President of the Rabbinical Assembly, editor of *Judaism: A Quarterly Journal*, and Chair of the Commission on the Philosophy of Conservative Judaism, Robert Gordis wrote on issues in biblical scholarship, contemporary social issues, and on the philosophy of Conservative Judaism. He articulated his own theology primarily in his books, *A Faith for Moderns* (1960) and *Dynamics of Judaism* (1990).

ARTHUR GREEN

Arthur Green is Philip W. Lown Professor of Jewish Thought at Brandeis University. His most recent book, *Honest Talk: Teachings of the Sefat Emet,* is published by the Jewish Publication Society.

IRVING GREENBERG

Irving Greenberg is president of Chaverim Kol Yisrael (Jewish Life Network) and founding president of CLAL—The National Jewish Center for Learning and Leadership. He is the author of *The Jewish Way: Living the Holidays* (1988) and of *Living in the Image of God* (1998).

DAVID HARTMAN

Rabbi David Hartman is the founder and director of the Shalom Hartman Institute in Jerusalem and a former Professor of Jewish Philosophy at the Hebrew University. His books include *Maimonides: Torah and Philosophic Quest* (1976) and *Conflicting Visions: Spiritual Possibilities of Modern Israel* (1990).

ABRAHAM JOSHUA HESCHEL (1907–1972)

A scion of several of the great Hasidic dynasties of Eastern Europe with a doctorate in philosophy from the University of Berlin, Heschel succeeded Martin Buber in 1937 as the director of the Hochschule für des Wissenschaft des Judentums (the adult education institute that Hermann Cohen had founded). He fled to London in 1939 and then to America in 1940, where he served first as a professor at Hebrew Union College in Cincinnati (1940–1945) and then at the Jewish Theological Seminary of America (1945–1972). Active in interfaith and civil rights efforts, Heschel wrote on those matters, the prophets, Rabbinic theology, Jewish practice (most notably, the Sabbath and prayer), Hasidism, and Maimonides. His own phenomenological theology is articularted most fully in his *Man Is Not Alone* (1951) and *God in Search of Man* (1955).

LOUIS JACOBS

Dr. Louis Jacobs is rabbi of the New London Synagogue and Visiting Professor at Lancaster University. He is the author of many books on Judaism, including *A Jewish Theology* (1973) and *Principles of the Jewish Faith* (1988).

MORDECAI KAPLAN (1881–1983)

Founder of the Reconstructionist Movement in Judaism, Rabbi Kaplan served as a professor at the Jewish Theological Seminary of America from 1909 to 1963. He also founded and served as the rabbi of the Society for the Advancement of Judaism, the first congregation to embody the principles and practices of Kaplan's emerging theology of Reconstructionism. Until the founding of the Reconstructionist Rabbinical College in 1968, however, Kaplan resisted those who would make Reconstructionism a separate movement, preferring instead to see it as a school of thought rooted in Conservative Judaism but potentially affecting all movements. A prolific writer, his own theology is best articulated in his *Judaism as a Civilization* (1934); *The Meaning of God in Modern Jewish Religion* (1937); *Questions Jews Ask: Reconstructionist Answers* (1956); and *The Religion of Ethical Nationhood* (1970).

ABRAHAM ISAAC KOOK (1865–1935)

The first Ashkenazi Chief Rabbi of the modern Israeli community (1921–1935), Kook's studies of philosophy and, especially, of mysticism prompted him to find value in every Jewish soul, religious or not. His mystical outlook also made him see the Jewish return to Israel as "the beginning of the flowering of our redemption," and so, unlike most Orthodox rabbis of his time, he was a staunch Zionist. He maintained, though, that secular Zionism was incomplete, wrongfully ignoring or openly rejecting the critical religious component of the national revival. Although a copious writer, he never created a comprehensive system of thought. His speculative writings are chiefly contained in his *Orot Ha-Kodesh (Lights of Holiness),* 3 vols., 1963–64; and his *Iggerot Ha-Re'ayah (Letters of Rabbi Abraham Isaac Ha-Kohen,* where *Re'ayah* is an acronym for Rabbi Kook's name that also bears the meaning *Letters of Testimony* or *Letters of Proof*), 3 vols., 1962–1965.

YESHAYAHU LEIBOWITZ (1903–1995)

After moving from his native Riga to Palestine in 1935, Leibowitz was appointed Full Professor of Chemistry and Neurophysiology at Hebrew University in Jerusalem in 1961. He was also an outspoken advocate of the view that Judaism must be based on a recognition of the duty to serve God according to Jewish law for its own sake, not to achieve physical or spiritual perfection, and that Israel must incorporate that form of Judaism to be a true Jewish state. His Jewish writings are found mostly in Hebrew periodicals.

EMANUEL LEVINAS (1906–1996)

Professor of philosophy at Poitiers, Nanterre, and, after 1973, at the Sorbonne, from 1946 on Levinas also served for several decades as director of the Ecole Normale Israelite

Orintale, the school established by the French Jewish community to train teachers for its schools in the Mediterranean basin. Disillusioned by Nazism in his original faith in a strict universalism, Levinas believed that the specificity of Judaism was necessary for the well-being of the world, and much of his thought is devoted to the relationship between the traditions of the "Greek" and the "Jew." A scholar of Heidegger and Husserl, his own theology has now been translated into English in, among others, *Ethics and Infinity* (trans. Richard Cohen), *Nine Talmudic Readings* (trans. Annette Aronowicz), and *Difficult Freedom* (trans. Sean Hand), in addition to the volume from which the selection in this anthology comes.

DAVID NOVAK

David Novak holds the J. Richard and Dorothy Schif Chair of Jewish Studies at the University of Toronto. He is the author most recently of *Jewish Social Ethics* (1992) and *The Election of Israel: The Idea of the Chosen People* (1995).

PETER OCHS

Peter Ochs is Edgar Bronfman Professor of Modern Jewish Thought at the University of Virginia. He is cofounder of the Societies for Textual Reasoning and for Scriptural Reasoning and coauthor, with Steven Kepnes and Robert Gibbs, of *Reasoning after Revelation: Dialogues in Postmodern Jewish Philosophy*.

JAKOB J. PETUCHOWSKI (1925–1991)

Born in Berlin, Jakob J. Petuchowski emigrated to England before World War II and was ordained by Hebrew Union College in 1948. He joined the faculty of that institution in 1956, and served as a professor of rabbinics until his death, devoting much of his academic career to the study of Jewish liturgy. In his book, *Ever Since Sinai: A Modern View of Torah* (1961), he articulated a theology that attempted to link Reform Jews to a sense of being bound by Jewish law and to the Jewish people.

JUDITH PLASKOW

Judith Plaskow is Professor of Religious studies at Manhattan College. She is the author or editor of numerous books and articles on feminist theology, including *Standing Again at Sinai* (1990).

FRANZ ROSENZWEIG (1886–1929)

Born in Kassel into a highly assimilated Jewish family, Franz Rosenzweig studied philosophy and history at several German universities and, later in life, established the Freies Juedisches Lehrhaus in Frankfurt. He studied under Hermann Cohen at the Hochschule in Berlin, which Cohen had founded, and there met Martin Buber, who became a lifelong friend and colleague. In addition to a rich philosophical correspondence with his cousin, Eugen Rosenstock-Huessy, Rosenzweig collaborated with Buber on a groundbreaking

German translation of the Bible. From 1922 until his death he was almost completely paralyzed, yet managed to maintain an active correspondence. His magnum opus is *The Star of Redemption*, written on postcards from the front where he was stationed during World War I, in which he articulates his existentialist philosophy of Judaism.

RICHARD RUBENSTEIN

Richard Rubenstein is President of the University of Bridgeport and author of *After Auschwitz* (second edition, 1992) and *The Cunning of History* (1974).

GERSHOM SCHOLEM (1897–1982)

The leading authority throughout his life on the Kabbalah and Jewish mysticism, Gershom Scholem served as librarian of the Hebrew University from 1923–1933 and as Professor of Jewish Mysticism and Kabbalah from 1933–1965. The author of hundreds of translations and studies of kabbalistic texts, he also wrote widely on political and social issues facing Jews in the post-World War II era. In addition to the book from which the selection in this volume was taken, he was author of *Major Trends in Jewish Mysticism* (1941), *Jewish Gnosticism, Merkabah Mysticism and Talmudic Tradition* (1960), *On the Kabbalah and Its Symbolism* (1965), *Sabbatai Sevi* (1973), and *The Messianic Idea in Judaism and other essays in Jewish Spirituality* (1971).

HAROLD M. SCHULWEIS

Harold M. Schulweis is founder of the Jewish Foundation for the Righteous, author of *For Those Who Can't Believe* (1996), and spiritual leader of Valley Beth Shalom in Encino, California.

STEVEN SCHWARZSCHILD (1924–1989)

Professor of philosophy at Washington University in St. Louis for most of his life, Schwarzschild, a member of both the Conservative and Reform rabbinical associations, served as editor of *Judaism: A Quarterly Journal* from 1961 to 1969 and produced more than 200 publications—in history of philosophy (including books on Hermann Cohen and Franz Rosenzweig), philosophical analysis, theology, and socialist, pacifist, and Zionist polemics. His own theology, based on his conviction that Judaism is a consistent, rational system, possessed of authoritative, normative character and susceptible to clear-cut exposition in a neo-Kantian mode, was articulated in many of his Jewish essays.

BYRON SHERWIN

Byron Sherwin is Vice-President and Professor of Jewish Philosophy and Mysticism at Spertus Institute of Jewish Studies, Chicago, Illinois. He is the author or editor of twenty books and over one hundred articles and monographs, including *Sparks Amidst the Ashes: The Spiritual Legacy of Polish Jewry* (Oxford 1997).

JOSEPH SOLOVEITCHIK (1903–1995)

Talmudic scholar and religious philosopher, from 1941 until his death Rabbi Soloveitchik influenced a whole generation of rabbinical students at Yeshiva University and, through them, the entire modern Orthodox movement. He also served as the rabbi of a congregation in Boston and founded the Maimonides School there. Following his family's tradition, he was reticent to put his thoughts into written form, preferring instead the format of oral expositions and sermons, but his own theology, heavily influenced by his doctoral work in neo-Kantianism and Hermann Cohen, appears in two extended essays, "Halakhic Man" (*Talpiyot* [1944], pp. 651–735; translated and published as a book in 1983) and "The Lonely Man of Faith" (*Tradition* 7:2[1965], pp. 5–67).

ELLEN M. UMANSKY

Ellen M. Umansky is the Carl and Dorothy Bennett Professor of Judaic Studies at Fairfield University. She is the author of *Lily Montagu and the Advancement of Liberal Judaism* (1983) and coeditor of *Four Centuries of Jewish Women's Spirituality* (1992).

DAVID W. WEISS

David W. Weiss is a professor in the Department of Immunology at Hebrew University in Jerusalem and, prior to his move to Israel in 1966, Professor of Bacteriology and Immunology at the University of California, Berkeley. He has also written and taught in areas of Jewish law and philosophy, most notably in his book, *The Wings of the Dove: Jewish Values, Science, and Halachah* (1987), from which the selections in this volume were taken.

MICHAEL WYSCHOGROD

Michael Wyschogrod is Professor of Religious Studies at the University of Houston. He is the author of *The Body of Faith: God and the People Israel* (second edition, 1996) and numerous books and articles on Jewish thought.

A. B. YEHOSHUA

One of Israel's foremost novelists, Abraham B. Yehoshua is the author of *The Lover* (1977), and *The Five Seasons* (1989), as well as *Between Right and Right* (1981), a collection of essays on Israel and Zionism.